THE CENTENNIAL HISTORY OF ILLINOIS
VOLUME THREE

THE ERA OF THE CIVIL WAR
1848-1870

BY
ARTHUR CHARLES COLE
UNIVERSITY OF ILLINOIS

CHICAGO
A. C. McCLURG & CO.
1922

TABLE OF CONTENTS

CHAPTER		PAGE
I.	The Passing of the Frontier	1
II.	The Coming of the Railroads	27
III.	Agitation and Compromise, 1848–1852	53
IV.	Prairie Farming and Banking	75
V.	The Kansas-Nebraska Act	101
VI.	The Origin of the Republican Party	125
VII.	The Lincoln-Douglas Debates	153
VIII.	The Election of 1860	181
IX.	The Growing Pains of Society	202
X.	Church and School, 1850-1860	230
XI.	The Appeal to Arms	253
XII.	Recruiting Ground and Battlefield	273
XIII.	The New Abolitionists and the Copperheads	290
XIV.	The Reëlection of Lincoln	312
XV.	Population in Wartime	330
XVI.	The Industrial Revolution, 1860–1870	354
XVII.	Agriculture and the War	373
XVIII.	Reconstruction and the Military Politician	387
XIX.	The Spoils and the Spoilers, 1867–1870	404
XX.	Religion, Morality, and Education, 1860–1870	420
XXI.	Play and the Press	436
	Bibliography	459
	Index	477

LIST OF ILLUSTRATIONS

	PAGE
ABRAHAM LINCOLN	*Frontispiece*
FOREIGN BORN POPULATION, 1860	16
RAILROAD DEVELOPMENT, 1850-1860	34
PRESIDENTIAL ELECTION, 1848	60
VOTE FOR TREASURER, 1854	132
STEPHEN A. DOUGLAS	156
VOTE FOR CONGRESSMEN, 1858	178
PRESIDENTIAL ELECTION, 1860	200
RICHARD YATES	256
VOTE ON THE CONSTITUTION, 1862	270
LYMAN TRUMBULL	294
VOTE FOR CONGRESSMAN-AT-LARGE, 1862	298
POPULATION OF ILLINOIS IN 1860	330
PRESIDENTIAL ELECTION, 1868	414

PREFACE

THE development of Illinois out of the frontier and through the storm and stress of Civil War is the story of an evolving western democracy in a period of grave transition; it was then that the hopes of the pioneer were finding buoyant expression in the prosperity of the prairies and in the assumption of a full share of responsibility in the nation's burdens. The story of Illinois thus striving to be "first in war and first in peace" is complicated by the place taken by Illinois leaders on the roll of national heroes; indeed, the historian of this period finds himself torn between the demands of the common people for an interpretation of their democratic influence over against the looming influence of the statesman on the hustings, in the national legislature, or in the presidential chair. In the synthesis here presented the author has tried to weigh with care the proportions due to every phase of the stirring life on the prairies of Illinois.

The author is greatly indebted to several institutions which have responded generously to his appeals for assistance by the loan of source material: The Library of Congress, the Illinois State Historical Library, the Chicago Historical Society, McKendree College Library, the Belleville Public Library, the Joliet Public Library, the Rockford Public Library, and Reddick's Library of Ottawa. A large number of individuals and newspaper offices have cooperated by placing at the disposal of the author their private files of newspapers which were otherwise unavailable. Acknowledgments for such favors are due the publishers of the *Rushville Times*, the *Carthage Republican*, the *Jonesboro Gazette*, the *Canton Register*, the *Jacksonville Journal*, *Quincy Whig*, *Aurora Beacon*, and to Mrs. Grace Scripps Dyche of Evanston for a copy of her father's *Gem of the Prairie* for 1848 and 1849. The trustees of the Cairo Trust Property have loaned valuable materials now under their custody, as have Mr. W. T. Norton and Mr. J. True Dodge of Alton, Mr. Judson Phillips of Jonesboro, and Mrs. James W. Patton of Springfield.

In the accomplishment of this essay in historical writing, I have been aided by the facilities offered by the Centennial Commission. Mrs. Jessie Palmer Weber of the Illinois State Historical Library and Miss Caroline M. McIlvaine of the Chicago Historical Society have been exceedingly helpful in many ways. I am especially indebted to those who have served me in the capacity of assistants: Mr. Jacob Hofto, Miss Jessie J. Kile, Miss Jeannette Saunders, and Miss Agnes Wright. The usual editorial acknowledgments are due to my chief, Clarence W. Alvord.

ARTHUR CHARLES COLE.

URBANA, *July 1, 1918.*

THE ERA OF THE CIVIL WAR
1848-1870

I. THE PASSING OF THE FRONTIER

THE year 1848 marks the beginning of a new epoch in Illinois history. Not only had the polity of the commonwealth found it necessary to lay aside its swaddling clothes for a new constitution, but its citizens began to move forward in strides that rendered obsolete existing institutions and prevailing methods in almost every phase of the life of the times. Agriculture was revolutionized in many of its aspects; urban life discarded more and more of the traces of the frontier; the prairies were filled up by a progressive population which flowed in from every corner of the new and the old world; industry developed into new and untried fields; and the state came to take a front rank among Mississippi valley commonwealths. The way was prepared for the leading rôle Illinois was to play in bearing the burdens of the union in the storm and stress of civil war.

The outstanding feature of life in Illinois during the fifties was the passing of the frontier. Every aspect of its social and economic make-up declared that the spirit of western pioneering could not perpetuate its dominance over the growing commonwealth. Every stroke of a hammer, every rattle of a farm machine, every puff of a locomotive, was a blow at the peace and calm of the untamed prairie wilderness, still the haunt of the rabbit, the deer, and even the wolves—a taunt to the slow and inefficient man power of the primitive first settlers.

The upbuilding of towns and cities was one of the strongest indications of the rapid development of the state. Illinois of 1850 boasted only ten incorporated cities: Chicago, Alton, Springfield, Beardstown, Pekin, Quincy, Peoria, Bloomington, Galena, and Rock Island. Inasmuch, however, as several of these had been insignificant hamlets in 1840, this represented a remarkable development toward a more highly civilized commonwealth. There were in addition, moreover, towns of from three to five thousand inhabitants in places to which ten years before not so much as a trail had led.[1] It was noted that the growth of towns and villages seemed to run parallel with the growth of grain; cities grew up only at points of special vantage for the penetration of interior districts by incoming settlers and for the ready exchange of farm products for the finished output of the factory and workshop. For this reason the river towns of the forties had swelled into thriving cities, their life supplied by the sonorous breathing of steam engines; and a business formerly confined to the barter of hazelnuts, butter, and eggs, for buttons, beads, cap ribbons, powder, and shot, was replaced by a business of thousands of dollars in merchandise and produce.[2] For this reason, too, the network of railroads that came to traverse the states developed the municipalities in the fifties; while the smaller communities were receiving new accretions by the hundreds, Chicago increased from a city of 29,963 in 1850, to 80,028 in 1855, and 109,260 in 1860.

Rapid accumulation of population prevented the municipal improvements that might well have been expected of places of such size, for in most senses the cities and towns were mere overgrown villages. Housing facilities could not keep pace with such rapid growth; dwellings were small and crude, often mere shacks. Bloomington erected over 250 new dwellings in 1850, and a scarcity was still noted, while newcomers to Springfield, after looking in vain for some place of residence, passed on in hopes of finding a more favorable location.[3] Home-owning was fairly general among the older townspeople; but rents for the newcomers were uniformly high, sometimes exorbitant. There was a steady shortage of dwellings in Alton, and houses were "worth from fifteen to twenty per cent. per annum on their cost."[4] In Chicago houses that cost $500 sometimes rented for $300 and $400 a year; "a moderate little tenement which might be got in the suburbs of

[1] *Chicago Daily Journal* clipped in *Illinois State Register*, June 22, 1850.
[2] *Naples Observer* clipped in *Belleville Advocate*, September 12, 1850.
[3] *Illinois Journal*, May 18, 20, 23, 1850.
[4] *Alton Courier*, February 7, 1854; see also September 27, 1852, March 9, 1853, March 20, 1854.

London for £25 per annum here fetches £200," reported a visiting Britisher.[6]

Alongside these conditions, however, were others which showed how hard it was for Illinois to outgrow entirely the frontier atmosphere that had shortly before prevailed in most parts of the state. The backwoods pioneer was not wholly out of his element in the cities, still less in the towns and villages. Even the editor of the *Charleston Courier* protested at the "enormous rent" he had to pay for his newspaper plant, $60 a year. At the same time the sturdy shoemaker at Morris had high hopes of establishing his economic prosperity on a capital of $50; he proposed to build a "small house 12 by 12 middling lumber nails, doors, windows, $12.00 put up by a few neighbors gratis. $25.00 for stock in my line of business which is shoemaking and the Ballance as a reserve and i am certain of doing well." Both men applied to the governor of the state for the necessary loans, the one as a political backer, the other as a stranger whose only security was "the word of a man of honor," and who submitted as a text Raleigh's lines, "True nobleness is not confined to palaces alone."[6] It is to be hoped that Governor French was able to justify their confidence — the sublime confidence of the pioneer in the spirit of democratic coöperation.

No town or city was sufficiently urban to develop a drainage system. In bad weather the streets approached the condition of a quagmire with dangerous sink holes where the boatman's phrase "no bottom" furnished the only description. An absence of civic pride made them the dumping ground of the community rubbish so that the gutters were filled with manure, discarded clothing, and all kinds of trash, threatening the public health with their noxious effluvia.[7]

In Chicago the drains in the streets, the alleys, and the

[5] *Chicago Weekly Democrat*, April 7, 1855. Special correspondence of *London Times* clipped in *Chicago Tribune*, November 12, 1860; see also *Chicago Press and Tribune*, April 2, 1859. Missionary effort in the west was discouraged by rents of $200 or $300 for houses that would bring only $60 in the east. *Presbytery Reporter*, 4: 74.
[6] J. J. Brown to French, April 3, 1849; James Campbell to French, July, 1851, French manuscripts.
[7] The square at Springfield always seemed in a disgusting condition. *Illinois State Register*, March 17, 24, 1853; *Illinois Journal*, September 13, 1853.

vacant lots were "reeking with every description of filth;" "all the slops of the houses, and the filth of every kind whatsoever, incident to cities, are emptied in the gutters, and offend the nostrils of every traveler, either on the sidewalks or the streets," complained a zealous advocate of clean streets. Michigan avenue was decorated with manure heaps while the contents of stables and pigsties were deposited upon the lake shore, a horrible stench arising from that "Gehenna of abominations." The rain washed this filth into the lake to be mixed with the drinking water supply of the city, for nothing short of frogs or fish seemed to clog the supply pipes of the city water system. The zealous apostle of cleanliness was often served with "chowder" in his bathtub. Some improvement was made in the later years of the decade; paving with planks, macadam, or cobblestones reduced the problems, although only a few dozen miles were paved out of the four hundred miles of city streets.[8]

Then, too, every city had its hog nuisance or some equivalent. The streets, squares, and parks seemed public hogpens; hog holes with all their filth met the eye and nose at every turn. Springfield wrestled with this problem long and earnestly; the controversy came to a climax in 1853, when an ordinance allowing the hogs to run at large was successively passed and repealed, followed by the requirement that they be rung if allowed to run at large. The city council was equally divided over this question and the mayor pursued a vacillating course in casting the deciding vote; while the hog and anti-hogite forces wrangled, his swineship contentedly pulled himself out of the mushy batter of his gutter-wallow, threatening to upset pedestrians as he carefully chose a freshly painted fence against which to plant himself and transfer the unctious matter with which he was loaded. In the fall of that year swine were more numerous on the streets of Springfield than in the pens of the state fairgrounds. Urbana had a record of more hogs in the community than people, and the porker had equal rights with citizens upon the streets. Decatur's anti-

[8] *Chicago Democrat*, March 30, May 7, 1849, August 7, 1851; *Free West*, June 22, 1854; *Chicago Press and Tribune*, October 8, 1858, March 25, April 2, 1859.

hogite forces triumphed by a narrow margin in 1859. For a time cows ran at large on the streets of Chicago, often passing the night on the sidewalks. Quincy prided itself on the use of geese instead of hogs as street scavengers.[9]

At the beginning of the decade not one of the cities of the state was provided with public utilities. Chicago almost immediately, however, arranged to have its streets lighted by gas and shortly afterwards provided itself with a sewerage system and a water system, though the latter was far from carrying out the original plan to supply the city with pure and wholesome water. Pekin and Rockton prepared to install a water system in 1853, while Quincy and Peoria put their energies into gas companies. Not until two years later were Springfield and Quincy able to arrange for water systems; by that time gas, light, and coke companies were organized in all the more progressive cities. Soon primitive wooden mains were installed and the decade brought to Illinois the beginnings of the so-called "modern conveniences."[10]

Chicago, the "garden city," became in this period a cosmopolitan metropolis, the commercial emporium of the Lake Michigan region and the adjacent states. The foreign born population came to outnumber the native born, with a considerable representation for every national group. After the completion of the Illinois and Michigan canal the current of trade which formerly flowed down the Mississippi was turned eastward, making Chicago the great market place of the west to the disadvantage of St. Louis which had previously dominated the situation. Excellent and extensive railroad connections next brought additional advantages; in 1854 seventy-four trains a day tapped the upper Mississippi and the whole northwest. By 1851 the total value of the trade of the lake port reached nearly $30,000,000; in 1855 it had a grain trade of 20,487,953 bushels, nearly twice that of its rival on the Mississippi. It had already become the greatest primary wheat depot in the world; in spite of a chronic com-

[9] *Illinois State Register*, May 5, 12, June 30, 1853; *Illinois Journal*, May 12, September 7, November 9, 1853; *Urbana Union*, September 27, 1855; *Chicago Democrat*, September 19, 1849; *Quincy Whig*, August 15, 1853; June 26, 1854.
[10] *Quincy Whig*, August 15, 1853, June 26, 1854; *Private Laws of 1853*, p. 417-422, 504-505, 510-511, 516-517; *Private Laws of 1855*, p. 544 ff.

plaint of a shortage of capital, by 1860 over five million dollars of capital were invested in Chicago.[11]

This precocious western city presented many incongruities. In 1850 it had several impressive public edifices, "large warehouses and stores, five or six stories high, splendid hotels, five public schools and dwellings, frequently magnificent churches;"[12] ten years later it had taken on even more metropolitan atmosphere. Yet at the same time these massive stone and brick stores, warehouses, and factories, even "palatial" hotels, were surrounded by wooden huts and shanties. Rough stumps of pine trees were set along the roads in all directions to carry telegraphic wires. On the occasion of the visit of the Prince of Wales in 1860, the *London Times* correspondent reported that Chicago was an "extraordinary *mélange* of the Broadway of New York and little shanties of Parisian buildings mixed up in some way with backwoods life."[13] The streets, though filthy, were generally broad and pleasant; and a commendable zeal for planting rows of shade trees furnished the beginnings of city beautification. An extensive park system was planned and given authorization by the state legislature. Regular omnibus service was started on the principal thoroughfares in 1850, while the State street horse railroad was opened in April, 1859. The community supported seven daily papers in 1853, besides weeklies and monthlies. With the westward march of the American people, Chicago came to have a central location; equipped with fifty-seven hotels in 1855, eight of which were "first class," it had come to be a point of attraction as a convention city.[14]

Springfield, the state capital, a city of 4,533 in 1850 and of 9,320 in 1860, was a place of few attractions. It had little civic beauty, was famous for the wretched condition of its streets, and for a long time lacked a single good hotel. Citi-

[11] *DeBow's Review*, 15:374; *Chicago Daily Democratic Press*, January 7, 1856; *Illinois State Register*, December 21, 1854.
[12] *DeBow's Review*, 15:374. It was called "the city of churches;" it laid claim to having more free public schools than any city of its size in the world. *Chicago Democrat*, May 4, June 5, 1849.
[13] *Chicago Tribune*, November 12, 1860.
[14] *Chicago Press and Tribune*, March 5, April 2, 1859; *Chicago Democrat*, April 21, 1855.

zens talked of a waterworks system during the entire decade without accomplishing anything; nor did it acquire any other public utilities. It was amazingly slow in starting a system of public schools. Yet it had all the optimism of the day; lots on the public square sold as high as $100 a foot and farming property on the outskirts was worth up to $100 an acre; its citizens always vigorously opposed the numerous proposals from rival cities to move the state capital to a more suitable point.[15]

Alton, an important port on the Mississippi, struck out aggressively for a railroad connection with Chicago and for a cross-state line to Terre Haute; these brought so important a westbound traffic to the city that, with the rush of settlement to Kansas, a direct steamship line to that territory was established which, as the easiest route, gave the city many of the economic advantages that St. Louis had previously secured from this movement. Peoria was a beautiful young city in 1860 with an important commerce sustained by a tributary agricultural region of unsurpassed fertility and first-rate facilities for manufacturing.[16] In the decade it had passed Galena, to become, with a population of 14,045, the second largest city in the state.

Cairo was in this period Illinois' great city of prophecy, the speculation of a company of eastern capitalists. Situated at "the most important confluence of rivers in the world" and at the center of the American republic, at the southern terminus of the Illinois Central, it was expected — as the *entrepôt* between the northern and southern markets — to dominate commercially the Ohio, Wabash, Tennessee, and Cumberland valleys as well as the great northwest, becoming, as a great inland emporium, the largest city in the world. In 1850, however, it was an embryo city of 242 inhabitants, living largely in wharf boats and small temporary shanties, waiting for the marshy bottom lands to be reclaimed from the over-

---
[15] *Illinois State Journal*, February 28, 1861; *Illinois State Register*, August 25, September 1, 8, 1853. The only change they ever would concede was that the name "Sangamo" or "Illini" was more suitable than Springfield for the state capital.
[16] *Presbytery Reporter*, 3:247; *Western Journal*, 1:113-114, 2:267 ff; *Chicago Daily Democratic Press*, July 12, 1855.

flow of the rivers.[17] With the beginning of active work on the Illinois Central, rapid developments took place, so that by 1860 the city had an enthusiastic population of 2,188, with the neighboring towns of Mound City and Emporium competing for a share of the expected prosperity.

Some of the more important centers of that period were places which after a few decades ceased to find favor with Dame Fortune. In 1860 Quincy was a bustling river port of 13,718 which prided itself on its gas plant and other civic improvements. Belleville, "a firm city of brick," with half a dozen breweries, was a prosperous community of 7,520, famous throughout the west for its lager beer. It sold great quantities of dry goods, hardware, and groceries to the Illinois back country; its place with reference to St. Louis corresponded to that of East St. Louis of today, then the insignificant village of Illinoistown.[18] Beardstown, thriving on the transportation facilities furnished by the Illinois and Michigan canal, was an important market for grain and provisions, but won its right to public attention chiefly through the busy scenes at its hogpens and slaughterhouses. Peru was for a time the successful competitor of its near neighbor, La Salle, for the benefits of the termination of the canal. Separated by only a half-mile, connected by river steamers with St. Louis and by the Illinois Central with Chicago and Galena, and crossed by the Rock Island and Chicago route, the two places promised to furnish the location for an important trade emporium. The spokesman of the sister town of Ottawa was compelled to admit that there was "more enterprise in a half dozen men in Peru than in the whole of Ottawa put together." The latter, however, soon began a rapid development so that real estate boomed and farms two or three miles out sold for from fifty to one hundred and fifty dollars an acre.[19]

These cities and towns were the focusing points of a population of 851,470 that had by 1850 found homes in the midwest commonwealth. The state had already given proof of

[17] *DeBow's Review*, 19: 683; *Illinois Organ*, April 26, 1851; *Chicago Daily Journal*, June 10, 1851.
[18] *Belleville Advocate*, February 22, 1849, March 2, May 4, 1859.
[19] *Ottawa Free Trader*, November 30, 1850, May 13, 1854; *Beardstown Gazette*, April 30, 1851.

having attained its majority by showing a natural increase of a native born population of 333,753. This generation which had played no direct part in the westward march of the pioneer bade fair to outgrow the ideas and ideals of their sires. Already names of native Illinoisians began to appear on the roll of the houses of the general assembly,[20] although as candidates for important offices they were still rare.

Another decade during which the population of the state increased to 1,711,951 was to work important consequences in obliterating the more important frontier survivals. So rapid, indeed, did the forces of progress move in Illinois that the growing sophistication drove out the restless pioneering spirits to the frontier regions of the far west. In the period after 1848, they contributed largely to the development of California, Kansas and Nebraska, and Colorado. With the discovery of gold in California the "gold fever" attacked Illinoisians; "Ho, for California!" became the rallying cry everywhere. In the winter of 1848-1849 companies began to form at various points ready to move west in the spring.[21] These companies, organized under strict regulations which excluded all but persons of industry and good reputation, usually elected a captain, lieutenants, sergeant, and wagon master and hired a guide to conduct them on the Overland trail. Stout wagons were procured, drawn by horses, a double team of mules, or three or four yoke of oxen. At first the young men were the victims of the California fever, then the infection spread to the older generation—for the romance of the gold fields made a wide appeal. In certain districts about Quincy, by February, 1849, a majority of the males were making preparations to leave. Prosperous farmers and settled artisans joined the restless youths; 10,000 to 15,000 were scheduled to leave that year. Illinois seemed the banner state in its contribution of "forty-niners;" a majority of the wagons on the Overland seemed to hail from Illinois. Plans for a company of fifty or sixty were made in Alton in January; by March one hundred and twenty selected emigrants took

[20] *Alton Courier*, March 11, 1853.
[21] *Illinois Journal*, December 20, 1848; *Quincy Whig*, December 26, 1848; *Beardstown Gazette*, December 27, 1848; *Illinois Globe*, January 6, 1849; *Chicago Democrat*, January 9, 1849.

the trail as the "Sucker Mining Company." Companies from Springfield, Jacksonville, and other points in western Illinois were soon off in parties of fifty, one hundred, or more. Many small groups left without flourish or display; on the trail they seemed to outnumber the organized companies. "Every wagon is apparently an independent nation of itself — every emigrant a captain," reported an enthusiastic emigrant.[22]

The progress of the emigrants on the trail was reported by the newspapers and aroused new interest. Finally, in 1850, however, as a result of editorial warnings, of discouraging letters from unsuccessful adventurers, and of the complaints of "California widows," a dismal picture of life in California replaced the glittering mirage; and contentment with prevailing conditions was restored in Illinois. The beginning of 1852 saw a serious recurrence of the California fever, but after another season of heavy migration the movement to California was gradually restored to a normal basis.[23]

No sooner had the gold fever subsided, however, than another diversion came when the fertile fields of Kansas and Nebraska were thrown open to settlement in the spring of 1854. An important movement had already begun the previous year; but now old rangers prepared in companies to go west to establish land claims in the new territory.[24] The genuine hard-fisted yeomanry of the older portions of southern and eastern Illinois yielded to the temptingly high prices offered for their own farms and transferred their families to the new pioneer field. The attention of the land speculator was also attracted to the new opportunities for investment.

A different incentive, however, soon came to dominate this emigration; in the fight between the north and the south for the control of the new territory under squatter sovereignty

[22] *Quincy Whig*, February 6, 1849; *Illinois State Register*, May 31, 1849; *Alton Telegraph*, March 23, 1849.
[23] *Illinois Journal*, October 17, 1849, February 8, 1850; *Illinois Globe*, December 22, 1849; *Ottawa Free Trader*, March 16, 1850, January 31, 1852; *Alton Telegraph*, March 22, 1850; *Beardstown Gazette*, February 11, 1852; *Quincy Whig*, March 16, April 26, 1852. The *La Salle Standard* reported the passage of at least a hundred wagons a day with three to five persons each. Five to twenty-five persons passed through Peru daily.
[24] *Chicago Weekly Democrat*, November 26, 1853; *Urbana Union*, March 23, 1854; *Illinois Journal*, April 13, 1854; *St. Clair Tribune*, April 22, May 13, June 3, 1854; *Belleville Advocate*, June 14, 1854.

the people of Illinois began to take a hand to preserve Kansas from the institution of slavery. An advance guard of one hundred and fifty New Englanders sent out by the Emigrant Aid Society had passed through Illinois en route for Kansas in July and aroused considerable attention;[25] when other companies followed, alongside the pioneer who sought the more fertile prairies of the west and alongside the restless adventurer, there marched from the sober homes of the northern counties, from the rich Military Tract, the garden of Illinois, the sturdy pilgrim who proposed to plant and water the seeds of freedom in that fresh soil.

In the beginning no special encouragement to emigrants was necessary; emigrant wagons passed through the state with the letters "Kansas" and "Nebraska" boldly chalked on their canvas coverings. The first mission from Illinois went from Quincy; a "Nebraska Colonization Company" was organized in that neighborhood in March, 1855, to found a city named Fontenelle, in which the moral and intellectual atmosphere of a free community should be preserved in a literary society and other institutions. But when blood began to flow upon the soil of Kansas, the more timid held back. Then companies of young free-state men were organized and conducted to the field of "bleeding Kansas," prepared, with Sharpe's rifles in their hands and the plow and sickle among the baggage, for either peace or war.[26] Following them whole communities were aroused to take part in these ventures; the material means to transfer these companies to Kansas were collected in the spring of 1856 by Emigrant Aid or Kansas Settlers' societies in Chicago, Rockford, and other towns.

Excitement began to quicken when, in spite of their military preparations, the Chicago company was held up by a superior force of Missourians, disarmed, and sent back to Alton under guard; while the outrage fanned the zeal for aiding Kansas sufferers, the company was again fitted out and sent to Kansas by a safer route.[27]

[25] *Alton Weekly Courier*, July 27, 1854.
[26] *Rockford Register*, February 23, March 8, 1856; *Rockford Republican*, March 5, 1856; *Chicago Weekly Democrat*, March 31, December 22, 1855.
[27] *Chicago Weekly Democrat*, July 12, 19, 1856; affidavit of Charles H. Wood, August 1, 1856, Trumbull manuscripts.

A state Kansas aid committee was created in Illinois to dispense relief, and local committees were organized and set to work. Upon the arrival of the news of the destruction of Lawrence, the free-state stronghold in Kansas, a meeting was held at Rockford at which $1,000 was easily raised as the nucleus of a fund to represent that community. At the same time a Chicago meeting raised $15,000 to aid persons willing to go to Kansas as actual settlers. Not to be outdone, the ladies of Chicago organized a "Kansas Women's Aid and Liberty Association," with active auxiliaries in the important towns and villages of northern Illinois, and sewing societies worked for the relief of their distressed sisters in Kansas.[28]

Enthusiasm thus aroused caused a general revival of unassisted emigration in the spring of 1857.[29] Thus did a state which a few years before had been the El Dorado of agricultural pioneers, give up a part of her settlers and their descendants to fill up the still farther "great west."

In the closing year of this decade, the rumor of the discovery of gold again reached Illinois, and the lure of the gold fields aroused the spirit of adventure in the manhood of Illinois. Soon the old scenes of 1849 were renewed; a rush to Pike's Peak attracted companies of young men from all sections of the state, usually in smaller groups than in the California gold rush. Thousands left for the gold fields and many others had completed preparations before the news came in May that the gold hunters were returning in droves with the cry of "humbug."[30]

The place of these citizens lost by Illinois to the trans-Mississippi west had been more than filled by a great influx from without which was still bringing in a great diversity of population. There was the Yankee stock from the rugged

---

[28] *Rockford Republican*, May 28, 1856; Peter Page to Trumbull, June 3, 1856, Trumbull manuscripts; *Chicago Weekly Democrat*, June 21, 28, 1856.
[29] *Rockford Republican*, February 26, 1857; *Aurora Beacon*, March 9, 1857; *Illinois State Journal*, April 1, 1857; *Chicago Daily Democratic Press*, June 5, 1857.
[30] *Quincy Whig*, January 28, March 19, 1859; *Ottawa Free Trader*, April 2, 1859; *Chicago Press and Tribune*, March 28, 1859; *Rockford Register*, May 14, 1859; *Ottawa Weekly Republican*, May 14, 1859; *Alton Courier*, May 19, 1859.

farms of New England, enterprising fortune seekers from the seaboard states as a whole, and, coming from the old world at the same time, the restless, ambitious, and freedom-loving refugees from the political and economic oppression of the European states—all destined to do their part in the development of the hospitable prairie commonwealth and by the diversity of the cultures they introduced to hasten the passing of the frontier.

Of the American born immigrants it was in large measure the northern elements that made up the westward movement. The Yankee immigrants found a special welcome because of their "good old New England character for thrift, morality, and intelligence;" furthermore they usually brought enough means to purchase improved farms, thus freeing the true pioneer to exploit other pieces of the prairie wilderness.[31] The Yankees showed a strong tendency to migrate in parties or even in well-organized colonies, groups of from twenty to forty families being fairly common. In 1855 two hundred families came from the vicinity of Rutland, Vermont, under the auspices of the Vermont Emigrant Association and, on the lands opened up by the Illinois Central, established a new Rutland in La Salle county. New England groups first sought their kind and kin in the northern counties, but it was not long before they turned to the attractive fields of middle and southern Illinois. In those regions the colony grouping was even more marked. Near the junction of the Ohio and Mississippi with the Illinois Central was Hoyleton, a Yankee colony of Congregational temperance men and republicans; in their zeal for education they included in their plans the scheme of erecting a seminary of learning.[32]

In Egypt, Yankee enterprise, industry, and frugality were welcomed, for they promised to bring about the development of the enormous wealth that lay latent and unused in south-

[31] *Illinois Journal*, May 19, 1853; *Carthage Republican*, clipped in *Chicago Daily Democratic Press*, November 24, 1855; *Belleville Advocate*, November 26, 1856; *Cairo Gazette*, April 29, 1859; *Rock River Democrat*, April 28, 1857; *Alton Courier*, February 4, 1854.
[32] *Ottawa Free Trader*, May 2, 1857; *Rockford Republican*, May 7, 1857; *St. Clair Tribune*, May 22, 1857; *Chicago Daily Democratic Press*, July 18, 1855; *Cairo City Times*, July 25, 1855; Ovid Miner to Trumbull, May 31, 1860, Trumbull manuscripts; *Central Illinois Gazette*, June 8, 1859.

ern Illinois. Many a local poet paid tribute to this vast transforming force:

> "And westward ho! on either side,
> See towns as if by magic rise;
> What Genii then the wonder works?
> Why, none — but Yankee enterprise." [33]

Both the Egyptian and the New England pilgrim, however, realized the absence of congeniality in their interests; the one frankly voiced his execration of "Yankee 'kinks' in politics," while the other deplored the survival of "intemperance accompanied with ignorance and indolence" that dated from the earlier settlers from the south.[34] "One thing is certain," declared a new arrival, "that where New England emigrants do not venture, improvements, social, agricultural, mechanic, or scientific, rarely flourish, and seldom intrude."

New Yorkers, Pennsylvanians, Ohioans, and even Hoosiers also came to play an important part in the settlement of central and southern Illinois. First, the Wabash valley, claimed by boosters to be the garden of America, was the region of attraction; wagons crossed the river at Terre Haute almost as fast as the ferryboats could carry them. With the opening up of railroad communication, however, settlers spread over the entire lower half of the state, which the best classes of immigrants previously passed by. Two hundred Pennsylvanians came in a group to settle in Adams county near Mendon. Joseph and M. L. Sullivant, wealthy land owners of Columbus, Ohio, purchased many thousand acres of Illinois prairie and sent out several well-equipped parties

---

[33] *Belleville Advocate*, February 8, 1849. The Yankee bard paid his respects to the attractions of Illinois in the *Boston Post*:

> "Westward the ☆ of Empire takes its Course."
> Come, leave the fields of childhood,
> Worn out by long employ,
> And travel west and settle
> In the state of Illinois:—
> Your family is growing up,
> Your boys you must employ.
> Come, till the rich prairies
> In the state of Illinois.

Clipped in *Belleville Advocate*, April 25, 1850.

[34] *Cairo City Times*, July 25, 1855; unsigned letter to Trumbull, January 11, 1858, Trumbull manuscripts; see also *Western Citizen*, August 3, 1852.

PASSING OF THE FRONTIER 15

of industrious farmers and mechanics to develop them; ex-Governor William Bebb of Ohio bought an extensive tract in Winnebago county.[35] These and similar ventures testified to a new era in Illinois settlement, when the advanced stages of the frontier had been pushed well across the Mississippi.

A novel feature of the immigration movement was the assisted migration of women and children. Missionary societies in cities like Springfield and Danville sent agents to the east to select worthy orphans to place in Illinois homes; groups of twenty-five to fifty were brought west and distributed among the farmers, to whom they were indentured until they became of age. It is evident that the problem of labor supply entered into this charity, and such an element is even more apparent in the scheme to secure for the west the surplus female population of eastern cities. In 1858 the agents of Women's Protective Immigration societies in New York and Philadelphia placed groups of fifty as servants in each of the towns of Decatur, Springfield, and Urbana.[36]

Only a slight immigration entered Illinois from the southern states. North Carolina made some contributions, while Virginia, Tennessee, and Kentucky sent many settlers across the Ohio; but they were outnumbered even in Egypt by northern born settlers. These new southern immigrants were superior to the old stock; they seemed "a better class, accustomed to think & act for themselves."[37]

The distracted state of affairs in Europe, with economic oppression increasingly unbearable and with liberal and revolutionary forces crushed under the iron heel of reactionary authority, promoted a spirit of restlessness that made the thoughtful, sober-minded workers

"Turn from the old world their anxious eyes, ·
To seek a home beneath the western skies."[38]

[35] *Illinois Organ*, June 28, 1851; *Terre Haute Journal* clipped in *Illinois State Register*, October 11, 1849; *Chicago Daily Democratic Press*, March 6, 1855, April 18, 1857; *Belleville Advocate*, July 18, 1855.
[36] *Illinois Journal*, August 4, 1855; *Illinois State Journal*, January 13, March 17, 24, 1858; *Urbana Union*, February 21, 1856, March 18, 1858; *Aurora Beacon*, April 20, 1857; *Belleville Democrat*, April 17, 1858; *Belleville Advocate*, November 20, 1857; *Our Constitution*, March 13, April 3, 1858.
[37] Edward Holden to Trumbull, March 9, 1858, Trumbull manuscripts.
[38] *Chicago Daily Journal* clipped in *Illinois State Register*, July 5, 1849.

Crowded cities of the old world poured forth a mighty stream of immigrants, whom Illinois received with enthusiastic welcome. With almost every national element already represented in the population of the state, Illinois offered the bewildered immigrant a hospitable asylum among friendly fellow-countrymen. The hardy workmen found places on the vast system of public works just being undertaken; to the more prosperous newcomers were offered the fertile farms of the state.[39]

Of the European nations, Germany and Ireland made the largest contributions to Illinois; in 1860 there were in the state 130,804 Germans and 87,573 Irish. Illinois drew so large a quota of the immigrants from all countries that even before 1850 it could boast of 111,860 foreign born settlers, or one-eighth of the total population of the state; by 1860 their number had nearly tripled, reaching a total of 324,643. Chicago, rapidly becoming an important immigration depot, retained so large a number of the new arrivals that the foreign born population of the city actually outnumbered the natives.

For a considerable period Illinoisians seem to have been unaware of the size of this foreign element. In January, 1854, however, the ice in the Mississippi held up fourteen steamers loaded with two thousand German and Irish immigrants, who, landed near Cairo and suffering greatly from cold, want of food, fever, and cholera, drew attention to the fact of the heavy foreign immigration. It became evident that the German and Irish emigrant societies of St. Louis who aided in the relief work had no effective Illinois counterpart, although a few local German societies had their agents on the ground. It became widely published, also, that of the emigrants landing at New York in 1856 seven per cent went to Illinois, but they brought with them over fourteen per cent of the "cash means" listed with the immigration authorities. Inducements to foreign immigrants to come to Illinois were therefore urged; a proper immigration system at Chicago was especially favored.[40]

[39] *Belleville Advocate*, May 1, 1851.
[40] *Chicago Daily Democratic Press*, January 24, 1854; *Illinois State Register*, January 26, 1854; *Peru Daily Chronicle*, February 1, 1854; *Rockford Register*, February 7, 1857; *St. Clair Tribune*, February 13, 20, 1857; *Illinois State Journal*, January 12, 19, 1859; *Chicago Democrat*, July 24, 1857.

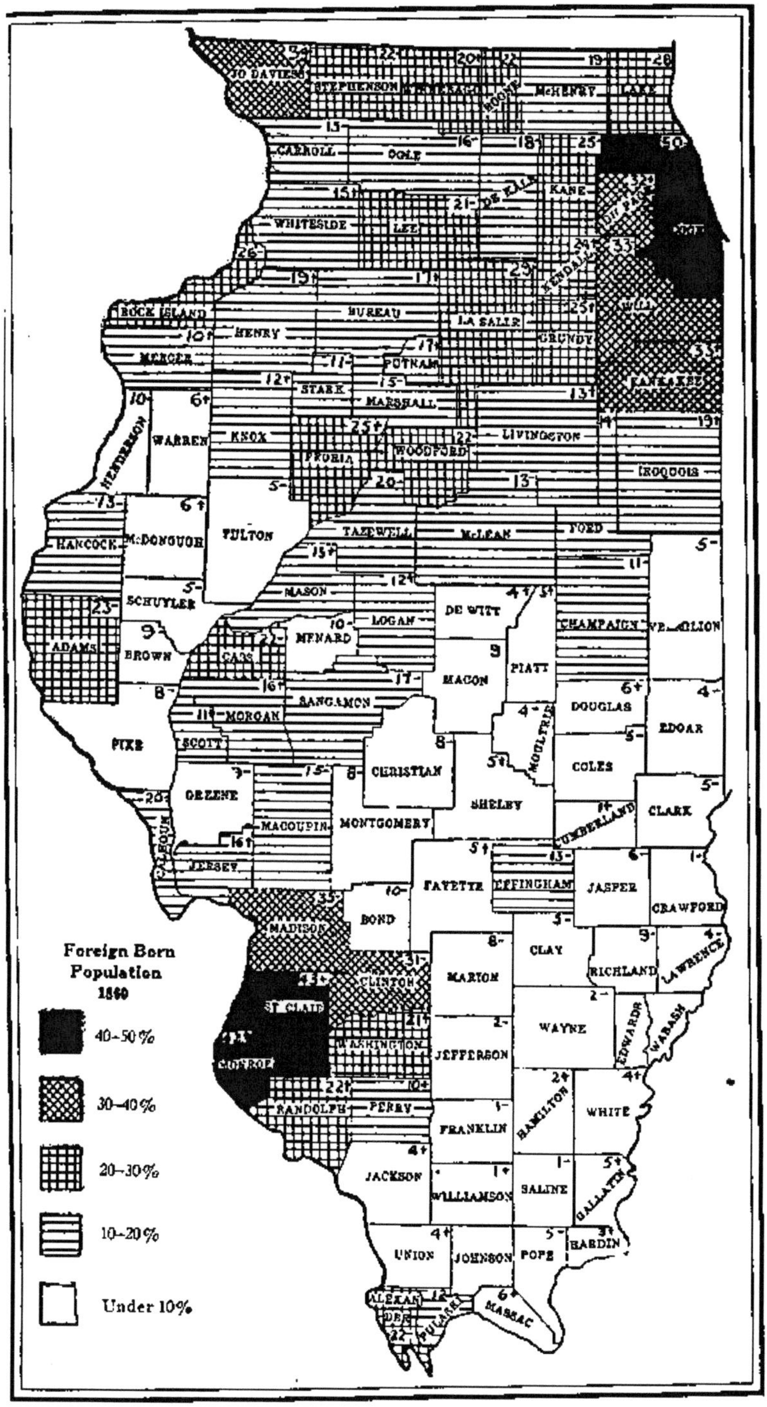
Foreign Born
Population
1860
40–50%
30–40%
20–30%
10–20%
Under 10%
JO DAVIESS
STEPHENSON
BOONE
McHENRY
LAKE
CARROLL
OGLE
KANE
WHITESIDE
LEE
KENDALL
ROCK ISLAND
BUREAU
LA SALLE
GRUNDY
WILL
HENRY
MERCER
PUTNAM
STARK
MARSHALL
KANKAKEE
HENDERSON
WARREN
KNOX
PEORIA
WOODFORD
LIVINGSTON
IROQUOIS
HANCOCK
FULTON
TAZEWELL
McLEAN
FORD
MASON
SCHUYLER
ADAMS
BROWN
CASS
MENARD
LOGAN
DE WITT
CHAMPAIGN
MACON
PIATT
SANGAMON
MORGAN
SCOTT
PIKE
DOUGLAS
EDGAR
CHRISTIAN
COLES
GREENE
SHELBY
MACOUPIN
MONTGOMERY
CLARK
CUMBERLAND
JERSEY
FAYETTE
EFFINGHAM
JASPER
CRAWFORD
BOND
MADISON
CLAY
RICHLAND
LAWRENCE
CLINTON
MARION
ST CLAIR
MONROE
WASHINGTON
WAYNE
JEFFERSON
EDWARDS
WABASH
RANDOLPH
PERRY
FRANKLIN
HAMILTON
WHITE
JACKSON
WILLIAMSON
SALINE
GALLATIN
UNION
JOHNSON
POPE
HARDIN
PULASKI
MASSAC

A considerable accession of French and French Canadian settlers was made during the fifties. The sons and daughters of *la belle France* increased so rapidly in Chicago that just when the influence of the old régime had about disappeared they became numerous enough to erect a church of their own where services were performed in their own language. French confectionery establishments began to make their appearance and even a French hotel. Nearby was the strong French Canadian settlement at Kankakee. It had steadily grown with fresh additions from lower Canada, the emigration becoming so considerable that the Canadian government took alarm. In 1857 a French paper, the *Journal de L'Illinois*, started publication at Kankakee with a subscription list of 1,200 persons. Twelve miles up the Kankakee river, at St. Anne, a new settlement of French families from Montreal and Quebec was started in 1852 by Father Chiniquy, a Roman Catholic priest and temperance apostle of note, who acted as a spokesman of French Canadian discontent; by 1860 these two settlements included over 1,500 families. The settlement at St. Anne was then just recovering from a period of hard times and financial embarrassment. Father Chiniquy, moreover, had become involved in a long and bitter contest with the Catholic bishop of the Chicago diocese; as a result of his increasing impatience with hierarchical authority a majority of his parishoners withdrew from the Catholic church and in 1860 joined the Presbyterian or Baptist churches.[41] Father Chiniquy himself with 1,000 communicants from the French churches of St. Anne and Kankakee became a part of the Presbyterian organization, and thirty-six young men of his flock offered themselves as candidates for the ministry.

Other French settlements were scattered over the state. A company of Trappist monks, direct from France, located

[41] *Chicago Daily Journal*, November 13, 1850, June 18, 1851; *Illinois State Register*, March 9, 1849; *Quebec Gazette* clipped in *Gem of the Prairie*, December 23, 1848; *Joliet Signal*, November 11, 1851; *Belleville Advocate*, September 1, 1852; *Chicago Press and Tribune*, December 1, 1859, January 18, 1860; *Presbytery Reporter*, 5:126; *Canton Weekly Register*, September 18, 1860. Eight months after the establishment of the *Journal de L'Illinois*, it was transferred to Chicago. *Chicago Daily Democratic Press*, January 6, September 9, 1857.

near Beardstown in 1849, while Ottawa, already something of a French settlement, in 1859 welcomed the arrival of a large number of families of Waldenses from the Vaudois. Another Waldensian colony was established near Odell, in Livingston county, on the line of the Chicago and Alton railroad. At the same time a large body of French Canadians were assisted by wealthy French planters in Louisiana in establishing themselves at Tacusa on the Illinois Central to serve as a central depot for the deposit and distribution of the staples of Louisiana.[42]

Probably the most interesting French settlement in the state was the company of French communists who acquired the property of the Mormons at Nauvoo. In 1849, under the leadership of A. Charles Cabet, an Icarian colony established itself there; soon upon the fifteen acres of ground with its outlying farm 340 colonists were housed; the settlement, with the remodeled old Mormon temple as headquarters had excellent educational facilities, a good library, together with workshops, mills, and a store in St. Louis for the sale of their textile manufactures. The progress of the colony was chronicled in its official paper, the *Popular Tribune*, edited by M. Cabet; later a German and a French weekly paper were added.

So well did the experiment succeed at the start — with a net profit of $9,000 for the year 1852 — that it was arranged to make Nauvoo, as the parent colony, a place for the preparation of new colonists who would found similar establishments in Iowa and elsewhere. Soon, however, discussions arose over administrative matters, and the authority of Cabet was challenged by opponents who sought his overthrow; the opposition acquired a majority and deposed Cabet shortly before his death in November, 1856. In resisting the leadership of Cabet, the rebels insisted upon the failure of the colony so aggressively that in spite of a considerable degree of prosperity, they succeeded in convincing even themselves of the truth of their assertions. They claimed that Cabet with his wild theories had fleeced fifteen hundred victims; they, there-

[42] *Beardstown Gazette,* January 10, 1849; *Chicago Daily Democratic Press,* March 7, August 20, 1857; *Quincy Whig,* March 5, 1857.

fore, petitioned for the repeal of the act of incorporation and removed to St. Louis.[43] This brought the complete ruin of Icaria; the faithful remained at Nauvoo but without spirit; farming operations were abandoned, and the property became heavily mortgaged. In August, 1859, they disposed of some goods at a public sale to satisfy a debt of $10,000 and a month later realized $10,000 on the remaining properties. Thus out of a factional opposition to the authority of Cabet, an end came to this promising experiment in the realization of a nineteenth century communistic Utopia.

During this decade Illinois acquired two Portuguese settlements, one in north Springfield and one in the vicinity of Jacksonville. In each case they were Protestant Portuguese exiles from the island of Madeira; the first company of 200 arrived November 1, 1849, followed by groups of from 60 to 150, until each settlement numbered 500 persons. These exiles proved to be thrifty and industrious workers and rapidly attained material prosperity. They promptly built homes for themselves and the Springfield group established a Portuguese school and church where they zealously guarded the cultural atmosphere of their native land.[44]

So considerable an increase in the Scandinavian population was made during the fifties that by 1860 it numbered well over 10,000. The Norwegians located largely in and around Chicago. They began to arrive in numbers about 1848; a year later there were nearly 600 in Chicago and by 1853, a Norwegian paper, the *Banner of Freedom*, was started in that city. Toward the end of the decade the Norwegian population of Chicago was variously estimated at from two to twelve thousand, with three Norwegian churches in the city. Chicago acted as a great distributing station from which Norwegians were supplied to other regions of the state; Norse groups gathered at "Old Sangamon Town" and in the "Kincaid neighborhood" north of Athens. Most of them, however, hired out with the farmers, who were so well satisfied with their work that some sent money to Norway to contract

[43] *New York Tribune* clipped in *Chicago Daily Democratic Press*, November 18, 1852; *ibid.*, April 10, 1855, February 21, 1856, February 16, 1857.
[44] *Illinois Journal*, November 13, 14, 1849; May 1, 10, 1854; October 9, 1855.

in advance for further help.[45] In 1850 the chief Swedish settlements were in Chicago, Rockford, Galesburg and Victoria in Knox county, Bishop Hill and Andover in Henry county, Lafayette in Stark county, Berlin, later Swedona in Mercer county, and dispersed throughout these northern counties. Swedish churches were to be found in Rockford, Andover, and in Chicago with congregations in Moline, Galesburg, and in other communities. A newspaper printed in the Swedish language, the *Swedish Republican*, was published at Galva in Henry county for over a year, but was removed to Chicago in 1857.[46]

The Bishop Hill colony five miles west of Galva was a settlement made in 1846 by hardy pioneers who left their native land with their leader, Eric Janson, to secure a religious toleration denied to them at home. The original settlement of 400 increased to 700 or 800 by the end of 1850, although over a hundred were lost in 1849, the cholera year, when sixty persons died in one week; the migration continued until 1854 by which time 1,000 Swedish exiles had chosen to join this colony. Here was another interesting experiment in communism. With a tract of 12,000 acres large scale agriculture was successfully practiced; in 1860 the settlers raised 3,000 acres of broom corn, 2,000 acres of wheat and of corn, and 2,000 in mixed crops, besides a considerable acreage of hay and pasture. Besides the brick, leather products, and other materials needed for local consumption, they manufactured 5,000 dozens of brooms annually, and produced some famous table linens, towels, and other needlework articles from flax raised by the colony. The society attained its greatest economic prosperity in 1860, just before its dissolution and the repeal of its charter of incorporation. Its collapse was occasioned by internal dissension and a factionalism that in-

---

[45] *Chicago Democrat*, January 10, 1848, July 14, 15, 1852, August 15, 1859; *Chicago Daily Journal* clipped in *Illinois State Register*, August 9, 1848; *Chicago Press and Tribune*, September 4, 1858; Robert H. Clarkson to W. H. Swift, October 1, 1849, Swift manuscripts. Many Norwegians were inclined out of a sense of superiority to resent being confused with the Swedes, whose special susceptibility to "ship fever" or cholera on the ocean trip, they declared arose from a want of cleanliness and from an addiction to strong liquor.

[46] *Illinois State Register*, January 10, August 22, 1850; *Chicago Daily Democratic Press*, April 15, 1856.

creased until the community feature was abandoned in 1860 and 1861.[47]

The scattered English element in Illinois was promised an important accretion as a result of the building of the Illinois Central railroad. English capitalists interested in the Central first used every possible means to direct the attention of emigrants to the lands of the company; as a result in 1859 a large body of English farmers and mechanics began to settle in companies along that road south of Centralia; meanwhile the agents of the largest English stockholders elaborated a plan for making such settlement more attractive. A little later in the same year steps were taken in London toward the organization of the "Prairie Land and Emigration Company" with a capital of $2,500,000, the object of which was to purchase prairie land in Illinois and colonize it with English farmers.[48] Such inducements encouraged English emigrants until the Civil War began; by 1860 they had reached a total of 41,745.

The great works of internal improvement of the forties had brought vast hordes of brawny Irish to the Illinois prairies, many of whom took their place in the permanent population of the state. A Chicago Hibernian Benevolent Emigrant Society was organized in January, 1848, to encourage and assist immigrants seeking locations in the west. The railroad construction work of the fifties now offered employment to those still on the ground and attracted a new immigration, mainly of those unfortunates driven from home by the potato famine.[49] The Irish remained to a large extent a restless floating population, little attracted by agricultural opportunities, but looking primarily to the cities for the essence of real life; in 1860 they constituted four times as large an element of the population of Chicago as of the agricultural regions of Illinois.

[47] *Chicago Democrat*, August 2, 1850; *DeBow's Review*, 9:330; *Chicago Daily Journal* clipped in *Rockford Forum*, October 9, 1850; *Chicago Press and Tribune*, July 17, 1860; *Rockford Register*, November 24, 1860; *Private Laws of 1853*, p. 328-329; Kiner, *History of Henry County*, 638-645; Stoneberg, "The Bishop Hill Colony," *ibid.*; Mikkelson, *The Bishop Hill Colony*.

[48] *Belleville Advocate*, April 16, 1859; *Mound City Emporium*, May 12, 1859; *Our Constitution*, May 14, August 6, 1859; *Chicago Press and Tribune*, May 17, August 5, 1859.

[49] *Gem of the Prairie*, January 29, February 5, 1848; *Illinois State Register*, March 24, 1853.

There seemed to be two strains, sometimes combined in the same individuals, in the Irish population of the state. There were on the one hand the brilliant idealists who supported the cause of civil liberty and liberal institutions in all its forms and expressions, whether in the Irish struggle for independence or in the European contests for self-government. Their local and state Hibernian societies were important agencies for the expression of this high ideal as well as of the feeling of brotherhood among the Irish. Irish relief work was carried on, and men like Senator Shields held themselves in readiness to join in the redemption of their native land when the hour to strike should come.[50]

But to the people of Illinois the Irishman more often appeared in another guise. To them he was pictured as the noisy, quarrelsome seeker after excitement, who found it in the company of John Barleycorn, in bloody street brawls, and even in the lower depths of crime. When an overwhelming majority of the visitors at police court were repeatedly reported to be Irishmen, it was not surprising that the public should make such adverse deductions.[51] The common practice of contemporary journalists was reflected in the point raised by the *Chicago Tribune*, December 23, 1853: "Why do our police reports always average two representatives from 'Erin, the soft, green isle of the ocean,' to one from almost any other inhabitable land of the earth? . . . . Why are the instigators and ringleaders of our riots and tumults, in nine cases out of ten, Irishmen?" There followed the report of a riot at La Salle and of the murder of a contractor by a set of Irishmen. The *Tribune*, aroused to the point of approving action under lynch law, declared: "Had the whole thirty-two prisoners that were taken been marched out and shot on the spot, as the citizens did the Driskells in Ogle County, some years ago, the public judgment would have sanctioned it at once."

A more careful analysis, however, revealed a situation that scarcely warranted such a superficial judgment. The railroad contractors were often shrewd schemers and hard

[50] *Aurora Beacon*, September 14, 1848; *Illinois Journal*, January 22, 1849.
[51] *Chicago Democrat*, December 17, 1849.

men who sought to impose upon the ignorant Irish laborers and to direct matters to their own advantage. Palpably unfair treatment was almost certain to arouse the temper of the hot-headed Irishman. As it was, however, thousands quietly submitted to conditions upon the public works that brought death or ill health, "from exposure to miasmi, bad accommodation in camps and shanties, and from improper diet;" when sickness fell upon them they were discharged and turned loose upon the world.[52] It is to be remembered, moreover, that the Irishmen who drew the fire of public criticism were largely members of the sturdy band of humble toilers, brutalized by the religious and political oppression and economic exploitation of their native Ireland and, in this land of opportunity which they had so eagerly sought, deprived of contact with the finer forces.

The German "forty-eighters," the unsuccessful revolutionists of 1848, fled to America in a steady stream and were led to Illinois by Friedrich Hecker, the organizer of the revolt in Baden. Conditions continued favorable to a heavy emigration of refugees from the political and economic oppressions of the fatherland. The German population of Illinois in 1860 was 130,804, with Chicago, Belleville, Galena, Quincy, Alton, Peoria, and Peru as the chosen places of settlement. This influx was directed to Illinois by the guidebooks of John Mason Peck and similar works. Charles L. Fleischman, United States consul at Stuttgart, prepared in 1850 to write an emigrant's guidebook exclusively on Illinois, having previously written two general works.[53]

Early in 1854 a number of prominent Chicago business men enlisted their support in a movement in favor of a law to create the office of commissioner of emigration, whose principal duty it should be to travel through Germany for the purpose of directing the stream of German emigration to Illinois. The *Illinois Staats-Zeitung*, however, opposed the move as a sharp business transaction and a political maneuver in the interest of ambitious local politicians. Nothing developed along this line; instead, taking their cue from the Irish,

[52] *Illinois State Register*, December 22, 1853.
[53] Charles L. Fleischman to French, March 20, 1850, French manuscripts.

Chicago Germans organized a society for the protection of German immigrants arriving at that city and employed an agent to devote his time to the care of the new arrivals.[54] Similar societies were organized, as the need for them was felt, at other points of German settlement and carried on an important relief work.

In this period a new center of German culture was developing at Chicago. There the Teutonic immigrants created a set of social institutions in which the familiar atmosphere of the fatherland was transplanted. German Lutheran churches and parochial schools under Lutheran preachers — the only schoolmasters — had appeared at an early date to perpetuate their fundamental social traditions. Now the refinements which they had sorely missed in their new western home were enthusiastically added: a German theater which made brilliant the dramatic atmosphere of Chicago; an orchestra which built up a musical reputation for the city, and a Männerchor, in which the lusty "liedersingers" vied with each other in the attempt to produce a spirited ensemble. The German brass band, the German militia companies of black jäger rifles, of Washington rifles, of Washington grenadiers, and of Washington light cavalry were features of many a gay procession. A German Odd Fellow lodge fostered the fraternal spirit among these settlers in true American style. Meantime other German settlements actuated by the same cultural impulse were acquiring the same institutions and stimulating the spiritual development away from frontier conditions.

There was much of an atmosphere of revolutionary democracy in these German circles. The forty-eighters were full of the failure of their cause. Many were downhearted, but others looked upon their residence in the United States as a training for future revolutionary attempts. In 1852 they invited Dr. Gottfried Kinkel, the German revolutionist, to include different Illinois groups in his tour of the country to collect funds for the German revolutionary committee which they hoped would soon strike another blow. This erstwhile professor of history and literature at Bonn was welcomed at

[54] *Chicago Daily Democratic Press*, February 2, June 19, 1854, November 5, 1857; *Free West*, February 23, May 18, 1854.

Chicago and Belleville with elaborate orations, and generous contributions were made to his fund.[55]

The hopelessness of the revolutionary cause, however, caused the German population in general to settle down into more conservative channels. The Turnverein was introduced into Illinois in 1851 with a company at Peoria and Chicago; Belleville and Springfield soon had their own German gymnastic companies. The Northwestern Turnerbund held its annual meeting in 1858 at Belleville, and in the following year the United States *Turner* organization met in convention as the guests of the Chicago society. The social democratic atmosphere of this movement, however, had not been transplanted to America; and the political significance of the movement was very slight. The meeting at Belleville was addressed by Friedrich Hecker of that city, one of the originators of the *Turner* movement in America; his brilliant attack upon Douglas and his plea for the republican party showed that American issues had replaced the problems of the fatherland in the minds of leading revolutionary exiles. In 1850, however, the centennial of Schiller's birth was commemorated in festivals at Chicago and Belleville which did much toward arousing a feeling for German nationality on a democratic basis.[56]

Rich as was the cultural atmosphere of their communities and content as they were with the surroundings they were able to create, these Germans could not confine their influence within these narrow barriers. Politically courted by both parties, their leaders took a prominent part in democratic politics and later transferred their allegiance to the new republican movement. Gustave Koerner continued a prominent figure in the politics of Illinois; with him were associated men like Caspar Butz, a prominent Chicago politician; George Schneider, editor of the *Illinois Staats-Zeitung*, and one of the founders of the republican party of Illinois; Friedrich Hecker, a republican elector on the Fremont ticket in 1856; and George Bunsen, an early advocate of a public school system, and an important influence in the educational development of the state.

[55] Koerner, *Memoirs*, 1: 576, 580; Bess, *Eine populäre Geschichte der Stadt Peoria*, 434.
[56] Koerner, *Memoirs*, 2: 45-50, 69.

The German voters held the balance of power between the whig and democratic parties before 1856 and between the democratic and republican parties after that date. The democrats rewarded them by giving Koerner the lieutenant governorship in 1852, and the republicans in 1860 honored in the same way Francis Hoffman, a Chicago banker and a former whig. The Lutheran and Catholic clergy exercised a strong political influence upon their congregations; being conservatives like the rest of their profession, they were slower to see that they were acting "*wickedly,* and against God's Holy will, by their supporting the Democratic party." Those in the outlying towns of Washington and Clinton counties were a unit for Buchanan in 1856, but in 1860 their ranks were broken as the result of an aggressive campaign by republican agents.[57]

The German press of Illinois, firmly grounded in this decade with a daily in every important center, showed better than anything else that the Germans had turned their backs upon Europe and taken up the political issues of the state and nation. These papers were naturally democratic organs until the slavery issue led them into the new republican party. The *Illinois Staats-Zeitung* was established at Chicago in 1848 and, under the editorial direction of George Schneider and his associates, wielded an important influence. It became a daily in 1851. Other experiments to establish German papers in Chicago inevitably failed after a short struggle. This was true in other Illinois German centers where a single paper was successfully established, and other attempts to enter the field fell stillborn.

As thus these different racial elements began to make potent their distinctive contributions to the evolution of the prairie state, it became increasingly evident that the simple society of the frontier state was giving way to the complexity of a mature commonwealth.

[57] William H. Pickering to J. Gillespie, July 20, 1860, Gillespie manuscripts.

II. THE COMING OF THE RAILROADS

DURING the decade preceding the war, the coming of the railroads revolutionized life on the prairies of Illinois. The advent of the "iron horse," his rapid multiplication, and his fiery plunges through the unsettled wildernesses that separated the river valleys, trampled under foot the trappings of the frontier state and furnished the power which produced industrial Illinois of today. There is romance in the story of how those changes were wrought; it is a wild and confused tale of lofty idealism smothered by lust for wealth and for power, of a spirit of public service buried in zeal for self-aggrandizement, of popular will compromised by factionalism and intrigue. It is the tale of human life in natural reaction to the complex economic institutions of modern society in which public welfare is at the mercy of men tempted to confine their vision within the narrow horizon of self-interest.

The great need of the pioneer west had always been good transportation facilities to connect the sturdy farmer with an *entrepôt* in which to market his surplus and from which it might be transported to the agents of the ultimate consumer in the industrial centers in the east. The facilities of Illinois in 1848, however, were limited either to the use of muddy prairie roads by the mud wagon, the prairie schooner, the stage, and other wheeled vehicles, or to the navigation of river systems that networked the state. Neither of these methods had been brought up to a high state of efficiency: river improvement was a prime necessity, but the state treasury did not permit of expenditures in that field, and the federal government had been dispensing "pork" with considerable economy. The general assembly did continue to create state roads by legislation, laying them out by stakes in the prairie and blazes on the trees, but experience demonstrated that even a sovereign state could not legislate a mudhole into a turnpike. Attempts at road improvement by local authorities and by private corporations availed little.

Coincident with the revival of railroad agitation, the plank road fever seized Illinoisians.[1] A general law was enacted in 1849, with later revisions to make easy the incorporation of plank road associations.[2] Companies secured charters and ambitiously organized to give the cities of their state the advantages of improved transportation over "farmer's" or "poor man's roads." From a provoking indifference that prevailed in 1848, the farmers aroused themselves to a state of tremendous enthusiasm. Hundreds of plank roads were located, and stock was eagerly taken up. Chicago entered the field with the Southwestern plank road toward Naperville and the Northwestern road toward Elgin; in the first six months of only partial operation of the latter the toll receipts were so heavy that the road paid expenses and forty-two per cent on the money invested.[3] Another project was that of building a road from the southern limits of the city to the north line of Will county; $53,000 of stock was subscribed on the first day, and three months later teams were rattling over the first mile and a half.[4] So it was all over the state. A traveler up the Illinois river reported almost every town and landing "engaged in constructing plank roads to the interior. Florence is building a road to Griggsville and Pittsfield—Beardstown to Virginia—Frederic to Rushville and Macomb—Copperas Creek to Canton—Liverpool to Canton, also Pekin to Bloomington. Peoria has several in contemplation. So also has Peru, La Salle and Ottawa. The plank road fever fully keeps pace with the railroad excitement."[5] By the middle of 1851, six hundred miles of plank road were said to have been built or laid out; at a cost of approximately $15,000 a mile, this involved an investment of nearly a million dollars. While mere child's play compared

---

[1] *Joliet Signal*, April 10, 1849; *Illinois State Register*, January 24, 1850; *Chicago Democrat*, July 31, 1850.
[2] *1 Laws of 1849*, p. 138-146; *Laws of 1851*, p. 11-12, 15-18, 146-147.
[3] *Prairie Farmer*, July, 1850; *Illinois State Register*, January 31, 1850.
[4] *Chicago Daily Journal*, May 28, 1850.
[5] *Chicago Tribune* clipped in *Illinois State Register*, March 13, 1851.

with the difficulty and expense of railroad construction or with the facilities thereby afforded, these projects brought immediate results in the improvement of transportation conditions. More significant by far was the completion of the Illinois and Michigan canal in the spring of 1848. This important connection between the Illinois valley and the Great Lakes was the dream-child of the prophets of the pioneer west, and its achievement meant the fulfillment of a long cherished vision. Heavy traffic began immediately, and a line of packets went into regular operation between Chicago and Peru. In the 180 days of navigation in that season nearly $88,000 was collected in tolls from 162 licensed boats on the canal. Navigation opened again in April, 1849; and in spite of complaints of mismanagement made by Chicago commercial interests,[6] receipts averaged nearly fifty per cent more than the previous season. By 1850 and 1851 the limits of the canal were so nearly reached that it was necessary to restrict its use to boats drawing no more than four feet and three inches. Though boats carrying nearly six thousand bushels of corn passed through the canal, the suggestion was made that it ought to be enlarged into a ship canal navigable by steamers of three to five hundred tons.

As a result of the canal traffic the entire upper river valley experienced a tremendous awakening. Lockport became a bustling town with large freighting and boat-building interests; and Joliet, Ottawa, La Salle, and Peru shared in the general prosperity. To Chicago, however, went the special advantages of the trade that followed the new route. The contents of the enormous granaries on the banks of the Illinois, which previously had no other outlet than the Mississippi river, now took advantage of cheap transportation by way of the canal. Unless a clear margin of from five to eight cents a bushel prevailed in favor of St. Louis, corn almost invariably took the cheaper northern route; and Chicago received the huge profits of the middlemen.[7] It was not evident, how-

---

[6] *Ibid.*, July 3, 1849; *Chicago Daily Journal*, April 15, 16, 1851.
[7] *St. Louis Intelligencer* clipped in *Illinois State Register*, April 1, 1852; *ibid.*, April 18, 1852.

ever, that the canal could endure the competition of paralleling railroad lines.[8]

A natural complement to this development was the growing importance of Chicago as a lake port. In 1850 a fleet of 145 sail and four steamers, totalling 20,637 tons, was registered in the district of Chicago. Inasmuch as the commercial supremacy of that port depended not upon the railroads but upon the superiority of its lake marine for the economical interchange of products with the east, energetic efforts were made to maintain the advantage even after the building of the trunk roads opened a sharp competition. Before the coming of the railroads, the various companies operating steamships on the lakes had in 1848 and 1849 taken advantage of the favorable situation to fix uniform and increased rates. Such arrangements could not hold later, however, when it was seen that only by low freight rates could there be a steady increase in the tonnage of lake commerce. A policy was pursued of furnishing more and more extensive accommodations, which finally led to the consideration of a ship canal for direct trade with Europe by way of Georgian Bay to Lake Ontario.[9]

One essential to extensive water transportation was the matter of river and harbor improvement; regardless of party affiliations, federal aid was invoked by Chicagoans and citizens of northern Illinois. A river and harbor convention was held at Chicago in July, 1847, which declared the constitutional authority of congress over improvements of a national character; the Great Lakes, and the Ohio and Mississippi rivers were designated as within the purview of congressional powers. Since financial embarrassment prevented the state itself from undertaking internal improvements, a northwestern Illinois river convention at Peoria in November, 1851, unanimously urged the national government to assume the expense of removing the obstacles to navigation from the Illinois river. Public sentiment in the west became too strong on this subject to brook the opposition of democratic leaders, who diplomatically

---

[8] See letters to W. H. Swift in the Swift manuscripts.
[9] *Chicago Democrat*, April 20, May 8, 1848; September 17, 1849; *Chicago Daily Democratic Press*, October 17, 1855.

COMING OF THE RAILROADS

yielded to the prevailing demand. True, southern Illinois chose democratic orthodoxy on this point and sustained the policies of President Polk and other party leaders; but the predominating voice of upper Illinois determined the course of Douglas, who championed river and harbor appropriations and stoutly contended that even an appropriation for the improvement of the Illinois river fell within the principles laid down by Andrew Jackson. In 1852, however, Douglas hit upon the expedient of state tonnage duties as a method of eliminating political bargaining in the raising of funds for such improvements. A year later during the agitation for the conversion of the Illinois river into a national thoroughfare of trade, Douglas brought his tonnage duty scheme aggressively to the fore, but suddenly the whole issue was pushed completely aside by the all-absorbing interest in the slavery question.[10]

The telegraph was the true forerunner of the railroads. By the beginning of 1848 the outposts of the eastern telegraph lines had been pushed westward to Chicago, Springfield, and St. Louis. Under the act of February 9, 1849, for the establishment of the telegraphs, connecting lines were soon sent out in every direction, so that by 1850 the outlines of an extensive telegraph system networked the state. In December, 1848, the first presidential message was relayed to the Illinois border at Vincennes; two years later almost every town and village had been placed in touch with current happenings by the aid of "lightning wires." The Illinois system was largely controlled by Judge John D. Caton, who rapidly became "the telegraph king of the West."[11]

Many improvements in land and water transportation and of telegraphic communication resulted from the stimulus of railroad agitation and the completion of new rail connections. These did not come, however, until the state had learned the full lesson of the collapse of public finance and of private enterprise that followed the panic of 1837. The reaction that had then set in placed the advocates of railroad construction

[10] *Chicago Weekly Democrat*, July 6, 13, 1847; *Illinois State Register*, July 16, 1847, December 4, 1851; *Ottawa Free Trader*, November 15, 1851; *Chicago Daily Journal*, November 15, 1851; *Chicago Democrat*, November 29, 1851; Douglas to Matteson, *Alton Courier*, January 28, 1854.
[11] *Chicago Weekly Democrat*, November 5, 1853; Koerner, *Memoirs*, 1: 509.

upon the defensive and engendered a new caution and soberness of judgment that augured rather better for the future development of the state. But the rich resources of Illinois, increasingly evident, could not be ignored; railroad schemes, accordingly, began to reappear to run the gauntlet of public opinion; and in the closing years of the forties a serious railroad fever began to infect the people of the state, for it was becoming more and more apparent that lack of adequate transportation facilities alone held back development; thirty-six counties with over two-fifths of the population of the state had only unimproved mud roads over which to market their crops. Extremely fertile regions little more than twenty miles from the canal, the lake, and the rivers, however, lay isolated and untouched because of the lack of cheap internal transportation. Without adequate market facilities, the rich prairie loam of the east central counties could not begin to compete with the less fertile soil in Egypt or northern Illinois. Moreover, the settlement of the state had gone on apace, the agricultural output had more than doubled in a decade, while industrial conditions showed that the atmosphere of the log cabin and of homespun had yielded to the march of progress. There was still fabulous mineral wealth to be tapped, and a large part of the state was virgin soil — one-third of the land remained in the hands of the federal government.

Two policies were involved in this new discussion: the need of tying together the various parts of the state and opening up the resources of unsettled areas by one or two north and south routes and by corresponding crosslines suggested projects of considerable dignity and expense which might be utilized to connect with trunk lines to the Atlantic seaboard and with the Mississippi water route; there was also the natural ambition on the part of isolated localities for short but necessary connections with undeveloped mineral deposits, with nearby markets and with adjacent water routes. The one need was theoretical and prophetic, the other practical and immediate. To realize these policies, a number of projects now seemed to warrant support: a central railroad beginning at Cairo, the southern point of the state, and running north to the terminus of the Illinois and Michigan canal with branches to Galena and Chicago; a connection between Chicago and Galena in the northwestern corner of the state, which would connect the Atlantic coast with the Mississippi as a continuation of the Michigan Central; an extension of the Northern Cross line from Springfield and from Meredosia so as to complete the lateral bisection of the state, and a line between Springfield and Alton with the possibility of a later extension northward to Chicago.

The interests of the chief towns of the state were linked with this system. Cairo was expected to become the southern *entrepôt* of Illinois; Springfield a halfway station in the whole system; Alton and Galena were to profit as termini, while such places as Rockford would be rescued from their isolation in the country. To Chicago, however, went the peculiar benefits of the projected system. A Chicago branch of the Illinois Central was counted on as a prime necessity, for, like the Illinois and Michigan canal, it would divert trade from St. Louis. The wretched condition of the Galena road out of Chicago constituted an effective argument when it was again pointed out that this made the lake-shore city unable to compete with the freight rates by way of St. Louis. In both instances the water routes of Chicago were tied up for several months by the freezing of the lake and canal, whereas St. Louis had no such handicap.[12]

This "Illinois plan" for a system of railroads was advocated as the embodiment of true "state policy" for the development of the state and its interests; projects not included in the plan met with prompt opposition. An Ohio and Mississippi route running across the state from St. Louis to Vincennes and Cincinnati, with eastern connections, was condemned on the ground that it would violate "state policy;" Illinois could not afford to contribute to the building up of a city of an outside state at the expense of all the small towns along the route. A similar argument was urged against the Atlantic and Mississippi railroad, a proposed line from St. Louis to Indianapolis or Terre Haute; most objections disappeared, however, with the suggestion that Alton be made the terminus.[13] It was

---

[12] *Chicago American*, June 25, 1840; *Chicago Daily Journal*, February 4, 5, 1847.

[13] *Alton Telegraph*, February 5, 19, 26, March 5, 1847.

suggested that a railroad might connect the Mississippi river at the Rock Island rapids to the canal and slack water navigation of the Kankakee, but for a long time Chicago interests were neutral.[14] Opposition to "state policy" was fairly well localized in the southern quarter of the state, a region directly tributary to St. Louis.[15] There it was felt that every facility ought to be afforded by the state to all companies desiring charters, and sentiment developed in favor of a general railroad incorporation act. In reply the people of Egypt were told by advocates of "state policy" that they were about to cut their own throats by favoring a course which would prevent the building up of an important city in their own section.[16]

The quarrel over "state policy" became especially heated in the summer of 1849. The supporters of the Ohio and Mississippi road were anxious to secure legislative authority for their project and welcomed the idea of a special session of the legislature which was then being urged to fill the seat in the United States senate left vacant as a result of Shield's ineligibility. The question of a called session aroused general interest; the northern counties were strongly opposed,[17] while the southern section was anxious to secure the railroad connection in question. Local railroad meetings, followed in June by a general railroad convention at Salem, were held by advocates of a rail connection between St. Louis and southern Illinois. This convention, termed by its opponents a *"Rebellion Conclave, a Rebellion against our own State,"*[18] was attended by Governor French, who was himself interested in the St. Louis road; he and the Springfield democratic machine were opposed to the "state policy" propaganda and were carefully canvassing the situation. When it became evident that the discussion had aroused a general popular interest in

[14] *Chicago Daily Journal,* June 5, 1847.
[15] *Belleville Advocate,* October 14, December 9, 1841, November 19, 1846. A line to connect Belleville with Illinoistown which would make the first town a suburb of St. Louis and a summer resort for transients was too local in interest to attract favorable notice from outside.
[16] *Cairo Delta* clipped in *Illinois State Register,* March 3, 1849; *Illinois Journal,* May 29, 1849.
[17] *Chicago Democrat,* August 27, 1849.
[18] Pickering to French, June 16, 1849, French manuscripts.

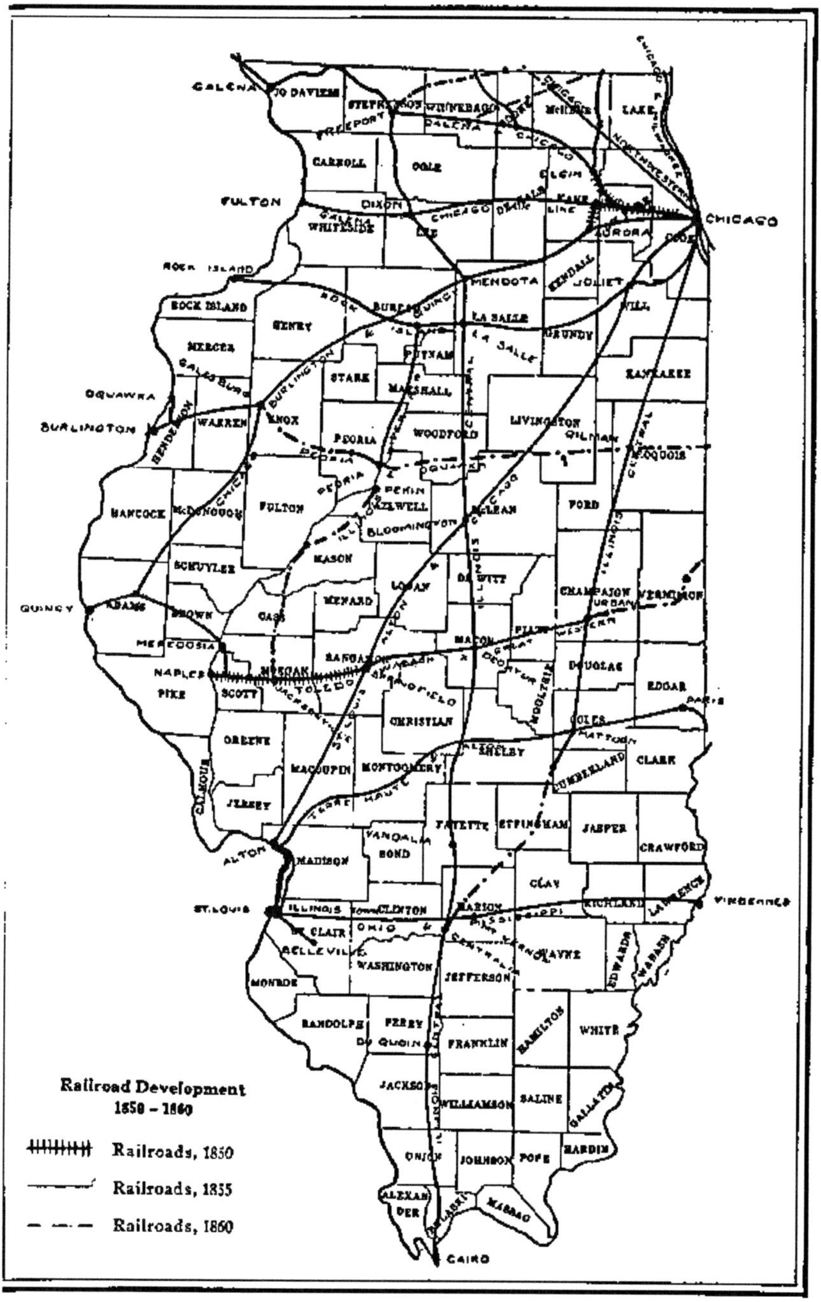

Railroad Development
1850 – 1860
Railroads, 1850
Railroads, 1855
Railroads, 1860
GALENA
JO DAVIESS
WINNEBAGO
McHENRY
LAKE
FREEPORT
CARROLL
OGLE
FULTON
DIXON
WHITESIDE
LEE
CHICAGO
AURORA
COOK
ROCK ISLAND
MENDOTA
KENDALL
JOLIET
WILL
HENRY
LA SALLE
GRUNDY
MERCER
PUTNAM
STARK
MARSHALL
KANKAKEE
OQUAWKA
BURLINGTON
WARREN
KNOX
PEORIA
WOODFORD
LIVINGSTON
GILMAN
IROQUOIS
HANCOCK
McDONOUGH
FULTON
PEKIN
TAZEWELL
BLOOMINGTON
McLEAN
FORD
MASON
SCHUYLER
LOGAN
DE WITT
CHAMPAIGN
VERMILION
URBANA
QUINCY
ADAMS
BROWN
CASS
MENARD
MEREDOSIA
MACON
PIATT
NAPLES
MORGAN
SANGAMON
DOUGLAS
EDGAR
PIKE
SCOTT
CHRISTIAN
MOULTRIE
PARIS
COLES
GREENE
SHELBY
MATTOON
MACOUPIN
MONTGOMERY
CUMBERLAND
CLARK
CALHOUN
JERSEY
FAYETTE
EFFINGHAM
JASPER
CRAWFORD
ALTON
MADISON
VANDALIA
BOND
CLAY
ST. LOUIS
ILLINOIS
CLINTON
SALEM
RICHLAND
LAWRENCE
VINCENNES
ST. CLAIR
BELLEVILLE
WASHINGTON
JEFFERSON
WAYNE
EDWARDS
WABASH
MONROE
RANDOLPH
PERRY
DU QUOIN
FRANKLIN
HAMILTON
WHITE
JACKSON
WILLIAMSON
SALINE
GALLATIN
UNION
JOHNSON
POPE
HARDIN
ALEXANDER
PULASKI
MASSAC
CAIRO

COMING OF THE RAILROADS

railroads and that the state was about to be swept by a veritable railroad fever, the governor issued a proclamation calling for the special session and enumerating railroad legislation among its objects.[19] He was at once bitterly assailed for taking this step and dubbed the tool of St. Louis and of a clique of railroad speculators. The *Charleston Globe*, a democratic paper from French's home district, edited by a personal friend, was convinced that St. Louis, Cincinnati, and Vincennes were "tricking Illinois out of interest and privileges which are of vast import."[20]

A bitter struggle was now under way. The advocates of "state policy" held railroad meetings and called for a general railroad convention to meet at Hillsboro. At this meeting, which was held on the fourth of October, eight or ten thousand persons coming from fifteen or more counties decided to terminate the tribute to St. Louis and passed resolutions aggressively demanding that no legislation be attempted in the interest of Missouri connections.[21]

When the legislature assembled, Governor French called attention to the authority of that body to pass general laws regarding internal improvements and recommended a general railroad law to end the disputes that had been occupying so much attention in politics and legislation. The "state policy" men were able to defeat any direct form of the St. Louis proposition. Their opponents then came out for "liberal general laws" and made sufficient headway to cause the moderate "state policy" men to support a bill "for a general system of railroad incorporations" which was passed and immediately approved by the governor. This act, however, was considered a triumph for "state policy," as it required every road to secure a special grant of a right of way and legislative action to fix its termini.[22] For this reason both the demand for a

---

[19] Preston to French, April 12, 1849, and Casey to French, August 23, 1849, French manuscripts; *Illinois State Register*, September 4, 1849.

[20] Latshaw to French, December 4, 1848, French manuscripts; *Illinois Globe*, September 15, 1849.

[21] Latshaw to Keating, Buckmaster, Smith, *et al.*, May 27, 1849, Gillespie manuscripts; *Illinois Globe*, June 16, 1849; *Alton Telegraph*, August 10, October 10, 1849.

[22] *Illinois State Register*, October 25, December 20, 1849; *Laws of 1849*, 18-33, 33-35; *Illinois Globe*, November 10, 1849.

cross-state road to St. Louis and for a "real" general railroad law continued.

The most popular railroad project in Illinois was clearly that for a great central highway connecting the northern "Yankee" counties with the region of "Egyptian darkness." It found its advocates in all parts of the state and, while looked upon as a primary feature of "state policy," was also warmly supported by the "anti-state policy" party. A company had been organized and incorporated in 1836 to build such a road; it was the backbone of the system provided for under the internal improvement act of 1837, under which a considerable amount of preliminary work was done; and it was revised in 1843, when the rights of the state were transferred to the Great Western Railway Company, incorporated to construct a railway from Cairo to the Illinois and Michigan canal. Confidence in this undertaking, however, had become impaired as a result of continued ill-fortune; and in 1845 the company yielded its charter and its work reverted to the state.[23]

The disastrous failure of railroad undertakings in general and of this central project in particular seemed to furnish convincing evidence that large and expensive enterprises could not succeed without material aid from the national government. Senator Sidney Breese was from the start a champion of the Illinois Central railroad; his favorite scheme was to induce congress to grant to the builders of the road preemption rights to a portion of the public lands through which it should pass.[24] This would enable the railroad company to market the lands at a profit, which would insure an income on the investment. Breese seemed to have secured little assistance, however, from other members of the Illinois legislature. With the entry of Stephen A. Douglas into the United States senate an important advance was made in the preparations for successful railroad construction in Illinois. Douglas was also an ardent supporter of the central road, but differed with his colleague's preemption policy in that he advocated a direct

[23] Brownson, *History of the Illinois Central Railroad*, 17 ff.; Newton, *Railway Legislation in Illinois*, 21 ff.; Ackerman, *Historical Sketch of the Illinois Central Railroad*.
[24] *Congressional Globe*, 29 congress, 1 session, 208.

grant of land to the state of Illinois, which was to be responsible for the construction of the road.[25] This form of national aid in internal improvement made allowance for the tenderness of democratic feeling on the subject of state rights.

Both Breese and Douglas had personal interests in this great undertaking. Both were strongly inoculated with the western fever of land speculation; Breese, one of the original incorporators in 1836 and a director of the Great Western Railway Company, sought to satisfy his ambitions in connection with the construction of this railroad, while Douglas, moving to Chicago in the summer of 1847, shrewdly foresaw the development of a western metropolis at this commanding position on the lower end of Lake Michigan and hazarded his available capital in a heavy investment in Chicago real estate.[26] Moreover, Douglas was more keen than his less able colleague in the analysis of political benefits; he realized the growing seriousness of the sectional line of cleavage between the northern and southern parts of the state and the threat at his own political ambitions involved therein; accordingly, a scheme that promised to contribute so effectively to a greater unity and harmony in party politics was certain of a hearty welcome.

Douglas now stressed the Chicago connection, which had been subordinated in previous schemes. He undertook to draw on the natural interests of the business men of that city, of shippers along the Great Lakes, and of eastern capitalists to secure support for the central project. He featured it, therefore, as a trunk line connecting the Atlantic seaboard with the Mississippi river at Cairo by way of Chicago and the lakes. Thus destroying some of the sectional character of the enterprise, he added eastern support to the general western demand for the inaugurating of government aid to railway construction. As a result his land grant bill easily carried the senate, although the south and the landless states, western as well as eastern, combined to effect its defeat in the house on strict

---

[25] See correspondence between Douglas and Breese in Breese, *Early History of Illinois*, appendix; also see *Illinois State Register*, January 23, March 13, 1851.
[26] Breese to Douglas, *Illinois State Register*, February 6, 1851. Governor French also had a "private interest" in the Chicago branch. Sturges to French, August 7, 1851, French manuscripts.

construction grounds.[27] Breese's proposition then had the same legislative experience.

Douglas' measure was lost by such a close vote in the house that the railroad promoters concluded that it was only a matter of time before the measure could be passed. The Illinois legislature, therefore, was induced by the members of the former Great Western Railway Company, the most formidable aggregation of capital in the state, to renew their charter, into which a clause was smuggled surrendering to the company whatever lands the federal government might grant to the state.[28] Knowledge of this situation in Illinois embarrassed Douglas and the Central advocates at Washington until the company was induced to surrender its corporate rights temporarily. Then Douglas, aided by Shields, who had succeeded to Breese's seat, and by John A. McClernand, John Wentworth, and William H. Bissell of the house delegation, pressed the land grant proposition in congress; by making provisions for similar grants to Alabama and Mississippi, the hostility of the south was allayed, so that the "Chicago and Mobile railroad" measure was able to survive a bitter opposition in the lower house[29] and become law on September 20, 1850.

The question immediately arose as to how the central road should be constructed. The corporate interest concerned was a group of capitalists, dominated from the beginning by Darius B. Holbrook, who were organized as the Cairo City and Canal Company for land speculation at the southern Illinois terminus. This "Holbrook company" was anxious, under the charter of the Great Western, to secure the benefits of the federal land grant by constructing the road; it had, indeed, pursued a policy of watchful waiting until favorable action by congress was assured before taking the steps required under the charter for the construction of the road.[30]

The company was, therefore, unwilling to yield its charter

---

[27] Brownson, *History of the Illinois Central Railroad*, 25; Johnson, *Stephen A. Douglas*, 170-171.
[28] This act was not published in the session laws of 1849; see, however, its repeal, *Laws of 1851*, p. 192-193.
[29] *Congressional Globe*, 31 congress, 1 session, 1838.
[30] Holbrook to French, December 24, 1849, September 2, October 8, 1850, French manuscripts; see also Greene and Thompson, *Governors' Letter-Books, 1840-1853*, p. 235.

unless reincorporated in another form. But Douglas was sufficiently irritated by the grasping ambitions of the speculators to suggest that it was not a bona fide construction company but on the contrary was planning to profit by the sale of the charter in Europe. It was suggested that if the work were to be done by a private corporation, a more disinterested group of eastern capitalists might be found to do the work under proper restrictions. This proposition does not seem to have grown out of any rival interests, as it was some time before any definite project was placed before the people. Another suggestion was that a company composed of holders of state bonds be given the right to construct the road under semi-legislative management, thus simultaneously reëstablishing the credit of the state. Though many advocates of direct state construction were still to be found, the lessons of the past weighed heavily against such an experiment; Senator Shields especially argued against the practicability of this method.[31]

When Senators Douglas and Shields returned in triumph from Washington they received the gratitude of the state for their sturdy devotion to the land grant; about the banquet table the victory they had secured was celebrated, and its significance proclaimed in the flowery language of the after-dinner speaker. The adherents of all the various ways of using the land grant soon clashed in a free for all political fight; with no definite provision for the route of the road, every village and hamlet along the line sought to influence the choice of route favorable to its development. In each legislative district the practical obligations of the next assembly were carefully considered; but the schemes for state ownership and for the continuance of the Holbrook company, being concrete and definite, were so vigorously assaulted that they were worsted by their opponents. The newly elected legislature showed a triumph of the forces of negation. When that body met, however, and proceeded to clear the way for action, it was found that no satisfactory substitute proposition was available. This

[31] Bissell to Gillespie, December 22, 1850, Gillespie manuscripts; *Chicago Democrat*, January 11, 1851; *Illinois Journal*, November 30, 1850, January 29, 1851.

situation was relieved when Robert Rantoul of Massachusetts in behalf of a group of eastern capitalists offered to build the road and, on condition of a surrender to it of the federal land grant, to pay the state in return a percentage of the gross receipts. The offer was regarded as very fair; it was favorably received by the friends of the central road; and Governor French promptly recommended it to the legislature. An act of incorporation fixing the share of the state at seven per cent of the gross revenues was passed almost unanimously and became law on February 10.[32]

The builders of the Illinois Central thus undertook to construct a road over twice as long as the largest railway system of that day, the New York and Erie. The charter allowed the company four years to complete the main line and six years for the branches; as a problem in contemporary engineering this required most careful planning. The organization was promptly completed,[33] and within a few months a preliminary survey was under way. A hotbed of agitation, bribery, and litigation developed along the general line of the Central where rival points struggled to secure the railroad for their own particular districts; the survey, however, went forward on considerations of engineering and administrative policy.

In regions not directly influenced by the Central system, attention was centered on securing other railroad facilities. The project of the Galena and Chicago railroad incorporated in 1847 was popular with both Chicagoans and residents of northern Illinois generally, who put it actively in the field with subscriptions to over a quarter million of stock; in one day President William B. Ogden of the company secured $20,000 on the streets of Chicago from farmers who were selling wheat. Early in 1848 contracts were let and construction was started on the section from Chicago to Elgin, and by the spring of 1849 fourteen miles were in operation; the thirty-five miles to Elgin, however, were not completed until February 1, 1850, when a grand celebration took place. On

---

[32] *Illinois Journal*, January 22, 1851; *Senate Journal*, 1851, p. 237, 265, 266. The act is not printed in the session laws.
[33] Schuyler to French, March 24, 1851, French manuscripts.

COMING OF THE RAILROADS 41

August 1, 1852, the cars made their entrance into Rockford amid the firing of cannon and ringing of bells, while on the fourth of September, 1853, the road was opened to Freeport, 125 miles west of Chicago. This was for a time the western terminus, the Illinois Central being used to cover the remaining fifty miles to Galena. With the completion of branches to the Wisconsin line from Elgin and Belvidere, the Galena and Chicago was ambitious enough to project an air line across the state to Fulton on the Mississippi; this was over half completed by the end of 1853, and by the beginning of 1856 it went into complete operation furnishing through service as the shortest line between Chicago and the Mississippi. The early operations of the road were very extensive and profitable, with net earnings varying from ten to twenty per cent. Such earnings in 1849 on less than twenty miles of road were $25,000. Dividends of ten per cent and eight per cent were declared in February and October, 1850. The road soon paid a higher percentage to stockholders than any road in the union, with semiannual dividends of from eight to twelve per cent.

Another early Chicago connection was the Aurora branch or Chicago and Aurora railroad, chartered in 1849. It used the Galena and Chicago track for thirty-three miles, while the remaining ten miles down the Fox river valley to Aurora it completed in 1850. Books were then opened for stock to continue it forty-three miles farther to Mendota on the projected Galena branch of the Illinois Central. This was completed in the fall of 1853.

By this time stable foundations had been laid for the Rock Island and Chicago, originally the Peru and Rock Island. Work was commenced in the fall of 1851;[34] a year later the line was opened to Joliet; in February, 1853, the rails were laid to Ottawa, and the road was hurried westward at a rate of nearly a mile a day, progressing more rapidly than any railroad in the state. On February 22, 1854, the completion of the road was celebrated with pomp and ceremony at Rock Island, for this made the first continuous connection of the Great Lakes with the Mississippi. Steamship connections with St. Louis and St. Paul were immediately established, and a

[34] *Ottawa Free Trader*, October 4, 1851.

bridge built across the river to tap the central Iowa country.[35]

During these years the Illinois Central was making rapid progress. The surveys were completed by the beginning of 1852 and the work was promptly put under contract; a force of 10,000 laborers prosecuted the work with vigor from the terminal points toward the center. By the end of 1853, 175 miles of track had been laid; the Chicago branch was opened to Urbana in midsummer of the following year; on the first of January, 1855, all the main line and most of the Galena and Chicago branches were in operation. Connections with other lines enabled the company to open through passenger and freight service, although the formal laying of the last rail and the driving of the last spike did not take place until September 27, 1856.[36] With additional improvements the Illinois Central became almost immediately the best built and equipped railroad in the west.

The Springfield and Alton railroad, another north and south line authorized in February, 1847, began operations in the middle of 1850. In September, 1852, through trains were running from Springfield to Alton, where they connected with fast steamers for St. Louis, making the total distance in four hours. Before that time an extension to Chicago had been planned; and the general assembly on June 19, 1852, changed the name to Chicago and Mississippi Railroad Company. On October 18, 1853, the road was completed to Normal; and the first communication by railroad from New York City to the Mississippi river was established by way of the Chicago and Rock Island to La Salle, and from there to Normal by the Illinois Central. Then, in the flowery language of the railroad celebration after-dinner orator, the iron horse that sipped his morning draught from the crystal waters of Lake Michigan could slake his evening thirst upon the banks of the Mississippi. By October, 1854, with the complete installation of its own train service, the "Alton" road had opened another through connection between the Father of Waters and the

---

[35] This bridge became a subject of serious controversy with the federal government, incited in part by rival St. Louis interests.
[36] *Chicago Daily Democratic Press*, October 2, 1856.

Great Lakes. Before 1860 a railroad extension from Alton to St. Louis was completed.

The downstate interests were engaged in converting their own cross-state projects from mere paper schemes into substantial railroad lines. The neglected Northern Cross line, the sole railroad remnant of the internal improvement orgy of 1837, was transferred to a private company and became known either as the Springfield and Meredosia, or Sangamon and Morgan railroad; in 1853, however, the legislature changed the name to the Illinois Great Western, and in 1860 it became a part of the Toledo, Wabash, and Great Western. This road was overhauled in 1848 and opened for regular passenger service to Naples in the summer of 1849. For a time energies were concentrated on securing a federal land grant to aid its completion across the state. In 1853 the eastern extension was brought to within a dozen miles of Decatur; the track was slowly carried forward until in 1857 the Indiana state line was reached, putting into operation 174 miles of road. The connection across the state, however, was not completed until 1858.

The Central Military Tract railroad was built in 1854 and formed an extension of the Aurora branch railroad from their common junction with the Illinois Central at Mendota to Galesburg where it connected with the Quincy and Galesburg branch of the Northern Cross railroad. In 1856 the Central Military Tract was consolidated with the Chicago, Burlington, and Quincy railroad, which also secured the Northern Cross line from Galesburg to Quincy. The Peoria and Oquawka railroad, incorporated to carry out the project of a great central railroad, was slowly carried forward in the period from 1853 to 1857.

The railroad problem of southern Illinois was complicated by rival cross-state enterprises. Alton and the backers of "state policy" continued to fight the St. Louis interests in their alliance with the rival land speculators, and the advocates of more southerly routes. The "state policy" forces had held their own down to 1850, although their opponents could match their professions of principle. The latter championed as true liberal "state policy" the privilege of railroad construction for every part of the state where the people were willing to undertake the enterprise and supply the capital.[37] Men like Governor French, Governor Matteson, Ben Bond, Bissell, and Koerner zealously pleaded for a free field for all enterprises; and Douglas was induced to go on record as in favor of a free field for cross-state lines.[38] The rival factions accordingly marshalled their forces in railroad conventions. The contest became so keen that even political issues were at times subordinated to the railroad question; a bipartisan combination at Alton supported "state policy" legislative candidates while elsewhere politics were sacrificed to the hopes of the backers of the roads.

The "railroad war" continued to be waged in each successive session of the legislature. Alton interests back of the Terre Haute and Alton were especially zealous in their hostility toward the Atlantic and Mississippi line, as it prepared for an aggressive campaign under the presidency of Colonel John Brough. In spite of a powerful backing, however, Brough's road repeatedly met with defeat even after the Ohio and Mississippi railroad from Vincennes to Illinoistown secured legislative sanction on February 12, 1851. In 1853 the assembly granted charters for enterprises totalling several thousand miles of railroad, but rejected the bill for the "Brough road" and tabled a resolution in favor of a general railroad law.[39] The authorization of the Vincennes road placed an additional obstacle in the way of the Atlantic and Mississippi; although it had previously rallied the liberal policy forces on the basis of the sectional resentment of Egypt to northern selfishness, the Vincennes backers now came to look upon the "Brough road" as a possible competitor for financial support.

[37] *Belleville Advocate*, January 12, 1853.
[38] Banks to French, January 10, 1850, Manly to French, August 28, 1851, French manuscripts; Douglas to Manly, December 28, 1850, *Illinois State Register*, January 16, 1851.
[39] It was even proposed by Joseph Gillespie that in return for a payment of one per cent of their gross earnings, the railroads already chartered should be given a virtual monopoly under state supervision, their consent being necessary to any charters for new roads running within twenty-five miles of any road already incorporated; all the territory between the Terre Haute and Alton and the Ohio and Mississippi roads was to be closed to east and west roads. *Illinois State Register*, February 3, 10, 1853.

By the fall of 1853, however, after the Ohio and Mississippi had sold its bonds and was on a firm financial footing; the "Brough road" supporters decided that the time was ripe to press their project by a combined opposition against "the narrow contracted policy of Alton." They immediately began an active campaign for an extra session as confident of the support of Governor Matteson as they had been of that of Governor French.[40] Breese, McClernand, Reynolds, Logan, Casey, and Morrison were active in organizing the forces that favored the call. At the close of a vigorous newspaper fight between northern and southern Illinois journals, an extra session convention was held at Salem on November 25, 1853, which, with twenty-four counties represented, proved the reality of the demand. Governor Matteson responded in January with his proclamation. Downstate interests began their campaign for a liberal railroad policy and were finally able to secure the charter for which its supporters, including two governors of the state, had been laboring for over five years. St. Louis gave the Illinois legislature a festival in honor of the passage of the bill that marked the end of the great Illinois railroad war.

A survey in retrospect revealed the fact that for four years countless controversies over applications for special railroad charters had wrecked the dispatch of legislative business.[41] "State policy" was therefore shelved even by its advocates as having fulfilled its purpose and become an obstacle in the way of progress.

The construction of two of the three southern lateral lines was completed in the latter half of the decade. The Terre Haute and Alton was organized for active work in 1850, but the road was not built until the period from 1853 to the end of 1855. Before it was completed, however, it secured a collateral branch to Illinoistown. This direct connection with St. Louis, like that of the Chicago and Alton, robbed Alton of the special advantage that her backers had expected to enjoy as a railroad terminus; they had to be content with the posi-

---

[40] *Belleville Advocate*, September 28, 1853. Lieutenant Governor Koerner went on record as in favor of the special session. Koerner, *Memoirs*, 1: 607-608; *Chicago Daily Democratic Press*, October 28, 1853.

[41] *Ibid.*, January 17, 1855; *Illinois Journal*, January 3, 1855.

tion of an important way station, while the St. Louis interests chuckled over the advantages that accrued to their city.

The Ohio and Mississippi road was opened from Illinoistown to Vincennes in July, 1855, although the connection with Cincinnati was not completed until nearly two years later. This road traversed a rich belt of country and brought important advantages to St. Louis as a direct east and west line of communication. It failed, however, to draw from Chicago the trade that was now accustomed to go east by the lake route. After energy had been expended in securing the charter for the Terre Haute and Illinoistown line, this project fell through and was not taken up again until 1865; St. Louis was thus deprived of another important eastern connection.

Belleville had contributed in Gustave Koerner, John Reynolds, and Don Morrison some of the most enthusiastic backers of both the Ohio and Mississippi, and Mississippi and Atlantic lines. They expected that their city would be made a station on both lines. The first disappointment came when the Ohio and Mississippi line decided, because of the land holdings of St. Louis investors and of Illinois speculators,[42] to pass four miles to the north of Belleville; bitterly did the Belleville leaders denounce the land sharks and speculators in bounty land warrants and tax titles. In their chagrin they hit upon the scheme of building a road to Illinoistown, which they were able successfully to execute by the fall of 1854, after which they carried a northern extension to Alton there to connect with the Alton and Terre Haute. This saved them from excessive disappointment over being left off the line of the road from Terre Haute and over the later failure of that project.

At the end of 1850, the completed portions of the Northern Cross line and of the Galena and Chicago Union railroad had given the state only a little over one hundred miles of railroad, yet in the first six years of the decade Illinois built a larger mileage than any other state in the union. With 2,235 miles of track it outranked all the states of the middle west.[43] By 1860 with important eastern connections running into Chi-

---

[42] Including even Don Morrison. *Belleville Advocate,* June 30, 1852; Koerner, *Memoirs,* 1: 565, 586, 587.
[43] *Urbana Union,* February 19, 1857.

cago, with the Chicago and Milwaukee (1855), and with the Chicago and Northwestern railroad systems tapping the state of Wisconsin at different points, Illinois was adequately provided with railroad communication with the outside world.

Yet the story of Illinois railroad development in the fifties is not finished without a mention of the numerous projects dreamed of by those who wished to have a hand in networking the state with railroad lines, for nowhere perhaps did the railroad fever rage more violently than in the state of Illinois. It seemed that the people would not be content until a railroad was located on every four miles of the state. Thousands of miles of road were authorized by the general assembly that never passed the state of paper projects; others were begun only to collapse of their own weight, worthy as well as merely ambitious enterprises going to ruin with the rest. At the beginning of 1851, the legislature petitioned congress for federal aid in behalf of the Alton and Mt. Carmel line provided for in the internal improvement act of 1837; but by the end of the year a lone Irishman working under the direction of General William H. Pickering, its indefatigable proprietor, was making the last effort to rescue this important project from oblivion.[44]

A tremendous array of forces gave to Illinois its railroads and railroad schemes. Local investors and land speculators conceived an enterprise and rallied the support of the community; farms were mortgaged to assist in the accumulation of capital; counties and municipalities voted to subscribe stock. In addition, the aid of eastern capitalists was called in. But such capital, even in the case of one of the more promising enterprises, was supplied only when special privileges were conferred upon the easterners who took every advantage of the Illinoisians. "Swarms of hungry cormorants" clamoring for special legislation besieged the state capitol. It was said that the bills pressed by these lobbyists "were prepared in New York, and were first canvassed by Wall street men before they

[44] *Laws of 1851*, p. 204; Allen to French, December 9, 1851, French manuscripts; a manuscript note to Pickering by Joseph Gillespie, 1879, is appended to a letter from Pickering to Gillespie, July 20, 1860, Chicago Historical Society manuscripts.

were sent to Springfield to secure legislative endorsement."[45] At times western investors were refused directors to represent their interests. In 1853 rumors circulated of a corruption fund of $80,000 to defeat the Mississippi and Atlantic railroad. Only the general enthusiasm for railroad development prevented a strong reaction in line with democratic prejudices against corporations and corporation influence.[46]

The service furnished by these newly built railroads varied according to circumstances. Most of them were constructed to meet a long felt want; the heavy freight and passenger traffic that immediately began often taxed the roads to their utmost capacities. When earnings ran as high as sixteen per cent roads like the Galena and Chicago were able to add new accommodations in response to the growing demands. All lines ran daily freight and passenger trains in each direction and in instances the time-table gave the traveler a wide range of choice. Good time was made by passenger trains; thirty miles an hour was a common speed, and Chicago and Alton trains were able to average twenty-two miles and rarely vary ten minutes from schedule. When the traveler, accustomed to a ride of three days and nights from Chicago to Springfield in Fink and Company's stages, made the trip by rail in twelve hours, it seemed "more like a sketch from some part of the Arabian Nights, than a matter of stern reality."[47] The element of luxury in travel was introduced into Illinois with the appearance of the sleeping coach on the Illinois Central line. Rates were very reasonable; while varying greatly passenger fares in most cases did not exceed three cents a mile. During the later fifties the Galena and Chicago and the Northwestern roads competed for traffic between Chicago and Rockford and both cut the passenger fares to one dollar.[48] Accidents, however, were frightfully common at the start especially because of

---

[45] *Chicago Daily Democratic Press* clipped in *Illinois State Register*, August 4, 1853.
[46] *Belleville Advocate,* March 30, 1853; *Chicago Daily Democratic Press* clipped in *Alton Courier,* April 12, 1853. As it was, a sober vote of warning came from papers like the *Chicago Daily Democratic Press, Illinois State Register,* July 28, 1853, and others.
[47] *Alton Courier,* June 3, 1853, February 22, 1854.
[48] *Chicago Democrat,* April 2, 1855; *Rockford Republican,* December 1, 1859; *Rockford Register,* January 7, 1860.

the want of fences along the right of way to keep out the cattle.[49]

The railroads rendered obsolete the prevailing methods of handling the mails. Very few of the 861 post offices located in Illinois in 1850 enjoyed regular daily mail service. Transported by the stage lines over unimproved and often impassable roads, the mails suffered serious delays from schedule as a result of washed out bridges and flooded roads. River mails were next adopted and worked a considerable improvement for the regions able to take advantage of them. But the railroad made possible the general and prompt transmission of the mails at all seasons. It took time, however, to perfect arrangements; in 1853 a traveler from New York could carry the city papers to Alton and deliver them four days in advance of the mails.[50] In a few years, however, a letter from New Orleans could be delivered in Chicago within three days.

The coming of the railroads hastened the forces that were revolutionizing the prevailing social and economic practices of the day. The railroads brought a great influx of population, first of laborers to participate in railway construction and later of immigrant passengers. The consequent heavy demand for both the food and other products of the state improved the local market. Reduction in the cost of transportation coupled with the new element of reliability, automatically increased the producer's share in the market prices of his crops. Prices in the east and west were now more nearly equalized.

The whole field of agriculture experienced a remarkable stimulus.[51] The new inducements to immigration attracted many men of means who often came to Illinois demanding improved lands; as a result farm values experienced a rapid rise of almost fifty per cent. The new availability of large tracts of unimproved lands offered tempting fields for land speculation; many a fortune was made on a gambler's risk of a successful guess of adequate railroad communications for the

---

[49] The Chicago and Alton superintendent issued an order that section masters pass over their respective sections in hand cars within an hour of train time and drive off any cattle that might be on the track. *Illinois State Register*, November 10, 1853.
[50] *Alton Courier*, August 1, 1853.
[51] *Hunt's Merchants' Magazine*, 27: 759.

land warrant locations. Methods of getting stock to market were improved; special stock-train service was furnished by certain roads at a great saving. Perishable fruits and vegetables now found a wide market which gave added attractions to horticulture; railroad communication placed the tomatoes and berries of southern Illinois upon Chicago dinner tables weeks before the home crops were harvested.

In the towns and cities changes took place which paralleled those of rural life. Merchants found new demands for their goods both from the railroad workers and from the farmers who found it easier in every sense to keep in touch with the distributing centers. Manufacturing experienced a remarkable stimulus with the advent of the railroads; both the raw material and the markets were brought nearer the factory. The railroad further rendered accessible the inexhaustible supplies of mineral wealth with which Illinois was blessed. The railroads soon discovered that coal burning locomotives were far more economical than those that used wood; by the end of the decade, the Illinois Central began to adopt the former type.[52] The process of supplying the railroads with coal promised to open up a new mining industry of equal importance to the manufacturing establishments and to the households of the timberless state. Thus it was that many a sleepy town or village of log huts and shanties was aroused and converted into a bustling city.

Towns sprang up with mushroom rapidity along the railroad lines that intersected the open prairies. In 1854, West Urbana was a depot on the Illinois Central; in another year it was a hamlet of a hundred houses with four or five hundred inhabitants, while three hundred buildings were in process of erection, including "two large hotels, six stores, a large furniture ware-house, four or five lumber yards, and a large ware-house for forwarding purposes," besides a Presbyterian church and a large school house costing some $4,000.[53] A census taken sixteen months later revealed a population of over 1,200. In 1861 this was the thriving town of Champaign with a separate corporate existence. A little to the south at

[52] *Quincy Whig*, April 16, 1858; *Chicago Democrat*, January 24, 1859.
[53] *Ibid.*, May 5, 1855.

the junction of the Central and Alton and Terre Haute railroad, the town of Mattoon sprang up almost overnight; in April there was not a sign of human life, by August there was "a large hotel," with another in process of erection, a post office, a dry goods store, and two groceries to supply a rapidly increasing population.[54] The hamlet of Earlville, thirty-five miles west of Aurora on the Chicago, Burlington, and Quincy railroad, in a short time grew from a settlement of six or eight dwellings, a store, blacksmith shop, and a tavern into a place of a thousand inhabitants, with over a score of stores, three public houses, and four church organizations. Favorably situated older settlements received similar benefits; Hillsboro and Carlinville were instances of towns that rapidly forged ahead when provided with railroad connections. Immigration poured in from every direction, merchants did a thriving business, the streets were often impassable because of the presence of farmers' teams.[55]

The greatest advantages, however, were derived by the termini of the roads, particularly Chicago, Alton, and St. Louis. In 1856 thirteen railroads centered in or were connected with Chicago which was served by 104 trains daily. Alton had dreamed of superseding St. Louis as a western metropolis; and in the economic domination of central and southern Illinois, a sharp competition for control of the field ensued.[56] In the summer of 1848 St. Louis tried to improve her harbor facilities by altering the channel of the Mississippi river with a dyke that would compel it to flow on the west side of Bloody Island. As this threatened to divert the channel away from the Illinois shore, Governor French was induced to exercise his authority to prevent the work; he accordingly authorized the sheriff of St. Clair county to use military force or a civil posse to enforce an injunction against the St. Louis authorities. The supreme court of Illinois sustained the governor in the dyke controversy, though later a compromise

[54] *Chicago Weekly Democrat,* September 1, 1855; *Presbytery Reporter,* 4: 327-328.
[55] *Aurora Guardian,* December 9, 1853; *Carlinville Statesman,* July 8, 1852, clipped in *Illinois State Register,* July 15, 1852; *Hillsboro Mirror* clipped in *ibid.,* March 31, 1853.
[56] *Review of the Commerce of Chicago,* 31; *Alton Courier,* September 18, 1852, April 4, 1853.

arrangement permitted the work to be completed.[57] While Alton and St. Louis continued their squabbles over the Ohio and Mississippi and over the "Brough railroad," other railroads were being constructed, and these cities suffered greater and greater losses to the metropolis on the lake. Not Alton, but Chicago — the key to the railroad system of the northwest — was to succeed to the economic leadership of St. Louis. Railroads reënforced the canal and even competed with it for the lighter freights.[58] When the rail connections with Rock Island and Peoria were completed, the process of making the Illinois valley tributary to Chicago was rounded out. The Chicago and Galena diverted from St. Louis and the Mississippi route the lead traffic and the agricultural products trade of Minnesota, Wisconsin, and northern Iowa as well as of northwestern Illinois. The Illinois Central brought forward to Chicago quantities of products from central Illinois, though it carried enough to Cairo to threaten to build up another rival to St. Louis at the southern extremity of the state.[59] At the beginning of the decade with five-eighths of the agricultural trade of St. Louis drawn from Illinois and with Illinoisians taking in return nearly three-fourths of the merchandise sold in St. Louis, the Missouri legislature was able to levy a tax of $4.50 on every $1,000 worth of foreign products and merchandise sold in that state and on articles purchased by outsiders; in the closing years St. Louis bent all her energies toward saving what remnants she could from the grasp of Chicago.[60]

With Chicago as the hub of a vast transportation system, Illinois promised to become the great railroad center as it was the geographical center of the nation. Prophets felt little boldness in predicting a leading rôle in the future for Illinois.[61]

[57] Reynolds to French, June 17, 1848, Reynolds *et al.* to French, June 23, 1848, Reynolds, Koerner, P. Fouke, William H. Underwood *et al.* to French, July 12, 1852, French manuscripts. Correspondence covering every side of the dyke controversy may be found in this collection.
[58] See E. S. Prescott to W. H. Swift, January 30, 1851, Swift manuscripts.
[59] *St. Louis Republican* clipped in *Illinois State Register*, May 8, 1851; *St. Louis Intelligencer* in ibid., May 22, 1851; see also *DeBow's Review*, 24:212.
[60] *Illinois State Register*, October 30, 1849, January 17, 1850; *Belleville Advocate*, November 29, 1849.
[61] Lee, "Transportation: A Factor in the Development of Northern Illinois previous to 1860," Illinois State Historical Society, *Journal*, 10: 17-85.

III. AGITATION AND COMPROMISE, 1848-1852

IN THE midst of the excitement of a successful war, with the distractions attendant upon a heated agitation of the slavery question, Illinois in 1848 entered upon a new era in her political development. Forces of more recent origin, however, were relegated to the background while old party alignment and orthodox political issues were revived in the discussion of candidates for the presidential office. In the country at large, as well as in Illinois, all omens pointed to the success of the democratic party, which, having generously fed the people's voracious appetite for expansion, had a claim to gratitude not to be matched by their empty-handed opponents. Party leaders for a long time would admit an uncertainty only as to who should represent the democracy in receiving from the tribunal of public opinion a formal recognition of the party's valued services.

Whig leaders, in desperation, consequently began to cast about for the most effective means of recovering their recent losses. "All the elements of party strife will bubble in the caldron," warned Orlando B. Ficklin, congressman from the third district. "War, pestilence, and famine, slavery & freedom, military and civil claims, will each and all lend their influence to the strife of '48."[1] The democrats, shaken in their confidence of victory, set about to rally their full strength about their strongest candidates. President Polk, though the official party leader in those days of storm and stress, was not the authoritative embodiment of democratic principles: there was little reason why he should be continued in the executive office in the face of the natural ambitions of party chiefs like Lewis Cass and James Buchanan. He had seriously offended many elements in the northern states by his silence on land reform and by his veto of the river and harbor bill as well as

[1] Ficklin to French, January 6, 1848, French manuscripts.

by his subserviency to the south.[2] Nevertheless, since he had not allowed himself to become entangled in the Wilmot proviso issue, he could still run a fair race. If Cass and Buchanan should wear each other out, those who opposed Polk's nomination feared that he might forget his declared lack of ambition for reëlection and avail himself of the opportunity to come up from behind as a compromise candidate; Congressman "Long John" Wentworth thought he detected a skillful Polk electioneering campaign on the part of Springfield politicians.[3] Wentworth himself advocated Douglas as a representative of the youthful spirit of the west which alone could carry the party to victory. But "Long John's" aggressive personality had created strong enemies within the party, who seem to have gradually gained the ear of even the cautious Governor French, and they combined with the Springfield machine politicians, who, disgusted by Wentworth's antislavery activities, were determined to block his control at all hazards.

Soon a contest developed in which the two factions measured their strength against each other. The point at issue was the manner of selecting delegates to the national convention. Wentworth wanted to have them elected by conventions in each judicial circuit, while the members of the state machine insisted on a state convention. The latter would secure a harmonious, unified delegation to represent the state on the principle of majority control; the district scheme, on the other hand, recognized a situation which clearly existed: the democrats of the state were radically divided on many questions and each district would in this way have the right of self-determination.[4] "We Barnburners believe in free opinion, free speech & free discussion as well as free labor and free soil," said Wentworth.[5] In the northern section of the state democrats were strongly devoted to the Jeffersonian slavery restriction policy initiated in 1787; they declared frankly in favor of "free soil once, free soil forever,"[6] and for river

---

[2] *Congressional Globe*, 29 congress, 1 session, 1181.
[3] Wentworth to French, March 5, April 13, 1848, French manuscripts.
[4] *Chicago Democrat*, January 31, 1848; Wentworth to French, March 5, 1848, French manuscripts.
[5] Wentworth to French, April 13, 1848, *ibid*.
[6] *Chicago Democrat*, April 18, 1848.

and harbor improvements without qualification. As one left the northern region, however, for the middle and southern counties, increasing democratic hostility to all these propositions appeared. Wentworth and his following succeeded in controlling the local party organizations in the vicinity of Chicago but failed to secure the recognition of his principle of "live and let live," worked out through district conventions. The state convention, accordingly, met on April 24 and 25 to perform the work of selecting delegates to Baltimore, as well as to place a state ticket and an electoral ticket in the field. The convention expressed a decided preference for General Cass but did not formally instruct the delegation to support him. The resolutions adopted condemned all intemperate discussion and unnecessary agitation of the slavery question and ignored other issues over which democrats differed. The state ticket scheduled Augustus C. French for reëlection as governor and William McMurty for lieutenant governor.[7] The state platform was not at all satisfactory to antislavery democrats, and the national convention a month later, by nominating Lewis Cass on a platform silent as to slavery, added to their unrest.

Democratic dissensions gave little encouragement to the whigs, who faced even more serious embarrassment. They, too, were divided on the slavery issue. There were "conscience whigs" or "wooly-heads," who rallied to the Wilmot proviso standard; but in the state, as in the nation, they were outnumbered by those who would avoid new and distracting issues. The whig party, moreover, already suffering from regularity of defeat, had further declined in prestige as a result of its opposition to the Mexican War and to territorial expansion.

Under these circumstances it was not easy to map out a program. Orthodox whigs felt that a consistent adherence to party principles and existing leadership would carry the day; these were Henry Clay men who hoped that the war had so weakened the democracy that Clay could easily swing the winning vote in 1848. Others felt that a policy of opportunism under a standard bearer who possessed real "availability"

[7] *Illinois State Register*, April 28, 1848.

was the only course to pursue. The brilliant exploits of Generals Taylor and Scott had given them a popularity that promised an assured response to their leadership. Early in 1847, therefore, promptly after the battle of Buena Vista, papers like the *Quincy Whig* and the *Morgan Journal* hoisted the name of General Taylor as a candidate for the presidency. Lincoln was one of the active group of Taylor congressmen who upheld the general's cause at the national capital.

General Taylor had no real political interests or beliefs; party lines had thus far concerned him but little, and there had already arisen an increasing nonpartisan demand for his nomination. Here was a candidate to offer the nation. "Old Zach" was the hero of the Mexican War; hampered as he had been by official democratic jealousy, he was the man to wipe out the whig stigma of opposition to a popular war. A struggle was soon under way between availability, as represented by Taylor, and orthodoxy, as identified with Clay; the result was a Taylor victory and a grave disappointment for Clay supporters.

Whig energy in Illinois was directed exclusively toward the national convention; after the ticket of Taylor and Fillmore was launched in June, it was discovered that no preparations had been made to contest the state election. This reflected the prevailing disorganization; the *Illinois Journal* frankly admitted that the party had no hope of carrying the state election in August, and that a defeat would detract from whig strength in the November election.[8] On the other hand, many whigs objected to letting the state election go by default because it would keep them from ascertaining the actual strength of the party; accordingly the *Quincy Whig* and other papers hoisted the names of Pierre Menard for governor and J. L. D. Morrison for lieutenant governor.[9]

The administration of Governor French had been eminently satisfactory to all impartial men of the state. He had displayed no unfair partisanship, with the result that even many whigs desired his reëlection.[10] He had, moreover, kept

[8] *Illinois Journal*, June 19, 1848.
[9] *Quincy Whig*, June 6, 1848.
[10] Turner to French, no date, 1848, French manuscripts.

fairly clear of the factionalism that had prevailed in his own party. Even John Wentworth, the ubiquitous critic, approved the absence of official dictation and pointed to the unwonted harmony in the ranks of the state democracy as justification of French's reëlection.[11] When finally the cry of "Springfield clique" was raised, it seems to have referred to the *Illinois State Register* following rather than to the state administration. For all these reasons, the opposition to the French state ticket was very feeble and the election in August went off very quietly.

The newly elected legislature was strongly democratic; anti-war whiggery proved a millstone for the whig legislative triumvirate, Stephen T. Logan, Isaac Williams, and William Thomas, who sank in political waters normally favorable for a plunge.[12] The complexion of the Illinois congressional delegation was unchanged, Edward D. Baker being elected as the lone whig member. Thomas L. Harris, a democrat, was elected to Lincoln's seat in a close contest; William H. Bissell without opposition replaced Robert Smith in the first; John A. McClernand, Wentworth, and William A. Richardson were all reëlected over their opponents, with Timothy R. Young in the third district.

The atmosphere having thus been cleared, all energies were thrown into the presidential canvass. The whig leaders set out to develop a dramatic hero worship of General Taylor, the "people's candidate." The spirit of 1840 was revived in their ranks. Processions, mass meetings, and barbecues became the order of the day. The rank and file were urged to keep up the "grape" that the hero of Buena Vista, the general who "never surrenders," might bring the enemy to his knees.[13] The disaffection of Clay whigs gradually subsided and terminated when Clay formally declined to allow his name to be used independently. Little was said of concrete whig principles. The bank issue was declared obsolete; since the land warrants of Mexican War veterans would absorb the public domain for years to come, there would be no proceeds of the

[11] Wentworth to French, December 19, 1847, April 13, 1848, French manuscripts.
[12] *Illinois State Register*, August 18, 25, 1848.
[13] *Beardstown Gazette*, September 13, 1848.

public land for distribution; with the heavy demands created by war debt, the tariff could no longer be a party matter. The great and vital issue, therefore, was the question whether the people or one man should rule. In the past the vetoes of democratic presidents had thwarted the public will; had not Polk in this way defeated a crying need for river and harbor improvement?[14]

The democrats replied by challenging the meager qualifications of the whig candidate for political preferment. Wilmot provisoists were reminded of the fallacy of voting for a planter and slaveholder. The German and Irish were played upon by the customary charge of whig hostility to foreigners; Taylor, it was claimed, was in league with the nativists.[15]

In counter attacks the whigs ridiculed the attempt of the democrats to write General Cass into a military hero. Abraham Lincoln from the floor of the house of representatives made a burlesque of his own military exploits and those of General Cass, drolly suggesting that neither had seriously qualified for the presidency on that score.[16] Cass's position was declared to be no more satisfactory on the slavery question. Originally inclined toward the Wilmot proviso doctrine he had found it expedient to expound in his canvass a noncommittal doctrine of popular sovereignty for the territories, a doctrine which was promptly attacked as a Janus-faced appeal to both antislavery and proslavery democrats. The genuineness of his democracy was challenged by referring to a statement in which he was alleged to have favored "whipping and selling poor white men and stubborn servants."[17]

With the increasing seriousness of the sectional controversy, it became evident that the restless antislavery elements would hold the balance of power. There was widespread discontent with both national parties for their consistent evasion of the slavery issue; both in their national conventions had just rejected propositions to check the extension of slavery's domain. In New York, where an explosion had been threatening for some time, the antislavery democrats, or "barn-

[14] *Beardstown Gazette*, October 4, 11, November 1, 1848.
[15] *Chicago Democrat*, June 22, 1848.
[16] *Works of Abraham Lincoln*, 2: 104.
[17] *Illinois Journal*, September 16, 1848.

AGITATION AND COMPROMISE 59

burners," were so disgusted with the proceedings of the national convention that they launched an independent movement, summoning all antislavery forces to meet in convention to agree upon common cause. The result was the organization of the free soil or free democratic party at Buffalo on the ninth of August, 1848.
Illinois delegates led by Owen Lovejoy, Isaac N. Arnold, C. D. Wells, Samuel J. Lowe, C. Sedgwick, and Charles V. Dyer, attended this convention but took no conspicuous part in the proceedings.[18] Immediately, therefore, the question arose as to whether or not the movement would take root in Illinois, where the weak and despised liberty party polled only 4,000 votes.[19] The "barnburner" movement, however, quickly gathered strength. An Illinois free soil convention, with sixteen counties represented, assembled at Ottawa on August 29; they prepared an electoral ticket of their own and made ready to take an active part in the canvass.[20] Five or six new papers were started to advocate the election of the free soil candidates, Martin Van Buren and Charles Francis Adams.[21]

Shrewd political prophets predicted a free soil vote of 20,000 in Illinois. Managers of both old parties were deeply concerned over the inroads that were being made into their ranks: which would suffer most heavily?[22] Democrats were frightened to see some of their best men, like Norman B. Judd, Dr. Daniel Brainard, Isaac N. Arnold, Mahlon D. Ogden, and Joseph O. Glover bolt the Baltimore nominations to go for Van Buren.[23] When Wentworth was renominated by a district convention controlled by "barnburners" which refused

---

[18] *Gem of the Prairie*, August 12, 1848; cf. Smith, *The Liberty and Free Soil Parties in the Northwest*, 142.
[19] *Illinois Journal*, September 6, 1848. This was the congressional vote of 1848, just the size of Birney's vote in 1844. Owen Lovejoy polled 3,130 votes in the Chicago district.
[20] *Illinois State Register*, September 8, 1848; *Beardstown Gazette*, September 13, 1848.
[21] Prospectus of *Alton Monitor* in Shurtleff College scrapbook. A free soil league at Chicago fitted up a club with a reading room and displayed considerable activity. *Chicago Democrat*, September 8, 1848.
[22] *Quincy Whig*, September 5, October 10, 24, 1848; *Illinois State Register*, September 15, 1848.
[23] Reddick to French, July 12, 1848, French manuscripts; *Joliet Signal*, October 16, 1848; *Rockford Forum*, October 24, 1848.

to sustain the national ticket,[24] it was rumored that he, too, had bolted the Baltimore nominations. Wentworth at once replied, however, that since he believed in making his objections before a convention and not afterwards, he had never even considered bolting; he also declared that he preferred Cass to Taylor on the slavery question.[25] Under democratic representation that David Wilmot and all true Wilmot proviso men were supporting Cass and that Van Buren stood no chance of election, former democrats like David Kennison of Chicago, the 112-year-old survivor of the Boston tea party, gave up their free soil predilections to sustain Cass.[26]

Whigs reversed the argument to favor their candidates: Van Buren was an ancient ally of slavery; every vote given by a whig to Van Buren was half a vote given to Cass. "The abolition party under the cloak of Van Burenism," they declared, "are attempting to play the same game" that defeated Clay in 1844;[27] the free soil question "is a cardinal principle of the Whig party."[28] Abraham Lincoln, campaigning in behalf of General Taylor, stressed these points in indicating the policy and duty of all anti-extensionists. Many old liberty party men, it was boldly suggested, "prefer Gen. Taylor to Van Buren — believing him sounder and entitled to more confidence on the free soil question, than the Buffalo convention."[29]

These paradoxical and unconvincing arguments reflected the fears of party politicians as to the outcome of the election. Cheered by the encouraging results of the October elections in Pennsylvania, whigs counted the chances of carrying Illinois. Several items were listed in their favor; a hostile Mormon vote of 3,000 had been withdrawn from the state, the "barnburners" were expected to carry off thousands from Cass, while his position on river and harbor improvement and other issues would cause further democratic losses.[30] Even the least sanguine democrats, however, relied upon being able to hold their

[24] Galloway to French, June 9, 1848, French manuscripts.
[25] Wentworth to French, June 23, 1848, ibid.
[26] *Chicago Democrat*, November 6, 1848.
[27] *Aurora Beacon*, September 27, 1848.
[28] *Beardstown Gazette*, November 1, 1848.
[29] *Quincy Whig*, October 31, 1848.
[30] *Ibid.*, August 15, 1848; *Aurora Beacon*, September 13, 1848.

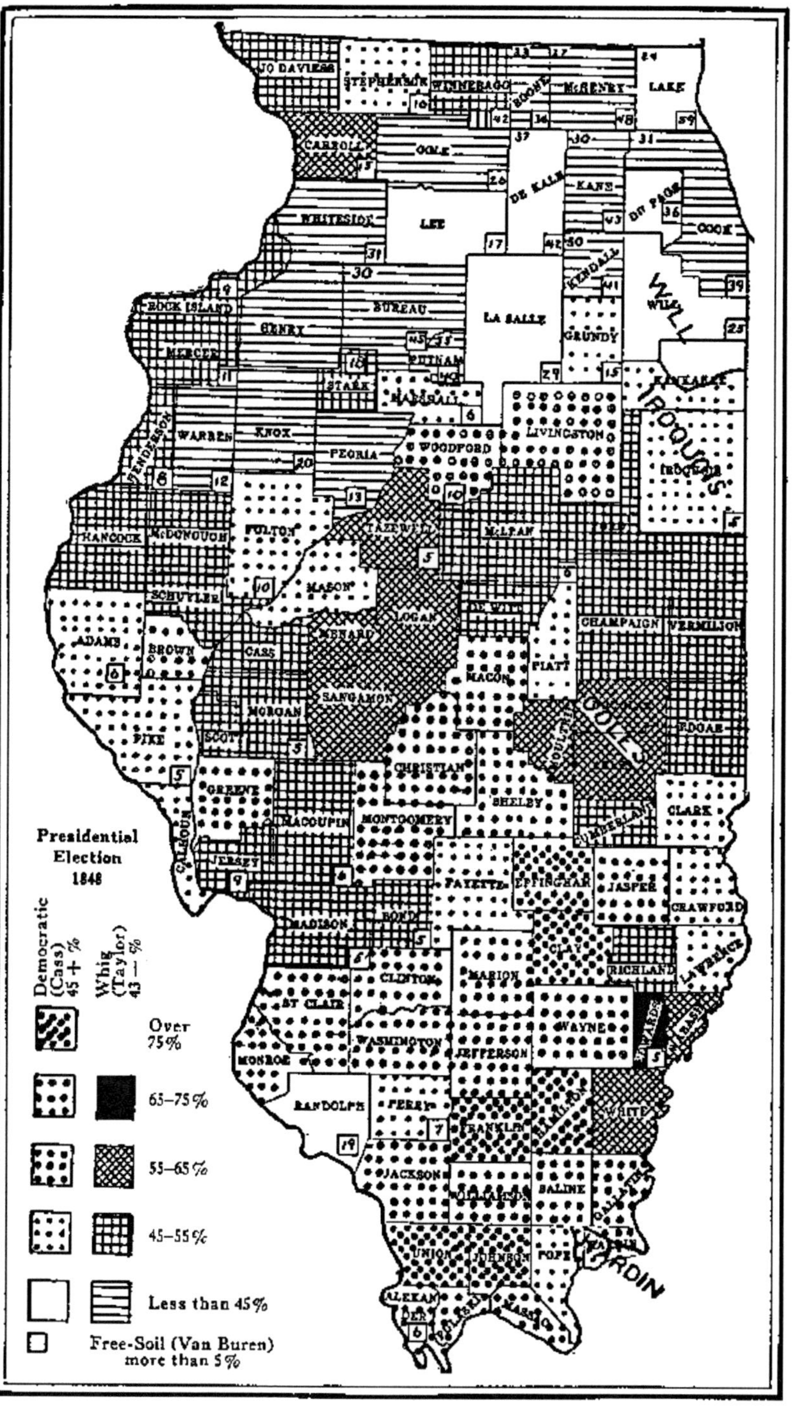

Presidential
Election
1848
Democratic (Cass) 45 + %
Whig (Taylor) 43 — %
Over 75%
65–75%
55–65%
45–55%
Less than 45%
Free-Soil (Van Buren) more than 5%
JO DAVIESS
STEPHENSON
WINNEBAGO
BOONE
McHENRY
LAKE
CARROLL
OGLE
DE KALB
KANE
DU PAGE
COOK
WHITESIDE
LEE
KENDALL
WILL
ROCK ISLAND
BUREAU
HENRY
LA SALLE
GRUNDY
MERCER
PUTNAM
STARK
MARSHALL
KANKAKEE
IROQUOIS
HENDERSON
WARREN
KNOX
PEORIA
WOODFORD
LIVINGSTON
HANCOCK
McDONOUGH
FULTON
TAZEWELL
McLEAN
MASON
SCHUYLER
DE WITT
CHAMPAIGN
VERMILION
ADAMS
BROWN
CASS
MENARD
LOGAN
MACON
PIATT
SANGAMON
MORGAN
PIKE
SCOTT
CHRISTIAN
EDGAR
GREENE
SHELBY
CLARK
MACOUPIN
MONTGOMERY
CALHOUN
JERSEY
FAYETTE
EFFINGHAM
JASPER
CRAWFORD
MADISON
BOND
CLAY
RICHLAND
LAWRENCE
CLINTON
MARION
ST CLAIR
WAYNE
WASHINGTON
MONROE
JEFFERSON
RANDOLPH
PERRY
FRANKLIN
WHITE
JACKSON
WILLIAMSON
SALINE
GALLATIN
UNION
JOHNSON
POPE
HARDIN
ALEXANDER
PULASKI
MASSAC

existing strength and upon using a normal democratic majority to carry the state. The returns showed that Taylor had carried the nation. The whigs of Springfield celebrated this victory with bonfires, cannon, a torchlight celebration, and an illumination of whig residences and places of business. Nevertheless, in the state the democrats had been correct in their calculations. Cass was given a plurality of 3,099 — less by 9,000 than that for Polk four years before. Both parties suffered heavy losses to the free soil movement, which netted 15,702 votes. In the vicinity of Chicago the Van Buren vote was especially heavy; a free soil plurality was returned in the city and in Cook and seven adjacent counties, besides many other single precincts. This was largely at democratic expense, the result, said Wentworth, of Cass' announcement, at the dictation of Georgia politicians, of the doctrine of popular sovereignty.[31]

The logical result of the campaign that had just closed was a demand for concrete and tangible evidence of the much heralded devotion of both old parties to the principle of the Wilmot proviso. The free soil whigs promptly undertook to place the legislature on record in this matter. A drastic whig proviso resolution, however, was rejected in the house by a party vote, only a dozen democrats voting with the whig delegation. A long debate began on the Wilmot proviso and kindred propositions. Several resolutions were discussed; finally a mild resolution offered by Senator Ames was adopted in the senate by a vote of fifteen to ten. The house accepted the joint resolution and it was spread on the record.[32] It was voted, however, that it was not a resolution of instruction relating to any specific proposition then before congress;[33] accordingly Douglas, despite the clamors of the whig press at this "rank federalism," quietly ignored it.

It was the task of this legislature to elect a successor to Senator Sidney Breese. The whigs were clearly out of the race and democratic sentiment was divided between Breese and

---
[31] Hereafter, he urged, "let the North stand firm and she will compel southern men to announce themselves against slavery extension in order to get northern votes." *Chicago Democrat*, November 20, 1848.
[32] *1 Laws of 1849*, p. 234.
[33] *Quincy Whig*, January 16, 1849.

General Shields. Breese was an experienced legislator but not a statesman of eminence; Shields laid claim to neither qualification but had powerful personal friends, popularity as an Irish champion of liberty, and the reputation of a military hero in the Mexican War. Breese was the favorite of the conservative Egyptian democracy and found favor with the national administration at Washington; Shields was popular with Wilmot provisoists and with advocates of river and harbor improvement in the northern portion of the state.[34] As a result, this immigrant from the Emerald Isle, still ready, when Ireland should prepare to strike for liberty, to aid in the redemption of his native land, secured the nomination in the democratic caucus and was promptly elected by the legislature.

General Shields presented his credentials to the special executive session of the senate following Taylor's inauguration. His eligibility was promptly challenged on the score of his inability to meet the constitutional requirement of nine years of citizenship. It was recognized at once that the challenge had been made in behalf of Sidney Breese, his unsuccessful and disappointed rival;[35] but since he actually lacked a few months of fulfilling the requirement, the senate was compelled to reject him as ineligible. The democratic party in Illinois was racked by the controversy; both Breese and Shields seemed to have worn each other out, but no strong neutral candidate was available to take the place.

Governor French was in no sense disposed to play the part of arbiter in this dispute. Finding himself in a tight place, pressed by the two rivals on the one hand and on the other by compromise candidates, he held, in opposition to the opinion of Douglas, that as no election had taken place, he had no power to appoint.[36] He therefore called a special session of the legislature to select a senator.

By this time democratic politics had become hopelessly

[34] *Rockford Forum*, January 17, 24, 1849; *Quincy Whig*, January 30, 1849.
[35] Shields to French, March 17, 1849, French manuscripts. A heated correspondence took place between the two leaders.
[36] Douglas to French, May 16, Douglas to Lanphier and Walker, August 13, *Illinois State Register*, August 30, 1849; French to Manly, June 8, *ibid.*, June 21, 1849. Robert Smith and Thomas J. Turner also offered themselves as candidates for the appointment. Robert Smith to French, March 9, 1849, Turner to French, May 17, 1849, French manuscripts.

AGITATION AND COMPROMISE 63

entangled. The friends of John A. McClernand, of lower Egypt, put him forward as a compromise candidate on the ground that the two rivals had worn each other out; they welcomed the idea of a special session as favorable to his ambition.[37] Advocates of special legislation requested the governor to include their schemes in his proclamation summoning the legislators to Springfield. Free soilers at first feared the danger of having their Wilmot proviso instructions withdrawn; later they made their plans to have them formally renewed.[38] The sectional division of the state over railroad development served as a leading line of cleavage between the advocates and opponents of a called session. When in October the session finally convened a hot contest between Breese, Shields, and McClernand took place in the democratic caucus. Shields was able to draw upon McClernand's following and win out on the twenty-first ballot; whereupon his election was formally accomplished in joint session.[39]

The attention of the Illinoisians was now drawn from these petty factional disturbances to the lowering cloud on the horizon threatening to deluge the nation in the flood tide of disunion. North and south had grown more and more defiant in their intention to stand by their respective views on the slavery question, the north to prevent the spread of the hated institution to another inch of soil already consecrated to freedom, and the south to enter the new territories with slave property on equal terms with the free states. Southerners, pushed to the wall and losing their hold on national politics, showed a disposition defiantly to insist upon their position. Should this be denied them, they were prepared to withdraw to secure their rights and to defend them with the sword.

[37] *Illinois State Register*, July 3, 1849; *Chicago Democrat*, September 3, 1849; *Illinois Globe*, October 20, 1849.
[38] John Wentworth led the northern democrats in their opposition to the called session. Wentworth to French, June 28, 1849, French manuscripts; see also *Chicago Democrat*, July, August, and September, 1849.
[39] *Illinois State Register*, November 1, 1849. Breese quietly acquiesced in the result; McClernand's organ, the Shawneetown *Southern Advocate*, however, burst out bitterly claiming that "McClernand was defeated and betrayed by the free soil members of the legislature." "When such men as McClernaud and Breese," it commented, "are beaten by an arrogant, vain, ignorant, *lying* Irishman, it is high time that all men, who respect their characters should retire in disgust from the political arena." *Illinois Journal*, November 8, December 11, 1849.

This ominous situation was closely followed in Illinois. The northern section was strongly committed to free soil; Egypt, still seeking some middle ground, helplessly decried agitation. The closing months of Polk's administration saw Oregon organized under a policy of slavery restriction; the Illinois votes in favor of this action were given on the ground that it was not an application of a new policy but a moral obligation created by the Missouri compromise line.[40] The question of the disposition of California, of New Mexico, and of Utah remained as a bone of contention between the hostile sections.

Illinois had contributed large numbers of her citizens to the settlement of California and naturally watched with great interest developments on the Pacific coast. Great was her applause, therefore, when a constitution was drawn up in the new territory which refused to make provision for the institution of slavery. This was a development even more satisfactory than congressional prohibition of slavery because it promised to add a new free state to the union and to destroy the even balance between the north and south in the senate. Taylor's annual message and his special California message urging the admission of this new state were warmly received by the Wilmot provisoists and furnished them with a practical working platform.

The situation naturally provoked bitter hostility in the south. The admission of California as a free state, it was declared in alarm, would be followed by New Mexico and Utah. Even sober-minded southerners, influenced by a new and more aggressive generation of leaders, began to calculate the value of the union; separation was threatened in terms of more or less passion and violence. In the tense and heated atmosphere legislators at Washington became overwrought and excited. Illinoisians were for the first time convinced that there were southern politicians "determined, if possible, to bring about a dissolution of the Union."[41] Their reply was that it was the duty of the state, of the entire west, to

[40] Illinois whigs were flattered that the office of governor of Oregon was tendered to Abraham Lincoln, although he found it necessary to decline the honor. *Illinois State Register*, October 4, 1849.
[41] *Illinois Journal*, February 1, 1850.

prevent the accomplishment of this foul plan. "The great and patriotic West," declared the *Alton Telegraph*, "has become strong enough to strangle the monster of disunion the moment it shall venture to raise its head."[42] It was denied that ground for disunion existed.[43] William H. Bissell, the Alton representative in congress, maintained an admirable self-control under these trying conditions; but on the floor of the house on February 21, he declared after an analysis of the southern threats that the people of Illinois and of the northwest would spring to arms to save the union.[44]

Douglas eloquently claimed for his section a deciding rôle in this stirring controversy: "There is a power in this nation greater than either the North or the South—a growing, increasing, swelling power, that will be able to speak the law to this nation, and to execute the law as spoken. That power is the country known as the great West—the Valley of the Mississippi, one and indivisible from the gulf to the great lakes, and stretching, on the one side and the other, to the extreme sources of the Ohio and Missouri—from the Alleghanies to the Rocky mountains. There, sir, is the hope of this nation—the resting place of the power that is not only to control, but to save the Union. . . . . This is the mission of the great Mississippi Valley, the heart and soul of the nation and the continent."[45]

John A. McClernand, Douglas' right-hand man in the lower house, felt that the situation demanded that the west prepare to display her strength. On the seventy-fourth anniversary of American independence he greatly feared for the continuance of the union; Texas was making ready to defy the federal government by force of arms; such action many felt to be the signal for a disunion movement on the part of the whole south. McClernand, therefore, confidentially giving his view of the interests of Illinois to Governor French, advised the governor to take measures immediately to give the state militia the greatest efficiency: "I would prepare for the storm—I would provide against portentous violence. This

[42] *Alton Telegraph*, February 1, 1850.
[43] *Chicago Democrat*, April 8, 1850.
[44] *Congressional Globe*, 31 congress, 1 session, 225-228.
[45] *Ibid.*, 365; Johnson, *Stephen A. Douglas*, 175-176.

as a citizen of Illinois and a lover of the Union, I call upon you to do."[46]

Thus did the "raw head and bloody bones" of disunion leer over the horizon to terrify the more timid. Soon a union-saving cry arose promising to checkmate the strong sectionalism that had been dominating the situation. Henry Clay, the great compromiser, had left his retirement at Ashland to play the rôle of peacemaker; his bold leadership made the idea of compromise popular, and all sorts of schemes were brought forward under that guise. Senator Douglas, though calm amid the prevailing hysteria, became one of the union savers. His clear fresh vision enabled him to foresee the failure of any single comprehensive compromise proposition such as Clay had recommended. Northern supporters of a California admission bill, aided by advocates of popular sovereignty in the south, might easily enact that measure; propositions for territorial governments for New Mexico and Utah on the same principle would receive support from moderate men in both parties; and in both sections, after extreme sectional devices had failed, the slave trade in the District of Columbia and the fugitive slave evil could be dealt with on their merits; but to tie all these into a single bungling scheme as Clay had urged would bring defeat because of the unanimity of opposition to specific objectional features. He commended the self-sacrificing spirit of Clay and of Webster, but optimistically declared: "The Union will not be put in peril; California will be admitted; governments for the territories must be established; and thus controversy will end, and I trust forever."[47]

Douglas held that the effective solution of the slavery question would come through "the laws of nature, of climate, and production" recognized and ratified by the people of a state or territory, not by act of congress. He stressed the great democratic principle of leaving each community to determine and regulate its own local and domestic affairs in its own way. This was a safe road to freedom because the vast territory stretching from the Mississippi to the Pacific was rapidly filling up with a hardy, enterprising, and industrious population, des-

---
[46] McClernand to French, July 4, 1850, French manuscripts.
[47] *Congressional Globe*, 31 congress, 1 session, 364 ff.

tined by the laws of nature and of God to dedicate the new territories to freedom.

For these reasons Douglas offered his solution on March 25 in the form of a California bill and a territorial bill; they were drafted after conferences with Richardson and McClernand, who introduced the same bills into the house.[48] Clay arranged to incorporate these bills as the first part of the omnibus bill which the select compromise committee of thirteen reported. Douglas' territorial bill was silent on the slavery question; the committee's measure contained an additional clause, prohibiting the territorial legislatures from legislating on the slavery question. This Douglas attacked as a restriction on the right of the inhabitants of the territory to decide what their institutions should be, for he was already in the lists as a champion of popular sovereignty.[49]

Congress began a long discussion of the Clay compromise, of President Taylor's proposal to await the action of the people of the territories in question, and of the northern and southern schemes for the disposition of slavery. Douglas' proposal and other plans were subordinated to these leading propositions. Douglas was frequently on his feet in the senate; Shields, his colleague, usually followed his lead, while McClernand, Richardson, and Harris urged the same course in the house. Douglas carefully explained his objection to the Wilmot proviso but found it necessary in accordance with the instructions of the Illinois legislature to vote with Shields for propositions embodying that principle;[50] he was always much relieved to find himself in the minority. The house delegation was under no such formal obligation; its vote was usually divided, with a majority against congressional intervention to restrict slavery. John Wentworth, the strongest Wilmot proviso man in the delegation, voted consistently for that principle; he seldom took the floor, however, except to press the passage of the California bill at times when its success was threatened by other distracting questions.[51] Edward D. Baker, the lone

[48] McClernand offered them, however, as parts of a single bill, a plan "not of my authorship." *Ibid.*, 628.
[49] *Ibid.*, 1114 ff. He was later gratified by the dropping of this clause.
[50] *Senate Journal*, 31 congress, 1 session, 375.
[51] *Congressional Globe*, 31 congress, 1 session, 1444, 1468.

whig, usually voted with Wentworth, while the other five democratic members opposed congressional restriction.

Douglas, preferring the separation of the various items in the omnibus bill, had the satisfaction of witnessing the failure of that measure in line with his predictions. By midsummer, the omnibus had jolted over the rocks of sectionalism until all its occupants had been spilled out save one—the Utah territorial proposition. Then Douglas, in accordance with his original plan, began to press the items separately. The Utah bill was given the right of way and rushed to passage. Then in quick succession came the enactment of the New Mexico territorial law, the California admission bill, and measures for the more effective rendition of fugitive slaves and for the abolition of the slave trade in the District of Columbia.

The Illinois representatives at Washington voted solidly for the California and the District slave trade measures; but Wentworth and Baker opposed the Utah, New Mexico, and fugitive slave laws, which the other congressmen supported. Douglas and Shields voted in favor of every one of these measures of adjustment except the fugitive slave law. On the days when it was brought up for final action, Douglas was absent from Washington on business, but his colleagues knew that he was in favor of the bill.[52] Shields, however, had no alibi; the evidence suggests that he was one of the vote-dodgers with whom Douglas was classed in the popular mind.[53] It is bootless to attempt to apportion the exact amount of credit due to the different advocates of an amicable adjustment of the slavery controversy, but Douglas was able to claim in all modesty that he had played "an humble part in the enactment of all these great measures."[54]

Coincident with the struggle in congress the same forces in Illinois were fighting for a decision. Whig journals that had led in the demand for slavery restriction as essentially part of the whig creed issued the call: "Rally! friends of

[52] *Congressional Globe*, 32 congress, 1 session, appendix, 65.
[53] At any rate he answered roll call on other propositions on two different days when he abstained from voting on the fugitive slave bill. *Senate Journal*, 31 congress, 1 session, 565, 581.
[54] Senator Jefferson Davis declared to his colleagues in these words: "If any man has a right to be proud of the success of these measures, it is the Senator from Illinois."

the Union, rally!!" Whigs were divided into advocates of the Clay compromise and supporters of the president's no-action plan; both groups, however, agreed to waive the Wilmot proviso policy as one no longer necessary.[55] The democrats, moreover, welcomed the opportunity to heal the division in their own ranks over the slavery issue.[56]

The union savers at an early date began organizing to influence public sentiment in favor of compromise. Belleville, a town where the populace gathered in mass meeting at the slightest provocation — usually ex-Governor John Reynolds — was one of the first cities in the country to hold a union meeting; on January 24 it adopted resolutions offered by Reynolds that the union be saved at all hazards.[57] A little later union mass meetings in Jacksonville, Edwardsville, and a few small towns voiced the same sentiment; the large Illinois cities, however, remained inactive until the middle of June. When, finally, a Springfield meeting indorsed the report of the compromise committee of thirteen, it was in numbers scarcely representative of that community.[58] The Jacksonville compromisers again summoned the voters of Morgan county to a union gathering, but three days later the Wilmot provisoists were able to arrange an equally successful meeting.[59]

The cry of "compromise" stimulated the activity of the agitators throughout the nation; in Illinois such excitement on the slavery question had never been known as prevailed in March of 1850. Proviso meetings were held at Waukegan, Ottawa, and other places.[60] A considerable stir was caused by a nonpartisan free soil meeting at the city hall in Chicago presided over by Mayor J. H. Woodworth, in which resolutions were adopted expressing utter abhorrence at all compromises that permitted the further extension of human slavery; condemning a compromise scheme attributed to Douglas by the press; and firmly declaring in favor of the Wilmot proviso and of the abolition of slavery in the District of Columbia.

[55] *Illinois Journal*, May 2, 1850; *Joliet Signal*, May 28, 1850.
[56] *Belleville Advocate*, May 30, 1850.
[57] *Alton Telegraph*, February 8, 1850.
[58] *Illinois Journal*, June 18, 1850.
[59] *Morgan Journal*, June 22, 1850.
[60] *Chicago Democrat*, March 15, April 6, 1850; *Ottawa Free Trader*, March 16, 1850.

In spite of the "no-party" appeal, whig provisoists were disappointed because Henry Clay's name was received with coldness while Benton's brought an outburst of applause; democrats, moreover, claimed that it was the work of fanatics and of political opponents of Senator Douglas—a charge corroborated by the *Illinois Journal,* which disapproved of this "knot of politicians .... bent on driving Mr. Douglas from the Senate."[61]

The free soilers sought to utilize the opportunity to strengthen their independent party organization; local and district conventions were arranged and the propriety of a state convention discussed. This activity was sufficient to douse completely the interest of old-line party men, who, for fear of embarrassing their own organizations, withdrew from the movement. Finally the *Chicago Tribune,* for two years a free soil organ, announced its decision to sever its ties with the free democratic organization.[62]

By this time, moreover, the union antidote had begun to work; the suggestion that it was "THE UNION VS. THE WILMOT PROVISO" left no alternative but to yield the principle of congressional intervention in the territories to the preservation of the compromises of the constitution.[63] Webster's seventh of March speech, though characterized by the *Belleville Advocate* as "profound but soulless" and "lacking in honesty," circulated in large editions, and strengthened the argument of those who held that slavery could never go into New Mexico or Utah. Clay's compromise scheme began to win support as an arrangement which despite its defects was likely to allay the excitement that was pervading the country.[64]

The main obstacle in the way of the union savers was the hostility to the proposed fugitive slave legislation. Douglas was known to be in favor of the measure as simple justice to the south under the constitution; papers like the *State Register,*

[61] *Chicago Daily Journal,* February 22, 1850; *Illinois Journal,* February 27, 1850; *Illinois State Register,* February 27, 28, 1850; *Joliet Signal,* February 26, 1850. Douglas repudiated the alleged compromise proposition and denounced the resolution of censure. Douglas to Woodworth, March 5, *Illinois Journal,* March 26, 1850.
[62] *Chicago Tribune,* May 29, clipped in *Western Citizen,* June 4, 1850.
[63] *Quincy Whig,* February 19, 1850.
[64] *Alton Telegraph,* March 1, 8, 22 and other numbers, 1850.

therefore, came out in support of the proposed measure.[65] This only served, however, to arouse protests from those who denied that they were so destitute of humanity and feeling as to accept such a clear violation of the principle of common justice. The news of its passage inflamed these objectors to action; the measure, they declared, had no moral or constitutional justification and ought to be resisted.[66] Petitions for its immediate repeal were widely circulated. Thirteen thousand copies of an anti-fugitive slave bill pamphlet were sold in three weeks at the rate of five cents per copy. "In our candid judgments," declared the *Ottawa Free Trader,* "there has not been, during the present century a law passed, or an edict issued by any government claiming to be free, which outrages justice as this law does." "The law will be a dead letter. It cannot be enforced."[67]

The friends of the Negro rallied to express their opinion in indignation meetings. Kenosha citizens on October 18 appointed a vigilance committee and listened to a deputy marshall assert that he would not serve a writ for the arrest of a fugitive slave.[68] The Congregational church at Aurora became the meeting place of a similar assembly. From many pulpits and ministerial associations were thundered violent denunciations. Chicagoans in mass meeting assembled spoke in strong, earnest condemnation of the obnoxious law.[69] Reflecting the popular indignation, the Chicago common council, with only two dissenting votes, formally pronounced the law cruel, unjust, and unconstitutional, a transgression of the laws of God, and declared that congressmen from the free states who assisted in its passage or "who basely sneaked away from their seats, and thereby evaded the question," were "fit only to be ranked with the traitors;" it was formally resolved that the city police would not be required to render any assistance for the arrest of fugitive slaves.[70]

[65] *Illinois State Register,* September 19, 26, 1850.
[66] *Western Citizen,* October 8, 29, November 5, 19, 1850.
[67] *Ottawa Free Trader* clipped in *Chicago Democrat,* October 14, 1850.
[68] *Ibid.,* October 23, 1850.
[69] *Aurora Beacon,* October 24, 1850; *Chicago Journal,* October 26, 1850.
[70] *Illinois State Register,* October 31, 1850; *Joliet Signal,* December 3, 1850.

Shields and Douglas, returning to their homes while public opinion was in this state of ferment, tried to stem the tide of protest, the former at a speech in Springfield on October 29 and the latter in an address at Chicago on the evenings of October 21 and 23. In spite of his absence at the final roll call Douglas, greeted by the hisses and jeers of a hostile audience, assumed the full responsibility of an affirmative vote; in his speech he so boldly and eloquently reminded his hearers that refusal to return a fugitive slave to his master was a violation of the constitution and a blow at the permanence of the union that at its close occurred one of those remarkable instances of mob spirit dropping a set of old idols for a new shrine at which to worship. Douglas presented a series of resolutions declaring the obligation of all good citizens to maintain the constitution and all laws enacted in accordance with it; these were adopted without a dissenting vote, whereupon a bolder step was taken and the audience was actually induced to vote an express repudiation of the resolutions of the common council.[71]

This unexpected indorsement of Douglas' position may be interpreted as a personal triumph of a masterful statesman in the very citadel of fanaticism, the laurels won by the persuasive eloquence of a lion-hearted orator. Time, however, showed that it had a deeper significance. Public opinion, wearied of agitation, was especially susceptible to any appeal for political quiet; the practical man realized the difficulty of effecting a repeal of legislation that had formally reached the statute books, while the agitator exhausted himself in futile condemnation of the most strenuous nine months of legislative controversy in American history.

The revival of party allegiance was a potent force in this process of readjustment. Party leaders finally came to realize that interest in the struggle at Washington had interfered with normal political activity at home. The closing weeks of congress and the period following adjournment, therefore, witnessed a general attempt to get the party machinery into

[71] Sheahan, *Life of Douglas*, 186; Flint, *Life of Douglas*, appendix 30; *Chicago Daily Journal*, October 24, 1850. The author of the other resolutions was B. S. Morris, a prominent old-line whig. Shields also introduced resolutions supporting the fugitive slave law. *Illinois State Register*, October 31, 1850.

AGITATION AND COMPROMISE

running order for the state and congressional elections in November, though it was too late to hold state conventions to nominate candidates for state treasurer. The democratic state committee, therefore, took the responsibility of offering the name of John Moore,[72] while the whigs made a feeble effort to rally to the support of John T. Knox. Democratic forces were badly split in the northern districts; but party leaders and party journals eloquently pleaded for union and harmony, for dropping past differences and uniting under one banner.[73] So zealously was this matter pressed that the separate free democratic candidate in the Chicago district was compelled to withdraw from the field. "Long John" had found his place in congress too unattractive to run again,[74] so that the party united on Dr. Richard S. Moloney, a Wentworth protégé of strong antislavery feelings; the *State Register*, however, struck his name from the list of democratic candidates that it posted.[75] This made the contest in that district, as elsewhere, a straight-out whig and democratic duel with only a handful of abolitionists in an independent movement. In the Springfield district Richard Yates, the whig candidate, defeated Thomas L. Harris in his campaign for reëlection and was the only whig member returned to congress.

Old party allegiance had thus crushed the very existence of the promising free soil movement of 1848. Strong antislavery activities were regarded as inconsistent with a proper loyalty to the union; they had been proved, moreover, in a party sense, to be disorganizing and party politicians now opposed them more than ever on that score. No sooner, therefore, had the legislative session organized in January, 1851, than a joint resolution was introduced declaring that inasmuch as the constitution was created and adopted in a spirit of compromise, and as slavery was one of the principal sub-

---
[72] *Illinois State Register*, September 5, 1850; Zarley to French, August 30, 1850, French manuscripts.
[73] *Ottawa Free Trader*, August 17, 30, September 28, 1850; *Chicago Democrat*, August 26, 30, September 6, 1850.
[74] Wentworth to E. W. Austin, July 1, 1850, *ibid.*, July 19, 1850; *Chicago Daily Journal*, July 10, 1850.
[75] *Illinois State Register*, October 17, 1850. Wentworth's opponents were planning to establish a rival conservative democratic paper in Chicago. Galloway to French, July 24, 1850, Harris to French, July 27, 1850, French manuscripts.

jects of compromise, as the constitution did not conflict with the divine law and as there was no higher law than the constitution, therefore, all controversy upon the subject of slavery was to be deprecated; for these reasons the measures of adjustment passed by congress in 1850, including the fugitive slave law, were given a hearty approval, the Illinois delegation in congress was instructed to use their best abilities and influence in resistance to any attempt to disturb this settlement, and the Wilmot proviso resolutions of instruction of 1849 were rescinded.[76]

This resolution, which was promptly passed, is an indication of the spirit that dominated party politics in Illinois up to the enactment of the Kansas-Nebraska bill. Especially was this true of the Illinois democracy, which was able to congratulate itself, despite antislavery resolutions of county and district conventions in the northern part of the state, that the state organization had never become contaminated with free soilism but had succeeded on the principles laid down by Thomas Jefferson and Andrew Jackson, while the party in other states had been divided by schisms and overwhelmed by defeat.[77] This remained a source of party strength until 1854 when it suddenly became a serious element of weakness with the reopening of the slavery controversy.

[76] *Laws of 1851*, p. 205-207; Underwood to Gillespie, January 15, 1851, Gillespie manuscripts.
[77] *Joliet Signal*, July 22, 1851.

IV. PRAIRIE FARMING AND BANKING

WITH the rush of immigration into Illinois new blood and energy was injected into all phases of agricultural activity. While the rest of the industrial population of the state increased only twenty per cent, the agriculturists more than doubled in the decade ending in 1860. The new settlers brought with them their own notions of successful farming, but their enthusiasm for the new environment tempered their devotion to old methods and inclined them to select only those features which might make for improvement. With the prairies thrown open for agricultural development and prairie farming only in its infancy this spirit of experimentation contributed to the important progress made in the last decade of the antebellum period.

Already by 1850 the adaptability of Illinois soil for specialization in corn culture had been demonstrated; a crop of 57,646,984 bushels of this staple represented an output nearly three times that of other grain crops. This emphasis on corn continued and was reflected in even stronger terms in 1860 when an output of 115,174,777 bushels moved Illinois from third rank as a corn growing state to the head of the column. In this decade the corn belt began to shift from the Illinois valley to the prairies of the eastern counties in the central division. Besides its supremacy in corn production, Illinois, the fifth wheat growing state of 1850, by more than doubling its wheat production, carried off first honors in 1860 with 23,837,023 bushels. In the early fifties the belief spread that the risks in wheat culture were less in southern Illinois where the grain matured earlier and was saved from the blight and rust caused by the June and July rains; and Egypt, which had been steadily losing ground during the forties, recovered with a sixfold increase while the northern and central divisions doubled their crops. The northern counties, however, still produced over one-half the wheat of the state. Northern Illinois also raised nearly three-fourths of the 15,220,029 oats crop of 1859, which represented a fifty per cent increase for the decade, and two-thirds of the rye crop of 951,281 bushels, and of the barley crop of 1,036,338 bushels, both of which represented tenfold increases.

With these important gains in the agricultural output of the state, Illinois became one of the most important granaries for the supply of the industrial centers of the Atlantic seaboard and Europe. Illinois flour began to find its way into eastern and European markets, the southern Illinois product being especially favored. Chicago came into its own as the grain emporium of Illinois and the west, an "agricultural weathercock" "showing from whence comes the balmy winds of prosperity." Soon it was the largest primary grain depot in the world.[1]

Grain buyers from Chicago scoured every section of the state, including even the extreme southern portion, and arranged to ship the crops northward. In order to hurry the grain to the eastern markets, eighteen of the most prominent mercantile houses organized a "Merchants' Grain Forwarding Association" in September, 1857. This represented a division of labor which changed the Board of Trade, organized in 1848, into a general commercial organization. Heavy grain speculation began to develop at Chicago; the operators worked incessantly at the exchange at the Board of Trade rooms and at a certain street corner known as "gamblers' corner." Many a fortune of $20,000 or $30,000 was made within a few weeks, though numbers of "lame ducks" appeared at the same time.[2] The general effect upon the business of the city was extremely good, but the farmers were restive under this system and throughout the decade continued a spasmodic agitation for coöperative associations for the disposal of their produce. Finally in 1858, local agitation led to a farmers' congress at the state fair at Centralia which adopted a declaration in favor

[1] *Illinois State Journal,* September 6, 1855; *Ottawa Free Trader,* February 18, 1854.
[2] *Cairo Times and Delta,* July 15, 1857; *Quincy Whig,* October 3, 1857; *Chicago Daily Times,* October 7, 1857; Guyer, *History of Chicago,* 23; *Chicago Democrat,* May 5, 1857; *Chicago Press and Tribune,* July 4, 1859.

FARMING AND BANKING

of the formation of wholesale purchasing and selling agencies in the great centers of commerce "so that producers may, in a great measure, have it in their power to save the profits of retailers."[3] It was another matter, however, to translate this resolution into action.

Good crops prevailed generally throughout the decade except in 1854 when a general drought did especially heavy damage in the southern part of the state. Vegetation in many districts was entirely burned up, wells and creeks dried up, and farmers unable to secure water often sold their stock to be driven where feed and water could be had rather than see it perish. The corn crop was seriously damaged, but small grains suffered less. Although there was no danger of a food shortage, the food speculators were soon at work forcing prices up to new records. High prices had been prevailing since the European famine year of 1847 which drove wheat up to $1.25 a bushel; a gradual drop had ended with the Crimean War news in early 1854 which, followed by the activity of foreign buyers, brought back $1.10 and $1.25 wheat. By that time prices which had previously varied considerably were becoming standardized by Chicago and New Orleans markets. The summer drought sent prices of breadstuffs higher than they had been for eighteen years, wheat selling at $1.25, corn at 40 cents and potatoes at $1.50. Normal prices had not been entirely restored when the panic of 1857 arrived. Speculators began to talk of short grain crops and of the rot in potatoes, but crowded cellars and bursting grain ricks contradicted their statements. They were able, however, to keep the bottom from falling out of the market, although the farmer suffered from the depression; the price of foodstuffs was prohibitive for the poor of the cities.[4]

It was obvious to the more aggressive and progressive agriculturalists of the state that education could work a vast improvement in prevailing methods and practices. Even con-

---

[3] *Rockford Register*, October 16, 1858; *Rockford Forum*, July 18, 1848; *Western Citizen*, January 8, 1850; *Our Constitution*, June 26, 1858.
[4] *Joliet Signal*, August 29, September 5, 1859; *Chicago Daily Times*, September 3, 1857. While exorbitant prices prevailed in Chicago, corn was burned for fuel at Kankakee as cheaper than coal. *Rockford Republican*, January 21, 1858.

temporary critics characterized the methods of cultivation as "most slovenly." "This is especially true in the Southern counties. The best farmers plough only four or five inches deep, never use a hoe, but do perhaps once in a season run a cultivator between the rows of Indian corn. Under such circumstances it is not probable that much more than half of what might be is raised." This was obvious, when in contrast with the general average of 35 bushels such large scale progressive farmers as B. F. Harris of Champaign county and David Strawn of La Salle county could raise over 60 bushels of corn per acre. B. F. Harris in 1855 harvested 700 acres of corn at 65 bushels per acre, 70 acres of oats at 30 bushels, 20 of wheat at 20 bushels, and 2 of potatoes at 75, besides raising 100 tons of hay, 360 head of cattle, 21 horses, 200 hogs and 12 sheep. In the same county Michael L. Sullivant planted over 7,000 acres in corn. There were farms with an acreage of 10,000 and even 27,000, one of the latter having 3,000 acres of corn in a single field. These large farms attracted considerable attention, but little was known of their methods by the small holders.[5]

With the decade of the fifties, however, the Illinois agriculturist began for the first time seriously to analyze his weaknesses and to determine his future needs. Out of the agitation for industrial education came the proposition to organize a state agricultural society. Farmers' associations and agricultural societies already existed in several counties, and under the leadership of the Sangamon County Agricultural Society the Illinois State Agricultural Society was launched at Springfield on January 5, 1853. One function of the new organization was to encourage the formation of additional county agricultural societies; it drafted a model constitution; and by the direct coöperation of its officers new societies were formed, first in the northern and central counties and later in southern Illinois. The legislature was induced to appropriate an annual sum of fifty dollars to each county society having an active existence. By the end of the decade, therefore, eighty-eight agricultural societies were to be found in Illinois, twenty more

[5] *Prairie Farmer*, July, 1855; *Western Journal*, 2:254; *Urbana Union*, October 25, 1855; *Our Constitution*, June 12, 1858; *Illinois Globe*, September 22, 1849.

than in any other state in the union. At the same time a broader connection was established when Illinois came to take part in the sessions of the National Agricultural Society, and when the Northwestern Agricultural Society established its headquarters at Chicago in 1859.[6]

Both the state and county societies placed especial emphasis on their annual fairs; the first state fair was held at Springfield, October 11-14, 1853. It was the policy of the society at this time to pass the state fair around among the various cities of the state; a movement gathered considerable force to localize it at Springfield with permanent grounds, purchased with a legislative appropriation; but it was defeated by the combined opposition of rival places.[7]

The premiums offered by the State Agricultural Society aroused general interest in new agricultural machinery. Several Illinois reapers were on the market, including, besides the Cyrus H. McCormick machine, the manufacture of which had come to be concentrated at Chicago, the inventions of Obed Hussey of Chicago, J. H. Manny of Freeport, Jerome Atkins of Will county, Charles Denton of Peoria, and G. H. Rugg of Ottawa. It was said that three of the four reaping machines that took prizes at the Paris exhibition in 1855 were owned and manufactured by residents of Illinois. Reaper trials were arranged to test the respective merits of the various machines; the State Agricultural Society held a trial at Salem in July, 1857, followed a few days later by a privately arranged contest at Urbana in which five reapers were entered. Advantages continued in favor of the C. H. McCormick machine which enjoyed special patent rights.[8] The success of mowers

[6] *Chicago Daily Democratic Press*, October 25, 1852; *Prairie Farmer*, December, 1852; *Illinois State Register*, January 13, 1853; *Peru Daily Chronicle*, January 6, 1854; *Chicago Weekly Democrat*, April 8, 1854; *Chicago Press and Tribune*, September 19, 1859, April 13, 1860.
[7] Illinois State Agricultural Society, *Transactions*, 1:43 ff.; *Aurora Beacon*, January 27, 1859.
[8] When, in 1852, McCormick applied for the renewal of certain patents that had already expired, considerable opposition developed on the part both of reaper inventors and of farmers who were unwilling to pay the patent fee of $30 which McCormick was able to collect under his monopoly. *Ottawa Free Trader*, February 7, 12, April 17, 1852; J. D. Webster to Trumbull, August 7, 1856, Trumbull manuscripts. See article "Illinois — The Reaper State," *Chicago Advertiser* clipped in *Illinois State Register*, November 6, 1851; also *ibid.*, September 4, November 13, 1851, September 13, 1855.

and reapers was so evident that inventive genius was next directed toward raking and binding attachments; L. D. Phillips of Chicago patented such an invention in December, 1857. Others brought out improvements in old machines with special devices of their own. The desire to develop a "steam plow" which might be used to turn the prairie sod with more economy than the use of horses, oxen, or mules would permit, furnished an interesting field of experimentation. At a trial at Decatur on November 10 and 11, 1858, a demonstration was made under unfavorable conditions, which was voted satisfactory by the newspaper correspondents. Another trial was made at the state fair at Freeport in 1859 with the Fawkes' steam plow, which had been awarded the grand gold medal at the United States Agricultural Fair the preceding year; the committee, however, was unable to arrive at a decision as to its success.[9]

By this time a considerable amount of agricultural machinery had been introduced on the large farms in certain regions along the Illinois river and in the upper counties, so that cultivators, seed drills, reapers, and mowers became fairly common while even a threshing machine was occasionally seen.[10] The value of farm implements and farm machinery increased from $6,405,561 in 1850 to $17,235,472 in 1860.

One of the chief difficulties of the Illinois farmer was that of securing a cheap and efficient fencing. Wood was too scarce and too expensive for its limited wearing qualities; wire and specially prepared sheet iron strips nailed to posts in the ground proved not altogether satisfactory; ditching and banking schemes and sod fences met with slight success, and though various kinds of hedges were tried, they were usually too slow of growth. Then Jonathan B. Turner introduced the Osage orange which had all the qualities most needed for a successful hedge — cheapness, certainty, quick growth, and unlimited endurance. By 1848 he had tried out two or three miles of hedge on his farm; and though it cost him $150 a mile for a three years' growth, he was able to sell plants at $10 per thou-

[9] *Chicago Daily Democratic Press,* January 8, 1858; *Chicago Press and Tribune,* November 15, 1858, September 13, 1859; *Belleville Advocate,* November 24, 1858; Illinois State Agricultural Society, *Transactions,* 3:99-100; 4:23.
[10] *Chicago Daily Democratic Press,* September 17, 1857; *Alton Courier,* August 2, 1858.

sand. Turner immediately called the attention of leading agriculturalists to his experiments, and by 1851 so many were converted to the Osage orange hedge that it threatened to supersede all other kinds of fences in a few years.[11]

Signs of a growing diversification of agriculture appeared during the fifties. Northern Illinois was raising potatoes in increasing quantities while in the southern counties castor beans became a favorite crop. The pioneer farmer and the recent settler had lacked the time to set out fruit trees and had later neglected this means of varying their hog and hominy diet. In 1850 there were few signs of fruit culture in Illinois. "Where the strawberry-bed ought to be, you will perhaps find a tobacco patch, and the hog-pen has usurped the place of the currant bushes,"[12] commented a thoughtful traveler.

Illinois farmers gradually became alive to this neglect of horticulture, especially as the demand arising for fruit and vegetables brought exorbitant prices for the available supply. Soon important developments were evident in the extreme southern counties of the state; by 1860 apples, peaches, and melons were shipped in large quantities from the southern fruit farms. Alton became an important fruit market with large exports; its peaches were sometimes ordered direct by New York fruit houses. Peach orchards of 1,000 trees became fairly common. Isaac Underhill of Peoria had on his "Rome Farm" of 2,200 acres an orchard one mile square with 10,000 grafted apple trees and 6,000 peach trees. William Yates had a four hundred acre farm in Perry county with over 4,000 peach, pear, and apple trees besides a wide assortment of smaller fruits. Mathias L. Dunlap's nursery near Urbana came to have a wide reputation for its excellent fruit and filled orders from every part of the west. Grape culture flourished in the German districts around Alton and Belleville; many

---

[11] J. B. Turner to French, May 24, July 7, 1848, French manuscripts; *Prairie Farmer*, January, 1851; *Western Journal*, 5: 190; *Joliet Signal*, January 14, 1851; *Illinois Journal*, April 2, 1851. Wire fences cost $181.80 per mile; rails $149.60, according to J. D. Whitely in *Prairie Farmer*, October, 1848.

[12] *Chicago Tribune* clipped in *Illinois State Register*, March 13, 1850. Potato prices hovered around the dollar mark during the earlier years of the decade but later dropped to twenty-five and thirty-five cents a bushel and became in truth the "poor man's comforter." *Alton Weekly Courier*, August 24, 1855; *Mound City Emporium*, May 13, 1858, March 17, 1859.

temperance advocates began to look to the use of native wines as the most satisfactory way of banishing drunkenness from the land.[18] In October, 1851, the Northwestern Fruit Growers' Association was organized; and, supported almost entirely by residents of Illinois, it met in annual session until 1857, when it decided to merge itself into the Illinois Horticultural Society, organized in 1856.

There were, of course, some unsuccessful attempts at diversification. In 1848 an enthusiastic campaign was inaugurated to develop hemp growing to the point of successful competition with the Missouri farmers; in a few years, however, the movement collapsed. Experiments were attempted with flax culture but without marked success, while the cotton crop of southern Illinois rapidly declined in spite of the previous success with it in that region.

The most exciting venture in the field of agriculture during the decade was in the cultivation of the ".Chinese sugar cane." The whole northwest nourished the ambition to convert itself into a sugar-growing district. In 1856 J. M. Kroh and a few other farmers in Wabash county planted small plots of this "Chinese millet," "sorgo sucre" or "northern sugar cane" as it was variously called, and reported great success with an output of forty-five gallons of syrup from a half acre notwithstanding many unfavorable factors. Immediately the keenest interest was aroused in this new discovery. Kroh alone sold seed to over 2,000 persons, and his neighbors distributed their surplus; seed was also distributed by congressmen as political favors to their constituents. In the next season the cane was planted in every county in the state; in many districts nearly every farmer planted at least a few rows by way of experiment; and Kroh's neighbor, Edwin S. Baker of Rochester Mills, tried the experiment on the largest scale, with twenty acres. The success of these various enterprises aroused enthusiasm for the new crop; sorghum molasses was immediately enrolled as an Illinois staple, and successful experiments in granulation made domestic sugar merely a question of the cost of manufacture. An Illinois State Sugar Cane Convention was held at Springfield, January 7, 1858; after an organization

[18] *Chicago Weekly Democrat*, August 6, 1853.

of the sugar growers was perfected, experiences were exchanged and important data assembled.[14] The result was an increased acreage and harvest. Sugar mills were installed, and although the production of sugar was found impracticable, the extraction of syrup was very successful; one mill in Springfield was operated in season day and night with a three hundred gallon daily output. The Illinois advocates of the Chinese sugar cane were exultant; nowhere in the United States had its cultivation been so successful and so encouraging.

Stock raising was an especially important interest in central Illinois where it proved a most profitable business when practiced on advanced principles. Three of the most extensive cattle raisers were Isaac Funk of Bloomington, who in 1854 sold in a single lot 1,400 head of cattle averaging 700 pounds for $64,000; Jacob Strawn, who fed the first steers in Morgan county and who "has probably fed more since that time than all other men in the county together;"[15] and B. F. Harris of Champaign county who made a fine showing at the World's Fair at New York in 1853; in 1855 he raised 500 head of cattle and 200 hogs and marketed a drove of 100 bullocks averaging 2,373 pounds. In the early days large cattle feeders like Jacob Strawn had to scour all central and southern Illinois and the settled parts of Missouri and Iowa to secure stock; now in the fifties cattle was brought in droves from Missouri, Texas, and even Mexico to convert the immense yield of Illinois corn into marketable form.

The more enterprising farmers of central Illinois were with decided advantage beginning to introduce blooded stock to improve the breed of cattle raised. It was next suggested that a joint stock company be organized to import first grade cattle from the east and from Europe. This suggestion was acted upon in December, 1856, when the Illinois Stock Importing Company was organized at Springfield with an immediate subscription of $12,700 worth of capital stock. A few months

---

[14] *Western Journal*, 4:14 ff.; F. S. Frazier to Trumbull, February 5, 1857, John H. Bryant to Trumbull, February 12, 1857, Trumbull manuscripts; *Illinois State Journal*, January 13, 1858.
[15] *Prairie Farmer*, November, 1854; cf. *Chicago Weekly Democrat*, December 23, 1854. His cattle sales in that season exceeded $96,000. Strawn for years either supplied or controlled the St. Louis beef market.

later its agents headed by Dr. H. V. Johns, former president of the Illinois Agricultural Society, were sent to England to make purchases. Some eighty head of imported stock arrived in Springfield in August, 1857, and were sold at auction to citizens of Illinois on the understanding that they should remain in the state for two years.

For pork growing few regions were as favorable as the Illinois prairies. Allowed to run at large upon the open plains as well as in the few timbered districts, hogs multiplied so rapidly that it was often a matter of difficulty to decide to whom a lot of grunting porkers owed allegiance. For this reason there were many advocates of a law for their confinement.[16] Since this was the only problem in hog raising—for there seemed to be no hog cholera or other disease until the spring of 1859—hogs were the chief means of converting the corn of the state into good marketable form. In 1850, 1,915,-907 hogs were raised; by 1860 the number had increased to 2,502,308.

Woolgrowing met with less success than other livestock interests in spite of the fact that Illinois seemed admirably adapted for sheep raising and although for some time the annual output of wool, chiefly from the northern counties and certain central districts, showed an increase. Extensive woolgrowers like Truman Humphreys of Peoria and James McConnell of Sangamon county insisted that wool could be grown in Illinois more profitably than anywhere else in the United States. With uncertain prices for wool, however, and with a more certain reward in other fields, most farmers were content to leave these opportunities to the advocate of woolgrowing. In the census of 1850, 894,043 sheep were listed with a wool crop of 2,150,113 pounds; but by 1860 an actual decrease of 14 per cent was indicated in the census total of 769,135 sheep.

The total value of the livestock of the state in 1850 was $24,209,258 and consequently meat packing had become an important industry; in that year animals to the value of $4,972,-286 were slaughtered. Pork brought in this decade prices ranging from $2 and $2.50 per hundred in the early years to

[16] *Cairo Weekly Delta,* November 23, 1848; *Prairie Farmer,* November, 1848.

FARMING AND BANKING

$5 and $6 in the latter part. For an average pork packing town 20,000 was a fair season's packing, and nearly a half million were packed annually in the state. In Alton and in the towns along the Illinois, notably Beardstown — the original Porkopolis — and Peoria, thousands of hogs were slaughtered each year; but with the opening of the canal and of the railroads more and more of the hogs were taken to Chicago to be slaughtered. By 1859 this tendency was so marked that Chicago had become the third pork packing city in the west and promised shortly to eclipse its rivals in the hog trade. The same development in the beef packing industry made Chicago in 1860 the greatest general meat packing center in the west.

The decade of progress along agricultural lines increased 5,039,545 acres of improved lands in 1850 to 13,096,374 ten years later. Unimproved holdings of 6,997,867 acres increased to 7,815,615. This represented an increased acreage of 73.7 per cent. The number of farms nearly doubled and the value of farm property nearly quadrupled. These statistics reflect the extraordinary demand for land that prevailed throughout the decade. Illinois, indeed, was still in the whirl of land speculation. The inpouring of settlers and the opening of the canal and of the railroads combined to produce a heavier demand and a greater accessibility for unoccupied holdings. Generally speaking, land sales came to involve fewer and fewer direct transactions between the government and the actual settler.

The unique event of 1848 was the placing upon the market of the Illinois and Michigan canal lands, an event which had been delayed by the interests of a clique of Chicago speculators. Prominent Chicago politicians claimed preëmption rights which held up some of the most valuable pieces;[17] and, with money scarce and the speculative feeling supposedly not very high, the sales went off with little spirit. The remaining lands, increased by 35,000 acres under a new construction of the federal grant, were offered to the public in annual sales. A rush to these sales began in 1852 and 1853; Chicago hotels

[17] Colonel Charles Oakley to French, August 26, September 6, 1848, French manuscripts.

were crowded, considerable excitement and competition among purchasers developed, and the bidding was prompt and spirited. By 1855 the best of the lands had been taken, although the sales continued to be held each successive year until the end of the decade.

On September 28, 1850, congress donated to the several states in which they lay, the public swamp lands and lands liable to overflow. These lands, which eventually totalled 1,833,413 acres, were promptly surveyed; and the general assembly of Illinois granted them to the counties in which they were located for the construction of the necessary levees and drains to reclaim them; the balance, if any, was to be distributed among the townships equally for education or roads and bridges as the county authorities might decide. These lands had been placed on sale and many disposed of when the federal government intervened on account of certain technicalities, which were not adjusted until after the purchasers had gone through a long siege of uncertainty. When in 1857 the rights of the states were confirmed by congress, the lands were again placed on the market; and all sales were later formally approved by the general assembly.[18]

In 1851, the assembly first directed the auditor to withhold from sale state lands along the more important railroad lines and later suspended the sale of all state holdings until two years later when they were again placed on the market, the proceeds to be devoted to the liquidation of the state indebtedness, with preëmption rights for squatter settlers.[19]

The state, however, was not the most important factor in the land sales of this period. The various federal land offices dispensed tracts from the millions of acres still in the possession of the federal government. Cash sales continued to be heavy while thousands of acres were entered with Mexican War land warrants and with warrants under the bounty land act of September 28, 1850. The lands along the Illinois Central were withheld from sale for a year while the selections

[18] *Laws of 1852*, p. 178-186; *Laws of 1859*, p. 201, 202; see petitions in Trumbull manuscripts for 1856.
[19] *Laws of 1851*, p. 23, 204; *Laws of 1853*, p. 231-234. These preëmption rights and sales in general were extended under acts of February 15, 1855, and February 16, 1857.

were being made for the Illinois Central railroad under its grant of 1850, after which there was a heavy rush both by actual settlers and by speculators; soon all lands within the grant were entered. Sales were especially brisk in southern Illinois, where the best lands were soon exhausted. The poorer lands, however, spurned in the open market, were quickly taken up, when, in 1854, congress passed a graduation act which permitted land entries at as little as twelve and one-half cents an acre.

As a result of these activities the public lands rapidly disappeared. The Quincy land office was closed up in June of 1855; already the Shawneetown district was rapidly approaching the 100,000 acre minimum which would terminate its claim to a separate land office. It was not long before the books of the general land office showed only a little over one quarter of a million acres remaining unsold.[20]

This left the Illinois Central the greatest landed proprietor of Illinois. An immense tract of two and a half million acres scattered over forty-seven counties and equal to ten counties of over four hundred square miles was transferred by the federal government to the railroad through the state as an intermediary. The selections were made and the titles completed by the spring of 1852 when the company prepared to open up its land office. The lands were divided into four classes: about 50,000 acres — valuable either as especially suitable for town sites or as containing mineral wealth — were to sell at not less than $20 per acre; 350,000 acres of superior farming land at $15 an acre; 1,300,000 acres at $8; and the remainder at $5. These prices were to be applied to land which, lying on the unbroken prairies, had previously been undesirable at $1.25 an acre; and while this schedule was being fixed, the government was selling its adjacent holdings at a maximum of $2.50 an acre. On September 27, 1854, the company opened its Bloomington office which in the first month reported the sale of 15,242 acres in McLean county at an average price of $9.97. In another year the company was aggressively pushing the sale of its lands in all parts of the state. By

[20] *Chicago Weekly Democrat*, June 23, 1855; *Chicago Daily Democratic Press*, March 22, 1858.

1857 with its grant half sold the company had realized $14,000,000.[21]

Thousands of squatters who had developed improved farms were found in southern Illinois on the lands along the Illinois Central. The general assembly recommended to congress that squatters on the federal domain be granted preëmption rights for a period of twelve months; the company, left to itself, pursued a policy of similar generosity toward the bona fide settler. In addition it extended long credits to settlers generally and was lenient to purchasers who found themselves unable to make their payments.[22]

The speculator also had his innings in all this confusing race for control of the soil. Thousands of acres in every county remained the unimproved property of purchasers who were holding them for a rise in value; extensive feeling among the settlers was aroused against these land monopolists, many of whom were eastern capitalists.[23]

The great bulk of the speculators, although they often followed outside leadership, was found in the local residents—successful farmers, lawyers, business men, and politicians. Governor French in his second term took advantage of the renewed agitation in favor of the Illinois Central railroad to buy up warrants and locate lands through a dozen friends and agents all along the probable route. His interests were also linked with the supporters of the Atlantic and Mississippi, a group of southern Illinois democratic leaders, who, while pressing its claim before the people and in the legislature, avidiously bought land about the strategic points on the line. Uri Manly, one of them, after having waited twenty years for such an opportunity, was fortunate enough to secure the land at the intersection of the Illinois Central and this proposed railroad; when the legislature refused a charter in 1851 and

---

[21] *Beardstown Gazette*, July 30, 1851; *Peru Daily Chronicle*, May 5, 1854; *Ottawa Free Trader*, September 5, 1857.

[22] *Laws of 1851*, p. 207-208; M. Brayman to Noah Johnston, November 4, 1852, in *Illinois State Register*, December 2, 1852; *Chicago Press and Tribune*, March 18, 1859.

[23] The Munn Illinois Land Company, an eastern concern, declared a dividend of $15 a share in 1851. *Cairo Sun*, May 22, 1851. The proverbial acumen of poets was proved by William Cullen Bryant, who sold his holding on the Rock Island railroad for $10 per acre shortly before it rose in value to many times that amount. *Boston Post* clipped in *Illinois State Register*, June 29, 1854.

again in 1852, he complained that he had lost a $15 accretion on two pieces of 4,000 acres in Effingham county, besides 2,300 acres in Clark county. "I had made a town — a city where our Road & the Central crossed," he lamented to his colleague in misfortune, Governor French.[24] With the rapid disappearance of the public domain and with the inflated prices of speculative holdings, agrarian movements began to take form in Illinois. Many citizens came to decry, with John Wentworth of the *Chicago Democrat*, the trend toward "the tenant system, under which Republicanism is impossible. This system," they held, "tends to separate classes in society; to the annihilation of the love of country; and to the weakening of the spirit of independence."[25] Already by 1850 the landless were the most numerous class of people in Chicago. The remedy agreed upon by all advocates of land reform was the free grant of homesteads to actual settlers, thus taking from the capitalist his last stronghold, the monopoly of the soil. Such reformers were numerous within the ranks of both political parties; in his zeal for his party, however, the whig politician often claimed a homestead policy as "true whig policy" while the democrat claimed the same honor for his party.

Radical land reformers, who were usually also aggressive abolitionists as well, spurned the advance of the old political parties and organized independent land reform associations, carrying on an aggressive propaganda of their own. In 1848 the "national reformers" held a national industrial congress and chose as their presidential candidates, Gerrit Smith of New York, and William S. Wait of Illinois. In the fall of that year the "national reformers" held a meeting in Chicago in which they repudiated the newly organized free soil party and its reform platform because it failed to assert "man's inherent and inalienable right to a limited portion of the soil upon which he subsists" as the real and only ground of "free soil." Later, however, when Van Buren placed himself on satisfactory ground and the free democracy of Chicago adopted

[24] Uri Manly to French, September 3, October 27, December 17, 1851, January 29, March 2, 1852, French manuscripts; see also French manuscripts for 1850 and 1851.
[25] *Chicago Democrat*, January 22, March 28, 29, 31, 1848.

90 THE ERA OF THE CIVIL WAR

" the true free soil principle," they were able to effect a working agreement. They immediately undertook an active campaign which culminated in an Industrial Congress at Chicago on June 6 and 7, 1850, which adopted resolutions offered by H. Van Amringe, a prominent lecturer and reformer, declaring that "the free land proviso would everywhere, on the cotton plantations of the South, and in the cotton factories of the North, unite all lovers of freedom and humanity, against all haters of freedom and humanity, and would strip the question of liberty of all prejudices resulting from sectional and partial agitation." These reformers saw the folly of fighting an autocracy that dominated the southern half of the nation while supporting in their own midst, " Factory Lords, Land Lords, Bankers, Speculators, and Usurers."[26]

Independent thinkers like John Wentworth had always seen the issue of land monopoly behind the slavery question; from this point of view the Wilmot proviso was "but a modification of the great principle, that the earth was given for the uses of man; and that, like the other essential elements to existence, no portion of its surface should be the subject of monopoly." For that reason he was a supporter of the preëmption policy and in the spring of 1848 introduced into congress a resolution for the extension of three years of the time for payment under the preëmption laws; later he presented many Illinois petitions for land reform and on January 22, 1850, laid before the house a resolution passed by the lower house of the Illinois legislature in favor of a homestead law.[27]

With this official sanction from the most representative body in Illinois, it was now obvious that a radical reform had become popular. Douglas had introduced a homestead bill on December 27, 1849, and defended it with eloquence; Richardson and other members of the Illinois delegation also accepted the principle of free grants to actual settlers and were kept busy presenting memorials of Illinoisians in its favor. When therefore, in the congressional campaign of 1850 the "Na-

[26] *Gem of the Prairie*, May 20, July 1, 22, October 7, 14, 21, November 25, December 9, 1848. Wait, however, declined the nomination and was made elector at large on the ticket of the "national reformers." *Chicago Democrat*, November 3, December 12, 1848, June 7, 8, 17, 1850.
[27] *Ibid.*, November 20, 1848; *Congressional Globe*, 31 congress, 1 session, 302.

tional Reform" Association of Chicago questioned the various candidates on their attitude toward land reform it received without exception favorable replies.[28] In 1851, the general assembly adopted a joint resolution urging congress to enact a homestead law. With another land reform convention at Chicago on October 13, 1851, the reformers had completed their work and were gratified to see their views adopted by the lower house at Washington. In the senate the fight continued without success until June, 1860, when the law was blocked by the veto of President Buchanan. With the organization of the republican party and the incorporation of a homestead plank in its platform, the republicans claimed special consideration as the champions of the homestead bill; challenging the devotion of their opponents on all occasions, they were able to make effective use of Buchanan's veto as an argument in favor of the election of Lincoln in the campaign of 1860. On the basis of their success they were able to carry out their promises in the homestead law of 1862.

Railroad construction and the land boom of the fifties had an important effect upon the state of the public treasury. At the beginning of this period the state, with an indebtedness of $16,661,795, was still virtually bankrupt and unable to pay the accumulated and long overdue interest. Under the refunding act of 1847, however, the conversion of the internal improvement indebtedness was started under the direction of Governor French, and confidence in the credit of the state began to develop in the financial world. The constitution of 1848 placed the state on a basis of strict economy in the matter of salaries and general expenditures and article fifteen authorized a two mill tax to be applied to the state indebtedness. With the authorization of the Illinois Central and various other railroads, moreover, Illinois stock began to take a rapid rise. New York bondholders for some time urged that the Central road be constructed by a company composed of bondholders under special favors from the state.[29] The last install-

---

[28] *Ibid.*, 31 congress, 1 session, 87, 262-267; *Chicago Democrat*, November 4, 1850.
[29] *Aurora Beacon*, September 26, 1850; *Beardstown Gazette*, April 30, 1851; James Holford to French, December 10, 1850, William Osman to French, April 29, 1851, French manuscripts.

ment of the $1,600,000 canal loan and interest was paid in October, 1853, when the canal passed to the exclusive direction of the state. The state debt had just reached its maximum and was officially reported at $16,724,177. The two mill tax was being applied to the payment of interest on outstanding bonds; a proposed constitutional amendment to appropriate it to the purchase of state bonds failed of receiving popular ratification in November, 1852. Matters improved, however, so that internal improvement bond quotations began to approach par. In December, 1855, the first payment of the state's share of seven per cent of the profits of the Illinois Central railroad was made with the sum of $29,000. By 1859, certain Illinois indebtedness was commanding a premium of three per cent in certain markets, and it was no longer found necessary to collect the two mill tax.

In 1859 the fraudulent redemption of nearly a quarter million of 1839 ninety-day canal scrip was discovered, and ex-Governor Matteson was found to be the chief beneficiary. Inasmuch as he had been chairman of the senate finance committee before his election as governor in 1852, it was hard to prove his plea of ignorance of the fraud involved. He was allowed, however, to give security for refunding the money to the state within a period of five years.

The same year witnessed certain irregularities that led to the resignation of Secretary of Treasury James Miller; simultaneously Governor Bissell under a misapprehension of the law ordered the funding of a portion of the Macallister and Stebbins bonds, but his mistake was discovered in time to withdraw his action without injury to the state. With the public finances rapidly attaining bedrock soundness, therefore, these frauds and charges of frauds became subjects of political discussion.

One obstacle to the free and untrammelled development of the state along economic lines was the absence of adequate banking facilities. The need of capital was a fundamental factor in the plans of the merchant, manufacturer, or farmer for expansion. The legal rate of interest was advanced to ten per cent in 1849, but little money could be had even at that price. Money handlers were able to violate the law with impunity and demand fifteen, twenty, and even twenty-five per cent. Little specie appeared in circulation, and the uncertain paper money of foreign banks — that is, of banks organized in other states — had the field. Agricultural and business progress naturally was held back by these conditions.

Yet the outlook in 1848 was anything but encouraging. The attempt to extend the charter of the State Bank for two years had failed in 1848; and arrangements were made to wind up the affairs of that institution — a result that called forth from the Illinois democracy, the political majority, a sigh of relief that suggested vivid recollections of fingers burned in the banking debauch of the thirties. Although the bank democrats were evident in the commercial districts of northern Illinois, democratic leadership insisted that banks and the banking issue be relegated to oblivion to save the party from their contaminating influence; a hard money policy was defined as an essential test of genuine democracy. Whig politicians shortly undertook to make their party the distinctive champion of the banking facilities for which the business interests clamored; this alignment stood out in the election of the constitutional convention and in the discussions of the banking issue in that body.

When the new constitution was drafted, though every attempt to secure a constitutional prohibition against banking failed, an article shaped by radical anti-bank democrats was adopted which required every bank charter authorized by the general assembly to be submitted first to the people for their acceptance or rejection.

This was an ironclad guarantee against special legislation in the interest of favored business interests; at the same time it conveyed to bank advocates the hint that they might secure their ends in a general banking system such as might parallel the "free" banking systems recently inaugurated by New York, Ohio, and other states. From this point of view the bank forces hailed the adoption of the new constitution as a favorable indication of popular acceptance of their viewpoint. Soon an active campaign was launched; the Chicago Board of Trade framed a bill for the authorization of general banking privileges to be submitted to the legislature, while the business interests in other cities organized meetings to agitate in favor of banks.[30]

The faithful and vigilant sentinels on the democratic watchtowers of Illinois sounded the warning of this new danger. The party, therefore, incorporated in its 1848 platform a plank declaring "HOSTILITY TO A UNITED STATES BANK, AND ALL KINDRED INSTITUTIONS, WHETHER OF A STATE OR A NATIONAL CHARACTER, AUTHORIZED BY EITHER GENERAL OR SPECIAL LAWS." The interests of Illinois were declared by downstate democrats to be agricultural and not commercial. Governor French in his message of January, 1849, expressed himself explicitly and unreservedly against the introduction of banking institutions; and for a time the tide was stemmed.[31]

Then began a war of words between the bank and anti-bank forces, the one finding in the presence of banks the explanation of every economic ill with which banking states were afflicted, the other attributing the economic backwardness of Illinois and the dullness of business to the absence of banking facilities. Meantime, it was discovered that there was no constitutional or legal provision against insurance companies that might furnish money for loans and add to the facilities for carrying on trade by issuing some form of evidence of indebtedness as a circulating medium. The paper of the Wisconsin Marine and Fire Insurance Company, an institution located at Chicago and controlled by George Smith, had a wide circulation in northern Illinois. Chicago business interests considered the expediency of utilizing the Chicago Fire and Marine Insurance Company to this end. Springfield interests advocated the establishment of a local company to supply money to local borrowers.[32]

This eagerness for paper currency stimulated the organization of unincorporated private banking companies whose issues began to circulate at a variable discount. It also brought into the state a flood of foreign paper: Ohio "red backs."

[30] *Western Journal*, 4:211 ff.; *Illinois State Register*, May 5, December 29, 1848; *Joliet Signal*, January 2, 1849.
[31] *Illinois State Register*, May 5, 1848; *Joliet Signal*, January 16, February 27, 1849.
[32] *Chicago Democrat*, February 19, April 19, May 8, December 6, 1849; *Illinois Journal*, April 27, May 11, 1850; *Illinois State Register*, June 21, 1849.

Indiana "shinplasters," and all sorts of "rag" money of outside banks of unknown soundness. It was estimated that in 1850 St. Louis had a bank circulation of nearly half a million dollars in Illinois, while the people of the state paid annually in the form of interest not less than $600,000 of tribute money to foreign financial institutions.[33]

The laws of trade had proved stronger than the laws of Illinois; as a result Illinois suffered from all the evils of a paper circulating medium without receiving any of the benefits which banks conferred. "The present system has driven capitalists from the State to invest their wealths elsewhere, and domestic enterprise hobbles about on crutches, being forced to pay the unlicensed usurer twenty and twenty-five per cent. interest, for the poor privilege of moving at a snail's pace," complained the spokesman of the bank forces.[34] "Since we cannot prevent the bank paper of other States from flooding ours," he reasoned, "and since we must pay so enormously for its circulation, does not necessity and self-preservation call upon us to doff our scruples about banking for the present — make our own Banks, use our own money, and pay the profit to our own States."[35]

The bank forces concentrated their energies on a plea for a system of free banking that would provide a safe and reliable currency by which every dollar issued would be secured by real estate or other good, safe, and reliable property; a general banking law similar to the one prevailing in New York was urged. The issue was fought to a decision in the legislative session of 1851, after a large number of bank men had been elected to the general assembly. Governor French and downstate democratic leaders threw their entire strength against the movement; several professed anti-bank assembly men from the northern counties, however, including E. B. Ames and Peter Sweat, voted for the law because of the strong

[33] *Illinois Journal,* January 3, October 12, December 19, 1850.
[34] *Rock Island Advertiser* clipped in *Illinois Journal,* January 3, 1850.
[35] *Tazewell Mirror* clipped in *ibid.,* October 12, 1850. Said the *Journal,* November 23, 1850: "If banks are to furnish the medium of exchange of property, we can see no reason why we should not have them under our control; and we can see many reasons why such institutions would consolidate scattered funds, collect capital, and thus furnish facilities for doing the heavy produce business of our State."

demand of their constituents for banking facilities. Senator Joel A. Matteson cast the deciding vote in the upper house on the principle that it had become a question for the people to decide. When the bank bill passed both houses it promptly met the gubernatorial veto. Upon reconsideration, however, the assembly overrode the suspensive veto of the governor and enacted the measure over his head in the closing hours of the session.[36]

This law provided for the incorporation of banking associations on a minimum of fifty thousand dollars of capital stock. They were authorized to do a general banking business and were to receive from the auditor circulating notes to the market value of state or federal bonds deposited with him. The prevailing uncertainty as to the stability of Illinois securities occasioned a discrimination against them in the requirement that they be listed at twenty per cent less than their average market value. Banks were limited to seven per cent interest on loans, three per cent less than the current rate. The banks were to operate under the supervision of the auditor and of three banking commissioners.[37]

It remained for the measure, in accordance with the constitution, to go before the people for their approval. A stirring contest followed. Invoking the shade of Andrew Jackson, democratic leaders fought the "hydra headed monster," throwing themselves in the way of "the great oligarchy of money" that was said to rule Chicago. The New England and New York elements in northern Illinois, however, had brought with them preferences for banks which even local democratic leaders could not defy. This fact came out clearly in the canvass and proved the undoing of democratic leadership. The election in November, 1851, returned a fifty-four per cent vote in favor of the law: only four counties north of Springfield went anti-bank, while the counties about Chicago returned bank majorities of from eighty-five to ninety-five per cent; southern Illinois, except the old whig strongholds, voted overwhelmingly against the law. The democrats soon found

[36] E. B. Ames to French, December 22, 1851, Peter Sweat to French, December 22, 1851, French manuscripts; *Illinois Journal*, February 12, 17, 27, 1851; *Laws of 1851*, p. 163-175.
[37] *Ibid.*, p. 163 ff.

FARMING AND BANKING 97

themselves embarrassed by the question as to whether they could still make hostility to banks a test of party orthodoxy.[38] A number of banks were promptly organized throughout the northern part of the state under the law of 1851. The law was so construed, however, as to result in two types of institutions: those engaged in a general banking business under the supervision of the auditor and issuing non-secured notes, and those depositing securities with the auditor and obtaining notes for circulation. Only two banks issuing secured paper were organized by the summer of 1852, so that secured bank notes furnished but a small part of the circulating currency. For this reason there was much complaint and considerable talk of repeal in the session of 1853, the senate formally acting in favor of a repeal measure. This caused a rush for bank applications; within a few days twenty-seven were filed with the auditor. At the end of 1852 the first bank in southern Illinois was established at Belleville, St. Clair county; so eagerly did this district, which gave the largest numerical vote against the bank law, seek to embrace the opportunities created by it that a few months later four other companies were organized in that county with an aggregate capital of eight and a half millions, although none of these passed the stage of paper projects. By 1854, however, the banking commissioners, headed by ex-Governor French, reported only twenty-nine banks operating under the law, ten of which were located in Chicago, and two each in Springfield and Naperville, with other cities supplied with a single institution; these had an authorized capital of seventeen millions and resources totalling over six millions. Notes to the amount of over a million dollars were issued during the first year of the general banking act. They constituted, however, but a small fraction of the entire circulating medium of the state. Illegal issues by both private banks and certain of the newly authorized banking associations together with the notes of foreign banks comprised the vast

[38] *Joliet Signal*, September 9, 1851; W. Reddick to French, November 27, 1848, F. C. Sherman to French, December 6, 1848, E. B. Ames to French, December 16, 1851, William M. Jackson to French, January 2, 1852, French manuscripts. William Reddick, Joel A. Matteson, Norman B. Judd, Plato, Charles V. Dyer, John Hise, and Benjamin F. Hall were among the democratic bank men. '*Chicago Democrat*, December 3, 1851.

bulk. At the recommendation of Governor French and his successor, Governor Matteson, the legislature undertook in the supplementary act of 1853 to drive out all unauthorized issues, whether domestic or foreign. This was successful in eliminating the Illinois lawbreakers; but in spite of the drive, paper of non-specie paying foreign banks continued in the field, largely pandering to the demand for small notes which grew out of the high premium on silver coins. In 1854, over two and a quarter million secured notes were in circulation, but these were estimated as furnishing only thirty per cent of the entire volume of circulation in Illinois.[39]

The domestic issues, however, furnished a very reliable currency[40] amply protected through the cautious policy of the auditor in regard to the securities deposited with him. In the fall of 1854 Illinois banks were put to their first test when panic conditions began to appear in the west as a result of overdevelopment in railroads. When Virginia and Missouri bonds, which constituted two-thirds of the bank securities, dropped several points below par, a general alarm seized the holders of Illinois currency, especially of that based on Virginia and Missouri securities. The panic struck Chicago in November; runs on various institutions commenced; thousands of dollars of notes were presented for redemption; and several banks were compelled to close their doors. In a few weeks, however, after assurances by two of the bank commissioners, the excitement subsided, although money continued to be very tight. The auditor's report for December 1, 1854, showed three banks permanently closed by the panic; five others still in a state of suspension were later forced into liquidation under the supplementary act of 1855.[41]

By 1856 banking operations had expanded until $6,480,873 of notes were in circulation. Even then this paper constituted

[39] *Illinois Journal*, February 12, 1853; *Belleville Advocate*, December 8, 1852, February 16, 1853; *Illinois State Register*, June 15, 1854; *Bankers' Magazine*, 9: 102-113. Many bankers preferred to circulate their notes outside of the state in order to postpone the necessity of redeeming them; domestic needs, therefore, had to be cared for largely by recognized foreign paper.
[40] *Thompson's Bank Reporter* clipped in *Ottawa Free Trader*, May 20, 1854.
[41] *Alton Weekly Courier*, November 23, 1854; *Chicago Daily Democratic Press*, November 17, 1854; *Free West*, November 23, 1854; *Illinois Journal*, November 24, 1854; *Aurora Guardian*, December 7, 1854; *Bankers' Magazine*, 9: 822.

but a minor part of the currency of Illinois. Much foreign paper, especially the notes of Georgia banks, circulated in the state. Several of the Georgia banks were institutions owned by Chicagoans. George Smith had opened two banks in Georgia to take advantage of the opportunity of circulating paper unhampered by bond deposit restrictions and by limited interest rates. Although bitterly attacked by regulation bankers and by the journals of the state almost without exception, Smith's Georgia operations had sufficient stability not only to weather the storm of abuse but for a long time to thrive upon it as an excellent advertising medium. The war on the "Georgia red dogs and wild cats" took the form of prolonged runs on the bank of issue and of a boycotting agreement in which the leading merchants and business men of Chicago urged the banks to refuse to receive Georgia paper on deposit.[42] Smith, however, held his own until declining profits hastened his retirement in 1858.

The banking system was given a thorough overhauling in an act of February 14, 1857, which provided for more adequate regulation and at the same time sought to encourage legitimate banking by increasing the legal rate of interest from seven to ten per cent. This revision in part reflected the signs of an approaching storm in the financial world. The warning of 1854 had not stemmed the tide of overspeculation in the west, nor had it pointed out the danger of overexpansion of loans, discounts, and note issues, in the banking world. Two-thirds of the securities of the stock banks consisted of the bonds of Missouri, whose credit was now almost ruined by its wild fling at internal improvements. All these factors undermined the banking and currency situation in Illinois, and signs pointed to a financial collapse. The state was saved, however, by the solid foundations laid during the first six years under the banking act of 1851 and by the coöperation of the various forces in the financial world in making the necessary adjustments. The banks retired a part of their note issues and reduced the

---

[42] *Belleville Advocate*, October 4, 1854. "George Smith ought to pay the editors for abusing his bank of Atlanta. They have abused it into credit all over the United States. It is current all over the Union." *Chicago Weekly Democrat*, July 2, 1853; *Rockford Republican*, January 2, 1856; Andreas, *History of Chicago*, 1: 546, 547, 2: 617.

outstanding circulation by nearly a million; Chicago bankers agreed to receive the notes of Illinois banks at par despite steady depreciation. Auditor Jesse K. Dubois called for additional securities to cover the decline in the value of state bonds. The action of St. Louis merchants in voting to reject all Illinois currency offered at their counters caused general alarm, but they were shortly induced to recall their decision and to accept Illinois paper at a slight discount.[43]

In this way Illinois was saved from the full effects of the panic of 1857. Six banks out of fifty-four failed; but with a single exception, all redeemed their notes without loss to the holders. Business for a time came to a complete standstill in Chicago, 117 establishments failing out of 1,350; in the rest of the state, however, conditions were far from serious, with 199 failures out of 11,459.[44] The early months of 1858 showed rapid recovery; but with a short grain crop in that year, it remained for another twelvemonth to initiate the complete restoration of normal conditions. The bank commissioners, reporting in January, 1859, proclaimed the fact that the banking system had withstood the test of two trying years of financial depression and was therefore entitled to public approval. Governor Bissell subscribed to this fact in his message, and the legislature on this ground acquiesced in the decision to allow the system to stand without change. The decade, therefore, gave the state the experience of passing from a puerile hostility to banking institutions through a successful experiment with the institutions of a complex economic order.[45]

[43] *Illinois State Journal*, April 1, 1857; *Ottawa Republican*, April 4, 1857; J. K. Dubois to Trumbull, October 5, 1857, Trumbull manuscripts; *Quincy Whig*, October 5, 1857; *Chicago Daily Democratic Press*, October 6, 9, 14, 1857; *Cairo Weekly Times and Delta*, October 14, 1857.
[44] *Bankers' Magazine*, 12:681.
[45] *Illinois State Journal*, January 5, 1859; Dowrie, *The Development of Banking in Illinois*, 131-158.

V. THE KANSAS-NEBRASKA ACT

IN THE closing decade of the ante-bellum period no political issues remained vital enough to hold voters rigidly to old party affiliations. In Illinois local issues had changed with three decades of statehood; new problems in banking, railroad development, and education scarcely permitted an alignment that would coincide with old party divisions. In the main these questions came to be settled on their merits exclusive of the possibility of making political capital out of them. National politics in spite of the senility of orthodox leaders and issues was forced to furnish the chief basis of party alignment. Andrew Jackson, the popular champion of western democracy, had passed away without leaving any successor to continue the old traditions in their former vigor. Surely President Polk had not done so, nor was Franklin Pierce to meet with any more success. The leadership of Stephen A. Douglas was an acknowledged factor in Illinois but not in the nation at large. Even this was more than any whig could claim. Henry Clay had closed his career in a blaze of glory, not as a party chieftain, but as a national leader. No one fell a clear heir to his mantle, not even Abraham Lincoln, the aggressive Illinois orator who following Clay's death delivered the commemorative eulogy in the statehouse at Springfield.[1] Lincoln, indeed, was just reappearing from the obscurity forced upon him by his unpopular opposition to the Mexican War.

Whiggery was now upon its deathbed; anaemic democracy, desperately seeking a blood transfusion from political movements of youthful vigor, hoped to save itself from a like fate. The national bank issue was dead and buried; it was no longer politic to resurrect it either as a Cerberus to protect the nation's treasure or as a dragon to call forth a new American St. George. The tariff was discussed by all in terms of the revenue needs

[1] *Illinois State Register*, July 8, 1852.

of the government and the prosperity of American industry. Land policy was debated only in reference to the great agrarian reform demanded by the whole west to give land to the landless. Eyes were fixed on Washington, the federal capital, to be sure, but largely to judge of the nearness of the political storm that was gathering, a menace to all existing party lines. Illinoisians watched, ready to take refuge under the new standard of "liberty and union."

Before the crisis of 1850 the general desire of the northwest that the new territories should not be disgraced by the incubus of the enslaved African had expressed itself in an outburst of political independence which had threatened to arouse the south, regardless of party allegiance, to battle in defense of its institutions. The danger of disunion brought a reaction in which zeal for liberty was replaced by an even keener devotion to the union; even the professional politician decried that agitation out of which he had hoped to secure so much profit and sent forth the rally cry of loyalty to party.

This reaction was carried to completion in the course of 1851, undisturbed by the unexciting contests for city and county offices. The new bank law which was submitted to the voters for ratification aroused some democratic anti-bank prejudices. Party activities that sought to defy the general lethargy were directed toward the coming presidential and state election. Democrats early began to discuss the relative merits of their available candidates. Almost all were agreed upon Senator Douglas for the presidency, so that livelier discussion took place concerning the gubernatorial nomination. An array of names was suggested including those of David L. Gregg of Cook county, then secretary of state, Colonel John Dement of Lee county, and Joel A. Matteson, a well-known politician and contractor upon public works.[2] It was generally agreed,[3] that the nominee of the party must be a democrat ready to eschew with a holy abhorrence all Wilmot provisoism or free-soilism. Others, in line with traditional democratic anti-bank doctrine, held that the recent revival of the bank question also required

---

[2] Matteson to French, November 18, December 15, 1851, French manuscripts.
[3] *Chicago Democrat*, February 10, 1852, spoke for the few dissenters to this policy.

THE KANSAS-NEBRASKA ACT 103

the old test of orthodoxy and that only anti-bank men ought to be considered.[4] To the Egyptian democracy anti-Wilmot provisoism and anti-bankism were cardinal principles. When Dement, their early favorite, came out against the bank question as a party issue, they abandoned him for Gregg, who seemed to have a clean bill of health on both points.[5] Northern democrats, satisfied with the abortive death of an attempt to apportion the state convention on the basis of the democratic vote of 1848 as against total population, bided their time.[6] When the state convention opened at Springfield in April, Gregg was easily the favorite candidate. For six ballots he led the field; then his opponents began to concentrate on Matteson, whose strength grew until finally he was nominated on the eleventh ballot. The ticket was completed by the selection of Gustave P. Koerner for lieutenant governor, Alexander Starne for secretary of state, and Thomas H. Campbell for auditor.

Steam roller tactics seemed to dominate the convention, making possible the harmony that prevailed. All new business had to pass through the hands of a special committee, so that the introduction of various disorganizing resolutions was prevented. This accounted for the silence of the convention on the bank and slavery questions and explained the passage of resolutions approving the democratic principles of '40, '44, and '48, declaring for full obedience to the laws of the country, especially the recent compromise legislation, and seriously deploring all sectional agitation.[7] It was further agreed that

[4] The new bank law submitted to voters for ratification in 1851 aroused some democratic anti-bank prejudices but at the same time met with support from large numbers of northern Illinois democrats, who saw no harm in coöperation with whig bank men. [Lewiston] *Illinois Public Ledger,* clipped in *Chicago Daily Journal,* March 18, 1851; *Jonesboro Gazette,* May 21, 1851; *Cairo Sun,* December 4, 18, 1851.
[5] *Canton Weekly Register,* January 24, 1852; *Illinois Journal,* January 7, February 6, 1852; Breese to French, January 5, 17, 1852, French manuscripts.
[6] *Illinois State Register,* February 5, March 4, 1852.
[7] *Ibid.,* April 22, 1852. There was only one attempt to disturb the prevailing harmony; one of the southern delegates was prevailed upon to offer a set of resolutions indorsing the compromise laws, declaring ineligible to seats any person known to have been and still to be hostile to those measures and closing by proclaiming John Wentworth a political renegade and expelling him from the convention. *Chicago Democrat,* April 24, 28, 1852; *Quincy Whig,* April 26, 1852. The resolutions had such a smack of Cook county factionalism, however, that they were tabled by a large majority.

all future state conventions ought to be based solely upon the democratic vote of the state.[8]

The nomination of Matteson caused much astonishment. He was a capable business man, "a man of integrity, & a man of property," but it was an unexpected victory for the bank men and for the moderate antislavery democrats of northern Illinois.[9] Matteson's private convictions on both points were well known, although he was publicly noncommittal to a degree very acceptable to the entire party. The shelving of Gregg, however, caused such dissatisfaction as to require some explanation, especially when a rumor began to circulate that he was discarded because of his Roman Catholicism. The whig press immediately attacked their opponents for such bigotry.[10] Gregg was, therefore, induced to write a letter in which he denied the assumption that the convention had been actuated by such motives; "it is doubtless true," he said, "that a few men in the convention and out of the convention, sought to stir up religious prejudices with a view of accomplishing my defeat. But does that afford a reason for branding the convention with improper motives? Are the democracy of Illinois to be held responsible for the unworthy course of an inconsiderable number of knaves or bigots?"[11]

The whigs were meantime reorganizing in an attempt to "hold their own" in the coming contest: a tacit recognition by party enthusiasts of the inroads time had made into the party's strength; a grim and determined effort must be made to drive away the growing apathy and despondency even among the old stand-bys. A preliminary state convention was held at Springfield, December 22, 1851, which nominated delegates to the national whig convention and appointed a provisional state central committee to coöperate with committees to be appointed in every county.[12]

[8] *Illinois Journal*, April 29, 1852.
[9] *Illinois State Register*, May 13, 1852; *Illinois Journal*, June 22, 1852; Wentworth to French, March 5, 1848, French manuscripts.
[10] *Illinois Journal*, April 24, May 15, 1852; *Quincy Whig*, April 26, May 3. 1852; *Rockford Forum*, May 12, 1852.
[11] Gregg to Morris, May 12, in *Quincy Whig*, May 24, 1852; *Illinois Journal*, May 26, 1852; *Illinois State Register*, May 27, 1852. "Governor" Zadoc Casey had argued against Gregg on the score of his religious connections. Preston to French, January 20, 1852, French manuscripts.
[12] *Quincy Whig*, December 9, 30, 1851, April 12, 1852.

The county conventions in the spring months developed considerable whig enthusiasm and prepared the way for the state and national elections. The party recovered from a severe fright when Ninian W. Edwards, assemblyman from Sangamon county, after abjuring his whiggery and resigning his seat, was defeated for reëlection by James C. Conkling, the regular whig candidate. A state nominating convention was held on July 7; its deliberations resulted in agreement upon a ticket with Edwin B. Webb of White county for governor, Colonel J. L. D. Morrison of St. Clair county for lieutenant governor, Francis Arenz for treasurer, and Charles A. Betts for auditor.[13]

The presidential canvass was now well under way and attention was diverted from the state contest. It seemed in the spring of 1852 that the young and able Stephen A. Douglas was to come into his own by receiving the highest honor within the gift of his party, a nomination which was equivalent to an election. For a year the state democratic press and the rank and file of the Illinois democracy had been shouting for Douglas. His rapid promotion from a "favorite son candidacy" attested his leading place in the national councils of the party. He was supported as emphatically "a national man;" "he was born in New England and reared in New York, resides in Illinois and was married in North Carolina, and it can be truthfully said that he is connected with every section of the Union." "Place of birth accidental; of rearing, arbitrary; of immigration, choice; and of marriage only indicating his love for the Union."[14] Such was the rôle assigned to him by his enthusiastic followers.

Only one important democratic paper looked elsewhere for a candidate. This was John Wentworth's *Chicago Democrat*, which declared that Douglas was not the party's strongest candidate. The antislavery predilections and radical western sympathies of the editor made him favor a less orthodox candidate. He turned, therefore, to that great western figure,

[13] *Illinois Journal*, April 9, 27, 30, May 11, July 9, 10, 1852; *Illinois State Register*, April 29, May 6, June 10, 1852; *Quincy Whig*, July 19, 1852; see also Koerner, *Memoirs*, 1: 587.
[14] *Freeport Prairie Democrat* and *Knoxville Journal* clipped in *Quincy Whig*, July 22, 1851.

Thomas H. Benton of Missouri, the veteran senator recently denied reëlection because of his bold stand against the southern fire eaters. But the *Cairo Sun* and other journals speaking for the southern democracy promptly declared that Benton could command no real support south of Mason and Dixon's line, where his "political trickery and faithlessness," and "his pandering to the wishes of northern fanatics" was held in abhorrence. This revelation with the astounding strength that Douglas developed swept the *Chicago Democrat* into line. Since Douglas as a young man was likely to be more liberal, if not more radical, than some of the old fogies, Wentworth was content.[15]

This was precisely the strength of Douglas outside of Illinois. He was looked upon as the candidate of "Young America." An active group of young progressive democrats were booming Douglas, using the *Democratic Review* as their organ.[16] They defined the ideal candidate in terms of Stephen A. Douglas. No broken-down politician would do, no second or third rate general, no conservative representative of "old fogyism." He must be a "statesman who can bring young blood, young ideas, and young hearts to the councils of the Republic." "Old fogyism," however, still sought to continue its leadership; the delegations sent to Baltimore showed their skill in keeping young America out of control of the party machinery. Cass and Buchanan were the chief contenders; the former might easily have been nominated but for the customary two-thirds rule. It was expected that the northwest would go strongly for Douglas. The Illinois democracy was urged by Douglas to be represented in force at Baltimore.[17] Only eleven delegates, however, presented themselves; while they clung loyally to their favorite they received too little support from outside. Douglas started out with twenty votes, only four from the west in addition to Illinois. His total reached ninety-two on the thirty-first and thirty-second ballot, when he was leading the field, but without the slightest prospect of securing the nomination. His vote dropped off imme-

[15] *Chicago Daily Journal,* April 29, May 6, 1851; *Illinois State Register,* May 16, 1850; *Cairo Sun,* May 29, 1851; *Chicago Democrat,* March 31, 1852.
[16] *Democratic Review,* 30: 12.
[17] Douglas to Lanphier, February 25, 1852, Lanphier manuscripts.

diately; on the thirty-fifth, delegations began to break for Franklin Pierce, who received the nomination on the forty-ninth ballot. Douglas, ready to prove himself a good loser, generously accepted his defeat with good grace. In his congratulatory telegram to the convention he promised that Illinois would give Pierce a larger majority than any other state in the union. The promise, however, was not redeemed; Illinois voters were too little content with convention politics to acquiesce so easily in a victory over their favorite by a dark horse. Instead there were wry faces all over the state and disgusted ejaculations of the inevitable question, "Who is Franklin Pierce?"

The general gloom did not disappear until it was demonstrated in the national convention of the whigs that they were to enter the campaign with little more harmony and enthusiasm. Illinois whiggery, however, was less affected by factionalism than many sections of the party. No marked preference for a presidential candidate had been expressed; President Fillmore's administration was generally indorsed even in county conventions that recommended General Winfield Scott as their first choice. At Baltimore the Illinois delegates, who had generally supported Scott, rejoiced in his nomination. The conservative whig forces had first insisted on the adoption of a resolution acquiescing in the finality of the compromise measures; when after a stirring debate the vote was taken the Illinois delegation supported the resolution, though by the barest majority.

Approval of these proceedings was passed by the whig state convention in July. The nomination of Scott was indorsed as the first choice of the whigs of Illinois.[18] It seems to have been the intention of the leaders to give the "finality" resolution of the Baltimore platform the "go by." A ratifying resolution, however, was introduced which the convention did not dare to reject; it was adopted because of the danger of alienating union men if defeated. One of the members proposed that it be omitted in the published proceedings. It happened that it did not appear in the official proceedings, when first

[18] *Illinois Journal*, July 9, 10, 1852.

published in the *Illinois Journal*, although they were later reprinted in corrected and finished form.[19]

Relatively slight success attended the determined effort of whig politicians to arouse enthusiasm for the famous hero; Scott clubs with their "soup songs" did not overcome an apathetic indifference. Actual and open disaffection was rare. Alfred Dutch, editor of the *Chicago Commercial Advertiser*, was one of the few disgruntled Fillmore and Webster conservatives. He had found himself outmaneuvered by his rival, Charles Wilson, of the *Chicago Journal*, when a Scott delegate was appointed to the national convention and when Cyrus Aldrich was selected as congressional candidate for the Chicago district. Condemning "the rotten machinery of primary elections and delegate conventions," he announced himself as an independent candidate for congress, but failed to make much of a race.[20]

With the congressional nominations the troubles of the democrats increased. In the Chicago district, because "Long John" Wentworth seemed inclined to repudiate the Baltimore platform, Ebenezer Peck bitterly fought his nomination.[21] In the Alton district the rift threatened to be even more serious. After William H. Bissell, the popular congressman, had announced himself a candidate for reëlection, Sidney Breese undertook to challenge his claims. Under the influence of Breese a legislative caucus of half the members from the district called a convention to meet at Carlyle, the town of Breese's residence. This call received little publicity and did not give Bissell time to return to exert a personal influence. Meantime a new democratic journal, the *Alton Courier*, began to oppose Bissell's nomination on the ground of his neglect of duties in order to serve the Illinois Central railroad in the capacity of attorney. The friends of Bissell consequently decided that there was not time for an adequate representation at the Carlyle convention; when that body met, therefore, it was a bobtail meeting without delegates from certain counties. After a hard

---

[19] *Illinois State Register*, July 15, 1852.
[20] *Joliet Signal*, May 25, 1852; *Chicago Democrat*, September 22, October 13, 1852; *Illinois State Register*, September 30, 1852.
[21] *Illinois State Register*, July 29, September 30, 1852; *Chicago Democrat*, September 16, 1852.

race, in which Breese led for thirty-one ballots, Philip B. Fouke of Belleville was nominated, probably to pacify Bissell's friends at that place. The latter, however, condemned the clique management and scheming and brought out their favorite as a bolter. The hot fight which ensued encouraged the whigs, whose candidate, Joseph Gillespie, made an active canvass.[22]

These local contests diverted attention from the presidential canvass, in which cudgels were being vigorously wielded. Pierce was represented by his opponents as the bitter enemy of the west: had he not turned his face against appropriations designed to obtain for the people of the west secure harbors and navigable rivers? No river and harbor bills would become laws in case Pierce were elected.[23] Such doctrine appealed to southern Illinois, which insisted that all the benefits went to the northern part of the state; but along the upper Mississippi, the Illinois, and the lake front, Wentworth and democrats generally held that this was not a party issue and boldly championed river and harbor improvements, ignoring the record of the democratic candidate. Douglas sought to appeal to this same demand on democratic ground; in his "tonnage duties" scheme he proposed that the improvements be made by each town and city on the basis of the duties collected, thus taking the "pork barrel" out of politics.[24] Pierce and King were pictured as the enemies of the landless poor, voting against a homestead policy which was solidly supported by western members of congress.[25] On the tariff question there was no clear party issue; the democratic party, however, was designated as the "British party," because the English press was favoring Pierce's election in order to connect a democratic tariff with British interests.[26]

Charges of nativism and abolitionism were the two effective points scored against General Scott. On account of a "native

[22] *Belleville Advocate*, July 21, 28, August 4, 11, 18, September 8, October 20, 1852; *Alton Courier*, August 4, 5, 12, October 11, 13, 14, 19, 23, 25, 29, 1852.
[23] *Illinois Journal*, June 28, September 3, 22, 1852; *Alton Telegraph*, August 2, 17, 1852; *Chicago Daily Journal*, June 23, August 27, 1852.
[24] *Chicago Democrat*, April 10, 1851; *Chicago Daily Journal*, October 2, 1851; *Joliet Signal*, September 21, 1851; *Alton Courier*, July 31, August 3, 6, October 30, 1852; *Jacksonville Constitutionist*, November 6, 1852.
[25] *Illinois Journal*, July 20, 1852; *Chicago Daily Journal*, August 27, 1852.
[26] *Illinois Journal*, August 31, 1852.

American" letter he was charged with being tinctured with an "ism" that would be fatal to the success of any candidate in the northwestern states. Scott's supporters countermoved by pointing out that Illinois democrats had considered Catholicism sufficient to disqualify their leading candidate for the gubernatorial nomination.[27] In the meantime German votes were solicited on the strength of Koerner's name on the democratic state ticket, while the nomination of Arenz made a similar appeal for the whigs. Again, Scott was accused of abolitionism; it was pointed out that Senator Seward of "higher law" fame was his sponsor, that he was unwilling to give an unequivocal indorsement of the finality of the compromise measures. Both parties in Illinois made a two-faced campaign. In the upper counties they appealed to the free soil voters for their support on strong antislavery grounds; in Egypt they talked in terms of the finality resolutions adopted by their respective national conventions and deplored further agitation. The politicians in the central districts were called upon to show a skill in political gymnastics for which many of them were too inadequately trained. It was no easy matter to know when to designate one's party as the true free soil party, or the true compromise party, or when to keep mum on the slavery issue.

When in November the returns slowly came in, it was found that Pierce and the state ticket had carried in Illinois by over 15,000 votes, that the new legislature was overwhelmingly democratic, but that the whigs, under the new redistricting of the state, had won three additional seats in congress. The *Illinois Journal*, November 19, commenting on the election, ascribed the result of the presidential contest to the disappointment of Fillmore's friends and to the disastrous effects upon the whigs of the "isms" of the day. "Every ISM was against them — Free soilism, Abolitionism, Native Americanism, Secessionism, Anti-Rentism, Free Public Landism, Interventionism, Filibusterism — in a word, all the little factions in the country." This was doubtless true of the national election, but in the northern districts of Illinois the whigs had profited by their free soilism and their bids for antislavery votes. It

[27] *Illinois State Register*, June 17, 1852 ff; *Illinois Journal*, June 4, 12, 21, 1852.

was there that the new seats in congress were gained; Richard Yates was returned from the Springfield district over John Calhoun, who suffered somewhat from democratic defection; but Elihu B. Washburne's victory in the first district, Jesse O. Norton's in the third, and James Knox's in the fourth were made possible by free soil pledges, just as John Wentworth's victory in the Chicago district was made possible by his antislavery views. In the three new whig districts, the majorities were less than the difference between the free soil vote for president and for congressmen; only one had a whig presidential plurality.

This election proved to be the fatal crisis for whiggery in Illinois. It had never secured a strong hold on the pioneer population of the western prairies. It was the party *par excellence* of the wealth and intelligence, the respectability and dignity of the state. Though it drew upon the industrial dependents of whig employers, and upon the socially and politically ambitious elements of the population, it was unable to develop real strength outside of industrial centers except as it came forward with a "log cabin and hard cider" or "military hero" appeal.[28] No new popular reform ever emanated from the party to save it from withering decay under its proud record for aristocratic conservatism.

The year, 1853, was a year of general political calm — the lull before a storm. Political activity in Illinois was confined to the general assembly, where the democrats outnumbered the whigs nearly four to one. The whigs deplored blind servitude to party leadership; even the democrats were not in a humor to utilize their majority to draw party lines. Local and private rather than general or party considerations determined the issues presented and their fate at the hands of the legislators.[29] Liquor and bank legislation had their advocates and opponents. Railroad development was the chief subject of discussion, emphasizing the sectional interests within the state.[30] The quarrels of rival sections even threatened for a time to jeopardize Douglas' reëlection to the United States senate by involv-

[28] Brown to French, December 8, 1851, French manuscripts; *Illinois State Register*, February 5, 1852.
[29] *Illinois Journal*, January 8, 1853.
[30] See chapter II.

ing him in the quarrel over railroad policy.[31] The session had no sooner closed before the disappointed faction began to agitate a called session, which was approved or condemned, not according to party lines, but according to local interests. When Governor Matteson finally summoned the legislature the struggle was resumed under the new nonpartisan alignment.

Democratic politicians concerned themselves chiefly with the fruits of victory. The numerous spoilsmen engaged in a mad scramble at Springfield to secure the indorsement of the electoral college for their respective claims upon the Pierce administration. Soon the obvious disappointment of the unsuccessful began to find expression. Some voiced it calmly in a demand for the popular election of postmasters. In Egypt, however, feeling became intense because it was felt that Wentworth and other northern politicians were dictating the appointments and that the plums were going to democrats of antislavery proclivities. Many of the democratic papers of the state were soon engaged in a guerilla warfare in which the "old hunker" forces sought to drive the free soil element out of the party. Meantime party interest waned to the extent that in this "off" year a special judgeship election in Chicago went to the whig candidate by default, in spite of the efforts of the *Democrat* to get a candidate into the field. Critics of the convention system began to appear, while some persons condemned all party organization on the score of corrupting and anti-republican tendencies.[32]

Whig dissolution was well under way. In central and southern Illinois, numbers of "silver grey" conservatives were leaving the ranks upon the evidence that in the northern part of the state most whigs were trying to effect a union with the free soilers. This movement even split the party in some of the northern counties, where "silver greys" refused to permit such leadership. Other whig reorganization plans were in the air, in Illinois as in other parts of the union. There was some inclination to take up the temperance issue, while the more vague "people's party" was the favorite dodge of many.

[31] *Chicago Weekly Democrat*, January 1, 1853.
[32] *Ibid.*, January 15, April 9, 23, 30, 1853; *Illinois Journal*, July 14, August 18, 1853; *Southern Illinoisan* clipped in *Alton Courier*, August 12, see also May 10, 1853; *Joliet Signal*, September 6, 1853, February 7, 1854.

THE KANSAS-NEBRASKA ACT

Democratic leaders naturally welcomed this opportunity to whip party laggards into line and played up these tendencies to revive the old fear of the opposition.[33]

It was into this atmosphere of party disorganization that Douglas exploded the issue that killed off the whig party and left the democratic ranks rent in twain. Almost without warning came the crash as the territorial issue was launched in a form more insidious than had ever appeared in American politics. The land across the Missouri river was still the hunting ground of the American redskin, but emigrants from Illinois and neighboring states were beginning to pour in to dispute their rights. Douglas now proposed to open up the territory of Nebraska to all settlers — to the Yankee pioneer of the north and northwest, to the immigrant from European oppression, and to the southern planter with his drove of ebony-hued retainers. Proclaiming the broad principle of local self-government, of popular sovereignty, he hoped to ignore a solemn pact of nearly a quarter century's standing which dedicated to freedom the very territory into which he now sought to establish an unqualified "open door."

The possibility of such an issue was foreseen two months before Douglas' famous report on the Nebraska situation. A government diplomatic agent had been sent in to arrange treaties with the Indians to secure their lands, but he seemed to procrastinate and merely reported the Indians ready to sell out. A shrewd observer saw in the situation the reflection of a heated contest between two Missouri rivals, ex-Senator Benton, the champion of westward expansion on free soil, and Senator Atchison, the proslavery fire eater, who was anxious to prevent the growth of the political strength of the north. But the quarrel was now in danger of assuming "such a degree of importance as to threaten a renewal in Congress, with all its fury, of the 'Wilmot Proviso' agitation which it was hoped was settled by the compromise measures of 1850."[34]

The question of the origin of the repeal of the Missouri compromise is a controverted one. Senator Douglas is looked

---

[33] *Aurora Guardian,* October 12, 19, 1853; *Joliet Signal,* October 18, 1853; *Chicago Weekly Democrat,* July 23, 1853.
[34] *Ibid.,* November 12, 1853.

upon by orthodox historians as the responsible party, although they differ as to his motive: did he act on the high and broad ground of principle—the principle of local autonomy, of popular sovereignty; was he, because of his presidential aspirations, throwing out a sop to the south; or, because of his interest in and zeal for a transcontinental railroad, was he anxious to see the new territory opened to railroad development under any form of organization which could pass both houses of congress, particularly the senate?[35] Another view of the matter is that Senator Atchison of Missouri is entirely to be credited with the authorship of the repeal, with Douglas nothing more or less than his tool.[36]

In the fall of 1853 Douglas returned to Washington after a summer abroad and immediately took up the political problems he had temporarily laid aside. While analyzing the work which would come before the session of congress to meet in December he wrote his well-known letter of November 11 to the editors of the *Illinois State Register*.[37] In this letter he first disposed of rumors concerning his presidential candidacy. Stressing the obligations that were due to the party in its "distracted condition," in order to secure the consolidation of its strength and the perpetuity of its principles he waived aside all talk of the coming contest and declared his intention of remaining entirely noncommittal.

In this announcement he let fall the mysterious statement: "I think such a state of things will exist that I shall not desire the nomination." What, then, did this mean? The issues that would require attention were tariff reduction "to a legitimate revenue standard," the river and harbor question, which he proposed to solve by a well-devised system of tonnage duties, and the Pacific railroad, which he felt the federal government could aid only by a land grant modelled after the Illinois Central precedent.

No mention was made of the organization of Nebraska territory or of popular sovereignty. Does this silence warrant

[35] Hodder, "The Genesis of the Kansas-Nebraska Act," *Wisconsin State Historical Society, Proceedings*, 60: 69-86.
[36] Ray, *Repeal of the Missouri Compromise*.
[37] Douglas to Walker and Lanphier, November 11, 1853, Lanphier manuscripts.

the conclusion that Douglas was not alive to the significance of the territorial issue in its new form? This is scarcely possible inasmuch as the organization of Nebraska had been repeatedly before congress and had been a leading question in the last session, when Douglas, as chairman of the senate committee on territories, had exerted his influence in favor of the proposed legislation.[38] Letters may have gone forward to his confidants at Springfield taking note of the territorial issue. At any rate, the editors of the *State Register* were able on December 16 to publish an editorial condemning the agitation in the south for the establishment and in the north for the prohibition by congress of slavery in the new territory. "The territories should be permitted to exercise, as nearly as practicable, all the rights claimed by the states, and to adopt all such political regulations and institutions, as their wisdom may suggest. This liberty is calculated to attach them to the Union. .... We therefore hope that no slavery provisos will be attached to any territorial bill."[39] By this time a Nebraska bill had been introduced by Senator Dodge of Iowa and referred to the committee on territories; inasmuch, however, as the measure was referred on the afternoon of the fourteenth, the interval was not sufficiently great for Douglas to react on the bill and influence the editorial cited if he had waited for the measure to reach his hands. The editors, moreover, would have realized the danger of embarrassing the senator, whose confidence they enjoyed, if they had attempted to formulate a policy for themselves in the absence of some statement from Douglas. It seems, therefore, that an opinion must have developed in his mind at a rather early date and that the editors of the *Register* were promptly informed of his views.

This evidence reduces the possibility that outside influence, whether from Senator Atchison or from some other source, directly influenced Douglas in reaching this decision; it eliminates almost entirely the element of deliberate presidential ambitions as the motive. Douglas had, in a spirit of opportunism, resurrected an old principle which accorded with his

[38] Johnson, *Stephen A. Douglas*, 226, 228; Ray, *Repeal of the Missouri Compromise*, 186; *Congressional Globe*, 32 congress, 2 session, 1116-1117.
[39] Published in the weekly issue of December 22, 1853. Professor Allen Johnson does not distinguish between the different parts of the weekly issue.

desire to see Nebraska thrown open to settlement and to railroad development and to a practical experiment in the realm of this much flaunted principle of popular sovereignty. Thus it was that Douglas and Atchison actuated by different motives worked side by side lending each other aid and comfort in their efforts to reach a common goal.

Douglas made his report on January 4, 1854, presenting the bill in a somewhat amended form. The purpose was to apply the principles of the compromise measures of 1850 to the new territory of Nebraska. Douglas, speaking for the committee, held that the Nebraska country occupied "the same relative position to the slavery question, as did Mexico and Utah, when those territories were organized." Inasmuch, therefore, as the validity of the Missouri compromise restriction was seriously questioned by eminent statesmen, without attempting to affirm or repeal that restriction as the matter in controversy, the report held that the principles of 1850 ought to be carried into operation; the bill, accordingly, provided in the language of the Utah and New Mexico acts: "And when admitted as a State or States, the said Territory, or any part of the same, shall be received into the Union, with or without slavery, as this Constitution may prescribe at the time of their admission." "In order to avoid misconstruction" the famous twenty-first section was attached to the bill as the result of an eleventh hour decision by Douglas.[40] It specified the principles of the compromise measures, which were to be applied in this new legislation, particularly "That all questions pertaining to slavery in the Territories and in the new States to be formed therefrom, are to be left to the decision of the people residing therein, through their appropriate representatives."

This section was always interpreted by Douglas as having the effect of repealing by supersedure the Missouri compromise line of 1820. In this evasive way, purporting to stand for a great principle, he was prepared to wipe out that compromise which in 1849 he had formally declared to the Illinois legislature had "become canonized in the hearts of the American people, as a sacred thing, which no ruthless hand would

[40] Johnson, *Stephen A. Douglas*, 232-233.

THE KANSAS-NEBRASKA ACT

ever be reckless enough to disturb."[41] There were others, however, both friends and enemies of the proposition, who desired a less ambiguous reference to the legislation of 1820 and who prepared to compel Douglas to come into the open. Senator Dixon of Kentucky on January 16 moved an amendment which forced Douglas' hand. Under the pressure of southern democratic leaders, Douglas prepared amendments, for which as a party and administration measure he secured the approval of President Pierce; they provided for two organized territories, Kansas and Nebraska, in which, it was announced, the prohibition of slavery in the act of 1820 was specifically "declared inoperative and void; it being the true intent and meaning of this act not to legislate slavery into any Territory or State, nor to exclude it therefrom, but to leave the people thereof perfectly free to form and regulate their domestic institutions in their own way, subject only to the Constitution of the United States."[42]

For this measure Douglas waged a brilliant fight upon the floor of the senate, aided in the house by his trusted lieutenant, William R. Richardson, of the Quincy district of Illinois, who now occupied Douglas' old post of chairman of the house committee on territories. Honors were high for Illinois, if with all the seeds of agitation that it sowed, the Kansas-Nebraska act can be looked upon as bestowing honor. Little was said by Senator Shields, Douglas' colleague, or by the Illinois democratic delegation in the house. Wentworth, who opposed the measure, but was so dazed by it as to be unable to determine its party effect, remained silent; his journal, the *Chicago Democrat*, did not commit itself against the bill until the issue of March 11, when it credited Douglas with a sincere and consistent devotion to the doctrine of the Nicholson letter.

Douglas was at his best when, in a brilliant speech on March 3, he closed the debate in the senate by summing up the arguments in favor of the bill. He courageously and fairly met the thrusts of his opponents and cleared the way for giving the measure a place in a long series of struggles for the American principle of self-government, of popular sovereignty. "This

[41] *Illinois State Register*, November 8, 1849.
[42] *Statutes at Large*, 10:277-290.

was the principle upon which the colonies separated from the crown of Great Britain; the principle upon which the battles of the Revolution were fought, and the principle upon which our republican system was founded."

None of the Illinois delegation signed Chase's appeal of the "independent democrats" against the Kansas-Nebraska bill. The northern districts were represented by whigs except for Wentworth from Chicago. The Egyptian representatives were party regulars ready to take orders from the administration — all except William H. Bissell from the Alton and Belleville district. He was firmly opposed to the measure, but did not attempt to participate in the attack upon it. When a final vote was reached in the house on May 22, Wentworth went on record with the four whig congressmen, Elihu B. Washburne, Jesse O. Norton, James Knox, and Yates, as unwilling to follow Douglas in his new lead. Colonel Bissell was confined to his room by illness, but authorized Wentworth to state that had he been present, he would have voted against the bill; as it was, if his vote could bring about its defeat, he was ready to be carried to the house on a cot to cast it. William A. Richardson, Willis Allen of the Cairo district, and James C. Allen of the seventh, cast their votes in favor of the bill.[43] The house vote, therefore, would seem to indicate that Illinois was not ready to accept the new Douglas doctrine with all that it implied.

Douglas, however, had declared in one of his speeches that there was a universality of appeal in the principle of the Kansas-Nebraska act that would make it "as popular at the North as at the South, when its provisions and principles shall have been fully developed and become well understood."[44] If this were true there should have been no question as to Illinois, a border state, with a large southern population, trained to follow the lead of the "little giant." Yet there were signs that the adverse vote in the house spoke more correctly for the state than did the two senators — that Douglas in the rôle of prophet was doomed to disappointment.

---

[43] *Alton Courier*, June 9, 1854; *Cairo City Times*, June 21, 1854; *House Journal*, 33 congress, 1 session, 919-920.
[44] *Congressional Globe*, 33 congress, 1 session, appendix, 338.

The *Illinois State Register* and the *Quincy Herald* were the only papers to come out with a prompt indorsement. The *Register* followed up the editorial of December 16, 1853, with careful explanations of all the forces and principles involved.[45] The *Quincy Herald*, zealously hailing Douglas as the real author of the compromise of 1850, commended the "sacred" principle for which he stood, "one that lies at the root of all governments founded upon the maxim that the people are the true and rightful source of all political power."[46] It labored to show that slavery could never go into Kansas and that the measure was one to extend freedom, not slavery. The *Peoria Press, Eastern Illinoisan,* and *St. Clair Weekly Tribune* next entered the thin ranks of active Nebraska supporters. Other of the party journals merely acquiesced in the new test of party orthodoxy and allowed Douglas to defend his policy in their columns by printing his speeches. When at length the measure was enacted into law, the *Joliet Signal* abandoned a colorless support to break out in rejoicing at its triumph.[47] The *Cairo City Times* was aroused to declare: "The Constitution has been vindicated, and the rights of man reasserted."[48]

The immediate response of the whig opposition in Illinois to the introduction of the Nebraska bill was a shout of protest. Led by their central organ at Springfield, the *Illinois State Journal,* they spoke in no uncertain tone. Referring to the reopening of the slavery agitation, the *Journal* on January 13 declared: "to deliberately raise the flood-gates of those old damned up waters, because Mr. Douglas wants to be President, is too much of an infliction for the most forebearing patience." The *Chicago Tribune* claimed that Douglas' proposition put an end to the disposition of citizens to pay passive obedience to the fugitive slave law: "the violators of the Missouri Compromise had forfeited all right to appeal to law to sustain them." The *Alton Telegraph* declared that

[45] *Illinois State Register*, January 19, 26, February 2, 1854 *et seq.*
[46] *Quincy Weekly Herald*, January 30, see also January 16, February 6, 20, 27, March 6, 27, 1854, *et seq.*
[47] *St. Clair Weekly Tribune*, March 8, April 22, 1854; *Illinois State Register,* February 16, 23, 1854; *Morris Gazette* clipped in *ibid.*, March 2, 1854; *Ottawa Free Trader*, February 11, 1854; *Joliet Signal*, March 7, May 30, 1854.
[48] *Cairo City Times*, May 31, 1854.

Douglas had "sprung a mine which will forever blast all his presidential aspirations and cripple his political power."[49] Neutral journals took up the hue and cry. The *Canton Register*, March 2, announced its regret "that a Senator from our own State should exhibit such recklessness in regard to public feeling and public peace, and such a want of judgment and forethought as has been exhibited by Senator Douglas in this case."[50]

More significant, however, were the announcements from democratic journals that they could not follow Douglas in his new lead. Some came out after a considerable delay in which the full consequences of political heresy were considered. The *Chicago Democrat* waited until March 11 to express an honest difference of opinion with Douglas. When the measure passed, however, the editor declared with feeling: "The wall of 'compromises' has been broken down — the 'finality' is final no more — the 'wind has been sown' and it may be that the sowers shall reap the whirlwind."[51] The *Alton Courier* published the documents in full and the speeches of Douglas, Seward, and Everett in its successive issues from February 13 to March 4; then in a facetious article on April 11 it stated its refusal to be committed on the Nebraska question; but finally, after the passage of the bill, it made the unequivocal declaration: "It sanctions what we recognize as a great principle, but our objection is that in giving this sanction, it opens the door for a great outrage upon human rights, the introduction of slavery into Territory now free, and which we would be glad to have ever remain so."[52] The *Belleville Advocate* showed the inconsistency of Douglas' position on the Missouri compromise and the extent of the opposition to his new policy.[53] Even the *Chester Herald* and the *Greenville Journal* came out in opposition in the more truly Egyptian atmosphere of those two towns. The *Urbana Union* had spoken out with remark-

---

[49] *Illinois State Register*, February 2, 1854; *Chicago Tribune* clipped in *ibid.*, March 3, 1854.
[50] *Canton Weekly Register*, March 2, June 1, 22, 1854; the *Bloomington Pantagraph*, however, deplored the vituperative abuse of Douglas and declared that the logic lay in his course, *ibid.*, March 9, 1854.
[51] *Chicago Weekly Democrat*, May 27, 1854.
[52] *Alton Courier*, May 24, 1854.
[53] *Belleville Advocate*, March 1, 8, April 5, 26, 1854.

able promptness; on January 26 it questioned the ability of Douglas to settle this matter against all traditions since 1787. A few weeks later it frankly declared the introduction of the new issue "a very wrong and impolitic act unworthy of the head and heart of our distinguished Senator," and prepared to wage war on his bill.[54] At the same time the *Rock River Democrat* and *Galena Jeffersonian* announced themselves out of sympathy with Douglas in his course and washed their hands of all support of such demagogical proceedings. The *Aurora Guardian* protested: "It is scarcely a wonder that the people are arising in their majesty to protest against the Bill of Senator Douglas which bids African slavery welcome to the Territory of Nebraska, when it is considered that the boundaries include an area equal to ten States of the size of New York." "As a bid for the Presidency, Douglas introduces this fire brand."[55]

All this opposition was contrary to the belief of Douglas that he had applied a principle which would make the party "stronger than ever" because "united upon principle." "The principles of this bill will form the test of Parties, and the only alternative is either to stand with the Democracy or to rally under Seward, John VanBuren & Co."[56]

The official expression of the state through the general assembly, however, was more favorable to Douglas' course. Early in February, at the "little giant's" orders, it was later charged by Lincoln, resolutions indorsing the Nebraska bill were introduced by Senator Omelveny to whip the lukewarm and recalcitrant democrats into line. Inasmuch as it was represented as a mere vote of confidence in the two Illinois senators, the resolutions passed with only a handful of democratic votes in opposition. In the senate the vote of 14 to 8 found five democrats, James M. Campbell, Burton C. Cook, Norman B. Judd, Uri Osgood, and John M. Palmer voting with the three whigs in the negative; in the house eight democrats, thirteen whigs, and one free soiler went on record as opposed to the thirty-three democrats and three whigs who

[54] *Urbana Union*, February 16, 23, June 1, 1854.
[55] *Rock River Democrat*, February 14, 21, 1854; *Galena Jeffersonian* clipped in *Belleville Advocate*, March 8, 1854; *Aurora Guardian*, February 16, 23, 1854.
[56] Douglas to Lanphier, February 13, 1854, Lanphier manuscripts.

approved the resolutions adopted by that body, while thirteen democrats and five whigs comprised the list of those not voting. Many an assemblyman, with the rising storm of opposition and agitation, came shortly to regret his vote in favor of the resolutions; John Reynolds, "the old ranger," publicly recanted his vote.[57]

The Kansas-Nebraska measure was from the start the subject of heated discussion and angry controversy throughout the state. Douglas was burned in effigy on the streets of his home city and huge anti-Nebraska mass meetings were held in Chicago, Ottawa, Rockford, Alton, and Belleville. Although the Nebraska forces countermoved by attempting similar demonstrations in favor of the measure, it was without great success.

The pulpit burst out in wrath against this great assault on freedom; a protest signed by five hundred clergymen of the northwest denounced Douglas for his "want of courtesy and reverence toward man and God."[58] Three preachers in the legislature, to be sure, supported the Nebraska resolutions and the clergy of Egypt were but little affected; but twenty-five Chicago ministers met in March to protest against the Nebraska bill, while Colonel Bissell on April 18 presented in congress the remonstrance of S. Y. McMasters and nineteen other clergymen of Alton against the repeal of the Missouri compromise, and the Reverend W. D. Haley made the chief address of the Alton anti-Nebraska meeting of June 2.[59] John Mason Peck, the sage of Rock Spring, held that, while there was a general misunderstanding among the clergy of the north concerning the sacred character of the Missouri compromise, the Nebraska act was "unwise, uncalled for and ill-timed, with a direct tendency . . . . to revive all the sectional jealousies, strife, disunion, and *Abolitionism*, and even much more than existed in 1850."[60]

[57] *Works of Lincoln*, 2:245; *Chicago Weekly Democrat*, March 11, 1854; *House Journal*, 1854, p. 168; *Belleville Advocate*, March 22, 1854.
[58] *Congressional Globe*, 33 congress, 1 session, appendix, 654.
[59] They passed a set of strong resolutions to which Douglas replied in a long letter of eight columns in the *Washington Sentinel*; *Illinois State Register*, April 20, 1854; *Alton Courier*, May 6, June 8, 1854.
[60] John Mason Peck to the editor of the *Belleville Advocate*, March 21, in *Belleville Advocate*, April 12, 1854.

THE KANSAS-NEBRASKA ACT 123

Among the most sturdy opponents of the repeal of the Missouri compromise were the German voters of Illinois. They had at once been alienated by the Clayton amendment which denied to foreigners any political rights in the new territories. The German press of the state promptly rejected Douglas' pet measure. Before the end of January, George Schneider, editor of the *Illinois Staats-Zeitung*, aggressively committed his organ to the repudiation of the Douglas program. The *Quincy Tribune* placed its opposition on record in the issue of February 22, followed by the *Alton Vorwärts* and the other journals.

It has been claimed that the first protest mass meeting to be held was an indignation meeting held by Chicago Germans, January 29, under the leadership of George Schneider. However this may be, the Germans in Cook county promptly placed themselves on record as unwilling to swallow the Nebraska bill. When the legislature visited Chicago in February a committee of German citizens waited upon Lieutenant Governor Koerner and placed in his charge a petition to the legislature signed by several hundred against the repeal of the Missouri compromise. Judd presented in the general assembly a similar petition representing eight hundred German voters of Chicago. On the evening of March 16 a mass meeting of German citizens, in which Edward Schlaeger, George Schneider, Alderman Francis Hoffman, and others participated, unanimously condemned Douglas as "an ambitious and dangerous demagogue" and agreed to take the offensive against the slave power. A later meeting of former German supporters burned Douglas in effigy.[61]

Thus did the issue of freedom versus slavery become clarified in the minds of Illinoisians, and thus did they refuse to follow the lead of their popular senator when he seemed ready to give the advantage to the peculiar institution of the south.

The German stronghold around Belleville and Alton showed similar defection from Douglas democracy, led by Lieutenant Governor Koerner and others. The Germans of Taze-

[61] *Chicago Daily Democratic Press*, February 20, March 17, 1854; *Illinois Journal*, February 21, 1854; McLean County Historical Society, *Transactions*, 3: 53; Illinois State Historical Society, *Transactions*, 1912, p. 156-157.

well county held a spirited meeting at Pekin in which they selected delegates to represent them at a proposed German anti-Nebraska state convention to be held at Bloomington on the twelfth and thirteenth of September, simultaneously with the proposed state "republican" convention.[62] The *Illinois Staats-Zeitung* took a leading part in all these moves; in its issue of September 20 it made an appeal for a republican party, a great American "liberty" party.

[62] *Pekin Mirror* clipped in *Chicago Daily Democratic Press*, September 13, 1854.

VI. THE ORIGIN OF THE REPUBLICAN PARTY

THE Kansas-Nebraska act proved a most distracting question for the democratic organization in Illinois. A new issue had been raised, not by fanatical abolitionists or free soilers but by one who had ever declaimed against agitation. Was this then "a charlatanism as thin as it is contemptible?"[1] So at least large portions of Douglas' constituency promptly declared. The *Rock River Democrat* openly repudiated Senator Douglas and "his pampered allies" and declared: "We forbear an expression of our deep indignation, and shall choke the utterance of our abhorrence of the men who have insanely given us as a Democratic party to the contempt of the world."[2] The *Chicago Democrat* lapsed into pessimism concerning the future of the democracy: "Throughout the North we behold but one prevailing sentiment, and that is in opposition to a great measure which has just been consummated, the responsibility of which the democratic party of the nation will be compelled to bear."[3] When Wentworth, who always prided himself on his party regularity, returned to Chicago, however, and the sense of disappointment at the success of the Kansas-Nebraska act subsided somewhat, the announcement followed that the policy of the democrats was to "beat the enemy handsomely—carry the state gloriously, and thus continue the ascendancy of Democratic principles in her councils." All this might be done if the Nebraska issue was ignored, if the slavery question was left where.the national convention of 1852 left it. There were too many signs that this was not to be.[4] Some Nebraska democrats were inclined to urge a policy of generosity, but under the influence of Doug-

---

[1] *Galena Jeffersonian* clipped in *Belleville Advocate*, March 8, 1854.
[2] *Rock River Democrat*, May 30, 1854.
[3] *Chicago Weekly Democrat*, May 27, 1854.
[4] *Ibid.*, June 24, 1854; *Chicago Daily Democratic Press*, May 24, 1854; *Joliet Signal*, May 30, 1854.

las a disposition developed to require approval of the new statute as proof of party orthodoxy. Through the pressure of Douglas' control over federal appointments and under the sting of the party lash, this spirit gained much headway in Illinois.

The issue was fought out in the county conventions preparatory to the fall elections. The anti-Nebraskaites pleaded against the application of new tests, but hamstring politicians by press-gang methods generally secured the desired indorsement of the Kansas-Nebraska act and of its author. Morgan county seems to have been the only central county where a convention frankly laid aside the new issue and applied only the traditional tests of democracy.[5] The Nebraska test was applied everywhere in Egypt except in the Alton district; there the convention refused to indorse the Nebraska bill or even to pass a simple resolution of compliment to Douglas and was disrupted before making a nomination.[6] In the Chicago district and elsewhere in the northern tier of counties, the Nebraska and anti-Nebraska forces fought out the issue in primary meetings and county conventions with varying results. When the Nebraskaites could not secure their way in open convention they often seceded and held rival meetings of their own to carry the contest up to the next step in the party organization. The *Galena Jeffersonian* disgustedly proposed a state democratic convention to consider "formally excommunicating the adherents of Douglas' Nebraska scheme, from the great Democratic brotherhood."[7]

It was not surprising that the younger democratic leaders—Lyman Trumbull, John M. Palmer, Colonel E. D. Taylor, John A. McClernand, and Jehu Baker—took issue with Douglas on the Kansas-Nebraska act; but it came with a shock when old conservatives like John Reynolds and Sidney Breese spoke out with equal vigor. Breese "repelled with scorn the attempt to foist this bastard plank into the Democratic creed." Even Senator Shields began to waver and the rumor

[5] *Morgan Journal*, July 6, 1854.
[6] *Alton Courier*, September 9, 1854; *Chicago Daily Democratic Press*, September 30, 1854.
[7] *Galena Jeffersonian* clipped in *Ottawa Weekly Republican*, September 16, 1854.

circulated—which he felt in honor bound to deny—that in voting for the bill he merely obeyed the instructions of the legislature.[8] Whig leaders directed a bold attack on their enemy; since assemblymen James W. Singleton, William H. Christy, and James M. Randolph had voted for the Nebraska resolutions, the *Illinois Journal* read the trio out of the party and, with the *Chicago Tribune*, proclaimed the whig party as the anti-Nebraska stronghold. Singleton unsilenced by the assaults of his party associates, O. H. Browning, and Archibald Williams, continued to defend the Kansas-Nebraska act in the neighborhood of Quincy. Minor whig politicians, restive under the yoke of the party moguls, protested as "national whigs" against the attempt to convert the party to any brand of abolitionism; a group of them formally renounced their connection with the old party to go for "*Douglas, Kansas, and the Union.*"[9]

The idea of common cause for all anti-Nebraska forces, regardless of former party lines, made its appearance at an early day. A large and enthusiastic mass meeting at Rockford on March 18 passed a resolution that "The free States should now blot out all former political distinctions by uniting themselves into one great Northern Party."[10] The Pekin *Tazewell Mirror* suggested that a state convention be held of all parties opposed to the repeal of the Missouri compromise, and the *Morgan Journal* heartily indorsed the proposal; the *Illinois Journal*, however, frowned upon the idea, complaining that as the whigs were a unit on the Nebraska "outrage" there was "no necessity of breaking up their organization for the purpose of becoming a new political party, with a single object in view."[11] It preferred that anti-Nebraska democrats should adopt an independent organization. But anti-Nebraska democratic papers acceded neither to the idea of their own perma-

---
[8] *Alton Weekly Courier*, October 12, 1854; *Alton Courier*, October 26, 1854; *Illinois Journal*, October 17, 1854.
[9] *Illinois State Register*, September 7, 14, 1854.
[10] *Rock River Democrat*, March 28, 1854. A meeting of "respectable farmers and mechanics" at Freeport went on record in favor of uniting as one party in common cause against the extension of slavery. *Illinois Journal*, April 5, 1854.
[11] *Ibid.*, July 27, 1854; *Morgan Journal*, July 27, 1854.

nent organization nor to that of a fusion party; instead they directed their energies toward healing the schism.

Many confirmed free soilers and abolitionists, however, eagerly embraced the idea of fusion, or "coöperation," as their organ, the *Free West*, preferred to call it.[12] Ichabod Codding, a well-known antislavery evangelist, toured the state during the summer months in the interest of the new dispensation. Influenced by similar movements in Wisconsin and Michigan a mass meeting of antislavery independents at Ottawa, August 1, assumed the name "republican" as the title by which the new party was to be known; they passed a resolution recommending that a state mass meeting of the opponents of slavery extension be held later at Bloomington. Later "republican" conventions were held in La Salle, Will, Putnam, and other counties, followed by a congressional convention for the third district at Bloomington, September 12, which was attended by full delegations from ten counties.[13] There the name "republican" was formally adopted. A mass convention in the first district at Rockford, August 30, agreed to coöperate in defense of freedom "as republicans," while a "people's" mass convention at Aurora, September 30, acting for the second district assumed the name of republican; both of these put republican candidates for congress into the field. In the first and third districts whig and republican fusion was complete while the only obstacle to such a combination at Aurora was the difficulty of agreeing upon terms.

The republican state convention finally met at Springfield on the fourth and fifth of October. Though the state fair was at the same time in session, hope of political capital to be made thereby was extinguished when it was found that in spite of a public invitation by Lovejoy to the assembled throng, only a small band of twenty-six tested antislavery men appeared in the convention. Ichabod Codding, Owen Lovejoy, H. K. Jones of Morgan county, and Erastus Wright of Sangamon were the leading spirits. To their disappointment Abraham Lincoln carefully avoided the meetings though he

---

[12] *Free West*, May 4, 1854.
[13] *Ottawa Free Trader*, August 12, 1854; *Ottawa Republican*, August 12, 19, September 16, 1854.

had made a thrilling anti-Nebraska speech at Springfield just before the opening of the convention. This effort was highly commended; "Ichabod raved and Lovejoy swelled, and all endorsed the sentiments of that speech," sarcastically commented the editor of the *State Register*. Aggressive antislavery extension resolutions were adopted, after which John L. McClun of Bloomington, a whig member of the legislature, was named as the republican candidate for state treasurer.[14] McClun's name was posted by the *Illinois Journal*, October 9, and other papers, but was shortly withdrawn in favor of James Miller, an anti-Nebraska leader who, as the nominee of a whig convention, was of more orthodox stripe.

A state central committee was appointed by the convention, including Lincoln as the Sangamon county representative. Lovejoy vouched for Lincoln's agreement with the principles enunciated in the platform, but the wily whig leader, unwilling as a candidate for the United States senate to incur the political unpopularity that would follow association with abolitionists, had absented himself from the city in order not to be identified with the convention and later repudiated the use of his name.[15] It was this douche of cold water, probably, that prevented the organization of the state committee, and a similar party loyalty deterred all except discredited "abolitionists" from participating in the movement. It was that fact, rather than any radicalism in the proposed course of action, that caused the prompt death of this "republican" state organization.

Seldom in the history of Illinois had there been such confusion in the congressional canvass as in 1854. The Chicago district presented one of the worst tangles. Strongly democratic and antislavery in tone, it had been repeatedly represented in congress by the able but demagogical "Long John" Wentworth, a noted champion of river and harbor improvement, of land reform, and of freedom. Dominating the party machine in the district, he was not without his rivals, who frankly dubbed him a corrupt knave, "an unscrupulous demogogue and political Ishamelite," and denounced the abuses of

[14] *Illinois State Register*, October 12, 1854; McLean County Historical Society, *Transactions*, 3:43-47.
[15] Herndon and Weik, *Abraham Lincoln*, 1:40-41; Nicolay and Hay, *Abraham Lincoln, Complete Works*, 1:209.

the convention system, that prevailed under his "misrule." Several independent anti-Nebraska candidates, therefore, were announced to dispute his control long before the democratic convention was held; but strangely enough the *Free West* decided to support Wentworth on the strength of his sturdy fight against the Nebraska act.[16]

During this pre-convention canvass by democratic forces, the local anti-Nebraska "people's" movement was gathering headway. At a district convention at Aurora representative leaders decided to repudiate all previous party attachments and "hereafter coöperate as the Republican party;" James H. Woodworth, a free soil democrat since 1848, former mayor of Chicago and member of the general assembly, was nominated for congress. A whig convention simultaneously placed a capable candidate, R. S. Blackwell, in nomination. These developments fostered democratic humility. Wentworth's anti-Nebraska rivals withdrew; and he announced that, though his election was as certain as his nomination, he would step aside in favor of any true democrat who might be nominated. Again, Aurora became the scene of bustling political maneuvers. "Long John" and his men found their control disputed by a rival camp of Douglasites who held a convention of their own. Wentworth's cohorts merely reaffirmed the Baltimore platform of 1852 and repudiated all new tests of democracy as heresy. They nominated E. L. Mayo of De Kalb county, an old-time democrat, while the Nebraskaites put up a political unknown, John B. Turner of Chicago, president of the Galena and Chicago railroad. A four-cornered fight was thereupon waged which terminated in the success of Woodworth, the republican candidate.[17]

In the first and third districts, Elihu B. Washburne and Jesse O. Norton, the whig members of congress, were nominated as the candidates of the republican party; both had excellent free soil records that had stood out above their national whiggery. In the first district the democratic convention split

---

[16] *Chicago Daily Democratic Press*, August 12, September 22, 1854; *Free West*, September 7, 1854.
[17] *Ibid.*, September 21, 1854; *Chicago Weekly Democrat*, October 7, 1854; *Aurora Guardian*, October 5, 1854; *Chicago Daily Democratic Press*, October 6, 1854; *Illinois State Register*, October 12, 1854.

on the Nebraska issue with the result that rival democratic candidates contested for Washburne's seat.[18]

In the Alton district the democratic party found itself embarrassed by the numerous candidates for the nomination. The Nebraska faction seemed to control the organization but the anti-Nebraskaites served notice that they would not coöperate under any new test or issue. The result was a split in the district convention before a nomination was effected. Joseph Gillespie had been in the field as a whig candidate; but when Lyman Trumbull, a prominent democrat, came out in bold defiance of Douglas and the "new test" even the whigs rallied with enthusiasm in favor of his election to congress.[19] Trumbull made a brilliant campaign against Philip B. Fouke, a Nebraska democrat, and won a handy victory.

In the Springfield district, the democrats nominated Thomas L. Harris, a Douglasite, to make the contest for Yates' seat. Yates was, therefore, supported by the anti-Nebraska forces. He was doubtless injured, however, by the participation of Ichabod Codding in the canvass and the charge that he was the candidate of the abolitionists. Harris showed great confidence in his support of the principle of popular sovereignty; he permitted himself to be placed on record as willing on this principle to admit a state with a constitution recognizing and permitting polygamy.[20] But fear of abolition at their doors was so strong in the hearts of the conservatives that even "Polygamy Harris" was able to win, though by a small vote. In the remaining districts, the anti-Nebraska forces were under whig leadership. James Knox was easily reëlected in the Knoxville district. Archibald Williams made an unsuccessful contest for Richardson's seat in the Quincy district. William R. Archer ran James C. Allen a neck and neck race in the Decatur-Olney region, while no effective opposition was organized against Samuel S. Marshall in the Cairo district.

These signs of an impending political revolution in Illinois summoned Douglas from his triumph at Washington to avert

[18] *Free West*, September 21, 1854.
[19] *Belleville Advocate*, August 2, 1854; *Alton Courier*, August 30, September 9, 1854; *Illinois Journal*, September 30, 1854; *Alton Telegraph* clipped in *Alton Weekly Courier*, October 26, 1854.
[20] *Illinois Journal*, September 28, 1854.

the crisis. The announcement that he would address his constituents at Chicago, Saturday, September 1, caused a public demonstration of the unpopularity of his recent course. At one o'clock on the appointed day, the flags in the harbor were lowered to half-mast; later at six o'clock the bells of the city were tolled for an hour. Then eight or ten thousand persons gathered near North Market Hall; in spite of Mayor Milliken's admonition to remain quiet, the crowd greeted Douglas with a storm of hisses and groans, that overwhelmed the plaudits of his supporters. Unable to proceed he announced his intention to stay until he could be heard, whereupon the mob broke into the chorus: "We won't go till morning, till morning, till morning, till daylight doth appear."[21] Douglas defiantly faced the mob, "The spirit of a *dictator* flashed out from his eye, curled upon his lip, and mingled its cold irony in every tone of his voice and every gesture of his body."[22] He and the mob defied each other until midnight when at length the "little giant" was compelled to acknowledge his defeat. Shaking his fist at the audience, his face distorted with rage, he shouted: "It is now Sunday morning—I'll go to church, and you may go to Hell!"[23]

This incident gave Douglas an opportunity to travel over the state and say that he had been refused a hearing by the abolitionists of Chicago. He met with very little more success, however, throughout the northern counties. At Geneva he was compelled to leave off speaking until his opponent, Ichabod Codding, responding to the calls of the audience, graciously urged that Douglas be heard through.[24] Undaunted, he continued on his canvass, dashing from point to point in the country of the enemy and in the more favorable territory in central Illinois. The climax came at Springfield during the state fair, where his supporters hoped to score heavily by arranging for a formal address. The anti-Nebraska forces made their preparations to meet Douglas; Judge Trumbull, Judge Breese, Colonel McClernand, Judge Palmer, Colonel

---

[21] *Free West*, September 7, 1854.
[22] *Chicago Daily Democratic Press*, September 4, 1854.
[23] See *Chicago Tribune* account in *Illinois State Register*, September 7, 14, 1854.
[24] *Free West*, September 28, 1854; *Aurora Guardian*, September 21, 1854.

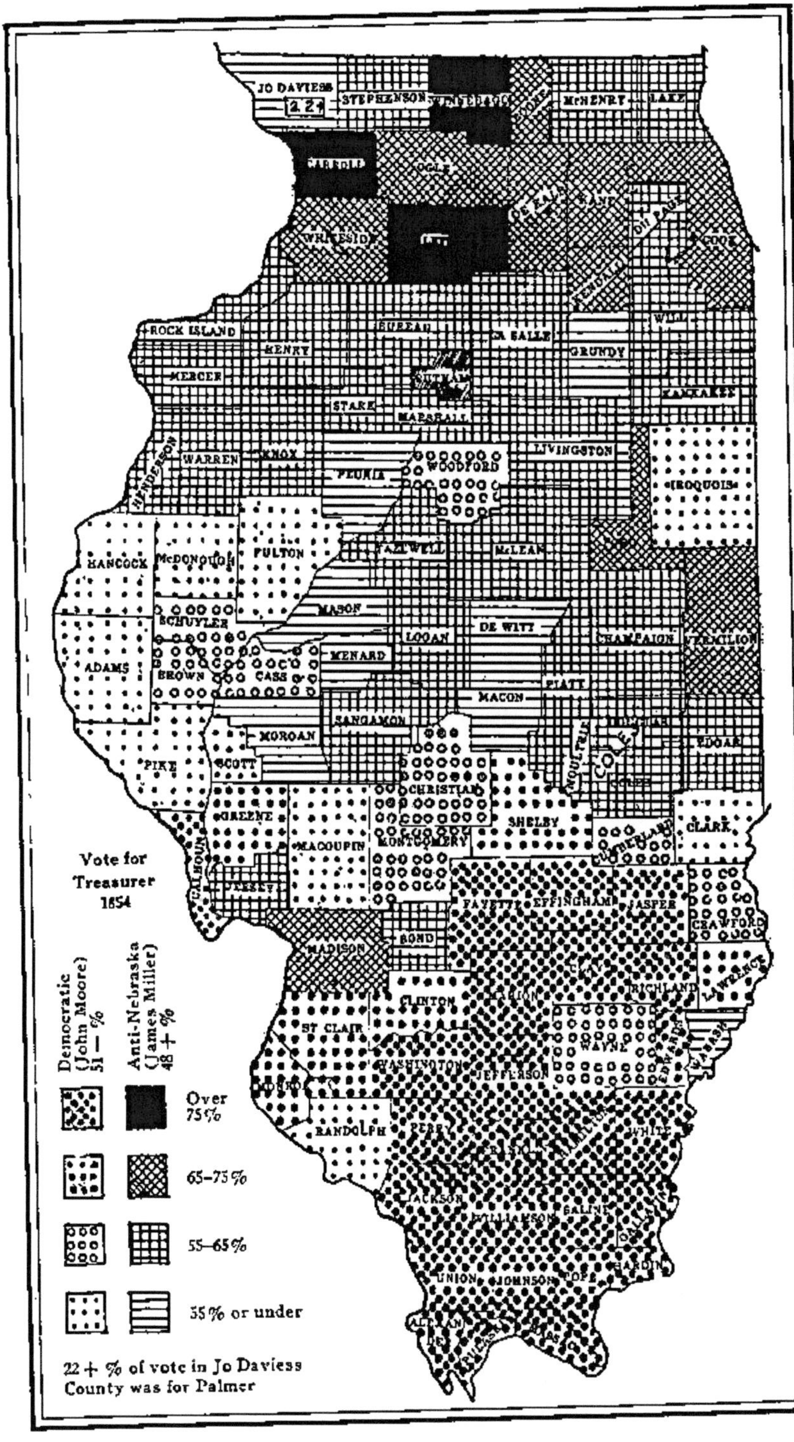
Vote for Treasurer 1854
Democratic (John Moore) 51 — %
Anti-Nebraska (James Miller) 48 + %
Over 75%
65–75%
55–65%
55% or under
22 + % of vote in Jo Daviess County was for Palmer
JO DAVIESS
22+
STEPHENSON
McHENRY
LAKE
CARROLL
OGLE
KANE
DU PAGE
COOK
WHITESIDE
ROCK ISLAND
HENRY
BUREAU
LA SALLE
GRUNDY
MERCER
PUTNAM
STARK
MARSHALL
KANKAKEE
HENDERSON
WARREN
KNOX
PEORIA
WOODFORD
LIVINGSTON
IROQUOIS
HANCOCK
McDONOUGH
FULTON
TAZEWELL
McLEAN
MASON
SCHUYLER
LOGAN
DE WITT
CHAMPAIGN
VERMILION
ADAMS
BROWN
CASS
MENARD
PIATT
MACON
SANGAMON
MORGAN
EDGAR
PIKE
SCOTT
CHRISTIAN
MOULTRIE
COLES
GREENE
SHELBY
CLARK
CALHOUN
MACOUPIN
MONTGOMERY
CUMBERLAND
JERSEY
FAYETTE
EFFINGHAM
JASPER
CRAWFORD
MADISON
BOND
RICHLAND
LAWRENCE
CLINTON
MARION
ST CLAIR
WAYNE
WASHINGTON
JEFFERSON
EDWARDS
WABASH
MONROE
RANDOLPH
PERRY
WHITE
JACKSON
SALINE
WILLIAMSON
GALLATIN
UNION
JOHNSON
POPE
HARDIN
ALEXANDER
PULASKI

E. D. Taylor, and other democrats, were easily prevailed upon to be at hand to make reply. With them enlisted Abraham Lincoln, the whig anti-Nebraska champion. Douglas made his main address on October 3 and was answered the next day by Lincoln in behalf of the anti-Nebraska group. Douglas replied in a "brief" hour and a half speech. On the fifth, with McClernand and Palmer standing by ready to measure lances with Douglas, Breese, Trumbull, and Taylor fell upon their erstwhile leader.[25] Douglas himself, with no opportunity to deliver a formal speech, had to content himself with brief answers to the assaults of his opponents with such assistance as could be given by his Sangamon county lieutenant, John Calhoun. All this opposition seems to have made no impression upon the fighting senator; he was soon off to other battle-grounds to get in his blows during the remaining weeks of the canvass.

Loudly and aggressively did the democrats fling the charge of "abolitionism" at their opponents, pointing to the active participation in the campaign of such antislavery extremists as Ichabod Codding and Owen Lovejoy, the brother of the martyr, Salmon P. Chase and Joshua R. Giddings, the well-known Ohio leaders; even Cassius M. Clay, and Frederick Douglass, the Negro abolitionist, invaded the state on short anti-Nebraska speech making tours. "Hired gangs of abolitionists of the Horace Greeley and Garrison school," warned the *Cairo City Times*, "are traversing the State, addressing the people and telling them *how to vote.*"[26]

The returns in November showed a sweeping democratic defeat. "Never before have the democracy of Illinois been so completely vanquished," lamented the *Joliet Signal* of November 14. A clear anti-Nebraska legislature was elected; and though democrats elected John Moore state treasurer, it was only by a policy of silence on the Nebraska question. The congressional elections went against their regular candidates by five to four. The shout of triumph in the anti-Nebraska camp brought humility to the Douglas democracy,

[25] *Illinois Journal*, October 10, 1854; *Alton Weekly Courier*, October 12, 1854.
[26] See the *Free West*, June-November, 1854; *Cairo City Times*, October 18, 1854.

which at length showed a disposition to let the Nebraska issue rest.[27]

The biggest stake in the elections of 1854 was Shield's seat in the United States senate. The anti-Nebraska majority in the legislature seemed to assure his defeat, though party allegiance still called loudly to democrats of all stripes. Among Shield's competitors were Governor Matteson, Lyman Trumbull, and Abraham Lincoln. Lincoln, still clinging to the obsolete whig tradition, was a champion of antislavery whiggery; and the main body of anti-Nebraska legislators supported him mainly because they themselves were of whig sympathies. But could the anti-Nebraska democrats support a candidate who hailed from the camp of the traditional enemy? Yet success depended upon the support of these democratic heretics. They were inflexibly committed against Shields, instinctively preferred Trumbull, but regarded Matteson a very moderate Nebraska man, as second choice. Matteson, indeed, might well have been elected had it not been that Lieutenant Governor Koerner, a foreigner and an anti-Nebraskaite, would then have been automatically promoted to the gubernatorial chair.

The house promptly elected anti-Nebraska officers. In the senate, however, the Douglas men delayed organization with obstructive tactics, while the anti-Nebraska democratic senators including Norman B. Judd, John M. Palmer, B. C. Cook, and Uri Osgood, refused to participate in the democratic caucus on organization. A joint resolution disapproving of the repeal of the Missouri compromise and instructing the Illinois senators to support its restoration was introduced but failed to progress to final passage, although in one vote the house committed itself to the resolution.

Hoping at least to prevent the choice of an opposition candidate, if only by preventing the election of a senator, Douglas tried to sow discord among the anti-Nebraska forces. His organ, the *Chicago Daily Times,* January 10, patronizingly exhorted the whigs to bear proudly their ancient name and principles, as embodied in Lincoln, rather than yield to the solicitation of democratic anti-Nebraska malcontents.[28] Lin-

[27] *St. Clair Tribune,* November 11, 1854.
[28] Douglas to Charles A. Lanphier, December 18, 1854, Lanphier manuscripts.

coln was opposed by some of these democrats, because of his "shortcomings on the Republican basis." Besides his connection with a conservative "mummy of a party," his unwillingness to oppose the fugitive slave law and to pledge himself in opposition to the admission of any more slave states, was regarded as evidence of too much conservatism for the old time abolition forces.[29] In the early balloting, Lincoln received the vote of every member of whig antecedents but still lacked a few votes. The anti-Nebraska democratic bolters supported Trumbull on the ground that as a majority of the legislature were democrats in old party allegiance, a democrat ought to be elected. Tremendous pressure was brought to bear upon them to vote for Shields or Matteson. One of the participants later charged that bribery as well as persuasion was attempted upon him. Just when the bolters, Judd and his colleagues, were on the point of abandoning Trumbull and joining their brethren to elect either Shields or Matteson, Lincoln, convinced that it was impossible to secure his own election, instructed his whig supporters to unite at once on Trumbull as a candidate who could be elected.[30] As a result the tenth ballot showed Lyman Trumbull the choice of the state legislature for United States senator. His election was hailed with universal satisfaction by the entire anti-Nebraska press of the state. Douglas and his followers, considering it preferable to a whig victory, promptly acquiesced.

While the Kansas-Nebraska question was the chief issue of 1854 and 1855, other problems competed with it for attraction and contributed to the general political chaos. Whig disintegration and democratic schism provided a favorable atmosphere for the many "isms" that sought a hearing. The tem-

[29] *Free West*, December 14, 1854; *Aurora Guardian*, January 11, 1855.
[30] *Chicago Daily Democratic Press*, January 13, 1855. George T. Allen claimed in 1866 that he was offered by the democrats through L. F. Mebrille, their agent, "all they could give" "to buy any vote for Gov. Matteson." George T. Allen to Trumbull, June 14, 1866, Trumbull manuscripts. See also *Chicago Weekly Democrat*, February 17, August 11, 1855; *Illinois Journal*, February 9, 1855. As it was, five anti-Nebraska members voted for Matteson on the last ballot; two of these were William C. Kinney and Albert H. Trapp of St. Clair county in Trumbull's own district, who incidentally wanted to see Koerner become governor as a result of Matteson's election. *Belleville Advocate*, February 14, 1855; *St. Clair Tribune*, February 17, 1855; Koerner, *Memoirs*, 1:624-625; Johns, *Personal Recollections*, 75-76; Lincoln to Henderson, February 21, 1855, Illinois State Historical Society, *Journal*, 4:73.

perance agitation, split though it was into various factions, suddenly acquired a magnetic appeal; after a surprising display of strength in connection with the proposed liquor law of 1855, however, the movement collapsed with equal abruptness. An attempt was made also to force an alignment on the issue of political nativism when a wave of native Americanism swept over the country to the hospitable prairies of Illinois; but since it sought to ignore the ever present slavery question, this became a centrifugal force which in time threw apart the elements of the conglomerate mass.

The "know nothing" party was the name given to this revival of native Americanism which, in its political aspect, was a protest against the part that the foreign born citizen was allowed to play, whether legally or fraudulently, in the practical workings of the American political system. It also involved some objection to the Roman Catholic allegiance of the foreign immigrant, particularly the Irish. Arising in the form of a secret political organization which concealed even its name and existence and holding up the high ideal of protecting American institutions from the "insidious wiles of foreigners," it made a strong appeal to various political groups in the state. It furnished an opportunity for a dark lantern exodus from old party bondage both to the whigs, who came to feel quite like men without a party, and to democrats, who were permanently alienated by the unfortunate leadership of Senator Douglas; at the same time its novelty, its secrecy, and its mystery as a ritualistic secret organization attracted hundreds of converts. The new nativist movement claimed to herald an era of political reform which should rid the country of the corruption that had crept into high places, which should substitute devotion to the union of the fathers for slavish devotion to party. To the conservative who had grown weary of the excessive sectional agitation, it promised an opportunity to steer clear of the unfortunate slavery controversy.

During the early weeks of the canvass in 1854, the *State Register* and other Douglas journals issued warnings: "Beware of the Know Nothings," and "Beware of secret societies." This was clearly an attempt to rally the foreign voters, particularly the Irish, in favor of the Nebraska party. Inasmuch

ORIGIN OF REPUBLICAN PARTY

as the democratic party had always been the chief beneficiary of the foreign vote the effect was to encourage nativism in the ranks of the opposition which inherited some of the whig traditions.[31] Soon evidences were discovered of local organizations in Joliet, Ottawa, Grayville, Canton, Vermont, Farmington, Alton, and other communities. A know nothing journal entitled the *American Era* was started at Grayville, while the *Canton Register* among others showed strong nativistic inclinations; it challenged the "disgusting" flattery bestowed on foreigners to secure their votes and declared that only Americans, including naturalized Protestant citizens, should rule America. By August the order numbered over three hundred in Alton and was preparing for the coming city election. One of its meetings was held "in the culvert under Prisa street." When the votes were counted on September 12 it was found that a closely contested election had quietly taken place which resulted in a complete know nothing victory. "The officers elected are among the best men in our city," declared the *Alton Courier*.[32]

It is difficult to state to what extent the November elections were influenced by this new issue. Richard Yates was said to have lost enough foreign votes to forfeit his seat in congress, as a result of the false charge that he was a know nothing. In the Belleville-Alton district hundreds of Germans and Catholic Americans, fearful that they might vote for some know nothing candidate, remained at home or "allowed themselves to be persuaded to vote against Mr. Trumbull under the representation that every anti-Nebraska man must necessarily be a Maine Law liquor man and a Know Nothing."[33] Similar reasons were said to have accounted for the defeat of the anti-Nebraskaites in the Quincy district. On the other hand, Norton and Knox in the third and fourth congressional districts and Allen in the seventh succeeded with the indorsement of the nativists. It was claimed that many members of the newly elected legislature were know nothings as well as anti-Nebras-

[31] *Illinois Journal*, August 2, 1854; *Ottawa Weekly Republican*, October 7, 1854; *Joliet Signal*, July 4, 1854.
[32] *Canton Weekly Register*, August 3, September 14, 21, 1854; *Alton Courier*, August 17, September 14, 1854; *Illinois Journal*, November 14, 1854; *Free West*, December 14, 1854. Lincoln was similarly believed to be one of the nativists.
[33] "An Adopted Citizen," *St. Clair Tribune*, November 25, 1854; see also *Alton Courier*, November 8, 1854.

kaites; disgusted democratic editors therefore called it a "heterogeneous mixture of niggerism, Native Americanism, black republicanism and intrigue," a compound of "Fusion, Know Nothingism, and Whiggery." The tabling of a resolution opposing any change in the naturalization laws and the defeat of Senator Shields, because a son of Erin, was offered as proof of the charge. "The Nebraska fight is over and Know Nothingism has taken its place as the chief issue of the future," declared Douglas anent the senatorial election.[34]

The next year was an off-year in Illinois politics; the know nothings utilized it to perfect their organization for more aggressive political activity. Recruits were enlisted in such numbers that the heterogeneous character of the local councils and the state organization became apparent. Nebraska and anti-Nebraska men were now joining the order without any strong conviction that nativism was the dominant issue of the day. Soon there was wrangling within the brotherhood; a general disposition to soften the proscriptive features of the know nothing platform betrayed a desire on the part of both the radical and conservative groups to build up strength for themselves even at a sacrifice of some of the fundamental tenets of the order. Each side charged the other in public with a monopoly on bigotry. It soon became a fight between "Sam" and "Jonathan." "Sam" represented the original and orthodox brand of nativism; "Jonathan" was the champion of an antislavery brand which welcomed all foreigners who would disavow temporal allegiance to the pope.[35]

These were insuperable obstacles to a strong and harmonious state organization.[36] Jonathanism, with an antislavery extension plank, made rapid progress in Illinois, preparing to resist the action of the southern know nothings. At a stormy two day session of the Illinois Grand Council at Chicago in May, Sam and Jonathan came together in a heated contest in

[34] *St. Clair Tribune,* February 17, 1855; *Joliet Signal,* January 16, 1855; Douglas to Lanphier, December 18, 1855, Lanphier manuscripts.
[35] *Alton Courier,* May 8, 1855; *Chicago Weekly Democrat,* May 5, 1855.
[36] Municipal activity presented the best field. In March, 1855, the know nothings elected their entire municipal ticket in Chicago and Rockford, while in April they lost the Quincy city election by 250 votes; *Urbana Union,* March 15, 1855; *Rockford Republican,* March 14, 1855; *Alton Courier,* April 21, 1855.

which the only gains were made by the latter.[37] A state convention at Springfield, in July continued the fight: the anti-Nebraska forces prevented the adoption of the Philadelphia national platform with its approval of the repeal of the Missouri compromise. The majority report of the committee on resolutions, which included a clause calling for the restoration of the Missouri compromise, was adopted by a vote of 74 to 35. The nativistic declarations were mild and ambiguous. It contained, indeed, less nativism than it did antislavery doctrine; congress was declared to have full power under the constitution to legislate on slavery in the territories. "The platform," complained a conservative opponent, also "contains enough of treason to the South and the Constitution to suit the Abolitionists." Jonathan seemed to have dealt Sam a death-blow and to have arranged for his burial. So true was this that the rival "know something" order, which welcomed the foreign votes on an anti-Nebraska platform, fell for want of *raison d'être*.[38]

Pursuant to an order of this state convention, a know nothing organ, the *Daily Native Citizen*, was established at Chicago by W. W. Danenhower. In its first numbers it took strong antislavery ground; after a few months, however, its tone changed somewhat; and it adjusted itself to a more conservative nationalistic position. At the same time its nativism was diluted to the point where it was able to commend the idea, as promulgated by the German press of the state, that Gustave Koerner be given the republican nomination for governor.[39]

It was obvious from all these signs that political nativism did not constitute a basis for party organization in Illinois. The most important question of the day was the question of slavery extension; the northern view, that slavery was a moral and political evil and that congress had a duty to prevent its extension into the territories was brought into vigorous asser-

---

[37] The *Chicago Democrat* charged Douglas with being a lobby member of the Grand Council, consulted by a large number of members of the proslavery tendencies, whom he advised to hold to their allegiance to Sam. *Chicago Weekly Democrat*, May 5, 1855.

[38] *Illinois Journal*, July 11, 1855; *Ottawa Weekly Republican*, July 14, 21, 1855; *Cairo City Times*, July 25, 1855; *Chicago Weekly Democrat*, October 27, 1855.

[39] *Daily Native Citizen* clipped in *St. Clair Tribune*, December 22, 1855.

tion by the enactment of the Kansas-Nebraska act. It was evident that various fragments lay upon the political scrap-heap which might be cemented together into an effective opposition to democratic domination. But blind adhesion to deceased or expiring parties together with infatuation for novelty and change had first to disappear, and this required time. Whigs almost convinced themselves at intervals that old issues were returning and that the day of resurrection was near at hand. At such times they were unwilling to abandon their "broad, tried, and natural platform" and their conservative friends in the south in order to be swallowed up in a republican fusion of democrats, whigs, and abolitionists. The *Illinois Journal* was convinced that the republican movement had degenerated into a sectional party; accordingly, it clung to its old whig connections but played the part of apologist for the native American party.[40]

John Wentworth, still proud of his democratic connections, took a long forward step when he permitted his journal to declare: "The North is all split to pieces upon matters of minor moment compared with the great question at issue. Now we think the North should unite as well as the South. If slavery can unite the South, certainly, freedom should unite the North." This was followed by an indorsement of the proposition made by the *National Era*, the old free soil organ, for united action by the north in 1856. The *Ottawa Republican* was at the same time conducting a propaganda to the same end.[41] The *Galena Advertiser* next recommended an anti-Nebraska mass state convention at Chicago in October in connection with the state fair. The idea of mixing politics and agriculture was first frowned upon, especially in view of a protest against such distractions by the executive committee of the State Agricultural Society, though a little later, when the proposition was renewed, it was widely indorsed.[42] Still it was felt that the responsibility for calling the convention

---

[40] *Chicago Daily Democratic Press*, December 22, 1854; *Quincy Whig*, July 7, 1855; *Illinois Journal*, December 12, 1854, January 27, August 4, October 5, November 23, 24, December 6, 1855.
[41] *Chicago Weekly Democrat*, June 30, 1855; *Ottawa Weekly Republican*, June 30, 1855.
[42] *Illinois State Journal*, September 1, 1855; *Quincy Whig*, September 11, October 9, 1855.

ought to be taken by some organization in the central part of the state and none of these had the courage to issue the necessary call. As a result, all that was done in the field of republican party politics during that year was the perfection of local organizations in the northern counties, where successful contests were made in the local elections. Again Ichabod Codding took the stump with the republican propaganda and Joshua R. Giddings journeyed from Ohio for a speech-making tour in the hopes of being able to participate in the christening of an Illinois republican party.

Meanwhile Douglas was energetically at work trying to bring unity and harmony into the councils of the democratic party. At the end of summer he took the stump, appealing to his erstwhile followers to rally for democracy and to beware of know nothingism and Maine lawism lurking behind the veil of anti-Nebraska. He tried to bully his opponents into acquiescence in the Kansas-Nebraska act by daring Trumbull to make a joint agreement to risk their seats in the senate on this issue in the coming state election. When his proposal was ignored, however, Douglas concentrated on side issues wherever he found himself in hostile territory. Douglas and Trumbull met in joint debate at Salem, September 26; and the two spoke on consecutive days at Chicago during the state fair. In general, however, Douglas tended to center his attention on Egypt where the party was solidly reorganized on Nebraska ground with old time whigs in the place of the few anti-Nebraska seceders.[43]

Party organization in Illinois was still in a most chaotic condition when the time arrived to consider the coming presidential election. All democrats believed themselves the true

[43] *Chicago Weekly Democrat*, October 6, 1855; *Cairo City Times*, October 24, 1855. A single outspoken Nebraskaite objector to Douglas leadership was found in the Shawneetown *Southern Illinoisan*, which declared that his visit had " not only evidenced the breach between himself and the people, but drawn upon him the bitter hatred of many who a short time ago numbered among his best friends." " What is Democracy? " it asked. *Ottawa Weekly Republican*, November 3, 1855. " In Illinois it means just now, to hallo for Douglas — get in office, gain wealth by the dishonest means afforded by your official standing, and retire to some secluded spot and spend your remaining days in princely style, considering yourself one of the ' luck dogs ' of the earth." *Belleville Advocate*, December 19, 1855.

protectors of the principles of their party, although it was apparent that the Douglasites controlled the organization. There were anti-Nebraska whigs who had learned to coöperate with some of their former opponents in the fight on Douglas; there were others who had entered the camp of the enemy believing that only in this way could they do effective battle for nationalism and conservatism; there were "old-line" whigs, who clung dreamily to the conservative traditions of the party; but there was no longer a whig party in Illinois. Know nothings found themselves driftwood on a tide that, having carried them to the high water mark, was now rapidly receding; the expediency of working toward an old or, if possible, some safer new haven was obvious to them.

Many whigs, democrats, and know nothings would have been glad to welcome the republican party, which had swept all before it in the neighboring states of Michigan and Wisconsin.[44] They were convinced that henceforward there could be but one issue, that of slavery, and that there were to be but two national parties — the slavery restrictionists, or republicans, and the slavery extensionists, or democrats. When in February, 1856, the combined anti-Nebraska forces in congress succeeded in electing Nathaniel P. Banks speaker of the house of representatives, they hailed this first national "republican" victory and summoned the republicans in their neighborhoods to celebrate it.[45] Anti-Nebraska democrats generally rejoiced at Banks' election, but seldom looked upon it as a "democratic victory" as did Wentworth in his *Chicago Democrat;* many, however, as reluctant as he to part company with old associations, did share his hope of being able to convert the party to slavery restriction — a hope which they would never relinquish unless the national democratic convention should record itself in favor of the principle embodied in the Kansas-Nebraska law. This was the position of William H. Bissell, Gustave Koerner, Lyman Trumbull, and hundreds of other prominent anti-Nebraska democrats.[46] But such anti-

---

[44] These democrats felt that they had made "a happy escape from a den of thieves, drunkards, gamblers, and blackguards." George T. Allen to Trumbull, January 19, 1856, Trumbull manuscripts.
[45] *Rockford Republican,* February 13, 1856.
[46] D. S. Phillips to Trumbull, January 15, 1856, Trumbull manuscripts.

Nebraskaites as John Reynolds, John A. McClernand, and William H. Underwood were democrats first and last; they would never falter in their allegiance. The persistence of party loyalty was a blow to the hopes of an effective state republican party. The party had its local and county organizations in the northern part of the state but lacked the aggressive support of just such democrats in central and eastern Illinois. It threw the burden of organization upon the whig elements with their reputation for lack of real organizing ability and energy. For this reason it was natural that when a caucus of anti-Nebraska men was held during the session of the supreme court at Springfield, it was decided under the leadership of Koerner and others that no separate anti-Nebraska organization or nominations should be attempted.[47]

Just at this time, the anti-Nebraska press of the state was agreeing upon a proposition of prime significance for the future of the antislavery extension group in Illinois. The *Morgan Journal*, edited by Paul Selby, a participant in the Springfield "republican" convention of October, 1854, suggested a meeting of the free state editors to consider "arrangements for the organization of the anti-Nebraska forces in the state for the coming contest." This move was seconded by the *Winchester Chronicle*, edited by John Moses, and warmly supported by William J. Usrey of the Decatur *Illinois State Chronicle;* Usrey suggested a meeting at Decatur on the twenty-second of February. The final call was signed by twenty-five of the leading anti-Nebraska journals; this did not include the *Rockford Republican*, although its editor had indorsed the proposition and appeared at Decatur in time for the opening meeting.[48] A dozen arrived at the appointed time and a few others, delayed by a severe snow storm, participated in the later proceedings. The meeting was organized with Selby as chairman and Usrey as secretary. Abraham Lincoln came

[47] Thomas Quick to Trumbull, January 24, 1856, *ibid.*
[48] *Rockford Republican*, January 30, 1856; list in Selby, "The Editorial Convention, February 22, 1856," McLean County Historical Society, *Transactions*, 3:36; Selby, "The Editorial Convention of 1856," Illinois State Historical Society, *Journal*, 5:343 ff. The *Chicago Democrat* and the *Chicago Daily Democratic Press* were the leading anti-Nebraska journals who ignored the call. The *Chicago Weekly Democrat*, March 22, declared it had approved the object but opposed the time.

up from Springfield as the only outsider present and actively conferred with the committee on resolutions headed by Dr. Charles H. Ray of the *Chicago Tribune*. Lincoln and Ray framed resolutions which, though protesting against the repeal of the Missouri compromise and against the further extension of slavery, were designed to be truly national and conservative on the slavery question. George Schneider of the *Illinois Staats-Zeitung* insisted in behalf of his fellow countrymen upon a moderate anti-know nothing plank.[49]

The convention appointed a state central committee and recommended a state delegate convention at Bloomington on May 29. One of the two appointees to the central committee for the state-at-large was Lieutenant Governor Gustave Koerner. Koerner, reluctant to break with his old party associations, declined to serve on the committee; he indorsed the principles adopted by the convention, however, and hinted that if they should be repudiated by the approaching state and national democratic conventions, he would feel free to act with another organization.[50]

Preparations followed rapidly for the state convention. The democratic victories in the March municipal elections in Chicago, Springfield, and other Illinois cities only spurred on the anti-Nebraskaites; by the end of April the tide was beginning to turn following the defeat of the erstwhile whig, Colonel Singleton, whom the democrats nominated for mayor of Quincy. Local anti-Nebraska and antislavery extension clubs were formed; county conventions followed, drawing together all the opposition odds and ends.[51] In some instances they frankly adopted the republican label, although this aroused the protests of those who, wishing to stress the larger appeal, called attention to the fact that the word "republican" did not

[49] The satisfactory character of the platform was obvious from its approval by the *State Journal* as "neither 'Know Nothing' nor 'Republican'" while the *Rockford Republican* in its turn declared: "There is not a plank in the platform but what is made of sound-live-oak Republican timber." *Illinois State Journal*, February 25, 1856; *Rockford Republican*, March 19, 1856.

[50] Koerner to the editor of the *Belleville Advocate*, March 6, 1856, clipped in *Quincy Whig*, March 14, 1856; Koerner, *Memoirs*, 2:3-4. These were the sentiments of other anti-Nebraska democrats like John M. Palmer and John Wentworth. *Chicago Weekly Democrat*, March 22, 1856.

[51] The *Chicago Democrat* and *Chicago Daily Democratic Press* gave the movement encouragement.

ORIGIN OF REPUBLICAN PARTY

appear in the calls of the state central committee. Leaders like William H. Herndon, George T. Brown of the *Alton Courier*, William H. Bissell, Orville H. Browning, in conference with Senator Trumbull, sought to direct the movement and keep it in the control of moderate men and conservative influences. It was felt that even the leadership of the Decatur convention would kill the movement.[52]

At the appointed time, the anti-Nebraska delegates assembled at Bloomington. About 270 delegates, outnumbering the official apportionment of the central committee, responded to roll call, although about thirty southern counties were unrepresented. "Old line Whigs, Jefferson and Jackson Democrats, Republicans, American and foreign born citizens, laying aside all past differences, united together there in one common brotherhood to war against the allied forces of nullification, disunion, slavery propagandism, ruffianism and gag law, which make up the present administration party of the country."[53] The democratic state convention had already taken place on the first day of the month and had adopted under Douglasite influences an aggressive Nebraska platform as a test of party orthodoxy; it nominated for governor Douglas' aid-de-camp in the passage of the Kansas-Nebraska act, his "man Friday," Colonel Richardson.[54] This was sufficiently decisive to absolve John M. Palmer and the more restive anti-Nebraska democrats from all party allegiance.

Judge Palmer accordingly presented himself at Bloomington as a delegate from Macoupin county. He arrived sufficiently early to participate with Lincoln, Washburne, and others in the speech-making on the night preceding the convention and made such a favorable impression that he was called to the chair by way of honor to the new accessions from the democracy. The convention adopted a platform of principles which closely followed the Decatur platform and made plans for a permanent organization.[55] William H. Bis-

[52] W. H. Bissell to Trumbull, May 5, 1856, O. H. Browning to Trumbull, May 19, 1856, Trumbull manuscripts.
[53] *Illinois State Journal*, May 31, 1856.
[54] *Ibid.*, July 14, 1856; *Chicago Daily Democratic Press*, July 13, 1856.
[55] *Illinois State Journal*, May 30, 1856; McLean County Historical Society, *Transactions*, 3: 148 ff.

sell, the old democratic war horse of St. Clair county, was nominated for governor by acclamation, to head the state ticket. An electoral ticket with Lincoln and Friedrich Hecker for electors-at-large was adopted. Illinois republicanism had even a few months previously been strong enough to participate in the preliminary national convention of the republican forces at Pittsburg, February 22. Owen Lovejoy and J. C. Vaughan attended as representatives of the more radical elements in the state. That body had called a national nominating convention at Philadelphia in June, and selections were now made of delegates to represent Illinois. After the completion of business the convention listened to addresses by O. H. Browning, Owen Lovejoy, B. C. Cook, and Abraham Lincoln, who "made *the* speech of the occasion."[56] Huge ratification meetings at Chicago and Springfield suggested the enthusiasm with which the work of the convention was received.

Next came the national conventions. At Cincinnati on June 2 the democrats selected James Buchanan on a squatter sovereignty platform; although Douglas had allowed his name to be placed in the field and had received the support of Illinois and Indiana politicians,[57] it was clear that the Kansas-Nebraska act had not advanced his availability. The republican national convention with a heavy Illinois representation met at Philadelphia June 17 and nominated John C. Fremont and William L. Dayton as the antislavery extension candidates. The Americans or know nothings had already nominated Fillmore and Donelson, who were later indorsed by the remnants of whiggery.

The Philadelphia convention was in many ways a struggle between former democratic and whig elements for a leading place in the new republican party. The whigs put forward Judge McLean of Ohio, a free soil whig; while the democrats settled on Fremont, whom the *Chicago Democrat* had advo-

[56] *Chicago Daily Democratic Press,* May 31, 1856. Herndon wrote later that he forged Lincoln's name to the document that got him to go to Bloomington. "Whiggery & Know Nothingism tried to hold him, but they couldn't," he wrote to Z. Eastman, February 6, 1866, Eastman manuscripts.
[57] W. D. Latham to Lanphier, November 9, 1855, Lanphier manuscripts. Douglas' Chicago organ, the *Times,* decided in December not to advocate the claims of any candidate for the presidency. *Cairo Weekly Times and Delta,* December 19, 1855.

cated for the democratic nomination as a "Union and constitutional candidate." But the news of the nomination of the conqueror of California, with a whig for the second place on the ticket, brought forth a general outburst of enthusiasm. "Fremont, the gallant, the indomitable, the hero of our western wilds, his name is a household word throughout the Union, and his active sympathy with Freedom has endeared him to the heart of every free man," was the motto of welcome.[58] Westerners forgot any disappointment they may have anticipated in their enthusiasm over the republican declarations for river and harbor improvements, the great desideratum of the west; and for the Pacific railroad, the great national highway.

The camp of the enemy immediately sent up the cry that the "black republicans" were a sectional party; if democratic "dough-faces" were trucklers to the slave power, then the "kinky-heads" were converts to rank abolitionism! Developments conspired to destroy the force of that charge; early Illinois republicanism had been repudiated because dominated by old-line abolitionists; the latter now in turn rejected the new brand because it would not measure up to their standard. The ultra abolitionists assembled in state convention at Joliet on July 31 and August 1 to nominate an electoral ticket to support Gerrit Smith.[59] This in effect stripped the republican party in Illinois of the stigma of abolition fanaticism.

Soon a spirited canvass was under way, with Illinois as one of the chief battle-grounds of the campaign. Here Douglas, reënforced by Horatio Seymour and John Van Buren of New York, Governor Henry A. Wise of Virginia, and Lewis Cass of Michigan broke lances in the ancient stronghold of "doughface" democracy with John P. Hale, the veteran abolitionist leader, Nathaniel P. Banks and Anson Burlingame of Massachusetts, Francis P. Blair, of Missouri, and Governor Charles Robinson of Kansas. The main work for the republicans, however, was done by local talent and it was of a high order. Trumbull and Lincoln, Koerner and Bissell, Owen Lovejoy

[58] Browning to Trumbull, May 14, 1856, Trumbull manuscripts; *Chicago Weekly Democrat*, February 8, 1856; *Rock River Democrat*, June 24, 1856.
[59] *Ottawa Weekly Republican*, July 26, 1856; *Illinois State Journal*, August 7, 1856.

and John Wentworth, Richard Yates and John M. Palmer led valiant charges on the "Buchaneers."

The republicans made effective use of the story of "bleeding Kansas." Illinois followed developments there with tense interest. The state contributed thousands of emigrants to the battle-ground of popular sovereignty, who either brought back in person livid tales of the outrages committed by the border ruffians, or kept their relatives and former neighbors informed through written communications. The republican newspapers eagerly garnered all fresh details while campaign orators equipped themselves with the "tyrannical laws of the bogus territorial legislature," and cudgelled their opponents, the "nigger-drivers," into silence or apology.[60]

The drive and energy of the republicans astounded their opponents. Huge parades and processions with gay banners and gorgeous floats preceded the meetings. At Peoria thirty-one young women dressed in white with wreaths of flowers about their brows, with one in mourning garb to represent Kansas, were embarked on a boat, drawn by eight splendid white horses; it was "The Constitution," "bound for the White House."[61] This device was adopted all over the state; often the young women were led by one more beautiful and splendidly attired than the rest to represent "the queen of hearts," the "adored Jessie," dashing wife of Colonel Fremont. Free dinners and barbecues, widely advertised in staring posters, drew together crowds of thousands; the roar of artillery, the fluttering of banners, and the melody of bands of wind and stringed instruments, aided in attaching the sturdy yeomanry of the Illinois prairies to the republican cause.

Northern Illinois with its Yankee prejudices became the base of the republicans. Egypt was the stronghold of the "unterrified" democracy, who shouted for "Buck and Breck;" only along the Mississippi, in the counties of Madison, St. Clair, Monroe, Randolph, Clinton, and Perry, where the German vote was strong, did the work of the Bloomington and

[60] A. H. Herndon to Trumbull, June 16, 1856, Trumbull manuscripts; *Illinois State Register*, September 13, 20, 1855.
[61] *Rushville Times*, September 26, 1856; *Chicago Daily Democratic Press*, October 11, 1856.

Philadelphia conventions find supporters.[62] The central section where old time whigs and Americans were numerous and an uncertain political quantity, was disputed territory. The antislavery whigs, led by Lincoln, Yates, Conkling, Browning, and others, had joined the anti-Nebraska cause. But many old Clay whigs of southern antecedents felt a strong impulse to affiliate with the democratic party as having the strongest claims to nationality. Don Morrison, E. B. Webb, Colonel Singleton, Robert S. Blackwell, and C. H. Constable were some of the leaders in this march into the open arms of the democracy.[63]

The know nothing situation provided a true political conundrum. Although the national convention had brought out the American ticket in February, Illinois supporters hesitated before ratifying the nominations. Under the leadership of men like Joseph Gillespie of Madison county — who had, however, been a signer of the Bloomington anti-Nebraska convention[64] — a state convention was held in May which drew up a state ticket and selected a group of Fillmore electors. The American nominee for governor was Colonel Archer, the anti-Nebraska whig candidate for congress in 1854 who had been defeated by one vote. Archer declined the nomination, declaring it folly for antislavery know nothings to throw away their strength on a third ticket, when the Nebraska know nothings were generally going for the Buchanan and Richardson ticket.[65] Buckner S. Morris, an old-line whig, a southerner by birth and a slaveowner by marriage, was then brought out as the Fillmore candidate for governor. In the end the American movement courted by both parties and torn between the argument

---

[62] Koerner, *Memoirs*, 2: 22-23; Parmenias Bond to Trumbull, June 28, 1856, Trumbull manuscripts.

[63] Constable was made elector-at-large on the Buchanan ticket, though he was known as a nativist and as an anti-Nebraska man with bitter feelings toward Douglas and the "political incendiaries" whose "wicked ambition drove them rough shod over everything sacred to patriotism in the accomplishment of their selfish and factious designs." C. H. Constable to T. B. McClure, January 6, 1856, *Belleville Advocate*, August 20, 1856. Blackwell had been an anti-Nebraska whig candidate for congress in 1854. *Rushville Times*, June 27, 1856.

[64] *Ottawa Free Trader*, May 24, 1856.

[65] *Rock River Democrat*, June 3, 1856. Alfred M. Whitney, an elector from West Urbana, declined to serve for the same reason. *Chicago Weekly Democrat*, September 13, 1856.

that a vote for Fillmore and Morris was either a vote for black republicanism or for the Buchaneers was stripped to its nucleus of old-line whigs and bitter-enders.[66]

The republicans elected their candidates for congress from the four northern districts, while the democrats returned the other four. An interesting contest took place in the third district. Reverend Owen Lovejoy, the abolitionist, was nominated by the republicans over Jesse O. Norton, the sitting member, and over other conservative candidates. Lovejoy had participated in fugitive slave rescues, and the circuit court records showed several suits against him for harboring runaway slaves; he was also said to be an uncompromising know nothing. The delegates from the southern and eastern portion of the district objected to Lovejoy's antecedents on the slavery question and accordingly decided to bolt the nomination and run a candidate of their own. A separate convention was held at Bloomington and T. L. Dickey of Ottawa nominated; he had the support of former whigs led by Churchill Coffing and Isaac Funk.[67] Judge Dickey later decided to leave the field whereupon the democrats fell upon Lovejoy with the charges of the bolters and waged merciless war upon him. Much to their surprise, however, Lovejoy carried the district by six thousand.

These circumstances complicated the problem of the foreign vote. The Irish controlled by the adroit politicians of their race, were generally firm in their democratic allegiance and strongly hostile to nativism. The Germans, like the Scandinavians, were, on the whole, anti-Nebraska but not clear as to the party alignment that this required.[68] The word "democrat" was still magic to their ears, while charges of the know

[66] B. S. Morris to B. D. Eastman *et al.*, August 12, 1856, *Illinois State Register*, August 21, 1856. *Canton Weekly Register*, September 23, 1856. The leading light in Illinois nativistic movements was W. W. Danenhower, editor of the *Native Citizen*, which came to be printed at the office of the *Chicago Times*. Danenhower encouraged by Douglas, started on an aggressive campaign in which he deplored the possible success of Fremont, the "sectional candidate."

[67] *Chicago Daily Democratic Press*, July 19, 1856; *Danville Independent* clipped in *Our Constitution*, July 24, 1856; *Joliet Signal*, July 22, 1856.

[68] On July 4, a Swedish paper, *Den Svenska Republikanen I Norra Amerika*, was started by the Bishop Hill colony at Galva to support Fremont and Dayton. It was the only Swedish journal in the west. Koerner to Trumbull, July 29, 1856, Trumbull manuscripts.

ORIGIN OF REPUBLICAN PARTY 151

nothingism of many republican nominees made them suspicious of a new attachment. Beset by arguments from both sides they usually followed the leadership of spokesmen like Gustave Koerner, Friedrich Hecker, Francis Hoffman, and George Schneider, who supported Fremont and Bissell. Koerner usually declared himself still an old-line democrat, working for the original aim of democracy, opposition to slavery extension.

The fall elections generally seemed to point to the election of Buchanan, although uncertainty existed in the three-cornered fight. Interest in the outcome became more intense as November fourth approached. When finally the votes were registered and counted, it seemed that Fremont had rolled up a vote in northern Illinois that must overwhelm the Egyptian democracy.[69]

As the returns came in, however, Buchanan showed an unexpected strength in the southern districts, which smothered the republican majorities of the northern counties. Winnebago county was the banner republican county, Fremont having polled 89 per cent of the total vote; dominated by Rockford, where three republican newspapers flourished, it was a Yankee stronghold in the west. St. Clair was the lone star republican county in lower Egypt, where conservative democracy piled up powerful majorities for Buchanan. The republicans consoled themselves, however, that this stronghold of democracy was a true "land of darkness" with a monopoly on the illiteracy of the state. Republicanism failed primarily in being unable to draw off a sufficient number of the whig and American voters in the center of the state and in the military tract. It was felt, however, that Fremont had done nobly; the *Illinois Journal* declared that while it had not favored Fremont's nomination, the election had "proved it right."[70]

The election was in one sense, moreover, a humiliating democratic defeat. Colonel Richardson and the state ticket went down before Bissell and his associates. Bissell had been a remarkably strong candidate. He was popular with everyone, with his former democratic associates, with the whigs,

[69] *Rockford Republican*, November 6, 1856; *Rock River Democrat*, November 18, 1856.
[70] *Illinois State Journal*, November 19, 1856.

who had helped to send him to congress in 1852, with the foreigners, and with the nativists in spite of his Catholic faith. Northern and southern Illinois united to support his candidacy. The *Southern Illinoisan* upheld Bissell as a democrat of the Jeffersonian school along with the democratic national ticket; Egypt was urged to enlist on his side, rather than that of the "burly demagogue and sottish blackguard of the north," in order to show that its neck no longer yielded to the yoke of Douglas domination.[71] Bissell, therefore, led the state ticket to victory with a plurality of nearly five thousand.

When the contest was finally decided and the governor-elect turned his attention to the problems of his administration, he found himself confronted by a democratic legislature opposed to republican policies. It was necessary for him in his inaugural address to begin the task of bringing this hostile majority to accept at least some of his measures. The problem was one not easily solved. Bissell had gone on record as opposed to slavery extension, was elected on that principle, and was bound to vindicate it; the charges that the republicans were largely know nothing had to be met by a liberal policy toward foreign born citizens, if the party was not to suffer from a loss of their vote as in the late election. Finally, the injustice of the existing division of electoral districts made it highly advisable to remind the legislature of its constitutional obligations to pass a law districting the state according to the population of the census of 1855. After long and serious consultations over portions of the message, these matters were agreed upon; the final wording left to Bissell "whose mastery of style was undisputed."[72] The first republican state paper in Illinois was a challenge to the very existence of the weakening democracy.

[71] *Southern Illinoisan* clipped in *Belleville Advocate*, July 9, August 20, 1856; *Chicago Daily Democratic Press*, October 14, 1865.
[72] Koerner, *Memoirs*, 2: 37-38.

VII. THE LINCOLN–DOUGLAS DEBATES

THE fruitage of the democratic victory in 1856 was a demand promulgated through the supreme court in the famous Dred Scott decision that the country at large accept the extreme southern doctrine—the right of slavery to go into the territories without restriction either from congress or from any other source. Here was a blow aimed not only at republican slavery restriction ground but also at negative action under the squatter sovereignty doctrine. The consequences of that decision were so serious that Dred Scott, the Negro slave, became a freedman and passed from view on the stage of history long before Illinois politicians had evolved satisfactory solutions to the problems that were raised.

The republican journalists sought to cover party embarrassment involved in this blow to their doctrine of congressional restriction by proclaiming the decision as an infamous attack upon the cause of freedom. "Where will the aggressions of slavery cease?" asked the *Illinois State Journal*, March 11, 1857. "Freedom and white men are no longer safe." "The infamous decision of the Dred Scott case, has aroused the whole North to a realization of the danger which our free institutions are subject to, at the hands of the slave power, and their adherents in the Supreme Court," commented the *Aurora Beacon*, March 6, 1857. "It now devolves upon the people," declared the *Belleville Advocate*, April 8, "to say whether they will submit to this revolution, or take their government into their own hands." Greater determination was conspicuous in all this comment; little consolation was sought in the fact that the blow had been struck in the form of what was clearly an extrajudicial opinion, "which even Judge McLean and Judge Curtis declined to recognize as authority."[1] Convinced that the decision was rendered "through political chicanry [sic] &

[1] *Illinois State Journal*, March 25, 1857.

fraud for corupt [sic] and political purposes,"² they set to work with greater zeal and energy to fight the battles for republicanism.

Democrats received the decision with a silence that betrayed their bewilderment and uncertainty; naturally inclined to resent the principles proclaimed, they hesitated to declare themselves in opposition to the president whom they had just placed in the executive office. Better to wait for a cue from some one who might discover an escape from the dilemma; they awaited the return of Senator Douglas to secure the advice of the champion of popular sovereignty. Meanwhile they sought to forget their own troubles by enjoying the discomfiture of their opponents whom they accused of being repealers if not rebels;[3] they pointed out that the decision declared unconstitutional nearly every point sought to be accomplished by the republican party.

Upon invitation Douglas on June 12 addressed the grand jury at Springfield on the topics of the day. He declared his acceptance of the Dred Scott decision; it was now the law of the land and should be obeyed. He insisted, however, that the great principle of popular sovereignty and self-government was sustained and firmly established by the authority of this decision. The right to enter the territories with slaves, he explained, "necessarily remains a barren and worthless right, unless sustained, protected, and enforced by appropriate police regulations and local legislation, prescribing adequate remedies for its violation. These regulations and remedies must necessarily depend entirely upon the will and wishes of the people of the Territory, as they can only be prescribed by the local legislatures."

Lincoln replied to Douglas in behalf of the republicans on June 26, also at Springfield. Suggesting that the merits of the case lay with the dissenting opinions of McLean and Curtis rather than with the decision of Chief Justice Taney, he declared that republicans had no intention of resisting the decision. They acknowledged that the decisions of the supreme court on constitutional questions, when fully settled, should control not only the particular cases decided but the general policy of the

[2] T. P. Cowen to Trumbull, May 26, 1857, Trumbull manuscripts.
[3] *Ottawa Free Trader*, March 14, April 18, 1858.

country. More than this would be revolution. "But we think the Dred Scott decision is erroneous. We know the court that made it, has often over-ruled its own decisions, and we shall do what we can to have it over-rule this. We offer no *resistance* to it." Lincoln, however, claimed the right for his party to treat this decision, made by a divided court with strong evidence of a partisan bias, as not having yet established a settled doctrine for the country.[4]

Douglas playing on the natural disgust in the minds of nearly all white people at the idea of an indiscriminate amalgamation of the white and black races had championed white supremacy. Lincoln asserted that the guarantees of the Declaration of Independence were intended to include the Negro and met Douglas' specious reasoning squarely: "I think the authors of that notable instrument meant to include *all* men, but they did not declare all men equal *in all respects*. They did not mean to say that all were equal in color, size, intellect, moral developments, or social capacity. They defined with tolerable distinctness in what respects they did consider all men created equal — equal with 'certain inalienable rights, among which are life, liberty, and the pursuit of happiness.' This they said, and this [they] meant."

Senator Trumbull paid his respects to the Dred Scott decision in a speech which his supporters felt surpassed the efforts of Lincoln. Gustave Koerner regarded Lincoln's speech as "too much on the old conservative order;" Lincoln was "an excellent man, but no match to such impudent Jesuits & Sophists as Douglas." "Why D. nor the Democratic party ever submitted to the *principle* decided by the Supreme court in the case of the national bank. He is a pretty fellow to talk about the sanctity of such decisions further than as regards the case decided."[5]

The summer of 1857 was one of great uncertainty for both political parties. It was, moreover, not a year for important elections, and party lines were normally weak in local contests. The situation was one which would try even the most adroit politician who might be under the practical necessity of adjust-

[4] *Illinois State Journal*, July 1, 1857.
[5] Koerner to Trumbull, July 4, 1857, Trumbull manuscripts.

ing his position to the will of the sovereign people. Lincoln and the republicans stood pat in their hostility to the principle of the Dred Scott decision; unless they did so the new party had been organized in vain. Their attention was centered on holding existing strength and on adding recruits from the democratic and know nothing ranks. The support of know nothing voters was encouraged by the nomination of moderate members who had never been elected to office by that party. An organized campaign sought to get democratic readers and subscribers for republican papers. C. D. Hay was instrumental in securing a thousand subscriptions in upper Egypt for the *Chicago Tribune* and the *St. Louis Democrat;* John G. Nicolay and others also added hundreds of subscriptions to antislavery papers.[6]

Douglas, however, was in a quandary; the previous election had revealed a restlessness on the part of his democratic constituency which the existing uncertainty could scarcely allay. Could the voters swallow the Dred Scott diet without resulting nausea? Were they ready to follow him in any course save opposition to the democratic administration at Washington? These were questions to which Douglas sought to find answers; they meant a serious summer's task for the doughty senator and promised to determine his success or failure in the coming contest for his seat in congress. Quietly and unobtrusively he set about feeling the public pulse. The support of central Illinois was especially important; he sought to learn its will. In September he appeared at the state fair at Springfield and jovially greeted all persons whom he met with a shake of the hand or a slap on the shoulder; he joined groups conversing on the topics of the day and soon became the center of the discussion.[7] The evidences of a growing antislavery sentiment in Illinois could not escape so shrewd an observer.

Interest in the situation in "bleeding Kansas" was unusu-

[6] O. C. Dake to Trumbull, September 14, 1857, C. D. Hay to Trumbull, October 4, November 7, 1857, John O. Johnson to Trumbull, October 9, 1857, John G. Nicolay to Trumbull, December 20, 1857, Trumbull manuscripts.
[7] See O. M. Hatch to Trumbull, September 11, 1857, Trumbull manuscripts. The effect was to arouse the ire of zealous republicans, who resented having this "truckling politician turn the fair grounds into a political arena."

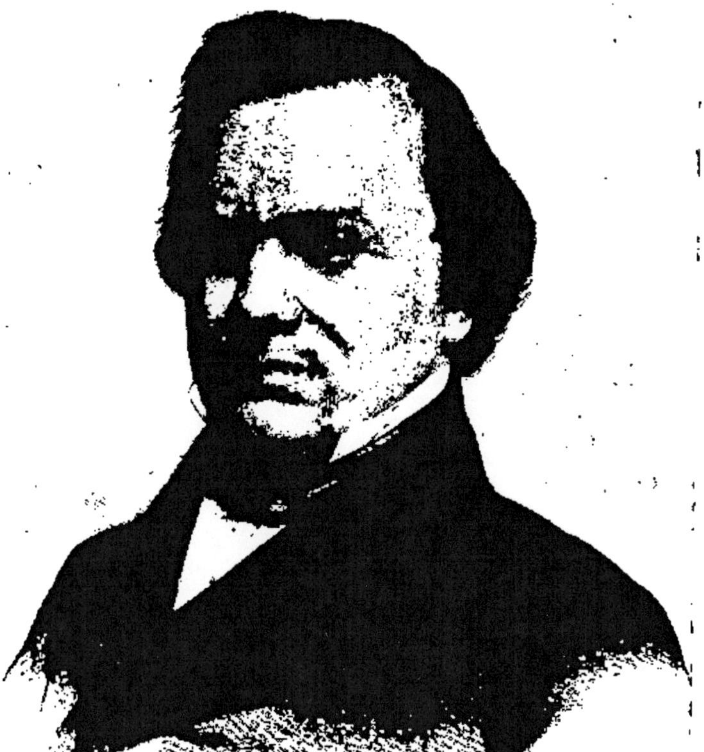

S. A. Douglas

ally keen and popular sympathy was generally with the free state party. Just after the November elections came the news of certain developments under democratic auspices in Kansas that threatened to be a source of embarrassment to Douglas and his followers in Illinois.[8] Under authorization of the territorial government, a constitution had just been drawn up at Lecompton authorizing slavery and providing for its continuance in the future state; the unique feature of the schedule was the arrangement for a popular referendum not on the entire document but merely on the slave state provision.

Douglas, however, either on principle or out of political expediency, soon decided to oppose the Lecompton constitution as a fraud against the doctrine of popular sovereignty. Brilliantly playing up the virtue of consistency, he was heralded by his henchmen and by his party organ as the champion of fair play, if not of freedom in Kansas.[9] At Washington he defied the authority of President Buchanan as a party leader by promptly announcing his anti-Lecompton position. Such a new and unexpected development tried the patience of the leaders in both political parties. What does he mean—is Douglas sincere?—was the question on everyone's lips.

Republican leaders were suspicious of his move. They could but wonder whether it was not an act of self-preservation, a ruse to guarantee the senator's reëlection. The conversion seemed too sudden to be sincere; to them it appeared merely a stand to attract support from the republican party.[10] By introducing an enabling bill into the new session of congress Douglas could assume the leadership in the fight against the proslavery forces on pure unadulterated popular sovereignty ground. But the "little giant" with an air of injured innocence undertook to inform republicans through various channels that they had unjustly accused him of selfish motives in his present position; was he not ready to combat the administra-

[8] *Washington Union*, November 17, 1857.
[9] *Chicago Daily Times*, November 10, 17, 18, 1857.
[10] "Let Republicans not be deceived by the treacherous 'little Joker!'" warned the *Urbana Union*, December 17, 1857. "Douglas has seven reasons for disagreeing with the President—five loaves and two fishes," explained the *Garden State*, clipped in *Urbana Union*, January 14, 1858.

tion to the bitter end in order to carry out the principles of the Nebraska bill?[11]

Republicans who felt no responsibility for the integrity of the organization swallowed this sop and began to shout for Douglas; Saul has at length got among the prophets, they said. Party leaders anxiously contemplated the difficulty of preventing former democrats from responding to Douglas' new appeal. A conference was called and held at Springfield in January, 1858, but no decision was reached except to "*keep cool* for the present."[12] Though it seemed best that the party should keep clear of all alliances, it was obviously good tactics to use Douglas as long as he could be of any service to them; they accordingly encouraged him and the democratic schism, hoping to profit by the "treason" without embracing the "traitor."[13]

It soon became evident that Douglas rather than the republicans had correctly judged the sweeping effect of his anti-Lecompton fight; not a split in the party but a mass transfer in democratic allegiance from the administration to the Douglas camp seemed imminent. The democratic press almost without exception came out for Douglas,[14] while the voters responded with enthusiasm to his bold leadership; only office-holders, office seekers, and ultra conservatives came out in support of the administration of President Buchanan. Southern Illinoisians wavered somewhat in their choice, but democrats of the northern section decided immediately for Douglas.

[11] Lest Douglas by raising the standard of rebellion should be able to rally to his leadership an important following of republicans, Chicago and Springfield editors of republican papers felt that their party ought to steal Douglas' thunder by having their own representatives at Washington introduce the enabling bill. C. H. Ray to Trumbull, November 24, 1857, C. S. Wilson to Trumbull, November 26, 1857; E. L. Baker to Trumbull, December 18, 1857, Trumbull manuscripts; see also Tracy, *Uncollected Letters of Abraham Lincoln*, 82, 83.

[12] *Aurora Beacon*, April 1, 1858; O. M. Hatch to Trumbull, January 14, 1858, Trumbull manuscripts.

[13] They were ready, however, to welcome him as a full-blooded republican if he could quietly content himself with a back seat. This most republicans did not expect, although the *Chicago Democrat*, March 9, 1858, forecast Douglas' conversion to republicanism to the extent of withdrawing from the senatorial race in favor of Lincoln. It was proposed also that Douglas might be run as the republican candidate for congress from the Chicago district. Ebenezer Peck to Trumbull, April 15, 1858, Trumbull manuscripts.

[14] In December 54 papers were anti-Lecompton; the *Joliet Signal*, whose editor was the local postmaster, sustained the Lecompton constitution, the *Menard Index* was willing to acquiesce in it.

A meeting of the Chicago democracy followed by a significant demonstration at Springfield on January 13, 1858, indorsed the anti-Lecompton position taken by Douglas in the senate.[15] Similar meetings and formal conventions were held in nearly all the counties, all of which adopted resolutions disapproving the policy of admitting Kansas under the Lecompton constitution.

The republicans seeking merely to apply the principle "divide and conquer," had aided inadvertently in this transfer of allegiance. They had found it necessary to admit that regardless of Douglas' motives, his present position placed him on the side of right; admiration of the man even prepared the minds of many for support of his political aspirations. The evidence of republican conversions forced the leaders to a reconsideration of their recent policy. They now returned to their original position and directed energy toward creating a real split. "We want to make it wider and deeper—hotter and more impassable," wrote W. H. Herndon. "Political hatred—deep seated opposition is what is so much desired."[16]

This policy required the discovery of a Buchanan or national democratic faction and its development into an effective organization. A nucleus for it could be found in the appointees of President Buchanan, all of whom had been active democratic politicians. It was obvious that the rebel Douglas would no longer be the dispenser of the administration patronage in the state; rumors began to circulate, moreover, that the political guillotine would shortly be set to work in earnest to lop off the heads of anti-Lecompton postmasters. Postmaster Price of Chicago was the first victim; others in fear and trembling awaited their turn. Republican leaders and journals labored industriously to bring democratic officeholders to a realization of the danger and office seekers to a sense of the rewards available for loyal administration men.[17]

Since the regular democratic journals were engaged in

[15] *Illinois State Register*, January 14, 1858; *Ottawa Free Trader*, January 2, 1858.
[16] Herndon to Trumbull, February 19, 1858, Trumbull manuscripts.
[17] *Rock River Democrat*, February 16, 1858; *Rockford Republican*, February 25, 1858; *Chicago Democrat*, March 15, 1858; *Chicago Daily Democratic Press*, February 19, 1858.

Douglas propaganda, the building up of an administration democratic press was essential to aggressive organization work. Federal officeholders were recruited as publishers and editors; during the spring the Chicago *National Union,* later replaced by the *Chicago Herald,* the *Illinois State Democrat* at Springfield, and several other Buchanan organs, entered the field. Before long a real administration party arose to dispute Douglas' triumph.[18]

The leading republican journals, finding that a portion of their own party press had been led to espouse the cause of Douglas, next labored to show that there was no more reason for supporting Douglas than for supporting the administration. The republican party has its distinct principles, they argued; to these principles Douglas is as much opposed as is President Buchanan; the only point of policy held in common by Douglas' friends and the republicans is opposition to the attempted fraud in Kansas. Even on that point Douglas, in contrast to republican adherence to principle, is influenced by selfish motives; his aim is to gratify his pique against Buchanan and to forward his own ambitions.[19]

To the dismay and embarrassment of republican leaders in Illinois the eastern spokesmen of the party seemed to have been taken in by Douglas' strategy. At the very opening of congress eastern republican members had entered into conference with Senator Douglas; he was given to understand that they would back him not only in his fight with Buchanan but even in his campaign for reëlection. Next, Horace Greeley, the editor of the *New York Tribune,* went to Washington to consult with Douglas. Shortly afterwards the *Tribune,* filled with eulogies of the "little giant," intimated that republican support of his senatorial candidacy was merely the preliminary step to Douglas' gradual identification with the republican party. Other eastern republican journals took up the idea, including even the *National Era,* the old free soil organ at

---

[18] *Chicago Democrat,* March 6, 1858; *Chicago Daily Democratic Press,* February 9, 11, 13, 1858; E. L. Baker to Trumbull, May 1, 1858, Trumbull manuscripts.
[19] *Urbana Union,* February 25, March 25, 1858; *Chicago Democrat,* April 15, 1858; *Rockford Republican,* April 1, 1858; *Rock River Democrat,* January 5, 1858.

Washington. In view of the influence wielded by these papers in the state of Illinois, their position caused republican politicians grave concern.[20]

Elihu B. Washburne, congressman from the Galena district, was sent to Springfield as a messenger from Greeley to propose that Lincoln be dropped in Douglas' favor.[21] Then came from Washington a proposition which was confidentially placed before leading republicans by Sheahan of the *Chicago Daily Times*, that in order to defeat the Lecompton legislative candidates in the doubtful districts, Douglas and the republicans should coöperate to elect the anti-Lecompton democratic congressmen, in return for which Douglas would retire in favor of the republican candidate for senator. Although this proposition was seriously considered by party leaders in Chicago and Springfield, it was finally agreed to call a state convention to reject the proposed bargain and to fight out those matters squarely with Douglas.[22]

The Douglas forces had been successful in setting the early date of April 21 for the democratic state convention at Springfield; though both factions busied themselves with the selection of delegates of the right stripe, everywhere the Douglas group succeeded in controlling the regular party organizations. In some places the only Buchanan democrat was the local postmaster, though in other regions, especially in Egypt, the "simon pure" Buchanan democrats did show some strength and activity. Challenging the regularity of the Douglas men, they undertook to read them out of the party and prepared to get up conventions of their own. An organization was established in Chicago, where the Irish led by Owen McCarthy and Philip Conley, inclined to stand by the administration; and meetings were held at Aurora, Springfield, and at various other places.[23]

[20] *Chicago Tribune* clipped in *Ottawa Weekly Republican,* April 24, 1858. Thurlow Weed and William H. Seward were apparently party to these negotiations, while Henry Wilson and N. P. Banks of Massachusetts approved the indorsement of Douglas. N. B. Judd to Trumbull, March 7, 1858, C. H. Ray to Trumbull, March 9, 1858, John O. Johnson to Trumbull, May 11, 1858, Trumbull manuscripts; Tracy, *Uncollected Letters of Abraham Lincoln,* 83-84.
[21] McLean County Historical Society, *Transactions,* 3: 123.
[22] J. K. Dubois to Trumbull, March 22, April 8, 1858, A. Jonas to Trumbull, April 11, 1858, Herndon to Trumbull, April 12, 1858, Trumbull manuscripts.
[23] *Chicago Democrat,* March 6, 1858; *Chicago Daily Democratic Press,* March 11, 29, 30, 1858.

The Douglasites appeared at Springfield in full strength. An aggressive anti-Lecompton platform was adopted, unanimously approving the principle of the Cincinnati convention of 1856 as applied by Senator Douglas; and his recent course was given a hearty indorsement. The convention decided, however, not to antagonize the Buchanan men by taking an emphatic stand against the administration. Even a resolution mildly censuring Buchanan for turning Douglas men out of office for opinion's sake was voted down. Besides the all-important nomination for senator, the convention named William B. Fondey as candidate for state treasurer and ex-Governor Augustus C. French as candidate for superintendent of public instruction.[24]

The national democrats had failed in their original scheme to send duplicate delegations to the convention to obstruct the work of the Douglasites. A squad of forty or fifty delegates was recruited, representing the formal organizations of five counties and informal representatives of twenty-three others; they were led by Isaac Cook, the postmaster of Chicago, who appealed to some with threats of removal from office and to others with promises of places. Since a preliminary caucus showed that they were hopelessly outnumbered, they presented no credentials to the convention, but assembled in a meeting of their own. A separate party organization was effected; after passing resolutions strongly indorsing the administration, they agreed to postpone the nomination of candidates until the meeting of a state convention on the eighth of June. This nominating convention of about two hundred delegates from thirty or more counties discussed Sidney M. Breese as a candidate for the senatorship, but took no formal action; they did put up John Dougherty for treasurer and the "old ranger," John Reynolds, for school superintendent.[25] Strangely enough on the point of principle both of these candidates had been anti-Nebraska men only four years before.

The indorsement of the traditional democratic faith by the Douglas convention made the duty of the republicans of

[24] *Illinois State Register*, April 22, 1858; *Illinois State Journal*, April 28, 1858.
[25] *Illinois State Register*, June 10, 1858; *Illinois State Journal*, June 9, 16, 1858.

Illinois exceedingly plain. On the night of the convention about thirty prominent republicans held a caucus which expressed a firm conviction that they were relieved of every obligation to Douglas and ought to have nothing to do with him. In an atmosphere of harmony and brotherly love the mutual suspicion of ex-whigs and of ex-democrats was allayed, while both elements acknowledged the moral obligation to support Lincoln in return for his withdrawal in 1855 in favor of Trumbull.[26]

The call for a republican state convention which followed the next day met an immediate and enthusiastic response. County conventions, after denouncing the treatment applied to Kansas often expressed a sense of gratitude to Douglas as well as to the republican congressman for their opposition to the Lecompton proposition; this was usually followed, however, by an announcement that Abraham Lincoln was the party's choice for United States senator. Ninety-five county meetings had given such an indorsement to Lincoln.[27] On June 16 there gathered at Springfield one of the largest delegate conventions ever witnessed in the state: one thousand five hundred delegates were said to be on the ground, all full of "electric fire." They adopted a platform of principles breathing a broad, liberal nationalism; it was based on the doctrine that free labor is the only true support of republican institutions. Exception was taken to the policies of the administration and to the Dred Scott decision.[28] A state ticket with James Miller for treasurer and Newton Bateman for superintendent of public instruction was selected. A resolution indorsing Abraham Lincoln as the first and only choice of the republicans of Illinois for the United States senate was greeted with shouts of applause and unanimously adopted.

Lincoln's nomination was so much a matter of course that he was prepared for the invitation which followed to address

[26] George T. Brown to Trumbull, April 25, 1858, E. L. Baker to Trumbull, May 1, 1858, Herndon to Trumbull, April 24, 1858, Trumbull manuscripts.
[27] *Rockford Republican,* June 17, 1858.
[28] Herndon to Trumbull, June 24, 1858, Trumbull manuscripts; Tracy, *Uncollected Letters of Abraham Lincoln,* 87-88. Support was promised to homestead legislation, to river and harbor improvement, and to a Pacific railroad by a central route. *Illinois State Journal,* June 23, 1858; *Alton Courier,* June 18, 1858.

the convention in an adjourned session in the evening. In a carefully prepared speech delivered without manuscript or notes, he laid before the assembled delegates a prophecy of grave moral and political import—a forecast of the logical result toward which events were hurrying the nation. "'A house divided against itself cannot stand.' I believe that this government cannot endure permanently half slave and half free. I do not expect the Union to be dissolved—I do not expect the house to fall—but I do expect it will cease to be divided." [29]

Was that undivided house to be all slave? The recent action of the supreme court in the case of Dred Scott was but one fragment of a mountain of evidence which revealed a design to make slavery national. "Put this and that together," he reasoned, "and we have another nice little niche, which we may ere long see filled with another Supreme Court decision, declaring that the Constitution of the United States does not permit a *State* to exclude slavery from its limits. . . . . We shall lie down pleasantly dreaming that the people of Missouri are on the verge of making their State free, and we shall awake to the reality instead, that the Supreme Court has made Illinois a slave state." In the face of this danger many had turned expectantly to the leadership of Douglas; but could he lead a real opposition to the advance of slavery, he who did not care "whether slavery was voted down or voted up?" That danger must be met by those who in their hearts did care for the result.

The senatorial canvass offered the republican party of Illinois an opportunity in the very crisis of its existence to establish itself politically in the state. Its weakness in 1856 had been concealed by the personal popularity of its gubernatorial candidate. Now with the discords of the opposition and with the feverish excitement that prevailed, it was hoped that Lincoln could snatch a real victory and terminate democratic control. The contest also promised to serve as a test of what the future had in store for the clever Springfield lawyer-politician whom political fortune had treated for twenty years with

---

[29] Nicolay and Hay, *Abraham Lincoln*, 1:240 ff.; *Lincoln-Douglas Debates*, 1; Sturtevant, *Autobiography*, 291.

LINCOLN-DOUGLAS DEBATES 165

all the fickleness of a courtesan. The senatorship was the prize which had dropped from his grasp in 1855 and which now promised to make or ruin his political career. Douglas' followers accepted Lincoln's nomination as a challenge which made the issue of the campaign the question of Lincoln's or Douglas' election. The Buchanan movement they sought to ignore as of little importance though policy suggested that the administration democrats be pacified, since party differences over Kansas were held to be no longer important.[30] The "national" democratic leaders, however, spurned all advances. They reminded each other of the epithets applied to them; they had been branded as hired minions, corruptionists, as "Buchaneers," the "Buzzardi and Lazzaroni;" Douglas himself had nicknamed them "Danites," whereas "stink fingers" was the coarse epithet applied to them by some Douglasites. All these terms rankled in their breasts. "We will not be insulted by them one minute and then embrace them the next;" said their organs, "they want to come into the Democratic party to enjoy those spoils they have been so much disgusted at lately. . . . *The arrant political traitors who sought to betray the Democracy must either go over to the Republicans, organize their new party, or retire to private life.*"[31] Let the bolters drop Douglas, and they would unite on any reliable democrat. Inasmuch as the Douglasites exhibited no willingness to accept this test, the "Buchaneers" brought out their own candidate for the United States senate; Judge Sidney Breese was carefully groomed by his followers in southern Illinois who claimed that Egypt was entitled to the next United States senator. Though Douglasites sought to induce Breese to leave the field, rumors of his withdrawal were authoritatively dispelled by him in a carefully prepared announcement.[32] Breese's aspirations were encouraged by the national

[30] The English bill had been passed allowing that territory a vote on the Lecompton constitution in full, with the offer of 500,000 acres of land in the event of favorable action. Douglas and the Illinois house delegation had voted with the republicans against the English bill as failing to provide open, free, and fair submission, but upon its passage the Douglasites acquiesced in the measure. Most Illinois democrats had preceded them in hurrying this issue.

[31] *Chicago National Union* clipped in *Illinois State Journal*, May 19, 1858.
[32] Belleville *Star of Egypt* clipped in *ibid.*, July 21, 1858; Breese to Reverend W. F. Boyakin, September 7, 1858, *Belleville Advocate*, September 15, 1858.

administration at Washington, which continued to use its control over the public patronage in Illinois to maintain the Buchanan organization.

Republicans for a time concentrated their efforts on maintaining the democratic split. The puny "national" organization still required attention; it was considered good policy to nurse the infant until it became strong enough to stand up and fight not only the Douglasites but even the republicans, since the latter could in any event easily knock it down. Separate democratic tickets would mean easy republican victory; the hopes of the Lincolnites fed upon the bitterness toward Douglas of prominent Buchanan men. Dr. Charles Leib of Chicago and even Colonel Dougherty lent aid and comfort in this direction by their assurances to both Senator Trumbull and Lincoln that the national democracy would without fail remain in the field with separate candidates in every county and congressional district.[33]

At the same time certain radical "black republicans" found indorsement of Douglas to be a valuable expedient to prevent the Buchanan men from harmonizing with the Douglas wing. M. W. Delahay, an Alton radical who bitterly hated Douglas, went on the stump for the "little giant" with the understanding of Lincoln and the republicans; he remained in the field until the Buchanan convention nominated its state ticket; then, according to arrangement, he came out for Lincoln.[34]

In playing policy to both democratic wings the republicans incurred the danger of overshooting the mark. Their interest in the "Buchaneers" was so marked as to make it necessary to deny charges of an alliance between the two groups, while their Douglas-espousing tactics actually encouraged lukewarm party men of democratic antecedents to break for Douglas. Old-line whigs, whose political connections for the past four years had been very uncertain, were already prone to choose moderate antislavery ground over "negro-equality republicanism," and welcomed such an opening, especially in view of recommendations in favor of Douglas coming from outside

---

[33] Joseph Medill to Trumbull, April 22, 1858, Herndon to Trumbull, July 8, 1858, Charles Leib to Trumbull, July 20, 1858, Trumbull manuscripts.
[34] M. W. Delahay to Trumbull, November 28, 1857, May 22, 1858, *ibid.*

republicans.³⁵ These developments forced republican leaders to change their tactics; they decided to concentrate their opposition on "the little dodger" as the real enemy to be met squarely and in the open. This was exactly to Douglas' liking; for the three-cornered fight practically ended with Douglas' return to Illinois to open his active canvass.

On learning of Lincoln's nomination, Douglas acknowledged the worth of his opponent by declaring: "I shall have my hands full. He is the strong man of his party—full of wit, facts, dates, and the best stump-speaker, with his droll ways and dry jokes, in the West. He is as honest as he is shrewd; and if I beat him, my victory will be hardly won."³⁶ With this compliment, Douglas buckled on his armor for mortal combat in the political arena. On July 9, just after the adjournment of congress, he arrived in Chicago. Enthusiastic supporters had met him in Michigan City to conduct him by special train to the splendid celebration of his homecoming. Chicago was in gala attire; cannon boomed, banners waved, and fireworks flashed, until the crowd—some said forty or fifty thousand people—was delivered over to the eloquence of the fiery senator, speaking from the balcony of the Tremont House.³⁷

Realizing that his rival, Lincoln, was an attentive listener within the hotel, the senator threw all his energies into his oratory. He pointed to the increased favor of his popular sovereignty principle, complimented the support that republican members of congress had yielded to that doctrine in the recent anti-Lecompton fight, and concluded with the assertion that he was the only rightful champion of the principle of local self-government as applied to slavery. Taking up Lincoln's house-divided speech he sought to make his rival the spokesman of a sectional abolition republicanism. He challenged Lincoln's plan to array section against section, to incite a war of extermination; he himself was not anxious for uniformity

[35] Tracy, *Uncollected Letters of Abraham Lincoln*, 87; *Chicago Democrat*, March 11, 1858; *Illinois State Register*, April 24, 1858; N. B. Judd to Trumbull, July 16, 1858, Trumbull manuscripts.
[36] Forney, *Anecdotes of Public Men*, 2: 179.
[37] Opposition journals claimed that the money for the expenses—$1,281— had been advanced to Douglas himself. *Chicago Press and Tribune*, July 10, 1858.

in local institutions—differences in soil, in products, and in interests required different domestic regulations in each locality. As to the rights of the Negro, in a government "made by the white man, for the benefit of the white man, to be administered by white men," anyone of inferior race should be allowed only such rights, privileges, and immunities as each state should judge consistent with the safety of society.

Lincoln replied from the same rostrum on the next evening, after a series of demonstrations in imitation of the Douglas celebration. He challenged Douglas' attempt to transfigure himself with the mantle of popular sovereignty by showing that any distinctive popular sovereignty doctrine had fallen before the assaults of the supreme court and that no one had ever disputed the right of the people to frame a constitution. Placed upon the defensive by Douglas' assaults of the previous evening, he undertook to explain his house-divided proposition as an experiment in the realm of prophecy and not as a program for practical political endeavor. "I did not even say that I desired that slavery should be put in course of ultimate extinction. I do say so now, however."[38]

After a week's rest Douglas started for the capital by way of Bloomington. There on July 16 he again attacked Lincoln's arguments to show that they were not worthy of the support of moderate men. Whigs and Americans, even honorable republicans, had found the true issue in the anti-Lecompton fight, while republican politicians, in order to defeat him, had formed an alliance with Lecompton men and betrayed the cause. Lincoln was present in the audience and when Douglas had concluded loud calls were made for a reply from him. Lincoln was induced to come upon the stand, from which he explained, after three rousing cheers, that as the meeting had been called by the friends of Douglas it would be improper for him to address it. He found his opportunity on the next day at Springfield when he replied to Douglas in what proved to be the most "taking" speech of the first part of his campaign.[39]

In all these preliminaries Lincoln was campaigning at a

[38] *Writings of Lincoln*, 3:49; *Lincoln-Douglas Debates*, 18; Tracy, *Uncollected Letters of Abraham Lincoln*, 86-87.
[39] *Ibid.*, 92-93; *Writings of Lincoln*, 3:67 ff.

distinct disadvantage. The democratic machinery gave Douglas' movements the atmosphere on a triumphal march: a train dedicated to the "champion of popular sovereignty" moved into a station heralding his arrival with the booming of a twelve-pounder mounted on a platform car, then came the flourish of trumpets, the roar of salutes, the music of bands, the parade formed with waving banners, until the festive crowd, forgetting the heat and dust of prairie midsummer, moved to the speech-making. This was good democratic enthusiasm. The republicans, with their more limited campaign funds and with too much of the lethargic whig spirit in their ranks, at best could only try their hand at imitation. Lincoln, trailing into town on the heels of Douglas, was lost in the immense audience that assembled to hear the "little giant" — an audience composed not only of loyal democrats but also of republicans, whigs, and know nothings drawn by the fame of the anti-Lecompton hero. Douglas usually succeeded in placing his rival on the defensive; seldom did he leave an opening which made possible an effective comeback. Lincoln's only chance came when, after the large holiday crowd had dispersed, the faithful of the faith rallied a handful of the populace to attend the lanky Springfield lawyer.

The republicans, perceiving their disadvantage, were shrewd enough to propose a joint canvass in true western style. The challenge was promptly sent;[40] Douglas, who for some time feared that the administration candidate might ask admittance in order to wage common cause against his seat in the senate, reluctantly indicated a willingness to meet his opponent in each of the remaining congressional districts. He reserved the right to dictate the details: they were to meet at the towns of Ottawa, Freeport, Jonesboro, Charleston, Galesburg, Quincy, and Alton; the opening speeches were to last one hour, the replies, one and a half, with a half hour rebuttal by the first speaker; Douglas was to have four openings and closes to Lincoln's three.

Meantime Douglas continued to meet his scheduled appointments and Lincoln followed in his wake. Recognizing that it was in the doubtful central counties that the battle had

[40] *Lincoln-Douglas Debates*, 59; *Illinois State Journal*, August 4, 1858.

to be won or lost, the speech-making tours carried them to almost every town in that region. Douglas, with Lincoln dogging him persistently, addressed his constituents in 57 counties, making 59 set speeches of from two to three hours in length, 17 responses of from 25 to 45 minutes to serenaders, and 37 replies of about equal length to addresses of welcome. Of these speeches all but two were made in the open air, and seven were made or continued during heavy rains. In this tour Douglas crossed, from end to end, every railroad line in the state, excepting three, besides making long journeys by means of horse conveyances and steamboats. His road travels amounted to more than 5,227 miles; by boat he made almost the entire western side of the state and all that portion of the Illinois river which was navigable by steamboats.[41]

The first joint debate took place at Ottawa on August 21. As was to be expected, the much heralded event attracted a large holiday crowd, the admirers of both contestants and the curious who were out for the excitement of the occasion. There was twice the noise and enthusiasm of previous meetings and after stirring preliminaries the debate began. This first encounter merely prepared the way for the contests that were to follow.

One feature of the debate at Ottawa was significant; Douglas in catechizing Lincoln respecting certain resolutions which he felt showed the dangerously radical character of the republican party, furnished a precedent that gave Lincoln his opportunity. At the second debate at Freeport he in turn put a set of four questions to Douglas; in the second he asked: "Can the people of a United States Territory, in any lawful way, against the wish of any citizen of the United States, exclude slavery from its limits, prior to the formation of a State Constitution?"[42] In this question, which demanded an affirmation or negative answer, Lincoln flashed before Douglas a two-edged sword; let Douglas seize it from either side to the destruction of his political ambidexterity! For him to deny the right would but confirm Lincoln's contention that popular sovereignty was as thin as broth made by boiling the

---

[41] *New York Times* clipped in *Illinois State Register*, November 23, 1858.
[42] *Lincoln-Douglas Debates*, 90.

shadow of a dove that had starved to death; while to affirm the right would alienate proslavery democrats in the south and in Illinois, who clung to the doctrine of the Dred Scott decision. From previous statements made by Douglas, there could be little doubt that, with certain reservations to evade the literal prohibition of the Dred Scott decision, his answer would be in the affirmative; he had already confronted and evaded the issue in his Springfield speech of June 12, 1857, and in his Bloomington speech of July 16, 1858, in both of which he had carefully elaborated the doctrine of local police regulations and of unfriendly legislation. Furthermore, since his immediate game was reëlection to the senate, he had to retain the support of Illinois democrats who had been won by his demand for a virile popular sovereignty. Obvious as should have been Douglas' attitude, Lincoln wanted the satisfaction of compelling him to promulgate it in as conspicuous a fashion as possible; he wanted once and for all to cut him off from the association and support of the proslavery democrats.

In his eagerness to lay the trap Lincoln seems to have overlooked the fact that at Freeport the audience was one of strong antislavery convictions; the more conservative voters were likely to be attracted by Douglas' explanation as to how slavery might be excluded. Since probably none of the other appointed places for joint debate would have been less favorable, it would, perhaps, have been the part of wisdom to select an audience more representative of the prejudices of old-line whig and national democrats, likely to be alienated by rather than attracted to Douglas' answer. But the Freeport crowd— 15,000 persons, report said—did furnish an opportunity to make Douglas expose his views to the light of pitiless publicity in a way that would make further evasion impossible.[43]

Douglas, without fear or hesitation, made a reply in terms of his doctrine of "unfriendly legislation" which became known immediately as the Freeport doctrine: "I answer emphatically, as Mr. Lincoln has heard me answer a hundred times from every stump in Illinois, that in my opinion the people of a Territory can, by lawful means, exclude slavery

[43] *Chicago Press and Tribune* clipped in *Illinois State Journal*, September 8, 1858.

from their limits prior to the formation of a State Constitution. . . . . The people have the lawful means to introduce it or exclude it as they please, for the reason that slavery cannot exist a day or hour anywhere, unless it is supported by local police regulations. These police regulations can only be established by the local legislature, and if the people are opposed to slavery they will elect representatives to that body who will by unfriendly legislation effectually prevent the introduction of it into their midst. If, on the contrary, they are for it, their legislation will favor its extension. Hence, no matter what the decision of the Supreme Court may be on that abstract question, still the right of the people to make a slave Territory or a free Territory is perfect and complete under the Nebraska bill. I hope Mr. Lincoln deems my answer satisfactory on that point." [44]

No opportunity remained in that debate for Lincoln to present his refutation of this doctrine. His silence was interpreted even by his friends as acknowledgment of his defeat before the logic of his rival.[45] At later meetings, however, he undertook to expose the fallacy of Douglas' reply: slavery did have the vigor to exist, had existed in the past without such local protective legislation as Douglas held to be necessary; was now, moreover, resistance to constitutional rights by unfriendly legislation a monstrous, anarchistic doctrine — as for himself he was for revising the decision; he could not believe there existed a constitutional right to hold slaves in a territory of the United States.

Over the map of Illinois, the struggle was waged. From the critical battle ground in the central counties they worked by slow stages down into Egypt as far as Jonesboro in Union county, where they faced the smallest audience of the joint debates. Then back they marched to Charleston in eastern Illinois; soon they were in the New England atmosphere of Knox county, which assembled in force at Galesburg. For pure oratory and logical synthesis the independent speeches often surpassed the joint debates: no debate was in itself a

[44] *Lincoln-Douglas Debates*, 95.
[45] Contrary to popular opinion neither Lincoln nor his friends and supporters at this time dreamed that the future had in store for him a presidential career.

unit, there were charges and countercharges, sturdy defense was followed by bitter attack, the opening of one debate was the rebuttal of the concluding speech of the preceding. With the closing words at the Alton meeting, October 15, some serious stock-taking could be attempted, but scarcely before that time. Then it seemed that there was neither victor nor vanquished; the two giants appeared only the stronger for the combat that had closed.

Lincoln had a valuable ally in the person of Senator Trumbull, whose analysis of Douglas' motives in opposing the Lecompton constitution was one of the most important features of the campaign. In speeches at Chicago, at Alton, at Jacksonville, and at other points in Illinois he charged Douglas with having changed from ground which would have required him to support the Lecompton document to a position of opposition out of purely selfish political considerations. In June, 1856, Douglas, as chairman of the senate committee on territories, had, after consultation with Senator Toombs, struck out from Toombs' bill for the future admission of Kansas a clause providing for the submission of the constitution to the people for their ratification or rejection, and had substituted certain other clauses to prevent a popular vote.[46] Corroborative evidence that such was formerly the devotion of Stephen A. Douglas to popular sovereignty was found in his speech at Springfield in June, 1857, and in the declaration of Douglas' personal organ, the *Chicago Times*, that there would be about as much propriety in submitting the Lecompton constitution to a vote of the inhabitants of the Fiji Islands as to the "free-state men" of Kansas. Eventually these facts were acknowledged by democratic organs but they were never satisfactorily explained by Douglas.[47]

The republican journals took up Trumbull's charges and pressed his point. Evidence was presented that suggested an original sympathy on Douglas' part with the Lecompton method of ratification. It was generally understood at Springfield and at other points that John Calhoun, the chairman of the

---

[46] *Congressional Globe*, 35 congress, 1 session, 127, appendix, 799.
[47] *Chicago Times* clipped in *Illinois State Journal*, July 29, 1857; *Chicago Daily Times*, August 13, 1858.

Lecompton convention, had written to Douglas in the month of September, 1857, asking the advice of his former chief as to the course to be pursued in the submission of the constitution. Representative Smith of Virginia made this charge on the floor of congress and declared that there was no evidence that Douglas had discouraged the Lecompton scheme.[48]

Why then had Douglas shifted to his aggressive anti-Lecompton ground? Republicans were prone to believe that he had planned the Kansas "fraud" so as to give himself an opportunity to win applause by opposing the abortion. They could make out a plausible case to show that the Buchanan administration had been seeking to destroy the "little giant," that his friends had been neglected in appointments, and the claims of Illinois overlooked; therefore, not intending to be crushed by the administration, Douglas was seeking a basis for new political popularity, that he might maintain his position and groom himself for the presidency.[49] Democratic critics, speaking with an air of authority of inside information, had added their testimony to confirm this explanation. Representative Smith of Virginia and Representative Burnett of Kentucky had told of a conference of the Illinois democratic delegation at the opening of the session to mark out a course to pursue in order to secure the reëlection of Douglas to the senate; in the conference it was determined that opposition to the Lecompton constitution was the only means by which Douglas could sustain himself at home.[50] Here, then, announced Trumbull, was the record of the man who stood as the champion of the fundamental principles of free government, of bona fide popular sovereignty; these were the motives

[48] *Illinois State Journal*, May 19, 1858. Two years later came unquestioned testimony from members of the convention that the form of submission determined upon was believed by them to have been suggested by Douglas and was known as the "Douglas plan;" they testified that Calhoun had repeatedly referred to a letter in his possession written by Douglas, which authorized a statement of his approval and of his willingness to advocate its passage through congress. Only one member, however, testified to having seen the letter; he was the proposed candidate for lieutenant governor under the new constitution. *New Orleans Delta*, October 16, 1860, clipped in *Canton Weekly Register*, October 26, 1860; *Aurora Beacon*, October 18, 1860.

[49] M. W. Delahay to Trumbull, November 28, 1857, Trumbull manuscripts; *Chicago Journal* clipped in *Illinois State Journal*, October 14, 1857.

[50] *Congressional Globe*, 35 congress, 1 session, 1392; *Illinois State Journal*, April 7, September 1, 1858.

of the hero who was braving unpopularity to declare the Lecompton mode of submission a mockery and an insult, who had recorded his preferences for private life in order to preserve his own self-respect and manhood to abject and servile submission to executive will.

While the romance of the campaign centered about the figures of Lincoln and Douglas, much of the real work had to be done by the journalists on both sides. Very inadequate reports of the debates and speeches were printed, but the more effective points made on the platform were sorted out and driven home to the rank and file through the medium of the editorial page. First, an analysis was made of the field of activity. Shrewd politicians on both sides recognized that the independent vote, of great strength in the central counties, where a slight shift would throw the majority to one side or the other, was certain to determine the outcome of the election. A circle of counties reaching not more than eighty miles from the capital—including especially Sangamon, Morgan, Mason, Logan, and Madison—constituted the real battleground; here lived many old-line whigs—timid, shrinking, but able men, from Kentucky, Tennessee, Virginia, and from other southern states.

Democratic editors expressed their confidence that old-line whigs were generally union men and opposed to sectional strife and the doctrine of Negro equality;[51] they could have but little sympathy with "nigger-stealers," "abolitionists," and "incendiaries." Whigs were assured that the republican machinery was under abolition control. Did not the nomination of Owen Lovejoy, the abolitionist, for congress over Judge Norton, Churchill Coffing, and T. L. Dickey prove it? Did not the revolt headed by Coffing and Dickey against the now abolitionized republican party prove it? Nine-tenths of the old-line whigs were for Douglas and democracy: there were such men as Cyrus Edwards of Madison who had repeatedly been the whig candidate for governor and United States senator; Edwin

---

[51] They tried to leave no doubt that the latter was a cardinal doctrine of the republican party. "Keep it before the people of Illinois," they shouted, "that the Abolition-Republican party headed by Abraham Lincoln, are in favor of negro equality, and claim that the Declaration of Independence included the negroes as well as the whites." *Illinois State Register*, October 13, 1858.

B. Webb, the last whig candidate for governor; Buckner S. Morris, the last American candidate for governor; John T. Stuart, once a whig representative in congress; and James W. Singleton, the confidential friend of Clay.[52] In Douglas they would find the true successor of Henry Clay; Lincoln was of the same stripe as William Lloyd Garrison, and believed in rooting out slavery from the union by fire and sword.

For their part, republicans pointed out that all Lincoln's past political connections had been with whigs and that he had been an ardent friend and supporter of Henry Clay; in 1844 he had stumped the state for Clay and traveled some four hundred miles on a speech-making tour in Indiana while Douglas was vociferating all over Illinois that Henry Clay had sold his country to Great Britain, that he was a drunkard, a liar, a gambler, and a grossly and notoriously licentious person. Lincoln had clung to that connection even after the anti-Nebraska revolt, down to the Bloomington convention itself. Identified all his life long with the old whig party, he now stood on true Henry Clay ground. He was not an impracticable abolitionist as misrepresented by Douglas; he conceded the right of each state to regulate slavery itself and had never accepted the Negro equality doctrine. Old whig leaders recognized the logic of an affiliation with Lincoln and the republican party — Joseph Gillespie, of Madison, had announced that the position of the republican party harmonized with that of old line whigs better than that of Douglas and the democracy; and W. W. Danenhower had written a strong letter urging Americans and whigs to vote against Douglas.[53]

Special appeals were made also to the remnants of the American party, for they together with the whigs had in 1856 cast a vote of over 35,000 for Fillmore; the support of this body of voters was absolutely necessary to develop a winning side. Douglas interlarded his speeches with praise of that

---

[52] *Our Constitution*, October 23, 1858; *Joliet Signal*, October 20, 1850; *Ottawa Free Trader*, August 21, 1858. Senator J. J. Crittenden of Kentucky, the friend and associate of Clay, having coöperated with Douglas in the anti-Lecompton fight, was named as a supporter of Douglas' candidacy. T. Lyle Dickey to Crittenden, July 19, 1858, Herndon to Crittenden, November 1, 1858, Crittenden manuscripts.
[53] Joseph Gillespie to Sidney Todd, August 20, 1858; *Belleville Advocate*, September 22, 1858; *Rockford Register*, October 30, 1858.

"noble band of Americans in the late Congress that opposed Lecompton;" republicans replied by reminding Americans that Douglas had been an early and persistent foe of know nothingism. The tendency of these conservative voters was to hold aloof from republican radicalism, and the democrats pressed their advantage by placing former know nothings on their legislative tickets. The republicans in alarm also threw out political sops to attract American support, while they pointed to the Roman Catholic allies of Douglas as evidence of the old union between popery and the slavery propaganda.

Meantime the foreign born voters were prepared for their part in the campaign. Most protestant Germans had by this time become thoroughly attached to the republican cause. They were still subject to appeals from the party of their former allegiance, but the eloquence of leaders like Koerner, Hecker, and Hoffman kept them from wavering. Carl Shurz, moreover, came to Illinois to take the stump and aroused considerable enthusiasm. Like most of their countrymen the French voters of Chicago, numbering about 400, were largely republicans; in Kankakee where they held the balance of power, their organ, the *Journal de L'Illinois*, insured for Lincoln the votes of the French population. The Scandinavians of Chicago were generally Lincoln supporters. Against all these, the democrats balanced the Irish vote which was a power in Chicago and in other centers.

The closeness of the fight in the central counties furnished a serious temptation to party politicians. In the closing months of the campaign, both republican and administration democratic journals detailed charges that the Douglas organization had made preparations to colonize doubtful counties with floating voters. Evidence was submitted that Irish laborers drawn from Chicago, northern Illinois, Wisconsin, Indiana, and St. Louis were being shipped by the railroads, ostensibly as railroad hands, to such points as Mattoon, Champaign, Peoria, Carlinville, Bloomington, and Virginia.[54] Governor Matteson, who was interested in the St. Louis and Alton railroad, was said to be party to these colonization schemes. Douglas was baldly characterized as the agent and tool of the Illinois Cen-

[54] Tracy, *Uncollected Letters of Abraham Lincoln*, 93-94.

tral, that giant monopoly whose interests would one day be found to be diametrically opposed to the best interests of the people of Illinois. It was extensively rumored that the agents of Douglas had appealed to the Tammany Society of New York for material aid and that this organization had set aside $50,000 for the Douglas campaign.[55] "Look out for fraudulent votes" was the warning cry sounded by republicans everywhere.

Douglas' chief problem, growing out of the split of the democracy, was to maintain control of Egypt, where there were numerous signs of administration strength. An eleventh hour attempt to play the rôle of peacemaker and to close the schism was undertaken by Alexander H. Stephens, the Georgia congressman, friend of Buchanan and of Douglas. When his mission failed, democratic leaders from the southern border states began to pour into Illinois; ex-Senator Jones of Tennessee, an ex-whig, was one of a large number of slave state democrats who mounted the hustings in Illinois in behalf of Douglas; by the first of November it was stated that "no less than 41 slave holders" were campaigning for the "little giant."[56]

Lincoln was pictured by his opponents as a politician having little claim to the support of the people of Illinois. In twenty years of unlimited opportunities for public service he had never initiated or seriously influenced the enactment of any measure which had contributed in any substantial fashion to the welfare of the state, or even of the nation. His most conspicuous stand in congress was declared to have been his emphatic opposition to the Mexican War; he was falsely charged with having even voted against sending supplies to the American army in Mexico.

Election day arrived November 2, cold, wet, and raw. The fair weather brigade, preferring the comforts of the fireside to a walk or ride of a mile or more in the rain, was with difficulty induced to present itself at the polls in force. This was especially disastrous to the republican party which seemed to

[55] *Rockford Republican*, September 16, 1858; *Chicago Press and Tribune*, September 10, 1858; *New York Herald*, September 15, 1858.
[56] *Chicago Democrat*, November 1, 1858.

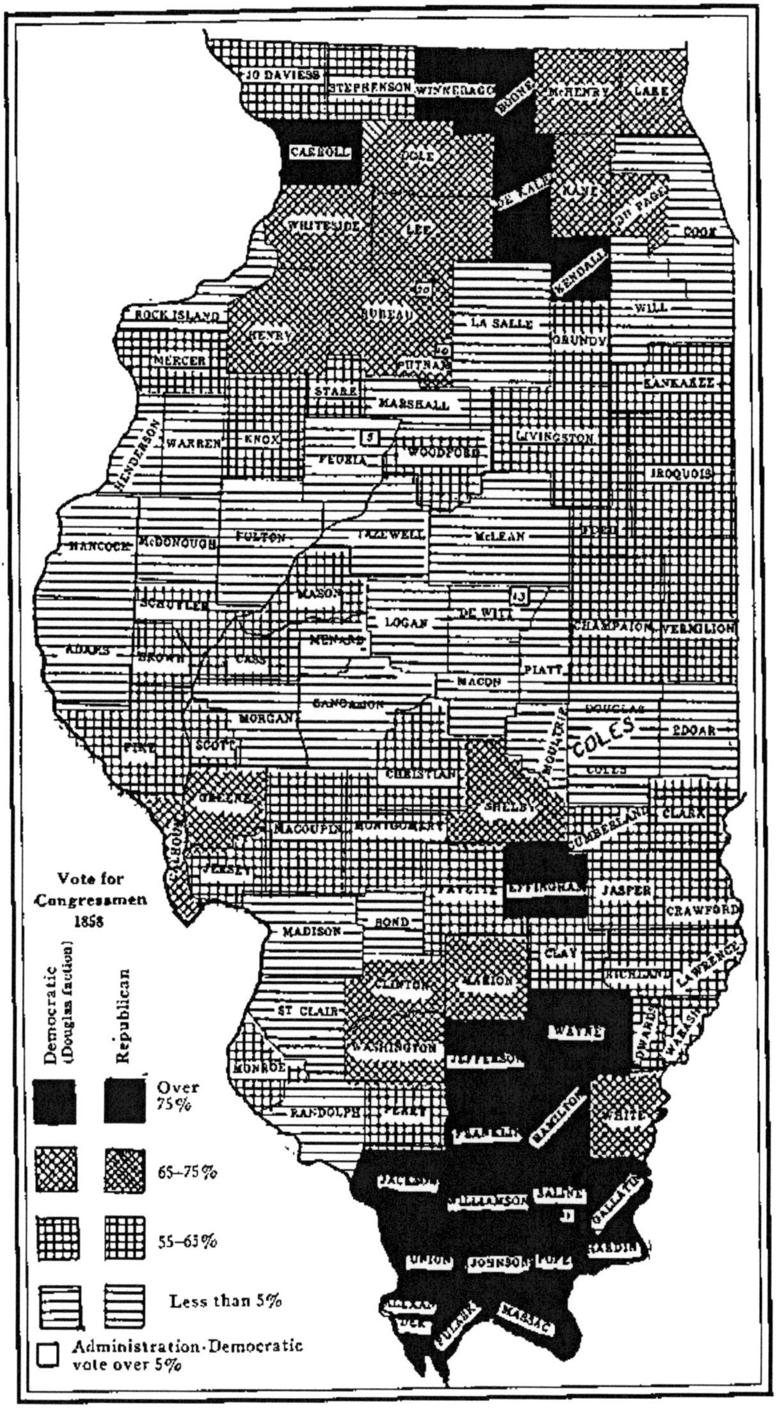
JO DAVIESS
STEPHENSON
WINNEBAGO
BOONE
McHENRY
LAKE
CARROLL
OGLE
DE KALB
KANE
DU PAGE
COOK
WHITESIDE
LEE
KENDALL
ROCK ISLAND
BUREAU
LA SALLE
WILL
HENRY
GRUNDY
MERCER
PUTNAM
KANKAKEE
STARK
MARSHALL
HENDERSON
WARREN
KNOX
PEORIA
WOODFORD
LIVINGSTON
IROQUOIS
HANCOCK
McDONOUGH
FULTON
TAZEWELL
McLEAN
SCHUYLER
MASON
DE WITT
ADAMS
BROWN
CASS
LOGAN
CHAMPAIGN
VERMILION
MENARD
PIATT
MACON
MORGAN
SANGAMON
DOUGLAS
EDGAR
PIKE
SCOTT
CHRISTIAN
MOULTRIE
COLES
GREENE
SHELBY
CLARK
CALHOUN
MACOUPIN
MONTGOMERY
CUMBERLAND
JERSEY
EFFINGHAM
JASPER
CRAWFORD
MADISON
BOND
CLAY
CLINTON
MARION
RICHLAND
LAWRENCE
ST CLAIR
WASHINGTON
WAYNE
MONROE
WABASH
RANDOLPH
PERRY
HAMILTON
WHITE
JACKSON
WILLIAMSON
SALINE
GALLATIN
HARDIN
UNION
JOHNSON
POPE
PULASKI
MASSAC
Vote for Congressmen 1858
Democratic (Douglas faction)
Republican
Over 75%
65–75%
55–65%
Less than 5%
Administration-Democratic vote over 5%

have inherited the old whig love of ease in bad weather; the loss of votes was reckoned at fully 10,000. As the election returns came in it became evident first that the republicans had carried Chicago, then that Douglas had been given a majority in both branches of the legislature, although the two republican candidates for state office were elected, indicating that Illinois had at length become a full-fledged republican state.

An analysis of the vote for legislature, moreover, showed that the republican members of the new assembly represented a population larger than the democratic members. This was because an antique apportionment law based upon data that had ceased to be facts eight years before compelled the northern counties to produce 1,000 votes to offset 750 in the southern section; this had made the election a contest of Egypt against Canaan; Egypt was returned the victor.

Douglas defeated the republicans for the right to take the lead in administering a rebuke to the proslavery position of the national administration. Republican leaders regretted that the profit to Douglas from the aid and comfort given him by their eastern associates had more than covered the loss of the "Buchaneers."[57] The latter indeed proved to be an impotent faction, strong in the post offices, but polling only two per cent of the total vote. The election of a democratic legislature did not absolutely guarantee the return of Douglas to the United States senate, for the "Danites" were determined to defeat Douglas and worked to tie up the legislature so that no choice of a senator could be made. Three holdover senators were said to be national democrats; and also, it was claimed that, while the "Danites" had failed to elect any of their own legislative candidates, three or four representatives might be induced to see the danger of supporting the ambitious man whom the Buchanan administration considered the most dangerous enemy of the democratic party. Agents of the administration were said to have been sent to Springfield to influence members to shelve Douglas.[58]

Most democrats were too well aware, however, that the

[57] J. M. Palmer to Trumbull, December 9, 1858, Trumbull manuscripts.
[58] *Chicago Herald* clipped in *Illinois State Journal*, November 17, 1858; *Ottawa Free Trader*, January 7, 1859.

defeat of Douglas meant playing too much into the hands of the republicans; to the relief of Douglas' friends the joint balloting on January 6 revealed a rigid party line with all democratic votes cast in his favor. "Glory to God and the Sucker Democracy, Douglas 54, Lincoln 41," was the word telegraphed to Douglas. "Announcement followed by shouts of immense crowd present. Town wild with excitement. Democrats firing salute. . . . . Guns, music and whisky rampant."[69] Back over the wires to Springfield flashed the laconic comment of the victor, "Let the voice of the people rule."

[69] C. H. Lanphier to Douglas, January 5, 1859, Lanphier manuscripts. The official vote was 54 to 46, *House Journal*, 1859, p. 32-33.

VIII. THE ELECTION OF 1860

DEMOCRATIC enjoyment of the fruits of the victory of 1858 was sharply interrupted by Governor Bissell's message of January 5, 1859. His review of the state's affairs—concise, clear, and convincing—revealed a sympathetic appreciation of all progressive movements at work in Illinois.[1] To the democrats it came as a painful reminder not only that the popular vote was now in the hands of the republicans but that as a result the control of the legislature might slip out of their hands and with it the choice of the next United States senator. The demand for a new apportionment law furnished them an opportunity to try to save themselves from this calamity; without consulting republican members of the committee, they at once constructed a gerrymandering apportionment bill that would sustain the ascendancy of their party and undertook to place it upon the statute books. Republican leaders fought it on the floor with every known filibustering device,[2] for the proposition was regarded as worse than the infamous old measure that had defeated Lincoln. Despite all opposition and protest, however, it passed both houses by strict party vote and was sent to Governor Bissell. After holding it in his hands for several days the governor returned it with a stinging veto message.[3] In order to leave the house without a quorum, most of the republican members had withdrawn so that the democrats were unable to pass the bill over the veto. This revolutionary action forced the adjournment of the session without action on various appropriation items and on several hundred proposed bills.[4]

---
[1] *House Journal*, 1859, p. 20-29.
[2] *Rockford Republican*, February 3, 1859.
[3] *Illinois State Journal*, February 23, 1859.
[4] B. C. Cook to Trumbull, January 14, Trumbull to B. C. Cook, January 20, 1859, Trumbull manuscripts; *Alton Courier*, February 25, 1859; *Chicago Press and Tribune*, March 3, 1859; *Ottawa Free Trader*, March 12, 1859.

The summer of 1859, an off-year as far as elections were concerned, was devoid of any real political excitement. The municipal elections, which were held in the chief cities of the state during the spring months, resulted in significant republican victories in Chicago, Quincy, and Rockford.[5] These were all regions of normal democratic strength, and these victories were held to foreshadow unmistakably the success of the republican ticket in 1860. County elections in November had little significance since personal considerations generally overbore political preferences and party rules. In Ottawa, however, excitement was aroused by an attempted fugitive slave rendition which ended in a famous rescue case and as a result the republicans rallied to the polls to reverse a normal democratic majority.[6] In the Springfield district a special congressional election resulted in a victory for John A. McClernand, democrat, over John M. Palmer, republican; in this as in the general political development the outcome was doubtless affected by the reaction that followed the John Brown raid on Harper's Ferry.[7]

Like wildfire the news of this astonishing attempt had spread over the country; John Brown, a fanatical abolitionist with some twenty men, black and white, had treasonably seized a United States arsenal, had raised the standard of revolt and liberation, had placed guns in the hands of Negroes — of slaves — and had sought to deal a blow at all the forces of law and order. Defeated in his mad purpose, he had fallen into the hands of the state authorities. What then did all this mean? Democrats, eager to exploit the incident for political purposes, inquired peremptorily whether this revolutionary attempt could be construed as anything but the logical fruit of republicanism, of the "irrepressible conflict" doctrine of Abe Lincoln and Senator Seward! The republican party, they declared, means nothing more nor less than open defiance of the laws and authority of the United States and in the end, as a natural consequence, revolution and anarchy. After all, is there any real distinc-

[5] *Illinois State Journal*, April 13, 27, May 18, 1859.
[6] *Ottawa Free Trader*, November, 1859; *Rockford Register*, November 19, 1859.
[7] *Illinois State Journal*, November 2, 16, 1859.

tion between abolitionists and "black" republicans on the subject of slavery?[8]

All this was extremely embarrassing to Illinois republicans, who had generally regarded the raid as the product of a disordered brain. Unable adequately to refute these charges, they involuntarily became admirers of the bravery and daring involved in the exploit; if it was not the result of an insanity, for which allowances should be made, it was a new brand of courage such as the country had rarely known. John Brown was pictured as a mild, inoffensive, peaceable citizen transformed by his sufferings in Kansas at the hands of proslavery cutthroats into a patriarchal, though misguided, champion of freedom who planned to wreak a bloody revenge upon the institution of slavery. When with Spartan courage the stern old Puritan paid with his life the penalty for his rashness, the reaction became even more marked. Solemn public meetings of protest were held in several northern Illinois cities on the day of the execution, prayers were offered up for his soul, and the church bells tolled in commemoration of the martyr to the "irrepressible conflict."

As the campaign of 1860 drew near, Douglas made plans for his own presidential nomination and election. His political success since the Kansas-Nebraska act had been the result of a two-faced interpretation of his pet doctrine which gave him the advantage of appearing both to break down and to uphold the slave interest. His republican opponents realized, however, that no ingenuity could long keep these antagonistic elements in harmony.[9] The Freeport doctrine had undermined his popularity in the slave states. Southerners who accepted, as well as those who rejected his explanation, pointed out that it merely demonstrated the need of congress giving more adequate protection to slavery — in the territories — a tacit demand that Douglas accept the idea of congressional intervention to protect slavery.[10]

[8] *Ottawa Free Trader*, October 22, 29, 1859; *Rockford Republican*, October 27, 1859; *Mound City Emporium*, November 3, 1859; *Belleville Democrat*, November 5, 1859; *Joliet Signal*, December 6, 1859.
[9] *Writings of Lincoln*, 5: 18, 19.
[10] *Richmond Enquirer*, September 10, clipped in *Illinois State Journal*, September 29, 1858.

Douglas was not prone to overlook the political necessity of courting the south. Promptly after his victory in November, 1858, he had left for the southland, ostensibly on business and in pursuit of health, but in part to feel the pulse of the slave states. All his energies were bent toward making himself agreeable to the hospitable planters who welcomed him; his references to the Dred Scott decision indicated unqualified acceptance, while the version of the Freeport doctrine which he presented was of innocuous innocence. He announced himself in sympathy with the manifest destiny of the United States to acquire Mexico, Central America, and Cuba.

When he found, however, that the south was so far ready to accept him at his word as to look to him for a champion of congressional intervention to protect slavery, Douglas made haste to backwater. Only on the matter of Cuban annexation, which he had always supported, could he stand squarely with the southern democrats.[11] For the rest he had hardly returned to Washington before he was breaking lances with Jefferson Davis and other southern democratic champions who argued in favor of protective legislation for slavery in the territories.[12] Douglas declared himself unwilling to support any proposition to interfere with territorial regulation of property rights, whether in horses, mules, or Negroes; he was even unwilling to indorse congressional intervention to prevent polygamy in Utah. Further, in the face of a growing demand in the south for the reopening of the African slave trade, he placed himself on record as opposed to the illicit traffic that was beginning to assume such large proportions. The fact that he was by such a course manifestly alienating political support was made more potent by President Buchanan's efforts to stir up the southern democrats against him. Douglas' leadership of the democratic party the president persistently challenged; upon his arrival

[11] His own party in Illinois backed him on this proposition. *Joliet Signal*, February 1, March 1, 1859. While republican leaders and journals naturally inclined to oppose, some felt that inasmuch as "acquisition is a trait of American character," it was good strategy to come out for territorial expansion and to lead off boldly for the spread of the free institutions of the country. *Belleville Advocate*, December 29, 1858, February 9, 1859; *Alton Courier*, January 21, 1859; J. M. Palmer to Trumbull, December 9, 1858; J. P. Cooper to Trumbull, December 14, 1858, Trumbull to B. C. Cook, January 20, 1859, Trumbull manuscripts.
[12] *Congressional Globe*, 35 congress, 2 session, 1243-1245, 1259.

in Washington the Illinoisian found that the democratic congressional caucus at Buchanan's instigation had deposed him from the chairmanship of the committee on territories.

Such a thrust must have rankled in the heart of the "little giant," especially since the practical issue before the country was the territorial question. To clear up his position on that subject Douglas wrote a labored exposition of his views for *Harper's Magazine*; obviously facing northward, he sought to establish firmer constitutional foundation for the Freeport doctrine.[12] Here at last, in Douglas' labors to maintain his strength north of Mason and Dixon's line, was a tacit admission of the effect of the attacks of Abraham Lincoln. Lincoln, meanwhile, pressed the offensive; campaigning in Ohio in the fall of 1859, he made the point that Douglas' doctrine of unfriendly legislation was equivalent to saying that "a thing may be lawfully driven away from where it has the lawful right to be."[14] At Cincinnati he analyzed Douglas' record in a speech which was printed with the title, "Douglas an enemy to the North. Reasons why the North should oppose Judge Douglas. His duplicity exposed." So scathing was the indictment that it was later circulated by Douglas' supporters in the south in order to win popularity there.

All these developments were bringing Lincoln into the limelight. Up to this time he had not been a prominent figure in national politics. To be sure, in the Philadelphia convention of 1856 he had displayed strength in the race for vice presidential nomination, second only to the victor, William L. Dayton. Yet his name was not mentioned in connection with the presidency. As late as June, 1858, the republican delegates journeying to the state convention at Springfield had found from a straw vote that their preferences for the presidency were overwhelmingly for Seward; Lincoln received only a casual vote.[15] The Lincoln-Douglas campaign, however, worked a revolution in sentiment, in large part because of the resentment of the Illinois leaders at the advice of eastern republicans that Douglas be returned to the senate. In view

[12] *Harper's Magazine*, 19: 519-537.
[14] *Chicago Press and Tribune*, October 6, 1859.
[15] *Missouri Republican*, June 24, 1858, clipped in Sparks, *Lincoln-Douglas Debates of 1858*, 3:24.

of the feeling that "Seward, Greeley & Co." had materially contributed to Lincoln's defeat, the decision was reached that Illinois ought to throw its strength to anyone rather than Seward.[16] Lincoln stock boomed immediately. After a few timid suggestions by party journals that Lincoln's name ought to have a place on the presidential ticket in 1860, the *Olney Times*, November 19, 1858, boldly printed "Abram Lincoln for President for 1860" at the head of its editorial columns. By the following summer Lincoln in the minds of Illinoisians had become first-rate presidential timber.[17] Impressed with this development by the little coterie of Springfield politicians, he allowed himself to be groomed for the coming race, though he modestly admitted that he did not consider himself "fit for the Presidency."[18] The radical edges were carefully smoothed off; he placed himself on record as opposed to the repeal of the fugitive slave law; in his Ohio speeches he sought to convince conservatives that his "house-divided" prophecy was neither novel nor sectional doctrine; he declared himself willing to support a national ticket in 1860 with the name of a southerner at either end. He assumed the rôle of peacemaker in the republican party. The German republicans were restless as a result of an amendment to the Massachusetts constitution, adopted, it was said, under republican auspices, which provided for political restrictions upon newly naturalized citizens. Lincoln therefore gave assurances that he was opposed to the Massachusetts provision; and the republican state committee through its chairman, N. B. Judd, published a strong letter of repudiation.[19] The conviction grew that "Old Abe" was the man about whom to rally to full strength of the republican party. The republican club of Springfield resolved itself into a "Lincoln club" to use all honorable means to secure the nomination of Abraham Lincoln.[20] The movement spread and Lincoln clubs appeared on every hand.

---

[16] E. Peck to Trumbull, November 22, 1858, Trumbull manuscripts.
[17] *Chicago Democrat*, November 11, 1858; *Illinois State Journal*, November 17, 1858; *Rockford Republican*, December 9, 1858.
[18] *Writings of Lincoln*, 5:31.
[19] *Ibid.*, 5:26; Koerner, *Memoirs*, 2:75.
[20] *Canton Weekly Register*, November 1, 1859; *Aurora Beacon*, November 10, 1859; *Central Illinois Gazette*, December 7, 1859; *Illinois State Journal*, January 18, 1860.

Chief attention in national politics was centering on the fate of Douglas at the hands of the democratic party; the family quarrel was steadily growing more bitter and the two wings voiced their open defiance of each other. Douglas, charged with apostasy from the party creed and with a desire for self-aggrandizement, was convinced that the proper method to clear himself was to secure the democratic nomination at Charleston upon such a platform as he could accept. Though he stood firmly against congressional intervention in the territories, he admitted the need of some measure to protect the states and territories against acts of violence like the Harper's Ferry conspiracy.[21]

The party machinery in Illinois was set in motion to enable Douglas to put his full strength into the field; a list of every able supporter who could be present at Charleston in the capacity of delegate or alternate was made up and completed at the state democratic convention.[22] In order to outmaneuver the "nationals" the Douglas wing had fixed an early date of meeting, lest the latter might act first and set up an embarrassing claim to speak for the Illinois democracy. On January 4, 1860, therefore, the Douglasite convention adopted resolutions which reaffirmed the Cincinnati platform of 1856, objected to any attempt to force upon the party new issues and new tests, and referred all controverted questions to the adjudication of the supreme court; it also pledged the Illinois democracy to support any candidate nominated at Charleston.[23]

The "Danites" held their conclave six days later and, as the Douglasites feared, selected a delegation to claim admission to the seats at Charleston allotted to Illinois. Their platform contained a clear-cut repudiation of the Freeport doctrine, affirmed the Calhoun theory, and upheld the decision of the supreme court in the case of Dred Scott; the policy of the Buchanan administration, especially on the slavery question, was given unqualified approval. There was a platform without equivocation: there was none of the trimming practiced by the

---

[21] See his speech of January 23, 1860, *Congressional Globe*, 36 congress, 1 session, 553-555.
[22] Douglas to Lanphier, October 1, 1859, January 1, 1860, Lanphier manuscripts.
[23] *Illinois State Register*, January 5, 1860.

Douglasites, "'here a streak of lean and there a streak of fat,' now 'a little turtle and now a little pork,'" as one critic put it;[24] but it was the work of an impotent and discontented minority destined to count for little in the active campaign.

These were practically the lines upon which the Charleston convention later divided and rent the party in twain. The Douglas platform underwent no change; it was the work of the Illinois democratic delegation in congress under the direction of Senator Douglas himself. It represented every concession that it was deemed possible to make to the south; the Illinois delegation, moreover, was selected so as to include the "men with the best *political record on the Slavery question*," men "especially favorably known at the South."[25] The platform supported by the southern wing at Charleston covered the ground of the "Danite" resolutions, with an additional plank incorporating Jefferson Davis' declaration of the duty of congress to provide adequate protection to slave property in the territories. The leader of the Illinois Douglas delegation at Charleston was Colonel William A. Richardson, whose abilities in political management and manipulation were sufficiently recognized to give him the larger rôle of leader of the Douglas forces in general. Fresh from Washington and from close contact with Douglas, he conducted an aggressive campaign to capture the machinery of organization. In the preliminary skirmishing the Douglas men drew first blood; technical points were decided in their favor, and the convention refused to admit the contesting "Danite" delegation from Illinois headed by Isaac Cook. The real test came on the adoption of a platform. Douglas had instructed Richardson to be prepared to withdraw his name in the event of a victory for the Davis doctrine. When, however, the southern majority report was rejected for the Douglas minority resolutions, the southern hotspurs voiced their defiance and promptly seceded. Under the two-thirds rule, the "rump" convention balloted in vain; Douglas led with a large majority until it was voted to adjourn to meet June 18 at Baltimore.

[24] *Illinois State Journal*, January 18, 1860.
[25] Douglas to Lanphier, October 1, December 31, 1859, January 1, 1860, Lanphier manuscripts.

THE ELECTION OF 1860

In the interim Lincoln had his innings. A fortunate combination of forces in Illinois operated to bring his name to the fore. There had been for some time a growing fear of Seward's radicalism with a consequent decline in the stock of the New York leader. Old-line whigs in the central part of the state had never been reconciled to Seward's strength; Egypt was beginning to break with the democracy, but any tendency to go over to the republicans would end if a candidate tainted with abolitionism headed the ticket. Conservative Illinois business men objected to Seward's analysis of "labor" states and "capital" or "slave" states, since there was more capital in good old New England than in the southern states combined;[26] they inclined to favor Edward Bates of Missouri, but his name could not be considered if the votes of the Germans were to be obtained. The German vote preferred Seward or Fremont but would go enthusiastically for Lincoln.[27] In fact Lincoln's moderation appealed to all factions, and his zealous supporters were meeting undreamed-of success. County convention after county convention indorsed his candidacy as the choice of the republican party. Encouraged by this success, his Illinois supporters began a quiet but active campaign in a larger field. They won a preliminary victory when Chicago was selected as the place of meeting of the national nominating convention, although at the time this city was considered fairly neutral ground, since Illinois was not yet, in national councils, regarded as having any strong presidential candidate. By March, however, not only Illinois but a steadily widening circle of states in the northwest were flying Lincoln's colors. "It seems as if the whole West was about to rise *en masse* in favor of the nomination of Abraham Lincoln by the Chicago Convention. Never did the proposal of any man's name elicit such an overwhelming testimonial to his fitness and the propriety of his nomination. Paper after paper throughout not only Illinois but the whole northwest, has put his name at the mast head, until the ones which have not done so are the marked exceptions."[28]

---

[26] Russel Hinckley to Trumbull, March 28, 1860, Trumbull manuscripts.
[27] G. Koerner to Trumbull, March 15, April 16, 1860, *ibid.*
[28] *Central Illinois Gazette*, March 28, 1860.

State politics temporarily attracted the attention of the republicans from the developments in the national canvass. The previous winter had witnessed a sharp struggle in republican circles over the gubernatorial nomination. Norman B. Judd, for sixteen years senator from Cook county, was put forward as the representative of the old democratic element of the party; his rival was Leonard Swett, who was championed by republicans of whig antecedents who claimed that the principle of rotation ought to be recognized in the governorship. Judd was the stronger and abler candidate but suffered from a set of scathing articles against him in the *Chicago Democrat*, which voiced the feelings of John Wentworth, his rival in the republican as of yore in the democratic ranks.[29] The preconvention contest furnished an excellent opportunity for a dark horse to enter the field; one appeared in the person of Richard Yates of Jacksonville, a devoted and capable republican, who had been a member of congress as a whig at the time of the passage of the Kansas-Nebraska act. To the surprise of almost everyone, Judd was defeated when the republican state convention was held at Decatur on May 9; and the nomination given to Yates. Francis H. Hoffman was nominated for lieutenant governor by acclamation to honor the German vote that he represented. The rest of the state officers were renominated for their respective stations. The general platform reaffirmed the Bloomington and Springfield platforms of 1856 and 1858, declared against change in the naturalization laws and against discrimination between native born and naturalized citizens, commended the proposed homestead law, and demanded an economical administration of the state government.[30]

The state convention also completed the arrangements for participation in the Chicago convention. Resolutions were adopted which instructed the delegation to the Chicago convention to use all honorable means to secure Lincoln's nomination. Thereupon, "for fifteen minutes, cheer upon cheer went up from the crowd."[31] Upon consultation with Lincoln, Gus-

[29] *Chicago Democrat*, November 7, 1859; *Joliet Signal*, December 13, 1859.
[30] *Chicago Press and Tribune*, May 11, 1860; *Illinois State Journal*, May 16, 1860.
[31] Arnold, *Life of Abraham Lincoln*, 162.

tave Koerner, Norman B. Judd, Orville H. Browning, and Judge David Davis were selected as delegates-at-large. A week later they were in Chicago, the center of a noisy bustling crowd at the Lincoln headquarters, assisted by Yates, Jesse K. Dubois, Palmer, Judge Stephen T. Logan, and others.

The metropolis of the northwest had enthusiastically accepted the obligations that accompanied the choice of that city for the national convention. A huge wooden structure, christened the "Great Wigwam," rose rapidly on Lake Street with a seating capacity of ten thousand persons. But even it was entirely inadequate for the accommodation of the tremendous crowds of hilarious holiday-makers that kept streaming in. The hotels, especially the Tremont House, where 1,500 persons were stored away, were largely taken up by various state delegations and by campaign headquarters. Private hospitality made up for what the hostelries were unable to provide; the latchstrings were all out in true western style. Every now and then above the uproar of the crowds would be heard the din of martial music, a band would come in sight heading a procession of Seward or Cameron or Bates supporters in uniform attire bearing banners and mottoes; there was marching and countermarching with friendly clashes between the rival paraders. The attitude of the convention crowd as a whole was that the republican party should wipe out a disgraceful reputation; neither the straight-laced puritanism of the antislavery movement nor the dignity and decorum of whig respectability should longer characterize it. On the contrary, it was now to show a spirit, an abandon that had heretofore been the monopoly of the democrats. To that end "Captain Whisky" was enlisted as evidence that the republicans had imbibed "the spirit as well as the substance of the old Democratic party;" accordingly, midnight processions, serenades, and champagne suppers drove dull care away in the satanic style "that would do honor to Old Kaintuck on a bust." [32]

Behind the scenes party workers were busy preparing their campaigns; there was caucusing and speech-making; there was scheming, intriguing, and bargaining. The uninstructed dele-

[32] Halstead, *National Political Conventions*, 121, 140, 145.

gates were courted on every side. When the convention opened, Edward Bates, Salmon P. Chase, Simon Cameron, and the others seemed to be getting nowhere, and current political gossip conceded but two important republican camps: the "irrepressibles" who backed the favorite, Seward, and the "conservatives" who talked of the unpopularity of Seward's ultraisms and gave their backing to "Old Abe."

Seward was opposed by all the doubtful states—Indiana, Pennsylvania, and New Jersey as well as Illinois; as yet, however, they had given their united support to no one candidate. But the favorable Illinois atmosphere was beginning to count for Lincoln. During the preliminaries of the convention the uninstructed Indiana delegation was gradually induced, aided by the logic and eloquence of Koerner and Browning, to throw their support to Lincoln rather than to Bates, while Pennsylvania, though committed to Cameron, its favorite son, gradually became more favorably inclined toward Lincoln. "Old Abe," the representative of conservatism, respectability, and availability, went the current of talk, will win the race.[33]

In the tense atmosphere, the convention was organized and quickly disposed of the regular business. The platform was then drawn up and adopted. It was in various ways influenced by the Decatur resolutions which were presented by Koerner, the Illinois member of the committee;[34] but the general draft, especially the forcible indictment of the sins of the democratic party, was the work of Judge William Jessup of Pennsylvania, the chairman of the committee. The easterners insisted on a tariff plank, but it was toned down into a very harmless declaration for incidental protection.

Though there was no definite alignment over the platform, Seward seemed to be gaining strength in a very subtle way. His opponents had hoped to down him by forcing the adoption of a rule that a majority of the whole electoral college should be required to nominate candidates. This was almost equivalent to a two-thirds rule; but although the majority report recommended this method, it was rejected by the convention

---

[33] Halstead, *National Political Conventions*, 122; Koerner, *Memoirs*, 2:88-89.
[34] With the aid of Carl Schurz he was able to secure the incorporation of a plank opposing any change in the naturalization laws and any legislation by the states to impair the rights of naturalized citizens. *Ibid.*, 2:87.

THE ELECTION OF 1860

for a simple majority rule. Although Seward's supporters were victorious in every preliminary skirmish, Lincoln's strength became immediately apparent when on the third day the convention began to ballot. The Wigwam was packed with a noisy Lincoln crowd, for the strategy of the Illinois workers had seen the emptiness of parades and of display on the city's streets; instead their time and energy had been utilized to provide Lincoln supporters with tickets before they were distributed to others. The Lincolnites had taken little part in the general celebrations, but were saved for the convention-hall orgies of sound, and when the time came they were ready to overwhelm their opponents with the reverberating Lincoln "yawp."

After an irritating delay the nominating commenced; Seward was named and applause filled the hall. Judd, in a few highly impressive words, offered the name of "Honest Abe" Lincoln; and the Illinois stalwarts cut loose with a deafening shriek. Other candidates were brought out — the crowd waited in expectancy. Caleb B. Smith of Indiana seconded the nomination of Lincoln and a deafening roar followed. Then Seward's candidacy was seconded, and his supporters shrieked their applause with an infernal intensity that surpassed their rivals; Lincoln's supporters were given another turn; and the hall became a riot of sound that defied description, while Henry S. Lane, republican candidate for governor in Indiana, leaped upon a table and madly performed with hat and cane. All this had its significance. The caucusing had continued during the whole night that preceded this session, and delegates had arrived but half convinced as to the nature of the first vote they should cast and without a program for the balloting that would follow. The shouting impressed even the most skeptical that the contest would resolve itself into a duel between Seward and Lincoln and that the westerner had a chance to win. The Indiana delegation became convinced that Henry S. Lane, their leader, was correct in his desperate insistence that their vote go as a unit to Lincoln, lest Seward be nominated and kill the hopes of the republican ticket in the hoosier state. The Cameron men were satisfied that their candidate had no chance and showed less uncertainty in their decision to throw their strength to Lincoln at the time when it would bring about his nomination by the convention. Assured by Lincolnites that their favorite would be rewarded with a cabinet appointment, the Pennsylvania delegation repeatedly retired for vote consultation and delayed the roll call much to the amusement and disgust of the convention throng.[35]

The first ballot was taken; Seward led with 173½, Lincoln was in second place with 102, while Cameron, Chase, and Bates each received approximately 50 votes. Seward lacked sixty votes of the required majority. As the balloting proceeded, Cameron's name was withdrawn and Lincoln gained 79 votes, bringing him within 3½ votes of his rival. Here was impressive evidence of the strength of his candidacy. Amid intense excitement the roll was called for the third ballot; busy pencils tabulating the vote counted a total of 231½ votes for Lincoln, within 1½ of the nomination.

A stuttered announcement of a change of front by the Ohio chairman turned the trick for Lincoln. The statement was made in a tense silence of expectancy; then again burst out the Lincoln "yawp," swelling into a wild hosanna of victory. It was followed by a stampede for "Old Abe:" ten Maine votes, ten Massachusetts votes, and the whole of the Missouri, Iowa, Kentucky, and Minnesota votes were changed. Amid the pandemonium, a man posted on the roof to signal the results to the huge crowd of ten or twenty thousand waiting anxiously outside demanded the meaning of the demonstration. One of the secretaries, tally sheet in hand, shouted, "Fire the salute! Abe Lincoln is nominated!" The message was relayed to the anxious mass of humanity below, which in turn took up the roar with insane energy, while the booming of the cannon scarcely made itself heard above the din.[36]

When the enthusiastic demonstration finally subsided, William M. Evarts, the Seward spokesman, moved that the nomination be made unanimous; this motion passed after the usual indorsements of the successful candidates, followed by a brief speech in behalf of Lincoln by Orville H. Browning. In concluding its work, the convention nominated Hannibal

[35] Halstead, *National Political Conventions*, 143.
[36] *Ibid.*, 149-150; *Illinois State Journal*, May 23, 1860.

THE ELECTION OF 1860

Hamlin of remote Maine as Lincoln's running mate. The news of the nominations was telegraphed broadcast, and before many hours almost every town and village in Illinois was reproducing in miniature the scenes of the western metropolis. Lincoln enthusiasts rallied their resources to concoct celebrations; processions formed of noisy youths bearing rails through the streets, tar barrels were heaped on blazing bonfires, drums were beaten, old cannons were dragged out to rend the night air with their disturbing blasts.[37] Hoarse throats were quenched with torrents of liquor, and the excitement continued until intoxication or exhaustion prostrated the joyous celebrants.

As a part of the Springfield festivities Lincoln was serenaded at his home by a large crowd of enthusiasts, who went wild at the appearance of his tall gaunt form and at the well-chosen remarks he addressed to them. The following evening the state capital held a formal jubilee when a committee headed by George Ashmun, president of the republican convention, came down from Chicago to notify Lincoln of his nomination and to receive his acceptance. An elaborate dinner was served to the committee; and, after the notification ceremony, a vast assemblage gathered in a ratification meeting in the statehouse square to listen to the speech-making. Brass bands marched through the streets; exploding fireworks sent out their lurid light; parties gathered in the hotels to drink toast after toast to the American union, to the republican party, and to its presidential nominee.

Republican enthusiasm continued undisturbed by the nomination of rival candidates at Baltimore. Douglas' friends triumphed and secured his nomination from the adjourned meeting of the democratic convention; the southern democrats, however, put their own candidate in the field in the person of John C. Breckinridge of Kentucky. Old conservative union men engineered a new movement which resulted in the formation of the constitutional union or national union party, with John Bell of Tennessee and Edward Everett as its candidates. The scattering Illinois supporters of each of these

[37] In Springfield church bells were enlisted to the disgust of the democrats. *Illinois State Register*, May 19, 23, 1860.

candidates hustled out their tickets for presidential electors and for state officers and entered the field with as much enthusiasm as they could rally.

The republicans of Illinois had the advantage of having harmonized on their state candidates and of having entered the field several weeks before their opponents. The Douglas candidates were not selected until June 13, when it was found impossible to agree on a state ticket of any real strength; James C. Allen of Crawford county was nominated for governor over Samuel A. Buckmaster and James L. D. Morrison; Lewis W. Ross for lieutenant governor, George H. Campbell for secretary of state, Bernard Arntzen for auditor, Hugh Maher for treasurer, and Dr. E. R. Roe for superintendent of public instruction completed the ticket.[38] The Breckinridge party was made up of the remnants of the Buchanan national democrats. It became more than ever a corporal's guard of officeholders. Its main strength lay in the southern counties where proslavery sentiment flourished.

The Bell-Everett movement in Illinois had a subtle importance in the campaign. It was the feeble successor of old-line whiggery and know nothingism; but it had a certain strength in southern Illinois, where there was no effective rival of Douglas democracy, and in the central counties, where a slight shifting of the vote might change the outcome of the election. The national union state convention at Decatur, August 11, nominated an electoral ticket and a full state ticket headed by John T. Stuart for governor; the most prominent delegate present was Judge Buckner S. Morris, a bitter opponent of republicanism; he had supported Douglas in 1858 and declared that Douglas had owed his election to American votes.[39] After declaring himself willing to support Douglas or any democrat in order to defeat Lincoln, Morris became a controlling force in the state central committee. This naturally confirmed republican suspicions that the union movement was a ruse to help Douglas accomplish the defeat of Lincoln.[40]

The campaign was now in full swing driven on by the

[38] *Illinois State Register,* June 15, 1860.
[39] *Illinois State Journal,* August 22, 1860.
[40] *Chicago Democrat,* August 15, 1860; *Belleville Advocate,* July 27, August 24, 1860.

THE ELECTION OF 1860

conviction that on the outcome in Illinois would to a large extent depend the result of the presidential contest. The gay holiday atmosphere of the canvass makes it stand out as one of the most picturesque of presidential elections; the prevailing enthusiasm duplicated that of the Lincoln-Douglas contest of 1858 with the situation reversed in Lincoln's favor. This time he had the advantage of being identified with the typical western spirit. The "rail-splitter" became the idol of the people; his early struggle in the wilderness carried more weight in the democratic west than the reputation of his rival. "Abe Lincoln; in Indiana he followed the plow and the path of rectitude; in Illinois he mauled rails and Stephen A. Douglas," was the eloquent motto on many a Lincoln banner.[41] Was he not too the representative of the party that stood for opening up the lands of the west to free settlement by the pioneer? In vain did his opponents point to the emptiness of his political career; it was more important that he embodied a spirit that the people of the frontier could understand.

Early in June republican campaign preparations had begun to take form. The unique feature of the canvass was the "wide awake" organization. A company of enthusiastic and "wide awake" Chicago republicans was organized to take a prominent place in the party parades and processions.[42] The idea was immediately taken up throughout the state until every village and hamlet had its "wide awakes," composed largely of young men, some under voting age. Shortly after nightfall one "hears the strains of martial music, and beholds a large body of men, bearing blazing torches, and marching in fine military order. Each man bears a thin rail, surmounted with a large swinging lamp and a small American flag, bearing the names of Lincoln and Hamlin. The uniform of the privates is a black enamelled circular cape, quite full and of good length, and a glazed military fatigue cap, with a brass or silver eagle in front. Some companies are uniformed with blue, red, drab and silver gray caps and capes, and relieve the monotony of the darker uniforms. The captains and non-commissioned officers are distinguished by an Inverness over-coat, with black

---
[41] *Illinois State Journal*, July 24, 1860.
[42] *Chicago Press and Tribune*, June 8, 1860.

cape and undress military caps. In some companies the captain carries a red, the aids a tri-colored, and the lieutenants a blue or green lantern; in others, the captain merely carried a painted baton. The measured tread, steady front and unbroken lines speak of strict attention to drill and the effective manner in which the various bodies are managed by their officers shows conclusively that men of military experience control their movements."[43]

A half million young men constituted the "wide awake" army of the union. They were the nucleus of parades, supplemented by marchers bearing banners and mottoes. Meetings of tremendous size brought together in impressive demonstrations the companies from neighboring towns. The great Springfield meeting at the fair grounds attracted a crowd of over fifty thousand people. Lincoln was present but refused to respond to the clamor for a speech except to say a few words of acknowledgment of the honor conferred upon him. Four thousand "wide awakes" marched in a procession that passed for nearly two hours before the local "wigwam." The celebration on the occasion of Seward's speech in Chicago in October is said to have attracted over one hundred thousand strangers to the city; the Wigwam was the center of the festivities, and 10,000 "wide awakes" carried their torches in the procession.[44] "The prairies are on fire," was the announcement that went out from republican headquarters.

Lincoln himself refused to take any direct part in the campaign. His record was subjected to careful scrutiny from every angle and old charges against him were revamped, but he was wise enough to recognize that he had capable friends campaigning in his behalf and that direct disavowal even of false charges would be playing into the hands of his opponents. He maintained his headquarters at the statehouse at Springfield and conferred with some of the campaign speakers, but at the same time displayed a leisurely hospitality toward all visitors with whom he conversed, not so much on political matters as on personal experiences and interests.

Effective work on the stump was done by Senator Trum-

[43] *Chicago Democrat*, September 24, 1860.
[44] *Ibid.*, October 3, 1860.

bull, Judd, Yates, Gillespie, Palmer, Koerner, Wentworth, and others, with outside aid from Senator James R. Doolittle and Carl Schurz of Wisconsin and Francis P. Blair of Missouri. It is to be noted that most of these leaders were former democrats disgusted with the subserviency of the "dough-faces" to the southern slave power; the talent of the democratic party had to a large extent been transferred to the republican organization. They carried with them the old fighting spirit, far superior to anything that old whiggery had been able to arouse in its ranks, and were always ready for the hard work necessary for the success of the new party. Jesse K. Dubois had frankly admitted: "My observation is that we old line whigs belonging to the Republican ranks are not worth a curse to carry on a campaign and its only life is in the Democratic part of the ranks."[45]

The democratic party started the canvass at a complete disadvantage. The republican campaign was well under way before Douglas' nomination was accomplished; then the news reached party members well-nigh nervously exhausted by the long-drawn-out fight at Charleston and Baltimore. An attempt was made at developing enthusiasm; much was accomplished but not enough to destroy the impression that whereas the democracy had occupied the position of vantage in 1858, it was now relegated to second place in the matter of popular favor.

Political oratory on behalf of Douglas was of a decidedly inferior brand. Realizing this, the "little giant" broke all traditions and entered the hustings in person, much to the disgust of his republican opponents.[46] He was soon in the midst of a most extraordinary canvass which took him on a tour through New England, into the southern seaboard states, and back to the region of the middle states, until, nearly exhausted by his strenuous efforts and convinced by the October elections that Lincoln's success was inevitable, he repaired to the southern states to labor in behalf of the union and the peace of the country.

The Douglas leaders in Illinois, left largely to their own

[45] J. K. Dubois to Trumbull, July 17, 1858, Trumbull manuscripts; cf. *Illinois State Journal*, May 23, 1860.
[46] *Belleville Advocate*, July 27, August 24, 1860.

resources, waged a spiritless campaign. The old charges as to Negro equality were rung against the republican party; the old wolf cry of abolitionism was shouted without effect. The German vote was courted on the strength of Arntzen's place on the state ticket; appeals were made to the Americans as union men. Since the legislative canvass which was to determine the possibility of Trumbull's reëlection to the senate was second in importance only to the presidential contest, there was a desire on the part of some of the more unscrupulous to save as much as possible from the ruins. In an effort to duplicate the victory of 1858 by capturing the middle counties the democrats colonized doubtful points with Irish laborers from Chicago.[47]

It proved, however, a losing fight. Election day on November 6 bore out the forecast of the October elections in the pivotal states of Pennsylvania, Indiana, and Ohio. Lincoln swept the north with a quarter of a million more votes than his doughty opponent. Illinois with a Lincoln plurality of 1,200 placed itself squarely in the republican column. Breckinridge and Bell each received only one per cent of the vote. Richard Yates and the entire republican state ticket were carried into office by 12,000 votes. Democratic control of the legislature was destroyed and the reëlection of Senator Trumbull was assured.

One of the most remarkable features of the campaign and election was the increase of republican strength in Egypt. In the region below Alton the party made a fourfold increase over Fremont's vote in 1856. Republicanism had fought an uphill battle in the southern counties, and these important gains were made against great odds. John A. Logan, the champion of Egyptian democracy, contested every inch of ground that was lost, sometimes by methods hardly scrupulous in character. It was by such tactics that the determined congressman acquired the cognomen of "Dirty Work" Logan. By threats of mob violence he compelled the editors and pub-

---

[47] Amos C. Babcock to Trumbull, August 27, 1860, Trumbull manuscripts; *Canton Weekly Register*, October 11, 30, 1860; *Illinois State Journal*, October 10, 31, 1860. S. G. Ward of Elgin explained in a letter to Trumbull, January 14, 1860 [1861], how he had colonized eleven Kane county republican voters in Peoria. Trumbull manuscripts.

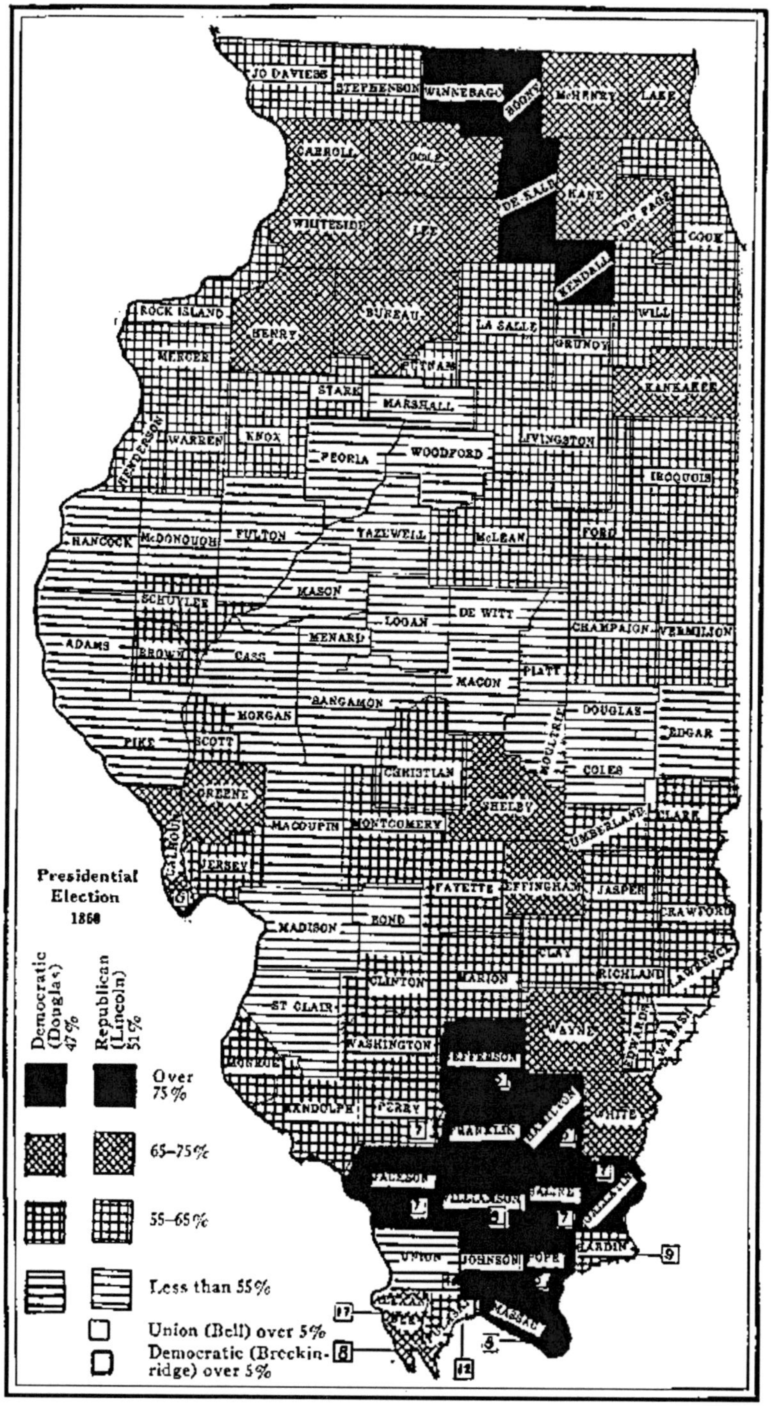
Presidential Election 1860
Democratic (Douglas) 47%
Republican (Lincoln) 51%
Over 75%
65–75%
55–65%
Less than 55%
Union (Bell) over 5%
Democratic (Breckinridge) over 5%
JO DAVIESS
STEPHENSON
WINNEBAGO
BOONE
McHENRY
LAKE
CARROLL
OGLE
DE KALB
KANE
DU PAGE
COOK
WHITESIDE
LEE
KENDALL
ROCK ISLAND
HENRY
BUREAU
LA SALLE
GRUNDY
WILL
MERCER
PUTNAM
KANKAKEE
STARK
MARSHALL
HENDERSON
WARREN
KNOX
PEORIA
WOODFORD
LIVINGSTON
IROQUOIS
HANCOCK
McDONOUGH
FULTON
TAZEWELL
McLEAN
FORD
MASON
SCHUYLER
DE WITT
LOGAN
ADAMS
BROWN
MENARD
CASS
CHAMPAIGN
VERMILION
PIATT
MACON
SANGAMON
MORGAN
DOUGLAS
MOULTRIE
EDGAR
PIKE
SCOTT
CHRISTIAN
COLES
GREENE
SHELBY
CALHOUN
MACOUPIN
MONTGOMERY
CUMBERLAND
CLARK
JERSEY
FAYETTE
EFFINGHAM
JASPER
MADISON
BOND
CRAWFORD
CLAY
CLINTON
MARION
RICHLAND
LAWRENCE
ST CLAIR
WAYNE
EDWARDS
WABASH
WASHINGTON
MONROE
JEFFERSON
RANDOLPH
PERRY
HAMILTON
WHITE
FRANKLIN
JACKSON
WILLIAMSON
SALINE
GALLATIN
UNION
JOHNSON
POPE
HARDIN
ALEXANDER
PULASKI
MASSAC
9
17
8
12

lishers of the *Franklin Democrat* at Benton to sell out at a ruinous sacrifice, because they had hauled down the Douglas and Johnson banner and were about to raise the standard of Lincoln and Hamlin.[48] Voters of republican leanings were reminded that schoolmasters had been dismissed for voting for Fremont in 1856; clergymen, antislavery propagandists, were threatened with an investment in the martyr's garb — tar and feathers; the Reverend Mr. Ferree of Lebanon was pelted with eggs on the streets of Cairo while making a republican speech.[49] In spite of everything, however, the conversion of a native occasionally took place, while an influx of intelligent immigration from the eastern states continued to carry the leaven of republican sentiment into "dough-faced" Egypt.[50]

[48] See statement of A. Sellers, Jr., and G. Sellers, in *Illinois State Journal*, September 20, 1860. A number of new republican papers made their appearance in the southern portion of the state following Lincoln's nomination. *Chicago Press and Tribune*, June 11, 1860. Thomas H. Dawson sold out the *Louisville* [Illinois] *Democrat* to undertake the publication of a republican paper and the *Mt. Carmel Register* took the Lincoln train.
[49] *Golconda Herald*, March 9, clipped in *Chicago Press and Tribune*, April 16, 1860; *Cairo Gazette*, July 26, 1860.
[50] B. L. Wiley to Trumbull, January 10, 1860, Trumbull manuscripts; *Chicago Press and Tribune*, October 16, 1860.

IX. THE GROWING PAINS OF SOCIETY

AN IMPERATIVE need in the development of Illinois was labor. Glowing words of welcome met the incoming settler or toiler; he was assured that "the product of labor is the only real wealth," and lecturers traveled about discussing "the dignity of labor." Yet the worker found himself allotted as a wage for eleven or twelve hours a day a sum which usually allowed him only to eke out a frugal existence and to prosper only barring misfortune or unemployment. The great mass of unskilled labor was paid at the rate of seventy-five cents a day in 1850, and this wage rose to a dollar and five cents average by the end of the decade. Immigrants from foreign countries sometimes found it difficult to find remuneration even at that rate, and in 1860 they constituted three-fourths of the paupers of the state. The more exclusive field of skilled labor, though it paid rather better than this, was closed to many youths by four and five year periods of apprenticeship.[1]

With uncertain periods of employment on works of internal improvement, with many engaged in seasonal occupations, the growing cities and towns of Illinois found themselves confronted with a new problem of poverty. Unemployment in a period of high prices brought the helpless, unorganized workers and their families to dire straits — and there were many such periods. Even the ordinary winter involved a severe strain upon the workers' finances; the unorganized poor relief of that day was ill prepared to cope with these demands. The winter of 1854, with a financial depression following a bad drought that sent wheat up to $1.40 a bushel retail, compelled the "friends of the poor" in the cities to recognize the prob-

[1] *Chicago Democrat*, May 17, 1848, April 9, 1849. According to the 1848 report of the commissioners of patents, wages of mechanics and laborers were $8 to $10 a week in central and southern Illinois and $15 to $20 in the northern section. *Illinois State Register*, March 10, 1848. At the same time serving maids received a dollar a week and, no longer content to possess a single calico dress, were reputed recklessly extravagant. *Ibid.*, August 18, 1848.

THE GROWING PAINS OF SOCIETY 203

lem and devise alleviative measures. Meanwhile the editor of the *Chicago Democrat* acutely analyzed the cause: "Reduction of the Wages of Labor — High Prices — High Rents, &c, &c." In the next two winters there was only the normal problem of poverty; but 1857, the panic year, brought a general state of unemployment. In the midst of plenty, with barns and storehouses full of grains and foodstuffs held back because of the low prices, twenty thousand workers in Chicago were without the usual means of earning a livelihood and with their dependents faced actual starvation; the other cities of the state confronted a similar problem. Though municipal works were advocated, municipal bakeries and soup-houses suggested, and the sale of foodstuffs at cost by the city administration was urged, little effective relief was rendered; and the workers struggled through the winter as best they could. Unemployment continued well into the spring. In June there was not nearly enough work on the streets of Chicago at seventy-five cents a day for two days a week to supply the demand; it was therefore decided to reduce the wage to fifty cents and put one-third more men into the city's service.[2]

Reformers who confronted these conditions usually found the explanation of poverty in the new difficulty of securing cheap or free land for the potential settler, who was therefore driven to the cities to seek a livelihood. Land reform, accordingly, was the cure-all put forward for the economic ills of the day.[3] Protection from exploitation by ruthless capitalists would come, they held, only when free homesteads were placed at the disposal of all would-be tillers of the soil.

Simultaneously with the appearance of a serious problem of poverty, the newspapers chronicled a great wave of crime in the larger cities of the state. The old offenses of the frontier were easily separated from these new developments; horse-stealing in the rural districts continued to arouse vigilance

[2] The tendency was to shift the responsibility for poor relief from the county to the town or township. *Laws of 1851*, p. 183-184, 194-195; *Laws of 1852*, p. 113; *Laws of 1853*, p. 261-262, 275-277, 464-465; *Alton Weekly Courier*, December 7, 1854; *Alton Courier*, December 12, 29, 1854, January 11, 25, 1855; *Belleville Advocate*, February 21, 1855; *Chicago Weekly Democrat*, February 10, 1855; *Rockford Register*, July 19, 1858.
[3] See pages 89-90.

committees which often dispensed lynch law to the thief as fearlessly as they applied a coat of tar and feathers to the violator of the community standard of morality.[4] These were not the urban crimes, however, the steady increase of which had been noticed in the cities. Various explanations for such growth had been given: some held that it was not real but merely the apparent result of improved facilities for knowing the evil transactions of society; some attributed it to the moral laxity that prevailed as a result of the growing inclination toward extravagance and dissipation; but an occasional critic soberly commented: "At the commencement of winter, especially in the large cities, there is the prospect of more suffering and poverty, and crime is more rife, than at other seasons of the year. And it is observable, that most of the criminal acts now-a-days are committed in the cities."[5] In the closing years of the decade the alarming increase of crime seemed to be accountable on no other basis.

Even the humble sociological observer of that day was able to discern some connection between this disorderly atmosphere of the cities and the "demon drink." Intemperance was a prevailing feature of community life. Grogshops and saloons were licensed as fast as applications were made; Belleville, a city of 4,000, had forty licensed retail liquor establishments with "probably as many more unlicensed." The danger of such conditions had already been realized in the more settled states of the east; a temperance movement swept over New England, producing the "Maine law" brand of temperance, a crusade for total legislative prohibition on alcoholic liquors. Appearing just when the objectivity of the frontier was yielding to the subjective analysis of more intensive civilization, it is not surprising that the movement now spread to the states of the Mississippi valley and had a profound sig-

---

[4] Horse-thief detecting societies were still common in certain parts of the state. See notice of a meeting in 1852 of the Brighton society in *Printer's Scrap Book*.
[5] *Belleville Democrat*, December 11, 1858. See editorials on the increase of crime in the *Rockford Register*, May 16, 1857; *Chicago Daily Times*, August 28, 1857; *Belleville Democrat*, January 23, 1858; *Chicago Democrat*, August 13, 1859; *Urbana Clarion*, October 29, 1859. In the lists of crime, thefts of food and clothing were quite common; many were juvenile offenders especially in the cases of food stealing.

nificance in Illinois life and politics. In 1849 John Hawkins, the father of the "Washingtonian" temperance movement, appeared in Chicago; in an address on the necessity of temperance effort in that city, he declared that after having carefully inspected the situation in the Illinois metropolis he could frankly state that in all his tours over the United States he had never seen a city or town which seemed so much like one universal grogshop as Chicago. A little later considerable interest was aroused by the temperance lectures of James E. Vinton of New York, known as the "Mohawk Dutchman." These men found a fertile field for their evangels and spread their propaganda throughout the state.[6]

Up to the year 1847 temperance agitation in Illinois had been feeble and unpopular. Small temperance groups, chiefly offshoots of the New England movement, had worked in obscurity in Chicago, Springfield, Jacksonville, and other points. In November, 1845, the Sons of Temperance, a secret ritualistic organization pledging its members to the practice of temperance, entered the state. Two years later when a state organization was formed there were only six divisions in Illinois; but before another six months 91 units had been chartered with a membership of 3,000, with new divisions rapidly forming. Their processions in the regalia of the order and their public exercises became a feature of all legal holiday celebrations. It was not long before temperance became "the order of the day;" a temperance paper, the *Illinois Organ*, was established, subsidiary organizations were formed — a "Temple of Honor" for the especially fervent Sons of Temperance, the Cadets of Temperance for the younger generation; and for zealous sisters local "Ladies Temperance Unions" and "Daughters of Temperance." In the course of four years of activity in the state the Sons of Temperance recruited only four thousand members; in the year of 1849–1850, however, 6,626 were enrolled, while the number of divisions rose to over 270. Although this pace could not

[6] *Belleville Advocate*, June 13, 1850; *Western Citizen*, August 28, 1849. Chicago had at that time 275 authorized drinking establishments, one for every sixty inhabitants; see *Chicago Democrat* clipped in *Illinois Journal*, July 21, 1849; *Alton Telegraph*, December 28, 1849; *Ottawa Free Trader*, October 19, 1850, March 8, 1851; *Illinois State Register*, October 14, 1852.

be maintained, steady progress continued in the years that followed.[7]

It is to be remembered that the temperance cause was not built up into a single organization; various societies carried on their respective lines of activity. The churches often undertook independent campaigns against intemperance; the Catholics had their Sons of Temperance order and total abstinence societies. A good deal of temperance activity was carried on without formal and permanent organization; mass meeting and temperance conventions were assembled with remarkable ease. General state temperance union meetings were held regularly each year and a national convention at Chicago on November 18, 1857.

The goal of the Sons of Temperance and similar societies was too vague for the more aggressive temperance advocates. Moral suasion, the approved method, did not promise entire reform and was thus unsatisfactory to those who wanted a complete purification of society. Many urged, therefore, that some form of political action ought to be undertaken which would strike at the root of the evil. The relative desirability of a high license system, with its "respectable" grog aristocracy working behind cut glass and mahogany cases, and of a low rate, producing a democratic system of bunghole dispensing "doggeries," was discussed by certain temperance forces, while others argued for the entire prohibition of liquor selling. The license system itself was scrutinized and attacked; the reformers pointed out countless infractions of the license laws both by the licensed dealers and by their unauthorized competitors. A vigilance committee in Ottawa kept a careful eye on the grogshops in the hope that it might eventually expel

[7] *Gem of the Prairie*, February 19, 1848; *Quincy Whig*, April 19, 1848; *Illinois Organ*, July 1, 1848, September 21, 1850. The movement now attracted favorable attention. "This institution bids fair to become one of the most efficient engines of social improvement ever devised by man, and all such as desire the amelioration of the condition of the human race, will not long withhold from it their aid and influence," was the commendation of the editor of the *Illinois State Register*, October 22, 1847. Its political rival, the *Journal*, also undertook to point out the advantages of the movement and commended the rescue work carried on by the Sons of Temperance. *Illinois Journal*, August 7, 1850. List of the 272 divisions on June 1, 1850, *Printer's Scrap Book*. *Illinois State Register*, October 22, November 19, 1847, February 11, 1848, August 1, 1850; *Ottawa Free Trader*, May 3, 1851; *Chicago Democrat*, May 8, 1851; *Beardstown Gazette*, March 31, 1852; *Alton Courier*, October 29, 1853.

every rumseller from town.[8] The no-license forces finally gathered strength to carry the elections in Quincy, Rockford, and Springfield in the spring of 1850 and barely lost in Ottawa.

Many, however, for various reasons desired general state wide action. A cry arose for the complete banishment of the liquor dealer from the state. So much strength was displayed by the temperance forces that the legislature in January, 1851 abolished the existing license law and prohibited the selling or giving away of spirituous liquors in less quantity than one quart; this law was expected to pacify temperance advocates, while the liquor forces were shrewd enough to see the impossibility of enforcement. The law justified the forecast and became immediately an absolute nullity until its repeal and the substitution of the license system in February, 1853.[9]

Disillusioned by this development, the temperance forces now took up Maine law prohibition, which was being vigorously agitated throughout the middle west. Hard-headed business men who had at first eyed it with suspicion as the propaganda of the traveling tract peddler and the would-be reformer, identified with all the incipient isms of the day, now came to look upon it as a force that might work incalculable good. As the Maine law came to be regarded as a preventive scheme more desirable than legislative interference in the field of morals and religion, the temperance movement underwent rapid reconstruction. Its most aggressive expression was now found in a newly created system of Maine law alliances with township and county divisions and an active state organization. By the beginning of 1854 forecasts were made that two-thirds of the voters of the state would be members of the different alliances and the enactment of the Maine law was regarded as a settled fact.[10]

A more careful analysis revealed the fact that the strength of this movement lay in the northern counties in the old New England districts; neither Egypt where, according to its

---

[8] *Ottawa Free Trader*, June 8, 1850.
[9] *Laws of 1851*, p. 18-19; *Laws of 1853*, p. 91-92, 127; *Belleville Advocate*, January 30, 1851; *Illinois Organ*, February 1, 1851; *Western Citizen*, February 11, 1851.
[10] *Joliet Signal*, March 9, 1852; *Alton Courier*, September 16, 1853; *Peru Daily Chronicle*, February 14, 1854.

spokesman, "the use of intoxicating drinks seems more natural than the use of water,"[11] nor the democratic strongholds in the north were effectively organized for the cause. Petitions, however, poured into the legislature from all sides requesting prohibition legislation. When a special committee in February, 1853, reported adversely upon a petition with twenty-six thousand signatures which had been referred to it, only greater activity was aroused among the Maine law forces. When in the session of 1854 the general assembly again ignored the demand that the Maine law question be submitted to the people, the temperance forces entered the field of state politics with a grim determination. Previous to this the most significant political action of the temperance forces was the canvass made by them in Chicago in the municipal election of 1852. Placing a city ticket in the field, they conducted an active canvass and ran second in the field of four mayoralty candidates, in spite of the fact that their original candidate for mayor was induced to leave the field. The contest was again attempted in 1854 with even greater success.[12]

Up to this time the great political stumblingblock for the temperance forces had been the democratic party. The Springfield machine was strongly opposed to the temperance propaganda and inclined to favor making it a party issue, inasmuch as nearly every whig paper in the state was out for temperance;[13] the democratic party had thereby acquired the nickname of "whisky party." There were democrats, however, who saw the evil consequences of the dictation that came from Springfield; they saw that the temperance issue had already counted subtly against them in county, legislative, and even congressional elections; this rebellious spirit helped to feed the anti-Nebraska revolt of 1854. In several districts, where the democratic party split over the temperance issue, independent temperance democratic candidates were placed in the field.

[11] *Cairo Weekly Times and Delta*, February 3, 1858.
[12] *Aurora Guardian*, January 19, February 23, 1853. The Illinois Central refused to transport spirituous liquors over any part of its seven hundred miles of railroad. *Belleville Advocate*, August 17, 1853; *Chicago Democrat*, February 9 to March 3, 1852; *Free West*, February 9, March 9, 1854.
[13] *Alton Courier*, November 18, 1853.

Temperance agitation at this time found an ally in the antislavery extension propaganda—the enemy of slavery the natural foe of rum. Some even declared that the Nebraska question was of no greater importance than that of the Maine law; in the northern section, temperance conventions nominated the congressional and legislative candidates put forward by the new republican movement.[14]

The anti-Nebraska victory of 1854 was, therefore, more than an anti-Nebraska victory, it was a reform triumph, a temperance victory. The new legislature was a strong anti-Nebraska temperance body, anxious to secure the enactment of the Maine law. The opponents of prohibition hoping to save themselves from certain defeat immediately suggested that any legislation ought to be submitted to the people for ratification. Finally, however, the temperance advocates were able to push to enactment a somewhat ambiguous measure for total prohibition; it provided for a popular referendum, at a special election on the first Monday in June, 1855.[15]

Thereupon an exciting three months' contest began between the Maine law and anti-prohibition forces. Both sides put their full strength into the field. Temperance workers stumped the state, copies of their organs were strewn broadcast, their organizations conducted a systematic campaign with the support of a majority of the regular newspapers. But the opposition revealed strength that was scarcely in accordance with calculations. They used to advantage both the fact that the Maine law had not been successful in the New England states that had given it a trial and that real temperance did not involve prohibition. Morality on compulsion was decried and the revolutionary interference with personal liberty that the law involved, while the farmer was reminded that the law would have a tendency to destroy the market and lower the price of corn. These arguments were used with telling effect in Egypt, in the German stronghold around Belleville, and

---

[14] The *Free West*, the antislavery organ, was one of the strongest temperance journals in the state. *Aurora Guardian*, September 14, October 19, 1854; *Canton Weekly Register*, October 11, 1854; *Free West*, October 5, 1854.

[15] *Alton Courier*, November 20, 23, 1854. Thomas J. Turner, the new speaker, was a "fiery liquor prohibitionist" as well as an "uncompromising abolitionist." *St. Clair Tribune*, January 13, 1855; *Laws of 1855*, p. 3-30.

among the Germans and Irish of Chicago, where some serious riots took place on April 21 and 22, 1855. Anti-prohibitionist papers were started in Chicago and Belleville, and the liquor dealers of Chicago subscribed a large fund with which to fight ratification. As a result the returns of the heaviest vote ever cast in the state shattered the hopes of the overconfident temperance forces. The northern counties lived up to expectations, but their "light" was smothered in what was called by them the "moral and intellectual darkness" of southern Illinois.[16]

This defeat, followed by the general shift of interest to the slavery controversy, took the wind out of the sails of the state wide temperance movement. Local eddies, however, made possible the adoption of prohibition ordinances in various towns and cities. Some victories had already been won in this field. Jacksonville, always a strong temperance center, passed a prohibition ordinance which was tested in the courts and resulted in a decision by the state supreme court in favor of local option without legislative authorization. Springfield had already enacted a prohibition ordinance in 1854; Ottawa, Rockford, Aurora, Joliet, Canton, Macomb, Princeton, and other cities also gave it a trial. All Winnebago county became dry territory.[17] But the general unwillingness to assume responsibility for law enforcement permitted first a stealthy evasion of these ordinances and later complete and open free trade in everything intoxicating with the result that public opinion fell back upon the old license system, under which the old evils continued unabated. Chicago, with some eight hundred liquor dealers organized to defend the traffic, never got any farther than a strict license ordinance. Gradually by the end of the decade, a reaction set in which relegated the cause of temperance into the dim background. Temperance societies were no longer

---

[16] Koerner, *Memoirs*, 1: 622-623; *Illinois Journal*, April 22, 26, 1855; *Aurora Beacon*, April 26, 1855; *Aurora Guardian*, June 14, 1855. The majority against prohibition was 14,447, Illinois election statistics manuscripts; cf. *Ottawa Weekly Republican*, July 7, 1855. The banner county was Winnebago with a vote of 2,163 to 363 for prohibition. The Germans of Chicago held a procession and meeting in celebration of the defeat of the liquor law. *Chicago Weekly Democrat*, July 7, 1855.

[17] *Aurora Guardian*, May 4, 1854; *Rockford Register*, April 9, 1859. Even villages in southern Illinois, including Carlinville, Jonesboro, Carbondale, and Metropolis, caught the contagion and experimented with prohibition. See *Central Illinois Gazette*, June 22, 1859; *Quincy Whig*, July 17, 1854.

heard of; even the "Sons" appeared to have left the field. The churches, formerly silent partners in the temperance movement, found themselves unable to revive interest in the lost cause.[18]

Throughout the struggle by the temperance forces for effective legal action, the more fanatical agitators now and again had recourse to mob action. Many a cask of liquor was absorbed by the thirsty soil when a storehouse was quietly entered and holes were bored into the containers to drain them of their contents. In other instances the work was done boldly and openly; "liquor riots" repeatedly took place in which bands of leading citizens attacked the hated groggeries, destroyed the liquor found on the premises, and threatened the proprietors with personal violence if they did not choose a more honorable calling. Inasmuch as there was a disposition to deplore such fanaticism, however, this work was often left for enraged feminine victims of the liquor traffic. Many an unnamed Carrie Nation came forward to lead her band of followers in a destructive assault upon the offending whisky shops; armed with hatchets, rolling pins, broomsticks, kitchen knives, and fire shovels, they routed the enemy, leaving empty barrels and broken glasses and decanters to decorate the streets.[19] The temperance forces generally extended their approval to such raids regardless of whether havoc was done to the property of licensed dealers or to illicit violators of prohibitory ordinances. This aggressive work of the women attracted more attention than their active and valuable services in the regularly organized temperance movement.

Up to this time the women's rights movement had found its strength largely in the east; Illinois as a western state had been somewhat slow to respond. Now, with the passing of the

[18] Father McGorrisk, the Catholic priest at Ottawa, was a prohibitionist until he made an investigation and found that the liquor sales increased considerably and the establishments increased from twenty to thirty licensed shops in 1855 to 143 illicit doggeries in 1857. *Ottawa Free Trader*, June 6, 1857. See also *Ottawa Weekly Republican*, July 26, 1856, June 13, 1857; *Presbytery Reporter*, 4:89.

[19] *Peru Daily Chronicle*, April 27, 28, 1854. These nineteenth century amazons did effective work at one time or other in Milford, Lincoln, Farmington, Canton, Plano, Tonica, Towanda, Liberty, and Winnebago. *Quincy Whig*, March 27, 1854; *Canton Weekly Register*, March 20, 1856; *Illinois State Journal*, March 25, 1856; *Urbana Union*, March 27, 1856; *Joliet Signal*, June 8, 1858.

frontier, there was an awakening. Men who represented other radical movements of the day had been the first to find courage to present this new propaganda before the public; the versatile H. Van Amringe of Chicago pleaded for woman's rights and listed the cause with land reform and abolition in his lecture repertoire. Next women propagandists took the stage, though at first limiting themselves to discourses to the members of their sex on anatomy and physiology. In 1853, however, Miss Olive Starr Wait, a native of Madison county, and niece of William S. Wait, the Illinois reformer, attracted widespread attention by her lectures on "Women's Rights" in southwestern Illinois. Two years later her lecture route included the state capital. Miss Wait had a happy faculty of presenting her subject in a manner which offended few and attracted many. "For chaste elocution, happy illustration, beauty of diction and depth of pathos, these lectures have been but seldom equaled," wrote a discriminating patron.[20] At the end of 1853 Lucy Stone visited Chicago and then started on a tour of the state on a feminist mission. In the discussion that followed, the removal of legal restrictions on women was advocated and even found supporters in the legislative halls at Springfield.[21]

There was a good deal of confusion as to just what the women's rights movement covered. Few advocated the bestowal of the franchise, and no one included political equality in the matter of officeholding. Admitting a distinct sphere for womankind, the women's rights forces insisted upon the injustice of contemporary legal discriminations as to propertyholding, and in addition claimed those rights, the denial of which would defraud woman's very nature. Confined to the narrow training of the contemporary female seminary or college, shut out of the high schools and colleges, many women labored to secure for their sex equality in education. "Let women be educated," urged one champion, "'Tis her right, not the fashionable education of the boarding school, an education too often, of the head, at the expense of the heart! There

[20] N. M. McCurdy to Joseph Gillespie, December 15, 1855, Gillespie manuscripts. Miss Wait later became the wife of Honorable Jehu Baker.
[21] *Illinois Journal*, January 24, 1853; *Chicago Weekly Democrat*, September 17, 1853.

THE GROWING PAINS OF SOCIETY 213

are five kinds of education which every woman has a right to: intellectual, moral, social, physical, and industrial."[22]

Such advocacy began to have its effect; although Illinois Baptists, like the Reverend R. F. Ellis of Alton, were scandalized at the news that Miss Antoinette L. Brown had been ordained as Congregationalist pastor of South Butler, New York, "in a Baptist house." Yet within five years a Mrs. Hubbard, one of the earliest women preachers in Illinois, was preaching to a crowded house of "hardshell" Baptists in a small meeting house in Madison county.[23]

One off-shoot of the women's rights agitation was the attempt to establish a more sensible costume for women, since it was the feeling of many that woman's inequality grew out of the evils of dress which by ancient custom make "our women feeble when they might be strong," "stooping when they might be straight," and "helpless when they might be efficient." Feminine dress would not permit the vigorous physical exercise which develops superior intellects, and man, thus deprived of the society of women in many of his avocations and diversions, regarded her as his inferior. This was the argument of the dress reformers, whose adherents demonstrated their seriousness in 1851 and again in 1858, when wearers of the bloomer costume, designed by Mrs. Bloomer at New York, made their appearance on the streets of various Illinois cities. For the "Long dangling street sweeper" which had constituted the female dress, there was substituted an abbreviated "skirt," reaching to the "courtesy benders." Bloomer parties were held to keep up the courage of the unterrified who braved the gaze of the curious and the sharp tongues of the town gossips. Many women, safe from the public gaze, enjoyed the convenience which the costume afforded for the performance of housework.[24] Soon, however, the number of conversions

---

[22] *Alton Courier*, January 27, 1854.
[23] In May, 1859, the first class graduated in the women's department of Sloan's Central Commercial College at Chicago, "the first class of ladies who have received a thorough commercial education in the West, if not in the United States," *Chicago Press and Tribune*, May 19, 1859. *Alton Courier*, October 13, 1853; Stahl, "Early Women Preachers in Illinois," Illinois State Historical Society, *Journal*, 9:484-485.
[24] See resolutions of dress reform meeting at Aurora, *Aurora Beacon*, April 8, 1858.

declined; and the traditions of centuries triumphed over the would-be reformers.

With the passing of the frontier atmosphere, the church struggled to hold its monopoly of the sabbath against forces of progress which made it difficult to cease worldly affairs on the seventh day and against a popular tendency toward kinds of relaxation that could not adjust themselves to a puritanical sabbath observance. Many stores and shops kept open doors on Sunday and seemed to take special pains to make as large a display as possible.[25] Sunday railroads, newspapers, and mail service had their beginning. Certain communities took on a gala atmosphere on Sundays; militia companies in uniform paraded to music while companies of young folk spent the day in merrymaking and the patrons of the liquor shops defied all attempts at Sunday closing.

All this offended the upholders of a sturdy backwoods puritanism. An organized movement for sabbath observance had existed in the state for several years; a Southwestern Illinois Sabbath Convention was organized in 1846 and a similar organization existed in the northern part of the state. In May, 1854, a sabbath convention for the entire northwest met in Chicago. These forces had secured the enactment of a state law for sabbath observance as well as many city ordinances prohibiting the sale of liquor on Sunday. They worked with zeal to stay the ever-alarming increase of sabbath desecration in all directions, but especially did they challenge the new encroachments of commercial enterprise. Attention was directed to the alarming desecration threatened by Sunday trains; a sabbath convention met at Chicago in May, 1854, and denounced this danger as more appalling than from any other source.[26] Objection was even made to the running of the Chicago horse railway or omnibus lines. Nevertheless, it became more and more evident that on this score the Sunday

---

[25] *Rock River Democrat,* July 5, 1853.
[26] "If business monopolies set the example, the effect of that example will be to demoralize the country, and destroy the influence of the Bible and its ordinances," declared the editor of the *Alton Courier* who was willing to place the ban on "telling the news, though from the latter good may indirectly result," *Alton Courier,* May 20, 1854; *Free West,* May 25, 1854. Many editors of political journals took the same stand; also *Ottawa Free Trader,* June 18, 1853.

observance movement was an abstraction that could not stay the hands of the clock of time.

The tendency toward democratic Sunday amusement gained headway in the towns and cities. This was especially true of the German element which in the summer months repaired to nearby picnic grounds or Sunday gardens and spent the day in merrymaking. To the Germans of Chicago, who associated with the sabbath not only the idea of religious worship but also the festive holiday atmosphere, the gayety of their Sunday gardens at Cottage Grove or of the Holstein picnic grounds three miles out on the Milwaukee road seemed an inalienable right. On the same principle the Belleville Germans assumed certain privileges in the parades of their military company and of their "gymnastic infidel company" that annoyed their fellow-citizens.[27] The Northwestern Sabbath Convention of 1854 therefore declared that "the vast influx of immigrants joining us from foreign and despotic countries, who have learned in their native land to hate the established religion and the Sabbath law as part of it, calls on us for special prayer and labor in behalf of this portion of our population, to reclaim them from this fatal error."[28] Such reclamation, however, made little progress; the socially-minded westerner, indeed, found an appeal in this new gospel of the joy of life that could not be offset by his own evangels. When, therefore, the German's right to his peculiar form of Sunday observance was threatened, sturdy champions among the native elements of the population came to his aid.

All the efforts of the restrictionists, therefore, seemed to end in failure. With the city clergy clamoring for the rigid enforcement of state laws and local ordinances,[29] conditions in Chicago were described as follows: "Here in Chicago, we have fifty-six churches open on Sunday, during the forenoon and evening, but at the same time, there are no less than eighty ball rooms, in each of which a band plays from morning till

---

[27] *Chicago Daily Times*, September 6, 1857; *Chicago Press and Tribune*, July 14, 1859. Protests were sent to Governor French by William H. Underwood and others under date of September 20, 1851, July 8, 1852, French manuscripts.
[28] *Alton Courier*, May 23, 1854.
[29] *Chicago Press and Tribune*, July 16, 1859.

midnight, and waltzing goes on without intermission. In addition to these festivities we have two theaters, each with its performers in tights and very short garments, rivaling Elsler in their graceful evolutions. Saloons have their front doors closed by proclamation, but do a thriving business through side entrances."[30]

Health conditions in this period reflected the survival of frontier optimism and neglect. Although the traditional ague and fever did not long trouble the pioneer, yet the new conditions of the more thickly settled towns and cities bred disease which spread in epidemics through the community. With back yards, alleys, and streets filled with filth and offal and giving forth a fetid odor, with the environs of the public buildings and stores especially offensive, with market houses strewn with "sheep feet, pieces of decayed meat and vegetables," immunity from disease could scarcely have been expected. Impure and contaminated water supply was the rule, while the children of Chicago and other cities were given the milk from cows "fed on whisky slops with their bodies covered with sores and tails all eat off."[31] Smallpox was a dread visitor liable to appear anywhere during the winter months; vaccination was possible only to a limited degree and was scarcely popular. Hydrophobia was the natural consequence of the packs of dogs that ran at large in the streets—for the city dweller of that day was not able to abandon in urban life the former guardian of the isolated farmhouse and the assistant of the shepherd.

But the pestilence which left behind the widest path of destruction was the cholera, the product of the filth that was accepted as a matter of course in the frontier settlement. A year of special calamity was 1848; cholera, making its appearance in the early spring, came to prevail all over the country and in Illinois decimated the population of many a town and village. Chicago, Springfield, and some of the larger cities under the lead of the local health authorities had taken simple precautions which greatly reduced the fatalities. In the crowded

[30] *Chicago Daily Times,* clipped in *Mound City Emporium,* November 12, 1857; cf. *Chicago Democrat,* May 13, 1858.
[31] *Alton Weekly Courier,* July 27, 1854. Editorial entitled "Why So Many Children Die in Chicago," *Chicago Weekly Democrat,* June 4, 1859. Nine out of every ten quarts of the milk drank in Chicago came from this source.

THE GROWING PAINS OF SOCIETY

portions of the smaller communities the victims were especially numerous. The mayor of Springfield appointed June 28 as a day of humiliation, fasting, and prayer in view of the probable advent of cholera in that city; by July death was so busy in their midst that a state of panic existed among the people of the city. West Belleville lost over fifty out of a population of 350. Where the disease raged at its worst a majority of the population left for the country, and most of the stores were closed, usually all the groceries. Almost everyone felt or affected to feel the unusual depression and other premonitory symptoms of the plague.[32] The streets were empty except for the doctors rushing from victim to victim and the coffin-makers and undertakers, following closely on their heels ready to carry the corpses to the cemeteries. Huge piles of wood were lighted to purify the atmosphere and the smoke hung low on the heavy oppressive air of the prairie midsummer. It was a never to be forgotten year for those who survived the long strain.

In the autumn the dread disease disappeared. Winter seemed to clear the atmosphere; and much of the old carelessness in sanitary matters returned, especially where the losses had not been heavy. As a result Chicago, Galena, and a few centers had serious visitations in the summer of 1850 with heavy mortalities. In 1851 the insidious disease reached into the interior towns of the state, many of which had been previously immune.[33] It presently subsided, however, and in later years reappeared only in isolated cases.

Medical service in the state improved steadily during these years. At the beginning of the decade Rush Medical College at Chicago with a full corps of instructors was turning out new physicians every year; Illinois College at Jacksonville for a brief period attempted medical education with a full medical faculty. In 1855 a Chicago homeopathic school, the Hahneman Medical College, was given a charter; and arrangements were made to open in October, 1860. At the same time Lind University at Lake Forest was organizing a medical depart-

[32] *Western Citizen*, July 31, 1849; Koerner, *Memoirs*, 1: 543-544.
[33] *Western Citizen*, July 30, August 6, 13, 20, 27, 1850; *Chicago Daily Journal*, August 23, September 3, 1850. Galena had fifty to sixty deaths in four days; the total of deaths by cholera in Chicago was 441. S. Sutherland to French, August 19, 1851, French manuscripts.

ment at Chicago. At a meeting in Springfield a State Medical Society was organized in June, 1850. There was a fine spirit of public service in the profession which usually worked incessantly largely on a credit basis. Chicago had a large city hospital under joint allopathic and homeopathic management. Meantime Dr. J. D. Freeman of Jerseyville had undertaken to propagate an eclectic movement throughout the state with an organ, the *Eclectic Advertiser,* "devoted to medical reform — and foreign and domestic news" in which he vigorously attacked the "shocking barbarity" of old school medical practice. The meeting of the Western Dental Convention at Quincy in 1858 also testified to the steady progress of the state away from pioneer conditions.[34]

Out of this vast ferment, in which the bacilli forming reactions of the frontier were furnishing the forces from which a twentieth century culture might develop, the abolition movement stood out most uncompromisingly. A sturdy band of idealists conducted their propaganda in utter disregard of the scorn and hostility of those who upheld the traditions of conservatism and respectability. Ichabod Codding, Zebina Eastman, Philo Carpenter and Charles V. Dyer of Chicago, C. W. Hunter of Alton, Shubal York of Edgar county, A. M. Gooding of La Salle county, and President Jonathan Blanchard of Knox College were a few of the brave spirits who with a transplanted New England idealism coöperated with Owen Lovejoy of Bureau county in maintaining the traditions of the movement of the thirties. Like Garrison and his followers they were thorough radicals, hospitable to every reform that came their way. They were enthusiastic believers in the brotherhood of man: they were champions of world peace and conscientious objectors to all war, they were staunch defenders of the rights of labor, they were advocates of land reform, of free soil as a check upon capitalists and monopolists, they were supporters of women's rights, and they took a leading part in the propaganda for educational reform.[35]

The popular free soil movement of 1848 tended to absorb

[34] *Illinois Journal,* June 5, 1850; Dr. E. N. Banks to French, July 2, 1851, French manuscripts; *Chicago Press and Tribune,* July 13, 1858.
[35] See their organs, *Gem of the Prairie, Western Citizen,* etc.

and obscure the activities of these liberty party men and further to discredit those abolitionists who held aloof, as "bitterenders." Dyer, running as the liberty party candidate for governor in 1848, secured only 4,893 votes while Van Buren polled 15,702. When the free soil movement collapsed in 1850, however, the abolitionists saw their opportunity to reorganize; taking advantage of the general hostility to the fugitive slave law, they framed the protestations of the various churches against that enactment on the basis of the fundamental sinfulness of slaveholding; a preliminary meeting at Chicago on December 9, 1850, opened the way for the organization of the Illinois State Antislavery Society at a convention at Granville on January 8 and 9, 1851.[36] The new movement was launched under favorable auspices; its sponsors promulgated an elaborate constitution and a declaration of principles which asserted that slavery was "a heinous crime against the laws of God and man" and as such should be "immediately repented of and abolished." Soon, however, the conservative reaction under the magic spell of the "compromise" brought about the collapse of the movement in so far as making a successful popular appeal was concerned. In the election of 1852 they found themselves compelled to make a common cause with the free soil remnants but polled slightly less than 10,000 votes. When the Kansas-Nebraska act revived the slavery agitation in 1854, the abolitionists were so discredited that the anti-Nebraska forces in Illinois refused to follow their lead for a new republican party, and only gradually did they work their way into positions of importance in the party that raised Lincoln to the presidency.[37]

In spite of the popular odium which prevented abolitionists from securing political control, they did wield an indirect influence upon the old parties by compelling them in northern Illinois districts to take more advanced antislavery ground. On account of the abolition leaven, too, the conservatives were never able to undermine the influence which their more liberal colleagues derived from this source. Indeed such shrewd politicians as John Wentworth, Jesse O. Norton, E. B. Washburne,

[36] *Western Citizen*, December 17, 24, 1850, January 21, 1851.
[37] Eastman, *History of the Anti-Slavery Agitation in Illinois*.

and others, who led boldly for freedom when the public mind was favorable but insisted on a strict party regularity until they definitely abandoned the old parties for the republican organization, openly advocated many propositions which were usually looked upon as the peculiar monopoly of the uncompromising abolitionists.[38]

With the growing importance of the slavery issue and with the serious moral issue raised by the abolition forces, the religious organizations furnished one of the most effective fields for abolition propaganda. As the national organizations had wrestled with this question and found it the rock upon which they had split into northern and southern wings, so within the state the fight was taken up by contending factions in almost every denomination. The clergy in general came to be divided into an antislavery camp and into a party that abhorred the menace of abolitionism.

Episcopalians believing that the conservative spirit of their church was one of the great bonds that held together the union, steered a safe noncommittal course between the Scylla of slavery and the Charybdis of abolition. The Methodist church in Illinois prided itself on its solemn and earnest protest against the evil of slavery and pointed to its vigorous anti-fugitive slave law resolutions; nevertheless, at the same time it acquiesced in the sanction of the institution in the slaveholding states to such an extent that zealous antislavery members from the northern part of the state demanded a separation of the church "from its criminal connection with slavery."[39] Most Congregational, Baptist, and Unitarian churches were controlled by elements unequivocally committed to abhorrence of the institution of slavery; they even formally adopted "higher law" ground in their denunciation of the fugitive slave law. The Western Unitarian Conference at Alton in May, 1857, almost unanimously adopted a strong antislavery report following the secession of the protesting St. Louis delegation.[40]

The old school Presbyterians continued along the lines of

---

[38] Eastman, *History of the Anti-Slavery Agitation in Illinois*.
[39] *Illinois Journal*, August 1, 2, 1855; *Chicago Tribune*, October 25, 1860.
[40] *Western Citizen*, November 5, 12, December 3, 1850; *Free West*, May 25, 1854; *Chicago Daily Democratic Press*, May 21, 1857.

their traditional conservatism and refused to give consideration to any form of the slavery question. Within the new school group there were many who sought to proclaim the wickedness of slaveholding and, in view of the vacillating policy of the general assembly, to effect a general withdrawal or separation from that body. A free Presbyterian organization with a constitution declaring slavery a sin against God, had been formed in 1847 out of seceders from both the old and new school bodies; to it were attracted many earnest antislavery men in Illinois whose convictions of duty threw them out of sympathy with the religious groups to which they belonged. Two free Presbyterian churches existed in Illinois in 1851, at Paris and Bernadotte.[41]

Most Illinois new school Presbyterians deplored the workings of the whole system of slavery as it existed in this country; they were divided, however, on the proposition to refuse the hand of the fellowship to the slaveholder in order "to free the Presbyterian church from all participation and communion with slaveholding."[42] Conservatives within the group even suppressed in their official publication antislavery resolutions agreed upon as a result of the persistence of the radical antislavery members. This issue led the synod of Illinois in 1849 to consider the expediency of withdrawing from the general assembly. The presbytery of Ottawa decided not to send commissioners until an unequivocal non-fellowship declaration was made. The presbytery of Illinois in session at Pisgah September 20, 1856, petitioned the general assembly to proclaim slaveholding "as *prima facie* evidence of unfitness for church membership," and several other presbyteries took the same stand in the following year.[43] The abolition group in the Third Presbyterian church in Chicago precipitated this issue in the spring of 1851 and carried a resolution declaring that as long as the unsatisfactory policy of the general assembly on this issue continued, the church would "stand aloof from all meetings of Presbytery, Synod, and Assembly

[41] *Western Citizen*, December 17, 1850, January 28, 1851.
[42] *Ibid.*, November 13, 1849.
[43] Reverend Lemuel Foster protested such suppression by the Alton presbytery in his little paper, *The Truth Seeker*, Alton, July, 1848; *Western Citizen*, January 8, 1850; *Presbytery Reporter*, 3:356, 504; 4:28.

and thus .... free and relieve itself of all responsibility." The pastor, a strong antislavery man but a stauncher Presbyterian, appealed to the presbytery which declared that the members who voted for the resolutions had disqualified themselves to act as members of the Presbyterian church and thus expelled a majority of the members of the church. The expelled members thereupon arranged to organize themselves into a Congregational church, the first to be organized in Chicago.[44]

An important figure in these church controversies over slavery was President Jonathan Blanchard of Knox College; convinced that "the heart of action in the Church" was the missions, he declared that from them "the foul spirit of Slavery must be dislodged before it will be *cast out of the Church*."[45] Accordingly, beginning in 1847 he had led a fight at the annual meetings of the American Board of Commissioners for Foreign Missions in favor of refusing to receive slaveholders into the mission churches. This fight he kept up until hope was abandoned that the American board would relinquish its partnership with slaveholders. Then the Illinois Wesleyan Missionary conference commended the uncompromising opposition to slavery of the American Missionary Association and urged affiliation with it instead of the formation of rival missionary societies among antislavery christians. President Blanchard showed, however, that the American Missionary Society and similar denominational organizations permitted the membership of slaveholders; antislavery Baptists even felt compelled to organize the American Baptist Free Mission Society. In July, 1852, therefore, a group of uncompromising opponents of slaveholding fellowship met at Chicago and formed the Free Mission Society for the Northwest. For the same reason the Western Tract Convention was organized in 1859 out of antislavery seceders from the conservative American Tract Society.[46]

This struggle tended to break down the denominational barriers that separated the christian antislavery forces. With

---

[44] *Western Citizen*, February 11, May 6, 20, 1851.
[45] *Ibid.*, March 18, 1851; see also issues of August 21, 1849, July 29, 1851.
[46] *Ibid.*, March 25, June 24, September 2, 1851, June 1, July 20, 1852, *Chicago Democrat*, October 19, 1859.

THE GROWING PAINS OF SOCIETY

the prevailing "adoption of the doctrine of expediency as a substitute for the law of Christ," [47] churchmen could not but feel at times that the slavery issue was of more importance than sectarianism. A state convention to consider the union of the Illinois Congregationalist associations and new school presbyteries was called in 1850 with the approval of Dr. Blanchard and a number of prominent clergymen, including the Reverend Flavel Bascom, pastor of the First Presbyterian church of Chicago, and L. H. Loss of the Third church of that city. But this movement, intended to "deliver those of us who are Presbyterians from our ecclesiastical connection with slaveholders, through the General Assembly, and enable us to withdraw Christian fellowship from them without incurring the charge of violating ecclesiastical constitution by so doing," [48] brought results.

Non-sectarian energy was in the end largely absorbed in the Christian Antislavery Convention which held a national meeting at Cincinnati in April, 1850. A Chicago meeting in preparation for the convention drew considerable support from prominent clergymen and laymen, and a large delegation was sent to Cincinnati. A Christian Antislavery Convention for northern Illinois met at Ottawa in May, with an adjourned session in September, to effect a permanent organization of all Illinois christians who believed in non-fellowship as the only proper christian position to assume toward slaveholders. The first regular semiannual meeting was held at Granville, Putnam county, in January, 1851. Dr. Blanchard and other Illinoisians on the general committee appointed by the Cincinnati convention arranged for the next interstate meeting at Chicago, July 3-5, 1851. Blanchard was chosen to preside over an enthu-

[47] *Western Citizen*, January 22, 1850. There were also direct apologists for slavery in the religious groups. C. H. McCormick, the reaper manufacturer, tried to counteract the antislavery tendencies in Chicago Presbyterianism. *Rockford Register*, October 3, 1857. The Chicago *Prairie Herald*, established in 1846 by J. B. Walker, a professed abolitionist, was taken over in 1851 by a new editor who published articles to show that slaveholding of the worst description was practiced by members of the first christian churches and that neither Christ nor his apostles denounced it. As a result many of the subscribers of the *Prairie Herald* shifted their support to the *Christian Era*, edited by Reverend Epaphras Goodman. *Western Citizen*, March 18, August 12, 26, 1851.

[48] *Ibid.*, January 21, 1851; Moses and Kirkland, *History of Chicago*, 2: 332-333.

siastic session of 250 delegates which the regular papers passed over as a meeting of fanatics and enemies of the country. The Illinois delegation consisted of 130 persons, of whom 60 were Congregationalists, 29 Baptists, and the rest scattered between a half dozen denominations. The only Chicago clergyman who actively participated in this meeting was Reverend A. M. Stewart of the Scotch Presbyterian church. A western branch of a similar organization known as the League of Universal Brotherhood was founded in Illinois and during its brief existence seemed to find favor with the Methodists of the state.[49]

The Christian Antislavery Convention disappeared from existence during the conservative reaction after 1851; but in October, 1859, it was revived at a general meeting in Chicago as the Northwestern Christian Antislavery Convention. Again Blanchard was a leading figure, calling the convention to order and explaining his support of the republican cause as nearer the truth than any other. By this time the activities of antislavery leaders were no longer unpopular, and the convention was regarded with favor by the spokesman of the growing republican party.

When the voice of protest came from the pulpit at the passage of the fugitive slave law and of the Nebraska bill, the democratic press and politicians began to deplore the tendency of the clergy to leave their sacred calling and enter into political strife. "When ministers enter the arena of politics, and associate themselves with the corrupt and lying hypocrites who lead the black republican party, and utter seditious harangues from the pulpit, they are no longer entitled to that respect which their sacred calling commands," declared the *Joliet Signal*, when four of the local clergy participated in a republican ratification meeting as vice presidents. Such a challenge did not, however, reduce the zeal of the antislavery clergymen for the republican cause. Many a radical abandoned altogether his aversion to mingling in politics. While the Covenanters of Coulterville were unable to enter politics or to

[49] *Western Citizen*, February 5, April 2, May 7, August 13, 20, 1850, March 18, June 17, July 8, 15, 29, December 30, 1851; *Ottawa Free Trader*, June 1, 15, 1850.

do more than lend their moral support to the cause of freedom, the Shakers of Lebanon held that when freedom was at stake, it became a duty to let their votes be given in its defense.[50] It was thus that many a black-frocked emissary of freedom found courage to spread the gospel of republicanism even to the remotest corners of Egypt.

Illinois of 1850 had a Negro population of 5,436, a persecuted group which increased to 7,628 by 1860. This increase was in large part the normal expansion of a fairly prolific race. Although the border slave states had a large free Negro population which they would gladly have seen transferred to Illinois, the state was after 1853 legally closed against Negro immigration, whether free or slave. Although no additions were made to the "black laws" of the state in the way of imposing further disabilities upon the Negro population, yet in the constitutional convention of 1847 there had been adopted after a struggle a provision which instructed the legislature to pass laws prohibiting the immigration of colored persons. This section was separately submitted to the people for ratification and was adopted by a vote of 50,261 to 21,297, the opposition coming chiefly from the northern counties. The state legislature did not act, however, until the session of 1853 when a drastic act was passed which provided for a heavy fine for every Negro bond or free who entered the state; in default of payment the Negro was to be sold at public auction to the person bidding the shortest period of service in return for the payment of the fine. The antislavery forces in the legislature were outnumbered nearly two to one and were impotent to do more than amend the bill to provide for jury trial.[51]

On the merits of this measure which the *New Orleans Bee* declared "an act of special and savage ruthlessness," public opinion in Illinois was divided. In spite of its defense by the *Register*, the central democratic organ, as just and necessary for the state to protect itself against the pauper, vagrant, and vagabond blacks who for twenty years had overrun the

[50] *Joliet Signal*, April 4, 1854, June 17, 1856; *Cairo City Times*, October 24, 1855; *Rushville Times*, September 5, 1856; *Illinois State Register*, January 7, 1857; William Edgar to Trumbull, January 27, 1857, Trumbull manuscripts; *Illinois State Journal*, October 13, 1856.
[51] *Public Laws of 1853*, p. 57-60.

southern part of the state, many democrats vigorously joined the whig press in assailing the law. The *Ottawa Free Trader*, claiming that it would establish a peon system more heartless and cruel than southern slavery, declared: "We should like to see the man that would mount the auctioneer's block in this town and sell a freeman to the highest bidder, and we should like to see the bidder." Less than a half dozen journals openly and unequivocally indorsed the law. Asked the *Jonesboro Gazette*, a democratic sheet published within thirty-five miles of Cairo: "How long will the people of this hitherto 'Free State' suffer this shameful enaction to disgrace their statute book?"[52]

There was a widespread feeling that the law was unconstitutional; some said that it could not be enforced against a hostile public opinion. The law was applied, however, to various cases; and Negroes seeking homes on the prairies of Illinois were put upon the block and sold to the highest bidder. In 1857 a free mulatto named Jackson Redman was arrested in St. Clair county and found guilty of violating the act of February 12, 1853; legal notices were accordingly posted up about the streets of Belleville offering Redman for sale at public auction. Only the interposition of Gustave Koerner, the German republican leader who advanced the sum of $62.50 to cover the fines and cost, saved the victim from the clutches of the black law. Such cases generally aroused widespread indignation, although apologists were to be found; D. J. Van Deren, the editor of the *Mattoon Gazette*, even advocated the reëstablishment of slavery in the state as preferable to the possibility of extending to the Negroes political and social equality.[53]

Sympathy for the Negro, whether the southern slave or the northern victim of the black laws, was aroused by the publication of *Uncle Tom's Cabin* in 1852. Hundreds of copies of every edition were avariciously consumed by interested Illinoisians. Proslavery sympathizers sneered at this "higher

---

[52] *New Orleans Bee* clipped in *Morgan Journal*, April 28, 1853; *Illinois State Register*, February 24, 1853; *Illinois Journal*, March 1, 1853; *Ottawa Free Trader*, February 26, 1853. Cf. *Galena Jeffersonian* clipped in *Quincy Whig*, April 11, 1853; *Alton Courier*, April 14, 1853.
[53] *Joliet Signal*, March 1, 1852; *St. Clair Tribune*, April 17, 1857; *Belleville Advocate*, April 22, 1857; *Chicago Daily Democratic Press*, August 6, 14, 1857.

revelation of an abolition prophetess," but the friends of the Negro in Illinois were inspired to undertake the work of securing for them equal rights before the law. In spite of ill-success bills were constantly introduced into the legislature to allow Negroes to testify in the courts, to abolish the distinction between Negroes and whites in the public schools, to repeal all laws making distinctions between the races. None of these propositions, however, received the necessary support. Public men of the day, nevertheless, were timid about the Negro question; many members of the republican party even were frightened by the specter of "Negro equality" paraded by their opponents. When in 1857 the Joliet *True Democrat* came out in favor of extending the right of suffrage to the colored men of Illinois, many republican organs bolted for cover, while others refused to commit themselves.

Northern Illinois was much more charitable to the Negro than Egypt. Race hatred often broke out in southern towns; in 1857 people of Mound City undertook to drive out all Negroes. Only in Chicago did the colored people display any aggressiveness in defense of their rights. There they held mass meetings and sent a delegate to the Colored National Convention at Cleveland in 1848; they urged that the black code be repealed to wipe out this injustice. In their Chicago Literary Society they openly condemned the fugitive slave law and the black law of 1853, urging the repeal of both. They even organized to protect each other from being borne back to bondage under the operation of the fugitive slave law, and in 1860 a colored military company was formed in Chicago. Although a state colonization society had an active existence in Illinois, receiving support from the leaders of all political parties, a colored people's convention at Chicago in 1853 rejected the idea of colonization in all its forms; in the closing years of the decade, however, the proposition of emigration to Hayti received considerable support from them.[54]

The Negro population of the state dwelt in true humility in obscure corners of the towns and cities, with their own

[54] *Mound City Emporium*, August 6, 1857; *Gem of the Prairie*, September 23, 1848; *Chicago Democrat*, October 9, 1850, June 20, 1851; *Illinois State Register*, November 6, 1853; *Central Illinois Gazette*, August 18, 1858; *Chicago Press and Tribune*, April 26, 1859.

churches and sometimes separate schools maintained with the assistance of white patrons; only now and then were appeals made for aid in purchasing the freedom of relatives in the south. The tranquillity of the black men's domicile was disturbed by kidnappers and slave hunters. Cases of kidnapping and carrying off of free Negroes were fairly common in the southern part of the state, where organized bands of kidnappers operated boldly under the knowledge that the Negroes would not be admitted to the witness stand. Matters became so bad in Cairo that the mayor called out the citizens to break up the operations of a local gang of armed kidnappers, who worked in league with a band of Missourians.[55]

In 1848 in the case of Illinois v. Sherman Thurston and Thomas Field, Judge H. T. Dickey of the seventh judicial circuit had declared unconstitutional the section of the code defining kidnapping as criminal. Fortified by the fugitive slave law of 1850 Missouri slave hunters made their appearance in Negro settlements in northern Illinois creating a panic among even the older colored residents, many of whom fled to Canada for protection; United States Marshal Benjamin Bond and his successors pursued various fugitives to Chicago only to find that their victims had been secreted or hurried off to safety in the Queen's dominion. While the law took its course in downstate communities, it became generally recognized that in the hostile atmosphere of Chicago, the Illinois terminus of the underground railroad, execution of the fugitive slave law was impossible except at the muzzle of the musket. When in June, 1851, a Negro resident of Chicago was forcibly arrested and claimed as Moses Johnson, a fugitive slave belonging to a Missourian, the city was alive with excitement. Special constables were created, and five companies of militia called out. A surging tide of humanity surrounded the hall in which the trial was carried on, contemplating a rescue if the case went against the alleged fugitive. The commissioner who conducted the trial, however, discharged the prisoner, and the pent up energies of the crowd found a harmless safety valve in the celebration of his release. Cases of fugitives being snatched from the custody of the officers were rather frequent, Negroes

[55] *Cairo Weekly Times and Delta*, July 29, 1857.

often constituting the rescuing parties; republican city officials winked at these affairs and treated them as good jokes. Meanwhile the conductors of the underground railroad were busily forwarding their human freight from the south on to Canada and freedom. Even consignments of fifteen and twenty passengers were successfully dispatched to their destination.[56]

The most famous rescue of the period was the Ottawa case in which a group of leading citizens on October 20, 1859, participated in the rescue of a fugitive from the custody of the United States marshal.[57] Seven of the rescuers were promptly indicted by the federal grand jury; John Hossack, one of the most prominent of the group, was tried first and found guilty by the federal district court. In October, 1860, he and his associates were given small jail sentences as well as fines. Even the republicans acknowledged an obligation to the constitutional guarantee; it is interesting to note that "the jury who convicted Hossack under the Fugitive Slave law, stood *Eight* Republicans and *Four* Democrats and were not over two hours in making their verdict."[58] The republican state central committee refused to involve itself in the case financially; but Mayor Wentworth of Chicago assumed responsibility for the payment of the fines and directed a popular subscription for the payment of the costs of the case so as to hasten the day of the prisoners' release. The local democracy washed their hands of this instance of mob violence so that the case played an important part in the closing weeks of the campaign for Lincoln's election.

[56] *Gem of the Prairie*, October 7, 1848; *Western Citizen*, November 5, 1850, June 10, 1851; *Chicago Democrat*, June 4, 5, 6, 7, 1851, October 10, 1859, *Chicago Daily Journal*, June 7, 1851; *Aurora Guardian*, December 7, 14, 1854; *Chicago Weekly Democrat*, January 6, 1855; *Chicago Democrat*, October 10, 1859.
[57] *Ottawa Free Trader*, October 22, November 5, December 31, 1859.
[58] "I was on the jury myself and know how hard it was to vote against my prejudices." Isaac R. Hitt to Trumbull, December 17, 1860, Trumbull manuscripts.

X. CHURCH AND SCHOOL, 1850-1860

DURING the fifties the foundations of a democratic educational system were firmly laid in Illinois. At the beginning of this decade, although the state boasted eighty-one private schools, the public school was lacking in many towns and cities; and in none of the rural regions, not even the counties of northern Illinois into which New England settlers were transplanting their township system and their ideal of free common schools, were there adequate educational facilities. The 1848 report of Secretary of State H. S. Cooley, *ex officio* superintendent of common schools, presented an incomplete list of 2,002 schools with an enrollment of 51,447 pupils.[1] Several of these, however, were private or select schools; at that time Chicago alone had nineteen and two years later about thirty, although only four public schools existed to justify its claim for generous provision in this field. Springfield likewise supported its quota of private schools, but nobody seemed disposed to push the matter of establishing a system of common schools.

In 1850 the federal census takers encouraged the advocates of public schools with a list of 4,054 schools and an attendance of 125,790; at the same time they fostered a wholesome concern over the illiteracy returns: 41,283 persons over 20 years of age were found who could neither read nor write, seven-eighths of whom were native born Americans. These, it was noted, were mainly residents of southern districts, the counties south of Springfield having three-eighths of the schools and five-eighths of the illiteracy. Not a single school or academy was to be found in such older communities as Logan, St. Clair, and Wayne counties, where true Egyptian darkness prevailed.

Public opinion was being prepared for the work of the coming decade. An "Illinois State Educational Society" was

---

[1] Superintendent of Public Instruction, *Report*, 16:clxvi; *Aurora Beacon*, May 31, 1849; *Alton Telegraph*, June 22, 1849.

organized in a protracted series of meetings in the winter of 1846 and 1847 in which resolutions were passed in favor of alteration of the school law and of the appointment of a superintendent of public instruction. The editors of the state were requested to devote a portion of their columns to "the deeply interesting and important subject of common school education."[2] Thomas M. Killpatrick, president of the society, was authorized to act as its agent in imparting and receiving information on the subject of schools in the absence of a state superintendent. He went about the state lecturing on the needs of the state along educational lines; and the second annual meeting of the society at Springfield, January 15, 1849, attracted wide attention to its aggressive program.[3] Local and county meetings to promote interest in education came to be held in various parts of the state at which permanent educational associations or societies were organized.

Some of the more prominent educators in the state, among them President Jonathan Blanchard of Knox College and the Reverend Francis Springer of Springfield, were brought out on the lecture platform. Professor Jonathan B. Turner of Jacksonville College, a minister and practical farmer, began to loom up as a prominent figure in this educational propaganda. He was already attracting state wide attention with a pet scheme for a state agricultural or industrial university, which received the support of the farmers and of many practical business men. The teachers, however, condemned this "wildcat" scheme as a "worse than Utopian dream," and centered their attention on a state normal school, at the same time trying to kill Turner's hobby by having professorships of agriculture established in the colleges of the state. But either faction, it was argued, could build only upon an efficient common school system, toward which the first step should be the creation of the office of superintendent of public instruction; the result was an agitation which bore fruit in the public school laws of 1854 and 1855. Matters came to a head in the winter of 1853 and 1854. At

[2] *Sangamo Journal*, April 29, 1847.
[3] *Illinois Journal*, September 29, 1848, January 26, 1849, July 25, 1850; *Gem of the Prairie*, October 14, 1848, January 6, 1849; *Beardstown Gazette*, October 25, 1848; *Rockford Forum*, January 3, 1849; *Illinois State Register*, January 23, 1849; *Aurora Beacon*, February 15, 1849; *Prairie Farmer*, March, 1849.

a common school convention at Jerseyville, December 19, 1853, arranged by Turner and his followers, he, as chairman of the committee on resolutions, presented a program which, except for its mention of a state industrial university, was everything that the strongest supporters of educational facilities could desire. On December 26 the leaders of the school teachers assembled a convention at Bloomington; after a struggle between the normal school advocates and the industrial college minority the meeting adopted resolutions for the establishment of a state normal school, of a state educational journal, and for the appointment of a state superintendent of public instruction; after the adjournment of the convention, a state teachers institute was organized to meet in annual session.[4]

The pressure of public opinion was now sufficient to secure legislative action. In the constitutional convention of 1847 the friends of educational reform had secured a favorable report from the committee on education, but the proposed article presented by John M. Palmer was finally defeated in the open convention. Since that time the assembly had enacted a few items on education, beginning with the act of April 13, 1849; the general trend was to make it easier to secure by taxation the funds necessary for the establishment and maintenance of public schools.[5] A bill to create the office of state superintendent passed the house in 1849 but failed in the senate. Finally, however, in a proclamation calling the special session of February 9, 1854, Governor Matteson included the proposition "to amend the school law and provide a superintendent of common schools for the state." After various propositions for a general free school system supported by a public tax had been defeated, a law was passed providing for an elective superintendent to hold office for two years commencing in 1856—a temporary appointee of the governor to serve until the election in November, 1855. Meantime, according to the law, this officer, Ninian W. Edwards, drew up a bill providing

[4] *Peru Daily Chronicle*, January 5, 6, 7, 1854; official proceedings in *Alton Courier*, January 3, 1854; Superintendent of Public Instruction, *Report*, 16: clxxvi-clxxix.
[5] *Journal of Convention of 1847*, p. 352-353; *Laws of 1849*, p. 153-179; *Laws of 1851*, p. 127-130.

for a general system of free schools which was presented at the next session of the legislature. Edwards recommended the use of the township as the unit for school purposes, with the township directors to combine in a county convention to elect a county superintendent; the legislature, however, retained the district system. Important gains, however, were made in the provisions for a state school tax, for unlimited local taxation, and for a free school in every district for six months in the year.[6]

This law was passed by the representatives of northern Illinois in spite of opposition from most of Egypt. St. Clair county, however, unanimously supported the proposition because of the popularity of education among the Germans there, led by men like George Bunsen, school commissioner of St. Clair county, who was later appointed a member of the first state school board. The wealthier northern counties of the state wanted education badly enough to pay more than their share for it; they proved this to the south by arranging the distribution of the two mill tax on the compound basis of population and territory—two-thirds according to the school children and one-third according to the number of townships. Some of the northern counties received less than half what they contributed, while southern counties doubled their contributions. This consideration, reënforced by the complaints from northern districts of the unfair distribution of the state funds, reconciled many parts of Egypt to the law, and the school fever began to carry all before it.[7]

The law, however, was criticized by Superintendent Edwards as containing many obscure and unjust features. On February 16, 1857, therefore, in the face of attempts to repeal the statute, an amendatory act was passed which cleared away many obscurities and added certain necessary details. In the

[6] *Laws of 1854,* p. 13-15; *Laws of 1855,* p. 51 ff. The supporters of J. B. Turner in a convention at Macoupin, February 24-25, recommended his appointment as state superintendent; he was regarded by many, however, as too visionary and too destructive in his interests. *Alton Courier,* March 9, 1854.

[7] Orwell Sexton to Trumbull, June 1, 1858, Trumbull manuscripts. In certain particulars it worked hardships in southern Illinois, because of the difficulty of getting teachers and of continuing the schools for the six months period required. See P. Knowlton to William H. Powell, September 22, 1857, and reply, *Illinois State Journal,* October 14, 1857.

same session provision was made for the establishment and maintenance of a state normal university, which was promptly located at Bloomington.[8]

Under this encouraging legislation, rapid strides were made. In 1850 poorly trained teachers conducted a large share of the few schools that existed, and the terms were often only three months. Two-thirds of the school buildings were log houses and only one-fifteenth brick or stone. Many of the rest were shanties or temporary shacks. The average worth of 21 school buildings in Stark county was $65. But in the two years of service of William H. Powell as superintendent for 1857 and 1858 three thousand schoolhouses were built, bringing the total well over 8,500, nearly two thousand school districts were organized with a total enrollment of 440,339, making only 1 child of school age in 15 not in attendance; the average school term was now six and five-sixths months.[9]

Considerable improvement was also made in the caliber of the teaching staff. Before 1850 almost anyone with a superficial knowledge of the most common and necessary branches of education was accepted for service. Under the new laws, however, prospective teachers had to pass examinations showing qualifications for the teaching of all the seven branches named in the laws. County commissioners found this work of examining candidates especially burdensome because so few were able to come up to the requirements. "It is a common occurrence for persons to apply who have taught school for years, and cannot answer the simplest questions, such as children twelve years old ought to answer, and generally can answer readily," wrote a conscientious commissioner.[10]

There was at all times a dearth of available teachers in the west. A considerable percentage of those already engaged were New Englanders or easterners, and in view of the growing demand the National Educational Society through their

[8] *Illinois State Register,* March 20, April 3, 1856; Superintendent of Public Instruction, *Report,* 2: 52-68; 16: cxcii; *Laws of 1857,* p. 295 ff.
[9] Cook, *Educational History of Illinois,* 85-86; Superintendent of Public Instruction, *Report,* 2: 8-9, 68-69.
[10] *Ottawa Free Trader,* May 3, 1851; N. H. Abbott to French, March 11, 1852, French manuscripts.

agent, ex-Governor Slade of Vermont, sought to transfer to the west well-trained classes of eastern young women as missionaries in the cause of education. In the period after 1847, when Slade secured the coöperation of the Illinois Education Society in the work of securing places for his protégés, he made regular visits to the state, bringing sixteen young women to Illinois in 1847 and eighteen in 1848, thirty per cent of the entire number sent west. The fourteenth class of teachers was sent west in September, 1853, and the work continued through the decade. The complaint of western advocates of education was that the young women were not brought on fast enough and that "instead of teaching other folk's children, [they] soon find employment in teaching their own."[11]

This importation of teachers naturally aroused objections from various quarters. Certain democratic politicians, including the great Douglas, who came to Illinois himself as a Vermont Yankee schoolmaster, pointed out the danger that these selected emissaries of abolitionism would try to convert the youth of Illinois into the likeness of "canting" "freedom-shrieking" New England demagogues.[12] Moreover, Secretary of State Cooley in his educational report of 1851 suggested that such teachers were bound to bring in a spirit of condescension growing out of their lack of sympathy with western habits, customs, and feelings. In both instances such ungenerous criticism proved unwarranted but furnished an argument for a local supply of teachers. The colleges of the state were heavily drawn upon but were never able to supply the demand, nor were their graduates specifically trained for the teaching profession. This situation finally led to the founding of a normal school at Bloomington, but the decade closed while its first classes were preparing for graduation.

In spite of the limited supply, teachers continued to be entirely too meagerly compensated, although salaries nearly

[11] *Illinois Journal*, November 28, December 1, 1848; *Illinois State Register*, December 2, 1851, August 4, 1853; Superintendent of Public Instruction, *Report*, 16:clv ff. It was found that they made excellent wives and mothers, two-thirds of them settling down to domestic life before a period of five years elapsed.
[12] *Belleville Advocate*, February 18, 1857; *Ottawa Free Trader*, March 15, 1851.

doubled during the decade, averaging in the case of male teachers about $35 a month. For financial reasons the general prejudice against "female teachers" began to decline, as they never received much more than half what was given to men. With the increasing professional spirit among Illinois teachers, county institutes were organized and in some places were aided by county appropriations. The State Teachers' Institute was organized at Bloomington in December, 1853; in accordance with its decision an educational publication entitled the *Illinois Teacher*, edited by members of the institute, made its appearance in 1855. From the outset it exercised an important influence on educational thought.

Higher education made some notable gains during the decade. Public high schools were established at Chicago, Ottawa, and Canton, though voted down as premature in Quincy; school associations undertook to provide similar facilities in Petersburg, Belleville, and other towns. A general act for the incorporation of academies and seminaries of learning became a law in February, 1851; academies and seminaries increased in number and improved in the facilities offered to their patrons.[13] The old established colleges of the state were in such a prosperous condition, especially the denominational schools, that many friends of education came to believe that the time when it was necessary for the state to foster a college had forever passed. Illinois College at Jacksonville suffered a $25,000 loss by fire in 1853, but the amount was replaced by local subscription and the institution continued out of debt with a generous endowment; $50,000 was added to its resources as a result of a two years campaign started in 1858. Shurtleff and Knox colleges were the other more flourishing older institutions — Knox with buildings and grounds worth $120,000 being "said to be the third institution of learning in point of wealth, in the United States."[14]

[13] The *Ottawa High School Journal* was published by the schools of that community, *Ottawa Free Trader*, May 16, 1857. A gymnasium was provided for the boys of the Chicago high school. *Chicago Press and Tribune*, May 27, 1859; *Laws of 1851*, p. 85-87.
[14] *Alton Courier*, January 19, 1853; Sturtevant, *Autobiography*, 274-276; *Quincy Whig*, January 17, 1853; *Presbytery Reporter*, 4:304; 5:284-285. See J. Blanchard to Turner, October 19, 1848, Turner manuscripts; *Chicago Daily Democratic Press*, July 14, 1857.

No less than two dozen institutions of higher learning were incorporated in the period from 1848 to 1860, of which six or eight succeeded in becoming permanent colleges. Illinois State University was the ambitious name of a Lutheran institution incorporated and located at Springfield in 1852, to replace the Lutheran college at Hillsboro; it started out inauspiciously, however, in spite of the able administration of its president, Reverend Francis Springer. Several other ambitious undertakings struggled along to final success. Illinois Wesleyan University, incorporated in 1853, began to get in running order by the close of the decade. Northwestern University was incorporated on January 28, 1851, as a Methodist educational enterprise. A site was selected on the lake front eleven miles north of the city of Chicago, and a university was planned which they hoped would become the equal in every respect of Yale and of Harvard, with a law department and biblical institute. Efforts at the start were confined to the department of literature, science, and arts. This promising enterprise was slow in getting started; instruction opened on November 5, 1855, with a faculty of two and hardly more than a dozen students, and two years elapsed before Reverend R. S. Foster assumed charge as president.[15] On January 30, 1857, the old University of Chicago was incorporated. Senator Stephen A. Douglas was able to subserve his own interests in land speculation and at the same time to pose as a patron of learning by offering to contribute ten acres of his holdings in the suburb of Cottage Grove to the projected Baptist University in Chicago on the condition that a fund of $100,000 should be raised for the erection of a college building and the endowment of the institution. Douglas was just then under fire from the republicans for denouncing the opposition of the clergy to his position on slavery. On July 4, 1857, the corner stone of the main building was laid; Reverend J. E. Roy in his prayer sent up a petition "for our poor colored brethren in bondage, even though Judge Douglas himself is present among us;" and I. N. Arnold, the orator of the day, a zealous republican leader, delivered an antislavery address taking

[15] Wilde, *Northwestern University*, 1:166-168.

exception to the policies of Douglas, who was seated near him on the stand. But with his surrounding lots increased in value some $20,000 by the location of the new building, Douglas could afford to remain silent amid these evidences of ingratitude.[16] Born in this atmosphere of political controversy and delayed by the financial crash of 1857, the university opened in temporary quarters; but under the aggressive leadership of President William Jones a department of law was organized and went into operation in the fall of 1857, shortly after the dedication of the new buildings. For many years the university led a precarious existence and did not find a place among the more important educational institutions of Illinois.

Many of the traditional earmarks of college life began to appear as the increasing attendance at all institutions brought together larger groups of students. Rates of tuition and living expenses were generally very moderate; a collegiate education could easily be acquired at from $80 to $100 a year. This was possible because the faculties were groups of patient, long-suffering, philanthropic enthusiasts serving for a bare living; McKendree College, the oldest institution in the state, paid to the instructors of eighty students, in house rent and in salaries, less than $1,500 a year. Other institutions made more generous compensation for teaching, but were frequently in arrears. Although the professors were said to be hard taskmasters, making excessive demands for intellectual work and turning out dyspeptic looking graduating classes, the students had the requisite physical energy for the traditional affrays with local town boys.[17]

The strong New England atmosphere of educational circles and the idealism of the instructional staffs made the colleges of the state hotbeds of antislavery feeling. Reverend Howard Malcolm was elected president of Shurtleff College, the Baptist institution in Upper Alton, after he had been compelled to resign the presidency of the college at Georgetown, Kentucky, because of having voted in favor of the gradual abolition of slavery. President Blanchard of Knox was one of the most

---

[16] *Our Constitution*, July 11, August 22, 1857; *Ottawa Free Trader*, July 11, 1857; *Rock River Democrat*, August 11, 1857.
[17] *Chicago Daily Journal*, January 11, 1850; *Alton Courier* clipped in *Chicago Weekly Democrat*, July 29, 1854; *Alton Courier*, February 21, 1854.

CHURCH AND SCHOOL 239

active abolitionists in the state. In 1848 he took part in the campaign as elector on the free soil ticket and engaged in other antislavery activities that finally aroused one of the conservative professors to organize a party in the board of trustees, of which he was himself a member, to oust Blanchard from the presidency. A stirring contest took place, with the board nearly evenly divided; but the fortuitous vacancy of six places in that body gave opportunity for adding six "good, honest, upright antislavery men" to safeguard Blanchard's position for the future. President J. M. Sturtevant of Jacksonville College took the stump in 1856 for Fremont and "bleeding Kansas;" the entire faculty there, notably Professor Jonathan B. Turner, were aggressive antislavery men. In 1857 they went so far as to expel a student who persisted against the advice of one of the professors in giving a political anti-republican address upon a public occasion. This, however, seemed too much like a sacrifice of that freedom of utterance that these educators claimed for themselves, too much like the prostitution of education to partisan politics.[18]

With the growing general interest in education, attention had turned to the rapidly accumulating "university and seminary fund" reserved out of the income from the federal land grant of 1818. By 1850 it had reached nearly $150,000, and there was a general demand that practical use be made of the money. The denominational colleges proposed that this fund be divided among them and that they be erected into a university subject to the visitation and control of a board of state regents, recommending honorary degrees "to be conferred by

[18] *Alton Telegraph,* September 21, 1849; *Illinois State Register,* April 8, 11, 1857; Sturtevant, *Autobiography,* 279-282; also Turner manuscripts. J. Blanchard to Salmon P. Chase, June 30, 1849, Chase manuscripts. The *Illinois State Journal,* April 15, 1859, undertook to justify the faculty declaring that "the tendency of the teachings of all our Colleges was to Republicanism," that almost all men of letters were republicans; "do you propose to fill the professorships with bogtrotters from Tipperary, in the same way that you fill the Police and the Post Offices?" it queried. Blanchard resigned in 1858 and after two years of pastoral work accepted the presidency of Wheaton College. This institution founded by the Methodists was in 1860 transferred to Congregational control by the election of a majority of orthodox Congregational members of the board. "This was done," according to Blanchard, "on condition that their testimonies against slavery and secret societies should be kept good, which condition has been faithfully fulfilled by the present Board." *Chicago Tribune,* April 2, 1867.

the University of Illinois in conclave assembled."[19] This arrangement, which would have a state as well as a collegiate dignity, was preferred to the placing of the fund at the disposal of any existing college or to the erection of a new competing institution. In furtherance of such an arrangement the college heads met at Springfield in the fall of 1849 and 1850 to influence legislation. President Blanchard of Knox College proposed that a common school professorship for the education of teachers, and perhaps an agricultural professorship, might be annexed to the various colleges out of their respective shares in the funds.[20]

The establishment of chairs of agriculture were proposed largely to offset the propaganda carried on by that exemplary democrat, Jonathan B. Turner of Jacksonville College, in favor of a state agricultural or industrial university. As a veteran student of the educational needs of Illinois, he claimed that the existing system of collegiate education was entirely unadapted to the needs of the industrial classes who comprised over ninety-five per cent of the entire population of the state: the colleges virtually shut out the mass of the people and, like Oxford and Cambridge, confined the advantage of a liberal education to the few. Turner proposed that, in addition to the usual branches, the system of education should be adapted to the particular callings of the industrial classes, especially that of the agriculturists. In October, 1850, he brought his plan to the attention of Governor French and suggested that he be given an opportunity to address the legislature on the subject.[21]

Turner soon secured a favorable hearing from a large portion of the people of the state and organized an active propaganda to secure the authorization of his project. He was a prophet without honor in his home city of Jacksonville; neither of the rival local papers gave him any real support. The *Morgan Journal* edited by Dr. E. R. Roe, later teacher in the

[19] See Richard M. Young to French, November 23, 1849, E. Wentworth to French, December 13, 1847, June 23, 1849, French manuscripts; see also *Illinois State Register*, April 14, 1848.
[20] J. Blanchard to French, December 23, 1850, French manuscripts; J. Blanchard to Turner, October 19, 1848, Turner manuscripts.
[21] Turner to French, October 11, 1850, French manuscripts; French to Turner, January 29, 1851, Turner manuscripts.

state normal university, vigorously attacked Turner while professing to approve of his main purpose of educating the masses in a thorough manner. Nothing daunted, he went about the state spreading his gospel through lectures, addresses, and contributions to the various newspapers and periodicals. His active campaign was opened November 18, 1851, in a convention at Granville which urged the establishment of an industrial university. Turner's hand was plainly visible in this move: he was made chairman of the committee which reported the resolutions that were adopted, he unfolded at length his plan for the establishment of the proposed institution, and he was placed at the head of a central committee appointed to call a general state convention of the friends of such an institution.[22]

In spite of this propaganda Governor French, a friend and supporter of McKendree College, but a believer in agricultural education, recommended the division of the university funds among the several colleges in his message of 1852; but the house committee refused to report in favor of any specific disposition of the money. The second industrial convention met at Springfield June 8, 1852; some of the opponents of the scheme attended, notably Professor John Evans of Chicago, one of the founders of Northwestern University, Dr. E. R. Roe of Jacksonville, and Professor Cummings of Lebanon College; but the aid of men like John A. Kennicott of Chicago, who was selected to preside over the convention, and William H. Powell of La Salle, its secretary, had been enlisted in favor of the plan; and a resolution to memorialize the legislature for a state industrial university was successfully passed. But opponents appeared on all sides among the friends of existing collegiate institutions; John M. Peck pronounced Turner's theory a "wild project," "fascinating, but impracticable and useless." The great need of the day, it was held, was more academies and common schools; enough colleges already existed; farmers, moreover, would not send their sons to one great central school; as to state schools, had

[22] *Morgan Journal*, January 10, 1852; *Illinois Journal*, February 12, November 29, 1851, January 3, 1852; *Prairie Farmer*, February, 1852; Turner, *Plan for an Industrial University for the State of Illinois.*

they not always proved wasteful and imbecile as to literary instruction?[23]

In November, 1852, another industrial university convention assembled at Chicago, and again preparations were made to place Turner's plan before the legislature. A committee consisting of Turner, L. L. Bullock, and Ira L. Peck was appointed to address the citizens of the state in its favor, while a memorial to congress asking for a grant of public lands to aid in the establishment of an industrial institution was later prepared by a committee headed by ex-Governor French. The convention adjourned to meet at Springfield on January 4 after the legislature convened. Meetings of farmers and mechanics were called at various points to be represented at this session; and delegates were present from Buel Institute, La Salle County Agricultural Society, the Northwestern Pomological Association, and other groups. An "Industrial League of the State of Illinois" was organized to disseminate information by lectures, articles, and other literature.[24]

The idea of federal aid by a land grant had been promulgated by Turner in an article in the *Prairie Farmer* of March, 1852, and had been taken up by the Springfield convention three months later. It became thereafter the most unique feature of the Turner plan for industrial education. Indeed, the only immediate result of this agitation was the adoption of a resolution by the legislature asking congress to appropriate 500,000 acres of lands to each state to aid in the establishment of an industrial university. Turner and his associates in this enterprise, moreover, entered into extensive correspondence with leaders in other states with the view of securing their coöperation for united action on the part of the states to secure such a donation of public lands from the federal government. Representative Washburne presented the Illinois resolutions in congress in April, 1854. Representative Richard Yates from the Springfield district, who had in 1851 and 1852 brought Turner's plan to the attention of the United States patent office and of the National Agricultural Society, now

---
[23] *Prairie Farmer*, April-August, 1852; Peck to French, June 7, 1852, French manuscripts. The *Eclectic Journal of Education* of Chicago opposed Turner's plan.
[24] Incorporated February 10, 1853, *Laws of 1853*, p. 514; Turner manuscripts.

CHURCH AND SCHOOL 243

prepared to secure congressional action and requested Turner to draft a bill. The industrial league, meantime, kept up an active propaganda; Dr. R. C. Rutherford was engaged to bring its proposition before the people of the northern counties; and Turner was induced to give his energies entirely to the lecture field for several months, beginning December, 1853. An informal indorsement was secured from a mass meeting of the Illinois State Agricultural Society on October 6, 1854. Another convention was held at Springfield in January, 1855; its committee, in consultation with legislative committees, prepared a bill which gave every promise of adoption when it was discovered that as a result of defalcation the treasury was exhausted and the measure had to be postponed.[25]

The advocates of orthodox education and the supporters of the existing colleges continued to wage an unrelenting war on this proposition. . Many lukewarm advocates of educational reform, moreover, were satisfied with the educational legislation of 1854 and 1855 and, with excitement increasing over slavery, shifted their interest to this new field. Some champions of the common people tellingly pointed out that the industrial league had a "monstrous scheme" which would stratify class lines and permit the favored few to be trained to do the thinking of the nation, while the masses, the "common trash," would be trained for the performance of their drudgery. Many denominational school teachers argued that the state was "incompetent to control the subject of education," that this was the function of the church.[26] Others like State Superintendent Edwards ignored the federal land grant proposition and objected to the use of state funds as involving heavy taxation, since the college and seminary funds had

[25] *Illinois Journal*, June 9, 1852, February 18, 1853; Carriel, *Life of Turner*, 104, 110-111; *Free West*, November 2, 1854; *Prairie Farmer*, May, 1855. Bronson Murray of Ottawa, who was president of the Third Industrial Convention at Chicago, had suggested the organization of the league and generously contributed to its support. Yates to Turner, June 25, 1852, April 14, 1854, Turner manuscripts. See Turner and Murray manuscripts.

[26] *Macoupin Statesman* clipped in *Ottawa Weekly Republican*, December 30, 1854. The *Joliet Signal*, however, dropped its support of the industrial university because it feared that the advantages would be restricted to the wealthy as it could not accommodate more than four hundred or five hundred students, *Illinois State Register*, February 9, 1854. George Lumsden to Murray, February 16, 1853, in Carriel, *Life of Turner*, 131-133.

already been borrowed by the state and used for other purposes. Some opponents professed to be opposed not to the proposition *per se* but to the employment of state funds upon a mere experiment. The *Chicago Democrat* was warmly interested in agricultural education but urged a totally different scheme; it proposed an agricultural college supported by an endowment of scholarships given by farmers, in sums of one hundred or one hundred and fifty dollars; two thousand scholarships would provide an annual income of $14,000, "a sum fully capable of sustaining an able and sufficient corps of professors in all the branches of science relating to agriculture, and of defraying existing expenses." [27] A Northern Illinois Agricultural College was chartered on February 12, 1853, by a group of Putnam county backers, but the proposition fell stillborn.

All these forces combined to make the local situation unfavorable for action by the state government. After 1856 less popular discussion took place, although Turner and his friends continued their activities. The new republican governor, William Bissell, in his message of January, 1857, displayed a favorable attitude toward the future establishment of an agricultural university. Interest, however, was now transferred to the national government, where the effort was to secure federal aid. The aid of a large number of educators, journalists, and politicians throughout the country had been enlisted in support of the scheme; a definite league was now organized to bring pressure to bear upon congress. In order to avoid encountering the ill-feeling of easterners, who had already come to regard with dismay the large grants to western states for school and other purposes, it seemed wise to arrange for the introduction of the proposition by an eastern representative. For this reason Representative Morrill of Vermont was induced to father a land grant measure for the endowment of an agricultural college in every state in the union. Its advocates had the disappointment of seeing the bill pass both houses of congress, only to meet the veto of President Buchanan on Feb-

---

[27] *Prairie Farmer*, January, 1855; *Chicago Daily Democratic Press*, January 9, 15, 23, 1855; *Chicago Weekly Democrat*, July 15, September 16, 1854, July 28, 1855; *Private Laws of 1853*, 407-410.

ruary 26, 1859. Three years later, with the nation torn by civil discord, the measure was again carried through congress and became law with President Lincoln's signature on July 2, 1862. So long a time had elapsed, however, since the project had first taken form that few of the participants in the legislation connected this important measure with the tireless activity of Jonathan B. Turner in the early fifties in behalf of an Illinois industrial university. Such, however, was the origin of a measure which has determined the nature of a large number of the higher educational institutions of this country; it was an "Illinois idea," or, as John A. Kennicott enthusiastically declared after its introduction in congress, " Illinois thunder." [28]

With this period of Illinois history came other refinements of modern civilization. Encouraging signs began to appear in the religious life in the state. The total number of churches had increased by 1850 to 1,223 and in the next decade exactly doubled, although the value of church property increased more than fourfold. The Chicago of 1850, with twenty-six institutions representing almost every denomination from Catholic to Swedenborgian, freethinkers to orthodox Jews, was known as the "city of churches." At the end of another decade the city had 61 Protestant churches with an attendance of over ten thousand, besides 59 sabbath schools and 31 mission schools. Quincy, a city of seven thousand, had 16 churches with 2 others in contemplation. Galesburg with a population of about five thousand in 1855 had 9 churches; three Presbyterian, one Baptist, one Congregational, one Universalist, one Lutheran, one Methodist, and one Swedish Methodist.[29]

Every denomination had a proportionate share in this growth with the exception of the Baptists and Presbyterians, who, however, with sixty per cent increases were able to retain their respective second and third places. The Methodists,

[28] Turner to Trumbull, October 7, 1857, Kennicott to Trumbull, January 25, 1858, Trumbull manuscripts; Trumbull to Turner, October 19, 1857, Turner manuscripts. It was first introduced December 14, 1857, *Congressional Globe*, 35 congress, 1 session, 32, 36-37.
[29] *Chicago Democrat*, September 19, 1848, May 4, 1849; *Chicago Daily Journal* clipped in *Illinois State Register*, December 25, 1849; *Presbytery Reporter*, 5:128. Eight hundred and ten dollars was paid for a single pew in the Second Presbyterian church of Chicago, *Western Citizen*, December 31, 1850. See also *Quincy Whig*, March 9, 1852; *Chicago Daily Democratic Press*, April 15, 1856.

increasing the number of their churches from 405 to 881 with a membership of nearly one hundred thousand in 1860, maintained their lead. Methodism in the west, however, still suffered from the neglect of the central organization; not a bishop, newspaper, or book-room had been provided by the General Conference for the Mississippi valley. The Illinois Conference recovered, however, from the slump of the forties and with the younger Rock River Conference enjoyed an active existence. The denomination was still influenced by the untiring energy and uncompromising antislavery conviction of its great leader, Peter Cartwright.[30]

The Baptists of the state, doubling in number in the decade, continued to be the radical force they had been in previous decades, even though the new generation of leaders showed no names comparable to those of James Lemen and John Mason Peck. In spite of strong southern ties, the church showed a pronounced antislavery leaning, which, together with an aggressive part in the temperance agitation of the day, continued to make a strong appeal to the democratic yeoman of Illinois. The Baptist organ, the *Western Christian*, published at Elgin but removed to New York about 1850, had a wide influence; it was radical, reformative in spirit, and democratic. The Christian churches, that most typical and at the same time most unique expression of the western pioneer spirit in religion, increased from 69 in 1850 to 148 in 1860; enthusiasm was inspired by the western tour in 1853 of the Reverend Alexander Campbell, the founder of the denomination, who filled a large number of Illinois appointments.[31]

The Presbyterians by their divisions gained attention which offset the energy lost in dissension. The radical wings established their devotion to freedom without challenge, although at times small groups left the denomination entirely because of the bitterness of their reactions. The census of 1860 returned 43 Cumberland, 18 Reformed, and 27 United churches as against 272 in the main camp. The total membership of all groups was 15,810.

[30] *Minutes of the Annual Conference of the Methodist Episcopal Church*, 4:486-490, 524-529; 5:654-659; *Free West*, May 31, 1855.
[31] *Alton Courier*, October 31, November 1, 1853; Moses, *Illinois*, 2:1077-1078

The heavy influx of the New England element brought numbers of Congregationalists into Illinois. In the thirties an agreement between eastern Congregationalists and the Presbyterians had arranged for the affiliation of Illinois Congregationalists with Presbyterian institutions; after a time, however, the Congregationalists abandoned this policy and began to establish congregations under their own name. The number of churches increased in a decade from 46 to 140; this registers the important growth in the northern tier of counties through which the membership more than doubled and reached the figure of 12,849. Not until April, 1851, was a Congregational church established in Chicago; then the first in the city was organized by the repudiated antislavery majority of the Third Presbyterian Church, most of whom had New England Congregational antecedents. Two other congregations were organized in Chicago during the decade. The Illinois association remained a sturdy upholder of orthodoxy in religion, if not in politics, and in 1859 excommunicated Reverend J. Mason of Hamilton for denying the doctrine of the trinity and the eternity of future punishment.[32] Members of this denomination were reached by the *Congregational Herald* of Chicago.

The strength of the Lutherans lay largely in the Germans and Scandinavians who settled in and around Chicago and Illinoistown.[33] Chicago added a Swedish Lutheran church in 1853 to the German and Norwegian congregations formed a half dozen years earlier. Some members of these Lutheran groups, however, withdrew to support Evangelical churches.

The Episcopal church maintained only a few dozen clergymen in the state in 1850, under the supervision of the pioneer Bishop Philander Chase; Chase died in 1852 at Jubilee College after having seen the parishes of his diocese increase from six to fifty-two. Five of the churches were located in the city of Chicago, one of them in a Scandinavian parish.

[32] *Illinois State Register*, January 6, 1860. Jonathan B. Turner in the same year accepted the challenge of the Reverend James C. Richmond of Milwaukee to defend Congregationalism against the doctrines of the Episcopal church. *Chicago Press and Tribune*, May 24, 1859.
[33] William H. Pickering to Gillespie, July 20, 1860, Gillespie manuscripts.

Bishop Chase was succeeded by Henry J. Whitehouse, who had been assistant bishop for a year. About fifty-two clergymen were in active service in the state in 1860, with forty-six churches numbering 3,070 communicants. The church was not in a healthy condition; several parishes including Palestine, Grove, Beardstown, Peoria, and Edwardsville, had to be stricken from the roll as deficient; several large rural parishes were vacant; and a heated controversy was waging between Bishop Whitehouse and low church critics who attacked him as "teaching Tractarian and Semi Romish Errors."[34] In 1858 the low church party set up an organ in Chicago, the *Western Churchman*, to combat the influence of the official publication, the *Chicago Herald*.

The Catholic church was gaining steadily in the larger cities from the heavy immigration of Irish and foreign Catholics. The Right Reverend James Oliver Van de Velde was installed as successor to Bishop William Quarter as bishop of Chicago in 1848, but gave way five years later to Bishop Anthony O'Reagan; neither of these, however, aroused the enthusiastic coöperation of the clergy or laity. The see of Quincy was established in 1852, followed in 1857 by the erection of the episcopate of Alton. At the close of the decade the Catholics established the *Western Banner* as their organ at Chicago.

Contrary to expectations, the less orthodox and more liberal denominations were showing, especially in the Yankee settlements, some ability to move westward with the pioneer. Eight Unitarian groups with four churches existed in 1850 and seven Universalists; the *New Covenant*, a successful Universalist publication, was established at Chicago in 1848. By 1860 liberal religion had spread in the cities to an extent that eleven Unitarian[35] and thirty Universalist churches were located by the census enumerators.

Religious activity, however, was largely confined to the

[34] Smith, *Life of Philander Chase*, 339-340; *Aurora Beacon*, October 25, 1860; *Illinois State Register*, July 27, 1854; *Chicago Record*, November 1, 1858; *Church Record*, January 1, September 15, October 1, 1859, August 15, November 1, 1860.
[35] *Alton Courier*, October 22, December 13, 1853; *Illinois State Journal*, July 1, 1857.

towns and cities. In the smaller communities there were often no church edifices and the various congregations alternated in the use of some public building. In Beardstown, the courthouse was the common place of worship; the Episcopalians conducted their services in the morning, the Presbyterians worshipped in the afternoon, while the Methodists took their turn in the evening; it was noted that about the same constituency was present at each meeting. A church at Joliet was occupied alternately by the Universalists and the Baptists. In other places societies labored zealously to secure funds for their own houses of worship. An occasional congregation was distinguished by the possession of a parsonage. Regularly educated and well-trained ministers were very rare in the west; generally speaking there was always a shortage of ministers, partly because of the expanding field of activity and partly because the rural congregations of the western states were almost continually in arrears with the salaries of their pastors. Many congregations were wholly without provision for regular preaching; but the humble and zealous itinerant preacher, the pioneer in the work of evangelizing the frontier, reached a large constituency by going his round among the sparse population. Dr. Cartwright, the quaint and fearless pioneer clergyman, was at the age of seventy years still stationed at Springfield, duplicating some of the feats of his prime. On one occasion he rode through almost incessant rain for ninety-four miles, preached to numerous congregations, and "received as quarterage 'fifteen cents,' and by way of table expenses, a dozen large apples." Since the great mass of the community were never seen inside of the churches, Chicago Methodists commissioned a city missionary to return to apostolic usages; soon an extensive system of street preaching was organized.[38]

A more far-reaching remedy was the provision of facilities for the education of a supply of specially trained religious

---

[38] *Illinois State Register*, April 28, 1853; Illinois State Historical Society, *Transactions*, 1901, p. 61-62. The West Urbana Congregationalists granted the use of their new church to the Baptists on Sunday afternoon and later shared their minister with the new school Presbyterian congregation. Graff, *The Record of Fifty Years*, 9. *Church Record*, December 1, 15, 1859; *Illinois Journal*, December 28, 1848; *Christian Review* clipped in *Ottawa Free Trader*, March 22, 1851; *Chicago Democrat*, August 22, 1859; *Autobiography of Peter Cartwright*.

leaders. The Northwestern Biblical Institute at Evanston, later the Garrett Institute, was inaugurated by the Methodists, January 1, 1855;[37] and after a few years it was attached to Northwestern University. The Chicago Theological Seminary was organized under Congregational auspices in 1854 and formally opened in October, 1858, while the Presbyterians in 1857 incorporated and erected Blackburn Theological Seminary at Carlinville; in 1859 McCormick Theological Seminary was located at Chicago. New school Presbyterians of the northwestern states started a project for a theological seminary at Galena which, like a proposition for a Baptist theological seminary for the northwest, bore no immediate fruit.

The Young Men's Christian Association made its way into Illinois during this period. The association was organized in Springfield in 1853 and soon had desultory beginnings in Peoria, Chicago, Quincy, and Rockford. The Chicago Association, permanently organized in 1858, provided a free reading room and arranged a series of lectures for each winter. This movement was greatly strengthened by taking advantage of a decided tendency upon the part of the young men of the cities to organize for their intellectual and moral improvement.

The large field for missionary work in Illinois was recognized by all religious denominations, most of which had formally accredited representatives in this field. The American Home Missions Society and the American Missionary Association had their agents in Illinois, but the positions were unattractive because of inadequate compensation. The missionaries, moreover, worked almost entirely in communities of fair size and left the rural regions practically untouched.[38] These were reached, however, by the agents of the American Bible Society and by the *colporteurs* sent out by the American Tract Society.

Local Bible societies were formed in the cities in the period after 1840 when the Chicago society was organized; active work, however, came largely in the period after 1848, commencing in the northern portion of the state. Before 1860

[37] *Chicago Weekly Democrat*, January 6, 1855.
[38] Reverend Joseph Gordon, the Presbyterian missionary for the Alton presbytery in one year preached 136 sermons, converted 25 new members, and traveled, 5,574 miles. *Presbytery Reporter*, 3:503; cf. *ibid.*, 4:74.

one hundred and six county Bible societies and eight hundred branch societies had been organized under the direction of Amasa Lord, general agent for the state; they acted through about 5,000 agents who without pay made personal visits to every house in their respective districts carrying the Bible with them.[39] Illinois was the second or third state in the Bible cause. Remittances from Illinois to the central treasury of the society were nearly equal to the total remittances of the six surrounding states; over $40,000 per annum was raised in the state by donations and sales.

In a somewhat different fashion the American Tract Society through its paid agents reached into the state from outside. The *colporteurs* dealt with precisely the same conditions as the agents of the Bible Society but attempted a somewhat more intimate religious contact with the people, making what were in many cases practically pastoral visits, the time being occupied in religious exhortation often accompanied with prayer. A sincere effort was often made to check intemperance, sabbath breaking, and general tendencies toward immorality; Illinoisians, however, frequently resented the highly colored tales of prevailing immorality and religious indifference that *colporteurs* incorporated in their letters to eastern publications.[40]

Although violent religious emotionalism was becoming more and more rare, the camp meeting and revival continued; in the closing weeks of the dreary Illinois winter, revival meetings began to be held in almost every country meeting house to continue until the arrival of Easter. It was an annual event on the religious calendar of the state. In the early part of 1858, however, an unusual spiritual awakening was perceptible throughout the country. Revival meetings attracted an unusual community wide interest, and a remarkable number of conversions was reported. Large daily union prayer meetings were held at Springfield, at Canton, at Metropolitan Hall in Chicago, and in other places. The freedom from sectarianism and the perfect cordiality with which the preachers and laymen of the different churches labored seemed remarkable;

[39] *Belleville Advocate*, March 25, 1857; *Rockford Register*, March 10, 1860.
[40] *Illinois State Register*, May 12, 1853.

another feature was the freedom from the extravagancies and the wild excitement that had usually attended such awakenings. Only in the little community of Avoca did the meetings produce the phenomenon known since the beginning of western revivals as the "jerks;" there about a hundred young persons were affected, producing the most ludicrous scenes. "Just imagine," said an eyewitness, "forty or fifty persons going through all the different postures, twistings, bendings, strikings, kickings, and other violent motions of which the human frame is capable, together with occasional barking and other unusual sounds, and you will have a faint idea of the scene exhibited here night after night."[41] When the general excitement was over and the statistics were calculated, it was found that Illinois with 10,460 converts was second only to New York in its share in the great awakening.

[41] *Chicago Daily Democratic Press,* March 16, 1858; see *New York Courier and Enquirer* clipped in *Illinois State Journal,* June 9, 1858.

XI. THE APPEAL TO ARMS

LINCOLN'S election was interpreted by southern fire eaters as a defiance of their threats to withdraw the planting states from the union in order to work out southern nationality in a separate confederacy. Disappointed democrats in Illinois could not forbear pointing out the phases of republican policy which seemed to justify an aggressive move from the south to protect its rights. "It is not worth while to conceal the fact, *that the North is hopelessly abolitionized,*" declared the *Belleville Democrat*. "*To submit* then, or *secede*, is forced upon the South. . . . Thus far, they have *justice* and right on their side. . . . We cannot see how they will ingloriously submit."[1] Even the *State Register* seemed to take the position set up by the southern disunionists that a state had the right to secede without infringing seriously any of the powers delegated in the constitution, while sympathy with the secession idea was especially strong in the southern counties. The *Cairo Gazette* sought to clear up all misunderstanding by announcing: "The statement that the inhabitants of Egypt are in favor of the perpetuation of the Union by force, is unauthorized. No such feeling exists. On the contrary, so far as our observations have extended, the sympathies of our people are mainly with the South." Since there was considerable evidence that the south was already putting into practice a non intercourse policy, the *Gazette* stopped to consider the effect of secession upon the future of Cairo and arrived at the conclusion that it would prosper whether the union was dissolved or not.[2]

Some republicans were prepared to support Greeley's recommendation to "let the erring sisters depart in peace." To

[1] *Belleville Democrat* clipped in *Belleville Weekly Advocate*, November 16, 1860; see also *Ottawa Free Trader*, December 8, 29, 1860.
[2] *Illinois State Journal*, November 21, 1860; *Cairo Gazette*, December 6, 20, 1860.

certain admirers of fundamental democracy, the south seemed to be claiming the rights of small nations to self-government; coercion, therefore, whether of the state or of individuals involved an offense to the conscience of the American people, which, according to the *Rockford Register*, "would be found to be as much opposed to the exercise of arbitrary power over a subjugated province, as they are to the transformation of this government into a slave-holding despotism. If a separation must come, let it be a peaceful one. Let all states that deliberately desire to go out of the Union, be permitted to do so in peace."[3] Such a radical antislavery man as the Reverend G. W. Bassett of Ottawa, issued a pamphlet entitled "A Northern plea for the right of secession" in which he maintained the "absolute and unqualified right of the people of any State of this Union to dissolve their political connections with the General Government whenever they chose." The *Belleville Advocate* would have been willing to relieve the union of the petulance of South Carolina and of the financial encumbrance of Florida, but, "believing it unwise and dangerous to admit in practice what we deny in theory," the best policy seemed to be to require those states to obey the will of the nation.[4]

The general body of Lincoln's supporters rallied to the task of preserving the union from the storm that was gathering upon the horizon. It devolved upon them to prove that the republican party was the party of the union. They reminded each other of the wisdom of restraint in the flush of victory, in order to convince the people of the south by their words and acts that they were not half so fierce and ravenous as represented, that they could be gracefully generous to a vanquished foe. The enforcement of the fugitive slave law was conceded as one of the rights to the enjoyment of which the south was justly entitled. At the same time they insisted on being "true to the North—true to themselves—true to the

[3] *Rockford Register*, December 8, 1860, March 16, 1861; A. W. Metcalf to Trumbull, December 18, 1860, Trumbull manuscripts.
[4] *Belleville Weekly Advocate*, December 14, 1860; *Ottawa Free Trader*, March 2, 1861. After the outbreak of the war Bassett delivered a sermon in the courthouse at Ottawa, which was later published, in which he again advocated the right of secession, and declared that "our country is at present engaged in an unjust and unholy war." *Ibid.*, September 28, 1861.

THE APPEAL TO ARMS

great interest of free labor — true to Republican principles."[5] If, then, the southern states insisted upon a disruption of the union in violation of the fundamental laws upon which the constitutional superstructure of the nation had been built, republicans would plant themselves upon Andrew Jackson ground and exhaust every resource for the enforcement of the laws. They made it clear that they understood that the constitution did not and could not operate directly upon the states; "it has to do with the people — with individuals."[6] "The Union, it must be preserved — execute the laws," was the republican rally cry.

In their rejection of compromise and concession these republicans were prepared for a test of arms. "I am in favor of 20 years of war," wrote one of Trumbull's correspondents, "rather than the loss of one inch of territory or the surrender of any principal [sic] that concedes the right of secession, which is the disruption of the government." "Petitions are circulating rapidly for a reorganization of the militia and everybody is signing them" announced Horace White. "We live in revolutionary times, and I say God bless the revolution!"[7]

Republican leaders held council as to the course of action required of them by the crisis. President-elect Lincoln took up quarters at the governor's office in the statehouse and held conferences in which were shaped the policy of constitutional rights for the south without compromise. The Illinois delegation at Washington promptly after the opening of the session assembled and unanimously resolved that "the Union must and shall be preserved."[8] Governor Yates, knowing that, as the governor of Lincoln's state, his views would have a special significance in the public mind, took counsel with men of wider political experiences as to the content of the inaugural address.

[5] *Illinois State Journal*, December 15, 1860; *Chicago Tribune*, November 8, 1860.
[6] *Ibid.*, December 20, 22, 29, 31, 1860. Gustave Koerner drew up an elaborate article to prove that there could be no constitutional right of secession; this was sent to the *Missouri Democrat* and widely circulated in the Illinois press and in pamphlet form. Koerner, *Memoirs*, 2:108; Koerner to Trumbull, December 10, 1860, Trumbull manuscripts.
[7] W. H. Hanna to Trumbull, December 19, 1860, Horace White to Trumbull, December 30, 1860, *ibid.*
[8] *Chicago Tribune*, December 19, 1860.

Entering on his duties as governor January 14, 1861, he insisted in a lengthy address upon the perpetuity of the union and declared that "the whole material of the government, moral, political, and physical, if need be — must be employed to preserve, protect and defend the constitution of the United States." Democrats and republicans, alike could not but believe that the document, produced under the nose of the president-elect, had a special significance in forecasting the policy that would obtain with Lincoln's inauguration.[9]

Compromise and concession found so few supporters in republican circles that the ranks of the party were thrown into consternation when news came from Washington that early in January William Kellogg, member of congress from the Peoria district, had introduced a compromise measure, involving amendment of the constitution. Kellogg's lead was bitterly denounced in public and in private by the controlling element in the republican ranks; and his followers, indignantly repudiating the proposition, assembled in convention to read him out of the party. To such republicans the word "compromise" soon became an "accursed" term which they regretted had never been eliminated from the English language.[10]

Although democrats were naturally more hospitable to the idea of preserving the union by compromise, yet on January 16, when a state convention met at Springfield to settle upon a policy for the party to pursue, it was revealed that party leaders were divided between advocates of strong union ground, followers of Congressmen John A. McClernand and Isaac N. Morris, and secession sympathizers like General James W. Singleton. Six of the latter were given places on the resolutions committee; the convention, however, agreed upon a platform advocating any plan of conciliation and compromise by which harmony might be restored, denying the constitutional right of

[9] Yates to Trumbull, December 21, 1860, Trumbull manuscripts; *House Journal*, 1861, p. 102; *Joliet Signal*, January 22, 1861.
[10] *Peoria Transcript*, February 9, 1861; *Joliet Signal*, February 26, 1861; *Aurora Beacon*, February 7, 1861; *Illinois State Journal*, June 24, 1861; J. H. Smith to Trumbull, January 7, 1861; A. P. Bartlett to Trumbull, February 9, 1861; J. H. Gallatin to Trumbull, February 11, 1861, Trumbull manuscripts. President Sturtevant of Illinois College held that rather than sacrifice principle to the union, it would be better that "the Union should be dissolved than made such a Union as the South intends to make it." J. M. Sturtevant to Trumbull, January 30, 1861, *ibid*.

[From photograph in possession of Mr. Richard Yates, Springfield, Illinois]

secession, and urging the limitation of military authority to the assistance of the civil authorities in the execution of the law. Republicans interpreted this as "an echo of the false and detestable position of southern traitors." Democrats, however, declared that it followed their illustrious leader, Stephen A. Douglas, in offering to concede and sacrifice everything to save the union.[11]

Senator Douglas, who had promptly joined the ranks of the union men after the news of Lincoln's success and his defeat, was laboring energetically to end the national crisis by an appeal to the spirit of compromise; he urged all loyal Americans to discard party lines and unite to save the country from impending disasters. As member of the joint committee of thirteen appointed to prepare measures of adjustment, he not only supported the Crittenden compromise and all other propositions based on the principle of mutual concession but submitted a plan of his own applying the doctrine of nonintervention and popular sovereignty. The republicans, on the one hand, however, persisted in their firm adherence to the Chicago platform while the secessionists, on the other, showed a disposition to reject even the opportunity to dictate all the terms that would enable them to continue within the union.

A mass of secession problems came before the general assembly when it convened on January 7. The state of Virginia had proposed the appointment of commissioners by the several states to meet in convention at Washington to consult about a peaceable settlement of the difficulties between the states. Leading republicans held a series of caucuses to deliberate on this matter; Lincoln, who stood firm against any concessions to the south, advised against any action by Illinois which would suggest that the state desired any constitutional changes. Even after Governor Yates was asked by the governors of Ohio and Indiana whether Illinois would appoint commissioners, Lincoln urged no action. "Lincoln said that he would rather be hung by the neck till he was dead on the steps

[11] *Illinois State Register,* January 17, 1861; *Chicago Tribune,* January 19, 1861; *Rockford Register,* January 26, 1861; *Joliet Signal,* January 22, 1861; Koerner to Trumbull, January 21, 1861, Trumbull manuscripts.

of the Capitol before he would beg or buy a peaceful inauguration."[12] Finally it became evident that provision for sending commissioners was a matter of political necessity "because if we had not united to do so, some of our knock kneed brethren would have united with the democracy, and would have given them sufficient strength to have carried the resolutions appointing by the General Assembly." Lincoln and Yates both opposed the step but, once taken, Yates gave the appointments, mostly of persons named by Lincoln, to ex-Governor John Wood of Quincy, Judge Stephen T. Logan of Springfield, Gustave Koerner of Belleville, and Congressman B. C. Cook of Ottawa and Thomas Turner of Freeport.[13]

Another proposition growing out of the disunion crisis was the organization of the state militia. Governor Wood, the successor to the unexpired term of Governor Bissell who had died in office in March of 1860, called attention to this need before turning the reins of office over to Governor Yates. The state could not then boast any efficient militia organization; a people loaded with the bounties and blessings of long continued peace had seen no occasion for diverting energy into either martial spirit or organization. Not more than thirty companies existed with any regular organization under the state law for the supply of arms to militia companies. Their occasional drills were "held more for exercise and amusement than from any sense of duty to the State." The young men who, during the campaign of 1860, had swelled the ranks of the Wide Awakes, the Douglas Invincibles, and other organizations of a political character had received a more valuable training than the military companies.[14]

In the face of a general demand that now arose for the reorganization of the militia and the full arming of the state, many democrats assumed a hostile attitude. "As Democrats,

---

[12] W. Jayne to Trumbull, January 21, 28, 31, 1861; W. H. Herndon to Trumbull, January 27, 1861, Trumbull manuscripts.

[13] E. Peck to Trumbull, February 2, 1861, W. Jayne to Trumbull, February 1, 1861, ibid. Joseph Gillespie of Edwardsville led the fight for compromise within the republican ranks. N. B. Judd to Trumbull, January 17, 1861, ibid.; *Ottawa Free Trader*, January 26, 1861; Koerner, *Memoirs*, 2:113.

[14] "Annual Report of the Adjutant General, January 1, 1863," *Reports General Assembly*, 1863, 1:467; *Chicago Tribune*, January 3, 1861.

we claim exemption from service in this Black Republican war," declared the *Joliet Signal*, January 15, 1861. "Let the Black Republicans of Illinois do the training, and fighting if necessary, for it was their party that brought the calamity upon the country. We trust that the Democratic members of our Legislature will vote against arming and drilling our people to prepare for murdering and butchering their Southern brethren." As a result of this democratic opposition, combined with the prevailing uncertainty, no effective legislative action was taken by the general assembly.

The legislature set to work upon arrangements for the constitutional convention ordered by the people at the last election and for the reapportionment of legislative districts which also required attention. The republicans hoped to perpetuate through reapportionment the supremacy won in the legislative victory of 1860 but were not nearly as enthusiastic as the democrats about a new constitution which might disturb the fruits of that victory. The two propositions, therefore, went through together as mutually counteractive, the democrats choosing to believe, after protracted filibustering, that, however infamous the apportionment bill might be, there would never be an election under it.[15] The assembly also formally ratified the decision of the people in favor of the reëlection of Trumbull to his seat in the United States senate, and the docket was cleared for the new problems that might arise when the republican president-elect should take his seat.

On a brisk bright day, March 4, 1861, Abraham Lincoln, the first Illinoisian to enter the White House at Washington, was inducted into the presidential office. Lincoln's inaugural address was an emphatic declaration of the duty of the president to maintain the supremacy of the laws against all resistance, in the same spirit in which "Old Hickory" had met the nullifiers in 1832. Douglas promptly designated it as a declaration of war and prepared to lead a factious opposition to the new administration.[16] Less than six weeks later, however, the secessionists at Charleston challenged the federal military authority at Fort Sumter and, in compelling the garrison

---
[15] *Ottawa Free Trader*, January 26, 1861.
[16] Koerner, *Memoirs*, 2: 118.

to haul down the flag, precipitated the bloody civil struggle which had been so long impending.

The day of compromise was now clearly over; here was evidence that all the labors of the peacemakers had gone for nought. President Lincoln sent out a clarion call for defenders of the union that ended much of the futile discussion and wrangling between the leaders of the two parties in the north. Senator Douglas was one of the first to respond to the leadership of his lifelong rival; with Lincoln's call for seventy-five thousand troops came the announcement that Douglas had formally agreed "to sustain the President in the exercise of all his Constitutional functions, to preserve the Union, maintain the government, and defend the Federal capital."[17] Personal policy was subordinated to the public safety; with obligations to his country paramount to those of his party, the partisan had been sunk in the patriot. Having rallied a large band of prominent "war democrats" around the administration, he confronted a serious defection in the southern counties of his own state and hurried off with Lincoln's blessing to secure the loyalty of this stronghold of democracy.

Early in February signs had pointed to the danger that traitors might become numerous in southern Illinois. Republican leaders, therefore, advised against the establishment of a federal court at Cairo, where the union forces would not have sufficient strength and influence to convict the most flagrant disloyalist.[18] The governor was informed of the growing strength of the disunion feeling. Secret meetings were held at various points; Pope county held an open mass meeting and declared the right of secession, while a meeting at Marion, Williamson county, on April 15, pledged itself to perform the task of effecting a division of the state and to attach Egypt to the southern confederacy. These resolutions were understood to have received the approval of Congressman John A. Logan, who was opposed to the coercion of the southern states; a speech in which he compared the secessionists with our forefathers struggling for liberty, was widely circulated. It was generally believed in Egypt that W. H. Green, A. J.

[17] Arnold, *Life of Abraham Lincoln*, 200-201.
[18] James C. Conklin to Trumbull, February 12, 1861, Trumbull manuscripts.

Kuykendall, and other leading democrats were advocating a secession of Egypt if matters developed as they predicted. Ex-Governor John Reynolds sympathized strongly with the confederate cause and was willing to pronounce before "God and man, that the revolution in the South is the greatest demonstration of human greatness and grandeur that was ever performed on the globe." [19]

To end this situation Douglas directed all his energies. Arriving at Springfield on April 25 he poured forth an eloquence which swept not only the assembled audience but penetrated to the farthest confines of the state. Frankly confessing that his own mistakes had been made "in leaning too far to the Southern section of the Union," he was in a position to warn his old following against continuing to commit the same errors.[20] Thus was he arousing the people of Illinois to the defense of the government and of the flag, when a fatal illness seized him and permanently silenced his eloquent pleas for the union on the third of June, 1861.

By this time the response of the people evidenced itself in the military preparations that were under way. Mass assemblages received with applause Lincoln's call for troops. A countless number of recruits immediately offered their services to the government, so that within a fortnight the governor became "greatly embarrassed by the number of volunteers."[21] Governor Yates had replied to the fall of Sumter by issuing a proclamation convening the legislature in special session. This began on April 23 and in the following ten days its work was rushed through. The drafts of new legislation had been pre-

[19] *Illinois State Journal*, June 10, 11, 18, 20, 1861; *Cairo Democrat*, September 25, October 2, 1866; *Shawneetown Mercury* and *Harrisburg Chronicle* clipped in *Chicago Tribune*, June 17, 1861; *ibid.*, September 18, 1861; *Central Illinois Gazette*, June 19, 1861; *Illinois State Register*, June 19, 1861. Logan wrote to the editor of the *Register*, June 18, 1861, branding as a "lie" the charge that he had brought forward and openly advocated a plan "to effect the separation of southern Illinois from the remainder of the state and attach it to the southern confederacy;" *ibid.*, June 21, 1861. See also *Jonesboro Gazette*, March 14, 1863; *Congressional Globe*, 36 congress, 2 session, 178-181; S. E. Flannigan to Trumbull, April 9, 1861, Trumbull manuscripts; *Belleville Advocate*, August 28, 1863.
[20] Johnson, *Stephen A. Douglas*, 483-485.
[21] Trumbull to J. R. Doolittle, April 27, 1861, Illinois State Historical Society, *Journal*, 2:44. "Three regiments too many have already assembled and thirteen regiments are pressing to get into service."

pared in the executive office with the advice of republican leaders like Gustave Koerner and Senator Trumbull, the latter having hurried home from Washington. A bond issue of two millions was authorized to provide a war fund; the old obsolete militia system was replaced by a new militia law which provided for an elaborate organization; additional regiments were authorized for state defense.

The forces raised in the state were distributed between the district opposite St. Louis, with encampments at Alton and Caseyville outside Illinoistown, and at Camp Defiance at Cairo. A main purpose was to curb the spread of secession activities throughout Egypt. Recruits from the southern counties were joining the confederate forces and in some instances receiving encouragement from democratic leaders who considered the possibility of taking part in person in the raising of companies.[22] The name of John A. Logan, who bitterly denounced Douglas for the betrayal of the democracy, was used in the interest of southern recruiting as late as June, 1861; but, finally confronted by the alternative of committing political suicide or of clearing up his position, he proceeded to Camp Yates to discourse eloquently on "the duty of all patriots to sustain the Government in its efforts to vindicate the Constitution."[23] Logan followed this up by joining the volunteer army; and though secession activity continued in Egypt, the effect of his leadership and that of McClernand, who had been a union democrat from the start, was seen in the heavy enlistments that in the summer of 1861 began through the southern counties.

From the military point of view, the chief danger lay in the uncertainty of the situation at St. Louis. Cairo, to be sure, was the one point directly exposed to attack by the secession forces; but a strong military force was stationed there under Brigadier General Prentiss.[24] The secessionists, on the other hand, were organizing in St. Louis and the danger was that

[22] Joseph Medill to Trumbull, April 16, 1861, Trumbull manuscripts. James D. Pulley, a member of the legislature was arrested on the charge of enlisting men for the southern army. *Illinois State Journal*, June 5, 1861.
[23] *Ibid.*, June 18, 20, 1861; *Illinois State Register*, June 19, 1861; Koerner, *Memoirs*, 2: 124, 134.
[24] Trumbull to J. R. Doolittle, May 10, 16, 1861, Illinois State Historical Society, *Journal*, 2: 45-48.

Missouri would be forced into secession by their armed strength; with that state out of the union the problem of defending Illinois would be doubled. Illinois was almost devoid of military equipment; but the federal arsenal at St. Louis had an extensive supply, liable on account of inadequate protection to fall into rebel hands. For that reason 21,000 stands of arms and supplies were stealthily transferred one night to the possession of the state authorities of Illinois.[25]

Illinois coöperated in the western governors conference at Cleveland early in May which memorialized the president to create a department of the west, to establish rules for the stopping of supplies to the south, and to emphasize military operations on the Ohio and Mississippi. Soon after the creation of the western department, it was enlarged to include Illinois, Indiana, and a part of Kentucky; as a result Illinois troops were soon scattered over Missouri fighting to control that state for the union. The Illinois authorities were next successful in having General Harney, who though a union man was a Virginia slaveholder, replaced in the command of the federal forces at St. Louis by General Fremont.

By the summer of 1861 Illinois had a powerful force of 20,000 men in the field in addition to its heavy German enlistment in Missouri regiments; with the Iowa, Minnesota, and Wisconsin regiments drawn off for service in the east and those of Indiana and Ohio in West Virginia, Illinois troops promised to be the dominating factor in the reconquest of the Mississippi valley.[26] This situation stimulated the ambitions of various Illinoisians to secure commands over the state troops. Lincoln had been so busy dispensing patronage to party leaders in general that his own state had received little consideration. The state administration, therefore, brought pressure to bear upon Washington as a result of which John Pope, Grant, Hurlbut, Prentiss, and McClernand received brigadier generalships. The name of John M. Palmer was at first passed over, although he received the recommendations of the state officials

---

[25] Koerner to Trumbull, May 31, 1861, Trumbull manuscripts; Koerner *Memoirs*, 2: 130-133.
[26] John Pope to Trumbull, July 6, 1861, Trumbull manuscripts.

and of the congressional delegation; Senator Trumbull considered Palmer "one of the bravest & in my opinion the coolest, most sagacious & ablest of them all." [27]

From the start there was a good deal of the impatience for results in the republican ranks, which as time went on made for a serious misunderstanding between Illinois republican leaders and President Lincoln. In particular there was sharp criticism of the administration of the war department under Secretary of War Cameron. Cameron, a Pennsylvania republican politician who had been a rival of Lincoln for the republican presidential nomination, had been appointed to the cabinet much against Lincoln's best judgment; Illinois leaders had resented the appointment of Cameron as "a man who could not obtain the votes of ten decent, sober, moral Republicans for any office whatever." [28] The supposed inactivity of the war department caused great disgust especially in view of the situation in Missouri. The *State Journal* voicing this impatience declared: "Our people venerate LAW next to GOD, but they are restive under the restraining operations of red tape. The idea of waiting for orders from Washington to defend ourselves or protect our outraged Union brothers in Missouri may not much longer be brooked." [29] Even the disaster at Bull Run, resulting from the general popular demand for action, did little to cool this ardor.

Another source of republican dissatisfaction in Illinois grew out of the treatment received by General Fremont from the national administration. Illinois was concentrating its attention upon the situation in the Mississippi valley and in particular upon Missouri where General Fremont had set to work to organize an efficient army. Fremont, however, from the outset was not given proper support by the administration; and, with limitations in the shape of a strong personal ambition and a tendency to make important assignments to irresponsible and dishonest subordinates, he rapidly widened the gap between

[27] John Pope to Trumbull, June 16, 1861, John M. Palmer to Trumbull, July 8, 1861, Trumbull to Lincoln, October 1, 1861, Trumbull manuscripts.
[28] Koerner, *Memoirs*, 2:114; William H. Herndon to Trumbull, January 27, 1861, William Butler to Trumbull, February 7, 1861, W. B. Plato to Trumbull, March 29, 1861, Trumbull manuscripts.
[29] *Illinois State Journal*, May 17, 30, 1861; *Canton Weekly Register*, May 14, July 23, 1861.

himself and the Washington authorities.[30] When in the late summer Fremont issued a proclamation declaring martial law in Missouri and authorizing the confiscation of the property of the rebels and the emancipation of their slaves, Lincoln instructed Fremont to withdraw the proclamation and upon the latter's refusal, the president as commander-in-chief formally annulled Fremont's action. Illinoisians, however, generally felt that Fremont had shown himself equal to the emergency. Lincoln's disallowing order was roundly denounced. Many did not hesitate to declare Fremont right and Lincoln wrong.[31]

It was obvious that a serious breach had developed between the president and the western commander; yet republican sympathies were with the latter rather than with the Illinois statesman in the White House. In September the report gained currency that General Fremont had been superseded. The editor of the *Rock River Democrat* described his feelings with utter frankness: "We felt like ripping and tearing things generally; in fact, we felt like saying, let the government go to smash if it has done so foolish a thing. . . . . It is the settled conviction of the people of the West that Gen. Fremont is just the right man in the right place, and is promptly and rightly doing his duty, and if the Administration desires to outrage that sentiment it can find no surer way to do it than by superseding Gen. Fremont."[32] When finally early in November the government did act to remove Fremont on the ground of incompetence, recklessness, and extravagance, a howl of indignation went up from the republican camp. Senator Trumbull had protested to Lincoln against the failure of the administration to give Fremont a proper support. Gustave Koerner, the German republican leader, claimed that there was universal satisfaction with General Fremont at St. Louis and that the policy of the administration was "outrageous;" "the administration has lost immensely in the Northwest," he declared.

[30] Trumbull to J. R. Doolittle, August 31, 1861, Illinois State Historical Society, *Journal*, 2:48-49; Trumbull to Lincoln, October 1, 1861, Trumbull manuscripts; E. B. Washburne to S. P. Chase, October 31, 1861, Chase manuscripts.
[31] *Joliet Signal*, September 3, 10, 1861; W. Kitchell to Trumbull, December 10, 1861, Trumbull manuscripts.
[32] *Rock River Democrat*, September 17, 1861; *Rockford Republican*, October 17, November 7, 1861.

Only from the democrats did the president receive a warm indorsement of his course; from the rankest copperhead sheets, even, came the assertion that the president deserved the praise of every honest union man.[33]

The first winter of the war came on with the deepest gloom prevailing among the staunchest union men of the west. Grant had led the Twenty-first Illinois into Missouri to participate in the expulsion of the rebels from that state and soon won promotion to the rank of brigadier general. He had next been assigned to the command of all the troops of southeastern Missouri and southern Illinois which included the management of the great depot recently established at Cairo, his headquarters. On November 7, 1861, in order to make a diversion to prevent a junction of two confederate forces, he led 3,000 men into the jaws of death at the battle of Belmont. Grant succeeded in effecting his main purpose but, after carrying the strong confederate position against great odds he was compelled to withdraw his raw troops among whom he maintained order with great difficulty. The withdrawal seemed an ignominious flight to many disappointed union critics upon whom the heavy union losses in dead, wounded, and prisoners had a most depressing effect.

Coincident with the news of the battle of Belmont came the returns of the November election. As in the case of the municipal elections in the spring, the telegraph told of democratic victories. This, too, was in spite of the appeal made by administration backers during the summer months to sink partyism in patriotism. "If we understand the matter rightly," declared the *State Journal*, "there are no parties. We are all for the Union, for the preservation of the government and for the speedy suppression of the rebellion." It had been argued that the amendment of the state constitution was an important work to be delegated only to leaders " able to rise superior to the excitements of feeling and exacerbations of passion that govern the labors of weak men." The democratic press resented such appeals, pointed to the instances where the repub-

---

[33] Trumbull to Lincoln, October 1, 1861, Koerner to Trumbull, November 18, 1861, Trumbull manuscripts; *Cairo Gazette*, November 7, 1861; *Jonesboro Gazette*, November 9, 1861; *Ottawa Free Trader*, December 28, 1861.

licans failed to carry these principles into practice, and rallied all democrats to their party candidates. The election, in which democratic candidates won out not only in the southern counties but also in Cook, Will, La Salle, Peoria, and other northern districts, was interpreted as proof that the people were opposed to the formation of a new union party. "If anything has been revealed by the election," declared the *State Register*, "it is the fact the people are beginning to discover that the democratic party is the only true Union party;" at any rate the election seemed to insure the framing of "a sound Democratic Constitution."[34]

Did the election indicate that the citizens of Illinois, protected in their private opinions by the secrecy of the ballot box, were unwilling to set their seal of approval upon the attempt to hold the southern states in the union by force? This was a question that no one dared to raise. It could not be denied that the convention movement had been taken up by the people in 1860 under republican auspices and that a year later republican leadership had been rejected. Nor was there indisputable evidence either of the republican claim that their strength had been undermined by heavy enlistments or of the democratic charge that "the corruption, usurpation, and villainy" of republican officials had caused the revolution in political sentiment.[35] Forty-five democrats, twenty-one republicans, seven "fusionists," and two members classed as doubtful composed the body which, according to republican comment, was controlled by the rebel elements in Illinois politics. "Secession is deeper and stronger here than you have any idea," reported Governor Yates after the body had assembled at Springfield on January 7, 1862. "Its advocates are numerous and powerful, and respectable."[36]

The convention was organized under uncompromising democratic officials, not one of whom hailed from the region

[34] *Illinois State Journal*, August 2, 1861; *Chicago Tribune*, August 14, September 25, 1861; *Illinois State Register*, July 20, 27, November 15, 1861; *Ottawa Free Trader*, August 24, 1861; *Joliet Signal*, September 17, 1861; *Cairo Gazette*, November 14, 1861.
[35] *Illinois State Register*, March 17, 1862.
[36] He felt that the situation required the stationing of a regiment of well-armed soldiers at Springfield. Yates to Trumbull, February 14, 1862, Koerner to Trumbull, December 12, 1861, Trumbull manuscripts.

north of Springfield. This led many to suspect that Egypt would attempt secession; to their surprise, however, the leaders lacked courage to take any open anti-war stand. Judge H. K. S. Omelveny's resolutions aggressively defining state rights and a definite denial of the right of secession was adopted as an item of the bill of rights.[37] They took pains also to make provision for taking the vote of the soldiers in the camps on the adoption or rejection of the constitution.

Not being committed to any very sweeping changes in the constitution, the democrats saw in the convention an opportunity to manipulate matters in the interest of party politics. They canvassed the conduct of the republican administration in war expenditures and showed that contracts had been let without legal warrant and at rates much higher than the federal government was paying for the same commodities.[38] An investigation of the treatment of Illinois troops in the field was authorized, but General James W. Singleton of the committee on military affairs returned a report vindicating Governor Yates and Quartermaster Wood. The convention framed an anti-bank provision and adopted a resolution instructing the auditor not to issue in the meantime circulating paper to any but specie-paying banks. A section was adopted, incorporating into the organic law the Negro immigration prohibition of 1853. A partisan apportionment arrangement gave equal representation to the smaller southern counties and attached small republican counties to large democratic districts. The articles on banks, admission of Negroes, and congressional apportionment were to be submitted separately. A special election was provided for to be held on the seventeenth of June so that in the event of the adoption of the constitution an election of all state officers could take place the following November.[39]

All these propositions aroused the ire of the republicans. They attacked the convention as an illegally organized body;

[37] In a speech on April 19, 1861, Omelveny had advocated permission for seceding states to retire peacefully. *Illinois State Register*, January 27, 1862; *Illinois State Journal*, March 3, 1862; *Ottawa Weekly Republican*, January 11, 1862; *Chicago Tribune*, January 10, 1862; *Journal of the Constitutional Convention*, 1862, p. 72, 1076.
[38] *Illinois State Register*, January 27, 1862.
[39] See the proposed constitution in full, *Journal of the Constitutional Convention*, 1862, p. 1072-1114.

had it not, instead of accepting the oath to support the state constitution as prescribed by the law providing for its call, substituted the one taken by the convention of 1847? But the democrats replied that the substitution had grown out of the suggestion of Elliott Anthony, a republican member from Cook county, because the body could not without absurdity support that which it was its duty to amend, if not to wipe out altogether. The effort was made to get the convention to adjourn to a later date, if possible until January, 1863. The alleged reason was that the people were too deeply engrossed in the rebellion to give a proper consideration to the question of the revision of the constitution.[40] The real motive was doubtless fear lest the republican state administration might be ousted in November, 1862. With the failure of these devices the republicans allowed the convention to drag out its work under protest, assuming that the people would dispose of the product as it deserved. When, therefore, the convention adjourned on March 24, the real fight began.

The republican press immediately assaulted the proposed constitution as a partisan work, "the new democratic bantling." It was grudgingly admitted by some that it contained provisions of merit but it was declared that in general they had not improved upon the document under which the state had prospered for nearly fifteen years and which was in reality "good enough;"[41] moreover, the transactions of the constitutional convention "were ungrateful, unpatriotic and treacherous." To the republicans the most dangerous feature of the constitution was the apportionment of the legislature; should the Egyptian minority rule the majority? "Shall the manufacturing, agricultural and commercial interests of northern Illinois be put into Egyptian bondage?" queried the *Aurora Beacon*.[42]

The new constitution with its provisions for increased salaries and for new offices was charged with extravagantly imposing new burdens on the taxpayers at a time when

[40] *Illinois State Register*, February 1, 17, March 3, 1862; *Illinois State Journal*, February 18, 1862; *Chicago Tribune*, January 29, 1862; *Rockford Register*, February 1, 1862.
[41] *Ibid.*, March 29, 1862; *Illinois State Journal*, March 27, 1862; *Ottawa Weekly Republican*, March 29, 1862.
[42] *Ibid.*, April 5, 1862; *Aurora Beacon*, April 24, 1862.

retrenchment was the order of the day. The bank and Negro articles were roundly denounced. The document was submitted to a general overhauling: "the new constitution .... changes the entire order of things, and sets everything afloat. We are satisfied under the present order of things," was a typical republican criticism.[43] They called upon the people "to reject the Constitution entirely, without regard to its merits or demerits, as a rebuke to the Convention for its officious intermeddling with the war, and its attempt to cast odium upon the administration of Gov. Yates." [44]

Almost all the corporations in the state joined the republicans in this war on the new constitution. Not only did the document openly defy the banking interests but also the Illinois Central railroad, which was forever bound by article IV to the payment to the state of the seven per cent of its earnings agreed upon in its charter. Associated capital in general was aroused by the provision that "all laws enacted after the adoption of this Constitution, which create corporations, amend existing charters, or grant special or exclusive privileges to individuals, shall be subject to alteration, amendment or repeal."[45]

The democrats tried to rally voters to the support of the constitution as a document in the interests of the people rather than of corporate privilege. They charged its opponents with having been "bought up" by the corporations, particularly the Illinois Central. John Wentworth, the Chicago republican leader, "the friend of the laboring people" and the opponent of banks, corporations, and special privileges, took the stump in favor of the new constitution.[46] Other republicans announced that they intended to support the document as a whole, while rejecting certain of the articles submitted separately.

The state officials from Governor Yates down set busily at work in a rousing campaign against the new constitution; speakers of both party antecedents were put into the field, from Owen Lovejoy representing the strongest antislavery

[43] *Aurora Beacon*, May 8, 1862.
[44] *Havana Battle Axe* clipped in *Illinois State Journal*, April 4, 1862.
[45] *Journal of the Constitutional Convention*, 1862, p. 1082; *St. Louis Republican* clipped in *Belleville Democrat*, April 5, 1862.
[46] *Joliet Signal*, May 6, 13, 1862; *Illinois State Register*, May 8, 1862. Wentworth had become estranged from the "state house clique" at Springfield, see Trumbull manuscripts.

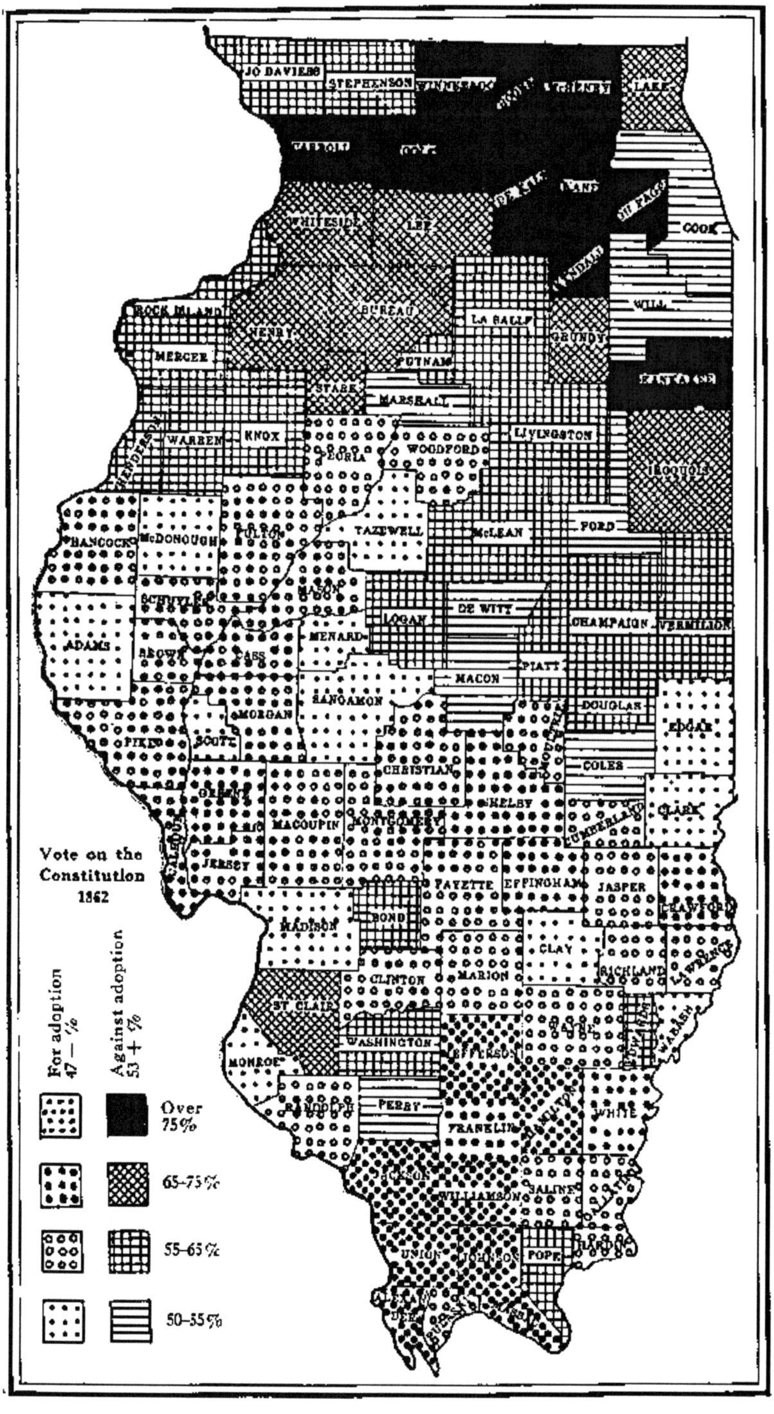
JO DAVIESS
STEPHENSON
LAKE
COOK
WHITESIDE
LEE
BUREAU
ROCK ISLAND
HENRY
MERCER
LA SALLE
GRUNDY
WILL
PUTNAM
STARK
MARSHALL
KNOX
WARREN
PEORIA
WOODFORD
LIVINGSTON
HANCOCK
McDONOUGH
FULTON
TAZEWELL
McLEAN
FORD
SCHUYLER
MASON
DE WITT
LOGAN
CHAMPAIGN
VERMILION
ADAMS
BROWN
CASS
MENARD
MACON
PIATT
SANGAMON
MORGAN
DOUGLAS
EDGAR
PIKE
SCOTT
CHRISTIAN
COLES
GREENE
MACOUPIN
MONTGOMERY
SHELBY
CUMBERLAND
CLARK
JERSEY
FAYETTE
EFFINGHAM
JASPER
CRAWFORD
MADISON
BOND
CLAY
RICHLAND
CLINTON
MARION
ST. CLAIR
WASHINGTON
MONROE
WABASH
RANDOLPH
PERRY
FRANKLIN
WHITE
JACKSON
WILLIAMSON
SALINE
UNION
JOHNSON
POPE
Vote on the
Constitution
1862
For adoption
47 — %
Against adoption
53 + %
Over
75%
65–75%
55–65%
50–55%

republicanism to John Reynolds, the incarnation of old democratic conservatism. They effectively played up in Egypt the bugaboo of increased taxes; and as the contest neared its close, they dragged out the bloody head and raw bones of treason in a sentimental appeal to the partiotism of the voters of the state. Every band of traitors in the state, they said, was working for this humbug constitution, this Vallandigham document. "Why is it that every rebel sympathizer in Illinois is open mouthed for the adoption of the new Constitution?" asked the *Illinois State Journal* on the day before election. "Down with the Secession Constitution," was the caption of the editorial in which the *Chicago Tribune* gave a final warning on election day.[47]

The commissioners appointed to take the vote of the Illinois troops outside of Illinois began their work early in April. With two regiments in Virginia, others on the remotest borders of Arkansas, besides the forces stationed in Missouri, Kentucky, and Tennessee, this was no small task. Early reports that the soldiers were going for the constitution caused considerable alarm; shortly, however, the returns went heavily against adoption. Sentiment throughout the state became increasingly hostile. Election day brought out a heavy vote except in Egypt where the fear of increased taxes and the charge of disloyalty rendered many democrats indifferent.[48] With a majority of 16,051 against ratification the work of the constitutional convention was rejected. The taking of the soldiers' vote was not completed until well into the summer but added substantially to this majority. The articles prohibiting banking and the congressional apportionment were rejected by much smaller majorities while the sections prohibiting the settlement of Negroes and mulattoes in the state and prohibiting them from voting were carried by the overwhelming majorities of 107,650 and 176,271 respectively. The section requiring the legislature to pass laws carrying the provisions of the last two sections into effect was ratified with a majority of 154,524. On the basis of the returns Governor

[47] *Illinois State Journal*, June 16, 1862; *Chicago Tribune*, June 17, 1862.
[48] *Jonesboro Gazette*, June 28, 1862. In eleven of the strongest democratic counties in Egypt the vote reflected a loss of nearly six thousand. *Canton Weekly Register*, June 24, 1862; *Chicago Tribune*, July 11, 1862.

Yates in August issued a proclamation announcing the rejection of the constitution.[49] This defeat was to prove but the beginning of a growing democratic discomfiture in state politics.

[49] Election returns from the secretary of state's office; *Illinois State Journal*, August 5, 16, 1862.

XII. RECRUITING GROUND AND BATTLEFIELD

TO THE call to arms Illinois responded with an enthusiasm that suggested the important part she was to play in fighting the battles of the union. Early in 1861 attempts had been made by the legislature to prepare the state for the civil strife that was impending. Governor Yates then called attention to the collapse of the militia system and to the failure of universal conscriptive enrollment which other states had discarded for voluntary organizations. In spite of a theoretical enrollment of all able-bodied males, the state could marshal less than 800 uniformed militia, with less than 200 serviceable muskets to represent the $300,000 outlay that the federal government had issued to the state.[1] Yet the legislature hesitated to raise the issue of militia reconstruction at a time when it was hoped that the south might be pacified if its tender feelings about coercion should not be offended. Democratic assemblymen from the southern counties called attention to the seriousness of the situation. William H. Green of Massac county suggested that his constituents "like a wall of fire" would oppose any attempt to invade the north; but "if the North were marched upon the South, her forces would be met on the prairies and made to march over the dead bodies of the men who people them." The senate, therefore, held up the bill for the reorganization of the militia — Richard J. Oglesby, chairman of the committee in charge, remarking that when the necessity should arise "the whole country, having the love of the Union at heart, would rise *en masse*, and, disregarding the hindrances of a militia law, volunteer their services to the proper authority of the State speedily and without delay."[2]

[1] *Reports General Assembly*, 1861, 1:10-11; 1865, 1:21; cf. *Senate Journal*, 1861, p. 26.
[2] See debate in *Chicago Tribune*, January 12, 1861; cf. report in *Illinois State Register*, January 14, 1861.

When the news from Sumter was received on April 15 Governor Yates promptly issued a proclamation calling for six thousand troops to fill the government requisition. In less than five days volunteers in excess of the quota had reported for duty, sixty-two companies having been offered to the governor. Mass meetings were called in many communities; the need of defending the union was eloquently placed before the assembled populace; and, after the speaking, volunteers for a local company were enrolled and the officers elected. Competition was keen between rival communities and competing officers, and the rush to recruiting stations was general. The first call, therefore, resulted in the organization of six regiments. The legislature summoned in special session responded to the further recommendations of the governor by appropriating $3,500,000 — $1,000,000 for organizing and equipping ten new regiments, $500,000 for purchasing arms and building a powder magazine, and $2,000,000 for general purposes of state defense — while an extra regiment of cavalry and four companies of artillery were also provided for. By June all ten regiments had been accepted by the national government, together with an additional regiment of infantry (commanded by Colonel Hecker), a battalion of light artillery, and one regiment of cavalry — making nineteen regiments in all.[3] Four other cavalry regiments were raised before the disaster of Bull Run in July which spurred the state to offer sixteen more regiments. Countless thousands of the lusty sons of Illinois only awaited further recruiting, and dozens of companies were tendered in anticipation of further requisitions upon the state, while most of the three months men reënlisted upon their return in August. So powerful was the flood of recruits that for a time, in spite of strong pressure on the war department, only one-fourth of the companies raised could be accepted; several companies, besides numerous individual recruits, therefore offered themselves to Missouri and other states.[4] By the first of October forty-three regiments were already in actual service, more than the state of New

[3] *Illinois State Register*, April 20, 1861; Grant, *Personal Memoirs*, 1:230-231; *Illinois State Journal*, May 1, 8, 1861; *Reports General Assembly*, 1861, 1:17-21.
[4] *Ottawa Free Trader*, August 17, 1861.

York had contributed, while enough men were enrolled in regiments in process of formation to give the state a total of nearly 70,000 troops. Before the end of the year Governor Yates was able to report in service fifty-eight regiments of infantry, eleven of cavalry, and eighteen companies of artillery, enrolling a total of 60,000 men.[5] Two artillery regiments supplied with James' rifled cannon were also accepted after Governor Yates obtained an order from the war department authorizing regimental organization. Although by the summer of 1862 the secretary of war had refused to accept any more batteries from Illinois, since it had more artillery companies in the field than any other state, yet when the call came for additional regiments of infantry the response was not only prompt but heavily in excess of the calculations of the war department. During the summer of 1862 sixty-one regiments of infantry were furnished together with two regiments of cavalry and six batteries, in all sixty-five thousand men. This made a total enlistment since the commencement of the war of nearly 135,000 men, divided between 125 regiments of infantry, 16 of cavalry, and 30 batteries.[6]

The heavy enlistments of the late summer of 1862 may be accounted for largely on the basis of the choice that was to be offered between volunteering or being conscripted. In the weeks following August 23, an enrollment of the entire militia force of the state was made in case a draft to fill up old regiments should be required. Meantime the republicans of Illinois stoutly supported the stand taken by Senator Trumbull in favor of federal conscription. He pressed the bill in congress against the opposition of the more timid and was rewarded by witnessing its enactment on March 3, 1863. The provost marshals and their assistants were soon at work preparing the rolls and making arrangements for the drawing. It was generally expected that the process of drafting would commence promptly, but hundreds of companies were sworn into service, and Illinois with volunteers far in excess of its quota was relieved from the operation of the draft.

[5] *Illinois State Journal*, December 14, 1861.
[6] *Ibid.*, September 13, 1862. The number on the muster rolls was 135,440. Adjutant General of Illinois, *Report*, 1861-1866, 1:22.

The same goal of keeping ahead of her quota was adopted by Illinois in the succeeding years of the war. Enlistment, with reënlistment of veteran regiments, was sufficiently heavy to delay the necessity of conscription. With a surplus of 8,151 under the draft quota, with an additional credit of 10,947 for volunteers discovered in a reëxamination of the rolls, and a net credit of 4,373 from the 6,032 Illinois citizens enrolled in Missouri regiments, recruiting placed Illinois on January 1, 1864, far in excess of the total quota under all calls of 145,100.[7]

Preparations were again made in 1864 for heavy drafts. The people of Illinois, flattered by previous reports, immediately set out to maintain this record, spurred on at times by warnings of the danger of conscription. In this way enlistments kept well ahead of quotas, reaching an excess of nearly 35,000 in the summer of 1864. This was a noble record; Governor Yates took just pride in the response to his energetic efforts to have Illinois take her full part in fighting the battles of the union.[8] When finally the south was crushed and the war record of Illinois was surveyed, it was found that the state had furnished under various periods of service over one-quarter of a million men.[9]

Great credit for the proud record which Illinois made dur-

[7] Adjutant General of Illinois, *Report*, 1861-1866, 1:30. Eight hundred and forty-eight Illinoisians were found in the Eleventh Missouri infantry and 670 in the First Missouri cavalry, *Illinois State Journal*, January 6, 1864; *Chicago Times*, January 6, 1864. Proclamation of Governor Yates, February 1, and report of Adjutant General Allen C. Fuller, February 1, *Illinois State Journal*, February 10, 17, 1864; Adjutant General of Illinois, *Report*, 1861-1866, 1:29-32. In the closing months of 1863 Adjutant General Allen C. Fuller thought he detected a disposition to hold back recruiting and incite the draft "as a good thing to have in this state."

[8] This excess, though large, was not sufficiently large to prevent some conscription under later calls. Only occasionally did a carping critic interpret the excess as involving a neglect of the welfare of the people, "a wanton waste of the lives and energies of the people of Illinois." *Cairo Democrat*, July 3, 1864.

[9] *Chicago Tribune*, September 14, 1864, October 20, 1866. Two hundred and twenty-five thousand and three hundred troops were enrolled in 150 infantry regiments, 17 cavalry regiments, and 33 batteries. This did not include Illinoisians enlisted in or recruited for the regular army, or in other organizations without the state, nor did it include colored troops. Provost Marshal General Fry of the war department on September 2, 1865, reported a total of 256,297 men furnished by Illinois without reference to periods of service, which varied from three months to three years. The total credit for the state on December 31, 1865, was 226,592 as against a total quota of 231,448. Adjutant General of Illinois, *Report*, 1861-1866, 1:157, 216; 8:777 ff. War department statistics published in the newspapers in 1866 placed the total figures at 258,277 and 279,006. *Chicago Tribune*, October 20, November 20, 1866.

ing this great national crisis is due to the aggressive leadership of her zealous and industrious commander-in-chief, Governor Richard Yates. His face was grimly set against the southern threats of disunion and when the test came he summoned forth with his eloquence the resources of the state of Illinois. Anxious to crush out the dread specter of disunion, he chafed under the caution exercised by the central government. "If I were Lincoln," he impatiently stated in February, 1862, "I would lead enough of the Potomac army to take Richmond—and this though Washington could not be saved—I would march to victory or death—Washington is nothing, if we remain an unconquered people with our institutions safe."[10] He was inclined to feel that, while he asked no credit from Lincoln for having gotten up the great Illinois army, the state did not receive full justice from the Washington authorities. Accordingly, on July 11 of that year, simultaneous with his response to Lincoln's new call for three hundred thousand, Yates sent an open letter to Lincoln demanding "the adoption of more decisive measures," the end of mild and conciliatory means to recall the rebels to their allegiance, and "greater vigor and earnestness" in military movements. "In any event," he declared, "Illinois, already alive with beat of drum and resounding with the tramp of new recruits, will respond to your call. Adopt this policy and she will leap like a flaming giant into the fight."[11]

So martial was the spirit instilled in the souls of peace-loving Illinoisians by stirring appeals to rally to the colors! War mass meetings were held in every village and town to encourage enlistments; subscriptions were taken to aid prospective recruits in making the decision; funds were raised to contribute to the relief of the families of volunteers; boards of supervisors and city authorities were called upon to offer bounties in addition to those held out by the general government. Recruits held back to see what bounties would be offered and where they would be most generously rewarded for enlistment. After a succession of increases Rockford volunteers in

[10] Yates to Trumbull, February 14, 1862, Trumbull manuscripts.
[11] *Reports General Assembly*, 1865, 1:15-16; Eddy, *Patriotism of Illinois*, 1:124.

1864 received a bounty of $400 from the city and county authorities. Sixty-nine counties alone had an expenditure of $15,307,074 for bounties in aid of raising troops.[12] The possibility of a state bonus even came up for discussion. In the closing months of the war taxpayers began to groan under the burden caused by these bounties. Special prizes were offered by local merchants and manufacturers, and draftees who were men of means were induced to pay the $300 fee, by which they could purchase exemption, to substitutes who would enlist in their behalf.[13] Funds were also raised to contribute to the relief of the families of volunteers.

The great spur to enlistment, however, was the desire to avoid the enforcement of the draft. This whip was held over the able-bodied men of the state, and arrangements were made repeatedly for the application of the law. In the summer of 1862 the draft seemed so near at hand that a rush for Canada was only checked by the requirement that traveling could be done only under passes issued by deputy marshals.[14] The democrats condemned the conscription law and challenged its constitutionality; they found special fault with the provision making possible exemption for those paying a fee of $300. The *Chicago Tribune,* which had originally defended this section as one essentially making for democracy, came to admit that "if the $300 clause is the *poor* man's fund we don't think *they* see it."[15] From the winter of 1863–1864 to the end of the war it seemed that the lottery of life and death would be drawn at almost any time; draft protection associations were organized in almost every community to raise funds to procure substitutes for members who might be drafted. The draft was actually ordered and the wheel set in motion in the fourth and

---

[12] *Rockford Democrat,* August 24, 29, 1864; *Ottawa Free Trader,* July 26, 1862; Adjutant General of Illinois, *Report,* 1861-1866, 1:137.

[13] The Chicago Board of Trade in July, 1863, raised $15,000 bounty money and recruited a full company of artillery in forty-eight hours; besides this Board of Trade battery, two Board of Trade regiments, the Seventy-second and the Eighty-eighth, were recruited. The Chicago Mercantile Association organized the Chicago Mercantile battery. *Ibid.,* 1861-1866, 4:553, 5:259, 8:732.

[14] *Aurora Beacon,* August 7, 1862; *Ottawa Weekly Republican,* August 23, 1862.

[15] *Chicago Tribune,* March 3, 1862, December 25, 1863. Three hundred thousand names were drawn in one instance and all but twenty-five thousand escaped, mainly under this clause.

tenth districts in October, 1864, and in most districts in March, 1865, when the order arrived in April to stop the draft and recruiting in Illinois.[16] Thus it happened that recruiting in Illinois involved a quota of only 3,538 draft men.

Strangely enough, the most satisfactory response to appeals for enlistment came from the democratic counties in southern Illinois. True, there had at first prevailed a disposition to regard the contest as an aggressive war on the part of a new president and therefore a corresponding reluctance to take up arms; but, the war having become a reality, the feeling grew among the people of Egypt that they had to "see the thing through." Even under the first call, the Cairo district in the extreme southern end of the state offered more companies than could be received. When in the summer of 1861 John A. Logan, "the little Egyptian giant," tendered his services to the stars and stripes, following the lead of John A. McClernand, who had already become a brigadier general, the tide was turned in favor of the union; the response to Logan's call for a regiment to follow him was immediate. Henceforth, Egypt, following the advice of the lamented Douglas, was tendering troops not by companies but by regiments; it not only filled its quotas but usually piled up a surplus. On the first of October, 1863, the ten extreme southern counties were officially credited with an excess of nearly fifty per cent. Old democratic strongholds charged with copperheadism, offered recruits with a generosity that shamed their opponents.[17]

Among the Illinois regiments were many representing select groups; they reflected the fact that the responsibility for early recruiting was assumed by individuals—civilians who rallied about them, fellow-workers, friends, and neighbors. Certain regiments consisted almost entirely of countrymen and farmers;

[16] *Rockford Register,* January 28, 1865; *Ottawa Free Trader,* February 4, 1865; *Cairo Democrat,* February 22, 1865; *Illinois State Journal,* April 15, 1865.
[17] *Ibid.,* May 15, 1861; *Illinois State Register,* August 19, 1861; *Jonesboro Gazette,* August 31, 1861, October 11, 1862; *Belleville Democrat,* August 30, 1862, January 23, 1864; *Cairo Democrat,* February 12, 1864. Within four months Alexander county, with a voting population of 1,047, including only a hundred (106) republicans, furnished seven companies; Union county in eighteen months furnished nineteen companies out of a voting population of 2,030, including but 157 republicans. At the same time Massac county had contributed five-sixths of its voting population.

the State Agricultural Society undertook in 1862 the organization of an entire brigade.[18] Railroad men at the same time took up the work of organizing another brigade; the Chicago railway battalion was part of the response in 1862 to the president's call for three hundred thousand more men. Early in the war Colonel C. E. Hovey, president of Illinois State Normal University, raised the "Normal regiment," to a very large degree composed of school teachers and advanced students, and he was soon seeking authority to expand it into a brigade. "The high intelligence and social cultivation which prevails among the privates makes discipline an easy task, while the pride of character & *esprit du corps* which is a matter of course among such men, will make them a very superior and effective regiment," wrote one of his captains.[19] Reverend B. C. Ward, the congregational pastor at Geneseo, raised a company of one hundred young ministers of the gospel "not for Chaplains, but to stand up for Christ on the field of battle;" it was incorporated, however, in a Missouri regiment. A project for a temperance regiment was set on foot with the idea of eliminating the demoralizing influences to which soldiers were exposed in camp.[20]

The adopted citizens in Illinois made an important contribution toward winning the battles of the Civil War. The Germans around Belleville responded enthusiastically from the start; a company was immediately organized by Augustus Mersy, a veteran officer of the Baden army of the German revolution of 1848, who promptly became lieutenant colonel. Friedrich Hecker, who had at first enlisted in Franz Sigel's Missouri regiment as a private, was given authority to raise an independent regiment, so that the Twenty-fourth Illinois infantry became known as the "Hecker regiment."[21] With the return of the three months men in July, Koerner offered to raise

---

[18] *Illinois State Journal*, August 16, 22, 1862; K. K. Jones to Trumbull, May 22, 1861, Trumbull to Governor Yates, September 27, 1861, Trumbull manuscripts.
[19] C. E. Lippincott to Trumbull, December 22, 1861, January 8, 1862, *ibid.*; *Belleville Democrat*, August 17, 1861.
[20] *Rockford Register*, September 28, 1861; *Joliet Signal*, October 8, 1861; *Illinois State Journal*, August 2, 1862.
[21] Koerner, *Memoirs*, 2:150-151. A second "Hecker's regiment," the Eighty-second, was recruited later in the war.

two German regiments, officered by men of experience. After considerable delay Governor Yates gave Koerner the necessary authority to raise one independent regiment, which was recruited in a few weeks and placed under the command of Colonel Julius Raith. This was the Forty-third infantry, or "Koerner regiment."[22] Many German recruits of that region joined Missouri German regiments, because of the failure of their leaders to secure prompt organization for exclusive German regiments. Companies were also organized in Springfield, Ottawa, and elsewhere, while the Chicago Jaegers, the Turner Cadets, and the Lincoln Rifles were ready from the start for incorporation in the union army. The Thirteenth cavalry regiment was the "German guides," organized at Chicago in December, 1861. Within a sixmonth, it was estimated that 6,000 Germans from Illinois were in the federal army.[23] This stream kept up during the war; it was possible as late as 1864 to recruit a German regiment in Chicago and vicinity. The Irish were not to be outdone. In a week's time they organized in Chicago the Twenty-third Illinois, otherwise called the Irish brigade, which was accepted as an independent regiment under Colonel James A. Mulligan. Irish companies from Springfield and Rockford also tendered their services. The following year the "Cameron guards" were recruited at the capital, while the "Ryan guards" from Galena and other companies were being organized for a Chicago regiment. The "Irish Legion," the Nineteenth infantry, was mustered into service at Chicago in the late summer of 1862. During the first two years of the war two so-called "Scotch regiments," the Twelfth and Sixty-fifth, were organized.[24] Even the Israelites of Chicago were aroused; in 1862 within forty-eight hours they raised a company together with a fund of several thousand dollars to put it in the field. The Portuguese in Springfield and in Morgan county enrolled large numbers in the companies recruited in those regions.

The idea of using Negro troops had long been urged upon

[22] Koerner to Trumbull, July 24, 29, 1861, Trumbull manuscripts; Koerner, *Memoirs*, 2: 161-165.
[23] *Rockford Republican*, October 10, 1861.
[24] The synonyms comprising the local names of military organizations are listed in Adjutant General of Illinois, *Report*, 1861-1866, 1: 217-223.

the national administration by Governor Yates and Senator Trumbull, and in the fall of 1863 the first Illinois regiment of Negro soldiers was finally authorized by the war department. Before this a colored company had been started in Galesburg, and recruits had been secured from Illinois for Rhode Island and Massachusetts organizations; a state wide canvass was now inaugurated which brought together five hundred recruits at Quincy in February, 1864. But failure to give them the same pay and bounty that was paid to white soldiers prevented Negro enthusiasm from developing; as a result less than two thousand colored troops were mustered into service and these naturally played little part in the fighting of this war.[25]

Back of the serried battalions that marched forth from Illinois there rallied legions of loyal women to minister to the physical and moral well-being of the fighters in the field. Nimble hands were set to work manufacturing the flags and uniforms with which the volunteer companies were outfitted. The scraping of lint and making of bandages was started at a rate that promised an oversupply; energies were thereupon partially transferred to the making of flannel shirts, drawers, socks, and other articles of clothing. The needs of the sick and wounded soldiers and of families left without support in nearly every community were met by local soldiers aid societies; an Illinois Soldiers' Relief Association was even organized at Washington by the Illinois colony in that city. Sociables and benefit concerts and performances were arranged as means of raising funds for supplies; sanitary stores were collected, funds were solicited from merchants, and farmers were induced to bring in their surplus of fruits and vegetables in the summer and wood in winter for the benefit of soldiers' families. In 1863 ladies union leagues began to spread all over the state. Members of these organizations often ventured into new fields of service, acting as substitutes for clerks who enlisted into service, and in certain instances turning out in a body to plant gardens and small farms in order to send the produce to the

[25] *Chicago Times*, October 6, 1863; *Rockford Register*, November 7, 1863; *Chicago Tribune*, October 20, 1866; Adjutant General of Illinois, *Report*, 1861-1866, 8:777-810. The records at Washington list 1,811 colored troops from Illinois.

soldiers.[26] A soldiers' home at Chicago was maintained during the later years of the war by the Ladies' War Committee; 46,284 arrivals were served during its first year.[27]

Other agencies also responded to the heavy demands for relief. Wealthy citizens and men in the workshops subscribed to funds for the support of the families of volunteers; the physicians of Decatur pledged their services without compensation.[28] County boards of supervisors and common councils in the cities designated certain funds for this work. Toward the end of 1863 the relief movement came to be organized more systematically: the Freemen's Aid Society changed its field of operations to that of supplying the wants of soldiers' families, while a movement was started to raise a fund for the maintenance and education of the children made orphans by the war.[29] There were various projects for orphans' homes which in 1867 culminated in the establishment near Bloomington of the Illinois Soldiers' Orphans' Home.

Illinoisians also coöperated in the support of two nation wide organizations which made substantial contributions to the physical and moral health of the soldiers. These were the United States Sanitary Commission and the United States Christian Commission. The latter sought to provide every soldier with a testament; it had stations in the army camps and at Cairo, where it maintained reading and writing rooms to counteract the contaminating and debasing tendencies of camp life.[30] The Sanitary Commission was extremely efficient in caring for the physical welfare of the soldiers. Governor Yates urged the formation of sanitary associations in each county to supply systematically such articles and funds as were necessary for hospital work. In order to replenish the exchequer of the Sanitary Commission, a great Northwestern Fair was held on October 27, 1863, at Chicago, the receipts of

[26] *Illinois State Journal*, May 11, 1861, July 18, 1862; *Rockford Register*, May 21, October 1, 1864; *Rockford Democrat*, December 15, 1864; *Carthage Republican*, January 14, 21, 1864. A grand wood procession was arranged at Carthage, which brought in eighty-eight loads of wood.
[27] *Chicago Times*, June 18, 1864.
[28] *Illinois State Journal*, April 19, 20, 23, 1861.
[29] *Ottawa Weekly Republican*, December 5, 1863.
[30] *Cairo Democrat*, February 9, May 8, 1864; United States Sanitary Commission, *Statement of the Objects and Methods of the Sanitary Commission*.

which were about $60,000; a year later a State Sanitary Fair was held at Decatur, and another Northwestern Fair arranged for May 1, 1865.[31]

The long casualty lists for Illinois created heavy demands for hospital facilities. This problem, however, was handled entirely without efficiency. Accommodations were provided only when heavy losses on the battlefield called attention to the need; this was especially true after the bloody battles of Fort Donelson and Pittsburg Landing, after the struggle for Vicksburg, and the battles about Chattanooga. Upon the receipt of the news of the capture of Fort Donelson, the constitutional convention assumed the unique responsibility for appropriating a half million dollars for the relief of the wounded;[32] and a year later the legislature set aside another fund of $10,000. Governor Yates, however, in his zeal for administering relief did not wait long for appropriations but rushed aid to the battlefields. In the fall of 1864, when the fighting in the Mississippi valley had practically come to an end, 700 Illinois soldiers lay in the hospitals about Louisville, 1,000 in Nashville, 1,500 in Chattanooga, and 3,400 below Chattanooga. In fallen heroes Illinois paid its toll to Mars: 5,857 were killed on the field of battle, 3,051 died of their wounds, and 19,934 died from the ravages of disease.[33]

With her vast levies of troops, Illinois was cast to play an important rôle in the work of suppressing the southern confederacy; their logical and self-appointed task was first to protect the state and then to carry out an offensive that would drive the rebels from the Mississippi valley. Early in the first summer Governor Yates secured for Illinois a fair representation in the Grand Army of the East, but the general body of troops remained in the department of the west.

Thirteen regiments, at first with no general officer in com-

---

[31] *Ottawa Weekly Republican*, September 6, 1862; *Chicago Tribune*, January 16, October 28, 1863; *Chicago Morning Post*, October 30, 1863; *Illinois State Register*, September 21, 1864; United States Sanitary Commission, *Financial Report from June, 1861, to October 1, 1865;* also *What the Sanitary Commission Is Doing in the Valley of the Mississippi*.

[32] *Illinois State Journal*, February 17, 1862; *Illinois State Register*, February 19, 1862; *Jonesboro Gazette*, February 22, 1862.

[33] *Illinois State Journal*, October 5, 1864; *Chicago Tribune*, October 20, 1866; Eddy, *Patriotism of Illinois*, 2:690. Higher figures are given in Bost, *Slavery and Secession in Illinois*, 79; Moses, *Illinois*, 2:731.

mand, were sent into Missouri to rid it of confederate troops. When finally Grant, Hurlbut, Prentiss, McClernand, and later Palmer were given their commissions as brigadier generals, decisive operations in Missouri as elsewhere were long restrained by superior officers and frequent changes in commands. General Fremont had been superseded in the department of the west early in November by General Hunter, who in turn ten days later yielded to General Halleck. In July, however, Illinois troops under Colonel Franz Sigel had fought valiantly against great odds at Carthage, and under General Lyons at Wilson's Creek; a little later, after Grant relieved General Prentiss at Cairo, his command faced the murderous confederate fire at Belmont, suffered heavy losses, but thereby prevented the junction of the confederate forces in Kentucky and Missouri. But for most of this period the western army lay idle, guarding railroad bridges, depots, engine-houses—chafing under their inactivity and reflecting the growing clamor at home for a movement "on to Memphis and New Orleans." General Palmer, complaining of the lack of progress, frankly assigned the blame to the constant change of commanders and to the prevalence in all armies of "Feather bed Generals, who run the machine by Telegraph and trifle away time."[34]

In the spring of 1862, however, more satisfactory results were evidenced when the work of saving Missouri to the union was completed, and the federal offensive began against the first confederate line. On January 27, 1862, Lincoln as commander-in-chief ordered the army and flotilla of armed river craft at Cairo to advance—a part of a general movement of the federal forces against the insurgents. The result was the capture first of Fort Henry on the Tennessee, and later of Fort Donelson on the Cumberland river. The latter feat brought glory to the Illinois troops who constituted a majority of the army of 30,000 men led by General Grant. Back of this victory, however, was the courage and heroism of any army that for three days and nights fought on in the midst of rain and snow and frost, without shelter and almost without food. Far-off Maine could not restrain her admiration for the work of these

[34] J. M. Palmer to Trumbull, February 3, 1862, Koerner to Trumbull, January 2, 26, 1862, Trumbull manuscripts.

brave volunteers; the governor and legislature of that state formally extended their congratulations to the victors, singling out the Illinois troops for special mention for their heroic conduct.[35]

This victory brought to Grant his first significant military laurels. A West Pointer who had seen service in the Mexican War and in the west, he had reëntered civilian life and in the crisis of 1860 was adjusting himself to the obscurity of a clerkship in his father's leather business in Galena. Then, as a Douglas democrat, he took the lead in the raising of a volunteer company at Galena and accompanied it to Springfield. His appearance on that occasion was not "very prepossessing;" "hardly of medium height, broad-shouldered and rather short-necked, his features did not indicate any very high grade of intellectuality."[36] His friends brought him to the notice of Governor Yates and secured an appointment as assistant quartermaster-general at two dollars a day. Soon his abilities as a military commander began to evidence themselves and led Governor Yates to assign him to the command of cantonments at Springfield, at Mattoon, and at Anna. Later he in all modesty accepted the colonelcy of the Twenty-first regiment; on August 23, after two months of efficient service in the field, he was promoted brigadier general with a commission dated May 17. Now following the capture of Fort Donelson, Grant received the rank of major general, his commission fitly dated February 16, the date of the surrender of the fort. Already his courage, his clearness of judgment, his knowledge of military science and of men, his ability to command the confidence of his subordinates had been demonstrated in a way that prepared the minds of Illinoisians for his future achievements.[37]

Simultaneously with Grant's movement against Fort Donelson, an expedition under General Pope moved down the Mississippi and captured the confederate positions of Island Number 10. A general advance was then made on the next confederate line from Memphis to Chattanooga; moving up the Tennessee, Grant's army was suddenly attacked at Pitts-

[35] *Rockford Republican*, February 20, 1862; see resolutions and letters of Governor Washburne, *Illinois State Journal*, April 8, 1862.
[36] Koerner, *Memoirs*, 2: 126.
[37] Eddy, *Patriotism of Illinois*, 1: 178-189.

burg Landing, and the battle of Shiloh took place on April 6 and 7. Only the arrival of reënforcements saved the hard-pressed union army, many officers of which charged General Grant and General Sherman with negligence. " Good generalship would have saved us thousands of valuable lives and have carried our army in triumph into Corinth," declared one Illinois officer.[38] John M. Palmer cursed the fates which brought the calamitous losses to the union army: " No sadder day will I hope ever come for Illinois than that sad Sunday when the flower of her soldiers were decimated at Pittsburg unless the day Grant was made a Brigadier General or that upon which he was promoted may be regarded as more unfortunate."[39] Grant was in a measure superseded by General Halleck, who assumed chief command for a time. Tales of Grant's addiction to drink began to circulate in camp, but seemed to be founded on small talk;[40] at any rate, the advance was successfully continued until Corinth was occupied, after which Memphis fell into the hands of the union forces. The federal army followed the retreating confederates, but operations were uneventful until they pressed hard upon the defenses of Vicksburg. Illinois troops to the number of about 20,000 accompanied Grant on this expedition against Vicksburg, and 25,000 more were with Rosecrans when he attacked Bragg at Murfreesboro on the last day of 1862. In both expeditions the Illinoisians acquitted themselves creditably and were in instances conspicuous for their gallant behavior.

Illinois troops under able leadership were winning fame everywhere. John A. Logan had a brilliant military career and won promotion to a brigadier generalship. Even his old republican antagonists supported the proposition to have him advanced to the rank of major general; and, since Grant and McClernand were rivals for the laurels of the Vicksburg campaign, the military leadership of the Illinois troops was thus, strangely enough, committed to democrats.[41] Party-minded

[38] George T. Allen to Trumbull, April 25, 1862, Trumbull manuscripts.
[39] John M. Palmer to Trumbull, April 24, 1862, ibid.; Koerner, *Memoirs*, 2: 214-220.
[40] George T. Allen to Trumbull, May 11, June 7, 1862, Trumbull manuscripts.
[41] H. McPike to Trumbull, February 23, 1863, ibid.; Koerner, *Memoirs*, 2: 205-206.

republicans challenged their devotion to the cause and doubted whether they possessed the stuff of which heroes are made, but were not willing to claim altogether superior endowments for their own leaders like gallant "Dick" Oglesby and General Hurlbut.

The surrender of Vicksburg, July 4, 1863, after it had been invested for months and repeatedly stormed with shot and shell, opened the Mississippi throughout its entire length. The capture was an undisputed victory for Grant; John A. McClernand had been eliminated during the campaign, for Grant, after severely criticizing his generalship, had relieved him of his command. McClernand never admitted any culpability on his part and claimed that a grave injustice had been done him; restored by order of President Lincoln and assigned to operations in Louisiana and Texas, he remained in the field until the early part of 1864, when he resigned his commission, claiming that he had been discriminated against in promotions.[42]

Illinois troops had taken their full part in the task, assumed at the outset of the war, of severing the confederacy along the line of the Mississippi river; but their services did not end there. Illinois regiments were an important factor in the capture of Chattanooga by Rosecrans in September, 1863; others marched with Grant a few weeks later to relieve the beleaguered union army there and to establish federal control in that region. Over seventy regiments then came under the immediate command of General Grant, only to be transferred to General Sherman when Grant was called to Washington to assume, under the military title of lieutenant general, the command of all the armies of the United States.

Nor had the volunteer soldiers of Illinois been idle elsewhere. Illinois regiments had participated in the Peninsular campaign; and they had met the enemy in the bloody battles of Antietam, Gettysburg, Fredericksburg, and Chancellorsville. Illinois cavalry had taken conspicuous parts in the fighting in the west and in Virginia, especially in April and May, 1863. The brilliant raid of the Sixth Illinois cavalry under

---

[42] John A. McClernand to Trumbull, January 14, 1864, Trumbull manuscripts; see correspondence in *War of the Rebellion, Official Records*, series 1, volume 17, part 2, p. 555, volume 24, part 1, p. 6, 169-186.

Colonel Grierson — from Tennessee through the states of Mississippi and Louisiana as far as Baton Rouge — astounded the rebel leaders, who saw the heart of the confederacy penetrated for the first time. The Eighth and Twelfth cavalry regiments tried to equal this exploit when in Stoneman's expedition they dashed into the rear of Lee's army, within a few miles of Richmond.[43] Illinoisians marched with Sherman "from Atlanta to the sea" and northward through the seaboard states. They backed up Grant in his "Wilderness campaign," steadily cutting down the distance to Richmond. By land and sea they operated in the department of the gulf under the command of Major General Hurlbut to complete the conquest of the lower Mississippi valley.

In the early months of 1865 they saw their efforts crowned with success on every hand. The battle-scarred veterans of the gulf poured into New Orleans with the well-earned laurels of their campaign; Sherman's forces pressed on toward the rear defenses of Richmond; while two regiments, the Thirty-ninth infantry, or "Yates Phalanx," and the Twenty-third, or "Irish Brigade," followed Grant into the streets of the confederate capital and were present at Lee's surrender at Appomattox. When the shouts of victory began to subside, Illinois was thrilled to learn that it was the silk flag of the Thirteenth Illinois regiment, a rebel trophy rescued and hoisted by a Massachusetts soldier, that was the first to proclaim the union occupation of Richmond.[44]

It was not long then before the regiments of war-weary boys in blue, their flags emblazoned with deeds of glory on scores of battlefields, began to return to their homes and peaceful callings. Glorious was the welcome which they received from friends and loved ones whom they had left to serve their country. Proudly did they recount exploits that brought honor to their state. Yet no more eloquent testimony to devotion to the union could have been offered than that which came from silent battlefields consecrated by the blood of fallen heroes.[45]

[43] *Rock River Democrat*, May 13, 1863.
[44] *Illinois State Journal*, May 23, 1865.
[45] The Eighty-fifth regiment of Peoria, which had started out in 1862 nine hundred strong to fight its way to Savannah and up to Richmond, returned with three hundred and fifty men in the ranks. *Ibid.*, June 17, 1865.

XIII. THE NEW ABOLITIONISTS AND THE COPPERHEADS

FROM the time the first call went out for volunteers through the years of fighting in the field President Lincoln wrestled with the colossal task of preserving the federal union. With unquestionable sincerity he grappled with the worst tangle of problems ever confronted by an American executive and with persistence, energy, self-control, and a high degree of tact, prepared to carry the nation through its greatest crisis. It was impossible, however, for his former associates in Illinois to gauge the difficulty of his position; as they impatiently awaited results which they felt ought to reveal themselves at once, they turned to each other with the question: "Is it possible that Mr. Lincoln is getting scared?"[1]

Within Illinois, as throughout the nation, the atmosphere of war had generated a passion for freedom quite novel to the sectional controversy; even before the clash of arms William H. Herndon had demanded that slavery be met boldly and extinguished. "Liberty & Slavery," he declared, "are *absolute* antagonisms; and all human experience—all human philosophy says—'Clear the ring & let these natural foes—these eternal enemies now fight it out—To separate them *now* is murderous to the men—women & children of the future.'"[2] Another Illinois republican had urged that the southern states be warned that in seceding and relinquishing their equality in the union, they would fall back "into territorial pupillage again," subject to the right of congress to prohibit or abolish slavery in the territories—a state suicide theory older than the war itself.[3] This suggestion furnished a way of striking directly at the institution of slavery; many who had been

---
[1] William Butler to Trumbull, March 14, 1861, Trumbull manuscripts.
[2] W. H. Herndon to Trumbull, December 21, 1860, *ibid.*
[3] W. B. Slaughter to Trumbull, February 15, 1861, *ibid.*

extremely conservative on the question of slavery had come to feel that, while the point in dispute was union *v.* rebellion, slavery was at the bottom of the whole situation and that its continued existence must become the real issue.

A line of cleavage appeared between the new abolitionists and the conservative defenders of the union. Congress, under conservative leadership, adopted the position presented by John J. Crittenden of Kentucky that the war involved the preservation of the union and not an interference with the domestic institutions of any of the states; and Lincoln and the Illinois congressional delegation excepting Senator Trumbull coöperated in giving the loyal slaveholders of the border states this assurance. At the same time, however, "radical republicans" in Illinois set up a plea for emancipation; they demanded that the real issue be dragged into the light — that the battle cry of freedom be proclaimed.

The belief spread that the war would have to continue until all the causes which produced it had been removed — slavery must be put in process of extinction. The *Chicago Tribune* was busy preparing the public mind for the first step, pointing out that, " every day the rebellion lasts increases the probabilities that slavery will receive its death wound before the struggle is ended."[4] When, however, democratic papers protested against making the object of the war the extermination of slavery, the very journals that were working toward emancipation denied categorically the existence of any such danger; it was shortly after such a denial that the *Central Illinois Gazette*, edited by a veteran abolitionist, urged that " freedom should be proclaimed to all the sons of Africa that would fight on the side of the Government."[5]

Just at this stage came the report of Fremont's proclamation providing for the confiscation and emancipation of the slaves of rebel planters in his military district. The news of this action met with an outburst of applause on the part of thousands of republicans, who welcomed it as an assault upon the institution of slavery; even independent papers were able

---
[4] *Chicago Tribune*, July 22, 1861; *Central Illinois Gazette*, June 26, 1861.
[5] *Ibid.*, July 24, August 28, 1861; *Jonesboro Gazette*, September 21, 1861; *Rock River Democrat*, October 8, 1861; *Ottawa Free Trader*, October 19, 1861.

to indorse it, on the principle that a slave owner forfeited all rights to protection of property when found in arms against the government.[6] When the news of President Lincoln's disallowing order followed, it brought bitter disappointment to those who had thought that a long step forward had been taken.

Although some Illinois republicans approved the president's decision, the great preponderance gave their support to General Fremont's proclamation. The *Rock River Democrat*, an opponent of a general emancipation policy, declared that " the Proclamation had received the endorsement of the free people of the West — it was just the thing needed, and Fremont was just the man to execute it. . . . We believe the principle enunciated in the Proclamation will yet have to be adopted by the Government — it is right, the magnitude of the stake for which we are playing demands it, and we say God speed the day."[7] John Russell, the Bluffdale educator, in his disappointment, expressed the opinion that " the repudiation by Mr. Lincoln of the clause of Fremont's Proclamation, manumitting the slaves of Missouri rebels, gave more '*aid and comfort to the enemy*' in that state than if he had made the rebel commander, Sterling Price, a present of fifty pieces of rifled cannon."[8] The Germans of Chicago and of the Belleville district, who had become noted for their zeal for liberty and fundamental democracy, were especially strong in their admiration for Fremont.

It seemed clear that Lincoln's policy was to preserve slavery intact. This was extremely vexatious. William H. Herndon, Lincoln's law partner, grew restive to the point of declaring: " Good God! if I were Lincoln . . . . I would declare that all slaves should be free. . . . What does Lincoln suppose he can squelch out this rebellion while he and the North in common are fighting for the status of slavery? Good Heavens. What say you?"[9] Many felt convinced that the government had " a higher and holier mission to perform, than to *lavish* hundreds of millions of Treasure,

[6] *Ottawa Free Trader*, October 19, 1861.
[7] *Rock River Democrat*, September 24, October 8, 1861.
[8] John Russell to Trumbull, December 17, 1861, Trumbull manuscripts.
[9] W. H. Herndon to Trumbull, November 20, 1861, *ibid*.

and to sacrifice tens of thousands of the lives of our noblest young men, to see how strong it can hold a Traitor's negro with one hand and how successfully it can fight his master with the other."[10] More and more was the argument brought forward that the abolition of slavery, a cancer which must be cut out and cauterized, was the only remedy that could save the union. "The South has made Slavery the issue," declared the *Central Illinois Gazette*, November 27, 1861, "and Congress must enable the people to throttle rebellion and break its head with this 'bone of contention.'"

Lincoln, however, again placed himself in the way of further progress. His first annual message to congress, on December 3, 1861, took no advanced ground on the question of emancipation; he contented himself with the suggestion that the states might be allowed to confiscate the property of rebel citizens and that congress might secure the forfeited slaves by crediting their value against their tax quotas.[11] To the root and branch abolitionist, which many republicans were fast becoming, this seemed "one of the most unjust, & humiliating propositions that could be conceived."[12] Disappointed Lincoln supporters voiced their sentiments in varied expressions of regret, disgust, and even anger. The editors of the *Chicago Tribune* condemned it as a piece of cowardice, "a horrible fiasco."[13] The radicals, becoming more and more violent in their hatred of the rebels and their cause, charged their bitterness to the extreme mildness with which the "giant crime" had been treated.[14]

Better things, however, were expected of congress. There Senator Trumbull, the author of the first confiscation act, led the fight for another measure which would drastically extend

---

[10] Shubal York to Trumbull, December 5, 1861, W. Kitchell to Trumbull, December 10, 1861, *ibid*. The *Rockford Republican*, June 24, 1862, objected to this "playing war," "with a tract in one hand and a rifle in the other," "for the purpose of giving the black-hearted cut-throats and scoundrels of the barbarous South a chance to repent."

[11] Richardson, *Messages and Papers of the Presidents*, 6: 54.

[12] Grant Goodrich to Trumbull, December 5, 1861, Trumbull manuscripts.

[13] C. D. Ray to Trumbull, December 6, 1861, *ibid*.

[14] See Cole, "President Lincoln and the Illinois Radical Republicans," *Mississippi Valley Historical Review*, 4: 422-423. One aggressive critic called it "a tame, timid, time serving common place sort of an abortion of a Message, cold enough with one breath to *freeze* h—ll *over*." Shubal York to Trumbull, December 5, 1861, Trumbull manuscripts.

freedom to slaves of all persons resisting the union. The republican voters of Illinois rallied to Trumbull's support in spite of the efforts of the democratic journals to arouse conservative republicans to their duty of resisting "the plot of Trumbull, Sumner, and Co."[15] Lincoln, in setting himself in opposition to the step advocated by Trumbull, aroused the impatience of those who felt that the administration was neglecting the very means best calculated to hasten the suppression of the rebellion. J. M. Sturtevant of Illinois College could not understand Lincoln's position, while John Russell of Bluffdale boldly denounced "the imbecility of President Lincoln," whom he accused of having "done more to aid Secessia than Jefferson Davis."[16]

Oblivious to these criticisms, Lincoln continued his efforts to attach the border slave states more securely to the union. In a special message to congress on March 6, he recommended the compensated emancipation of the slaves in the border states and was able to secure from that body a joint resolution favorable to that policy. This almost unexpected recommendation recognizing slavery as the cause of the rebellion was as warmly welcomed by the republicans as it was deplored by the democrats; and when next Lincoln agreed to the abolition of slavery both in the District of Columbia and in the territories, he won more golden opinions. Those, however, more thoroughly cognizant of his position on slavery found cause for impatience; they chafed at his persistence in pressing till midsummer the proposition for compensated emancipation and were nettled at his reluctance, on account of certain "objectionable" emancipation provisions, over signing the second confiscation act.[17]

Meantime, the pressure upon Lincoln in favor of some general emancipation scheme began to have its influence. His mind was already at work on this most serious problem of the

[15] *Illinois State Register*, September 11, 14, 21, December 15, 1861; *Ottawa Free Trader*, January 25, 1861.
[16] J. M. Sturtevant to Trumbull, December 28, 1861, John Russell to Trumbull, February 4, 1862, Trumbull manuscripts.
[17] *Joliet Signal*, March 11, 1862; *Chicago Tribune*, March 11, 1862; *Writings of Abraham Lincoln*, 6: 87-90, 94-99. He submitted his objections in the form of a proposed veto message which he had originally intended to submit to hold up this act.

Lyman Trumbull

[From photograph in possession of Mr. L. C. Handy, Washington, D. C.]

war. Inclining more and more to the position recommended by the radicals, he refused them the satisfaction of even a hint as to the new policy he was considering. He gave them no comfort when Governor Yates on July 11 formally addressed him to urge that sterner measures be used against the rebels. His reply to Greeley's plea for emancipation as the prayer of twenty millions was a mere equivocal unionsaving pronunciamento. When, as late as September 13, 1862, a delegation in behalf of a large meeting in Chicago presented an address in favor of an emancipation proclamation, he replied that, while the subject lay very near his heart, a decision was difficult on account of the practical difficulties involved and on account of the uncertainty as to the value of such a course when entered upon.[18]

The desire of certain republicans to see slavery put in process of extinction was reënforced by practical political considerations; they felt, indeed, that were emancipation postponed indefinitely, it would be fatal to the party. Discontent raged within the union ranks; the radicals criticized the Lincoln administration for its caution, and the conservatives looked askance at the steps leading toward emancipation. In the intimacy of republican counsels, charges were passed of mismanagement of army contracts and incompetence in military leadership. Members of the state administration complained of being "tired of traitors from West Point."[19] Even General Grant came in for his share of complaint. He was charged by republican army officers with being intemperately devoted to intoxicants. His abilities as a military leader were seriously called into question. With so much uncertainty as to the prowess of the federal armies and as to the political future of the republican party, republican leaders regarded an emancipation policy as the one clarifying agency; yet they confronted the unanswered enigma: why did not *Lincoln* see this and strike boldly?

It was probably only the irony of fate that during this summer so full of disappointment and uncertainty for the rad-

[18] *Ibid.*, 6: 123-124, 135-139; *Illinois State Journal*, September 17, 1862.
[19] D. L. Phillips to Trumbull, March 22, 1862, Trumbull manuscripts. They wanted to compel the democrats to "go before the people on the issue of reenslavement." Joseph Medill to Trumbull, June 5, 1862, *ibid.*

icals Lincoln was developing his plan for the inauguration of the very policy so insistently demanded by them. When, therefore, the battle of Antietam made possible the promulgation of the preliminary emancipation proclamation on September 22, 1862, it was received with mingled feelings of surprise, satisfaction, and relief. To some it came as a great act of justice, wisdom, and mercy which would immortalize the name of Abraham Lincoln and save the nation from destruction; others regarded the delay as so serious that, while they rejoiced at the actual course taken, only continued evidence of firmness, self-assertion, and energy on the part of the president could wipe out the disgrace of his protracted inaction.

It was Lincoln's expectation that in the congressional elections of 1862 the results of the emancipation proclamation might reveal themselves as favorable to his general policy. In Illinois, however, republicans had relaxed their efforts after the defeat of the new constitution and looked with favor upon the advice of prominent war democrats like John A. Logan, I. N. Morris, John E. Detrich, A. J. Kuykendall, Washington Cockle, and others that "party lines and partizan feelings should be swallowed up in patriotism."[20] Republican leaders, thereupon, arranged for the coöperation of all administration backers in a union fusion party. They agreed that an extra session of the legislature would be suicidal for the party, and there was much reluctance about holding a state convention. When finally a union convention did meet, Eben C. Ingersoll, a war democrat from Peoria, was given the nomination for congressman-at-large; and candidates representing both old party affiliations were put in the field in the various districts.

The impression prevailed that the democratic party, as such, was discredited. Old liners, like Richardson, James C. Robinson, and Anthony L. Knapp, who had not joined the war following, were consorting with Vallandigham, the notorious Ohio copperhead; and the democratic state convention of September 10 brought out a scant attendance with one-third of the counties entirely unrepresented. Yet in May, John A.

[20] *Illinois State Journal*, August 20, 22, 23, September 11, 24, October 13, 1862; Robert Smith to Gillespie, October 16, 1862, Gillespie manuscripts; Joseph Medill to Trumbull, June 25, August 25, 1862, Trumbull manuscripts.

Logan's vacant seat in congress was filled by William Joshua Allen, a peace democrat, who was elected over both another peace advocate and Colonel Isham N. Haynie, a war democrat.[21] The November election, moreover, resulted in a sweeping democratic victory: the state ticket netted a majority of 14,000, the state legislature came completely under democratic control, while James C. Allen, the democratic candidate for congressman-at-large, was returned victor with eight of the other thirteen members of the delegation. This triumph assured the election of a democratic United States senator to take the place of Senator O. H. Browning in Douglas' seat.

The democrats waxed jubilant over these glad tidings. "The party which triumphed two years ago in every Northern State," proclaimed the *Joliet Signal*, November 11, "and by sectionalism and slavery agitation provoked secession in the Southern States, and hurried us into a dreadful civil war, and caused our land to be drenched with the blood of its citizens, has been ignobly vanquished." More than this, the winners interpreted it as the rout of abolitionism and as a proper rebuke to the party that was trying to Africanize the north. The voter had registered his reaction to the democratic charge that the federal government was "seeking to inaugurate a reign of terror in the loyal states by military arrests and transportation to prisons out of the limits of these states, of citizens, without a trial, to browbeat all opposition by villainous and false charges of disloyalty against whole classes of patriotic citizens, to destroy all constitutional guaranties of free speech, a free press, and the writ of 'habeas corpus.'"[22]

Even the republican vote was not to be interpreted as an indorsement of Lincoln's policies, for the main body of the republicans was following the radical leadership of Senator Trumbull and Governor Yates. Governor Yates had thrown himself wholeheartedly into the struggle; and, disappointed with the president's reluctance to adopt more radical policies, he was inclined to question Lincoln's ability to lead the country on to victory. Lyman Trumbull even publicly proclaimed the

[21] *Illinois State Journal*, May 28, 1862.
[22] *Illinois State Register*, September 9, 1862.

incompetency of the administration.[23] This thoroughgoing champion of freedom, to whom Lincoln had in 1855 graciously yielded the senatorial laurels as a more conservative champion of the antislavery cause, had now been transformed into a leader of the radical republican following in congress. Trumbull was a man whose austere talents had little of that warmth that attracts a large circle of friends, yet his intellectual leadership and honesty, backed by a puritan conscience, won for him a political following that was a silent but effective tribute to his genius. As the author of the first confiscation act and as a leading figure in every movement for the effective prosecution of the war, every suggestion of his carried weight with those who were shouting the battle cry of freedom.

Trumbull's correspondents unburdened to him their disgust with the national administration. Lincoln seemed to place too much trust in conservative generals out of sympathy with the methods best calculated to bring the rebellion to a speedy close; in his cabinet he listened too much to timid, incompetent, and conservative advisors, like "Seward and proslavery Blair and Bates."[24] Even after the definitive emancipation proclamation of January 1, 1863, this dissatisfaction continued though checked slightly by the July victories at Vicksburg and Gettysburg.

Meantime the democrats proceeded to enjoy the logical fruits of their victory. These were garnered in the legislative session of 1863. First, Congressman William A. Richardson, who had developed into a bitter opponent of the administration, was selected for the vacated seat in the United States senate over Governor Yates, who had been given the complimentary republican nomination. The democrats then devoted their attention to their legislative program. Resolutions denouncing the policy of the federal administration, urging an armistice and a national convention at Louisville, in which Stephen T. Logan, Samuel S. Marshall, H. K. S. Omelveny,

[23] *Chicago Times* clipped in *Illinois State Register*, June 6, 1862; Yates to Trumbull, February 14, 1862, Trumbull manuscripts.
[24] T. Maple to Trumbull, December 28, 1862, Grant Goodrich to Trumbull, January 31, 1863, *ibid.* Senator Browning was the only prominent republican to support the conservative middle ground taken by Lincoln, but he was treated by republican organs as a renegade. *Chicago Tribune*, July 2, 18, 1862.

Vote for
Congressman-
at-Large
1862

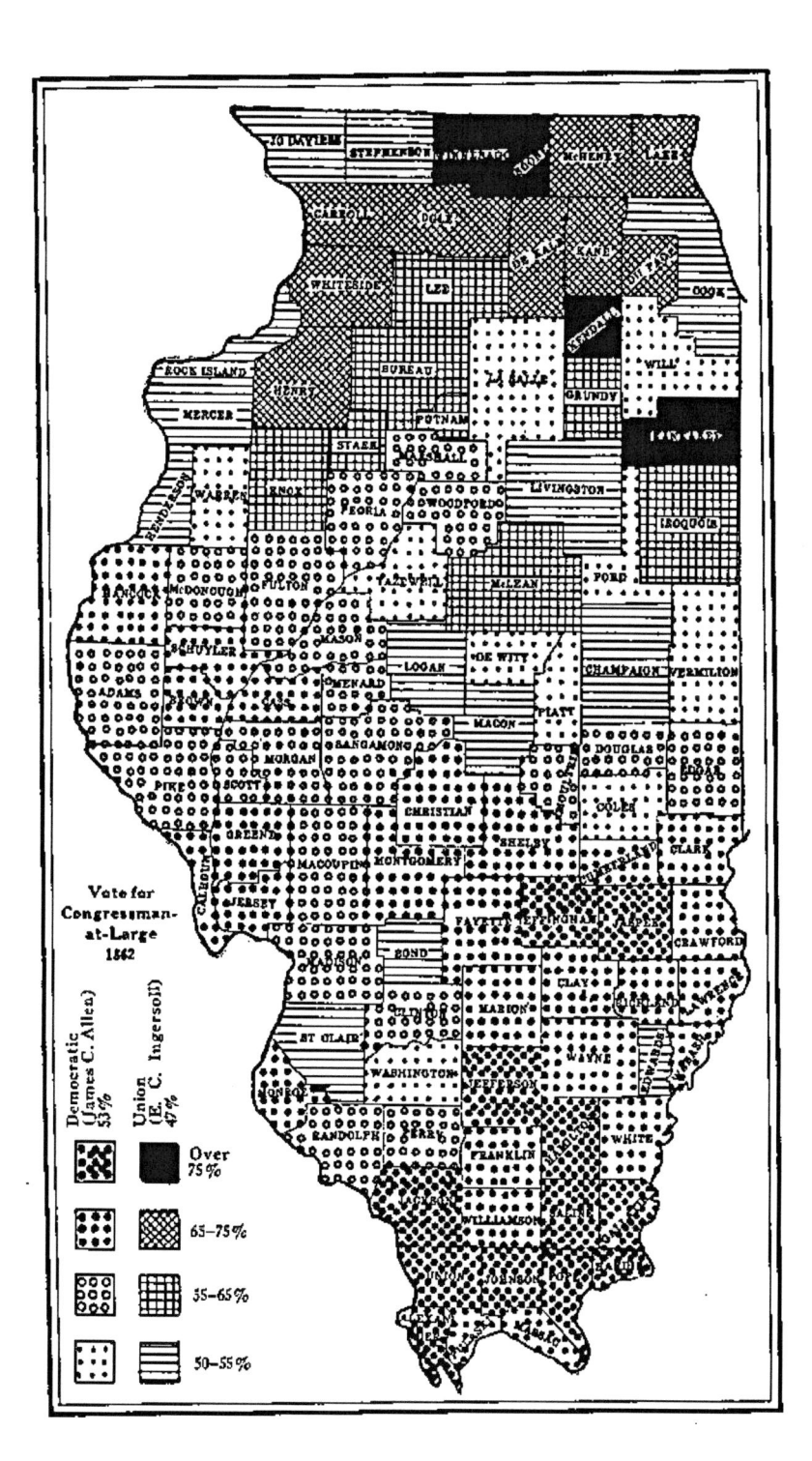

Democratic (James C. Allen) 53%
Union (E. C. Ingersoll) 47%

Over 75%
65–75%
55–65%
50–55%

William C. Goudy, Anthony Thornton, John D. Caton were named as commissioners, were pressed through the house and were blocked in the senate only by the withdrawal of the republican minority.[25] This filibustering ended only after assurances that the regular business of the legislature would be taken up until disposed of; after the apportionment and appropriation bills had been passed a recess was taken until June. Since Governor Yates had vetoed the apportionment bill, the democrats made their plans to pass it over his veto. A habeas corpus bill to prevent illegal arrests, a bill to prevent the immigration of Negroes, and resolutions reported by a joint committee on federal relations were also to be taken up. Irritated beyond endurance by his obstreperous opponents, Governor Yates interposed to end the session by proroguing the legislature — the first time in the history of the state that a governor had exercised this power. A vigorous protest against this action was drawn up and signed by the democratic members, who refused to recognize his authority; the house formally remained in session for a fortnight.[26]

While the democratic majority of the legislature was protesting at its prorogation, there was held at Springfield, June 17, 1863, a democratic mass convention which, it was estimated, brought together forty thousand enthusiastic anti-administration democrats and their most influential leaders. Following addresses by Senator Richardson, Congressmen S. S. Marshall, James C. Robinson, J. R. Eden, J. C. Allen, and other responsible democrats, resolutions were adopted affirming the supremacy of the constitution in time of war as well as of peace; condemning the violations of the bill of rights by the national administration; pronouncing the action of Governor Yates in proroguing the legislature an act of usurpation; then, in the famous "twenty-third resolution" declaring that as the "further offensive prosecution of this war tends to sub-

[25] These resolutions also denounced "the ruinous heresy of secession" and opposed recognition of the independence of the southern confederacy as inconsistent with the interests of the great northwest. *House Journal*, 1863, p. 373-375.
[26] The question of the legality of Governor Yates' act was taken to the state supreme court which, however, sustained the governor. *Illinois State Journal*, June 11, 1863; *Illinois State Register*, June 11, 1863; *Joliet Signal*, June 30, 1863; *Chicago Times*, October 30, November 7, 14, December 16, 25, 1863.

vert the constitution and the government, and entail upon this Nation all the disastrous consequences of misrule and anarchy" the convention was "in favor of peace upon the basis of a restoration of the Union" for the accomplishment of which it proposed a national convention to settle upon the terms of peace.[27]

This was the forerunner of a series of meetings in which the democrats of Illinois voiced their desire for the restoration of peace, and such meetings afforded republican leaders an opportunity to exaggerate the animus of the democratic forces in the state. It was easy enough to construe specific items in the democratic indictment of administration policies as incontrovertible evidences of disloyalty. Lincoln's proclamation was denounced in an imposing popular demonstration at Springfield as "unwarrantable in military as in civil law; a gigantic usurpation, at once converting the war, professedly commenced by the administration for the vindication of the authority of the constitution, into a crusade for the sudden, unconditional and violent liberation of three million slaves."[28] Democratic journals insisted that the proclamation, in giving the south something definite to fight for in place of an abstraction, had caused the prolongation of the war; the *Chicago Times* suggested that it was properly called a "war measure" as one which would "protract the war indefinitely."[29] The conscription bill of 1863 was vigorously opposed under the leadership of Senator Richardson; in its enactment the democrats of Illinois acquiesced mainly because their state had furnished thousands of volunteers in excess of its quota.

Democrats, moreover, were unsparing in their denunciation of the complete disregard of personal liberty evidenced in the arbitrary arrest of critics of the administration, and in the

---

[27] Moses, *Illinois*, 2:687-688; *Illinois State Register*, May 27, 29, 30, June 2, 4, 5, 18, 1863; *Illinois State Journal*, June 18, 1863; *Ottawa Republican*, June 18, 20, 1863; *Chicago Tribune*, June 20, 1863; *Joliet Signal*, June 23, 1863. A resolution denied that the democratic party was wanting in sympathy for the soldiers in the field; the evidence of the sincerity of this declaration, $47,400 was raised at the meeting by subscriptions and pledges which Colonel W. R. Morrison was directed to distribute in aid of sick and wounded Illinois volunteers.
[28] *Illinois State Register*, January 6, 1863; *Illinois State Journal*, January 7, 16, 1863; *Jonesboro Gazette*, January 10, 1863.
[29] *Chicago Times*, September 24, 1863; *Joliet Signal*, March 24, 1863; *Cairo Democrat*, September 20, 1863.

denial of freedom of speech and of the press. In the late summer of 1863 there took place a wide suspension under executive order of the writ of habeas corpus, the one remaining guarantee of personal liberty.[30] All administration supporters, even, could not agree with the *Illinois Staats-Zeitung* when it declared on April 19, 1862, that "Those who, in time like the present talk of the right of habeas corpus, sympathize with the rebels." The *Chicago Times*, October 1, 1863, therefore assailed the suspension of the writ of habeas corpus as "an act so bold, so flagrant, so unprecedented, and involving to so great an extent the rights, the liberties, and even the lives of the people, that its legality and propriety cannot be too thoroughly discussed." The *Belleville Democrat*, September 26, 1863, called it "the death of liberty;" it "makes the will of Abraham Lincoln the supreme law of the land, and the people, who have made him what he is, the mere slaves of his caprice." Claiming that President Lincoln had finally surrendered himself to the radicals and that the subjugation of the south to these radical policies was a practical impossibility, many began to urge the termination of the war if necessary by a compromise. The proposition for a peace conference at Louisville received wide support; it was suggested as a necessary preliminary that President Lincoln "with draw his unconstitutional emancipation proclamation."[31]

It was the task of administration officials to drive this opposition underground; but, since official action could not be thorough, the leaders of public opinion took it upon themselves to crush it by a skillful appeal to the patriotism of the masses. In favorable locations champions were easily found to administer severe thrashings as a rebuke to the anti-war spokesman. Neighbors who more quietly shared the same views left many a loose-tongued critic of the government to his own defense when some band of union regulators brought him to silence by threats and intimidation, if not by physical violence. Vigilance committees to hunt out and punish secession sympathizers were organized against the advice of the more levelheaded;[32]

[30] *Chicago Times*, September 17, 19, 25, 1863.
[31] *Joliet Signal*, April 14, 1863.
[32] *Chicago Tribune*, April 24, 1861.

they soon made free speech a byword, so far as criticism of governmental policy was concerned, and freedom of public assembly an obsolete right. It was generally believed that only such methods could hold back a flood of "copperheadism" that threatened to engulf the union cause in Illinois.

Every democrat who did not openly and actively support the administration and the war was labelled a venomous "copperhead," at once a southern sympathizer and a traitor to the union. At the beginning of the war, indeed, sympathy for the south was very widespread; democratic papers in southern Illinois had placed the blame for secession on the abolitionist rather than the slavocrat. This feeling continued and was often translated into action, varying from cheers for Jefferson Davis to active aid for the rebel cause; military companies were recruited to aid the south and prominent public men encouraged enlistment. A half dozen prominent democratic journals boldly suggested the division of the state so that Egypt might consider the possibility of joining the southern confederacy— William J. Allen, member of congress after 1862, openly proposed this to John A. Logan, at the same time advising men to go south to fight.[33]

The most outspoken opposition to the government was finally driven underground. By a system of wholesale arbitrary arrests, so offensive as to bring out protests from radical republican legislators, like Senator Trumbull, and army officers like General Palmer, the work of intimidating persons suspected of disloyalty had been given a good start. Among the victims of arbitrary arrests for disloyal practices were to be found many persons who in the previous decade had taken a prominent part in state politics. In September, 1862, Benjamin Bond, United States marshal under Fillmore and a prominent conservative, was arrested by Lincoln's appointee to the same office. In the course of time other state prisoners were rounded up, including W. J. Allen, member of congress, Judge John H. Mulkey, Judge Andrew D. Duff, Judge C. H. Constable, state senator William H. Green of Massac county, Levi

---

[33] *Canton Weekly Register,* January 29, April 9, 1861; *Central Illinois Gazette,* October 21, 1864; *Illinois State Journal,* July 30, 1862; J. H. Brown and S. M. Thrift to Trumbull, May 26, 1862, Trumbull manuscripts.

D. Boon, an old democratic wheel horse, and M. Y. Johnson and David Sheean, lawyers of Galena.[34] Several of these were "honorably discharged" after weeks of confinement, not, however, without the taint in reputation that in the public mind follows such treatment.

The suppression of opposition journals was attempted to check unrestrained defiance of governmental policies; few democratic editors followed the lead of James W. Sheahan of the *Chicago Morning Post* in supporting the war policy of the government without giving up the democratic point of view. Certain vigorous critics like the *Peoria Demokrat* were denied the privilege of the mails early in the war.[35] In July, 1862, the circulation of the *Quincy Herald* in Missouri was forbidden by military order on the assumption that it encouraged the rebel bushwhackers. In the same summer the arrests of the editor and publishers caused the temporary suspension of the *Paris Democratic Standard* while the *Bloomington Times* office was destroyed by a union mob. In December, John C. Doblebower, editor of the Jerseyville *Democratic Union*, fled to escape arrest.

Early in 1863 the Chicago Board of Trade and Y. M. C. A. started a boycott of the *Chicago Times,* and the Chicago and Galena railroad for a time prohibited its sale on the company's trains. In February, General Hurlbut at Memphis, and other post commanders forbade the circulation of the *Times* within their respective districts. On June 1, without waiting to confer with the war department, General A. E. Burnside, in command of the department of the northwest, issued general order number 84 which proclaimed the suppression of

---

[34] J. M. Palmer to Trumbull, January 3, 1862, Trumbull manuscripts; Koerner, *Memoirs,* 2:173; *Senate Journal,* 37 congress, 1 session, 40; White, *Life of Trumbull,* 191-200. Both Sheean and Johnson, however, successfully sued the federal marshal for arrest and false imprisonment, and Sheean was soon elected mayor of Galena. Johnson's case was carried in 1867 to the federal supreme court; the judges applied the principle of *ex parte* Milligan and pronounced decisively against arbitrary arrests; the court referred the case to jury trial in Jo Daviess county, where Johnson was awarded a judgment of one thousand dollars and costs. *Illinois State Register,* January 28, 1863, July 15, 1867; *Chicago Evening Journal,* November 15, 1865; *Chicago Tribune,* July 9, 1867; *Portrait and Biographical Album of Jo Daviess and Carroll Counties,* 192-193, 206-211.

[35] *Rockford Register,* October 19, 1861; *Canton Weekly Register,* October 22, 1861.

the *Chicago Times* and of the *Jonesboro Gazette,* " on account of the repeated expression of disloyal and incendiary statements." Before daybreak on June 3, a military detachment from Camp Douglas took possession of the *Times* printing establishment. Within a few hours a meeting of prominent citizens of both political parties presided over by the mayor unanimously agreed to request the president by telegraph to rescind Burnside's order—a request which was reënforced by the personal solicitation of Senator Trumbull and Representative I. N. Arnold of the Chicago district. The lower house at Springfield simultaneously passed a resolution condemning the Burnside order. In Chicago that evening a mass meeting of twenty thousand representative voters gathered and enthusiastically resolved that the freedom of speech and of the press should be upheld by the subordination of the military power to the civil authority. The next day, while sixteen carloads of soldiers from Springfield were on their way to Chicago to handle the crisis there, President Lincoln responded to the pressure of public opinion in Chicago by revoking the order suppressing the *Times.* At Urbana the troops were stopped by telegraph and informed of Lincoln's action, whereupon General Burnside wisely recalled the whole order.[36]

With that date official interference with freedom of the press came to an end, and public opinion was left to do the work of discouraging carping and disloyal criticism. One of the most irritating critics of the administration was the *Chester Picket Guard,* only a short distance from the military depot at Cairo; in July, 1864, just after it had been refitted and furnished with new presses, a mob of soldiers and civilians sacked and completely destroyed the whole equipment.[37]

The contemporary judgment of these cases of interference with freedom of press may be found in the silent disapproval voiced by subscribers to the persecuted journals; after its ill-treatment the circulation of the *Chicago Times* increased

---

[36] *War of the Rebellion, Official Records,* series 1, volume 23, part 2, p. 381; *Illinois State Journal,* February 14, 18, June 3, 6, 8, 1863; *Illinois State Register,* June 3, 5, 10, 1863; *Chicago Times,* June 30, 1863; *Writings of Lincoln,* 6: 306. The *Belleville Democrat,* June 13, 1863, suggested that Lincoln's action alone prevented civil war.

[37] *Cairo Democrat,* April 9, July 30, 1864; *Jonesboro Gazette,* July 30, 1864; *Belleville Democrat,* July 30, 1864; *Chester Picket Guard,* November 29, 1865.

ABOLITIONISTS AND COPPERHEADS

materially among the common people. Both war and peace democrats, moreover, challenged the gross usurpation of power by the military authorities and decried the recourse to mob violence. Other champions of civil rights came from among that body of spirited radicals who, while dissatisfied with the slow progress that was being made against the south and slavery, heartily disapproved interference. The *State Journal* had in anticipation undertaken to declare as early as June 25, 1861: "Public men are, to a certain extent, public property, and the people and the Press are free to praise or censure their actions. We would never see this right abridged."[38]

The justification for drastic action by individuals or by government authorities was found in the so-called "crimes of the copperheads," which terrorized not only individuals but whole communities. They were so numerous and varied that there was a fearful uncertainty as to when and how the copperheads might next strike. Many carried on an active and open propaganda to discourage enlistments and to obstruct the operation of the conscription law—the enrollment in preparation for the draft arousing widespread opposition. Fulton county and vicinity had more than their share of draft troubles; in June, 1863, the enrolling officers in certain districts were driven off forcibly by armed mobs, and after repetitions of this experience a military force was sent to protect the provost marshal and his deputies. In spite of such protection, however, the draft resisters attacked the officers and in two instances at least there were fatal shootings. Olney was for three days besieged by a mob of 500 men, who threatened to burn the town unless the enrollment lists were given up.[39]

Another serious offense charged against the copperheads was that of influencing desertion, which in the spring of 1863 became especially serious. Desertions were, indeed, the result either of the advice and aid of relatives and friends, or of any anti-war agency that stressed the view that this was an unholy and anti-democratic war — an attempt on the part of the "abo-

---
[38] *Illinois State Journal*, June 25, 1861; *Jonesboro Gazette*, January 31, 1863.
[39] *Canton Weekly Register*, June 29, 1863, October 31, 1864; *Rushville Times*, May 13, 20, 1869; *Evansville* (Indiana) *Journal* clipped in *Rockford Register*, August 1, 1863; *Biographical and Reminiscent History of Richland, Clay, and Marion Counties*, 422-423.

litionists" to break down the democratic party. From June 1 to October 10, 1863, 2,001 arrests were made in Illinois, and in the three following months 800 deserters were apprehended. By the end of the war there were 13,046 desertions of enlisted men from Illinois. In January, 1863, following wholesale desertions and fraternization with the rebels that assumed the proportions of a mutiny the One hundred and ninth regiment, recruited largely from the heart of Egypt, was arrested, disarmed, and placed under guard at Holly Springs, Mississippi. The One hundred and twenty-eighth regiment at Cairo suffered so heavily from desertions that there remained in March, 1863, only thirty-five men in the ranks.[40] Federal troops detailed to arrest the numerous deserters in southern Illinois counties often found themselves thwarted not only by the concealment of the renegades but by the armed opposition of mobs formed to prevent their arrest. In some instances backsliders were rescued from the custody of officers; in other instances they failed with a heavy loss in killed and wounded.

Armed resistance on the part of the anti-war forces was a constant fear in the minds of union men. A heavy demand for Colts' revolvers, guns, and ammunition was noticed by storekeepers whose supplies were drained by buyers from copperhead districts. Guerrilla bands, formed in the rural regions of southern Illinois, conducted demonstrations in places as large as Charleston, Jacksonville, and Vandalia; a band operating in Union county destroyed property of loyal men and assaulted unionists who fell in its hands. Armed rebel sympathizers often met in numbers for military organization and drill. Union men were seized and whipped and sometimes driven from their homes; in numerous instances they were shot down, even in their own homes, by rebel sympathizers.[41]

[40] *Chicago Tribune,* March 18, October 19, 1863, October 20, 1866; *Belleville Advocate,* January 1, 1864; *Cairo Democrat,* March 9, 1864; Halleck to Grant, August 11, 1864, *War of the Rebellion, Official Records,* series 1, volume 42, part 2, p. 112; *Illinois State Journal,* January 12, 13, 15, 28, 29, February 3, 1863.
[41] See list of murders in *Illinois State Journal,* February 8, 1864. General Wright issued an order prohibiting the traffic in arms and ammunition in the department of the Ohio. *Ibid.,* March 31, 1863. *Jacksonville Journal,* March 19, September 17, 1863; *Chicago Tribune,* August 3, 1862, April 18, May 5, 1863. Finally Jonesboro, the residence of a number of the marauders, and a town with only three union men, was seized by federal troops who made a large number of arrests.

Many of these acts, it must be remembered, were done in a spirit of retaliation for the lynch law visited upon more or less harmless peace advocates. The latter, indeed, had at the start the more ground for complaint against the outrages perpetrated on them by the super-patriots of the day. The democrats complained that Governor Yates had repeatedly condoned such acts of violence; and as "the arch-criminal who has 'sowed the wind'" they hoped for the sake of justice that he might "reap the whirlwind." They invoked the law of reprisals in their defense: having in vain counseled obedience to law and an appeal to it for redress in all cases of lawlessness, they felt that responsibility for having to organize for their own protection and to make reprisals in kind, rested upon their opponents.[42]

In the closing years of the war this organized retaliation became extremely serious. Gangs of bushwhackers from Missouri, horse thieves and deserters from both armies swelled the ranks of the copperhead desperadoes in the river counties and for a long time threw all central and southern Illinois into a panic.[43] Under the daring leader named Clingman one band of armed guerrillas, largely clad in butternut clothing or in gray rebel uniforms with white ribbons on their hats, did especial damage in the vicinity of Montgomery county until it was broken up in the summer of 1864.

Edgar and Coles counties were the seats of especial disturbances. On the outskirts of Paris a band of several hundred insurgents had its rendezvous and terrorized the neighborhood. In February, 1864, the town was threatened by attack until federal forces came to its relief; even then armed clashes between the copperheads and the soldiers took place.[44] On March 28, the storm broke loose in Charleston when a bloody affray occurred between armed backers of Congressman J. R. Eden and soldiers under Major York who were then on a furlough; Major York and two union men were killed while two copperheads met their death. The Fifty-fourth Illinois regi-

[42] *Chicago Times*, March 11, April 28, 1864.
[43] *Illinois State Register*, May 31, 1863; *Chicago Tribune*, July 28, 1864; *Illinois State Journal*, August 3, 1864; *Cairo Morning News*, January 12, 1865.
[44] *Chicago Tribune*, February 7, 1864; *Illinois State Journal*, March 2, 5, 1864.

ment was promptly dispatched from Mattoon, and the Forty-first Illinois and Forty-seventh Indiana followed as reenforcements. Although before their arrival the rioters had disbanded, numerous arrests were made and the city and county placed under martial law. For several days rumors circulated that a force of ten hundred to twelve hundred insurgents had collected outside the town, threatening to attack either Charleston or Mattoon; Sheriff John O'Hair of Coles county and the sheriff of Edgar county were said to be the ringleaders of the conspiracy. The unionists of Charleston organized to prevent a repetition of this experience, and little difficulty was experienced in this region for the remainder of the war. The Charleston "riots," however, loom up as the worst example of copperhead "outrages" in Illinois.[45]

A secret political society known as the Knights of the Golden Circle furnished the basis for unity of action by those anti-war forces that preferred to work under cover. This was originally an organization of young southern filibusters who had purposed to invade Mexico in order finally to Americanize and annex that republic; when first brought to the attention of Illinoisians in the spring of 1860, the newspapers warned adventuresome spirits against the "humbug." With the outbreak of the rebellion, however, it became the stronghold of secession sympathizers; it found a foothold in Egypt where conditions were most favorable and spread rapidly over the state.[46] Chicago was said to have established a lodge in the spring of 1861; the organization became a formidable factor in the political life of every section of Illinois. The activities of the various lodges remain obscured by the secrecy of meet-

[45] *Illinois State Journal*, March 30, April 1, 2, 4, 1864; *Charleston Plaindealer*, March 28, clipped in *ibid.*, April 16, 1864; *Chicago Tribune*, March 29, 30, 31, 1864. The brother of Sheriff O'Hair and the son of the sheriff of Shelby county were included in the list of prisoners arrested by the military. O'Hair was later murdered in retaliation for the "Charleston murders." The *Coles County Ledger*, a democratic paper, vigorously condemned the "votaries of Jeff Davis and slavery," but the opposition papers throughout the state treated the incident as a row between drunken citizens and drunken soldiers, which the union men used for political capital. *Chicago Times*, April 1, 1864; *Joliet Signal*, April 5, 1864; *Ottawa Free Trader*, April 2, 1864; *Carthage Republican*, May 5, 1864; *Cairo Democrat*, June 26, 1864; *Coles County Ledger* clipped in *Belleville Advocate*, April 15, 1864.

[46] *Cairo Gazette*, April 5, 1860; the ritual may be found in *The* (Columbus, Ohio) *Crisis*, December 30, 1863; *Canton Weekly Register*, May 21, 1861.

ABOLITIONISTS AND COPPERHEADS 309

ings protected by signs and passwords; evidence points, however, to an organization which covered anything from a dark lantern democratic reorganization as an anti-war party to actual constructive treason. In 1861, a number of persons in southern Illinois arrested as Knights of the Golden Circle were investigated before a commission appointed by Judge Samuel H. Treat of the federal district court; the commission reported, however, that membership in these organizations did not involve treason to the United States. A further investigation of the order followed the arrest of Congressman W. J. Allen and Judges Duff and Mulkey in the summer of 1862. The existence of the order and even the object of effecting the reorganization of the democratic party could easily be proved; but the charge that it was organized along military lines for armed opposition to the government and its policies could not be substantiated. A state convention or Grand Castle was held in Chicago, August 4, 1863, with seventy-one counties represented but its secrecy was not penetrated; another state convention met on March 4-8, 1864, after which the *Chicago Tribune* published what purported to be the newly adopted ritual of the order, but this, whatever its other points of vulnerability, furnished no proof of treasonable intentions.[47]

In order to combat the anti-war propaganda of the Knights of the Golden Circle, the unionists organized a secret oathbound political society of their own, known as the Union League. The first Illinois council was formed at Pekin, Tazewell county, on June 25, 1862; and the order was well under way by the end of the summer when the first state convention was held. In the following year the goal of a league in every township was set up. Lists of names and residences of "copperheads" were drawn up and sent to the league headquarters at Springfield, and the order went forth that "the council must be put on a war footing;" just what this meant was extremely indefinite, although their opponents thought they found — in

[47] In December, 1861, ten thousand members were said to have been enrolled. *Chicago Tribune*, November 12, 1861, August 26, 1862, March 27, 28, 1864; *Cairo Gazette*, November 14, 1861; *Belleville Advocate*, September 5, 1862; *Illinois State Journal*, August 27, 1862; *Carbondale Times* clipped in *ibid.*, December 7, 1861.

shipments of government arms and equipment from Springfield to local leagues — an answer of civil war.[48]

The Union Leaguers pointed ominously to a new danger on the horizon, the danger of a revolt to effect the establishment of a northwestern confederacy. This more dangerous venture had apparently become the undertaking of the reorganized Knights of the Golden Circle who had adopted the name of Ancient Order of American Knights or Sons of Liberty. This order, obviously political in its aims, was charged with arming and organizing its members for a revolt to detach the northwestern states. How far this purpose was accepted in Illinois is obscured by the secrecy of the methods of the day and by the lapse of time; many democratic leaders undoubtedly did believe in the desirability and inevitability of the detachment of the west from its New England connections, but they were not always prepared to secure this end through the work of secret political orders.[49] In August, 1864, however, a band of alleged conspirators was arrested; and when the trial was held at Indianapolis, evidence was submitted that a conference had been held at Chicago by a council of sixteen representing the states of Illinois, Indiana, Missouri, and Kentucky and, in order to clear the way for an uprising, had formulated the plan of overturning the governments of those states and releasing the rebel prisoners at the prison camps.[50] These plans, however, were not communicated to the body of the society; and the wild rumors that, out of a membership of 100,000 in Illinois, 40,000 or 50,000 armed knights stood ready to coöperate with the confederate forces to overthrow federal control, seem to have had little foundation in fact. When, moreover, on November 8, during the excitement of election day, copperhead leaders and confederate agents from Canada attempted to release the nine thousand rebel prisoners at Camp Douglas, they were thwarted and the so-called "rebel invasion" or "Chicago conspiracy" ended with the arrest of a

[48] *Canton Weekly Register*, April 20, 1863; the league ritual was published in the March 23, 1863 issue. *Belleville Democrat*, February 20, 1864; *Carthage Republican*, April 14, October 27, 1864.
[49] *Chicago Times*, July 30, August 1, 1864; *St. Louis Democrat* clipped in *Illinois State Journal*, August 6, 1864; *Jonesboro Gazette*, January 3, 1863.
[50] *Illinois State Journal*, November 2, 4, 8, 1864; Pitman, *Indiana Treason Trials;* Ayer, *The Great Treason Plot*, 56 ff.

half dozen alleged ringleaders. In the conspiracy trials at Cincinnati the following spring, two of these, Buckner S. Morris and Vincent Marmaduke, were acquitted but the others, including an English soldier, were convicted.[51] In this atmosphere of plot and counterplot, Illinois wrestled with the nightmare of civil strife.

[51] *Chicago Tribune,* November 8, 9, 1864, April 25, 1864; *Chicago Times,* November 8, 9, 1864; *Cairo Weekly Democrat,* April 27, 1865; *Atlantic Monthly,* 16:108-120; Ayer, *The Great Treason Plot,* 163-171; Rhodes, *History of the United States,* 5:324 ff.

XIV. THE REELECTION OF LINCOLN

THE time was rapidly drawing near when it was necessary to prepare for the elections of 1864. The heavy republican reverses of 1862 made the national political situation extremely uncertain, while in Illinois the democratic victories had been so sweeping that the republicans displayed considerable anxiety over the coming popular decision. The election was to be a test of the success of the Lincoln administration; yet, although it was logical for the republicans to name Lincoln as their standard bearer, it was by no means certain that he could lead their hosts to victory. While his success with difficult feats of political balancing compelled the admiration of many who chose to travel along middle ground, there were others who scorned his dispassionate efforts to maintain his political equilibrium. Democratic obstructionists on the one side and radical republicans on the other were convinced that Lincoln possessed "neither consistency, statesmanship or resolution;" the latter, however, could not subscribe to the partisan charge that "even the claim set up for his honesty was absolutely unfounded and that the country has never before been afflicted with a ruler so absolutely destitute of integrity and principles."[1]

In handling the problems of civil war, President Lincoln had assumed certain powers which made his rôle quite as significant as that of a dictator in the days of Rome's glory. Without legislative warrant and without precedent in American history, he had suspended the privilege of the writ of habeas corpus, one of the dearest of civil rights in the minds of the American freeman. He had given at least indirect approval to most arbitrary arrests at the direction of the secretaries of state and war. Even Senator Trumbull, the radical, openly condemned the imprisonment of citizens upon *lettres de cachet*

---

[1] *Illinois State Register*, February 28, 1864, cf. February 13, 1864.

THE REELECTION OF LINCOLN

while General John M. Palmer declared that it would mean the conversion of "this Constitutional Republic into a despotism."[2] There had been also arbitrary interference with freedom of speech and of the press even outside the zone of actual fighting, the responsibility of which Lincoln had to share. By executive order he had undertaken to strike the shackles from thousands of slaves and thus to destroy property rights to the amount of millions of dollars, though slavery was recognized, if not protected, under the constitution. He had recommended and officially approved, March 3, 1863, a conscription act which provided for compulsory military service by citizens selected at the turn of a wheel. These were only the principal features of a situation which made it possible for James Bryce to say: "Abraham Lincoln wielded more authority than any single Englishman has done since Oliver Cromwell."

These acts of the executive seemed indeed to involve infractions of the constitution, unless the war powers of the president could be interpreted to cover them—even their supporters could justify them only under the plea of military necessity. Here clearly was ground for wholesome and legitimate opposition on the part of the opponents of the administration, and the democrats sought on this ground to rally round their standards the defenders of personal liberty. "There is hardly a provision of the constitution which the President has not violated or treated with contempt," was the campaign slogan announced by the *Chicago Times*.[3]

The *Cairo Democrat*, July 14, 1864, took up the hue and cry with less restraint: "When a President will thus put aside the will of Congress, what are the people to expect from him? The freedom of the press and the *habeas corpus*, the two great bulwarks of our liberty, ruthlessly invaded. And last of all the voice of the ballot box has been crushed, and 'military necessity,' that bloody and envenomed queen, has seized upon its holy precincts. Great Heavens! how much more iniquity will the freemen of America stand from the usurper and tyrant

---

[2] John M. Palmer to Trumbull, January, 1862, Trumbull manuscripts. See also *Illinois State Register*, June 6, 1863.
[3] *Chicago Times*, February 22, 1864; *Illinois State Register*, February 28, 1864.

who is only fit to split rails." Democrats claimed that Lincoln had taken these steps because, ambitious of reëlection, he had allowed himself to be coerced and had surrendered to the guidance of the radicals. "Oh, Abraham," queried the tantalizing critic, "why do you let the radical tribe always badger you from three to five months, before they get you up to the good work?"[4]

While the democrats, on the one hand, were worrying Lincoln with complaints of executive usurpation, he confronted on the other the even greater problem of satisfying those of his party who, without the responsibilities of his office, sought to hurry things more rapidly along antislavery lines; chafing at his slowness of action, they were not certain as to their influence with the president and bitterly complained of the lack of real aggressiveness in his endeavor to conquer the south. Among the disgruntled in Illinois were leading republicans, influential party organs, the state administration from Governor Yates down, together with Senator Trumbull and members of the congressional delegation. Lincoln's friend Herndon charged him with trying to put down the rebellion by squirting rosewater at it, while Jonathan B. Turner, the Jacksonville educator, condemned Lincoln for too much reading of the New Testament instead of using the sword after the fashion of that Old Testament saint, Andrew Jackson.[5]

Other evidences of the republican party's lack of homogeneity were added to this clash between the antislavery element and the conservatives; survivals of the old alignment between whig and democrat revealed themselves in mutual mistrust and jealousy. Lincoln was charged with being too generous toward his former whig associates; disappointed ex-democrats questioned the honesty and sincerity of their colleagues of whig

---

[4] "We have a President, but he is merely a clerk for registering the decrees of Secretary Chase," bewailed the *Chicago Times*, December 11, 1863. "He is as good an Abolitionist as the best of them, but the great trouble is, '*he is always six months behind in acting the thing out.*'" *Cairo Democrat*, January 3, 1864.

[5] The editors of the *Chicago Tribune* were ready for a break with the president if developments should require it. Browning was the only conservative Lincolnite and Joseph Medill claimed that he represented "only the secesh of Illinois." See Medill to Trumbull, July 4, 1864, and other letters in Trumbull manuscripts; Cole, "Lincoln and the Illinois Radical Republicans," *Mississippi Valley Historical Review*, 4:430-431.

origin. There was also the problem of the foreign vote; could concessions be made to it without stirring up opposition from persons of nativist prejudices? To make matters even worse, Lincoln's cabinet was a hotbed of bickering, suspicion, jealousy, and rivalry; he could not secure the hearty support of a majority of it on any fundamental proposition or policy.[6]

Illinois republican leaders were baffled by the intricacies of the whole situation. They recognized that Lincoln had secured a strong claim to consideration by issuing his emancipation proclamation. The *Chicago Tribune*, cautiously presented his claims to reëlection with the warning: "Just so surely as their [the radicals] policy is abandoned by one who has been committed to it, ... just so sure will that one, thus guilty and thus foolish, be trodden under their feet."[7] In general, sentiment grew that the party could ill afford to refuse Lincoln the nomination, although the radicals were loath to acquiesce in the expediency of taking the lesser of two evils — that Lincoln might not win, but anyone else was even less likely to succeed.

There was, however, little real enthusiasm for Lincoln. Even in Washington, Senator Trumbull found that there was "a distrust & fear that he is too undecided & inefficient to put down the rebellion;" party leaders felt that if possible, some other man "supposed to possess more energy" than Lincoln ought to be nominated.[8] General Fremont had a considerable following of ultra radicals; Chase was eagerly seeking supporters to back his claims; other persons like Trumbull were frequently mentioned as available. A group of prominent republican senators and congressmen issued a pronunciamento charging the responsibility for the failure to suppress the rebellion on the president in whose ability to restore the union it was declared "the people have lost all confidence."[9] "A

---
[6] Secretary of the Treasury Chase became more and more independent and having presidential aspirations of his own, finally left the cabinet. *Diary of Gideon Welles*, 2: 102, 106-107, 166.
[7] *Chicago Tribune*, November 3, 1863. The *Tribune* concluded: "It is a great historical fact that in revolutions the radical party always wins."
[8] Trumbull to H. G. McPike, February 6, 1864, Trumbull manuscripts; Washington correspondence of *Chicago Times*, January 13, 1864.
[9] See Senator Pomeroy's circular in behalf of Chase, *Chicago Times*, February 26, 1864; *Illinois State Register*, February 28, 1864.

secret movement against Mr. Lincoln's renomination is extended all over the North," announced the *Chicago Journal.* "We hear of its workings in New England, New York, Illinois, Michigan, and Wisconsin. It has male and female traveling agents, correspondents, popular lecturers and newspapers, employed to promote its object."[10]

German republican voters, many of whom were radicals of the deepest dye, enthusiastically supported the claims of Fremont, an old favorite. They grew steadily bolder in their opposition to Lincoln and were encouraged by such papers as the *Missouri Democrat* and the *Chicago Telegraph.* They announced their inability to support Lincoln's reëlection and busied themselves with the organization of Fremont clubs. The *Illinois Staats-Zeitung,* to be sure, did urge an indorsement of Lincoln, but this was explained by the Fremont following as accomplished by flattery and official favors. Through the columns of the *Mississippi Blätter* many Germans announced their loss of faith in Lincoln and declared their unwillingness to be led or coaxed in the Lincoln camp.[11] The *Highland Union,* a German republican paper, hoisted the Fremont banner. The *Blätter,* March 4, 1864, indorsed the sentiment of the *Indiana Freie Presse:* "We cannot and dare not vote for Lincoln, unless we are willing to participate in the betrayal of the republic, unless we are willing to remain for all future the most despicable step-children of the nation."

This radical German opposition came to a focus in the state convention on May 25, 1864. There Friedrich Hecker led a futile fight against the instructions to support Lincoln. The convention was divided into determined factions of Lincoln and Fremont men, although paradoxically called the union state convention. The fact that it was far from a homogeneous body was seized upon with relish by democratic opponents. "It was literally what it purported to be — a 'Union convention'— an assemblage of incongruities," reported the *State Register.* "United on no principle, but brought together by the cohesive attraction of public plunder. . . . . There

---

[10] *Chicago Journal* clipped in *Jacksonville Journal,* March 10, 1864.
[11] *Chicago Times,* February 1, 13, March 28, May 3, 1864; *Mississippi Blätter,* February 14, 1863, March 13, 20, April 10, 1864.

was Jack Kuykendall and Jack Grimshaw—Deacon Bross and Deacon Haynie—the life-time abolitionist and the quondam Nebraska man—disciples of Calhoun and followers of Garrison—preachers and profanity. .... The millenium is coming, for we have seen the lion lie down with the lamb."[12] Even in this assemblage, however, the feeling grew that they could not afford to refuse Lincoln the nomination; and, when the committee on resolutions sought middle ground by commending Lincoln's administration without, however, indorsing him for reëlection, the resolutions were tabled and a new committee appointed. Granting Lincoln's inavailability, yet who offers greater? was a question no one could answer. When, therefore, resolutions damning Lincoln with faint praise and instructing delegates to vote for him were finally presented, they were, after a hot debate, adopted.[13]

The disappointed radicals then took up the movement for an independent nominating convention at Cleveland, a week before the regular meeting at Baltimore; there John C. Fremont and General John Cochrane were nominated as the true champions of freedom and of the union. The Illinois delegation largely represented the Germans; Ernest Pruessing was honored by being made one of the vice presidents, while Caspar Butz was a member of both the committee on permanent organization and of the committee on resolutions.[14]

The Cleveland convention cleared the republican ranks of a large group of obstructionists. The situation was thereby rendered more favorable for Lincoln's nomination at the regular republican, or union, convention at Baltimore on June 7. Chase still canvassed his chances, and his followers did not give up the field until an examination of the political situation at Washington on the eve of the convention indicated the hopelessness of the contest.[15] The delegates, catching the political

[12] *Illinois State Register*, May 26, 1864; cf. *Illinois State Journal*, May 26, 1864.
[13] See Joseph Medill's personal explanation, *Chicago Tribune*, May 15, 1868.
[14] *Illinois State Journal*, June 1, 1864. Butz, who was leader of the radical Fremont forces in Illinois, had been publishing at Chicago the *Deutsch-Amerikanische Monatschefte*, a journal on the plan of the *Atlantic Monthly*, with anti-Lincoln editorial policy. *Joliet Signal*, March 15, 1864. Ernest Schmidt as well as Butz and Pruessing signed one of the calls for the Cleveland convention. McPherson, *Political History of the Rebellion*, 410-411.
[15] *Diary of Gideon Welles*, 2:44, 45.

drift at Washington, passed on to Baltimore where, acting out of a sense of duty, they nominated Lincoln by acclamation but without any display of real enthusiasm.

The Fremont-Lincoln imbroglio rent the membership of the party. Lincoln's renomination was explained as the work of the spoilsmen: officeholders and contractors. In vain did the moderators praise the president and plead for union and harmony. The democratic papers fanned the fires of republican discontent by generous publicity for the Fremont movement.[16]

The republicans thus entered upon the campaign of 1864 under divided leadership. Nothing seemed to go satisfactorily during the summer months. With blunders on the sea, with failures in the land operations which in spite of a ruthless sacrifice of blood and treasure in Grant's attempted offensive, exposed Washington to capture by a small hostile force, more and more was said of the incompetency of the republican administration. Congress even went so far as to ask the president to set apart a day for fasting, humiliation, and prayer; when the appointed day arrived, August 4, Secretary of the Navy Welles soberly commented: "There is much wretchedness and great humiliation in the land, and need of earnest prayer." [17]

The break between Lincoln and the radicals was widened by conflicting views on the question of reconstruction. Republican leaders like Thaddeus Stevens and Senator Sumner held that secession had destroyed the statehood of the southern states which would have to accept the drastic jurisdiction which congress was authorized to exercise over territories. The "state suicide" theory found its advocates in Illinois, while others believed that the south would have to be subjected to the fate of conquered provinces.[18]

---

[16] *Cairo Democrat*, August 7, 9, 1864; cf. *Chicago Times*, June 6, 7, 9, 1864.
[17] *Diary of Gideon Welles*, 2:93; *Chicago Times*, June 29, 1864.
[18] See *ante*, 290; *Chicago Tribune*, October 3, 1863. One zealot proposed that " South Carolina be confiscated entire and become a territory to belong to the United States & be governed by the laws of Congress as the District of Columbia & let the whole state be appropriated to the blacks where they can cultivate the soil enjoy the benefit of schools and the institutions of the gospel preparatory to their carrying the same blessings to their fatherland and to the colonies they may form elsewhere." [no signature] to Trumbull, April 11, 1862, Trumbull manuscripts.

In an amnesty proclamation dated December 8, 1863, Lincoln had alarmed the radical republicans by assuming the restoration of the southern states under executive direction; but these advocates of congressional jurisdiction were pacified by his expressed willingness to abandon his own matured plan for one which might better "accomplish the great end of saving the Union, and redeeming the land from the curse of slavery."[19] When, however, in the early summer of 1864 the radicals in congress brought forward their own scheme in the Wade-Davis bill Lincoln, who considered it too drastic, defeated it with a pocket veto. This forced the issue; the radicals replied with a manifesto, crying out their defiance in a note that echoed over the prairies of Illinois.[20]

With all these elements of weakness in the administration party, it seemed to be doomed. Prominent supporters of Lincoln in Illinois, like Congressman Elihu B. Washburne, agreed with their associates elsewhere that they were fighting a losing battle. The republican national executive committee notified Lincoln of his probable defeat. Lincoln resigned himself to his fate and prepared "to so cooperate with the President-elect as to save the Union between the election and the inauguration."[21]

Out of the gloom of those depressing months of 1864 there rose before the American people a dread vision of the human lives destroyed by confederate bullets and camp disease, of widows and orphans, of more suffering and anguish and despair. The faith of many in "war to the finish" was shaken. "Peace! Peace!" was the cry that rose on every hand. Many distinguished and patriotic Americans believed and said that the war was a failure. Wendell Phillips undertook to remind himself and the nation that all civil wars are ended by compromises. Horace Greeley voiced the growing demand for a move to bring about an understanding with the south; so discouraged was he with the military situation that he was ready for peace at almost any price. Declaring that nine-

---

[19] *Chicago Tribune,* December 11, 1863; *Chicago Morning Post,* December 17, 1863.
[20] *Cairo Democrat,* August 13, 1864.
[21] *Writings of Abraham Lincoln,* 7: 196-197. Lincoln informed Gustave Koerner of his fears of defeat. Koerner, *Memoirs,* 2:432.

tenths of the people were equally anxious for an end to the war, he brought such pressure to bear upon Lincoln that the latter was compelled to sanction informal conferences with confederate agents at Niagara and Richmond. President Lincoln, however, submitted such an extreme ultimatum that, as he expected, it was straightway rejected; he was therefore denounced as an intolerant opponent of fair peace terms.[22] In Illinois the democrats found rich political capital in this situation. The administration party, declared the *Chicago Times*, July 25, 1864, "has been offered peace and Union, and has rejected the offer. It demands the wealth and lives of our people to prosecute a crusade against an institution whose rights are guaranteed by the law investing them with temporary power, and which they have sworn to defend and support." "The unceasing and still-recurring demands of Mr. Lincoln for more human lives is absolutely appalling. Where are the million and a half of human beings which the war has already swallowed up?"[23] "We are told," declared the *Cairo Daily Democrat*, July 31, "that we must fight on, fight ever, for the Union! We want the Union! None in the Lincoln army whether fanatic or Democrat wants the old Union more than we do. We would fight for it, die for it. But we must have peace."

The *Chicago Times* was explicit as to "how democrats would end the war:" "In detail, the policy of the democracy, after gaining possession of the government, and thus removing the cause of the secession of the South, would be to remedy one by one the grievances inaugurated by the republican administration, and against which the South is fighting. They would offer the South the constitution, and with it the guarantee that for all time the rights of the States under that constitution should be preserved inviolate. This would be a victory over the rebellion more potent than the taking of a dozen Richmonds or the slaughter of an hundred thousand rebels in arms."[24]

The organization of this peace propaganda the democrats

---

[22] This in Greeley's opinion was sufficient in itself to involve his defeat. Rhodes, *History of the United States*, 4: 513-514, 517; *Cairo Weekly Democrat*, January 3, 1864; *Cairo Morning News*, July 23, 1864.
[23] *Chicago Times*, February 5, 1864.
[24] *Ibid.*, July 2, 1864; cf. *Cairo Democrat*, July 29, 1864.

of Illinois had started openly in the late spring of 1863; under the lead of General Singleton, a series of democratic peace conventions had declared that peace was the creed of the democratic party. Conservative leaders sought to hold the party to this course; John Reynolds in "An appeal to the Democratic party of Illinois" urged peace, declaring that "Abolitionism is, and always was, the cause of the war." "The slave States," he stated, "have not now, and never had, any intention to dismember the Union, until Abolitionism forced them to defend their property."[25]

In line with this movement leading democrats made provision for an expression of opinion at a mass "democratic convention" at Peoria early in August, 1864. The meeting was arranged by the Illinois Order of American Knights and the list of 146 signers of the call included such peace advocates as James W. Singleton, Amos Green, Madison Y. Johnson, and David Sheean. Several thousand persons responded to the call — the *Chicago Times* said ten to twenty thousand, while the *Tribune* estimated the attendance as seven or eight thousand.[26] The convention adopted resolutions that declared the coercion and subjugation of sovereign states impossible as well as unauthorized by the constitution and urged an armistice, a convention of the states, and the repeal of all unconstitutional edicts and pretended laws as a preliminary to a final and honorable peace. The meeting resolved to reassemble at Springfield on August 18. Again the pilgrims of peace gathered in multi-

[25] *Belleville Democrat*, January 9, 1864. On November 25, 1863, a convention of war democrats from all parts of the union met at Chicago to establish a war democracy; on December 3, 1863, a "consulting convention" of peace democrats" from the northwestern states met there for special organization. The *Chicago Post* and the *Chicago Times* frowned on both of these abortive movements as unnecessary and harmful to the democratic cause. *Chicago Morning Post*, November 8, December 15, 1863; *Chicago Times*, November 26, December 12, 1863.

[26] *Illinois State Journal*, July 11, 21, August 6, 1864; the *Chicago Times*, July 8, 1864, protested the call of a democratic mass convention without reference to the regularly constituted authority of the party. Cf. *Canton Weekly Register*, July 18, 1864. The *Chicago Morning Post* (democratic) protested against the peace party's use of the name of the democratic party; it suggested that "love for Peoria whiskey" helped to explain the participation of at least certain politicians. The *Peoria Mail* said there were from twenty-five thousand to forty thousand people at the meeting, the *Illinois State Register*, August 6, said fifteen to twenty-five thousand, while the *Peoria Transcript* said less than two thousand.

tudes, arriving on horseback and in wagons bearing white banners with peace devices and mottoes; silver-tongued orators from neighboring states and from the different sections of Illinois charmed the large audience which was adorned with white rosettes and peace badges emblematic of the rôle of a triumphant democratic party.[27]

The democrats, without their having turned a hand, seemed to have victory within grasp. Posing as the watchful guardians of the constitution, they quietly enjoyed their steady gains and waited to organize their campaign. Yet within their ranks were all shades of opinion on war and peace, so that it was no easy task to figure out the strategy of their position. They finally held a state convention in June to select delegates to the national convention and to place an electoral ticket in the field; but postponed nominations for state offices to a later date. The state convention was clever enough to declare inexpedient the adoption of a platform since the national convention would make the necessary declaration of principles;[28] in this way it avoided a split over the issue of the desirability of a "war" platform or a "peace platform."

The date of the democratic national convention was postponed from July 4 until August 29. The party leader had carefully canvassed the field of presidential candidates; General Grant had been favored by many because of his availability as a military hero; though his democracy was dormant, it was sufficiently sound for the situation. Grant, however, repudiated the idea of presidential aspirations and a new candidate had to be found.[29] Governor Horatio Seymour of New York was the favorite candidate of many moderate democrats, while Pendleton of Ohio was supported by certain ultra peace advocates. General George B. McClellan was supported as having an availability similar to Grant's; he was a favorite with the army of the Potomac — personally liked and admired

---

[27] *Illinois State Journal*, August 19, 1864; *Illinois State Register*, August 19, 1864.
[28] *Ibid.*, January 25, June 16, 1864; *Chicago Morning Post*, January 29, 1864; *Jacksonville Journal*, June 16, 1864; *Chicago Times*, June 18, 1864.
[29] Grant to T. N. Morris, January 20, 1864, Illinois State Historical Society, *Journal*, 8: 592; cf. *Chicago Times*, January 6, 1864; *Ottawa Weekly Republican*, January 30, 1864; *Chicago Morning Post*, April 12, 1864.

THE REELECTION OF LINCOLN 323

by the soldiers. McClellan steadily gained strength throughout Illinois, although state democratic journals frowned upon this development. The *Chicago Tribune* claimed that McClellan's support came from the "bloated aristocrats of the democratic party," "the money-brokers of Wall street and the great railroad corporations of New York and New England," on the one hand, and from the "great unwashed of the Celtic persuasion," on the other; nevertheless, McClellan stock continued to climb.[30]

Inasmuch as General McClellan could not be charged with responsibility for any recent losses, the failure of the war was in August the most likely democratic rallying point. Accordingly, when the national convention met at Chicago, August 29, under the eye of fifteen thousand enthusiastic spectators, it nominated McClellan but permitted Vallandigham to draft a platform which declared the failure of the war and the need of peace. The immediate reaction was an outburst of enthusiasm that boded ill for Lincoln's hopes of reëlection.[31]

Republican leadership nearly collapsed at the signs of democratic unity and enthusiasm at Chicago. The withdrawal of both Fremont and Lincoln was suggested as a necessary preliminary to an effective reorganization of the republican campaign. Fremont's chances were known to be hopeless; Lincoln's apparent strength when nominated was declared fictitious. "I write you to have you use your influence to have Lincoln's name withdrawn," an Illinois constituent appealed to Trumbull. "Lincoln's course has not only dissatisfied but *embittered* many thousands of Republicans, particularly Germans, against him; the Fremont party, and the Chase and Wade-Davis movement, and the anti-slavery dissatisfaction in New England, weakens him greatly; there is no enthusiasm for him, and cannot be."[32] Many, though tried by Lincoln's course, continued

[30] *Chicago Tribune*, August 29, 1864; *Chicago Times*, August 18, 1864; *Jonesboro Gazette*, June 18, 1864; *Cairo Democrat*, August 17, 1864; John M. Palmer to Trumbull, January 24, 1864, Trumbull manuscripts; cf. Rhodes, *History of the United States*, 4:507n.
[31] *Illinois State Register*, September 1, 3, 1864; *Chicago Times*, September 1, 1864; Gershom Martin to Trumbull, September 3, 1864, Trumbull manuscripts. Even ex-Senator O. H. Browning, an old conservative supporter of Lincoln, commended the nomination of McClellan and declared that he should not feel at all distressed if he should be elected.
[32] Gershom Martin to Trumbull, September 3, 1864, *ibid.*

to feel that the country could not at such a time risk the upheaval entailed by change of presidents—so supported him without enthusiasm.[33]

Just at this crisis news arrived of Farragut's success at Mobile and, after a hard long struggle continued through weary months, of the capture of Atlanta by General Sherman.[34] The republicans became wild with sheer joy and spread the good tidings with enthusiasm. Then followed the report of a succession of victories by Sheridan in the valley of the Shenandoah. Republicans became still more jubilant; enthusiasts began in the same breath to predict the prompt suppression of the rebellion and the election of Lincoln. President Lincoln capitalized these developments politically by proclaiming a special day of thanksgiving to be celebrated in the churches, navy yards, and arsenals.

The democrats had just declared the war a failure; here was proof that they were in the wrong. The platform became impracticable and untenable; republicans called it "unpatriotic, almost treasonable to the Union."[35] So McClellan in his letter of acceptance repudiated the peace article in the platform, declaring himself unconditionally for the union, even to coercion. All democratic planning for the campaign was upset and gloom settled down upon their camp.

Even now it was evident that victory could come only to a united republican party; and Fremont was still in the field. His withdrawal, however, was arranged as a result of a bargain, to which Lincoln was at least indirectly a party; Postmaster-General Blair, a moderate, was sacrificed by the administration and asked to resign. Fremont in withdrawing took occasion to declare: "In respect to Mr. Lincoln, I continue to hold exactly the sentiments contained in my letter of acceptance. I consider that his administration has been politically, militarily, and financially a failure, and that its necessary continuance is a cause of regret for the country."[36] Republican

---

[33] G. T. Allen to Trumbull, October 4, 1864, Trumbull manuscripts.
[34] *Diary of Gideon Welles*, 2: 135-140.
[35] *Ibid.*, 135; *Cairo Democrat*, September 13, 1864.
[36] Fremont to George L. Stearns *et al.*, a committee, September 21, 1864, McPherson, *Political History of the Rebellion*, 426-427.

workers chose to forget the sting of this declaration and concentrated attention on the canvass.

It is hard to find a single constructive forward-looking issue in this campaign. The question of reconstruction, including the possibility of a thirteenth amendment abolishing slavery, might have been such an issue; indeed, some democrats, because of the troubles reconstruction had already caused the administration, did urge that it be made the momentous issue. Another possible issue, though not essentially constructive, was the question of the approval or disapproval of the Lincoln administration. For this the democrats were more ready than the republicans. The latter did not dare to indorse everything Lincoln had done — they could select certain features only and for the rest rely on his generally good intentions. The importance of the labor vote suggested another available issue, for it was in the Civil War period that modern labor problems had their beginning. Many republicans, therefore, wanted the president "to make the issue before the country distinctly perceptible to all as democratic and aristocratic;"[37] the whole purpose of the rebels, said they, was the establishment of an aristocracy of blood and of wealth. The administration, however, after its delay in assuming the same ground in dealing with the property of rebel leaders, was in no position to press this point. Besides, the republican party of 1864 was not that democratic force it had been in 1856: the fiscal needs and financial transactions of the government had not only drawn to its support but thrust into a prominent place in the party the representatives of another aristocracy of wealth — bankers, manufacturers, and government contractors. The democrats, moreover, as an opposition party, were able to make considerable progress with the argument that the industrial and laboring classes had been compelled to pay the greater portion of the taxes.[38] Legislation, they said, had been enacted on the old aristocratic policy that makes the rich richer and poor poorer. But the republicans in reply charged the democratic party with being an aristocracy

---

[37] *Diary of Gideon Welles*, 2:43, 141-142; *Jonesboro Gazette*, July 16, October 1, 1864; *Champaign County Union and Gazette*, October 14, 1864.
[38] *Joliet Signal*, July 19, 1864.

which had no place for "tailors, rail-splitters, mechanics, and laborers."

No republican argument on any topic, however, was complete without the illogical but effective declaration that under the best of circumstances democrats were copperheads if not traitors.[39] The Chicago platform was proclaimed unpatriotic — almost treasonable to the union. The issue was whether or not a war shall be made against Lincoln to get peace with Jeff Davis. A vote for McClellan would be a vote for slavery at a time when that crime had plunged the country into the sorrows and waste of war. It would be a vote for the rebellion at a moment when the rebellion was about to fail. It would be a vote for disunion at a moment when the union was about to be restored. All the south was hoping and praying for the success of the peace candidates. Had not the democrats imported as their leading campaign speaker the notorious Ohio disloyalist, Clement L. Vallandigham?[40]

Some of the democrats answered invective with invective. Could there be any real enthusiasm for the "widow-maker," for the "man of drafts," they asked. The American people, insisted the *State Register*, would never again commit the great blunder of placing "an abolitionist and a buffoon" in the presidential chair. Lincoln's three greatest generals were general taxation, general conscription, and general corruption. Evidence was offered that the republican campaign committee was collecting a large "corruption fund" by assessments upon officeholders; the formal demand for a quota of $67.44 from Captain Melancthon Smith, provost marshal for the second congressional district, was published with the news of Captain Smith's refusal. The authorities were charged with preparing to use the troops and returned soldiers to intimidate voters in the democratic strongholds; the warning was issued that union leagues were arming and organizing along military lines and that the free elective franchise was thereby threatened.[41]

The more levelheaded democrats concentrated on the argu-

---

[39] Koerner, *Memoirs*, 2:434-435. Koerner enlisted as a campaign speaker but found his audiences entirely unwilling to listen to sober political analysis.
[40] *Chicago Tribune*, October 22, 31, 1864; *Aurora Beacon*, November 3, 1864.
[41] *Illinois State Register*, September 4, 8, 25, October 6, 9, 15, 1864; *Cairo Democrat*, August 16, 1864.

ment that "our liberties are in danger through the action of the government in its efforts to put down the rebellion." They talked of martial law, of arbitrary arrests, of suppression of the press. They held that they, more truly than the republicans, were the real champions of "the Constitution as it is, the Union as it was."

The democrats were demoralized by the defection of prominent members of their party who as war democrats had supported the Lincoln administration and who now urged his reëlection. General John A. Logan, at the suggestion of the administration, returned from the front to participate in the canvass on the republican side. He was welcomed to Springfield by his former political opponents with a salvo of artillery and the music of a band; he and Governor Yates then made addresses at the statehouse in support of Lincoln.[42] Logan took the stump actively against William Joshua Allen, who was seeking reëlection to Logan's old seat in congress, and denounced him as the traitor who had tried to carry the southern half of Illinois into the southern confederacy.[43] General James D. Morgan, a lifelong democrat, was cited as having refused to indorse McClellan's candidacy because its chief strength lay among traitors. General John A. McClernand's name was often published as a supporter of Lincoln, but McClernand because of his disgust at the treatment he had received from the administration finally cleared up his position in a letter unequivocally in favor of McClellan.[44]

The wild enthusiasm inspired by the victories of Farragut, Sherman, Sheridan, and Grant had turned the political tide against the democracy. The army news discredited all prophets who proclaimed that the war was a failure. This was the undoing of the democrats; it was also a potent force to heal republican divisions. Radicals who had sworn never to repeat their 1860 votes for Lincoln buried their oaths in the republican celebrations; the German-American voters marched to the polls

[42] *Illinois State Register*, October 5, 1864; Dawson, *Life of Logan*, 86-87.
[43] *Chicago Tribune*, October 25, 1864; *Illinois State Journal*, October 29, November 1, 1864.
[44] *Illinois State Register*, October 7, 1864; *Chicago Times*, October 11, 1864. The republicans received another shock when Judge J. D. Caton of the state supreme court entered the campaign on the democratic side. *Aurora Beacon*, October 13, 1864; *Chicago Tribune*, October 26, 1864.

an almost solid Lincoln phalanx.[45] It was no wonder then that Lincoln swept all before him and that McClellan was buried in this famous landslide of November, 1864, when Illinois contributed 30,736 to the heavy popular majority piled up for her favorite son.

What, then, was the meaning of Lincoln's reëlection? It was the inevitable triumph of right, of the union, announced his supporters. Democrats, however, took a different view. "This result," declared the *State Register,* "is the heaviest calamity that ever befell this nation; . . . . [it is] the farewell to civil liberty, to a republican form of government, and to the unity of these States." "Lincoln re-elected himself in spite of the people," insisted the *Joliet Signal.*[46]

The republicans considered it a splendid victory, for the party, if not for the administration. They had thrown their entire strength into the national campaign knowing that upon it would depend the outcome of the state election and of the congressional contests. Thus it was that Lincoln carried the republican ticket for state offices to victory together with eleven out of the fourteen republican candidates for congress, while both houses of the legislature went strongly republican. Major General Richard J. Oglesby, of Decatur, was accordingly elected governor to succeed Governor Yates over James C. Robinson, the democratic candidate. The veteran "Long John" Wentworth was again sent to congress from the Chicago district, where he defeated Cyrus H. McCormick, the reaper manufacturer. Another notable republican congressional triumph took place in the heart of Egypt, where A. J. Kuykendall, aided by the work of John A. Logan, unseated Logan's former law partner, William Joshua Allen, the anti-war democrat. The logical fruits of the republican legislative victory were gathered in the election of Richard Yates to the United States senate to succeed William A. Richardson; this was the reward

[45] The *Chicago Tribune,* November 11, 1864, assigned an important share in the union victory to the German vote which finally lined up with the *Illinois Staats-Zeitung,* a consistent supporter of the Lincoln administration. Many Germans, however, like the editors of the Springfield *Illinois Staats Anzeiger* went so far as to support McClellan and Pendleton. *Chicago Times,* October 6, 8, 1864.
[46] *Illinois State Register,* November 10, 1864; *Joliet Signal,* December 6, 1864.

THE REELECTION OF LINCOLN

for four years of patriotic service as the war governor of the great prairie state.

The republican landslide of 1864 wiped out the troublous memories of democratic success in the two previous years, when the only real bond to the federal administration was to be found in republican control of the state executive offices. It was, indeed, at the very time, when the democratic party threatened to sweep the republicans from this last point of vantage, that the tide of war had turned and played havoc with the prognostications of the political prophets. Then the despaired of victory proved so sweeping that it laid the foundations for continued republican control of this old democratic stronghold and the traditions of the eighteen fifties and the early sixties yielded to a new order of things.

XV. POPULATION IN WARTIME

THE high water mark of the tide of humanity that swept out to the Illinois prairies was reached on the eve of the Civil War. Then came that upheaval that absorbed all the energies of the American people and repelled the stream of immigration that had been flowing across the Atlantic. America still continued to be symbolic of that large allowance of liberty for which so many Europeans longed; but, in view of the forecasts of the ruling class of Europe, they were fearful that it would be swept away in the torrent of blood in which the institution of slavery had deluged the American nation.

The traditions of northern freedom, however, still had a charm for certain Americans; from the slaveholding states there now poured a fresh stream of immigrants for whom the atmosphere of human slavery became as suffocatingly intolerable as any economic and political oppression in the old world. The lands along the Illinois Central had already become a lodestone for ambitious agriculturists from Tennessee and Alabama, even from far off Georgia — all eager to absorb the spirit that was transforming the prairies of Illinois into a garden state. With the first clash of arms the stream became a swollen torrent, bearing with it political refugees who refused to remain in a slaveholding republic founded upon the ruins of the old American union. The railroads developed a large business transporting families, with their furniture and agricultural implements, to points in Illinois, Iowa, and Wisconsin; steamers made their way up the Mississippi crowded with refugee pilgrims to the land of freedom; swarms of Missourians driven from their homes by secessionists crossed the river to Illinois bringing their teams, cattle, and remaining worldly goods[1] — though some of these exiles returned to their homes

---

[1] *Rockford Register.* February 16, 1861; *Rockford Republican,* April 11, 1861; *Jonesboro Gazette,* August 10, 1861; *Quincy Whig* clipped in *Rockford*

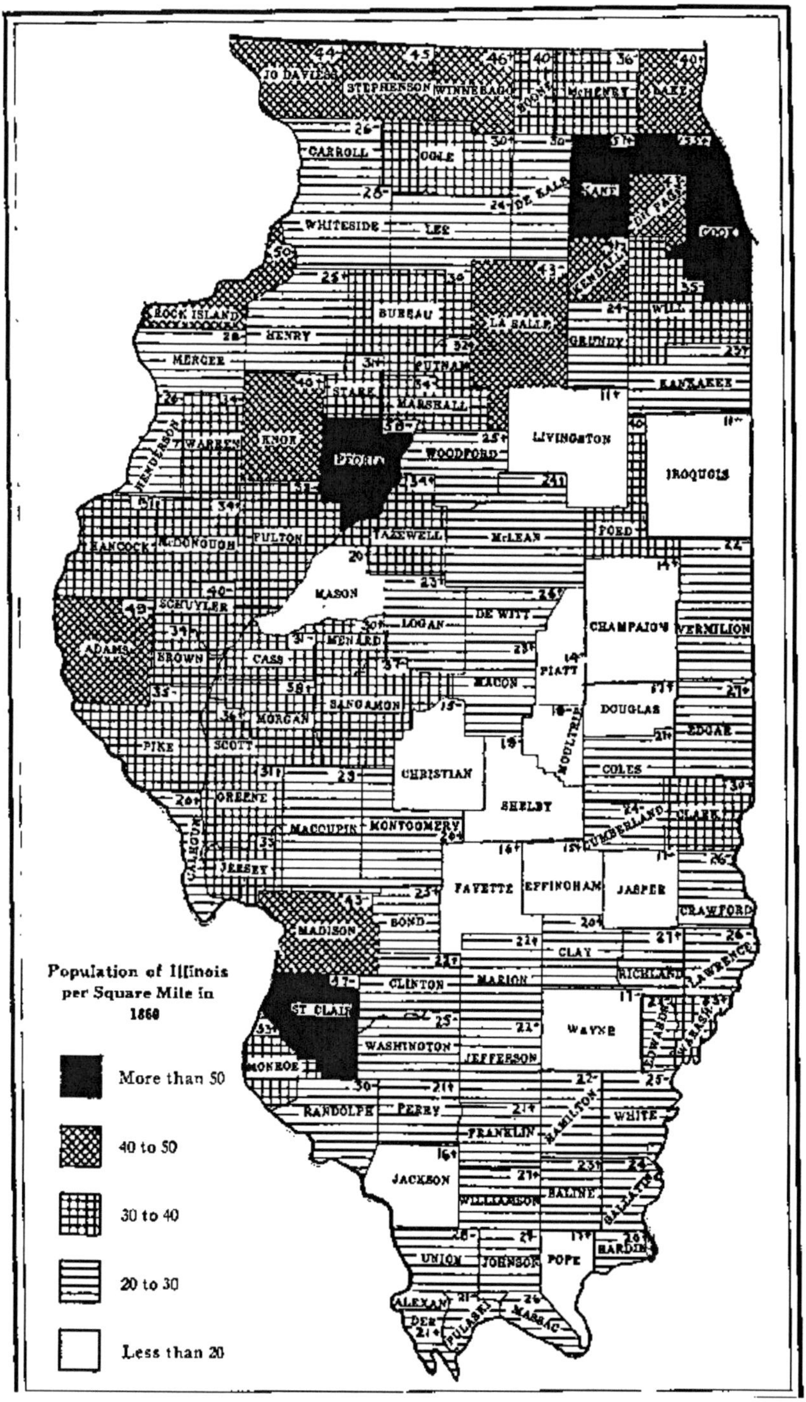

Population of Illinois per Square Mile in 1860
More than 50
40 to 50
30 to 40
20 to 30
Less than 20
JO DAVIESS
STEPHENSON
WINNEBAGO
BOONE
McHENRY
LAKE
CARROLL
OGLE
DE KALB
KANE
DU PAGE
COOK
WHITESIDE
LEE
KENDALL
WILL
ROCK ISLAND
HENRY
BUREAU
LA SALLE
GRUNDY
MERCER
PUTNAM
STARK
MARSHALL
KANKAKEE
HENDERSON
WARREN
KNOX
PEORIA
WOODFORD
LIVINGSTON
IROQUOIS
HANCOCK
McDONOUGH
FULTON
TAZEWELL
McLEAN
FORD
MASON
SCHUYLER
ADAMS
BROWN
CASS
MENARD
LOGAN
DE WITT
CHAMPAIGN
VERMILION
PIATT
MACON
MORGAN
SANGAMON
DOUGLAS
EDGAR
PIKE
SCOTT
CHRISTIAN
MOULTRIE
COLES
GREENE
SHELBY
CALHOUN
MACOUPIN
MONTGOMERY
CUMBERLAND
CLARK
JERSEY
FAYETTE
EFFINGHAM
JASPER
CRAWFORD
MADISON
BOND
CLAY
RICHLAND
LAWRENCE
CLINTON
MARION
ST CLAIR
WASHINGTON
WAYNE
EDWARDS
WABASH
MONROE
JEFFERSON
RANDOLPH
PERRY
HAMILTON
WHITE
FRANKLIN
JACKSON
WILLIAMSON
SALINE
GALLATIN
UNION
JOHNSON
POPE
HARDIN
ALEXANDER
PULASKI
MASSAC

in Missouri when the state was swept clear of secession and order was restored there. Victories of the union armies released new streams from all the border states; this was particularly noticeable in the spring of 1863, when the Illinois Central distributed hundreds of families from Virginia, Tennessee, Kentucky, and Missouri as candidates for the charity of the different communities. Friends and relatives in those parts of southern and central Illinois that had been settled by recent immigrants from the border states welcomed the new arrivals.[2]

Many of these refugees were women and children who represented the bone and sinew of the upper south; the men were usually in the southern or union armies, although some fled north to escape conscription. Many, too, belonged to the uneducated, non-slaveholding poor white class and presented a sorry appearance; even the women were usually snuff dippers or tobacco chewers and "a considerable sum of the money given to them, was immediately invested in snuff and tobacco."[3] All were received kindly, however, and treated charitably. The mayor of Centralia protested when General Buford "forced" one hundred and twenty paupers upon the city; but the union men welcomed them and the school directors placed at their disposal a large seminary building, the only vacant building in the city.[4]

Cairo was the Ellis Island for this immigration. Steamer after steamer arrived with cargoes of human freight and the nearby towns of Anna and Jonesboro received refugees until the people protested their inability to provide for more. Accommodations at Cairo were extremely inadequate and as the government did not assume complete responsibility for their welfare, great destitution and suffering often developed among the refugees. Families were sometimes left a good part of the night on the cold and muddy levee without shelter or even blankets, and even after aid had been dispensed in securing

---

Republican, October 17, 1861; *Illinois State Journal*, December 6, 1861; *Rock River Democrat*, March 11, 1862; *Mississippi Blätter*, June 8, 1862.
[2] *Illinois State Journal*, April 2, May 20, June 9, September 11, 1863; *Canton Weekly Register*, April 6, 1863; *Belleville Advocate*, April 17, 1863; *Cairo Weekly Democrat*, March 6, 1864.
[3] *Cairo Morning News*, June 25, 1863.
[4] *Cairo Gazette*, July 2, 1863.

quarters, the immigrants were often lost sight of in the endless stream that poured in; a relief committee found forty-two crowded into a single room of an abandoned barracks. Over three thousand, not including children, were given money contributions, clothing, and food by the local agent of the United States Sanitary Commission in the last six months of 1863. Some of these refugees were transported to Chicago and upper Illinois, where the adjustment to their new homes was often made under difficulties. One shipment of one hundred and fifty persons reached Springfield in January, 1865, after trying experiences; at Cairo they had been kept five days on an overloaded boat, without places to sleep, and with scarcely any food; the Illinois Central railroad agents then placed them in hog cars, which had not been cleaned since used, and they were transported in a severe midwinter temperature to Decatur, covering the two hundred miles in seventy-two hours, and thence they were brought to Springfield.[5] Although relief work was organized by the refugee relief committee in Chicago and in other parts of the state, yet it was always inadequate to the demand and numerous deaths among these poor folk resulted from the neglect and exposure which they underwent.

The problem of union refugees was complicated by bands of Missouri ruffians who came into Illinois representing themselves as expelled unionists; they were soon, however, under suspicion as akin to those bushwhackers who came over to carry on their depredations in copperhead districts. Again it appeared that the Missouri military authorities were often banishing convicted rebels to Illinois whose citizens protested against the "making of Illinois a 'Botany Bay' for the traitors of Missouri."[6] Moreover, the new Missouri constitution disfranchised certain classes as a result of which a number of noted

---

[5] *Chicago Times,* January 12, 1864; *Cairo Weekly Democrat,* January 13, 1864; *Rockford Register,* January 16, 1864; *Cairo Democrat,* February 3, June 1, 1864; *Cairo Morning News,* July 30, 1864; *Rockford Democrat,* January 5, 1865; *Chicago Tribune,* January 16, 1865. These refugees were expected to relieve the labor shortage. See *Mississippi Blätter,* March 6, 1864; *Cairo Democrat,* February 9, 1865. In 1865 an industrial home for refugees was established at Chicago. *Chicago Times,* February 23, June 27, 1865.

[6] *Jonesboro Gazette,* August 10, 1861; *Illinois State Journal,* February 17, March 28, 1864; *Chicago Tribune,* July 6, 1865.

POPULATION IN WARTIME

bushwhackers, guerrillas, and rebel soldiers moved over into the southern counties of Illinois.

Another species of immigrants came from southern climes to this new Canaan at the north. These were the Negro freemen, an element which the state in all its traditions had previously refused to welcome. At the outbreak of the war it was even a crime for a Negro to set his foot upon Illinois soil; a year later another constitutional provision to renew the mandate in the fundamental law was submitted to the people of the state by the constitutional convention of 1862; and the voters of both parties declared with a majority of over 150,000, out of an aggregate vote of 240,000, that they were still opposed to letting down the barriers to Negro immigration.

If Illinois was hostile to the free Negro, there could be no question as to its stand in regard to the fugitive slave, and it is not to be wondered that, in spite of southern prophecies, the inauguration of President Lincoln did nothing to open a haven of refuge for the fugitive slave in Illinois. Certain Illinois democrats were desirous that new guarantees to the south be furnished by state legislation in aid of the fugitive slave law, but Lincoln and the republicans were content with a faithful execution of the law and with preventing obstructions to its enforcement by northern legislation.[7] Lincoln's newly appointed federal marshals did not shirk their obligations; Marshal J. Russell Jones of the northern district was soon assisting the man hunters in recovering their property in Chicago; and, within a month of Lincoln's inauguration, considerable excitement was aroused when the family of Onesimus Harris was sent back to bondage in Missouri. Marshal Jones seemed in this case to surpass all his predecessors in office in his zealous enforcement of the law. As a result the colored population of the city, no longer regarding it as a place of safety, began to leave for her Majesty's dominions; within a week the exodus from the panic-stricken colored quarters became a veritable stampede.[8]

Under the federal confiscation laws, however, and under the

---

[7] *Belleville Advocate*, January 25, February 1, 1861.
[8] *Chicago Tribune*, April 4, 6, 1861; *Illinois State Journal*, April 4, 5, 1861; *Rockford Register*, April 6, 1861; *Prairie Farmer*, April 11, 1861.

policies of commanders in the field, slaves of rebel planters who were captured by the federal armies or had fled to the union lines were given a status as "contrabands" and their masters' claims were declared forfeited. Thereupon, large numbers of contrabands made their appearance at Cairo and began to distribute themselves over the state. This influx began just as the new constitution of 1862 was submitted to the voters of the state, and they spoke decisively. Yet in midsummer by arrangement between the secretary of war and the military commander at Cairo under the second confiscation act, the contrabands continued to pour into Cairo until the levees were "so dark with negroes that pedestrians found it difficult to peregrinate without lanterns."[9] From Cairo, which was under martial law and legally amenable to such a policy, the Illinois Central carried one to four carloads northward daily and distributed them in various parts of the state. Although republicans urged the farmers to welcome this source of cheap help, the democrats set up a howl about an impending reduction of wages and consequent distress among the laboring classes. When General Tuttle, commander at Cairo, formally invited the mayor of Chicago to coöperate in securing employment for Negro immigrants in that city, Mayor Francis C. Sherman, a democrat, with the approval of the city council, refused to act in violation of the state law "to the great injustice of our laboring population;" yet, refugees soon began to arrive in daily shipments of from eighty to one hundred and sixty.[10] Quincy and other Mississippi river ports were also receiving heavy consignments, and the people of Rock Island county therefore held a public meeting to consider the best mode of staying the influx.

Republicans were fast learning, to their sorrow, however, that race prejudice was no respecter of parties; they were greatly weakened, if not defeated, by this new issue in the election of 1862. Leonard Swett of Bloomington, republican candidate for congress, tried to stem the tide that was turning

---

[9] *Cairo Gazette*, August 19, 1862.
[10] *Joliet Signal*, September 23, 30, 1862; *Illinois State Register*, September 30, October 7, 8, 1862; *Champaign County Democrat*, October 9, 1862; *Jonesboro Gazette*, October 11, 18, 1862; *Rockford Register*, October 11, 1862; *Carbondale Times* clipped in *Belleville Advocate*, October 24, 1862.

against him by publicly announcing his belief that the importation of colored persons into Illinois would degrade white labor and demoralize the people. The republican press was indeed glad when it was able to announce, though already too late, that the war department had forbidden the sending of any more "contrabands" to Illinois; a few months later General Hurlbut transferred the contraband camp at Cairo to Island Number 10.[11]

With Lincoln's emancipation proclamation Congressman J. C. Allen rigorously attacked republican policy and declared his fears that the state would now be overrun with freedmen; and although the *Chicago Tribune* optimistically prophesied that the Negro would "shape his bearings and route by the Southern Cross instead of the North Star,"[12] only the prorogation of the legislature of 1863 prevented the enactment of new and more drastic guarantees against the impending immigration. The democrats, meantime, used the courts to enforce existing legislation; in February, 1863, six Negroes were convicted at Carthage of living within the state contrary to the black laws and were thereupon sold for their fines to the highest bidders. In July a Negro who returned with Dr. L. D. Kellogg, surgeon in the Seventeenth Illinois regiment, was sentenced and sold in like manner. The following month, Annie Long, a young colored woman who claimed that she had come into Edgar county merely to visit, was fined $50 and costs for violation of the law and advertised for sale until the funds were advanced by republican sympathizers.[13] Such action, together with the coöperation of the federal authorities at Cairo, for the time practically ended the influx of freedmen through southern Illinois.

In 1865 the repeal of the black laws after a campaign by

---

[11] *Illinois State Journal*, October 15, 22, 1862; *Cairo Gazette*, April 2, 16, 1863. William Yocum, superintendent of contrabands at Cairo, was later convicted of selling contrabands back into slavery in Kentucky; a Reverend Mr. Rodgers, chaplain of contrabands and General N. B. Buford were also accused of sharing in the profits of such illegal sales. *Cairo Democrat*, December 13, 1863; *Illinois State Journal*, June 25, 1864.
[12] *Belleville Democrat*, November 1, 1862; *Chicago Tribune*, December 6, 1862.
[13] *Rockford Register*, March 7, 1863; *Canton Weekly Register*, August 3, 1863; *Paris Beacon* clipped in *Illinois State Journal*, August 19, 1863; *Chicago Tribune*, August 21, 1863.

the radical republicans provided an open door to prospective Negro immigrants to Illinois.[14] Immediately they began to settle in various parts of the state, although new opportunities for the freedman in the south checked the northward flow. The new immigrants were distributed over the state by agents of the Northwestern Freedman's Aid Commission, which had been organized in 1863, for the relief of the colored population in the south.[15] The Negro population of the state increased more than threefold, reaching a total of 28,762. Of this population over four thousand out of sheer inertia remained behind in Cairo and its vicinity, where the ante-bellum population had been only fifty-five; in the main Negroes, however, sought the more hospitable atmosphere of Chicago and other antislavery centers like Quincy, Galesburg, Jacksonville, and Springfield. They thus became an urban population—the hewers of wood and drawers of water for their more prosperous white neighbors.

The war spirit served to break down some of the barriers against the Negro. Illinoisians were among the earliest advocates of Negro soldiers and hundreds of colored troops were recruited in the state as volunteers or as substitutes under the draft. In civil life, too, the Negro was given increased opportunities. Colored women were admitted to the Chicago Ladies Loyal League; Negro graduates appeared in the commencement exercises of Knox and Lombard colleges, while the doors of Shurtleff College and of the state normal school were opened to colored students.[16] The passage of the civil rights bill in 1866 guaranteed the Negroes against legal discrimination; the colored residents of Chicago and Cairo celebrated this event in a large meeting. In practice, however, the word "white"

---

[14] The author of the black laws of 1855 was John A. Logan, who introduced them in the lower house in 1853; they were presented in the senate by A. J. Kuykendall. These two men and S. W. Moulton, a prominent supporter, were then democrats, but in 1865 were prominent members of the union party, the last two having just been elected to congress. *Chicago Tribune*, January 16, 1865.

[15] *Carthage Republican*, July 27, August 24, 1865; *Central Illinois Gazette*, October 13, 1865; *Illinois State Register*, April 8, 1865; *Cairo Bulletin* clipped in *ibid.*, March 26, 1870. In 1864 the Quincy branch had a department at the local Sanitary Fair to raise funds to provide for the Negro refugees in that city in violation of the black laws. *Rockford Republican*, August 20, 1864, April 8, 1865.

[16] *Chicago Times*, July 1, 1864; *Chicago Tribune*, January 18, 1868; *Illinois Democrat*, March 28, 1868; *Belleville Democrat*, March 19, 1868.

remained in the school laws of Illinois; and although in some instances the Negroes were provided with segregated public schools, most communities excluded colored children from the schools with the provision that upon application the school taxes would be refunded to colored taxpayers.[17] These ostracized residents, already accustomed to religious worship in their own Methodist or Baptist churches, often raised funds for their own schools.

Much of the atmosphere of persecution began to disappear. There were still outbursts of negrophobia, but the maltreatment of inoffensive Negroes came pretty much to an end when civil rights were conferred upon that race. The regalia of colored secret societies, "white muslin belts and scarfs, embellished with blue, pink, black, yellow and white ribbons; large rosettes, sprigs of cedar, brass buttons, vari-colored tassels," began to appear on the streets on Sundays and holidays.[18] Negro military companies began to parade in uniform. Midsummer became a season of the festive picnicking and merrymaking, so compelling for the members of the race.

In the course of the decade the colored population of the state became more aggressive in the assertion of its rights. A mass convention at Springfield in January, 1865, petitioned the legislature to repeal "the laws now in force against us on account of our complexion;" a state delegate convention eight months later initiated their annual plea for impartial suffrage. The republicans not only agitated for Negro franchise but courted the prospective Negro vote by suggestions of future officeholding. In 1868 a group of local republican merchants urged the nomination of Captain James W. Brockway, of the Twentieth United States colored infantry, for the office of collector of South Chicago; a year later Governor Palmer explained to the colored residents of Springfield that they were eligible for any office under the constitution. The news of the ratification of the fifteenth amendment on March 30, 1870, resulted in grand demonstrations by the colored residents of the chief cities of the state; and on April 5, under the new dis-

[17] *Chicago Tribune*, April 13, 1866; *Cairo Times* clipped in *Belleville Advocate*, May 18, 1866; *Canton Weekly Register*, April 17, November 13, 1868. The annual taxes paid by colored residents of Cairo were about twenty dollars.
[18] *Cairo Democrat*, November 12, 1867.

pensation, they participated for the first time in Illinois elections.[19]

The war interrupted the westward movement of the native American population just at a time when the Illinois prairies were receiving a large share of hardy settlers. With the return of peace there came a renewed immigration from the eastern states, and Illinois had a special welcome for the Yankees who came to swell the New England towns and villages of northern Illinois. "You may know them by their neat churches and school-houses, and by the trees and flowers in their fenced yards," was the proud boast of a Massachusetts editor.[20] Theodore Tilton, editor of the New York *Independent*, traveling over the plains of Illinois on a lecture tour, was impressed with the thrift, energy, growth, and civil progress of the western communities; he came to feel that "the beauty of the New England character is not seen at its best till it ripens a while in the West. .... True, there is more wealth, more culture, more social refinement in the Eastern towns; but in the Western there is more of that indefinable quality which (for want of a better name) we call character. That is to say, there is more individuality, more freedom from conventional restraint, more independence in manners and opinions, more flavor of native originality."[21]

Peace removed the obstacles to foreign immigration to the United States; and of the throngs that came Illinois received more than her quota — its salubrious climate and rich and extensive prairies attracting the best of the home-seekers from the old world. In 1866 the tide was running strong, but the next year brought almost flood conditions; of the 25,000 immigrants landing at New York during each of the summer months of 1867, one-tenth indicated Illinois as their destination — more foreign emigrants sought homes in Illinois than

---

[19] *Chicago Tribune*, September 12, 1868, September 24, 1869. A few weeks later he appointed John Jones of Chicago the first colored notary public in Illinois. *Rockford Gazette*, November 25, 1869; *Illinois State Register*, March 31, April 4, 5, 6, 13, 1870.

[20] *Springfield Republican* clipped in *Chicago Tribune*, June 15, 1867.

[21] *Belleville Democrat*, January 4, 1867. It was still suggestive of the youth of the state, however, that the legislature did not show a single native Illinoisian in the senate and only eleven out of eighty-five in the house. *Chicago Tribune*, February 3, 1865; *The* (Columbus, Ohio) *Crisis*, February 15, 1865.

in any of the other states except New York.[22] After 1867 the flow of immigration to the United States was less spectacular, but the strong advantage for Illinois continued. In 1868, 34,625 immigrants arriving at New York gave Illinois as their destination, while at the same time 3,852 set out for Indiana. By 1870 there were in Illinois 515,198 foreign born residents.[23]

The attractions of the soil and climate, the natural resources of the state, and the relief from heavy taxation that Illinois promised, were now more systematically brought to the attention of prospective emigrants. Even during the years of the war, a Chicago Emigrant Agency prosecuted its activities, promising cheap passage from Ireland and England. With the return of peace an American Emigrant Company, with agencies in Europe and throughout America, appeared in Chicago; it imported skilled labor from Europe and supplied it at reasonable rates to manufacturers, railroad companies, and other employers of labor.[24] The Illinois exhibit at the Paris exposition in 1867 called the attention of Europe to the resources of the state, as did the European advertisements of the Illinois Central railroad. The bureau of immigration at Washington, recognizing the popularity of Illinois, secured data from Governor Oglesby for the benefit of the people of Europe. The German Emigrant Aid Society at Chicago continued its work but found its resources so strained by the heavy demand upon its good offices that it urged the state to make provision for direct assistance. Southern Illinois realized little or nothing from the immense tide of immigration until zealous citizens of Cairo formed an Emigrant Aid Society to attract settlers to that region.[25]

[22] *Chicago Tribune*, May 8, July 26, 1867; *Illinois State Journal*, Aug. 5, 1867.
[23] *Ibid.*, February 3, 1869. The decade of the sixties converted Illinois into a populous commonwealth of over two million and a half persons, a gain of nearly fifty per cent. The ratio of increase was lowest for the native American population. The natural increase within the state, however, was slightly above the general average, although there were in 1870 only 1,181,101 native born Illinoisians. The state failed to receive, however, a proportionate share of immigrants from other parts of the United States.
[24] *Chicago Morning Post*, April 1, 1864; *Chicago Tribune*, September 5, 1865.
[25] *Illinois State Journal*, February 3, 1869; *Chicago Tribune*, July 11, 1867, July 29, 1869; *Cairo Democrat*, November 16, 1866; *Cairo Evening Bulletin*, December 22, 23, 1868, January 9, March 30, July 1, 1869. The Irish of Chicago also moved to establish an organization to provide for newcomers from the Emerald Isle. *Chicago Tribune*, April 2, 1869.

In the decade the German born population of Illinois reached the number of 203,750, exceeding the Irish by over sixty-six per cent. The new German settlers, in contrast with the south German exodus after 1848, came largely from northern Germany. It was the old German centers in Illinois, however, that in large part received this accretion; they continued to be industrious, frugal, and peaceful communities. A new German center developed at Cairo, where a German theater, a school, and a German newspaper were established. The German residents of La Salle increased significantly and included the owners and most of the operatives of the local zinc factory. Their influence was expressed in furthering the cause of education in 1869 when they elected a school director and carried a bond issue of $20,000 for a new schoolhouse.[26]

The majority of the Norwegians who formed part of a heavy Scandinavian immigration passed through Illinois to either Wisconsin, Iowa, or Minnesota. Chicago and a Norwegian settlement nine miles out of Ottawa, however, received several significant increments during the closing years of the Civil War.[27] A Scandinavian Aid Society in Chicago was organized in 1866 to give assistance to bewildered immigrants. The Swedes, numbering 36,000 in 1870, were scattered all over the state, with a sprinkling in the southern counties and a considerable settlement at Paxton; but Rockford was the main objective of those who sought the atmosphere of old Sweden. At that place the Swedish Methodists undertook to publish the *Ambassador*, a religious paper; at Chicago in 1866 were launched *Den Svenska Amerikanaren*, a newspaper for the Swedish element of the northwest, and the *Skandinaven*, a Norwegian-Danish daily. Yet, while they sought papers in their own language, the Swedes of Rockford organized a literary society through which they proposed to acquire a fundamental knowledge of the uses of the English language — an action typical of this hardy, industrious class of settlers who longed to understand their new surroundings.[28]

[26] *Cairo Democrat*, December 10, 1863, June 14, 17, 1864, March 30, May 25, 1865, November 16, 1866; *Ottawa Weekly Republican*, August 19, 1869.
[27] *Ottawa Free Trader*, July 2, 1864; *Ottawa Weekly Republican*, July 2, 1864.
[28] *Rockford Gazette*, January 21, 1869. The Swedish residents of Galesburg

POPULATION IN WARTIME

Practically every foreign born element received increases during this decade. The Irish increased some 32,000, reaching the total of 120,162, but no longer competed very seriously with the Germans for the lead among the foreign born elements. The English immigration was light but included a colony of over three hundred families organized as the Durham and Northumberland Farmers' Club of England; their agent, Dr. A. R. Oliver, negotiated in behalf of this group for several thousand acres in Alexander and Pulaski counties. There was a hearty welcome for all; communities even competed with each other in trying to attract foreign settlers. The effort was even made in 1865 to attract to Illinois Polish political refugees from Russian autocracy; the newest contribution, however, to the cosmopolitan life of the state was a colony of six hundred Italian families who in 1866-1867 located a few miles from Pana.[29]

The foreign vote continued a formidable factor in the politics of the state. The different foreign elements went to the polls more or less as units and were often a decisive factor in an election; it was alleged that a half dozen canny Scots backed by only 75 to 100 Scotch voters controlled the republican vote of Will county, which numbered 3,000. In local contests a foreign group often put one of its nationality into the field and worked harmoniously for his election. The Germans, Scandinavians, French, Scotch, and Portuguese were mainly affiliated with republicans, the Irish adhered to the democratic party, while the Jewish vote seemed to be evenly divided.[30]

The German vote of Illinois and neighboring states was so powerful in 1860 that without its assistance Lincoln and

averaged $4,000 a month in remittances to the old country. *Rushville Times*, September 30, 1869.
[29] *Cairo Democrat*, November 26, 1867; *Illinois State Journal*, January 22, 1867.
[30] *Joliet Signal*, April 14, 1868. The French speaking population of Illinois organized a benevolent society which declared itself "in favor of a political union of all our elements to affirm our right and privileges" under the constitution; in 1867 they brought out Francis Pasedeloup for alderman of the seventh ward of Chicago. *Chicago Evening Post*, April 8, 1867. In 1868 the Swedes of Henry county nominated an independent candidate for sheriff. *Illinois State Journal*, June 24, 1868. Many Jews had not abandoned their democratic connections; with democratic aid, others remembered General Grant's order discriminating against them.

his party would have been decisively defeated; its support in the years that followed made it possible to carry the war to its logical conclusion. Yet the Germans were modest in their claims for a share of the spoils; for several weeks after applications for office began pouring in upon Lincoln not a single German office-seeker presented his claims. The services of even the most prominent Illinois leaders received only slight acknowledgment; Koerner, who had strongly nourished the hope of securing the Berlin mission, was given no recognition at all until he was sent as minister to Spain to succeed Carl Schurz, who preferred active service.[31] Theodore Canisius, editor of the *Illinois Staats Anzeiger*, was sent as consul to Vienna, while George Schneider was appointed consul at Elsinore, Denmark.

The German republican voters and their press were from the first firmly opposed to concession or compromise to prevent war; when the struggle came they were equally prompt to insist that it bring about the extinction of slavery. They were enthusiastic backers of Fremont's attack upon slavery; in a meeting in Chicago to sustain his proclamation they denounced the administration's attempt "to shirk the true issue of the contest."[32] This was the beginning of an estrangement from Lincoln that came to a climax in the campaign of 1864. Fremont had been one of their favorites in 1860, and after the events of the following year they continued to present his claims until his formal withdrawal in 1864. On the reconstruction issues they stood firmly for thoroughgoing southern adjustment to the consequences of secession and civil war; they, therefore, without hesitation, repudiated President Johnson and followed the radical leadership until the end of the decade.

A growing restiveness on the part of the German repub-

[31] Dodd, "Fight for the Northwest," *American Historical Review*, 16:786, 787, 788; White, *Life of Lyman Trumbull*, 103; Schneider, "Lincoln and the Anti-Know Nothing Resolutions," McLean County Historical Society, *Transactions*, 3:90; Selby, "Lincoln and German Patriotism," Deutsch-Amerikanischen Historischen Gesellschaft von Illinois, *Jahrbuch*, 12:523; *Illinois State Journal*, January 7, 1861; Koerner to Trumbull, January 21, February 22, March 13, 19, 1861, Trumbull manuscripts; Koerner, *Memoirs*, 2:114, 212 ff.

[32] Theodore Canisius to Trumbull, February 8, 1861, Trumbull manuscripts; Moore, *Rebellion Record*, volume 3, document number 142, p. 344-345.

licans appeared as the slavery issue began to wane. As local elections revived local issues, association in "the party of great moral ideas" with colleagues whose narrow vision precluded a sympathetic understanding of German social customs became distinctly embarrassing. The Puritanism of the Yankee now expended itself on a revival of the old demand for prohibitory liquor regulations and a strict sabbath observance. To the German, the seventh day brought the simple human joys of a jolly procession to the woods where the rifle club might have a shooting match, the singing club a *Gesangfest* echoed by the children in their frolic, and all a health to cherished memories and to the land of their adoption. To sip a casual social glass or to include in his meal one of the beverages of the fatherland seemed to the German a fundamental personal liberty which a free America could not deny him. To the scandalized Yankee the German's bottle of beer meant a drunken debauch and Sunday festivities meant a willingness "to sacrifice every principle or conviction in politics or morals" .... "for the precious privilege of getting drunk and carousing on the Sabbath."[33]

German leaders took counsel over this "adulteration" of the republican program by New England sectionalism. The democratic party had in its early days shown an ability to appreciate their distinctive traits; now again their old associates welcomed them with understanding: the Germans "are *Liberals* in the true sense, in religion, society, and politics. In this respect they are the exact antithesis of what is denominated the puritannical element in our country. The Germans believe in the largest liberty of conscience, of speech and social enjoyment."[34] Henceforward the word "republicanism" lost its magic; that the Teutonic allies did not desert *en masse* to the democracy was largely due to the strategy of the republican leaders: the policy was adopted of stressing the slavery issue in national and state elections and of answering republican

---

[33] *Cairo Democrat*, September 19, 1867.
[34] *Belleville Democrat*, September 26, November 7, December 12, 1867. On this crisis see *ibid.*, June 20, August 1, 29, October 3, December 12, 1867; *Cairo Democrat*, September 26, 1867; *Illinois Staats-Zeitung* clipped in *Carthage Republican*, November 21, 1867; *Joliet Signal*, September 24, 1867; *Ottawa Free Trader*, September 28, 1867; *Illinois State Journal*, October 3, 1867.

temperance crusaders with independent voting in the municipal contests.[35]

The Irish numbered forty thousand voters in Illinois in 1860. They controlled the elections in Cairo, Joliet, and other democratic cities and were largely responsible for democratic victories in Chicago. Because the republicans raised the anti-Irish shibboleth in order to enlist the prejudices of the Americans and Germans, the Irish in the main continued contentedly in the democratic fold.[36]

Most of the Irish were drawn into the ranks of the Fenian movement, probably the most significant national expression of the foreign born in American history. The Fenian brotherhood was a society of freedom-loving Irishmen passionately devoted to the mission of creating a sentiment of nationality among their countrymen, with a view ultimately of redeeming Ireland from English rule. In this brotherhood the most prominent and wealthy Irish citizens joined the laboring masses. Local societies called "circles" under officers designated as "centres" were formed in every Irish community, while the society was knit together by state conventions under "head centres" and by a national organization. In November, 1863, when the first national Fenian convention was held at Chicago, Illinois contained forty circles, and others were rapidly formed under the direction of organizers like A. L. Morrison and Michael Scanlan of Chicago; within a few months an Irish National Fair was held at Chicago, at which generous subscriptions to the cause were made by the friends of the Irish of every origin. By 1865, when the national organization had enrolled several hundred thousand members, Chicago had become the life and soul of the movement, regularly forwarding thousand dollar remittances to the New York office.[37]

---

[35] Bruncken, "Political Activity of Wisconsin Germans," Wisconsin Historical Society, *Proceedings*, 1901-1902, p. 200. In the election of members of the constitutional convention of 1870 German meetings adopted the policy of refusing to support any candidate who would not pledge himself to work against the introduction of prohibitory liquor regulations. *Joliet Signal*, February 2, June 15, July 27, 1869.

[36] *Ibid.*, April 14, 1868; *Joliet Republican*, March 7, 1868. Republicans claimed that one Irish republican in fifty was a high estimate. *Illinois State Journal*, September 15, 1868.

[37] P. W. Dunne of Peoria subscribed more money to the Fenian cause than any other man in America. *Chicago Tribune*, November 2, 1866; *Chicago Times*, November 4, 1863; *Chicago Post*, December 20, 1865.

The Fenian brotherhood came to encompass all the activities of the Hibernian population of Illinois. Their social life was shaped by the banquets, balls, and picnics arranged by the organization. Military drill was one of the objects of the society, and early in 1866 this motive became evident when the invasion of Canada under General Thomas W. Sweeney was attempted. A motley Fenian army including many veterans of the Civil War was raised, to which Illinois contributed generous quotas. Chicago had the finest regiment in the Fenian army—one thousand strong and nearly all veterans. In a few hours the Irish of the city raised $40,000 for their mobilization. Companies from all parts of the state were concentrated in Chicago, from which they moved eastward without any attempt at interference. Oddly enough there was little criticism of this attempt to accomplish by force, in spite of American neutrality regulations, what might more lawfully have been attempted by political methods. General Sweeney marshaled his forces in the neighborhood of Buffalo and gave orders to strike into Canada. A foray across the international boundary caught the Canadians unprepared and struck terror into the peaceful population. A company of Canadian volunteers from Chicago was raised by the Canadian society of that city and hurried across the border to assist in repelling the invasion.[38] The problem, however, had taken on an international aspect and forced the intervention of the American government. At this stage the Fenian movement collapsed and the would-be heroes were taken into the custody of the federal authorities.

After the fiasco certain republican papers were ready to confess their "infinite disgust and contempt for this whole Fenian business;" but before the attempted invasion, the only clear-cut opponent of the Fenian brotherhood was Bishop James Duggan of the diocese of Chicago, who placed it under the ban of the church against secret societies.[39] So formidable had been this Irish movement that no attempt was made within

---

[38] Finerty, *People's History of Ireland*, 2:878; *Chicago Evening Journal*, June 4, 22, 1866; *Chicago Tribune*, June 22, 1866.
[39] *Rockford Register*, March 16, 1867; *Chicago Evening Post*, February 23, March 11, 1867; *Rockford Gazette*, September 19, 1867; *Chicago Times*, February 3, 8, 19, March 2, 1864.

the state to check it. The democrats commended the zeal for liberty displayed by the Fenians and heaped encomiums upon the Irish, while the republicans saw no propriety in opposing it. Governor Yates and the state officers graced with their presence Fenian entertainments in Springfield and noticed invitations to other celebrations with letters of regret commending the principles of the organization.

The Fenians had early "disclaimed all notion of identifying themselves with any and all political organizations outside of the objects of the Fenian brotherhood;"[40] yet it was known that the organization served as a powerful auxiliary to the democratic party. A misstep by the *Chicago Times* in 1865 threatened this unquestioning allegiance; when that journal inadvertently published an article criticizing and ridiculing the types of Irish "squatters" in Chicago, the "United Sons of Erin" under the lead of John Comiskey and various Fenian circles denounced it as "an English spy sheet" "no longer worthy of the patronage of any Irishman."[41] Many Irishmen doubted whether they could go to the ballot box at the next election and vote the *"Times'"* ticket." The republicans eagerly availed themselves of this opening and, with a view of widening the rift, pointed out that by every principle of logic the Fenian advocates of freedom for Ireland ought to rally to the cause of freedom in this country. A recruiting agent for the republican party was found in John Pope Hodnett, a talented young Irish orator, who had participated in establishing the *Irish Republic* in Chicago to further both the Fenian cause and the republican party. The anti-democratic reaction became evident in July, 1866, when a meeting of a number of Chicago "centres" declared that thereafter on all occasions they would vote "for that party which finds no excuse in musty laws, in vested rights, and ancient prejudices for degrading and enslaving men."[42] A certain branch of Hibernian voters conceived a strong hatred for President Andrew Johnson, and when he stopped at Chicago on his famous "swing around the circle," Governor Oglesby and other

[40] *Illinois State Register*, April 4, 1865.
[41] *Chicago Tribune*, August 10, 1865; *Illinois State Journal*, August 21, 24, 1865.
[42] *Chicago Tribune*, July 12, 1866; *Joliet Signal*, July 17, 1866.

republican moguls made bitter anti-Johnson speeches at a great Fenian picnic at Haas' Park outside the city.[43] These latent forces of discontent found expression in an Irish republican vote in 1866, the harbinger of a larger republican following in later years.

Shortly before the election of 1868 came the first significant break in the democratic solidarity of the Irish voters. The continued harping of the republican press upon the "tyranny" to which the Irish tamely submitted in the democratic party— the clever insinuation that a small and corrupt native minority blandly exploited them to get into office—fanned into a blaze the smoldering discontent of the more restive Irishmen. They beheld certain attractions in the republican party with its fetish of freedom for the oppressed and with its anti-British tariff policy. In July, 1868, Hodnett, assisted by Alderman Arthur Dixon and J. F. Scanlan, organized an Irish republican club in Chicago to support the republican national ticket. Such a change in political alignment called forth a vigorous protest from standpat Irish democrats. The hall engaged by the republicans was invaded by members of Irish democratic clubs led by Aldermen Rafferty and Comiskey and a battle royal took place; in the *mêlée* stones, clubs, torchlights, and slingshots were freely used and several persons were seriously wounded. When similar republican clubs were organized in other cities they encountered the same hostility from the oldguard Irish. Nevertheless, the rebel movement could not be stayed until a significant minority was detached; on election day in Chicago nearly two thousand Irish voters marched to the polls and broke the chains that held them to the democratic party.[44]

These Irish republicans were jubilant in their new-found freedom; on July 5 and 6, 1869, an Irish national republican convention was held at Chicago, a nucleus which was expected to grow into a powerful party. It was evident that these Irish republicans looked at all questions from an anti-English standpoint; their platform of principles, though expressing a general

[43] *Chicago Tribune*, August 16, 17, 1866. The Irish republican leaders included L. O. O'Connor, J. F. Scanlan, and others.
[44] *Illinois State Journal*, August 11, September 12, October 30, 1868; *Chicago Tribune*, July 27, August 28, 1868.

sympathy for the downtrodden of all lands, specifically urged an anti-British foreign policy, denounced free trade, and insisted on the principle of protection. When they declared that free trade was "a cunning and selfish device of the enslavers of mankind," it was clear that they regarded a high tariff as injurious to British industry and commerce. This was too much even for the *Chicago Tribune,* which was insisting that tariff rates were already too high and should be reduced; it, therefore, advised the Irish republican politicians to temper their missionary zeal with political discretion, to drop the issues which tend to divide, and to "allow the Irish republican party to grow a little larger by being less vigorous in the restrictions and less crotchetty in the principles required as a test of membership."[45]

While Illinois was welcoming to its prairies the incoming emigrant, it was in turn making contributions to the western movement. Attracted by the gold mines of Idaho, the equable climate of Oregon and California, and by the new free lands of Kansas and Minnesota, Illinoisians of both native and foreign birth bundled their Lares and Penates into a prairie schooner to seek their fortunes on the frontier. In another very different way Illinois felt the influence of the western march of the pioneer; it lay directly across the highways that led to all parts of the northwest. These paths crossed the state at a half dozen places. Jacksonville citizens, for instance, could claim that "a constant tide of movers passed through our streets, going West."[46] Chicago, however, was the usual way station for this human traffic from the east. Hundreds of emigrants arrived daily and as they changed cars stopped to inspect the great metropolis of the west. They found Chicago's ninety-four hotels continually crowded in spite of extortionate rates.[47] Many took up residence in "the great Babylon of the West" who had originally sought a destination far beyond. So the city collected tolls in human lives as well as in the trade of a great *entrepôt.*

In the sixties Chicago nearly tripled in population, with an

[45] *Chicago Tribune,* July 7, 9, 1869.
[46] *Illinois State Journal,* October 15, 1868.
[47] *Chicago Times,* November 23, 1863, June 29, 1865; *Chicago Tribune,* May 28, 1867.

increase of 298,977, nearly one-half of which was of foreign birth. In spite of the fact that after 1866 business conditions were very discouraging in the other large cities of the country, Chicago prospered mightily. Buildings to the value of seven million dollars were erected in 1865, and the following years building was prosecuted with even more vigor; by the end of the decade, Chicago was running wild in real estate speculation.[48]

With its fine public buildings and private dwellings the city began to take on the true metropolitan atmosphere. A park was developed from Twelfth to Thirty-first street and the present Lincoln park system on the north side was started; at the same time the people of the western and southern divisions prepared to press their claims for civic improvement— for it became an accepted argument that without parks "no city is respectable or decent or fit to be the dwelling-place of men and women." Concrete sidewalks made their appearance, a wonderful improvement over the plank walks. Wabash and Michigan avenues were widened into fine drives lined with elegant residences, though the business district at the same time began to work eastward and to threaten encroachment upon these aristocratic boulevards. The streets were lighted by 2,500 gas street lamps, making it one of the best lighted cities of the country; this involved an annual expense of $75,000, however, which aroused an active movement in favor of the municipalization of this utility. The city was networked by an elaborate system of horse railway lines that ran along the chief thoroughfares; in 1865 they secured a ninety-nine year lease from the state legislature in spite of the veto of Governor Oglesby and the opposition of the *Chicago Tribune* to "the gigantic swindle." A few years later service was so inadequate that an elevated or "second-story" railway was advocated similar to the one then being experimented upon in New York.[49]

---

[48] *Chicago Tribune*, August 21, November 10, 1866, July 20, August 3, 1869; *Chicago Evening Journal*, November 25, 1865; *Aurora Beacon*, March 4, 1869. This included the new depot of the Michigan Southern and Rock Island railroads.
[49] *Chicago Tribune*, December 17, 1866, January 8, 9, 11, 16, February 19, 21, 1867, February 26, March 21, 1869; *Chicago Times*, May 7, 1864; *Chicago Evening Journal*, March 8, 1866.

Squalor and filth continued to litter the streets and combined with slaughterhouses to poison the air. "Everybody understands," insisted the *Chicago Tribune*, "that we have the foulest streets, the dirtiest river, the most inefficient police, the most nauseous water, the most fogyish Board of Public Works and Board of Health in the world, unless we look for their equal in Turkey, China, and Dahomey."[50] Finally, in October, 1866, after intermittent cases during the summer, cholera assailed the city in such a serious epidemic that a reorganization of the board of health under state legislative authority was made imperative. In 1866, too, a supply of fresh water was guaranteed by the completion of a tunnel running out two miles under Lake Michigan.

The prosperity of Chicago was the outgrowth of its superior transportation facilities. The city, now fifth among American cities in the volume of business, was not only the greatest grain, beef, and pork market in the country but the greatest lumber market as well;[51] asthmatic sawmills in Michigan and Wisconsin laboriously coughed out the cargoes of boards which were brought to Chicago by the three hundred lumber carriers that plied Lake Michigan. All the old advantages derived from lake navigation were enlarged by important additions to the harbor facilities along the lake front. When with the increase of railroad freight tariffs, St. Louis, with the natural advantages of its location on the Mississippi and with railroad connections of its own, threatened to draw more heavily upon the trade of the northwest, Chicago awoke to the importance of a navigable watercourse to the Mississippi river; throughout the decade its citizens urged the project of a ship canal which would guarantee its hegemony. The Pacific railroad also promised much for the future of the city; in order to be independent of tribute to the jobbers of San Francisco and New York, a bill was pressed upon congress to make Chicago a formal port of entry.[52]

[50] *Chicago Tribune*, July 4, 1865, January 10, August 28, 1867; *Chicago Evening Journal*, November 15, 1865, February 10, 1866.
[51] *Hunt's Merchants' Magazine*, 54:376-384; *The Lumber Industry of Chicago*, 7-8; Howe, *Yearbook of Chicago*, 1885, p. 241-243; *Chicago Times*, March 19, 1866, October 9, 1872; *Chicago Evening Journal*, November 17, 1865.
[52] *Chicago Tribune*, July 1, December 25, 1868.

Life in the other cities of the state began to quicken under the influence of the prosperity of Chicago. Peoria, with a population of 22,849, lost its place as second city and Quincy with 24,052 inhabitants succeeded to this position. Springfield nearly doubled in the decade to reach the figure of 17,364, while Aurora, Galesburg, and Jacksonville trailed some distance behind. Galena was the only important community of 1860 to experience a decline — it suffered a net loss of over one thousand. One important development was the rise of East St. Louis, incorporated in 1865; the atmosphere of old Illinoistown with "its disreputable floating population and its sink holes of iniquity where the moral filth of St. Louis could take refuge, to plan its deeds of crime" gave way to a thrifty and enterprising young town of 5,644.[53] In general, all these communities were prosperous and enlightened and were passing through a process of refinement which bespoke a steady modernization. This was especially true of Springfield, which awakened to its responsibilities when the demand for a removal of the capital was renewed by rivals like Peoria, Decatur, and Jacksonville.

The Civil War gave to Cairo the opportunity to realize on the promises brought by the building of the Illinois Central; inasmuch as it would be a feeder for Chicago, all Illinoisians had insisted that it was the most convenient depot for the distribution of the supplies for the army in the west. The advantages of this base became obvious in the winter of 1863–1864, when ice and low water closed the river below St. Louis and made Cairo the head of navigation on the Father of Waters. Business became brisk immediately: "Every house, cellar and shed on the levee, from one extreme of the town to the other, is occupied as a place of business and every occupant . . . is doing well."[54] At times buildings were almost unobtainable; "little shanties that people would not look at anywhere else, bring three or four hundred dollars per year, paying as much per cent. on their actual cost."[55] Five thousand steamers arrived each year to land and discharged

[53] *Belleville Advocate*, January 12, 1866.
[54] *Cairo Gazette*, August 20, 1864; *Cairo Democrat*, January 8, 1864; Mark Skinner to Trumbull, May 31, 1862, Trumbull manuscripts.
[55] *Cairo Democrat*, September 6, 1863.

their freight and passengers at Cairo and probably a million or more soldiers passed through the city during the war. The first fear of a prostration of business upon the withdrawal of government patronage after the war was succeeded by a lofty idealism which pointed to the geographical advantages in location and forecast a continuous position as the natural depot of exchange between the north and south — an emporium rivaling the great metropolis of the lakes. The last two years of the decade, however, showed the futility of this hope; the city had increased from 2,188 to ten or twelve thousand in 1867, but two years later the census enumerators could locate only 6,267 persons, and Cairo did not pass the 10,000 mark again until well toward the close of the century.

Why did Cairo fail to realize the expectations of the latter day prophets? Cairo was a house built upon mud; when the storms came and rain fell and the wind blew, portions of the city joined the murky waters of the Mississippi. True, the work of raising and widening the levee to save the bustling city, went on, so that in the flood years of 1862 and 1867 the levees held back the tide, while all the surrounding country was one vast expanse of water spread out like a sea. Yet flood conditions produced a menacing fear which endangered the future growth of the city. Rival communities chose to play upon this fear and coupled with it the general belief in the unhealthiness of Cairo. It availed little in meeting this impression that Dr. G. T. Allen, federal medical inspector, was able to report that "with filth enough in many of its streets to poison all the population of New York City, during the summer solstice, it is even then, in my opinion, as healthy as any place in the Union." With water everywhere, Cairo had at times literally not a drop to drink, except as it was hauled into the city in barrels to be retailed at from ten to twenty cents a pint.[56]

Chicago, the fulfillment of prophecy, the great city on the

[56] *Cairo Democrat*, February 17, 1864. See also *Cairo Daily News*, August 20, 1864: "Our streets, highways and byways abound, at the present writing, with a profusion of a slippery, sticky substance known to those who are familiar with its qualities as Cairo mud. It is found on the sidewalks and off the sidewalks, inside the house and outside the house — in the kitchen, parlor and bed chamber. No place is sacred from its intrusive visits, and it succumbs only to the sun and wind."

lakes, and Cairo, the city of blasted hopes, were the opposite poles of this great magnet in the middle west which was attracting the restive population of all parts of the globe.

XVI. THE INDUSTRIAL REVOLUTION, 1860-1870

MODERN industry in Illinois is built upon the foundations laid in the tumultuous era of civil strife. The transportation phase was marked by the extension to a point of greater adequacy of rail and water communication. During the war water transportation again became the great hope of all Illinoisians; they expected to revolutionize transportation facilities by improving the navigation of the Mississippi, Illinois, and Rock rivers and by building a ship canal to the Mississippi. They urged federal aid for the accomplishment of their ends and justified it as necessary to the efficient transportation of supplies and to the triumph of the federal arms. All projects found only local support, however, except as they connected themselves with the proposed ship canal. At first this meant merely the enlarging of the Illinois and Michigan canal so as to end the prevailing low water problems and permit the passage of ships of large draught between the Great Lakes and the Mississippi. The disunion crisis further emphasized the need, in order to reverse the course of trade and direct the products of the upper Mississippi eastward instead of toward the gulf. When war closed the Mississippi below Cairo the need became more definite. In the legislative session of 1861 the general assembly authorized an investigation of the possibility of an enlarged canal; when a favorable report was made appeals were sent to congress for federal aid.[1] The constitutional convention of 1862 unanimously adopted a formal memorial to congress; other memorials were sent in, including one from the Chicago Board of Trade.

In February, 1862, Colonel F. P. Blair, Jr., of the com-

[1] *1 Laws of 1861*, p. 277-278; R. P. Mori to Trumbull, June 6, 1861, Trumbull manuscripts; *Prairie Farmer*, November 24, 1861; *Joliet Signal*, November 19, 1861; *Ottawa Free Trader*, November 23, 1861; *Ottawa Weekly Republican*, November 30, 1861. In November, 1861, public meetings were held to call attention to the importance of this project.

mittee on military affairs of the house, reported a bill for the enlargement of the canal so that gunboats and other vessels drawing six feet of water might pass from the Mississippi to the lakes.[2] By this time the matter was squarely before congress. Representative Arnold from the Chicago district, a member of the committee on roads and canals, assumed the leadership of the Illinois delegation and made a favorable report to the house. In July, however, the project was killed on a test vote in which the eastern members lined up against the representatives of the west. Governor Yates, not to be thus silenced, then pressed the matter upon the attention of the president; in November he went to Washington for a joint interview in the company of Congressman Arnold. The war department was directed to examine into the practicability of the undertaking; meantime, the canal project was again pressed upon the attention of congress.[3]

Eastern selfishness, the canal advocates claimed, was giving force to the movement for the separation of the western from the eastern states and the formation of a northwestern confederacy. Even republican leaders declared that governmental policy was destroying the value of the agricultural products of the west, while manufactured articles from the east doubled and quadrupled in price. This discrimination could be removed by a restoration of the natural exchange of commodities by easy channels of commerce; and the canal was, therefore, a political as well as a military necessity. Governor Yates at the suggestion of western business and farming interests went so far as to send a commission to Canada to arrange for a Canadian route to the seaboard.[4]

While congress was wrestling with this problem, Arnold and other ship canal advocates arranged for a great national canal convention at Chicago to express the interests of the west. This body met on June 2 and 3, 1863, with Vice President Hamlin in the chair; it set out to secure the right of the

[2] *Congressional Globe*, 37 congress, 2 session, 902-903.
[3] *Illinois State Journal*, September 17, November 22, 1862.
[4] *Ibid.*, January 15, March 10, 31, April 20, 1863; *Aurora Beacon*, November 13, 1861; *Chicago Tribune*, November 27, December 23, 1862, June 2, 1863. Eastern transportation interests were said to be conspiring to prevent either waterways in the northwest or an aggressive policy to accomplish the reopening of the Mississippi.

states of the Mississippi valley to "national recognition as coequal sovereignties of the Great Republic."[5] It did not confine itself to the Illinois canal plan but adopted resolutions in favor of constructing different ship canals to connect the lakes with the Mississippi and the Atlantic. Although this was not exactly what Illinoisians wanted, yet, as the measure in congress had been given this larger scope, they welcomed the indorsement as a forward step. Again, however, congress took no action: not until January, 1865, was Arnold able to secure favorable action on the bill by the lower house; then the senate refused to lend its assistance, and with the close of the war one of the strongest arguments for federal aid came to an end. A survey was made, however, by the war department in 1867, and, though the engineers recommended the project, no action was taken.[6] Although traffic on the canal was declining rapidly, later efforts to secure federal action also failed to bear fruit.

The ship canal fever included a number of projects of more daring scope. In 1866 a widespread movement took place for the extension of the Illinois and Michigan canal to the Mississippi river at a point near Rock Island,[7] and a local following boomed a scheme for a ship canal from the Rock river to Lake Michigan. A series of conventions at Sterling, Geneseo, Dixon, Rock Island, Morris, and other points enthusiastically urged ship canals and river improvement. Some even advocated a canal under federal auspices around Niagara Falls to open up a more satisfactory route to Europe. The only tangible result that followed from all this activity was the act of the Illinois legislature of February 28, 1867, under which the state inaugurated the work of improving the canal and the Illinois river channel. As a sop to the advocates of other water routes the act referred to but made no provision for an extension of the canal to the Mississippi at Rock Island and the improvement of the Rock and other rivers.

[5] "The West," declared the *Chicago Tribune*, June 2, 1863, "will henceforth be a partner in the Union, entitled to all the immunities and privileges of her place."
[6] *Ibid.*, June 3, 4, 1863, July 20, 1867; Putnam, *Illinois and Michigan Canal*, 135; *House Executive Documents*, 40 congress, 1 session, number 16.
[7] *Chicago Tribune*, January 6, 8, 10, 17, 23, 1866; *Chicago Evening Journal*, January 8, 1866.

The strength of the agitation for water transportation reflected not so much the absence of rail communication as the dissatisfaction with the service which the railroads were furnishing. Some of the canal and river meetings were held as anti-monopoly conventions under the auspices of the movement which the farmers launched against the enormous freight tariffs of the railroads. The agriculturists claimed that they were at the mercy of the railroads, while Chicagoans held that these rates were "damaging Chicago to a degree that it is difficult to compute." [8]

There was a strong survival in Illinois of the sixties of the old frontier fear and hatred of monopoly; the railroad symbolized this hydra headed monster whose inroads had been dreaded since the days of Andrew Jackson. When the railroads, deprived of the competition of the Mississippi water route and encouraged by general economic and monetary conditions, steadily increased their passenger and freight rates to a point that seemed extortionate, a note of alarm and protest was sounded which showed the crystallization of widespread dissatisfaction; the year 1865 saw the crest of a high rate wave with a corresponding amount of complaint and indignation.[9] Transportation charges on shipments from Minnesota, Wisconsin, and Iowa, it was said, were retarding the development of the state and threatening the prosperity of the lake cities. The railroads were flourishing on tariffs like twenty-five cents on a bushel of wheat from Winona to Chicago; indeed, rates sometimes amounted virtually to an embargo upon the shipment of cereals by this route and forced trade to go through St. Louis and down the Mississippi river. Through freight, moreover, was often handled more reasonably than freight between two intermediary points.

A rumor began to spread of a great upper Mississippi railroad and steamboat combination; thereupon, two hundred and twenty of the leading mercantile houses of Chicago addressed a questionnaire to the railroad companies to learn whether they were in partnership with the elevators of the city,

[8] *Ibid.*, November 27, 1865.
[9] *Ibid.*, December 18, 1865; *Cairo Weekly Democrat*, January 19, 1865; *Paxton Record*, June 22, 1865; *Chicago Tribune*, December 15, 1865.

with express and transportation companies, or steamboat lines upon routes leading to Chicago, in such a way as to involve restraint of trade. The failure of the railroads to reply was interpreted as an admission of the combination; complaints became even more general and were summarized in February, 1866, in a report of a joint committee of the Chicago Board of Trade and the Chicago Mercantile Association.[10]

The result was a state wide revolt against the railway and warehouses "monopolies." In northern Illinois, farmers' mass meetings and commercial conventions urged that provision be made for new waterways and that the railway lines of the state be subjected to careful legislative regulation. As early as 1864, rate regulation had been proposed by farmers' organizations and in January, 1865, William Brown of Winnebago had proposed in the legislature a resolution subjecting all new railroads to a general law regulating freight and passenger rates. Within a year the demand for rate regulation became general; the supervisors of Winnebago county passed resolutions declaring that they would support no man for office who was not pledged to use his influence for the correction of this abuse.[11]

In January, 1867, the anti-monopoly forces came together at Springfield and formed a league which demanded of the legislature restrictions on railroad combinations, uniformity of freight rates, a three-cent passenger fare, and an annual report of expenditures and receipts of each road. Bills were promptly introduced into the legislature; but the railroad interests, aided by the unwillingness of downstate rail advocates to place any obstacles in the way of their own ambitions, blocked all attempts at legislation. In 1869 the cudgel was again taken up against the railroads. The blow was tempered, however, by a challenge at the constitutionality of such rate-fixing legislation. Southern Illinois spokesmen also pointed out that, since it would apply only to roads thereafter incor-

---

[10] *Chicago Tribune*, December 15, 26, 1865; January 11, 12, 1866; *Central Illinois Gazette*, January 19, 1866; *Illinois State Register*, January 12, 1866; *Chicago Evening Journal*, February 14, 1866.
[11] *Prairie Farmer*, December 24, 1864; *Rockford Register*, January 28, 1865; *Ottawa Weekly Republican*, January 28, 1865; *Chicago Tribune*, February 10, 1865; *Illinois State Register*, January 3, 1866.

porated, its sole effect would be to prevent the construction of new lines. A maximum rate bill introduced into the senate by General A. C. Fuller passed both houses but was vetoed by Governor Palmer; thereupon Senator Fuller introduced a new measure limiting all roads in the state to a "just, reasonable, and uniform" rate; this became law and went into force on March 10, 1869. The war between the people and the railroad ring continued and a point for the people was scored in the restrictions imposed by the new constitution of 1870.[12]

The remedy most strongly favored by the anti-monopolists was additional transportation facilities. Besides waterways new railway lines were welcomed to open up competition with those that were charged with indiscriminate pillage. Little, however, could be done in northern Illinois, which was dominated by the Chicago and Northwestern railway; this company, chartered in 1854 under the Illinois and Wisconsin laws, had first taken up the rights and franchises of the Chicago, St. Paul, and Fond du Lac railway company, then in 1864, after unsuccessful attempts to force out the Galena and Chicago Union railroad by competition, a consolidation of the two systems as arranged. A little later under the control of Henry Keep of New York and his associates, the Northwestern line absorbed the Chicago and Milwaukee railroad and with a mileage of 1,152 became the largest railway corporation in the United States; in 1868 evidence was published of a scheme to consolidate the Chicago and Northwestern, the Chicago and Rock Island, and the Milwaukee and St. Paul under one management; this, said the *Chicago Tribune*, "would practically deliver the whole territory north and west of Chicago over to the tender mercies of a Wall street ring."[13] Simultaneous with the election of three of the managers of the Milwaukee and St. Paul to the directorate of the Northwestern road, the Northwestern corporation tried to secure a majority of the

---

[12] *Chicago Tribune*, January 14, February 12, 19, March 13, December 6, 1869; *Illinois State Journal*, January 15, 1869; *Cairo Evening Bulletin*, January 16, 1869; *Ottawa Free Trader*, January 15, 1870; *Ottawa Weekly Republican*, June 30, December 1, 1870; *Laws of 1869*, p. 309-312.

[13] *Chicago Tribune*, March 6, June 4, 5, 1868, June 10, 1869; *Chicago Times*, June 2, 1864.

stock of the Chicago, Rock Island, and Pacific. It was no wonder that the people clamored for competing waterways, the only competition possible.

Southern Illinois, meanwhile, had been passing through another attack of the periodic railroad fever, and was now able to gratify some of its cravings for more railroads. Innumerable schemes were afloat many of which secured legislative sanction; work was commenced on twelve distinct roads, but only the more stable and conservative ventures were successfully executed;[14] through these, however, the railroad mileage of the southern third of the state was nearly doubled. The old St. Louis and Terre Haute project, revived and chartered in 1865 as the St. Louis, Vandalia, and Terre Haute railroad, was completed and opened in 1870. The Springfield and Illinois Southeastern was chartered in 1867; and the connection between the state capital and Shawneetown, except for the short link between Pana and Edgewood, was completed within the decade. The extension of the Belleville and Illinoistown toward Du Quoin produced the Belleville and Southern Illinois road which was not ready for use, however, until 1873. Plans were also well under way for a road between Cairo and Vincennes which was finished in 1872.

The central part of the state was almost equally fortunate in its new connections. The Toledo, Wabash, and Western was extended across Pike county to Hannibal, Missouri; and the St. Louis, Jacksonville, and Chicago between Bloomington and St. Louis, was opened for business in January, 1868, under a lease to the Chicago and Alton railroad. In 1869 the Indianapolis, Bloomington, and Western opened between Pekin and Danville. The western part of the state was traversed lengthwise by the Rockford, Rock Island, and St. Louis railroad which was finished in 1869 and soon became part of the Chicago, Burlington, and Quincy, a vast railroad combination which was steadily absorbing the roads of western Illinois. These larger systems built many branch lines most of which fell within the central tiers of counties. In many instances local connections were incorporated in the larger systems.

[14] *Cairo Evening Bulletin*, June 23, 1869; *Ottawa Weekly Republican*, July 8, 1869; *Chicago Tribune*, July 15, 1869.

By 1869 the mileage of Illinois roads had increased to 4,031 and Illinois remained the second railroad state in the union.[15]

One of the most significant developments of the decade was the building of the Pacific railroad. Illinoisians had always had a special interest in a trans-Atlantic rail line, especially a central route. This had been a leading factor in Douglas' eagerness to secure the organization of the territory of Nebraska in 1854; his opponents, moreover, had used a strong Pacific railroad plank in constructing the platform of the new republican party. When the Civil War created a new military demand, congress gave its approval to the undertaking and the president decided in favor of a Chicago connection. The effect upon such lines as the Chicago and Rock Island and the Galena and Chicago was immediate; the stock of the former rose twenty points in a few weeks. The Northwestern railway company, using the old Galena and Chicago air line to the Iowa boundary, was the first to complete an Omaha connection. In 1868, the Chicago, Rock Island, and Pacific undertook to build an extension of its line to Council Bluffs. At once Chicago began to tap the trade of the far west and in 1869, when the trans-Atlantic route was completed, an excursion of business men left Chicago for San Francisco to examine into the possibilities of commercial relations with the Pacific coast and the orient.[16]

Banking and currency problems divided with transportation the responsibility for clearing the way for the industrial prosperity of Illinois. The banks had just completed their recovery from the panic of 1857 when the sectional crisis precipitated by Lincoln's election brought the threat of financial chaos. Since the circulation of the state banks was mainly predicated upon southern securities, the banking interests at first reacted very conservatively and even recommended sacrifices of principle to pacify the south. The free banking system

---

[15] *Poor's Manual*, xliv-xlv. The *Rushville Times*, June 4, 1870, estimated the Illinois mileage at 5,200.
[16] *Ottawa Free Trader*, January 9, 1863, June 26, 1866; *Chicago Tribune*, October 11, 1866, July 1, 1869; James H. Bowen *et al.* to Trumbull, June 14, 1869, Trumbull manuscripts. The Chicago Board of Trade formally indorsed a Northern Pacific railroad from Lake Superior to Puget Sound. *Chicago Evening Journal*, April 23, 1866.

had created a machine for the issue of a circulating medium which was now endangered by the decline of southern securities. The banking commissioners in November, 1860, called for more securities from twenty-two banks, but before they were due the rapid drop of southern stocks had involved all but the fourteen or fifteen banks that had deposited northern state bonds.[17] Only the notes of these banks remained in circulation; the other paper was driven out and the auditor retired and destroyed the issues presented for redemption. Some specie, too, was forced out of its hiding places, and some foreign issues remained in the field, although their circulation was attacked.

The general assembly attempted to adjust the banking system to the new conditions under the banking amendment of February 14, 1861. This law provided for a central redemption system and quarterly reports, and restricted securities for deposits to United States and Illinois stocks. In consequence by the end of the year, Illinois bonds constituted the vast bulk of the holdings of the auditor. On the whole, however, this law failed to receive a fair trial. The large volume of federal greenbacks together with the later issues of national bank notes came to monopolize the field. By 1865 the office of bank commissioner was abolished and only $200,000 in state bank paper was circulated by twenty-three banks. On August 1, 1866, the federal tax on state bank notes succeeded in driving from circulation most of what remained. In 1869 the auditor's report showed only $531 in outstanding bank notes.[18]

In this way a system designed during the fifties to furnish Illinois with a supply of local bank notes collapsed under the double strain of the break with the south and of the competition with the new currency issues of the federal government. The national banking system received a hearty welcome from the business men of the state, and state banks learned to adjust themselves to the necessity of confining their operations to the

---

[17] *Illinois State Register*, November 16, 1860; *Chicago Tribune*, November 20, 1860; *Rockford Republican*, November 22, 1860; *Joliet Signal*, November 27, 1860; *Central Illinois Gazette*, November 28, 1860.

[18] *Reports General Assembly*, 1867, 1:115; 1869, 1:324; *1 Laws of 1861*, p. 39 ff.

receiving and transmitting of money and to a loan and discount business.

In the spring of 1862 the stream of greenbacks or federal legal tender notes began to flow into Illinois. There was little realization, however, on the part of citizens as to the significance of this influx. The previous winter had been extremely dull, the bottom had dropped out of the market. Now prices pushed up, trade became brisk, and prosperity seemed to prevail. A heavy demand was current for small change to which the government responded by authorizing the issue of a "fractional postage currency." Its distribution was managed inefficiently, however, and bankers found it necessary to secure consignments through senatorial intervention.[19] The government outlawed the use of tokens and checks which business houses issued to furnish a currency of small denominations. With the steady depreciation of the greenback, gold and silver disappeared from circulation and high prices began to prevail. For a time, however, the farmer complained of the great disparity between the price of his produce and the manufactured articles that he had to secure by purchase; the eastern money changers seemed to be deriving the peculiar advantages from these developments. Two years later, however, wheat was well over $2.00 with other agricultural products in proportion, a partial compensation for the fact that gold was approaching the 250 mark.[20] With the victories that closed the war the greenback recovered considerably in value, but prices remained ruinously high. The advocates of contraction placed the blame on the superabundance of money; yet in 1867 dull times and lower prices set in again without any explanation in a reduced supply of money. When contraction was suggested dozens of Chicago business men were found to oppose it. An outcry went up against heavy taxes. "The honest white men of the country are taxed and retaxed over and over again from the cradle to the grave, and are then taxed one dollar for dying,"

[19] E. March to Trumbull, November 28, December 6, 1862, J. Young Scammon to Trumbull, December 5, 15, 1862, R. Hinckley to Trumbull, December 13, 1862, Edward Abend to Trumbull, December 24, 1862, Trumbull manuscripts.
[20] *Ottawa Free Trader,* July 2, 1864; *Chicago Tribune,* July 20, 1864; *Joliet Signal,* December 16, 1862. The general increase in the cost of living was between two hundred and three hundred per cent.

complained the *Carthage Republican*.[21] Discrimination against the western agricultural states in internal revenue assessments was claimed at an early day; later when a tax of two dollars on a gallon of whisky threatened to decrease the consumption of grain, a general protest went up. A large body of republicans also agreed with the democrats that on the tariff the west was being "consumed by the good of New England & Pennsylvania" and a readjustment seemed essential.[22]

Then, however, the eastern creditors called up the currency issue in a new form by insisting on the payment of the interest on the federal debt in gold rather than in the legal tender paper. Illinois agriculturalists opposed the idea of special favors for "bloated bond-holders." The democratic party gained strength in 1868 when it seemed that George H. Pendleton would be nominated on his western greenback policy. When, however, he was rejected at New York for a hard money candidate, the issue was postponed to a later period in national politics.

Industrially, Illinois on the eve of the Civil War showed many frontier survivals; another decade, however, worked out a revolution that brought the state to the threshold of modern industrialism. The extended transportation system was one of the greatest factors in stimulating this progress; the other factors proceeded from the war itself. The war, in bringing high prices for grain and livestock, in bestowing protective duties that far surpassed the rosiest dreams of infant industry, gave a remarkable impetus to manufacturing industries. Cook county in 1860 had only 469 manufactories; another decade and this number had more than tripled.[23] In the same period the manufacturing establishments of the state had increased from 4,268 to 12,597 with the value of manu-

---

[21] *Carthage Republican*, June 27, 1867; E. W. Blatchford to Trumbull, February 27, 1867, Trumbull manuscripts; *Aurora Beacon*, February 7, 1867; *Cairo Democrat*, May 25, 1865, May 23, August 9, 1867; *Illinois Democrat*, December 21, 1867; *Chicago Times*, June 24, 1865; *Illinois State Journal*, July 24, 1865. Board in Chicago was ten to fifteen dollars per week.

[22] *Chicago Times*, April 23, 1864; *Illinois State Register*, April 28, 1866; *Chicago Tribune*, August 1, 1867, March 27, June 11, 1868; E. Peck to Trumbull, April 24, 1866, C. H. Ray to Trumbull, February 2, 1866, Trumbull manuscripts.

[23] Schoff, *Industrial Interests of Chicago*; Chamberlin, *Chicago and Its Suburbs*, 136-137.

factured products rising from $57,580,886 to $205,620,672. The number of operatives employed in the state increased from 5,593 to 82,979. These figures tell the story of a revolution which, after having broken out in England a century before, had irrepressibly swept on and on until it reached the prairies of Illinois.

The focusing point of the manufactures as well as of the railroads was Cook county. In 1870, although it contained just one-ninth of the establishments in the state, it listed about one-half of the employees; the industries, therefore, were not only more numerous but were organized on a larger scale. Chicago became a center for the manufacture of iron products, which received special protection under the tariff schedules; in 1860 there were 26 iron works in the city which increased in the decade to over a hundred, including about one-quarter of the capital invested in manufacturing. The large output of farm implements and machinery reflected the demand of the agricultural population of the northwest; Peter Schuttler's wagon manufactory, established in 1843, was known from Texas to Oregon, and McCormick's reaper works which were moved to Chicago in 1847 supplied a wide demand among western farmers. A factory started by Furst and Bradley in 1851 for the production of plows and other farm machinery was doing a thriving business before 1860.[24] Wood works to supply the building trades were second in importance followed by combined wood and iron establishments. Brick, stone, metal, and terra cotta works, together with leather plants, and textile factories were important in the industrial development of the city.

The milling of flour and grist was one manufacturing field that Chicago was gradually yielding to the smaller cities and towns of the state. In this field as well as in some of the other fundamental needs of farming communities, no serious attempt was made at large scale production; but the smaller centers were left both to supply the local demand and to export the surplus.

Every population center was ambitious to share in the new prosperity. Illinois claimed certain peculiar advantages for

[24] *Western Manufacturer*, May supplement, 1874.

manufacturing—nearness to the supply of foodstuffs, of raw material for the factories, and of coal for steam power; the cheapness of these commodities tended to offset the lower rates for capital and labor that prevailed in the east. Every city talked of its available coal deposits, its water power, or other advantages; in Peoria and elsewhere business organizations to promote their respective communities soon began to appear. A committee of Bloomington citizens studied the manufacturing towns of Ohio and pointed out ways and means to secure the same advantages to their own town; communities competed with each other in offers to secure new industries.[25]

Quincy, the second city in the state, specialized in stove foundries; during the war an important tobacco industry developed there by transfer from Missouri.[26] Peoria's prosperity was well grounded upon the distillery business; it had four distilleries in 1856, six in 1859, and nine in 1873. By 1871, moreover, it had two corn planter factories, two plow and cultivator establishments, and one starch factory.[27] Rockford claimed to have a manufacturing output of $3,000,000 per year. The other towns of 5,000 or over usually had grist and saw mills, a foundry and machine shop, a woolen factory, a wagon or plow factory, and certain more highly specialized establishments.[28] Certain communities boasted of rather unique manufacturing lines. The National Watch Company established its factory at Elgin in 1864; five years later the first watch factory at Springfield was established. La Salle had a flourishing zinc works and in 1866 the manufacture of glass was revived there in the only glass factory in the west; soon Ottawa promoters, headed by J. D. Caton, started to raise the

---

[25] At the beginning of the decade republicans advocated a protective tariff to foster manufactures; soon there was a surfeit and even the democrats urged the people to "quit raising corn and go to manufacturing" as "the true remedy for New England robbery." *Ottawa Free Trader*, October 14, 1865; *Carthage Republican*, January 18, May 3, 1866; *Paxton Record*, December 11, 1869; *Ottawa Republican*, December 15, 1870.

[26] *Western Agriculturist*, 11:6, 10; *The City of Quincy, Illinois*, 18-19.

[27] *Western Manufacturer*, 9:4; Board of Trade of Peoria, *Report*, 1873, p. 31; Dwyer, "Manufactures in Illinois," Department of Agriculture of Illinois, *Transactions*, 9:87.

[28] Over a dozen firms manufactured plows on a large scale. *Prairie Farmer*, December 10, 1864.

stock for a rival glass factory at that place.[29] Bloomington was unique in the possession of a melodeon factory.

Under the stimulus of war prices every town of any size made an effort to secure a woolen factory; at the end of the decade the census enumerators found twenty-four wool carding and cloth dressing establishments and eighty-five woolen mills in Illinois, many at obscure points like Dayton, Lacon, Augusta, and Fairbury. They represented an investment of $3,600,000 and employed 3,460 operators, one-fourth of whom were women.[30] This incursion into a new field met with limited success: almost all the new establishments were erected after the close of the war, yet before the seventies some of these were compelled to shut down. Cotton manufacturing, another venture that seemed equally promising, collapsed even more promptly; Henry W. Fuller of Chicago headed a concern to erect a factory in that city; in 1865, after two years of preparation, the Chicago Cotton Manufacturing Company secured an act of incorporation only to die a lingering death. The first cotton factory ever set in operation in Illinois was completed at Rockford in the summer of 1867;[31] Rockford had the only two establishments of the kind at the end of the decade.

Even these unsuccessful ventures into new fields testified to the industrial revolution. By the method of trial and failure the commonwealth that had in five decades risen from the wilderness ranked first among the states in its flour and gristmills and in its sirup and molasses factories, second in its manufactories of agricultural implements, and fourth in the number of establishments for the manufacture of carriages and wagons,

[29] *Ottawa Free Trader,* October 21, 1865, November 2, 1869; *La Salle Press* clipped in *Central Illinois Gazette,* December 22, 1865; *Illinois State Journal,* March 7, 1866.
[30] *Ibid.,* March 2, 1866; *Central Illinois Gazette,* March 3, 1866; *Champaign County Union and Gazette,* July 21, 1869; Illinois State Agricultural Society, *Transactions,* 8: 180. The woolgrowers, anxious to maintain the price of their product urged a protective tariff on the raw wool, but at the Cleveland wool tariff convention of 1866 the Illinois delegation recommended that the Illinois legislature pass a bill exempting from taxation all capital invested in woolen and cotton mills. *Chicago Tribune,* November 16, 27, 1866; *Jacksonville Journal,* November 19, 1866.
[31] *Prairie Farmer,* January 24, 1863; *Chicago Tribune,* January 16, 1866; *Chicago Evening Journal,* February 5, 1866; *Rockford Gazette,* December 31, 1868.

of saddlery and harness, of tin, copper, and sheet iron, of cooperage, of furniture, and even of millinery.

The Civil War decade also opened up some of the more important mineral wealth of the state — in 1861 the general assembly had passed an act to encourage mining in Illinois.[32] The use of coal in locomotives and manufacturing establishments caused a new stir in the coal fields. Informed by the state geological survey of 1860 that coal might be had for the digging anywhere in the state from Kane county to Cairo, prospectors appeared in every community to estimate the commercial value of the deposits. As a result the number of coal mines increased from 73 to 322 while the coal output of the state increased from 728,400 tons in 1860 to 2,624,163 in 1870.

The most thrilling event in the industrial world was the discovery of petroleum. In the early months of 1865, after important oil strikes at points between Knox, Jackson, and Lawrence counties, the excitement rose to such a pitch that it infected all parts of the state. "Petroleum is a fever, an itch, a mania, a madness with some," declared the *Chicago Journal*. "The very air is full of oil, the very pavement is slippery with it, as it were. All a man's five senses are assailed, conquered, carried by it. We cannot help seeing it, nor hearing it, nor feeling it, nor tasting, nor smelling it."[33] Little was accomplished, however, in the way of utilizing commercially this new resource.

One of the difficulties in the way of industrial development was the labor problem. The war had drawn off a large portion of the working population of the state and created a shortage of labor that not only raised wages everywhere but made skilled labor unobtainable for new enterprises. Yet increased wages could not keep pace with the rapidly increased cost of living. By 1864 living expenses had increased from 50 to 300 per cent, while wages had risen only 15 to 100 per cent. The burdens of war, therefore, fell more heavily upon the workers than upon any other class. An effort was made to solve this difficulty by introducing the principle of coöperative buying on

[32] *1 Laws of 1861*, p. 146.
[33] Clipped in *Belleville Advocate*, February 24, 1865.

the English plan; since there was no opportunity, however, to carry it beyond the experimental stage, it could not relieve the general situation.[34]

The result was a stimulus to organization such as never existed in the history of the state. Before the war organized labor had been represented almost exclusively by German workingmen's associations. German tailors, carpenters, and wagoners associations had been in existence in Chicago for some time and in 1857 the Chicago Arbeiter Verein was organized.[35] During that period, however, proximity to cheap lands offered a solution of the economic problem to many a hard pressed worker; this remedy still existed to a limited degree but the worker in a more complex society began to sense his own strength with a growing class consciousness — a consciousness that gave birth to the labor movement in Illinois.

In December, 1863, a mass meeting of Chicago workingmen representing nearly every field sent resolutions to the striking laborers of New York. Within a few months, in view of increased living expenses, Chicago workers were organizing into some twenty trade-unions with a "general trades union" to harmonize their relations.[36] With the same process going on in Springfield and the other cities of the state, strikes began to make their appearance in Illinois; March 1, 1864, was significant for the general railroad strike on roads entering Chicago in which the locomotive engineers sought, after having secured a $3.50 wage, to define their week's work in terms of a run of a specified mileage as against six ten-hour work days. The railroads stood their ground, backed by the newspapers, and the engineers one after another returned to their duty. In the same year short strikes took place among the coopers, carpenters, waiters, bakers, and other labor groups. The

---

[34] For coöperative stores and societies see *Prairie Farmer*, June 20, 1863; *Chicago Tribune*, November 21, 1863; *Chicago Evening Journal*, November 23, 1865; *Chicago Post*, January 3, 1866.

[35] The miners about Belleville were organized in 1860 under their leader, John Hincheliffe, with the German element sufficiently numerous to warrant a separate issue of the *Belleville Miner and Workman's Advocate* in German shortly after its institution. *Belleville Democrat*, February 2, 16, 1861; January 16, 1864.

[36] *Chicago Times*, December 29, 1863, April 25, May 6, 1864; *Chicago Morning Post*, December 30, 1863; *Chicago Tribune*, April 27, August 21, 23, 1864.

strike had taken its place as the favorite weapon by which the workers sought to secure their "rights."

With the growing class consciousness of the workers they began to recognize the influence they exercised in political life and soon launched a movement whereby labor definitely entered politics. In 1864 when many workers were alienated from Lincoln by his war policies, a Chicago mass meeting of workingmen proposed an independent "labor party." The republicans tried to head it off by references to their rail-splitter and tailor candidates while the democrats posed as the protectors of the laboring poor from the tyranny of capital and of the national administration. Cyrus H. McCormick, democratic candidate for congress, made a direct appeal to the workers through the columns of the *Workingman's Advocate*.[37] With such bids from the professional politician old party connections proved in every sense too strong for a new alignment. Indeed, politicians displayed unlimited zeal in trying to placate labor. In 1866, when the workers launched a widespread movement for an eight-hour law and organized an eight-hour league to support only eight-hour men, all candidates took up the idea. A legislature was elected which enacted the eight-hour law of 1867 providing that, in the absence of any contract, eight hours except in farm labor should be a legal day's work.

It was not to be expected that the employers would acquiesce without a fight in this new-found power of the workingmen. Indeed, they had not been sitting idly by; suddenly they showed their hand. Upon agreement they notified their employees that such as were unwilling to work ten hours might consider themselves discharged. The workers, in angry reply, organized themselves through the Illinois Labor Convention to secure the advantages of the eight-hour system. The law was to go into effect May 1; for that day they planned a grand demonstration in Chicago followed by a general strike. The newspapers, sensing a shift in public opinion in response to the uncompromising attitude of the employers, immediately attacked the program of the workers and aroused public opinion against them; nevertheless, on May Day the strikes broke out all over the state and soon work was generally suspended.

[37] *Chicago Times*, August 22, 1864; *Chicago Tribune*, October 30, 1864.

Chicago was the seat of special disturbances which at times went as far as serious rioting between the strikers and those who remained at work. Governor Oglesby, who had previously indicated his desire to see the state law enforced, was silent during the struggle; Mayor John B. Rice of Chicago, however, took advantage of the growing reaction against the law to issue on May 3 a proclamation calling attention to a statute which forbade preventing any person from working at any lawful business and combining to deprive the owner of property of its lawful use and management.[38] Under this policy the loosely organized workers were gradually compelled to resume employment; in only a few cases were they permitted to labor eight hours for eight hours pay. By the first week in June the struggle had pretty well come to an end and the law became a dead letter.

The eight-hour law and its failure stimulated experiments with the principle of coöperative labor. In some instances this meant the association of workers on a purely coöperative basis; in other cases old established firms, like Dillman and Company of Joliet, or newly organized joint stock companies, like the Northwestern Manufacturing Company of Chicago, introduced the new system into their plants.[39]

Deserted by the old party politicians, the more independent minded labor leaders began to consider an independent political activity to wield the influence to which their numbers entitled them. For them the blandishments of the old parties had come to an end; in the fall of 1867 preparations were made in various parts of the state for the launching of a labor party as a nation wide movement.[40] In the spring of 1868 plans were pushed aggressively. The republican leaders tried to check them by directing a labor movement within their party; a republican farmers' and laboring men's state convention at Decatur in April recommended Harrison Noble as the workers' candidate for the republican nomination as governor. When

[38] *Chicago Evening Post*, May 3, 1867; *Chicago Tribune*, May 4, 1867.
[39] *Ibid.*, April 29, May 7, 14, 27, 1867; *Joliet Signal*, June 11, 15, 1867; *Illinois State Journal*, September 3, 1867.
[40] Ottawa and Alton were centers of activity and in the latter a mayor was elected on the workingmen's ticket. *Ottawa Free Trader*, August 3, September 7, 21, 1867; *Ottawa Weekly Republican*, September 19, 26, October 10, 1867; *Illinois State Journal*, September 14, 1867.

this recommendation was ignored the movement became even more independent. Independent workingmen's candidates for congress were nominated, including Alexander Campbell of La Salle; possibilities of a presidential ticket were even discussed. The trade-unions of Chicago placed in nomination full legislative, county, and city tickets.[41] All these movements were abortive but they did not entirely discourage further efforts along these lines in succeeding years.

Some gains were made by the workers through political pressure. In 1869 an aggressive mechanics lien law was secured by the managers of the labor forces at Chicago which gave the workers a lien upon all buildings upon which they labored and also upon the lots upon which the buildings were erected. A bill requiring safety devices for the protection of coal miners in their hazardous occupation passed the lower house at Springfield in 1869 but, failing to become law, the proposition was passed on to the consideration of the constitutional convention of 1870.[42] Thus in a growing class consciousness and in an increasing sense of their power the labor forces of Illinois gave further testimony to the industrial revolution.

[41] *Illinois State Journal*, August 19, 1868; *Chicago Tribune*, April 8, 15, September 14, 1868; *Ottawa Free Trader*, August 15, 1868; *Ottawa Weekly Republican*, August 20, 1868.
[42] *Chicago Tribune*, January 27, February 8, April 12, 1869; *Illinois State Register*, January 26, 1870; *Du Quoin Tribune*, March 30, 1870; *Laws of 1869*, p. 255-259.

XVII. AGRICULTURE AND THE WAR

ILLINOIS had become by 1860 the center of the agricultural life of the nation. The Civil War brought with it an unique opportunity to place her resources at the disposal of the union cause and to develop a prosperity which made possible an important contribution to the sinews of war. As a result the agricultural life of the state was quickened; and, in spite of various handicaps, Illinois not only continued but strengthened her agricultural leadership of the northwestern states.

Much of this development was merely greater expansion along the well-established lines of wheat and corn production. Illinois profited from the new demand for foodstuffs to feed the union armies and, as a result of poor European harvests in 1860, 1861, and 1862, from the increased purchases by foreign countries. Despite the steady drain on farm labor with an army of over a quarter of a million men summoned to the colors, the acreage was increased and good crops were harvested. Corn production, with a harvest of 129,921,395 bushels in 1869, rose twenty per cent over the figures for the bumper crop of 1859, and Champaign, McLean, and La Salle counties took their place as the heart of the corn belt. They were more fortunate in their accessibility to markets than the counties along the Mississippi river, which had previously sent their corn crop to the slave states; these regions now converted their unprecedented corn harvests into the more marketable form of fat hogs, although at times local market prices dropped so low that large quantities were burned as fuel.[1] After the war, an important corn market was greatly weakened by the excise of two dollars per gallon on whisky, an article worth only thirty or forty cents; this was a factor sufficiently serious to cause considerable discontent among the

[1] *Hunt's Merchants' Magazine*, 48:400; *Galena Gazette* clipped in *The* (Columbus, Ohio) *Crisis*, January 10, 1866.

farmers. By strenuous activity in the wheat fields Illinois continued with an output of 30,128,405 bushels in 1869 to maintain her position as the first wheat raising as well as corn growing state. The price of wheat rose steadily and averaged over a dollar a bushel for the Civil War period. The high water mark was reached in 1867 when wheat sold for $3.50 and flour at $18.00 per barrel in the city of Springfield.[2]

A somewhat similar development took place in the production of the minor cereals. The output of oats leaped forward with an increase of over 180 per cent with the result that Illinois exchanged fourth place for ranking position in oats production.

The Civil War period brought to maturity the promise of the fifties for a wonderful horticultural development in southern Illinois. A region of less than one hundred miles along the Illinois Central railroad, centering in the district between Jonesboro and Carbondale, developed into an important fruit belt, containing over one hundred thousand bearing fruit trees in 1865 and three times that number in 1866; in that same year 716,375 apple, pear, and peach trees were set out. Willard C. Flagg of Madison county, secretary of the Illinois State Horticultural Society, had a 1,100 acre farm with 80 acres in orchard. A fruit farm near Cobden in Union county owned by J. L. and S. S. Sawyer, included 5,000 grape vines, 20,000 peach, and 7,000 apple trees, 7 acres of strawberries, 3,000 gooseberry plants, besides small fruits and vegetables.[3] In the summer of 1862 the Illinois Central was induced to inaugurate a special fruit express to avoid what was termed the rapacity of the regular express companies in bringing the fruit to the Chicago market. In the succeeding years at the demand of the Southern Illinois Fruit Growers' Association, a fruit train to St. Louis as well as Chicago became a regular arrangement; in the closing days of May a train of from ten to fifty cars transported the strawberry crop; in late July the peach trade began, followed shortly by pear and apple

[2] *Illinois State Journal,* April 26, 1867.
[3] *Illinois State Register,* August 10, 1866; Flagg's orchard included 4,500 apple trees, 150 pears, 1,200 peaches, 60 plums, and many others. *Belleville Advocate,* July 28, 1865; Illinois State Agricultural Society, *Transactions,* 6: 196-200.

shipments. In August, 1867, the Illinois Central cleared $40,000 on peach shipments alone; in that season it carried 8,692,200 pounds of fruit from twenty stations in southern Illinois.[4]

Egypt far surpassed northern Illinois both in the quality and quantity of its fruit harvests. The region about Quincy, however, was a good apple country—in 1867 shipping nearly fifty thousand bushels. The most successful grape culture of the state was carried on about Nauvoo, Peoria, and Bloomington; Dr. H. Schröder, the well-known horticulturalist of Bloomington, planted the first grape vines there in 1858 and soon had extensive vineyards; his exhibits were usually prize winners at the state fair.[5] By 1869 Illinois had nine local horticultural societies and four county associations, in addition to the societies based on larger territorial units.

The modern dairy industry of northern Illinois had its beginning in the Civil War era. Even during the fifties Chicago had come more and more to draw upon outlying towns for its supply of milk; in 1859 Elgin, with about twenty export dairymen, shipped 227,047 gallons of milk to Chicago. Eight years later though, with competition from Kane and neighboring counties, the shipment from Elgin had increased only to 296,197 gallons, yet its value had risen from nine to sixteen cents a gallon.[6]

Meantime, the dairy industry had become far more complex. A heavy butter trade developed: the little town of Wilmington in 1866 in addition to freight shipments sent out by express 16,912 pounds of butter in a single week. Butter sold at twenty-five to thirty-five cents a pound and was often in such demand as to leave unsupplied the local trade. In 1865 the Gail Borden and Company condensed milk factory was established at Elgin; at the end of the decade it was condensing daily from twelve to eighteen hundred gallons, or three to four thousand cans. In 1864 the first cheese factory in the west was established at Bloomingdale, Illinois; and within a few years

[4] *Illinois State Register*, September 18, November 14, 1867; *Cairo Democrat*, December 19, 1867.
[5] *Prairie Farmer*, January 30, May 14, October 1, 1864, January 12, 1867.
[6] *Chicago Press and Tribune*, February 8, 1859; *Illinois State Journal*, January 30, 1867.

there were such establishments in ten northern Illinois counties. McHenry county in particular promptly became a great cheesemaking center; in 1866 it contained no cheese factories; in 1867 eight factories in operation for a season of four to six months consumed 5,500,000 pounds of milk and produced 600,000 pounds of cheese. Two years later eleven factories made about 1,600,000 pounds. In 1870 nine counties in northeastern Illinois produced nearly sixteen million pounds of cheese with a capital investment of $1,667,500; cheese was then worth twelve and one-half cents a pound.[7]

What was probably the first dairyman's convention west of Ohio met at Rockford in March, 1867, for an interchange of ideas and comparison of experiences; this resulted in the organization of the Illinois and Wisconsin Dairymen's Association. Three months later a similar meeting at Elgin arranged for the organization of the Fox River Dairy Club.[8]

By doubling the value of all livestock Illinois rose in a decade from third to first rank as a stock raising state. The biggest gains were in the northern division of the state. In beef cattle production the increase for the state was only 8.7 per cent, since a 26.6 per cent loss in the southern division neutralized the heavy 38 per cent gain registered in the central counties. Though second to Texas in cattle production, Illinois beef began to take a leading place in the New York market; nearly one-half of the 165,000,000 pounds received in New York in 1862 was raised in Illinois.[9] This same record was maintained in the succeeding years with Illinois cattle often outnumbering those from all other states. Champaign county furnished large quotas; but Morgan county, with three of the largest cattle dealers in the country, held the palm. Jacob Strawn, until his death in 1865, had continued to be one of the leading Illinois stockgrowers, while John T. Alexander, the Jacksonville cattle king, sometimes sold single lots of 3,000

[7] *Illinois State Register*, December 5, 1865; *Ottawa Weekly Republican*, January 30, 1868, June 17, November 4, 1869, August 11, 1870; *Aurora Beacon*, January 30, 1868, October 9, 1869; *Ottawa Free Trader*, May 27, 1865; *Joliet Signal*, June 5, 1866; *Prairie Farmer*, February 22, 1868.
[8] *Rockford Gazette*, February 7, 1867; *Ottawa Weekly Republican*, February 6, 1868; *Prairie Farmer*, March 2, 23, August 10, 1867, February 1, 1868.
[9] *Rockford Register*, February 14, 1863.

head of cattle; he, together with William M. Cassell and George D. Alexander, in twelve months shipped over 65,000 head of cattle which at six dollars a hundredweight were valued at $5,000,000.[10]

The driving of cattle from Texas to Illinois for preparation for market revived with the close of the Civil War. The imported cattle often arrived in a sickly and exhausted condition, with their longhorned, shark-like carcasses resembling walking corn cribs. John T. Alexander after several trials finally found the business of fattening them for market decidedly unprofitable. Nevertheless, the shipping of longhorns to take advantage of the grazing and feeding facilities of Illinois continued by the thousands. One company in 1867 contracted for the shipment of over 70,000 Texas cattle. In 1868 the firm of Gregory and Hastings of Chicago grazed a herd of nearly 35,000 at Tolono. In that year sixty or seventy thousand came into the state by way of Cairo alone.[11]

These importations often brought with them a dread cattle murrain, the "Spanish fever," a disease that not only took a heavy toll from the longhorns but also infected fine herds of native cattle. In 1866 it caused so much complaint that in February of the following year a law was enacted "to prevent the importation of Texas or Cherokee cattle." Since, however, the law was ignored, with the result that in 1868 the disease again raged in Iroquois, Vermilion, Ford, and Champaign counties, vigilance committees were appointed at different stations to prevent the unloading of further importations. At the same time meetings were held and other movements initiated in favor of an effective state law against the importation of Texas cattle; a cattle convention at Springfield on the first of December advised a law the passage of which Governor Oglesby recommended in his message to the legislature. The result was legislative restriction on the importation of Texas cattle except between the first of November and the first of March.[12]

---

[10] *Illinois State Journal*, May 4, 1864; *Chicago Tribune*, August 2, 20, 1869.
[11] *Cairo Democrat*, September 17, 1867, July 14, 27, 1868; *Champaign County Union and Gazette*, August 5, 1868; *Illinois State Journal*, February 23, 1870; *Illinois State Register*, July 1, 1868, March 3, 1869.
[12] *Ibid.*, November 19, 1866, July 30, August 17, September 2, December

The war greatly stimulated the demand for pork, and prices continued steady between $5 and $6.50 per hundredweight. Illinois' output so increased as to place it in second place. At times the hog cholera prevailed in various parts of the state but never became epidemic. In 1867 an Illinois swine breeders' association came into existence.[13]

With the new demand for uniforms and with the widespread substitution of wool for the now unavailable southern cotton, the war offered a remarkable stimulus to the production of wool. In the five years ending in 1865 the number of sheep in the state more than doubled,[14] with Sangamon county as the center of the wool raising district. Although in 1861 wool was worth only twenty-five cents a pound, within a few years its value increased to eighty cents. As the demand from the government fell off with the close of the war and the price dropped to forty cents, sheep shearing exhibitions, fairs, or festivals were held to increase interest in the industry. In 1863 at the state fair at Decatur the Wool Growers' Association of the State of Illinois had been organized, and this body now undertook to secure a new stimulus to their industry by agitation in favor of a protective tariff against "inferior imported wool;" in 1866 and 1867 resolutions strongly urging protection were adopted.[15] Illinoisians also took a prominent part in the Wool Tariff Convention at Cleveland in 1866. In spite of the concessions they were able to secure, the price continued to drop; and the last five years of the decade brought a considerable decline in sheep raising.

The war cut off the normal supply of southern staples, and Illinois was one of the few states able to step in and take advantage of the situation. This was particularly true of cot-

[1, 3, 1868; *Illinois State Journal*, February 23, 1867; *Prairie Farmer*, March 9, 1867; *Champaign County Union and Gazette*, August 5, 1868; *Canton Weekly Register*, September 4, 1868; *Chicago Tribune*, January 5, 1869; *1 Laws of 1867*, p. 169; *Laws of 1869*, p. 237.
[13] *Hunt's Merchants' Magazine*, 54:376-384; *Ottawa Free Trader*, December 18, 1869.
[14] See the contradictory figures in *Cairo Democrat*, February 16, 1864; *Ottawa Weekly Republican*, July 29, 1865; *Canton Weekly Register*, February 5, 1866; *Aurora Beacon*, May 31, 1866; *Jacksonville Journal*, February 7, 1867.
[15] *Chicago Tribune*, October 6, 1863, January 9, 1867; *Chicago Times*, October 7, 1863; *Chicago Post*, February 22, 1866; *Aurora Beacon*, January 17, 1867; *Prairie Farmer*, January 19, 1867.

ton after the Mississippi river was closed. Previous to the war a considerable amount of cotton was raised in the southern counties but mainly by farmers' wives to add to their "pin money."[16] In the fall of 1861, after reports of successful experiments by certain individuals during the previous summer, preparations were made for extensive cotton growing in the following season. Although critics began to deplore the widespread "cotton mania," they were swamped by the "pro-cottonists." Immediately a seed problem arose; the federal government, however, undertook to secure seed and to distribute it in Illinois through John P. Reynolds, the corresponding secretary of the State Agricultural Society. As a result a crop estimated at twenty thousand bales was raised, when cotton was selling in the east at sixty cents a pound.[17] In the spring of 1863 the price had risen to eighty-seven and one-half cents, and the farmers of southern Illinois responded by securing cotton seed by the carload. Cotton culture on a large scale followed, and the 1864 crop was marketed when the eastern price was $1.50 per pound.

Many southern exiles and some Negro freedmen were drawn upon to aid in this new development. One of the former, Archie J. Elyutt, established the *Southerner and Cotton Planter* at Cairo in 1865 to attract southern emigrants and others to the possibility of cotton culture in southern Illinois.[18] The next harvest showed an unprecedented yield; Jonesboro and Carbondale with cotton in the air and on the streets seemed like southern cities. In season ten gins ran continuously in Carbondale, which shipped 4,000 bales. A region of southern Illinois which had produced only 1,416 pounds in 1862 three years later harvested over one and a half million pounds, marketed at the western price of forty-five cents a pound.[19] A high production cost, however, was involved in the raising of

[16] *Rockford Republican*, February 21, 1861.
[17] *Belleville Advocate*, February 14, March 21, November 21, 1862; *Illinois State Register*, February 11, 1862; *Illinois State Journal*, March 29, May 12, 1862; Lewis Ellsworth to Trumbull, February 19, 1862, Caleb Smith to Trumbull, February 20, 1862, Trumbull manuscripts; *Champaign County Patriot*, November 6, 1862.
[18] *Cairo Weekly Democrat*, March 23, 1865.
[19] *Chicago Tribune*, November 14, December 26, 1865; *Cairo Times* clipped in *Chicago Post*, March 14, 1866; Illinois State Agricultural Society, *Transactions*, 6: 191-194.

these crops; when, therefore, with the return of peace and competition with southern cotton a heavy 1866 harvest had to be marketed at one-half the 1865 price, the enthusiasm for cotton culture was promptly demolished; and by 1869 the production was only one-tenth that of 1865.

The scarcity of cotton during the early years of the war also stimulated the cultivation of flax. This was the opportunity of the northern district, and in 1863 it was seized upon with such keenness that a flax belt appeared centering in De Kalb county. Developments were less spectacular than in the case of cotton; but during the decade Illinois multiplied its output nearly fifty times, reaching a crop of 2,204,606 pounds in 1869. Factories for cleaning the flax fiber and for the manufacture of linen goods were established at Batavia, Ottawa, Sycamore, Mendota, and other points.[20]

Illinois also made wonderful progress in the field of raising saccharose crops to take the place of Louisiana cane sugar. The output of maple sugar had begun to fall off in the forties; but Civil War conditions stimulated a slight increase, while sorghum culture made great gains. Secession came just at the height of the enthusiasm over Chinese sugar cane, and during the first two years of the decade the output was almost doubled; such heavy sowings were made in southern Illinois that for a considerable time it was difficult to secure seed. Reduced prices after the war resulted in merely nominal increases so that the census of 1870 showed an output of only 1,900,000 gallons of sirup; the 1869 harvest had doubtless fallen off as a result of advice to force up prices by curtailed planting. Repeated efforts to produce a satisfactory granulated sugar from the Chinese sugar cane ended in failure; even such large scale ventures as the Northwestern Chinese Sugar Manufacturing Company which was incorporated in 1863 collapsed promptly.[21]

Interest in the possibility of beet sugar production was

[20] *Ottawa Weekly Republican*, February 21, 1863, December 16, 1869; *Illinois State Journal*, February 23, March 7, April 27, 1863; *Cairo Democrat*, October 8, 1863; *Aurora Beacon*, March 17, July 21, 1864.
[21] *Report of the Commissioner of Agriculture*, 1862, p. 140-147; *Jacksonville Journal*, November 13, 1862; *Chicago Tribune*, December 8, 1862; *Champaign County Union and Gazette*, April 1, 1868; *Ottawa Free Trader*, March 20, 1869; *Cairo Gazette*, April 2, 1863; D. C. Martin to Trumbull, February 1, 1862, Trumbull manuscripts.

aroused by the dissemination of information as to conditions in France and Germany; soon ventures were launched into this field. In 1862 an unsuccessful experiment was made by H. Belcher, a Chicago refiner; three years later nothing significant had been accomplished, though many people, including John P. Reynolds, the secretary of the State Agricultural Society, were convinced that the manufacture of sugar from sugar beets could be made to pay. Then a group of Chicagoans constituting the Illinois Beet Sugar Company undertook to investigate conditions in Germany and France through one of their number, C. E. Olmstead, whom Governor Oglesby appointed a special honorary agent for the state; but this brought no immediate results.[22] At the same time a beet sugar manufactory was being built at Chatsworth, in Livingston county, for the Germania Beet Sugar Company of which Theodore Gennert was superintendent. Gennert went to Germany where he secured the necessary machinery and three hundred mechanics and laborers. In 1867 this company manufactured and marketed one hundred thousand pounds of sugar and the following season was shipping a carload a week. This was the first successful beet sugar venture in Illinois.[23]

One of the most significant aspects of Illinois' marvelous agricultural contributions during the years of the war was the withdrawal of an army of a quarter million workers, a majority of whom went from the farms of the state; from certain agricultural districts over nine-tenths of the young and able-bodied men liable to the draft promptly went into service.[24] The shortage of farm laborers was soon reflected in increased wages and in appeals for help. Wages rose to $1.25, to $2.00, and were then forced still higher by the depreciation of paper money; in some instances farmers turned their cattle into their grain fields rather than pay the rates required to harvest. The revival of foreign immigration relieved the problem of upstate

[22] *Illinois State Journal,* June 21, 1865; *Illinois State Register,* September 25, 1865; J. D. Ward to Trumbull, September 19, 1865, Trumbull manuscripts.
[23] *Illinois State Register,* July 6, October 4, November 17, 1865; *Chicago Evening Journal,* December 18, 1865, March 8, 1866; *Prairie Farmer,* April 27, 1867; *Ottawa Free Trader,* January 4, 1868; *Champaign County Union and Gazette,* November 24, 1869.
[24] Fite, *Social and Industrial Conditions in the North during the Civil War,* 5.

farmers, while southern Illinois sent the Negro "contrabands" into the harvest fields. At an early day, too, women and children took their places as farm hands, and a grown man at work in the fields came to be pronounced "a rare sight."[25]

Invisible labor units were added by the installation of agricultural machinery, which saved many of the western crops;[26] even conservative farmers were forced to replace and supplement man power by machines. Oxen were found to be too slow for the hauling of expensive farm implements; and, in spite of the scarcity and high price of horses, the former were steadily discarded. The reduction of the number of oxen in the state in 1870 to about one-fifth of the 1860 figure offers peculiar testimony to the extensive introduction of farm machinery in the Civil War decade.

Illinois had prepared in the previous decade for this development in the use of farm machinery. In 1861 Illinoisians took out eighty patents, or over one-seventh of the patents for such machines granted by the government; seventeen for cultivators, fifteen for harvester machines, eleven for ploughs, and ten for corn planters.[27] In the decade the value of farm implements doubled, giving the state third instead of fifth rank among the states of the union. The prairie regions particularly came to be exploited by farm machinery: the value of farm machinery in Champaign county, for instance, increased from $25,000 in 1850 to more than $600,000 in 1870.

In 1860 the size of the average Illinois farm was 158 acres; in 1870 it had dropped to 127 acres, although there was still a gain in the amount of improved land. Against this general tendency on the part of farm units to decrease in size, many large farms held their own. Farms of several thousand acres were scattered over the state. M. L. Sullivant, who lived on an inclosed estate of twenty-three thousand acres called "Broadlands," eight miles south of Homer in Champaign county, was reputed to own "the largest farm in the United

[25] *Carthage Republican*, June 9, 1864.
[26] *Scientific American*, 9:9.
[27] U. S. Patent Office, *Report*, 1861, p. 637-648. In 1867 the first patent for a disc plow was granted to M. A. and J. M. Cravath of Bloomington. Hales, *History of Agriculture*, July 1, 1915, p. 47. Gang-plows had already begun to come into use as an important labor saving device. *Prairie Farmer*, June 4, 1864.

States, and probably in the world." He had an aggregate of 80,000 acres of land; one piece in Piatt county was a tract of 45,000 acres. At the same time John T. Alexander, a millionaire farmer of Morgan county, was said to own a tract of 80,000 acres without an acre of waste or poor land; 32,000 head of cattle fed in his pastures and 16,000 acres were put in corn for the 15,000 head of hogs that he was raising. In 1866 Alexander purchased "Broadlands" and established himself in Champaign county.[28]

In the Civil War era a new sense of professional pride in agricultural pursuits evidenced itself in a tendency toward more extensive organization. Farmers' clubs began to appear in all parts of the state for weekly neighborhood meetings and informal discussions, especially during the winter months. The county and state agricultural societies continued along established lines, although war conditions interfered considerably with their fairs and caused the omission of the 1862 state fair. The fairs and horse shows were assuming a more practical bearing; and important steps were taken toward the introduction of new breeds and the improvement of livestock in general. Moreover, the state society found new opportunities for practical service, in directing the adjustments in farm economy to war conditions and in conducting the discussion of problems connected with the establishment of an industrial university under the Morrill land grant act. In 1867 a very successful Illinois exhibit was made at the Paris exposition under the direction of John P. Reynolds, who was selected by the State Agricultural Society and commissioned by the governor to represent the state; in the awards the Illinois collection received several medals.[29]

The return of peace in 1865 terminated the advantage that the farmer had derived from war conditions. As war time markets were closed and prices on agricultural products dropped, although manufactured goods held their own, a rest-

[28] *Homer Journal* clipped in *Central Illinois Gazette*, June 22, 1866; *ibid.*, February 2, 1866; *Canton Weekly Register*, May 7, 1866; *Homer Journal* clipped in *Illinois State Register*, November 8, 1866.
[29] Illinois State Agricultural Society, *Transactions*, 7:616-708; *Ottawa Weekly Republican*, July 18, 1867; *Chicago Tribune*, July 29, August 1, 1867; *Illinois State Journal*, February 3, 1869.

lessness developed among the producing classes that threatened to break out into a serious farmers' revolt. The farmer had certain grievances growing directly out of the marketing of his products. First of all he confronted the difficulty of securing a fair price for his crops; then, with a growing dependence upon the railroads, he wrestled with the transportation problem. High rail rates and elevator charges conspired to rob him of what he regarded as a fair return upon his labor. The news of railroad consolidations and rumors of combinations between the railroad interests and the warehouses, followed by advanced rates of storage and transportation, acquired a new significance when it was found by that heavy stock subscriptions the railroads were controlling the grain elevators.[30]

Something of a crisis came in the winter of 1865-1866 when in parts of Illinois the price of corn fell to ten cents a bushel and was cheaper than wood for fuel purposes. At the same time railroad rates were so exorbitant as to cause cattle raisers to consider it more economical to drive their cattle to the Chicago market. Complaint became widespread among the producing classes; the cry of "monopoly" arose, "the people having become alarmed at the designs and usurpations of the Eastern oligarchs, who now own and control Congress"[31] — the issue was regarded by many as "eastern capital v. western labor." Then began a struggle between the agriculturists and the "monopolists" preliminary to the granger movement of the seventies. In 1862 an Industrial League had been formed by the farmers of La Salle county as the preliminary to this farmers' movement.[32] On October 22, 1865, a convention of over two thousand farmers of the sixth congressional district met at Grundy in the interest of cheap transportation; among other things it requested the executive board of the State Agricultural Society to call together a state farmers' mass convention at Bloomington on December 15. This was done; when the convention assembled it recommended an elaborate

---

[30] *Prairie Farmer*, April 2, May 7, August 13, 1864.
[31] *Galena Gazette* and *Monmouth Review* clipped in *The* (Columbus, Ohio) *Crisis*, January 10, 17, 1866; *Whiteside Sentinel* clipped in *Chicago Evening Journal*, November 20, 1865.
[32] *Illinois State Journal*, December 18, 1862; *Ottawa Weekly Republican*, January 24, 1863.

scheme of internal waterways and adopted a resolution "That it is expedient at this time to form a League of Illinois, with branch associations throughout the State, whose object it shall be, by legislative action, or, if necessary by constitutional provision, to restrict railroad, express, and warehouse charges within reasonable limits."[33] A similar mass convention was held at Bloomington June 29, 1866.

At the same time sentiment was developing against the so-called "live stock 'ring'" of Chicago. In the legislature of 1865 the Union Stock Yard and Transit Company had been incorporated with authority to manage a cattle yard, a series of branch railroads, a bank, and a hotel; many leading stock men had opposed it as a monopoly without knowing that $925,000 out of the capital of $1,000,000 was subscribed to by nine of the principal western railroads. In 1866 a group of commission men, calling themselves "The Board of Live Stock Commission Men," undertook to convert this largest and most important livestock market in the world into a secret exchange by suppressing the reports of sales of cattle in the daily newspapers. Though blocked by the local press, they were able at times to buy hogs at five or six cents live weight and sell pork, ham, and lard at more than double that price. In 1868 after wheat had been "cornered" three times, corn and barley twice, and rye and oats once, a corner on pork forced up the price of pork products to prices that aroused the wrath of the deluded farmer.[34]

Here was a hydra headed monster that must be slain. The people of the northwest were gradually awakened to the importance of legislative action to prevent these "moneyed monopolies from swallowing up the entire earnings of the producing classes, and reducing the country to poverty, that they may declare large dividends."[35] When new elevator companies found themselves unable to compete with estab-

[33] *Aurora Beacon*, November 20, 1865; *Chicago Evening Journal*, November 23, 27, 1865; *Illinois State Register*, November 29, December 23, 1865; *Jacksonville Journal*, June 1, 1866.
[34] *Illinois State Register*, January 29, 1865; *Chicago Post*, December 27, 1865; *National Live Stock Journal*, September, 1870, p. 29; *Chicago Tribune*, October 31, November 5, 1866; December 19, 1868; *Canton Weekly Register*, November 26, 1866; *Illinois Democrat*, September 11, 1868.
[35] *Paxton Record*, December 16, 1865.

lished concerns on account of railroad discrimination, the warehouse act of 1867 was passed in spite of the opposition of the warehouse men backed by the railroad lobbyists. This law established a set of regulations for warehouses, opened them to public inspection, fixed a penalty for "gambling contracts," and required the railroads to deliver grain to the warehouses to which it was consigned.[36] Members of the Chicago Board of Trade were arrested shortly for violating the clause prohibiting "gambling contracts;" their prosecution, however, was held up and the provision languished in innocuous desuetude until the next legislature restored trading in "futures." Repeated efforts at railway legislation resulted in the railroad law of 1869. Although no results followed the farmers' attack upon "the slaughter-house and cattle yard monopoly," repeated efforts at railway legislation bore fruit in the railroad law of 1869.

Thus did the farmers without adequate organization or direction show their strength in the politics of the state. But already the missionaries of a new order were preparing the soil for a more aggressive program of self-defense; in another decade under the more efficient organization of the Patrons of Husbandry Illinois agriculturalists were to take their part in a great revolt by the farmers of the northwest.[37]

[36] *1 Laws of 1867*, p. 177-182; *Chicago Tribune*, August 17, 1867, February 13, 1868; *Ottawa Weekly Republican*, August 22, 1867.
[37] *Prairie Farmer*, November 13, 1869, March 26, April 30, 1870; Kelley, *Patrons of Husbandry*, 245 ff.

XVIII. RECONSTRUCTION AND THE MILITARY POLITICIAN

THE brilliant military exploits of the autumn of 1864 were continued into the winter months. First General Sherman presented Savannah as a Christmas gift to the union and then, with scarcely enough opposition to relieve the tedium of the march, moved his unconquerable forces northward through the heart of Dixie; meanwhile Grant hammered away at the defenses of Richmond. This combination against the confederacy was enough to forecast its prompt suppression.

In January, 1865, General Richard J. Oglesby, the distinguished veteran of Donelson and Corinth, was called to the gubernatorial chair from the field of battle. His election and inauguration, therefore, forecast the transition that the nation was soon to experience when camp and battlefield were giving up their hosts and yielding to the constructive tasks of civil life. Governor Yates made his farewell in a message surveying the history of his administration and the war record of Illinois at such length as to break all records for state executive documents; Oglesby in his inaugural devoted himself largely to the national outlook—to problems which were in the large to assume greater importance than state politics during his administration. Like his predecessor he recommended the repeal of all laws bearing unequally upon Negroes and declared them entitled to the rights and privileges of the whites. The time was indeed ripe for reaping the harvest that republicanism had for a decade been preparing.

While awaiting the complete triumph of the federal arms the republicans undertook to make a final disposition of the slavery question by adopting a constitutional provision for abolition. Governor Yates had formally petitioned congress to take this step in January, 1864. An attempt was made early in the following June, but the proposition failed in the house of representatives where the Illinois democratic delegation voted solidly for its defeat.[1] The republicans, however, now interpreted their sweeping victory of 1864 as a mandate for abolition and insisted that five of the Illinois democratic congressmen had been instructed by the votes of their constituents to support the proposed amendment. The new legislature undertook to make these instructions formal in a set of joint resolutions, but before this action could be completed news reached Springfield of the passage of the amendment.[2] The Illinois congressional delegation, however, had again divided along party lines and voted against the amendment. On February 1, 1865, immediately upon the arrival of the news of congressional action, the Illinois legislature adopted a resolution of ratification, thereby winning the honor of being the first state to ratify the thirteenth amendment.[3]

As a very proper corollary to this signal step toward freedom for the Negro the Illinois legislature acted to repeal the "black laws" by which a free state had placed serious limitations upon the freedom of the Negroes within its limits. The republican assembly of 1861, to the disappointment of all radical antislavery leaders, had failed to eliminate these laws on account of the sectional crisis; then, having been driven from control by the democrats, the republicans had found their hands tied until the victory of 1864. Now, however, on February 7, 1865, the "infamous" legislation which the champions of freedom had so bitterly attacked but which had survived under democratic rule was wiped from the statute books. Next, confirming the prophecies of democratic critics, the "Negro equality" party began a discussion of the logic of Negro suffrage;

[1] The Illinois vote was five (all union men) for the measure and eight (all democrats) against it, with Anthony L. Knapp not voting; *Rockford Register*, July 2, 9, 1864; *Congressional Globe*, 38 congress, 1 session, 145, 522, 694, 2995; *Illinois State Register*, February 4, 1864.
[2] *Chicago Tribune*, November 20, 1864, January 24, 26, February 3, 1865; *Illinois State Journal*, February 1, 2, 1865; *Rockford Democrat*, February 2, 1865; *House Journal*, 38 congress, 2 session, 264-265. The most surprising vote against the amendment was that of John T. Stuart of the Springfield district, President Lincoln's former instructor and partner in law; Stuart like Lincoln had previously been a whig of the Henry Clay school, but while he now indignantly rejected any imputation of proslavery views, he could not reconcile himself to the political consequences of emancipation.
[3] *Laws of 1865*, p. 135.

THE MILITARY POLITICIAN

inasmuch as this suggested a new source of continued power, republicans promptly organized a campaign to attain that goal. To the end of reënforcing republican ascendancy in state politics the legislature enacted a voters' registration law and a soldiers' voting law, and considered a new congressional apportionment measure; although each had its merits in a nonpartisan sense, they all involved some peculiar party advantage, represented most clearly in the gerrymandering provision of the apportionment bill which sliced out the fifth ward of Chicago to attach it to a group of republican counties south of the city.[4]

Under the constitutional provision limiting the session to twenty-five days the last hours were characterized by hurry, confusion, and carelessness. Members of "the third house" or "lobbyists" busily plied their trade, especially the representatives of insurance companies of which seventy-one were incorporated. Party newspapers on both sides delicately hinted and then boldly charged fraud, bribery, and other corrupt practices, amid which 899 bills were passed, often without any knowledge of their provisions. These were mostly private or local bills, many of which were enacted as parts of omnibus measures which were jammed through by logrolling tactics. Everyone seemed to breathe a sigh of relief when the announcement of adjournment was made.[5]

On April 3, shortly after the legislative excitement subsided, the tidings reached Illinois of the occupation of Richmond by the union forces. The appearance of this dispatch in "extras" upon the streets caused the citizens to gather in wildest enthusiasm; flags were raised, church and fire bells began to ring, and cannon salutes reverberated upon the air. That night, brass bands and rockets summoned the people to further celebration; bonfires lit the sky with their glare and the intoxication of victory continued to a late hour.[6] Grant's and Lincoln's names were on everyone's lips. Citizens proudly

[4] *Chicago Times*, January 23, 1865.
[5] *The Tribune* considered it as welcome as the coincident announcement of the victory of an American horse on the French turf. *Chicago Tribune*, February 17, 24, 28, 1865; *Chicago Times*, February 18, March 4, 14, 1865; *Joliet Signal*, February 21, 28, 1865.
[6] *Illinois State Journal*, April 4, 1865; *Chicago Tribune*, April 4, 1865; *Carthage Republican*, April 6, 1865.

rejoiced that Illinois had contributed not only the largest quotas of men but two loyal sons who as civil magistate and as military leader had conducted the union cause to victory.

A week later public rejoicing was renewed upon the announcement of the surrender of General Lee's army. The people were happy in the belief that peace, with the beneficent blessings that follow in its train, was about to return to the republic. "There was a smile on every face—happiness in every heart. Booming guns, clanging bells, streaming banners, and the tumultuous cheers of a happy populace told the public joy and proclaimed it to the world. But in a few short hours all this was changed. The people went about the streets mournfully, the bells tolled, the flag of the Republic was hung at half mast, and the hope of immediate Peace, which made the country glad, vanished like a beautiful vision of the night—for ABRAHAM LINCOLN, who in the days of his triumph had become the champion of the pacification of the South by conciliation, had fallen under the hand of an assassin, just as he was about to accomplish the grandest and most solemn problem of statesmanship in the history of the world." [7]

Abraham Lincoln had been accorded a martyr's crown; friend and foe alike bore their tribute to his feet. "The great stateman, the pure man, the humane adversary of a wicked rebellion, the true christian, is assassinated," sorrowed the *Paxton Record*.[8] "A man upon whom, through four years of diversified hopes and fears, of doubtings and prayers, had at last centered the confidence and love of a nation, was stricken down in the hour of his triumph and vindication," eulogized the editor of the *Carthage Republican*, a political antagonist.[9] The *Chicago Times*, convinced that the presidential mantle had fallen upon the shoulders of a man in whom nobody felt confidence, proclaimed the sincere sorrow of all northern democrats: "Widely as they have differed with Mr. Lincoln,—greatly as their confidence in him has been shaken,—they yet saw in the indications of the last few days of his life that he might com-

---

[7] *Cairo Morning News*, April 20, 1865.
[8] *Paxton Record*, April 20, 1865.
[9] *Carthage Republican*, April 20, 1865.

mand their support in the close of the war, as he did in the beginning.[10]

No finer homage, perhaps, can be found than that paid by the *Cairo Democrat* which within a twelvemonth had proclaimed Lincoln as a "usurper and tyrant who is only fit to split rails;" it now commented: "Illinois claims Abraham Lincoln as her gift to the nation; and receives back his lifeless body, marred by traitors, weeping, like Niobe, and refusing to be comforted. Many of us have been active opponents of his administration — have warred against him with the determination of earnest enemies. . . . . In the past, we believed him to be pursuing the wrong path of public policy, and we told the world so, using language the strength of which was prompted by the passions of the passing moment; but when the end drew nigh, ... we saw this man whom we had condemned, rise above party, and disregarding his private anger, if he had any, become the great conciliator."[11]

The sincerity of democratic mourning was attested by the approval which had just been extended to Lincoln's policy in the matter of reconstruction. Indeed, the conciliatory measures projected by him for the restoration of the insurgent states received a warmer welcome from the opposition press than they were accorded by a large number of vindictive republican organs. In the last few weeks of his life his clemency and magnanimity toward the vanquished south had, in the minds of many democrats, absolved him from the trammels of party; with his martyrdom he attained an indisputable title to nationality.[12]

Democrats and republicans alike were skeptical of the qualifications of Andrew Johnson for the chief magistracy. The rumor had spread broadcast that on the occasion of his inauguration as vice president he had taken his oath of office and made his inaugural address in a state of intoxication; the *Chicago Tribune* undertook to verify the report and proclaimed Johnson's conduct a national disgrace. It demanded his resignation, declaring: "In the event of the President's death the

---

[10] *Chicago Times*, April 17, 1865.
[11] *Cairo Weekly Democrat*, May 11, 1865; cf. *ibid.*, July 14, 1864.
[12] *Chicago Times*, April 18, 22, 26, 1865; *Joliet Signal*, April 25, 1865.

Vice-President succeeds to his place. Who can measure the calamities that would befall the country if the Presidential chair were filled by a person who becomes grossly intoxicated on the gravest public occasion? Such a contingency may well appall us."[13] This opinion was shared by other republican journals of Illinois, while the democrats took pleasure in tracing Johnson's condition to "the license and corruption of his party."[14]

When, however, Johnson did become Lincoln's successor, his position was studied from a new angle. In him democrats saw an advocate of vindictive reconstruction who, from impotence as presiding officer of the senate, had advanced to the nation's highest seat of authority. Their horror at this turn of events was matched only by the satisfaction of radicals who had grown disgusted with the increasing soft-heartedness of Abraham Lincoln. From them came an outburst of applause at the very first announcement of the new president that he would be careful "not to pursue any policy which would prevent the government from *visiting punishment* on the guilty leaders who caused the rebellion." The *Chicago Tribune* opened its arms to Andrew Johnson. "That's the talk," it declared. "Johnson's little finger will prove thicker than were Abraham Lincoln's loins. While he whipped them gently with cords, his successor will scourge them with a whip of scorpions. He knows who they are and what they are. He hates slavery and has little affection for its high priests. There will be thorough work made of those who hatched and led the rebellion."[15] "The loyal heart of the people," explained the *Rockford Register*, April 22, 1865, "since the surrender and paroling of Lee's army, has been fearful that our late President was too full of the 'milk of human kindness' to enable him to deal justly with traitors. However this might have been, all the evidence we can gather as to Andrew Johnson's sentiments, points to the assurance that no such fears need be entertained regarding him."

[13] *Chicago Tribune*, March 14, 1865; *Rockford Democrat*, March 16, 1865; *Rockford Register*, March 18, 1865.
[14] *Chicago Times*, March 15, 1865.
[15] *Chicago Tribune*, April 18, 1865; *Aurora Beacon*, April 20, 1865; *Rockford Register*, April 22, 1865.

The democrats, however, reminded themselves that Johnson's political training had been in the democratic school; they hoped that, as a straightforward states rights democrat right up to the time of secession, he would administer the government in accordance with those principles. "He must rise above party and factions and act only for the people," they urged. "He must not be a hangman but a statesman." Then swift came the confirmation of their hopes; when Johnson took an early occasion to put his foot upon the state suicide doctrine, the democrats rejoiced that a point had been scored in their favor, and when in an amnesty and a reconstruction proclamation, both under date of May 29, he adopted and extended Lincoln's reconstruction policy, democrats exultingly proclaimed that he was taking " true democratic ground."[16] " May it not have been in God's providence," asked the *Cairo Democrat* in an editorial entitled " Radicalism Rampant," "that Andrew Johnson was raised from the level of the people to the high eminence which alone could check the before resistless flood?"[17]

The republicans were taken decidedly aback. For a time they held off open criticism, putting their energies into ridicule of the new born democratic faith in and Quixotic defense of Andrew Johnson. By July, however, they were ready to prophesy shame and disaster as the logical fruits of the president's policy. "We do not believe that he has 'Tylerized' — gone over to the enemy that only three months ago would have gladly hung him," was the dubious assurance of the *Chicago Tribune*.[18] By September certain republicans were preparing to read Johnson out of the party, although Dr. C. H. Ray of the *Chicago Tribune* protested against this lack of patience.[19] Democrats were also divided as to how much reliance they could place on Johnson; many opened their arms to welcome him to their ranks — a democratic meeting at Springfield called by prominent members of the party enthusi-

---

[16] *Chicago Times*, April 21, 25, 1865; *Joliet Signal*, April 25, 1865; *Cairo Democrat*, May 3, 1865; *Chicago Tribune*, May 2, 1865; *Carthage Republican*, May 11, 1865.
[17] *Cairo Democrat*, June 15, 1865; *Joliet Signal*, June 6, 27, 1865.
[18] *Chicago Tribune*, July 10, 1865; *Aurora Beacon*, July 27, 1865.
[19] C. H. Ray to Trumbull, September 29, 1865, Trumbull manuscripts.

astically indorsed Johnson's policies; others, however, held aloof, agreeing with the *Cairo Democrat* that "President Johnson is like the Irishman's flea, when you put your finger on him he is not there. One day he is held up as a model democrat, opposed to negro suffrage and all that, and the next day he is reported as an advocate of negro suffrage." [20]

Developments continued along these lines until the end of the year. The *Chicago Tribune*, seeking advantage from the situation, tried to disarm the democrats by proclaiming an era of good feeling: "The Copperheads vie with the Republicans of the North in fealty to a Republican and abolition administration, and denounce even friendly criticism as insidious treason." [21] The *Cairo Democrat* in alarm became more cautious and issued a warning that "the Democracy should be careful to not praise him [Johnson] beyond his merits." [22] Yet Johnson's first annual message, which has since been discovered to have been the work of George Bancroft, the historian, proved such a temperate and conciliatory document that it met with the formal approval of democratic as well as republican journals. The republicans, satisfied with the ferment at work among their opponents, again turned to consider the growing distrust of President Johnson in their own ranks. The problem of concealing it was becoming increasingly difficult; within a few weeks came the opening breach between Andrew Johnson and the radical republican majority in congress, and thereafter the democrats began to rally more and more to his support.[23]

Republican leaders continued to wrestle with the problem of their relations to Andrew Johnson. A band of radicals, including many German republicans, were in favor of throwing him overboard on the ground that he had "Tylerized" the government and gone over to the enemy. There were

---
[20] *Cairo Democrat* clipped in *Illinois State Journal*, September 15, 1865; *Cairo Democrat*, September 16, 1865; *Chicago Tribune*, September 12, 1865.
[21] *Ibid.*, October 26, 1865; *Rockford Register*, October 28, 1865.
[22] *Cairo Democrat*, October 30, 1865.
[23] *Illinois State Journal*, December 6, 1865; *Chicago Tribune*, December 6, 1865; *Rockford Register*, December 9, 1865; *Belleville Democrat*, December 9, 30, 1865; *Carthage Republican*, December 14, 1865; *Central Illinois Gazette*, December 15, 1865; *Canton Weekly Register*, December 18, 1865.

many, however, who still retained "faith in the enlightened patriotism of 'Andy Johnson'" and hoped that moderate counsels might prevail and save the party and the president from becoming involved in unnecessary and fatal antagonisms; this group included such notables as Senator Trumbull, Dr. C. H. Ray, and Newton Bateman, as well as General Allen C. Fuller, speaker of the house in the session of 1865, and D. L. Phillips, part proprietor of the *State Journal* and United States marshal for the southern district of Illinois.[24] Feeling that a break with the president would involve the overthrow of the party and leave Andrew Johnson cock-of-the-walk, they were for accepting the principles of his annual message and for avoiding the "consummate Folly" of "splitting hairs on the proposition, whether the rebel states are in or out of the Union."[25]

All republicans who took this view, however, were stout supporters of two bills that Senator Trumbull introduced on January 5, 1866, a freedman's bureau bill and a civil rights bill. These measures sought to secure to the freedmen provision for food, clothing, and shelter on the one hand and on the other the civil rights that were regarded as the corollary of the trumpet call of freedom. It was generally expected that the president would approve of the freedman's bureau bill and it was promptly pushed to passage; when on February 19 it was returned with the executive veto, Andrew Johnson lost the support of practically every wing of the republican party in Illinois; his veto of the civil rights bill on March 27 widened the breach and unified the republican opposition.

While the republicans in congress rallied to enact these measures over the president's veto, Illinois leaders marshaled their forces to defeat Johnson in the coming elections. In the contests of 1865, involving merely the local and county offices, republican politicians had been scandalized at the general tend-

[24] H. Schröder to Trumbull, December 23, 1865, Trumbull manuscripts; see letters from these and others to Trumbull in December, 1865, and January, 1866. "There is a strong disposition to make an issue with the President on the part of some, but for one I do not sympathise with it." Trumbull to Phillips, December 21, 1865, Phillips manuscripts.

[25] C. H. Ray to Trumbull, February 7, 1866, Jason Marsh to Trumbull, January 8, 1866, Trumbull manuscripts.

ency of the returned soldiers to criticize the union nominations as drawing too heavily upon civilians. In many counties rival "soldiers tickets" or republican "bolters" had been placed in the field and had received assistance from the democrats who often either made no nominations or fused with the soldiers. At the polls the independent tickets had usually been defeated; the republican leaders, after reading a sermon to the bolters rebuking them for attempting minority rule and for giving comfort to the common enemy in a way that would undermine the unity, harmony, and organization of the republican party, had promised to bestow a proper attention upon the soldiers in the future.[26]

The republicans redeemed these pledges in the elections of 1866, when the veterans of the Civil War came into their own. General John A. Logan, who had now taken up his residence in Chicago, was nominated by acclamation by the republican or "union" state convention for congressman-at-large. Logan was the idol of the soldiers, although many republican leaders were unwilling to believe that with his entrance into the republican ranks he had recovered complete respectability.[27] General G. W. Smith was nominated for state treasurer, to make the race as a teammate of Newton Bateman, candidate for state superintendent of public instruction. General Charles E. Lippincott and General Green B. Raum were named to lead the forlorn republican hope in Egyptian districts; but in general the old political leaders held to their berths in congress; on the other hand, in the contests for seats in the state legislature, the soldiers were given a generous share of the nominations.

The strength of the soldier wing was doubtless increased by the organization of the Grand Army of the Republic. This association like the Union League originated in the state of

[26] *Chicago Tribune,* November 9, 1865; *Joliet Signal,* November 14, 1865; *Central Illinois Gazette,* November 17, 24, 1865. In the spring of 1866 the Illinois Soldiers' College and Military Academy was incorporated and organized at Fulton, Whiteside county, to educate as many as possible of the 5,000 disabled soldiers in the state to earn a living by intellectual rather than physical labor. *Rockford Register,* December 15, 1866, July 6, 1867; D. S. Covet to Trumbull, May 7, 1866, Trumbull manuscripts.
[27] D. L. Phillips to Trumbull, December 26, 1865, George T. Brown to Trumbull, August 16, 1866, Trumbull manuscripts.

Illinois; after its beginnings in April, 1866, at Decatur, it rapidly spread over all the northern states. Its founder, Dr. B. F. Stephenson, surgeon in the Fourteenth Illinois infantry, served as provisional Illinois department commander for a few months until General John M. Palmer won out over General Logan for the post of regular head of the organization in the state. Illinois contributed in General Stephen A. Hurlbut, the first G. A. R. commander-in-chief. This association, though organized for fraternal, charitable, and patriotic purposes, exercised a formidable political influence.[28]

While the soldiers and republican politicians were busying themselves with campaign preparations, the democrats were arranging to take advantage of Johnson's apostasy. Johnson clubs were organized in Illinois communities from Chicago to Cairo;[29] in certain cities, moreover, the corporal's guard of republicans still clinging to Johnson were recruited into republican Johnson clubs which busily pointed out that the president's reconstruction policy was the same as that inaugurated by Abraham Lincoln — the only policy that could give peace and permanence to the divided and distracted country. The Johnson supporters, as "conservatives," appealed to all true union men to rally with them to oppose the machinations of the "radicals." A few prominent republicans led the exodus into the "conservative" camp. Congressman A. J. Kuykendall of the Cairo district, the only republican member of the Illinois delegation who sympathized with Johnson, who had voted against the freedman's bureau bill and whose absence alone had prevented a negative vote on the civil rights bill, yielded his claims to political preferment at the hands of the republicans.[30] Thomas J. Turner, chairman of the republican state central committee, supported "the president's plan of *restoration*" as against the congressional plan of reconstruction and on that account submitted his resignation, while the appointment of Orville H. Browning as secretary of the inte-

[28] D. L. Phillips to Trumbull, June 10, 17, 24, 1866, G. T. Allen to Trumbull, June 14, 28, 1866, George T. Brown to Trumbull, August 16, 1866, Trumbull manuscripts.
[29] *Chicago Tribune*, March 31, May 24, 1866; *Cairo Democrat*, April 13, 1866; *Jacksonville Journal*, July 2, 17, 28, 1866.
[30] John Olney to Trumbull, April 19, 1866, Trumbull manuscripts; *Chicago Tribune*, May 8, 1866; *Cairo Democrat*, January 9, November 22, 1867.

rior, as a reward for his support of Johnson was a distinct blow to the "radical" cause.[31]

Democratic preparations for the campaign were completed August 28 at Springfield at a state convention presided over by General John A. McClernand. This gathering of "conservatives," attended by Johnson republicans like T. J. Turner, selected a ticket of war democrats: for congressman-at-large Colonel T. Lyle Dickey, an old-time whig of Ottawa,[32] Colonel Jesse J. Phillips of Montgomery county for state treasurer, and, as a distinct "debt of gratitude" to the soldiers, Colonel John M. Crebs of White county for superintendent of public instruction. The convention approved the policy of President Johnson and rebuked the radical majority of congress for its ruthless disregard of the constitution; in order to secure the advantage of the republican rejection of an eight-hour resolution, it supported the claims of labor for a reduced working schedule; it urged the taxation of plutocratic bondholders and declared the greenbacks a safer and better currency than national bank notes; and, finally, proclaimed a sympathy for the people of Ireland and for the oppressed of every nationality. This platform anticipated many of the issues that were appearing on the political horizon.

One feature of the campaign was the visit of President Johnson, who, in the company of such notables as Secretary of State Seward, Secretary of Navy Welles, Admiral Farragut, and General Grant, came to assist in dedicating the Douglas monument at Chicago, and who, after an excursion of the presidential cortege to Bloomington, paid a visit to the grave of Lincoln at Springfield. This pilgrimage to the homes of the two foremost Illinoisians Johnson converted into an electioneering tour characterized by few formal addresses and numerous unmannerly stump speeches. Although this visit served to arouse the enthusiasm of the democrats and attached them more closely to their new standard bearer, yet Johnson's frequent passionate denunciation of his opponents and breaches of

---

[31] T. T. Turner to James R. Root, May 22, 1866 (ms. copy), Trumbull manuscripts; *Illinois State Register*, August 7, 1866; *Chicago Tribune*, July 2, 1866.
[32] *Illinois State Register*, August 29, 1866; *Ottawa Weekly Republican*, August 30, 1866; *Chicago Tribune*, August 31, 1866; *Cairo Democrat*, September 2, 1866; *Joliet Signal*, October 23, 1866.

the traditions of presidential dignity only confirmed the radicals in their opposition and made reluctant moderate republicans decide to repudiate the president whose administration they had sincerely desired to support. The city council of Springfield, while extending a formal invitation to General Grant and Admiral Farragut, went as far as to reject a proposal to give the president a public reception.[33]

If the democrats gained advantage from the presidential visit, the republicans had their turn when in October a group of southern union men from a convention at Philadelphia journeyed to Illinois to visit the grave of the martyred Lincoln; they followed the same route as that taken by President Johnson, whose " swing around the circle " they were intended to offset. Elaborate arrangements were made for their reception, in which the Grand Army of the Republic was marshaled in full strength. After a welcoming ovation in Chicago, October 1, they scattered over the state for a few days to contribute to the republican campaign. On the tenth, after visits to Kankakee, Peoria, Du Quoin, Mattoon, Cairo, Canton, Pana, and Alton, they came together for a grand celebration at Springfield, where they thrilled Illinois republicans with their testimonials of devotion to the simon-pure union cause.[34]

The visitors served to distract some attention from the interesting race between General Logan and Colonel Dickey for the privilege of representing the state in congress. Dickey's supporters made a feeble appeal to the soldier vote, which was reminded of his heroic deeds at Vicksburg. Logan, on the other hand, was the favorite of thousands of Illinois veterans who with him had bared their bosoms to the storm of war from Belmont to the victory of 1865. So strong was his political position that many had looked upon him as the logical successor to Trumbull's seat in the United States senate; indeed, Logan's nomination to congress was in part a device to eliminate him from the senatorial field, although he still continued to worry the friends of Trumbull.[35]

[33] *Jacksonville Journal*, September 6, 1866; *Cairo Democrat*, September 12, 1866; *Joliet Signal*, September 18, 1866.
[34] *Chicago Tribune*, October 1, 12, 1866; *Du Quoin Recorder*, October 5, 1866; *Canton Weekly Register*, October 8, 1866.
[35] George T. Brown to Trumbull, November 7, 1865, Trumbull manuscripts.

The democrats soon decided that the skeleton of Logan's past was one which they might well cause to stalk forth among his admirers. Although they found it impossible advantageously to play up the charges of cowardice made by Colonel Reynolds and others, they insisted that "Black Jack," the "renegade from the Democracy," had been selected to do "the dirty work for the radical party, as he used to do it for the democratic party."[36] When the "warrior orator" in a whirlwind campaign began drawing out by thousands the voters in every part of Illinois, his erstwhile associates brought out their heavy artillery in an attempt to shatter the bulwarks of his strength. Logan "would like to make treason odious," they said, "Well, so do we, and would suggest . . . . that Logan himself is a fit subject to commence on."[37] They charged him as a secessionist in 1861, having denounced the war as "a d—d abolition crusade" and with having drummed up an "Egyptian corps" of recruits to the southern army. Said the *Chicago Times*: "Almost every prominent journal in the state (the Chicago *Tribune* among the number) denounced him as a traitor and a rebel."[38]

Then "chapters from Logan's record" were published in the democratic press. He was charged with having made numerous speeches in the spring of 1861, denouncing the doctrine of coercion and declaring that he could never give aid, comfort, or countenance to an attempt at conquering the rebellion by force; he was pointed out as the sponsor for the resolutions adopted by a meeting in Marion, Williamson county on April 15, 1861, which demanded in the event of continued coercive policy, a division of the state to detach southern Illinois; he was charged with having denounced William J. Allen, his law partner, as a "dirt-eater" for having taken a leading part in movements to counteract the Marion resolutions; it was declared that, in June, 1861, on account of a general belief that he would be arrested for disloyalty, William J. Allen and

[36] The *Chicago Tribune* had before 1860 bestowed upon him the title of "Dirty-work Logan." *Illinois State Register*, August 14, 15, 1866; *Chicago Evening Journal*, November 4, 1865; *Joliet Signal*, October 24, November 7, 1865.
[37] *Mt. Vernon Free Press* clipped in *Jonesboro Gazette*, July 28, 1866; *Illinois State Register*, August 11, 1866.
[38] *Chicago Times* clipped in *ibid.*, August 14, 1866.

others advised him to wait upon General Prentiss with assurance that thereafter his conduct would be unobjectionable; that in purchasing a revolver from Thomas Wilson, who was mayor of Cairo in 1866, he had explained: "I am going to attend the extra session of Congress and make a speech, telling what I think about this d—d Abolition war, and I intend to blow out the brains of the first d—d scoundrel who questions my right to do so;" that it was generally believed in Egypt that Logan was raising his regiment to fight in behalf of the confederacy; that in June, 1861, after the arrest of Colonel James D. Pulley, Logan raised an armed force to drive off union soldiers who might come to assail the rights of the people of Marion; and that Logan bitterly denounced Douglas for his historic war speech before the Illinois legislature as no better than an abolitionist.[39]

The nine counts of this indictment were represented in every issue of the *Cairo Democrat* for October, 1866, and taken up by other democratic papers. Logan entered the war, they declared, for the same reason that he entered politics — to get office. "His love was for the ultra fanatics of secession, whose tool he had so long been — whose 'dirty work' he had so willingly performed. . . . . It was not till he found that the patriotic Democracy of Southern Illinois would not follow him into the ranks of the rebel army that he discovered that he was on the weather side. Thereupon, true to his office-seeking instinct, he turned a complete somersault, and entered the Union Army;"[40] now "in the desperate hope of seducing 'Egypt' into supporting the hellish schemes of the disunion Congress the Radicals placed the apostate Logan at the head of their ticket."[41]

The devoted wife of General Logan rose nobly to his defense. She journeyed to Marion and secured a statement signed by political opponents of Logan, some of whom had served in the southern army, which pronounced all the charges against Logan untrue. At the same time also his brother-in-law, Hibert B. Cunningham, wrote from Mississippi absolving Logan from

[39] *Cairo Democrat*, September 28, October 2, 1866.
[40] *Chicago Times* clipped in *Illinois State Register*, August 14, 1866; *Belleville Democrat*, September 1, 1866.
[41] *Chester Picket Guard*, September 5, 1866.

any responsibility for his going south to fight as a member of Captain Thorndike Brooks' company. Logan's opponents replied with a formal affidavit from one William M. Davis, who claimed that he had gone with Brooks' company "by and under the advice and influence of John A. Logan and his brother-in-law, H. B. Cunningham, who told me that Logan would join us in two or three months." Next a statement appeared over the signatures of six of the eight "signers" of Mrs. Logan's certificate, which declared that their names had been used "without our consent, for we are satisfied the charges are substantially true, as published in the Cairo *Democrat*, Chicago *Times*, and other journals. Any amount of additional testimony in reference to Gen. Logan's anti-war action and speeches here in 1861, can be had from the best citizens of all parties."[42]

These charges were taken up by various democratic stump speakers, while Dickey, Logan's opponent, conducted a clean campaign, concentrating mainly on the reconstruction issue. The two rivals met in joint debate at Carbondale and Decatur. General Logan displayed a good deal of fire and at times venom. "He abused the Democracy in most insulting language; blustered, talked loud, slapped his hands frantically, and shook his finger provokingly at the Colonel . . . . [he] bellowed invectives, and earned the reputation of being Brownlow's rival in the use of 'low-down' language."[43] According to an account of the Carbondale debate, when Dickey touched upon Logan's secessionist record, Logan declared that whoever made these charges were liars; thereupon his own sister, Mrs. Blanchard, rose and declared that he had furnished his brother-in-law with financial aid to assist the rebellion.[44]

It was in reply to the Carbondale denial by Logan that the editors of the *Cairo Democrat* drew up the nine specifications which they held themselves ready to prove. Whatever Colonel Dickey lacked in venom was more than counterbalanced by some of his supporters. The *Chester Picket Guard* hoped to

[42] *Cairo Democrat*, October 21, 27, 1866.
[43] *Ibid.*, September 30, 1866; *Chicago Tribune*, October 1, 2, 17, 1866; *Du Quoin Recorder*, October 5, 1866.
[44] *Salem Advocate* clipped in *Belleville Democrat*, October 6, 1866.

deliver the state already disgraced by "such a dishonest, radical, lecherous, blasphemous and drunken, dirty, beastly thing as Dick Oglesby" from "that low vulgar, dirty and hypocritical Logan. Maggots would sicken on him."[45]

The democrats capitalized to the full the desertion of Johnson republicans who joined the "conservative" forces. Besides T. J. Turner of Freeport and ex-Senator Browning, who was said to control the executive patronage in Illinois, a long list of converts was claimed, including Judge J. O. Norton, Judge G. D. A. Parks of Joliet, State Senator Green of Centralia, and T. L. Breckinridge, who in the union state convention had nominated Logan for congressman-at-large. The party sought to cement the attachment of the Irish to the democratic ranks by extending their approval to the Fenian brotherhood, which was now taking by storm the Celtic population of the state. The republicans at the same time made a strong bid for the Irish vote with a huge Fenian picnic near Chicago in August; although they made some converts, they were handicapped by the prevailing traditional allegiance of the Irish.[46]

In the fiercely contested canvass, the advantage lay with the republicans who had set out to win. From Senator Trumbull and Yates down the best campaigners entered the field. The full influence of the Union League organization was wielded for their candidates; the G. A. R. posts were sources of additional strength. When the democrats hurled at them the epithets of "nigger-equality party" and "miscegens," they replied with salvos against the "treason party" and "copperheads." When the bitter contest came to an end in November it was found that the republicans had won a sweeping victory, involving over fifty thousand majority for Logan, ten out of the other thirteen congressmen, and a two-thirds majority of the legislature. Illinois, an old stronghold of the democracy, became a citadel of republican power.

[45] *Chester Picket Guard,* September 12, 1866.
[46] *Aurora Beacon,* August 16, 23, 1866; *Joliet Signal,* August 7, September 18, 25, 1866; *Illinois State Register,* September 27, 1866; *Rockford Register,* August 18, 1866; *Chicago Tribune,* October 16, November 6, 1866.

XIX. THE SPOILS AND THE SPOILERS, 1867-1870

DURING the Civil War the people of Illinois had given themselves over entirely to national political issues; after the election of 1866, however, they wearily yielded to a reaction which reflected their satisfaction that the sectional issue had passed the crisis. The political majority came to feel that, with no effective opposition at home, they would do well to intrust Andrew Johnson and the tedious reconstruction problems to the care of the overwhelming republican majority in congress; the successive steps in the controversy between the president and the legislative department were mere journalistic details which they could follow in the newspapers. It was becoming high time, they realized, that problems vital to the future of the state — too long neglected and sidetracked — should receive full and earnest consideration.

When the general assembly convened on January 7, 1867, the legislators first cleared the way for their new rôle by disposing of the election of the United States senator. The claim of Trumbull's supporters that the republican victory was a verdict in favor of his reëlection was subtly challenged by rival candidates. The senator was criticized for "his lack of social qualities, his austerity of manners, his aristocratic sympathies and his natural tendencies toward conservatism."[1] For, strangely enough, Trumbull, the leader of the radical forces of Illinois during the Civil War, was a true conservative; and he had now to encounter the censure of certain "radical" critics.[2] General Logan, Governor Oglesby, and General Palmer, leagued together in common cause against Trumbull, were all ready to contest his claims. Palmer lay low for a time; but when Logan and Oglesby, in order to hold their

[1] *Jacksonville Journal*, January 8, 1867.
[2] Trumbull might not have broken with Johnson had not the issue become so direct and personal. *Chicago Post*, March 9, 1866.

own offices, transferred their claims to him he stepped out into the open. He fast gained strength for his election through the labors of the Grand Army of the Republic. Palmer's friends insisted that their favorite, and not Trumbull, had originated the civil rights act; Trumbull, however, succeeded in refuting this claim — indeed, as the people looked back upon his record in congress, they could not gainsay his title to reëlection. The factional contest came to an end in the republican legislative caucus on the test vote to proceed to the nomination of a candidate by viva voce vote, for Palmer's followers failed decisively in their plans to secure a secret ballot; thereupon Trumbull was nominated by acclamation.[3] The formal balloting in joint session gave the veteran statesman his credentials for another six years in the senate.

Governor Oglesby in his message to the legislature recognized that the day had passed when it sufficed to drag civil war issues across the political arena; indeed, he bespoke the needs of the state in a way that even secured the approval of many political opponents. "War, with all its scourges, has fled from our land, and gentle peace returns to heal its wounds," he pointed out. "A new career now opens to our State . . . . It is our duty to hold constantly in view every interest of the commonwealth; to bravely meet every requirement necessary to the full development of our natural advantages; to cherish the arts and sciences; to foster education, the soul of the State; and, with charitable hands, to meet and lift up the unfortunate."[4]

Before the assembly could consider the recommendations of the governor it found itself engulfed by demands for private legislation; lobbyists and logrolling forces were so active that just to meet their insistent demands would have more than consumed the forty-two days allotted by the constitution to the normal session. Batches of questionable private bills were forced through both houses without an adequate investigation of their contents; into one omnibus three hundred and twelve such items were bundled. A wave of criticism rose from

[3] *Illinois State Journal*, January 14, 15, 1867; *Chicago Tribune*, January 12, 14, 15, 1867; *Belleville Democrat*, February 14, 1867; *Cairo Democrat*, September 10, 1867.
[4] *Reports General Assembly*, 1867, 1:3, 4 ff.; *Joliet Signal*, January 15, 1867.

voters throughout the state and from the organs of both parties, together with a demand for a revision of the constitution to secure a longer session and to prohibit the creation of private corporations by legislative enactment. "About ten or twelve millions of dollars [have been] voted into the pockets of corporations, contractors, and speculators," announced the *Carthage Republican*, March 7, 1867. Charges of corrupt rings and bargains and of direct bribery began to circulate to such a degree that finally a special senate committee was appointed to make an investigation.[5]

Public legislation had to be scrambled through in the closing days of the session. Proposals for railroad legislation and for a constitutional amendment establishing "impartial suffrage" in the state died of sheer neglect. Before dispersing the legislature passed bills for the erection of a new penitentiary in the southern part of the state, for the construction of a new statehouse at an estimated cost of three million dollars, and for the location of the industrial university; provision was made for the regulation of warehouses and for the inauguration of a scheme of canal and river improvements, besides action submitting to the people the question of a constitutional convention.

Never had the adjournment of the general assembly met with such a widespread feeling of relief; democrats and republicans alike hailed the "blessed day" when "the most disgraceful Legislative body that ever convened in the State" came to an end. Not only were the legislators lacking in dignity—even the senate being the scene of frequent disorder with members shying books and paper wads at each other and at the speaker; but, more important, they seemed lacking in that essential virtue of honesty.[6] The shortcomings of the majority were admitted on both sides, by the democrats out

[5] *Chicago Post*, February 25, 28, 1867; *Ottawa Weekly Republican*, January 31, 1867; *Chicago Tribune*, February 18, 19, 1867; *Joliet Signal*, February 19, 1867; *Cairo Democrat*, February 26, 1867.
[6] *Ibid.*, March 1, 1867. In such a scene, with the clerks vainly attempting to read the bills then passing, the speaker, wielding the gavel with the grace of a stone-cutter, declared the senate adjourned *sine die*. *Chicago Tribune*, March 1, 1867; *Aurora Beacon*, March 21, 1867. The *Carthage Republican*, March 7, declared it "the most corrupt and imbecile legislature which ever disgraced the commonwealth of Illinois."

of partisanism, and by the republicans because in the contest for the spoils the party became divided into sectional groups and into "rings." Critics of both parties in Chicago and northern Illinois declared the statehouse and southern penitentiary legislation a "direct and open steal" engineered by an "industrial university–statehouse–penitentiary ring" which secured to Champaign the location of the agricultural college.[7] Reënforced by the disappointed ambitions of other cities like Decatur, which had looked to a transfer of the capital, they launched an especially aggressive attack against the "swindle" of the new statehouse law. The constitutionality of the legislation was brought before the courts; and although for a six-month the odds seemed to favor its rejection, the supreme court ended the controversy by upholding the law.[8] Springfield forces, regardless of party withstanding the opposition that came from every corner of the state, launched a counter attack against "the canal swindle" enacted by a "corrupt squadron" of northern Illinois interests. "A bigger steal upon the people of the State than is contemplated by its pet measure, the canal bill, can hardly be conceived," declared the *State Journal*. "What interests have the people of Central Illinois in widening the Michigan canal at an expense of twenty or thirty million dollars so as to make it navigable for boats? What interest have the people of Southern Illinois in such a project? *Not one cent's worth.* Their business and commercial relations all lead in another direction."[9]

In the midst of this confusing squabble Governor Oglesby whipped up the general assembly in two special sessions on June 11 and June 14 to adjust certain minor matters and to amend the assessment laws of the state so as to make the shares of national bank stock liable for taxes. The confirmation of his nominees for canal commissioners and southern penitentiary commissioners the senate recalcitrantly voted to postpone until

---

[7] *Chicago Post*, February 28, 1867; *Chicago Tribune*, March 6, 1867; *St. Louis Democrat* clipped in *Cairo Democrat*, March 3, 1867; *Aurora Beacon*, March 21, 1867.
[8] *Chicago Post*, February 25, March 15, 1867; *Chicago Tribune*, July 1, 8, 11, 13, 16, 18, 19, 1867; *Rockford Register*, February 23, 1867; *Illinois State Register*, October 29, 1867; *Jonesboro Gazette*, February 23, 1867; *Jacksonville Journal*, February 12, 27, March 2, 1867.
[9] *Illinois State Journal*, May 4, 14, 18, 1867.

the next session.[10] As a result two of the most important pieces of legislation practically became a dead letter. The statehouse appropriation was finally saved from destruction, and the location of the university at Urbana survived the opposition; a warehouse regulation act was the only important measure which was put through without a barrage of criticism.

These legislative developments are indicative of a period of serious party disintegration, especially in the ranks of the republican majority in Illinois. Side issues crept into the local and county elections of the year and often enabled the democrats to make important gains; republican majorities were reversed in Peoria, Fulton, Mason, and certain other counties. Illinois republicans, surveying these losses in the light of the approaching presidential campaign, promptly connected themselves with the movement for Grant's nomination, which they expected would draw out the full strength of the party. The democrats, alarmed at the republican enthusiasm for a man who had always been considered a democrat, now pointed out that Grant's candidacy was an indication of the fears of their opponents, who were willing to sacrifice principle for the sake of success. Sophisticated republican politicians, indeed, while conceding Grant's strength with the people and the Grand Army of the Republic, often had "serious doubts as to his fitness for a civil administration."[11] But as a fellow citizen, as a man with slight interest in partisan politics, and as a moderate on reconstruction, General Grant seemed on the score of availability to possess the formidable strength now imperative to the party.

Grant was not, moreover, a figure who would accentuate a line of cleavage in the republican ranks that had appeared during the impeachment proceeding against President Johnson; for, although the hatred of the president had reached such proportions as to suggest the desirability of his removal, all could not concede the honesty of such a course. Many Illinois republicans had been loud in their demand for impeach-

---

[10] *Aurora Beacon*, June 27, 1867; *Champaign County Union and Gazette*, July 10, 1867.
[11] Koerner, *Memoirs*, 2:480; *Ottawa Free Trader*, November 2, 1867.

ment, and Governor Oglesby had sent a formal demand to Washington for action.[12] When finally proceedings were instituted, John A. Logan took an active part as one of the managers in the prosecution. Some republicans, however, agreed with the democrats who characterized the impeachment as a partisan attack and the trial a farce; not many republicans were willing to acknowledge this, but the *Jacksonville Journal* admitted that it was a case of "the bluffer bluffed." "The impeachment trial of the president is a necessity, because he cannot be removed in any other way, but it must necessarily be, in some measure, a farce."[13] The *Chicago Tribune*, which admitted that the indictment was in part a political attack, insisted that Johnson be convicted only if found guilty as charged;[14] on the other hand, certain republicans flatly demanded a conviction. The *Tribune* received advance information of the probable acquittal of the president, which was borne out when Senator Trumbull and six other republicans, including erstwhile radicals, voted with the democrats to defeat conviction. Although Trumbull's vote was in line with his entire course on reconstruction, it fell like a blow upon many of his constituents, and a bitter attack was launched upon him.

Certain republicans reconciled themselves to the failure of the impeachment trial on the score that it would save the party in the midst of the presidential contest from another internecine war on the tariff question — a serious question for the Illinois branch of the party. They had yielded the principle of protection in 1860, but under the heavy demand for revenue the Civil War tariffs had carried the duties to a point where they threatened to strangle the agricultural and producing interests of the Mississippi valley. "We are being consumed by the good of New England and Pennsylvania," announced Dr. C. H. Ray. "If matters are not regulated and on a fairer and juster principle, the west will be badly injured before five years have elapsed. When will men see that legislative interference in trade as in religion or morals

---

[12] *Illinois State Journal*, January 8, 29, 1867; *Belleville Democrat*, December 12, 1867, March 12, 1868.
[13] *Jacksonville Journal*, March 5, 1868.
[14] *Chicago Tribune*, March 3, May 15, 1868.

is always mischievous?"[16] Early in 1866 a group of Chicago republicans, including the publishers of the *Chicago Tribune*, had organized a league for the protection to home labor as against foreign trade which bent its energies toward preventing increased duties. Joseph Medill, "the oracle of the Protectionists in the West," together with Horace White and other friends, threw their strength against such increases in 1866 and in 1867; they condemned the "gang of greedy speculators [who] seem to have got hold of the House of Representatives and are running the whole protection question into the ground."[16]

The party decided to bury its family quarrels in the love feasts of the Chicago convention, for Illinois was again honored by the republicans in the selection of the lake city. There on May 20 and 21 it was agreed that, in view of the general situation and in view of the demand that the party be held together for an approval of the votes of the thirty-five republican senators who held Johnson guilty as charged, no tariff plank should be inserted in the national platform.[17] There, too, General Grant was proposed by John A. Logan and unanimously nominated for the presidency, while Schuyler Colfax was selected as the party's other standard bearer. Grant was strong in the availability of a military hero, which more than covered his shortcomings as a partisan.

Illinois democrats had at first offered Sidney Breese, chief justice of the supreme court of Illinois, as their candidate for the presidency, but it became evident that this was largely a compliment to a favorite son; in the closing weeks of the pre-convention campaign they generally took up George H. Pendleton of Ohio as the western candidate, and the state convention formally instructed the Illinois delegates to support Pendleton. The national convention at New York, first making concessions to the western section of the party in the platform that was adopted, ran up the names of Horatio

---

[15] C. H. Ray to Trumbull, January 15, 1866, Joseph Medill *et al.* to Trumbull, February 7, 1866, Trumbull manuscripts; *Chicago Tribune*, May 16, 1868.
[16] Joseph Medill to Trumbull, July 1, 1866, C. H. Ray to Trumbull, February 2, 1866, E. C. Larned to Trumbull, July 2, 1866, Horace White to Trumbull, July 5, 1866, Trumbull manuscripts; *Chicago Tribune*, February 5, 1867.
[17] *Proceedings of the National Union Republican Convention*, 1868, p. 84-85 *et seq.*

Seymour of New York and Francis P. Blair of Missouri. Illinois democrats were decidedly disappointed with the nomination of Seymour, who represented the eastern point of view on the currency question, which was coming to have so much significance in the politics of the day. Illinois as a western state was strongly in favor of inflation; it looked with suspicion upon the eastern demand for the withdrawal of greenbacks from circulation in order to hasten the resumption of specie payments. Pendleton's strength in the west had in large part grown out of his pet scheme for the payment of bonds in greenbacks on an inflation policy, which was known as the "Ohio idea." W. J. Allen and the Illinois delegation had contended vigorously at the national convention in favor of Pendleton's position, and since the convention had incorporated a greenback clause in its platform, the democrats decided to interpret the nomination of Seymour, though a hard-money man, in this light.[18]

In state politics the old democratic leaders seem to have become so discouraged as to refuse the use of their names; the democrats, therefore, selected John R. Eden of Moultrie county to head their ticket against John M. Palmer, the almost unanimous choice of the republicans; and their candidate to oppose Logan for congressman-at-large was an unknown, W. W. O'Brien of Peoria. Most of the republican nominees were military men: besides Palmer and Logan, they named General C. E. Lippincott for auditor, General E. N. Bates for treasurer, Brevet General Bushnell for attorney-general, and Colonel Dougherty for lieutenant governor, an old Breckinridge democrat in 1860 and an early opponent of the war. Here was a dish entirely to the liking of all brands of Civil War veterans.[19] In the campaign that followed the advantage lay decidedly with the republicans. In addition to their disappointment at the national outlook, the democrats were disheartened at their failure to secure a stronger state

---

[18] *Cairo Democrat,* July 13, 1867, February 8, March 5, July 9, 16, 1868; *Illinois State Register,* July 12, 1867, February 11, 1868; *Joliet Signal,* July 16, 1867, February 8, 25, March 10, 1868; *Belleville Democrat,* July 25, 1867, July 16, 1868; *Paxton Record,* July 12, 1868; *Carthage Republican,* July 16, 1868.

[19] *Cairo Democrat,* May 12, 1868; *Champaign County Union and Gazette,* May 13, 1868; *Ottawa Free Trader,* May 30, 1868.

ticket. On most issues the democrats had to take the offensive, while the republicans could contentedly trust to past accomplishments. With little ardor the democrats took up the task, but duty drove them on. They began a campaign "to end the reign of the bond holders .... by paying off these bonds in the same kind of money which the law compels the farmer, the mechanic and the laborer to take for the proceeds of their honest toil;"[20] they asked the people of the state if they were willing "to swallow the negro-suffrage pill prepared for them" by the Chicago convention and asserted that it was "the holy mission of Democracy .... to restore political power exclusively to the Caucasian race."[21] The people were called upon to behold the "radical platform" with its "praises of the negro and promises to him but not a word from which the overburdened white toiler can derive any comfort;" it was the work of "a gathering of selfish and corrupt politicians, whose only object is to scheme for office and to devise means whereby they may be enabled to filch from the National Treasury the money which is wrung from the sweat and toil of the laboring white men of the nation."[22] The real issue, they proclaimed, was aristocracy versus democracy: "We have also an aristocratic class of citizens endowed with peculiar privileges, a bonded aristocracy, whose wealth is exempt from taxation for the support of Government, and who demand the interest due on their bonds paid in gold, while the laborer and the mechanic must take a depreciated currency for his labor." The new régime which would push on radical reconstruction at a terrific expense to the already overburdened taxpayer of the west would be "a *regime* of force, ... introduced by a shoulder-strapped President, to culminate in the long cherished hope of an empire."[23]

Seymour, on the other hand, would reduce the expenses of the government; would redeem the bonds in currency; would simplify the revenue laws, and cut down taxation; would modify the tariff laws, with a view to revenue, and not with a view to protection; and would make capital instead of labor

[20] *Carthage Republican*, July 23, 1868.
[21] *Rushville Times*, July 2, 1868.
[22] *Belleville Democrat*, June 25, 1868.
[23] *Rushville Times*, July 30, 1868; *Illinois State Register*, July 29, 1868.

bear the burdens of taxation. He would cut down the army and navy to a peace standard and put honest and efficient men in office.[24]

All these pleas fell on deaf ears. The republicans knew their strength and proceeded to consolidate it, taking their stand on past achievements. The *Chicago Tribune* of August 4 acknowledged that there were shortcomings within their party but proclaimed the policy: "In the present contest, the Republicans unite in demanding peace upon the basis of accomplished facts, and in consonance with lawfully-enacted statutes, and in requiring the payment of the public debt with 'the utmost good faith' to all: while the Democracy sound the tocsin of insurrection and threaten repudiation in one form or another. He who prefers a pacific and an honorable national policy will vote for Grant and Colfax: he who prefers internecine war and bankruptcy will vote for Seymour and Blair."

On this ground the republicans stood like adamant; they continued the canvass calmly and confidently, though some attempt was made to give the campaign the éclat which usually attached to a military hero candidate. Grant clubs were formed and uniformed companies of "tanners," recalling the former occupation of the general, and the torchlight processions of 1860 were repeated. These were popular movements which in bringing recruits further aroused the spite of the opposition. Democratic journals declared that Grant and his father had carried on another business during the war—that of trading in cotton; why not, they suggested, a cotton club with members clothed in cotton batting? Moreover, they asked was a man with "Grant's fondness for fast-horses, pup dogs, Havana cigars and Bourbon whiskey" a fit candidate for the chief magistracy?[25]

The republicans met these aspersions by pointing out that former members of the democratic party had forsaken their old associates to support Grant; not only did Thomas J. Turner of Freeport, whom the democrats had run for congress two years ago, return to his old allegiance, but such lifelong

[24] *Carthage Republican,* July 30, 1868.
[25] *Ibid.,* June 11, 1868; *Illinois State Register,* July 30, August 10, 13, 1868; *Chicago Tribune,* September 8, October 31, 1868.

democrats as Colonel I. N. Morris and Adolph Moses of Quincy, O. Pool of Shawneetown, Judge Quimby of Monmouth were listed as new republican recruits.[26] It was not strange, therefore, that the republicans not only swept the state for Grant with over fifty thousand majority but also turned the state government over to General Palmer and their state ticket to coöperate with a strongly republican legislature.

In January, 1869, Governor Oglesby turned the reins of government over to his successor, John M. Palmer, who brought to the gubernatorial office a reputation for calm, temperate, broadminded statesmanship which augured well for a clean administration. He had always been a moderate partisan, he had not forgotten his early democratic associations, and conditions generally were favorable to the maintenance of that popularity he had won as a military leader during the Civil War. His inaugural address, conceived in the spirit of nonpartisanship and progressivism, defined a sphere of state rights that made the republicans hold their breath in consternation, while the democrats hailed it as a model state paper.[27] In considering the general demand for corporation control and for regulatory railroad legislation, Governor Palmer called attention to proposals to enlist the national government in the creation of corporations for the construction of railroads in Illinois and adjacent states. Pointing out the confusion produced by the Civil War as to the relative powers and duties of the national and state governments, he declared: "Now that the war is ended, and all proper objects attained, the public welfare demands a recurrence to the true principles that underlie our system of governments, and one of the best established and most distinctly recognized of these is, that the federal government is one of enumerated powers. . . . . The state governments are a part of the American system of government. They fill a well defined place, and their just authority must be respected by the federal government."

---

[26] *Chicago Tribune,* June 9, 1868; *Joliet Republican,* June 13, 1868; *Illinois State Journal,* June 17, August 28, September 9, 12, 17, October 12, 1868; *Rockford Gazette,* June 18, 1868.
[27] *Ibid.,* January 28, 1869; *Illinois State Register,* January 12, 20, 1869; *Chicago Tribune,* January 12, 1869; *Cairo Evening Bulletin,* January 14, 1869; *Joliet Signal,* January 19, 1869; *Rushville Times,* January 21, 1869.

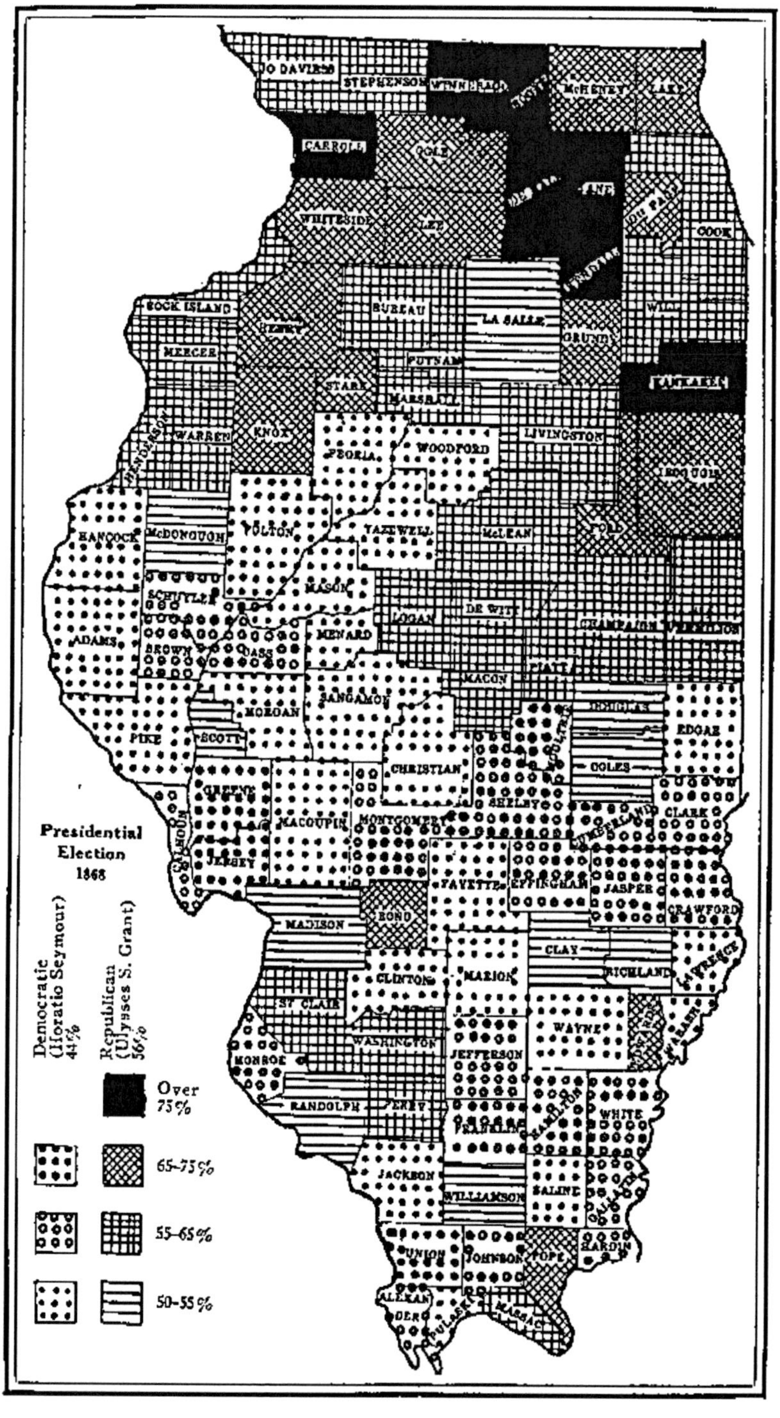

Presidential Election 1868
Democratic (Horatio Seymour) 44%
Republican (Ulysses S. Grant) 56%
Over 75%
65-75%
55-65%
50-55%
JO DAVIESS
STEPHENSON
McHENRY
CARROLL
WHITESIDE
LEE
COOK
ROCK ISLAND
HENRY
BUREAU
LA SALLE
GRUNDY
MERCER
PUTNAM
STARK
MARSHALL
KANKAKEE
WARREN
KNOX
LIVINGSTON
PEORIA
WOODFORD
IROQUOIS
HANCOCK
McDONOUGH
FULTON
TAZEWELL
McLEAN
FORD
SCHUYLER
MASON
LOGAN
DE WITT
CHAMPAIGN
ADAMS
BROWN
CASS
MENARD
PIATT
MACON
MORGAN
SANGAMON
PIKE
SCOTT
EDGAR
COLES
CHRISTIAN
GREENE
SHELBY
CLARK
MACOUPIN
MONTGOMERY
JERSEY
FAYETTE
EFFINGHAM
JASPER
CRAWFORD
MADISON
BOND
CLAY
CLINTON
MARION
RICHLAND
ST CLAIR
WAYNE
WASHINGTON
MONROE
JEFFERSON
RANDOLPH
PERRY
FRANKLIN
WHITE
JACKSON
SALINE
WILLIAMSON
UNION
JOHNSON
POPE
HARDIN

Palmer pointed to the appearance after each session of the general assembly of ponderous volumes "filled with acts creating corporations for almost every purpose, clothed with powers of the most extraordinary extent," and diplomatically suggested the problems growing out of this situation. In closing he emphasized the duty of the legislators: "The people of the State have confided to the General Assembly a great trust. They expect at your hands the most careful scrutiny of the operation of every department of the government. That abuses, if any are found to exist, shall be corrected. They demand the most rigid economy in the expenditures of the public money. I have no doubt your efforts to promote their happiness will meet their approval." [28]

The legislature, however, cared little for the advice handed out to it. Although Governor Oglesby upon retiring had left an excellent message stressing public needs, and Governor Palmer now added his suggestions for necessary legislation, the assembly callously set out to duplicate the orgy of 1868. Legislative "rings" and logrolling appropriation bills were prepared before the session formally opened; and rumors of "big steals" began to circulate, while the lobby, or "third house," assembled in force.[29] Special legislation of all sorts was jammed through; about seven hundred acts of incorporation were passed despite the constitutional provision which had sought to prohibit that class of legislation. Again talk of corruption and bribery filled the atmosphere until the legislature itself felt moved to order an investigation; this was a safe enough proceeding, according to the *Chicago Tribune,* because "the men who have 'money bills' in the Legislature are not so green as to pay anything beyond liquor, cigars and board until one day after adjournment — never in any case until the bill passes." When the legislature finally adjourned, opinions differed as to the amount of its political jobbery: the *Carthage Republican,* a democratic journal, was content to believe that "compared with the former, the legislature is a model of all virtues," although its dishonesty had been limited only "by

[28] *House Journal,* 1869, 1:202-208.
[29] *Bloomington Pantagraph* clipped in *Illinois State Journal,* January 7, 1869; *Joliet Republican,* January 9, 1869; *Illinois State Register,* January 9, 12, 1869; *Ottawa Free Trader,* February 20, 1869.

the impecunious character of the lobby;" the *Tribune* believed that with bipartisan combinations for special interests and with personal corruption which it was prepared to prove, it had been "reckless beyond precedent."[30]

Throughout the session Governor Palmer had conceived it his duty to check what seemed to be hasty, injudicious, and unscrupulous legislation with his veto; with the slaughtering of seventy-two bills he established a new record for the veto power of the governor of Illinois and won golden opinions from both democratic and republican critics of the legislature. Such interference did little to stem the flood of legislation; seventeen bills were hurried into law over the governor's merely suspensive veto. Besides four hundred pages of public laws, nearly three thousand five hundred pages of private legislation forced their way into the statute books.[31]

The more important items in the mass were: an appropriation of $400,000 for improvement in the Illinois river to permit the uninterrupted movement of boats by way of the Illinois and Michigan canal; the "penitentiary steal"—an appropriation of $300,000 to the "penitentiary ring" which had been unable to make a similar appropriation cover the previous biennium and which was accused of an administration which had resulted in a complete breakdown of prison discipline at the penitentiary;[32] a lake front act providing for the transfer of the submerged lands outside the tracks of the Illinois Central railroad to that company instead, as originally proposed, of releasing it to the city of Chicago, together with the lake front inside the tracks; and railroad legislation, including an act regulating railroad rates and an act which assigned a portion of the state taxes to assist in paying the remaining unpaid railroad debts of counties and municipal corporations. Two of the three last mentioned laws were enacted over the veto of Governor Palmer; in the case of rate regu-

[30] *Chicago Tribune,* March 2, April 17, 1869; *Carthage Republican,* March 18, 1869; *Ottawa Free Trader,* April 24, 1869; *Illinois State Register,* November 15, 1869.
[31] *Ibid.,* April 16, July 29, 1869; *Cairo Evening Bulletin,* March 1, 1869; *Illinois State Journal,* April 17, 1869; *Joliet Signal,* April 27, 1869; see also Debel, *The Veto Power of the Governor of Illinois,* 79.
[32] *Illinois State Register,* February 3, July 2, August 4, September 16, 1869; *Joliet Signal,* January 11, March 16, 1869.

lation, however, a veto pointed the way to modifications which met with his formal approval.[33]

While the legislature was at its work, news arrived of the passage of the fifteenth amendment giving the Negro the right to vote. This the assembly promptly ratified, although there was still a grave question as to whether Illinois was ready to admit its own Negro citizens to the polls. The issue of Negro suffrage had an interesting history in Illinois. The *Chicago Tribune* was one of the first papers in the country to advocate this principle; during the campaign of 1866 its editors, Senator Yates and certain other republican leaders, had boldly struck out for universal suffrage; but many in the party, especially republicans in Egypt, recognized that "the deep-rooted prejudices of the white masses can only be banished by the slow but certain process of time."[34] Democrats in the northern counties, too, came to accept the justice of Negro suffrage. The *Joliet Signal*, a democratic journal, declared itself ready to extend the franchise "as soon as the negroes shall prove that they are capable of a proper exercise of that privilege." After the campaign of 1866 was over the *Chicago Times* acknowledged Negro suffrage as so certain to be incorporated into the fundamental law that it became good policy, if not a public duty, to accept it without delay and in good faith. Democrats at the center and opposite end of the state, however, did not believe that their party could secure a new lease of life on that basis; and they soon silenced the *Times* by the storm of protest. A year later, by making plans for the establishment of a new party organ at Chicago, the democratic antis forced the *Chicago Times* to repudiate the heresy and chal-

[33] *Laws of 1869*, p. 245-248, 309-312, 316-321; Palmer, *Personal Recollections*, 290-291.
[34] *Central Illinois Gazette*, April 27, 1866; *Canton Weekly Register*, January 29, 1866; *Cairo Democrat*, October 20, 1866. "The prejudice against the negro is not wholly overborne," declared Dr. C. H. Ray, who was not in favor of imposing Negro suffrage on the south. "Say what we may, you and I share it; and what is true of us is doubly true of others. Because we have a sense of duty, a desire to be faithful to principles and a profound but not always active belief in that much talked-of 'brotherhood of men'. Where we *think* on this question, the masses give way to prejudice uncontrolled: and to dislike, I will not say hate, a negro is just as natural as to distinguish black from white." Ray to Trumbull, February 7, 1866, Trumbull manuscripts. So also Congressman Kuykendall of the Cairo district refused to follow his republican associates on the Negro suffrage issue. *Jonesboro Gazette*, January 5, February 9, 1867.

lenged the republicans to make Negro suffrage the issue for the next presidential campaign; the republican national convention, however, failed to put the issue squarely, though it continued an important feature of party politics. In the general assembly of 1869, as previously in 1867, considerable pressure was exerted in favor of an amendment to strike from the state constitution all discriminations against color and race in the matter of political privileges. When the fifteenth amendment, however, was given the approval of the state, the necessity of further action was eliminated, although democrats dared their opponents to strike the word "white" out of the new state constitution.[35]

Another act of the assembly of 1869 was to make the formal arrangement for the constitutional convention ordered by the people in the election of 1868. The election of delegates was set for the first Tuesday in November, and the convention was to assemble on the second Monday of the following month. This interjected a new atmosphere into the local elections of that year; inasmuch as none of the questions at issue, except the Negro suffrage matter, were political in character, the attempt was made to select capable representatives regardless of party affiliations. As a result the convention was made up almost equally of democrats and republicans, with a few republicans who ran as "people's candidates" holding the balance.[36] The party line, however, was also a sectional line, as the democrats were present in force only from Egypt, and the republicans from the northern half of the state.

The disintegration of the republican party, which bespoke the need for internal reorganization, found a wide range of expression. In the city and county elections of northern Illinois a certain puritanical reform element launched a political tem-

[35] *Illinois State Register*, November 13, 17, 1866, October 21, 1869; *Chicago Tribune*, November 13, 1866, January 10, 30, 1868; *Joliet Signal*, May 8, December 4; *Cairo Democrat*, November 14, 15, 16, 1866; *Carthage Republican*, November 15, 1866.

[36] The *Chicago Tribune*, November 4, 1869, rejoiced in the smallness of the republican majority, which it then estimated at ten: "This is as much as any party ought to have in any deliberative assembly. It is both safer and more reliable than a majority of twenty." It is quite evident that Joseph Medill's scheme of minority representation grew out of his disgust with the antics of the large republican majority in the sessions of 1867 and 1869. Cf. *ibid.*, November 13, 1869.

perance movement which placed separate candidates in the field; the democrats welcomed this movement as a division of the majority. In La Salle county a labor ticket was nominated on the platform of the National Labor Union; in Chicago, in Will county, and in Kane county, democratic and republican reformers united on "people's" or "citizens'" tickets to defeat the "ring tickets" put up by the local republican machines. All the republican newspapers in Chicago, except the *Post*, refused to support the regular party ticket; the *Chicago Times*, the leading organ of the democracy for the northwest, indorsed the "citizens'" candidates. The Kane county independent movement proved abortive, but victory was registered against "clique domination" in Will county, and in Cook county a stinging rebuke was administered to the corrupt gangsters who had for five or six years controlled the county offices and emoluments. The "barnacles," claimed the reformers, were being swept off the ship of state. Elsewhere, notably in Perry county, the result of dissension in the republican ranks had been either democratic gains or democratic victories.[37]

The republican party of 1870 had lost the spirituality that had characterized it in its early battles for freedom as a minority party. In that day the spoilsman had sought satisfaction for his ambitions in the ranks of the "unterrified" democracy, but the revolution of 1860 with its spoils of victory had drawn the professional politician into the republican ranks. After a decade of power the republican party was in need of much the same purification as that through which the democratic party had passed in the lean days of its failures during the Civil War.

[37] *Rockford Gazette*, February 4, July 15, 22, September 23, October 7, 21, 1869; *Ottawa Free Trader*, September 4, 1869; *Ottawa Weekly Republican*, September 30, October 14, 1869; *Chicago Tribune*, October 7, 1869; *The Nation*, 9:282; *Illinois State Register*, November 4, 1869; *Belleville Democrat*, November 11, 1869.

XX. RELIGION, MORALITY, AND EDUCATION, 1860–1870

IN SPITE of the lofty idealism of many northerners, who had welcomed the crusade against slavery, it cannot be denied that war conditions stimulated a moral degeneration sufficiently serious to command the attention of thoughtful observers. Later, when the champions of morality had secured perspective for adequate evaluation of the problem, they girded their loins for combat with the forces of darkness.

During the war normal habits of living were undermined by the incidents of poverty growing out of prevailing high prices and by the consequences of withdrawing a large percentage of the male population. Newspapers of every political stripe chronicled with horror the growing prevalence of licentiousness and crime. Besides the metropolitan vices of Chicago, crime seemed to find a safe refuge in cities like Springfield and Cairo, which had large military establishments. Rowdiness and bloody brawls among the soldiers grew at times into organized attacks upon persons and property. Street walks and corners were so infested by gay and flashing damsels, brazen-faced courtesans and their parasites, that the newspapers set up a howl of protest; the *Chicago Tribune* stated that there were known to be at least two thousand lewd women in that city. Cairo struggled helplessly with the problem, its citizens complaining that there was not another city in the country where the social evil was carried to such fearful and disgusting lengths. In 1865 matters came to a climax when the soldiers were being mustered out at Springfield. The city was so "overrun with blacklegs, burglars, garroters and harlots, (male and female) who have congregated to rob the soldiers . . . . of their hard earned wages,"[1] that Gen-

---
[1] *Chicago Tribune*, July 22, 24, 1865, January 9, 1866; *Cairo Democrat*, February 28, March 5, 1864, November 12, 22, 1865; *Cairo Evening Bulletin*,

eral John Cook detailed two additional companies to act as a provost guard whereupon the criminal business underwent a decided decline.

In attempting to explain this wave of crime, some held that there was no alarming increase — crime had merely concentrated in urban centers and was given the light of publicity by a press that had become microscopic; yet it was notably true that the state penitentiary at Joliet was unable to furnish satisfactory accommodations for the increasing number of convicts. To others the fact that in 1867 capital punishment was virtually abolished by the legislature explained the increase of crime; they therefore demanded the restoration of the death penalty. Still others proclaimed the wave as the legitimate and inevitable consequences of war; said the *Rockford Register*, a republican paper: "The restraints imposed upon evil propensities by society and by law, before the war, have been greatly weakened by the bloody scenes and lawlessness of the past four years."[2]

Coincident with the numerous reports of a general increase of drunkenness, a reviving temperance movement gathered strength, while the news of extensive frauds by Illinois whisky distillers who had evaded payment of a half million dollars of revenue tax played into the hands of reformers. But temperance had had its day in the fifties, and politicians were no longer amenable to the political pressure of the temperance forces. William H. Underwood, of Belleville, confessed in confidence to Senator Trumbull: "We have too many mere partizan drunkards and stump speakers now in office."[3]

The public man of the Civil War era must not be judged by the standards of today; indeed, it was only then that the traditional atmosphere, in which all important transactions were aided by alcoholic lubricants, was just beginning to pass away. To be sure, Lincoln could win the unqualified praise

March 30, May 28, 1869; *Illinois State Register*, April 16, 1862, February 10, 1864; *Chicago Times*, January 6, June 27, 1864; *Illinois State Journal*, July 25, 1865.

[2] *Rockford Register*, August 12, 1865; *Chicago Times*, January 21, 1864; *Illinois State Register*, February 24, 1864; *Chicago Tribune*, July 21, 1865, November 23, 1866; *Illinois State Journal*, March 14, 28, 1866, August 8, 1867; *Aurora Beacon*, December 13, 1866.

[3] W. H. Underwood to Trumbull, January 15, 1866, Trumbull manuscripts.

of a stern old puritan who proclaimed that "In old Abe is Combined the eloquence of an orator the fancy of a poet the Acuteness of a Schoolman the Profoundness of a Philosopher and the piety of a Saint for I am told that he neither drinks intoxicating drinks nor uses that nasty filthy dirty disgusting nauseating Poisonous weed called Tobbacco."[4] Yet because he was tolerant of the habits of his fellows he "*ran* smoothly in society—complaining of no immorality, no intemperance—no vice—no tobacco-chewing."[5] But some of the ablest representatives of the state at the Springfield capitol, in the halls of congress, and on the battlefields of the Civil War were given to overindulgence in intoxicating drinks. In 1868, when the resignation of a prominent United States senator, probably the most loved of all the public men of the day, was demanded by a large portion of his party's press on account of his intemperate use of liquor, he penned a solemn statement to the people of Illinois in which he frankly confessed the weakness that had brought "discredit upon my State and myself. . . . . During twenty seven years of political service—with the exception of ten of those years when I totally abstained—I have often yielded to temptation, and as often have suffered the pangs of unutterable remorse;"[6] the people of the state bade him a hearty Godspeed in his plans to reform.

In the first few months of the war many pious observers thought that it had worked out a purification—that the fear and cowardice of those who had stood by as silent witnesses to the martyrdom of the antislavery prophets had been stripped off and forever discarded. With the outbreak of civil strife it required little nerve to discourse on the moral evils of slavery and to set up a lusty shout for the union; the clergy, even those who had previously shrunk from the propositions of the abolitionist, now demanded the most up-standing loyalty of their fellows and of their congregations. Some had the courage of their convictions and, laying aside their frocks, rushed into the fray; a notable case was that of Reverend Jesse H. Moore,

---

[4] W. K. Kendall to Trumbull, January 7, 1860, Trumbull manuscripts.
[5] Herndon to Joseph Gillespie, February 20, 1866, Gillespie manuscripts. He continued: "Lincoln had no appetites, but *woman* must get out of his way."
[6] *Chicago Tribune*, March 30, 1868; *Rockford Gazette*, April 2, 9, 30, 1868; *Aurora Beacon*, April 30, 1868.

a Methodist pastor at Jacksonville, who raised the One hundred and fifteenth regiment in 1862 and graced his colonelcy so well that he was mustered out as a brevet brigadier general. Most clergymen, however, preferred to wage battle from the pulpit from which there now emanated a veritable barrage against the rebel and the copperhead. Loyalty resolutions were pressed upon all church conferences and conventions to such effect that they carried with practically no opposition. The Central Illinois Methodist Conference in September, 1862, adopted a resolution, drafted by Dr. Richard Haney, chaplain of the Sixth Illinois volunteers, requesting President Lincoln to free the Negroes from slavery; this resolution is claimed to be the first ecclesiastical action of the kind to reach the president.[7]

Although the Methodist conferences displayed unwavering loyalty—even suspending or expelling the few members who openly condemned Lincoln's emancipation policy—yet many felt politics to be too sordid a game to be mixed with true religion. The Illinois conference in session at Lima on September 2, 1863, adopted resolutions declaring affairs of state out of order in that conference, while at Carthage efforts were made to establish an independent Methodist church, where politics would not be tolerated in the pulpit; a call was even issued for a meeting of seceders from "abolition synagogues" who favored the organization of a society for christian communion free from political partisanship. The impetus of this feeling carried into existence a new organization called the "Christian Union" which within a year was able to send out a call to nearly twenty ministers to assemble in convention at Peoria.[8]

The democrats espoused and hotly defended the ministerial minority which abstained from politics and denounced the "degeneracy of the church" which allowed "political parsons"

[7] *Jacksonville Journal*, May 12, 1866; Adjutant General, *Report*, 1861-1866, 1:179. Haney had given thirty years of service to the ministry in Illinois and in September, 1866, preached the centennary sermon of American Methodism at Lexington. Ryan, "Antislavery Struggle in Illinois as it Affected the Methodist Episcopal Church," Illinois State Historical Society, *Transactions*, 1913, p. 75.

[8] *Chicago Times*, October 13, 1863, January 22, 1864; *Carthage Republican*, November 12, 1863; *Illinois State Register*, July 27, 1864; *Ottawa Free Trader*, November 26, 1864; *Canton Weekly Register*, December 19, 1864.

to outlaw "ministers who have conscientious scruples against preaching niggerism in the pulpit."[9] "It looks very much to an outsider," said the *State Register*, October 11, 1863, "as if the members of the conference, who approved of the desecration of the church in the manner stated, have their minds more upon the negro and politics, than upon religion and the salvation of souls." "Descending to the low squabbles of pot-house demagogues," commented the *St. Louis Republican*, "they have willfully placed themselves on the level with those who make politics their trade, or with those miserable creatures, found in some communities, who take delight in stirring up contentions among their neighbors."[10]

Whether this was spiritual degeneracy or the finest religious ecstacy, at any rate all denominations greeted the return of peace with an outpouring of old-time religion. Early in January and February, 1866, the meetings, followed by wholesale conversions, began and continued throughout the year. Never since the great revivals of 1858 had so many come to inquire, "what must we do to be saved?" At Springfield, which became the center of this great awakening with meetings at the state capitol and noon prayer meetings in the ward schoolhouses, the clergy, in October, called upon the people of the state to join in a five days prayer meeting to invoke "an outpouring of the Holy spirit upon the churches and people throughout the State."[11] The result was a great gathering of christians which aroused tremendous enthusiasm. All denominations made great gains during this bonanza year.

In contrast to the Methodists, Baptists, Congregationalists, and Christians, who quietly persisted along old lines of progress, was the internal strife that beset the other large denominations. Efforts were made to calm the conflicting forces tear-

---

[9] *Chicago Times*, October 12, 21, 1863; *Belleville Democrat*, October 17, November 7, 1863.
[10] *Cairo Democrat*, October 22, 1863. More complaint was made in 1866 when the Illinois Methodist conference bitterly arraigned President Johnson on political grounds. *Belleville Democrat*, October 13, 1866; *Ottawa Weekly Republican*, October 18, 1866; *Chicago Tribune*, October 31, 1866.
[11] This meeting had been called after consultation with representatives of all evangelical denominations throughout the state. *Illinois State Register*, April 11, 14, 1866; *Chicago Evening Journal*, May 10, 1866; *Joliet Signal*, October 30, 1866; *Chicago Tribune*, November 12, 1866; *Ottawa Weekly Republican*, November 15, 1866.

ing at the vitals of Presbyterianism. In 1865 even the old school synod for northern Illinois ratified the action of the General Assembly in refusing fellowship with unrepentant clergymen and laymen who had participated in the rebellion and who considered slavery a divine institution.[12] The next year Cyrus H. McCormick, an influential layman, began his labors to bring about a reunion of the northern and southern wings; the most definite response came from a southern Illinois Presbyterian convention at Centralia early in 1868, attended by representatives of the old school, new school, and the united and reformed branches, which approved of the so-called "Philadelphia basis" of union. In 1869 the question of reuniting the "new" and "old school" Presbyterians, after a division of thirty years, was decided affirmatively by the presbyteries.[13]

In the meantime the Episcopal diocese of Illinois was torn by the struggle between the high churchmen led by the rigid disciplinarian, Bishop Whitehouse, and the low church party which objected both to extremes of ritualism and to the introduction of cathedral worship. A climax was reached when the Reverend Charles E. Cheney of Chicago, a spokesman of the liberal forces, was severely disciplined before the bishop's court, although the case was later reviewed in Cheney's favor in a civil court. Out of this controversy grew the organization of the Reformed Episcopal Church under the leadership of Associate Bishop David Cummins of Kentucky, first known to Chicagoans through an anti-ritualistic sermon which he delivered during the controversy.[14]

The Catholics made progress in spite of the contentions that developed under the later years of Bishop Duggan's administration. Over one-half of the population of Chicago was Catholic; yet this included almost entirely persons of foreign birth or parentage since the increase was largely the result of immigration. One of the problems of the church was to Americanize the congregations; the Irish, however,

---

[12] *Galena Gazette*, October 24, clipped in *Chicago Tribune*, October 27, 1865.
[13] *Chicago Evening Journal*, May 16, 1866; *Jacksonville Journal*, March 2, 1868; *Ottawa Free Trader*, November 13, 1869.
[14] *Chicago Tribune*, July 15, 22, 29, August 4, 1869; *Belleville Advocate*, June 18, 1869; Andreas, *History of Chicago*, 2:412-415; 3:786-789.

often objected to the assignment of a priest who was not himself an Irishman.

The Catholics labored not only under the difficulty of internal heterogeneity but also of external criticism. In 1867 considerable anti-Catholic feeling developed in Illinois when the Reverend J. G. White of Jacksonville, a fearless champion of protestantism, went about the state lecturing on "Romanism." In Quincy he was disturbed at his first lecture and actually prevented by a hostile mob from delivering the rest of his series there. Mayor Pitman, a democrat, was appealed to for protection but he instructed the city marshal to prevent the lecture; Governor Oglesby, however, declared that the right of free speech should be maintained. White as well as several other "radical" protestant ministers continued to give his lectures in the following years with the result that disturbances took place at Bloomington in 1868 and Springfield in 1869.[15]

In general, however, the spirit of toleration was abroad. When colonies of Mormons appeared in various parts of northern Illinois they were allowed to carry on their affairs without interference; hundreds of Mormons returned to the region of Nauvoo; and Joseph Smith, the younger, passed the closing years of his life as the Illinois leader at Plano, Kendall county. The liberal sects, like the Unitarians and Universalists, grew in strength and went their way unchallenged. Citizens of Du Quoin took pride in the fact that one of the local churches opened its doors to an "infidel lecturer," for a series of ten lectures; and among the advantages of their city they held none so priceless as the "enlarged views, or liberality of our citizens. . . . It makes little difference here whether a man is Mohammedan, Christian or a Jew; Democrat Conservative, moderate or radical Republican, so long as he goes upon his own way."[16] Into the liberal atmosphere of such a state Lincoln's views on religion could be injected without much of a shock. Early in 1870 at a time when there was considerable current discussion as to Lin-

[15] *Jacksonville Journal*, April 26, 1867; *Quincy Whig*, April 24, 1867; *Chicago Tribune*, April 27, 1867, July 28, 1868, March 29, 1869; *Canton Weekly Register*, April 3, 1868; *Ottawa Weekly Republican*, August 26, 1869.
[16] *Du Quoin Tribune*, March 31, 1870.

coln's views, W. H. Herndon, his law partner, issued a lengthy newspaper statement on the matter. Lincoln he declared "*did not* believe in a special creation, ... he *did not* believe that the Bible was a special revelation from God, ... he *did not* believe in miracles, ... he *did not* believe that Jesus was the Christ, the Son of God, as the christian world contends." Lincoln was, he explained, a theist living in his moments of melancholy and gloom "on the borderland between theism and atheism." "I maintain that Mr. Lincoln was a deeply religious man at all times and places, in spite of his transient doubts," he declared. The fact that few were impressed with any incompatibility in the statement is a striking instance of growing tolerance.

One of the most significant moral educational issues of the late sixties was the question of woman's rights, which the Civil War revived in a more practical form than had ever appeared in Illinois — one in which forward-looking preachers were glad to coöperate with such assailants of revealed religion as Robert Ingersoll. At the outbreak of war the abstract question was abandoned while the "gentler sex" turned its energies into constructive work in the cause of the union; and after years of hard toil in the fields, in shops, in hospitals, and in relief work, the women felt that they had indeed earned a claim to consideration in the civil life of the state equal to that of the liberated Negro. Pioneer women editors, preachers, and physicians, emissaries from the east, appeared to demonstrate the ability of women to compete with the men for their traditional monopolies. Mrs. Mary A. Livermore, the author and reformer, was the active agent in the editing of her husband's *New Covenant*, the Universalist organ; she travelled to the hospitals and camps of the Mississippi valley as representative of the United States Sanitary Commission and in many ways prepared for her career as a woman's suffrage lecturer. Meantime Mrs. Myra Bradwell, as editor of the Chicago *Legal News*, and Mrs. Mary L. Walker, of the *Sorosis* and later the *Agitator*, became active propagandists for the cause of equal rights.

The new issue first gained recognition in 1867 and 1869 when state laws were enacted protecting married women in their property rights. Then, in spite of considerable objection, the trustees of the Illinois Industrial University on March 8, 1870, finally voted to permit the registration of women students. In February, 1870, after Governor Palmer, on account of legal obstacles, rejected the application of Mrs. Bradwell to be appointed a notary public, Mrs. Amelia Hobbs, probably the first woman chosen to hold office in Illinois, was elected a justice of the peace in Jersey county.[17]

It was commonly believed, however, that the caucus was not a fitting field for woman's endeavors, though women as well as men were ready to ask whether there was any ground in reason or justice why they should not vote.[18] In November, 1867, Susan B. Anthony, in coming to Illinois for a series of lectures which aroused wide interest, initiated an active suffrage propaganda that was aided in later years by Mary A. Livermore, Anna Dickinson, and other pioneers of the movement. The Illinois advocates of suffrage included Kate M. Doggett, Dr. Mary J. Safford, and Mrs. C. T. F. Stringer, and among the men, Judge C. B. Waite, Judge James B. Bradwell, Robert Ingersoll, as well as a number of clergymen. Soon woman suffrage associations were founded in various parts of the state; Judge Bradwell became chairman of the Illinois Woman Suffrage Association which conducted an active campaign to secure the elective franchise for women in the next constitutional convention. Strong local organizations were formed in all the large cities in the early months of 1870; and a state suffrage convention at Springfield, February 8-9, addressed an appeal to the constitutional convention to deal " as justly and fairly with the women of the State as . . . . by the negroes of the State."[19] Yet although the republicans toyed with the suffrage question, the only clear-cut indorsement received from any political group was from the Irish republican national convention at Chicago in July, 1869.[20] This, however, had little significance, and in the convention the woman

---

[17] *Chicago Tribune,* December 31, 1869; *Champaign County Union and Gazette,* February 23, 1870.
[18] E. C. Larned to Trumbull, March 10, 1866, Trumbull manuscripts.
[19] *Illinois State Register,* February 8, 10, 1870; *Illinois State Journal,* February 10, 1870.
[20] *Chicago Tribune,* July 7, 1869.

suffrage movement was consigned to the realm of futile propaganda.

More formal education was making progress upon the foundations laid in the fifties. The opportunity for education was eagerly embraced, and school attendance nearly doubled in the decade; some there were who would completely democratize the school system on the principle of compulsory education. Though this proposal was in advance of the times, in general champions of education now found their labors as easy as they had been difficult a dozen years before; it was a simple matter to secure from the constitutional convention of 1862 a satisfactory article on education and suggestions by Superintendent of Public Instruction Newton Bateman were placed before the convention of 1870 with every probability of a fair and favorable consideration.[21]

The more important gains came in securing physical conditions favorable to a greater degree of educational efficiency. The little red schoolhouse had had its day; and, with a steady reduction in the number of skeptics, the "big schoolhouse" policy adopted in Chicago several years before became general throughout the cities of the state. The increase of facilities, however, could scarcely keep pace with the new demand. Chicago in one year expended $341,145 for providing additional school accommodations, yet the enrollment increased so that "we are relatively worse off now than we were a year ago"[22]— even though in order to furnish educational opportunities to those unable to attend day sessions, several free night schools were inaugurated. In 1869 the Chicago board of education went to the legislature to secure authorization for a loan of $850,000 to build additional schoolhouses; and when, to quiet the complaint of extravagance it reduced its request to $500,000 it was with the proviso that no schoolhouse costing more than fifteen thousand dollars should be built until all the children in the city should be provided with school accommodations.

Jacksonville, with very generous provision for the educa-

[21] *Journal of the Constitutional Convention,* 1862, p. 766, 1093; *Chicago Tribune,* July 30, 1867.
[22] *Ibid.,* October 20, 1865, April 27, 1868, January 14, 18, 1869.

tional interests of the city, continued to live up to its reputation as the "Athens of the west," while Alton public schools attained an excellency that rendered private schools unprofitable.[23] Cairo discarded the "wretched rookery" worth only $400, which had been made to provide accommodation for eighty pupils; and within three years by substituting two splendid three-story brick structures and a spacious one-story frame building, caring for the educational needs of eight hundred children, the young city felt entitled to boast of one of the best public school systems in the northwest.[24] Belleville, although providing efficient instruction, could not display a single school building; the children were taught in "underground caverns [church basements] and rickety shanties." The *Illinois Teacher* boldly scored Belleville and Bloomington as disgracefully negligent in school accommodations.[25]

Among the teachers a growing professionalization was evident; county and state associations and institutes were managed with considerable smoothness, and a southern Illinois educational association was organized in 1868 with one of its purposes to agitate in favor of a southern Illinois normal school. The compensation for teaching was utterly inadequate; in spite of the fact that a six-month school session was the rule, and in the face of the war-time prices, salaries of $30 and $40 a month were common. One school director "made himself a name in history" by engaging a woman for the highest wages ever paid by his district to a man teacher, $30 a month. Cairo, it is true, paid wages of $100 to $150 to its male administrator teachers and $40 to $60 to the women, but the average monthly wage in 1868 was $42.40 for men and $32.80 for women.[26]

Much credit for improvement in the efficiency of the school system is due to Newton Bateman, who with only a two-year

---

[23] Norton, *Resources of Alton in 1873*, p. 28.
[24] *Cairo Gazette*, June 4, 1863; *Cairo Democrat*, November 14, 1864, November 13, 1866, September 10, December 4, 1867.
[25] *Illinois Teacher* clipped in *Belleville Advocate*, March 18, 1864.
[26] Nine month schools appealed to many as offering an opportunity to secure better teachers. *Du Quoin Tribune*, July 16, 1868, March 24, 1870; *Cairo Democrat*, November 14, 1866, May 15, 1868; *Jonesboro Gazette*, December 5, 1868; *Belleville Advocate*, August 6, 1869; *Cairo Evening Bulletin*, January 18, 1869; *Rockford Gazette*, February 18, 1869.

interruption served as state superintendent of public instruction for fourteen years between 1859 and 1875; his seven biennial reports constitute one of the chief sources of the knowledge of the early educational development of this state. For three years he served as editor of *The Illinois Teacher* and was one of a committee of three which prepared the bill adopted by congress creating the national bureau of education.

Higher education underwent considerable improvement in the Civil War decade. High schools became more common, although a few communities like Decatur could be found without either high school, academy, or seminary. Almost all the colleges of the state weathered the trials of the days when the students left the class room for the battlefield; and when, as in the case of Quincy College, even the school building was requisitioned by the government for use as a hospital. Politics in college made headway under war conditions: sometimes tense feelings gave rise to complicated situations, as when a professor of Eureka College ordered a student to remove a democratic badge and was sustained by his colleagues only to be forced to retract when the expulsion of twenty-seven students was followed by the withdrawal of as many more.[27]

The State Normal University went through the decade in a flourishing condition both in its finances and in the number of its students, of whom there came in 1868 to be 350. In 1869 the demand of the southern counties for a Southern Illinois Normal University bore fruit in a law for its establishment. After competitive bidding between rival points, the institution was located at Carbondale. In 1867 Cook county established at Blue Island the first county normal school in the state, but in 1869 it was transferred to Englewood.

In the storm and stress of Civil War, the dreams of Jonathan B. Turner and his associates for the foundation of an Illinois Industrial University found realization. After the defeat of the Morrill bill by the veto of President Buchanan, it long appeared to many advocates of agricultural education that the state would have to furnish the financial support for any undertaking that could be launched; accordingly, committees of the state agricultural and horticultural societies issued

[27] *Peoria Mail* clipped in *Belleville Democrat,* November 28, 1863.

a joint call for a convention to meet in the interest of agricultural education at Bloomington, June 27, 1860. Turner, however, who had not given up his scheme for a federal land grant system of colleges, attended the convention and presented his views; as a result, the resolutions adopted by the convention while urging the claims of agricultural and industrial education in all institutions of popular education, approved of the renewal of the agitation for a federal land grant.[28]

In July, 1862, news arrived of the enactment of the Morrill land grant measure, and great things were promised for the state; the legislature in the session of 1863 formally accepted the state's quota of 480,000 acres. As it had become evident that there would be a struggle between the advocates of industrial education and the supporters of existing institutions, in which the conservative forces would be strengthened by war conditions, a convention of agriculturists at Springfield, June 9, 1863, adopted a resolution presented by Jonathan B. Turner to defer the decision in regard to the proposed industrial university pending the collection of additional data for consideration by the next session of the assembly.[29] They also undertook to guarantee that the funds resulting from the congressional land grant should be devoted to the endowment, support, and maintenance of but one industrial college, independent of any existing institution, where a new and radical experiment in industrial education could be carried out. This program was announced in local and state agricultural conventions and in connection with the political contests of 1864.[30]

The advocates of classical education, however, wanted to use the land grant, according to Turner, "for the purpose of paying the debts or enlarging the facilities of mere classical or sectarian institutions." When Governor Yates appointed their champions on a committee to consider the proper use of

[28] J. H. McChesney of the state geological survey at Springfield announced to the meeting that Chicago University had just appointed him to organize an agricultural department; a year later, indeed, the course was announced to be given in connection with an experimental farm at Cottage Hill, fifteen miles out of Chicago. *Belleville Advocate*, June 22, 1860; *Illinois State Register*, June 30, 1860; *Aurora Beacon*, July 5, 12, 1860; *Illinois State Journal*, October 15, 1861; *Prairie Farmer*, September 19, 1861.
[29] *Ibid.*, June 20, 1863; *Illinois State Journal*, January 1, May 14, 1863; *Illinois State Register*, May 17, June 11, 1863.
[30] *Prairie Farmer*, January 16, February 6, September 10, October 1, 8, 1864.

the land grant, the agriculturists raised their voices in insistent protest. The editor of the *Prairie Farmer* turned his ridicule upon the "farce that 'our noble governor' and his friends are engaged in introducing for the amusement and *instruction* of the people." With clever mimicry he ushered in the actors: "'First come, first served.' Walk up, gentlemen, in regular order, and help yourself. Come, Alton, and Galesburg, and Jacksonville, and Chicago, and Bloomington, and La Salle, come up all you halt and maimed institutions, of whatever sect or denomination; here's a great sugar-plum to be divided between you. . . . . And you, million and a half of farmers of Illinois, you who never before saw in the dim distance the glitter of a dollar intended by the government for your especial benefit; . . . . just give us your *views*, and while we are deciphering the chirography of your stiffened fingers, the plum shall all be swallowed up by those having *claims* upon it." Turner was too much disappointed by the evidence that his life work was about to be undone to find any humor in the situation; "I am sick of this damnable trifling with every interest of the farmer," he burst forth, "making him only the hewer of wood and drawer of water for the miserable 'cusses' who manage by chicanery and dishonesty to usurp all places of trust and responsibility which should be occupied by honest men."[31] The advocates of agricultural education thereupon agreed to support for office only candidates favorable to their views; under this pressure, Governor Yates not only added the names of J. B. Turner and C. R. Griggs, of Urbana, to the committee but, together with Oglesby, candidate for governor, indorsed the scheme of the agriculturists.

Various forces, however, combined to endanger the ideal that Turner had for over twenty years held before the farmers and mechanics of Illinois. The "sectarians" in general were extremely industrious; Shurtleff and Knox colleges made an ill-concealed attempt to secure a division of the federal funds by transformation into the agricultural colleges of southern and northern Illinois, while Jacksonville boosters hoped to build the new institution about Illinois College. Chicago was

[31] *Ibid.*, September 10, 1864.

willing to join hands with some downstate point to split the university into a mechanical branch at Chicago and an agricultural college in a rural region.[32] This scheme appealed to the local ambitions of other cities — Bloomington, Peoria, Springfield, and the twin cities of Champaign and Urbana.

The agricultural forces of the state had appointed a number of committees which came together at Springfield in December, 1864, and, under the direction of Turner, drafted a bill for a land grant industrial university. Although the claims of rival points were presented, they were ignored by the committees; Turner then again carried the day for an undivided institution.[33] When, however, this measure was presented before the legislature, it was attacked by all its opponents, and action in the assembly of 1865 was found impossible.

The next two years were years of great activity by all forces. The agriculturists, continuing their meetings at Bloomington, authorized the preparation of another "farmer's bill;" the college presidents of the state, summoned together at Chicago in October, 1866, agreed to petition the legislature for a division of the funds among a select number of the colleges already in existence.[34] The plan for a division of the funds, however, was easily defeated; and on January 25, 1867, an act provided for the location of the university on the basis of competitive bidding.

This action brought to a climax the demoralizing wirepulling, logrolling, legislative scramble at Springfield. Through the masterful manipulations of the Champaign county representative at the capital, Clark R. Griggs, the twin cities of Champaign and Urbana secured the location on a bid of $285,000, though it was exceeded by all the other active competitors. The organization of the university in its newly chosen home was authorized on February 28, 1867. The board of trustees, including the governor, the state superintendent of public instruction, and the president of the State Agricultural Society, who were *ex officio* trustees, elected John M. Gregory of Kala-

---

[32] *Prairie Farmer*, August 6, 27, 1864; *Chicago Times*, January 13, 1865.
[33] *Illinois State Journal*, December 7, 1864; *Central Illinois Gazette*, December 9, 1864; *Prairie Farmer*, December 17, 1864.
[34] *Chicago Tribune*, October 30, November 1, 22, 1866; *Jacksonville Journal*, November 2, 1866.

mazoo, Michigan, "regent" or president; and the institution was formally opened on March 11, 1868, with an enrollment of seventy-seven students and four instructors.[35]

Grave doubt existed as to whether a great university could rise from the monotonous prairies of eastern Illinois. Turner, the educational pioneer, was bitterly disappointed with the choice of Urbana and with the prospects for his pet project. It was properly pointed out, however, that the best interests of the state now required the promotion of the establishment at Urbana, and the steady application of this policy has produced a great middle west state university.[36]

---

[35] *Reports General Assembly*, 1867, 1:443-445; 1869, 2:1-352.

[36] The Chicago interests still urged a polytechnical branch in that city and in 1868 offered the university $250,000 in bonds for the establishment of such a branch; although the university accepted the offer, the city found itself unable to carry out its proposal. *Chicago Tribune*, May 29, June 1, August 4, November 19, 20, 1868; *Illinois State Journal*, November 23, 1868. In 1870 Turner and Jesse Fell and Bloomington friends labored to influence the constitutional convention to establish a first-class university.

XXI. PLAY AND THE PRESS

THE use of leisure by a given society furnishes a measure of the height of its culture; surely nothing is a better index of the crudity of the frontier than the simple pastimes of the pioneer when temporarily freed from his task of conquering the wilderness. When, therefore, after three decades of statehood, the atmosphere of the frontier passed from the settled portions of Illinois, the refined amusements of a more highly civilized society filtered in to shape the cultural development of the state.

True, the wedding, with its festivities, the funeral, to which friends were invited by formal printed invitations, and the revival with its pervasive appeal still relieved the monotony of the rural community. A stirring reminder of the effective use of the rifle in the hands of the pioneer, who each week had devoted a day to target practice at the head of a turkey kept for the occasion, still persisted in the annual hunt of Upper Alton; the rival teams often brought in a bag of two thousand pieces of game which furnished a lavish barbecue for the assembled townspeople.[1] Another survival of an early sport was found in the fall races with their entry fees in corn. As late as 1851, too, Chicagoans found a touch of bygone days in the band of Potawatomi encamped on the prairie outside the city; for "their tents gleaming in the twilight, and the red glow of their camp fires, and their blanketed forms passing here and there, render it quite like a border scene, in earlier days."[2]

Into the towns, however, more highly developed amusements found their way to meet expanding needs. In these overgrown villages there was still much opportunity for continued expression of zestful living, and a conscious demand began to

[1] *Alton Courier,* October 10, 1853, September 28, 1854; *Belleville Advocate,* September 12, 1850.
[2] *Chicago Daily Journal,* March 29, 1851.

arise for the satisfaction of more directly cultural aspirations. This made for a hospitality toward all devices that promised to clear from the intellectual horizon some of the provincialism of the frontier.

Thus it was they embraced the opportunity to learn something of the surrounding country by taking the steamboat out on Lake Michigan and up or down the Illinois and Mississippi rivers. In the summer of 1849 two boats began to run between Galena and the falls of St. Anthony carrying visitors to Fort Snelling, to "a town called St. Paul's, which contains five hundred inhabitants," and to nearby fishing and hunting grounds.[3] With the completion of railroad lines and the celebrations that followed in each case, rail excursion trips were planned and well patronized.

In most instances, however, the outside world was brought to the eager seeker after diverson. Exhibits of wax figures, the forerunner of the dime museum, were financially successful and were carried from place to place. Picture exhibitions were arranged and extensively patronized—"Bayne's panorama," the "Panorama of Eden," the "Classical Panorama of Roman History," a "Panorama of China," and the "Moving Mirror of the Overland Route to California"—editors confidently recommended them to "those who have an eye, and a heart for fine delineations of beautiful scenes in this world of ours."[4]

An increasing realization of the importance of native artistic self-expression became evident, and in 1859 Chicago had so developed that it could plan a formal art exhibition. G. P. A. Healy, "the very pioneer of true artists in the Northwest," in 1862 initiated a movement to establish a free art gallery in Chicago; in 1865 it secured incorporation papers and organized to facilitate the collection of funds. In 1868 the "Academy of Design" brought together the largest collection of works of art ever exhibited in the northwest. By that time the *Art Journal* of Chicago was acknowledged to be "in some respects, superior to any other published in the United States."[5]

[3] *Illinois Journal*, February 14, August 7, 1849.
[4] *Chicago Daily Journal*, March 31, May 22, 1851.
[5] *New York Herald*, March 11, clipped in *Chicago Tribune*, March 14, 1868; *Chicago Evening Journal*, November 17, 1865.

Over the dusty roads of midsummer, the circus came to town: it might be Rockwell and Company's Mammoth Circus with two hundred men and horses, "the best managed and only perfectly organized Equestrian Establishment in the United States;" perhaps it was Welch, Delavan, and Nathan's; or Raymond and Company's Mammoth Menagerie; or E. F. and J. Mabies' Grand Olympic Arena; or Crane and Company's Great Oriental Circus; Dan Rice's Hippodrome, or any one of a host of others. Five of these performed at Springfield in two seasons, each one usually giving two daily performances in tents accommodating fifteen hundred to two thousand people. There was a magic about their appeal to old and young alike; no matter how wretched the performance, the newspapers heralded them with enthusiasm, and the people paid their annual tribute. At length criticism began; a Jacksonville paper made bold to ask: "We would like to know on what pretext the people is asked to patronize these performances. Is it because there will be a mutual benefit derived in a pecuniary point of view? .... Is it because they come to elevate our morals, or improve our intellects?"[6] When in 1853 Barnum's Grand Colossal Museum and Menagerie toured Illinois, papers in the northern part denounced his show for not coming up to the promises of the posters, but the papers of the state capital generously pronounced it "more than worth the price."[7]

During the fifties culture was imported into the state through the lecture platform by an array of talent. Horace Greeley, "the fearless champion of the masses, the poor and down-trodden of all nations," came to Illinois for frequent lectures. Emerson, Henry Ward Beecher, John Mitchell, the Irish patriot, Frederick S. Douglass, the former slave, Elihu Burritt, the advocate of universal peace through a congress of nations, George D. Prentice, the Louisville poet, humorist-editor, and politician — all carried their gospel to the prairie state. Lucy Stone, the woman's rights advocate, was offered $100 in 1853 to speak at Alton in the largest hall with "a larger audience than we can get into it" but was compelled

---

[6] *Morgan Journal* clipped in *Illinois State Register*, May 13, 1852.
[7] *Ibid.*, September 1, October 6, 1853.

to decline; a fortnight later, however, she lectured in Chicago on "the Bible position of woman" and on "social and political disabilities of woman."[8]

Special lectures on astronomy, electricity, physiology, and chemistry always seemed to attract attention. War times interrupted this lecture work but with the close of the struggle Wendell Phillips and Julia Ward Howe favored Illinois with their visits while William Lloyd Garrison toured the country to announce the discontinuance of the *Liberator* as having performed its mission. In 1869 Mark Twain, already "the well known humorist," lectured in Chicago on the "American Vandal abroad." It is doubtful, however, whether such lectures met a warmer welcome than the spiritualist lectures and mediums who after 1850 were busily distributing their propaganda; their influence was evidenced by the commotion which followed the numerous instances of "spirit rappings" reported in the early fifties.

Illinois also had a coterie of busy lecturers of her own. Probably Jonathan B. Turner of Jacksonville College was one of the busiest, turning from his propaganda on industrial education to speak on the "millenium of labor," on "wisdom and knowledge," or on some literary or religious topic. Editors, clergymen, and politicians were drafted for lecture work. Abraham Lincoln was one of the conscripts who got off easily; although he was scheduled for a lecture in Jacksonville in 1854 and in 1859 delivered one there on "discoveries and inventions," yet on the eve of his presidential nomination in 1860, he was able to say that he had "never got up but one lecture, and that I think rather a poor one."[9]

The wide range of lecture offerings was made possible by the library associations and the literary institutes that appeared in every town in the early fifties and established reading rooms and organized lecture courses. In 1850 there were 152 libraries in the state but only 33 were public libraries. These were scattered over northern Illinois, with three each in Cook, Du Page, and Adams counties. Quincy had a ten-year old

[8] *Aurora Beacon*, May 1, 1851; *Alton Courier*, December 23, 30, 1853; *Chicago Weekly Democrat*, January 7, 14, 1854.
[9] *Morgan Journal*, January 26, 1854; *Belleville Advocate*, February 23, 1859; Tracy, *Uncollected Letters of Abraham Lincoln*, 141.

library of 2,000 volumes. Then began a widespread movement for local libraries; in 1852, Springfield and Alton organized library associations. The forerunner of these more ambitious undertakings was the lyceum or debating society, a democratic force for intellectual improvement that required little in the way of talent or material equipment. Sometimes its members attempted ambitious discussions on education, temperance, or "Resolved that the geological assumption of the earth's immense pre-Adamic age is supported by reliable data" with a clergyman representing each side of the question.[10]

All these movements paved the way for more serious achievements. In 1856 Chicagoans organized the Chicago Historical Society, which after a year reported a collection of eleven thousand volumes, largely the gifts of members and friends.[11] In 1858 upon the recommendation of the State Teachers' Association an Illinois Natural History Society was organized at Bloomington to conduct a scientific survey. Chicago in this case again had in 1857 anticipated the state with the establishment of the Chicago Academy of Natural Sciences. The state society, however, tried a new departure by engaging a traveling agent to arouse interest by public lectures and to collect specimens for the museum at Normal University. In 1870 Illinois could boast of seven historical, literary, or scientific libraries; by that time 3,705 public libraries with 924,545 volumes placed Illinois ahead of all the states except New York and Pennsylvania.[12]

In the course of time a steady improvement was made in the musical and dramatic entertainment offered to Illinoisians. In the forties Chicago and Springfield had theaters in which local and traveling companies offered their performances; in Chicago Uncle Tom's Cabin drew unprecedented crowds whenever presented. The other towns had few theatrical facilities

---

[10] *Ottawa Free Trader*, November 4, 1854; Johnson, *Illinois in the Fifties*. Eighty-six sunday school libraries with 12,829 volumes constituted a strong force for education by reading.

[11] An effort to organize an Illinois historical society in 1848 ended in failure. *Chicago Daily Democratic Press*, April 4, 1856; *Chicago Press and Tribune*, November 26, 1857.

[12] Including private libraries there were 13,570 institutions with 3,323,914 volumes. The public libraries included one state, seven historical, literary, and scientific; fifty-three town or city, seventy-nine circulating, 135 law, 1,122 school or college, and 2,080 sabbath school. *Ninth Census*, 1:474 ff.

and had to be content with Shakespearean readings, with amateur performances, or with the efforts of roving performers. With the fifties the choice of entertainers included General Tom Thumb, "Yankee" Silsbee, the impersonator, Winchell, the humorist, Antonio Kaspar, the magician and juggler, and their kind, who were universally received with favor. "The Fakir of Siva," who for three days in 1852 held *soirées mystérieuses* at the Springfield courthouse before capacity audiences, left town without paying his bills; but most of the people regretted his departure for different reasons than those that motivated his creditors.[13]

Until 1857 Rice's Theater monopolized the field of the English drama in Chicago, but then soon found itself compelled to yield the field to the modern theater erected by James H. McVicker. In both Chicago and Springfield the Germans were credited with being "far more enterprising than the native portion of our population in the way of amusements."[14] In 1859 they supported three successful theaters in Chicago beside numerous so-called concert halls, and in Springfield they were more persistent in providing creditable dramatic entertainment than the English speaking citizens.

Entertainment of all sorts was placed at the disposal of music-loving citizens, though families and companies of strolling singers or musicians pretty well monopolized the field until 1850. The best known groups were the Antoni, the Newhall, and the Peak families, and the Columbians, and the Alleghanians, "universally acknowledged to be the best of the kind now travelling in the United States."[15] Negro minstrels — the Campbell Troupe of Ethiopian Performers, the Sable Melodists, the Algerines, and others were always greeted with marked approbation. Instrumentalists of all sorts were also favorably received; in 1853 eight hundred people went to the Springfield courthouse to hear the Swiss bell ringers, whereas on the previous night only some twenty

[13] *Illinois State Register*, April 29, May 27, 1852.
[14] *Illinois State Journal*, November 30, December 3, 1861; *Chicago Democrat*, August 15, 1859.
[15] The Peak family terminated a thirty year musical career in 1869 by which time they were said to have accumulated a million and a half dollars. *Cairo Evening Bulletin*, June 28, 1869; *Ottawa Free Trader*, November 30, 1850.

persons attended "the able and instructive lecture of Prof. Daggy upon the Science of Astronomy."[16]

On occasions the people of Illinois were favored with really rare musical treats. In 1851 the "Jenny Lind mania" prevailed throughout the state, and the merchants and business men of central Illinois on a sudden impulse went to St. Louis to hear the concert of the Swedish nightingale. Attempts to arrange a concert in Chicago in the later part of the year resulted in failure. The following season Ole Bull, the renowned violinist, attracted many Illinoisians to St. Louis. On several occasions in the years that followed not only he but also Adelina Patti and Marietta Piccolomini submitted their offerings to the music lovers of the state.

The effect was to stimulate effort at musical self-expression, and instruction in every department of music received its beginning. The music teacher and the dealer in musical instruments began to thrive; although it was still possible in 1853 to say that in Menard county just outside Springfield only one piano could be found, yet at the same time, "Professor" VanMeter at Alton was conducting a course in music with 500 pupils, 150 of whom performed in graduation recitals before crowded houses.[17] Bands were organized in various towns, although Grierson's band of Jacksonville was unique in that the members "played by the *card* instead of their own conception of what each particular piece of music ought to have been."[18]

These efforts at musical expression began gradually to take on an organized form. In 1850 there was a "Union Musical Association" in Morgan county; and, receiving an inspiration from the numerous German musical unions, philharmonic or choral societies began to appear in different towns. At Springfield in 1852 an Illinois musical convention held a several days session before which Professor Johnson of Boston delivered lectures and gave instruction; after that date such conventions were held with some regularity.

Chicago naturally became the musical center of Illinois. In the early fifties, when the Germans there had several musical

---

[16] *Illinois Journal*, September 24, 1853.
[17] *Illinois State Register*, September 22, 1853; *Alton Courier*, February 10, 1853.
[18] *Illinois State Register*, July 1, 1852.

societies, Julius Dyhrenfurth was laboring to develop a local orchestra. In 1852 the Chicago Philharmonic Society was formed, but, like other efforts, was not financially successful. The turning of the tide came in 1858: Julius Unger had a successful season in charge of Chicago's first full orchestra, which Henry Abner had organized in 1857; the Musical Union for vocal and instrumental music was organized and secured a hall opposite the courthouse for meetings and institutes; a Mendelssohn society was organized to rehearse and present choruses from the German composers under the conductorship of A. W. Dahn; and after two previous experimental seasons, Chicago came in 1858 to give grand opera a regular place upon its musical program.

The Chicago Musical Union steadily grew in its influence; at different times it produced the "Creation," "Elijah," and other oratorios, besides miscellaneous choral concerts. In 1859 it successfully presented the "Messiah" to celebrate the centenary of Handel's death. There were then two music halls in the city, one capable of seating over fifteen hundred people, in which musical entertainment was provided almost every night.[19]

The war suspended active musical development, although the Philharmonic Society gave a regular series of concerts, and progress was made in operatic production. With the return of peace, Chicago had not only the most brilliant amusement year in its history, but the first distinctive western opera season. Crosby's Opera House was opened for a notable season, and the impresario Grau was finally given full recognition for the brilliant array of talent with which he made the city acquainted. The honors were also shared by Leonard Grover's German operatic troupe which held forth at McVicker's theater, while a three weeks engagement of English opera opened in the hall of the Academy of Music. Another brilliant year followed in 1868, with sixteen weeks of English, German, and Italian opera and French *opéra bouffe*, with Edwin Booth and Edwin Forrest on the boards, and with a series of concerts inaugurated by the Orchestral Union, an organization

[19] *Chicago Press and Tribune*, October 13, December 24, 1858, April 30, 1859; *Chicago Democrat*, August 15, 1859.

built upon the ruins of the Philharmonic Society.[20] In 1868, also, Chicago was honored by its selection for the sixteenth annual festival of the North American Sängerbund, which was formally inaugurated "with speeches, processions, fireworks, artillery and music."[21] This festival was conducted by Hans Balatka of Chicago, the chosen leader not only of the German musical societies but of the Philharmonic Society and of the Oratorio Society.

Musical organizations catered to the social instincts of certain selected and highly trained groups; general opportunities for good fellowship were contributed by the social organizations that came into vogue. Club life had not found a real place as yet, but fraternal orders and secret societies became very popular.[22] The natural clannishness of a group having common traditions expressed itself not only in St. Andrew's, St. George's, and Hibernian societies, in the Société Française, and German clubs, but also in New England societies and Sons of the Pilgrims, the Excelsior Society, composed of natives of New York, the Sons of Penn, and similar groups that held at least annual meetings which involved considerable ceremony following sumptuous banquets.

The mystery of the secret society had an especial charm. Usually it was the Masonic order or the Odd Fellows, who were to be found in most of the cities; but even more compelling was a society which issued notices that "The Q. Z. K. in the ⊂⊃⊂⊃, 2° 38 3/4' will meet at the 6th rendezvous at the hour of the changes on the regular night of the calls of the Hing Hong."[23] This mysterious element was one explanation of the remarkable popularity of the know nothing political order and of the Sons of Temperance.

The appeal of the secret society was resented by the clergy, whom President Blanchard of Knox College aroused in a pam-

---

[20] *Chicago Tribune*, December 2, 1865, November 20, 1868. Dr. Florence Ziegfeld opened the Chicago Academy of Music in 1867 and in 1868 gave his first pupil's recital.
[21] *Ibid.*, June 17, 1868.
[22] In the rural districts the general store and post office continued as "a village club." See Johnson, *Illinois in the Fifties*.
[23] *Ottawa Free Trader*, February 9, 1850; *Illinois State Register*, October 2, 1851. There were ninety-four Odd Fellow lodges and 4,035 contributing members in Illinois in 1851.

phlet entitled "An Argument on Secret Societies;" he classed not only the social orders but the Sons of Temperance as "anti-Republican in their tendencies and subversive of the principles both of the Natural and Revealed Religion."[24] Blanchard abandoned this foe, however, to fight the battles of freedom; and not until after the Civil War and after fifteen years of silence, did he launch the new crusade; first he placed the Congregational General Association of Illinois on record as in opposition to secret societies, and then started an interdenominational movement which laid its plans to overthrow the secret order in conventions at Aurora in 1867 and at Chicago in 1869. Gradually, however, his opponents came out in direct attack upon "Blanchard's monomania;" and his propaganda, openly scored as an amusing pastime like barking at the moon, began to lose ground. The Masons, the special objects of attack, failed to decline in popularity and in 1869 boasted seven hundred lodges and over forty thousand members in Illinois.[25]

People began to step out into society in the cities, which became centers of gayety with banquets, balls, parties, and masquerades. The governor's levees set the pace for conservative folk; at a levee in honor of Douglas' reëlection to the senate in 1853 supper and music and dancing were generously provided for the 1,500 guests who attended. Soirées, cotillion parties, and balls were held periodically in every town with quadrilles, schottisches, polkas, and an occasional waltz before the supper interval. In 1854 the New Year's festival at Alton was a "promenade concert" with a band from St. Louis, to which seven hundred persons paid the admission of seventy-five cents and competed for seventy-five prizes.[26]

While the middle class was finding wholesome amusement along these lines, no provision met democratically the needs of all classes. For this reason the rougher elements and youths

---

[24] *Western Citizen*, October 1, 1850.
[25] *Chicago Evening Journal*, May 28, 1866; *Ottawa Weekly Republican*, June 7, 1866; *Chicago Tribune*, June 5, 1867, June 11, 1869; *Aurora Beacon*, October 3, November 7, 1867, June 17, 1869; *Joliet Signal*, June 29, July 20, 1869; *Cairo Evening Bulletin*, May 4, 1869.
[26] *Illinois State Register*, January 20, 1853; *Alton Courier*, January 2, 1854.

from fourteen to sixteen avidly responded to the appeal of the disreputable dance hall, which made its appearance in Chicago and spread to the other cities during the Civil War. The need which these dance halls emphasized caused some to advocate free places of public amusement in which innocent and elevating entertainment could be found. The idea of the modern institutional church appeared in a suggestion of a proposed "social union," "to combine religious teaching on the sabbath with weekly literary exercises, musical soirees, gymnastic performances, meetings for debate and political management, a library and reading room, social parlor, dramatic exhibitions, lectures, a museum, art hall, bathing rooms, refreshments, mineralogical cabinet, and chemical and philosophical apparatus;"[27] but such an institution was quite too ambitious for those days of long ago. It was nevertheless noted that "those cities which extend the largest amount of patronage to amusements, do the greatest amount of business and attract the most visitors."[28] Chicagoans, therefore, felt themselves justified in the expenditure of a half million dollars a year for the city's formally organized amusements.[29]

The rise of sport bore unique testimony to the departure of the frontier — to the need of formal exercise to take the place of the more strenuous physical demands imposed upon the pioneer. Military companies continued to attract the interest of youths who appreciated the magnetism of gay colored uniforms for the damsels; yet a declining interest was reflected in the growing demand for more active sport that organized athletics alone could satisfy. First came a transition period during the fifties, when the more exciting forms of sport were represented by a chess match played between the chess clubs of Chicago and Quincy by telegraph, pigeon-shooting matches, coincident with the formation of an Audubon club for the preservation of game, cricket games between teams from Chicago and Milwaukee, and the beginnings of pleasure boating and boat racing in Chicago. Chess was able to hold its own as a form of indoor amusement, but none of these out-of-

[27] *Chicago Tribune*, April 24, 1866.
[28] *Cairo Democrat*, October 1, 1863.
[29] *Ottawa Republican*, January 31, 1867.

door sports seized a firm democratic hold upon the sturdy westerner.

Although the rapidly growing population of Chicago encouraged experiments with gymnasiums on a commercial basis, yet even they had little real success; and when there was agitation in Alton for a gymnasium and for formal physical culture, the city fathers calmly shook their heads and pointed to the woodpiles in the back yards. Yet in 1859 Chicago youths, cadets in a local military company, were able to realize their ambition for a gymnasium which also served as a drill hall.[30] So also the Young Men's Literary Association of Ottawa in 1865 undertook a campaign for a "gymnasium and reading room;" Rockford moved in the same direction two years later; and the young men of Cairo established a gymnasium in 1869.

Meanwhile other forms of diversion were gaining ground; in 1869 the "cue-rious fact" was related that Chicago spent two millions of dollars a year on billiards.[31] The first billiard tournament in Chicago, which was the second in the United States, was held in April, 1863; five years later the city was chosen for a contest to decide the national billiard championship. The horse-racing instincts of the frontier were gradually supplanted by a craze for the great American game of baseball. The game had attracted informal attention ever since the formation of the National Baseball Player's Association in 1858; Chicago had a baseball club as early as 1856, but for some time the game had little real popularity. Ten years later the situation had changed: in 1865 a convention of baseball clubs with representatives from four states and eleven cities organized at Chicago the National Association of Baseball Players of the Northwest; in 1866 formal clubs were organized in Jacksonville, Cairo, and Rockford; the following year the Independent Baseball Club of Cairo issued a call for a baseball convention at Chicago on July 26, during the visit of the national club of Washington; the object was to secure recognition as members of the national association and to provide

---

[30] *Chicago Press and Tribune*, August 10, 1859; *Alton Weekly Courier*, July 6, 1854.
[31] *Jonesboro Gazette*, January 23, 1869.

for a state championship tournament. Then followed the first great baseball tournament in Chicago, in which fifty-four clubs were represented. It was not long before the game became "all the rage;" on October 23, 1866, the Egyptians trounced Magenta at Cairo by a score of 59 to 6, and soon all kinds of nines were organized — the printers played the clerks, the fats played the leans, the old challenged the young, the married the single, even rival boarding clubs pitted their strength against each other.[32]

Literary activities in Illinois were to a large extent confined to the journalistic field. Although the market for books increased rapidly after 1850, none but the humblest publishing ventures were undertaken in Illinois; one of these was *Uncle Tom's Cabin as it is*, by W. L. G. Smith, a reply to the popular classic by Harriet Beecher Stowe. No greater interest was shown in western periodicals; a few literary and "common novel publishing" journals had a slight circulation, but these were almost universally eastern publications.[33] All early attempts to develop western literary periodicals came to an untimely end. Such a case was that of the *Literary Budget*, 1852–1855, the monthly and later weekly bulletin of W. W. Danenhower, the Chicago bookseller, which soon developed into a literary journal of considerable merit. It announced editorially: "A new field is open to authorship. . . . . The West is full of subject-matter for legend, story or history. . . . . All that is lacking is the proper channel. This channel we offer. The *Budget* claims to be a western literary paper, and we invite writers to send us articles on western subjects, for publication."[34] Another interesting experiment was made by the *Chicago Magazine, the West as it is*, in 1857, a monthly edited by Zebina Eastman for the Mechanics' Institute of Chicago; beautifully and profusely illustrated and devoted to literature, biography, and historical reminiscences, it was considered a magazine of the "highest tone." There

---

[32] *Cairo Democrat*, October 24, 1866, July 12, 1867; *Rockford Gazette*, July 30, 1868; *Rockford Register*, April 27, 1867; Andreas, *History of Chicago*, 2:613-614. In an important game at Chicago in 1867 the victors made thirty-two runs in the last inning.

[33] *Canton Weekly Register*, April 20, 1854; *Illinois State Register*, July 8, August 26, 1852.

[34] Fleming, "The Literary Interests of Chicago," *American Journal of Sociology*, volumes 11 and 12.

was also the Chicago *Literary Messenger,* which had a short life in 1865 and after, the *Chicagoan,* 1868–1869, and the *Illustrated Chicago News,* 1868. Certain ventures having a degree of literary success were those incidental to other aims; besides Danenhower's *Literary Budget* there was *Sloan's Garden City,* 1853–1854, a paper edited by Walter Sloan, a vender of patent medicine, and later by his son; it became a pro-western literary organ of genuine merit. Stories and literary contributions by John Russell of Bluffdale and others appeared in the *Baptist Monthly* of Chicago, and serials and other "light literature" were included in the columns of the *Chicago Merchants' Weekly Circular and Illustrated News.*

The regular newspapers conveyed to their readers not only the event and comment of the day but also the vast bulk of products of the poetry, essay, and fiction writers; for nearly all courted support as purveyors of pure literature as well as politics. In general, it must be said that the scissors and pastebrush were wielded much more vigorously than the pen; yet, in the hot, dull midsummers, any editor, like George T. Brown of the *Alton Courier,* might be aroused to inject new literary attractions into his paper. In 1853 he held a prize contest for tales of western adventure, as a result of which Dr. E. R. Roe of Jacksonville was awarded the first prize of $100 for his story of the "Virginia Rose." Later in the year the *Courier* published *The Mormoness, or the Trials of Mary Maverick, a Narrative of Real Events,* which John Russell had written especially for that paper.[35]

Radical reform journals, like the *Western Citizen,* the *Illinois Organ,* and the *Gem of the Prairie,* were especially zealous in stimulating literary and educational progress. Edited by aggressive representatives of New England Yankeeism, they sensed more keenly than many of their contemporaries the importance of developing a truly western literature. "The West must have a literature peculiarly its own," declared the editor of the *Gem.* "It is here that the great problem of

---

[35] *Alton Courier,* July 15, 30, August 27, 1853; the following year the *Courier* published serially Russell's *Flora Jarvis: or the Young Wife's Plea for the Maine Law.* E. C. Banks to French, January 10, 1850, French manuscripts. An aggressive reader often took a dozen newspapers besides one or two ladies' or special magazines.

human destiny will be worked out on a grander scale than was ever before attempted or conceived of."[36]

Before 1848 central and southern Illinois were to a large extent dominated by the press of St. Louis; even the Springfield papers complained that they did not receive a patronage in the capital as large as did the "foreign" organs. After that date, however, self-sufficiency began to develop in this as in other fields. By 1854 the state could boast of over 150 papers, including twenty dailies and 118 weeklies. Chicago, the literary purveyor for northern Illinois, then had seven dailies and fifteen weeklies and all the six monthlies, bi-monthlies and semimonthlies published in the state. The southern counties suffered from a corresponding dearth; politics was lopsidedly democratic there and little interest was taken in things literary by the general public of a region high in illiteracy. In 1849 the *Southern Illinois Advocate,* published at Shawneetown, standing on the edge of Egypt for "universal liberty abroad, and an ocean bound republic at home," was alleged to be the only newspaper in some ten counties of that region.[37] With its premature death a few months later it yielded the palm to the *Jonesboro Gazette,* which has had a continuous existence to date and which for long was the most influential democratic paper in southern Illinois. Numerous attempts were made at Cairo and other points to establish other journals, but only a few were able to meet with success.

The quality of the leading Illinois press became such that it was complimented as surpassed by very few papers in the land; the modern newspaper was gradually developing during this period. With the westward extension of telegraph lines in 1848, daily issues, previously confined to Chicago, appeared in the other towns of the state. In 1848 the *Illinois State Journal* became a daily, and in the next year the *State Register* followed its rival. On account of heavy telegraphic charges the *Quincy Whig* and *Peoria Register,* after brief experiments in 1848, were compelled to suspend their daily issues. In 1850 there were eight dailies in the state; four years later the number had increased to twenty. There was considerable

---

[36] *Gem of the Prairie,* February 26, 1848.
[37] *Illinois State Journal,* May 18, 1849; Scott, *Newspapers of Illinois,* 315.

complaint of the news telegraphed from the east to western papers, that important matters were ignored and items forwarded such as: "a fire in New York destroyed a thousand dollars worth of property," or "Barnum's lilliputian elephant has eaten three apples and a pint of peanuts."[38]

In 1848 editors were still glad to receive payment for subscriptions "in Wood, Winter Apples, Potatoes, Cabbages, Turnips, Flour, Corn, &c."[39] For a time, too, the pioneer atmosphere was still reflected in the fisticuffs between rival editors. At uneventful seasons the editor was likely to write an editorial urging the planting of shade trees, at the same time apologizing "for the digression" on the ground that he was "troubled wherewithal to fill this sheet."[40] In the same period, however, the editor of the *Warsaw Signal*, ahead of the times, was planning a collection of newspapers and urging his fellow editors to send him three copies of their journals to be bound, one for his own use, one for the proposed Illinois Historical Society, and one for the Smithsonian Institution at Washington.

Other characteristics of the modern newspaper made their appearance. Detailed publication of the proceedings in criminal trials whetted the appetite of the public for sensational news. In the spring of 1850 editors and readers alike reveled in the mysterious and sentimentalities of the trial of Professor John W. Webster, a Harvard chemistry instructor who was convicted of and later confessed to having murdered and disposed of his most intimate friend, Dr. Parkman. Yet it was considered good editorial form to conceal such taste in announcements such as: "A fondness for the details of revolting crimes is characteristic of a brutal mind, and the experience of the past few years proves that the publication of trials, so far from checking crime has, paradoxical as it may seem, actually increased it. We pander to no such appetite for honor; though we are aware that this sin of omission on our part is regarded by many as altogether unpardonable. We

---

[38] *Illinois State Register*, August 25, 1848, July 31, 1851; *Vermont Chronicle* clipped in *Alton Courier*, April 9, 1855; *Seventh Census*, 736; Scott, *Newspapers of Illinois*, lxx-lxxi; *Illinois State Journal*, September 8, 1848.
[39] *Ibid.*, November 15, 1848.
[40] *Ibid.*, April 10, September 10, 1849.

give the following details solely because the telegraph furnished us, from day to day, during the progress of the protracted trial, with the particulars of the evidence as it transpired, and we do not like to leave the story half told."[41]

To such newspaper copy little influence leading to the increase of crimes can be traced, although it did call attention to developments that had seldom come to notice in pioneer days. Some editors held that there was no actual increase of crime and frankly declared that their methods had come to involve the dragging of all sensational news into the open. There is serious question as to whether there was actual fabrication of sensational news items; yet in dull seasons there was a suspicious tendency for news items to appear noting that an anonymous German had met his death by falling into the canal or river, had gone suddenly insane, committed suicide, or been convicted at some distant point of wife-beating.

Modern reportorial work had its beginnings in this period when the editor discovered that it had become his function to chronicle the local news of the region in which his paper circulated. This became a very laborious part of his work: "he must be a kind of Paul Pry," he noticed, "but he cannot be everywhere at once." Accordingly, he invited subscribers to assist him in becoming posted on all local developments and submit news items "when a new school-house, church or mill is built, a new store or shop opened, or bridge constructed, or a new road made, or when a political, literary, or religious society is formed, or meeting held, or when there is a ball, picnic, school examination, or any festive gathering."[42] When, however, the volunteer failed to respond with enthusiasm and efficiency, the professional reporter was sent out into the highways and byways to garner items.

Most of the papers were political organs, aggressively preaching to their readers the importance of an unwavering allegiance to their party leaders. The actual demand for such organs was artificially stimulated and greatly overestimated;

[41] *Illinois State Register*, April 4, 1850; *Joliet Signal*, April 16, 1850. On June 13, 1867, the *Jacksonville Journal* without hesitation pronounced sensationalism "the shame of the newspaper press."
[42] *Belleville Advocate*, June 19, 1863.

in the period after 1854 about thirty-five or forty new ventures were launched each year, a large percentage of which came to grief. Campaign papers, too, sprang up like mushrooms in every important canvass and supplemented the work of the regulars.

Whig editors labored under the direction of Simeon Francis, the veteran pioneer editor who since 1831 had directed the destinies of the *Illinois State Journal*. Francis retired with a handsome competency in 1853, having for a long time been dean of the editorial profession. Until his removal to Oregon in 1859, he gave his services to the State Agricultural Society, which he had been instrumental in organizing and which he served as recording secretary. Francis and his brother Allen, the junior editor, sold out to John Bailhache and Edward L. Baker, who had joined their fortunes in the editorial management of the *Alton Telegraph*, another leading whig paper. Judge Bailhache, a personal friend of Henry Clay, was nine years the senior of Francis and had begun his editorial career in Ohio in 1810; in 1836 he had come to Alton and taken charge of the *Telegraph*. His son, William Henry Bailhache, succeeded his father upon the death of the latter in 1857. Baker, a young man of twenty-six when he took up active editorial direction of the *Journal*, was identified with its editorial policy for nearly twenty years. Paul Selby, one of the organizers of the republican party while editor of the *Morgan Journal*, became associate editor in 1862 and was henceforth in various ways identified with the *Journal*. Other noteworthy downstate whig papers were the *Morgan Journal*, the *Quincy Whig*, and the *Aurora Beacon*.

In Chicago whiggery was upheld by Charles L. Wilson of the *Daily Journal*, by the *Tribune* company after 1852, and by the *Commercial Advertiser*. "Father" Alfred Dutch of the *Advertiser* was an iconoclastic spirit with much in common with John Wentworth, his democratic prototype. Some democrats were shrewd enough to support Dutch in his financial crises on the ground that he never attacked the principles of the democratic party nor the record of the party: "he picks out certain prominent men of the party for personal abuse and there his political warfare begins and ends," explained

Wentworth.⁴³ Dutch did not welcome the competition of the *Tribune* when it abandoned its nonpartisan position for whiggery; he charged its publishers with selfish motives and one of them with having said "that he didn't care a d—n about either whigs or democrats—but that a whig paper was the only one that could get a paying advertising business."⁴⁴ It is significant that all the prominent Illinois whig journals cast their fortunes with the republican party when it was formally organized in Illinois in 1856, and their editors did yeoman service for the cause.

The democrats looked to Springfield for journalistic as well as political leadership. Indeed, the patronage of the state printing was an important factor in the success of the *Illinois State Register*. It was controlled editorially by Charles H. Lanphier and George Walker until the death of the latter in 1858 and Lanphier's withdrawal in 1863. Lanphier was a journalist of no mean ability and directed the editorial policy in confidential relationship with Douglas. John Wentworth claimed that the *Register* controlled a number of sporadic democratic sheets in central and southern Illinois by hiring a traveling journeyman printer as local editor and sending him *Register* editorials to digest and quote back as public opinion in those sections.⁴⁵ The *Alton Courier*, founded in 1852 by George T. Brown, after the city had been without a democratic paper for over ten years, was an aggressive journal that soon claimed the largest circulation of any downstate paper. Other influential democratic papers were the *Ottawa Free Trader*, published by William and Moses Osman, the *Joliet Signal*, the *Charleston Globe*, edited by the second oldest democratic editor in Illinois, W. D. Latshaw, and the *Belleville Advocate*.⁴⁶

---

⁴³ He continued his explanation: "The democrats must see that he is kept as editor. For, if he abandons his post, some one will come here who will abandon all his personal abuse and vindictiveness, and advocate whig principles at length, and an entire organization of the whig party. And, with the aid of all the banks and other corporations, a whig editor who would advocate, with tact and ability, whig principles and a whig organization, to the exclusion of all personal issues, might for a time, at least, revolutionize the city." *Chicago Democrat*, April 5, 1852.

⁴⁴ *Chicago Weekly Democrat*, January 15, 1853.

⁴⁵ *Chicago Democrat*, May 24, 1849; see also the Douglas manuscript letters to Lanphier.

⁴⁶ *Alton Courier*, May 29, 1852; W. D. Latshaw to French, December 4, 1848, French manuscripts.

In Chicago, John Wentworth, the dean of the editorial profession, managed the fortunes of the *Democrat* in his own inimitable and irresponsible fashion, as ready to assert himself against opponents in his own party as in the opposition ranks. On July 24, 1861, he closed an editorial career of twenty-eight years, when the *Democrat* was absorbed by the *Tribune*. In 1852, John L. Scripps, one of the most talented journalists in the state, who had in four years built up the *Chicago Tribune* into a popular and influential paper, left the *Tribune* because of its new whig connections and founded the independent *Democratic Press*, which was later absorbed by the *Tribune*.[47] Wentworth's *Democrat* was able, however, to monopolize the regular democratic journalistic field in Chicago until Douglas, by introducing his Nebraska bill in 1854, was shorn of the support of some of his most enthusiastic followers; among them were not only the *Chicago Democrat*, but also the *Alton Courier*, the *Belleville Advocate*, and several others. As a result Douglas found himself face to face with the necessity of reorganizing his journalistic support. In Chicago, *Young America* was founded and converted in a few weeks into the *Chicago Times*, published by Isaac Cook, James W. Sheahan, and Daniel Cameron, with Sheahan, an able journalist, in editorial charge. Another Chicago democratic journal was added, when in 1858 Douglas set himself at odds with a large wing of his party, this time with the national or pro-southern democrats, who thereupon undertook to set up a rival press in Illinois.[48]

The *avant-courier* of the republican press was the radical antislavery journalism that gathered strength in the late forties: the *Western Citizen*, with its campaign supplement, the *Free Soil Banner*, the *Gem of the Prairie*, and its daily issue, the *Tribune*, and abortive ventures like the *Aurora Free Soil Platform*, the *Alton Monitor*, the *Sparta Freeman*, the *Rockford Free Press*, and *Galesburg Western Freeman*. In the editorial motto of the *Western Citizen*, " anti-slavery, universal freedom, universal brotherhood, fraternity of nations, reign

---

[47] *Belleville Advocate*, July 7, 1852.
[48] The result was the founding of the *Chicago Herald*, originally the *National Union*, and the *Illinois State Democrat* at Springfield. See p. 160.

of peace" they were influenced by W. L. Garrison, Whittier, and the eastern abolitionists for a more thoroughgoing pacifism than abolitionism.[49] Adopting mere non-extension of slavery ground, they served as valuable precursors to the anti-Nebraska revolt and to the republican party, in which they were joined by former whig and democratic journals. The union was formally cemented by the three elements at the editorial convention at Decatur on February 22, 1856.[50] Henceforth the press, heralding the crusade for freedom, remained a valuable asset in preparing the way for the republican victory of 1860.

The Civil War era was a period of storm and stress for the journalistic profession — a time when the more prosperous and worthy enterprises increased in strength and prosperity, while the weaker journals either declined in influence or collapsed and were buried with few mourners. When Chicago dailies, like the *Times* and *Tribune*, offered special correspondence and telegraphic news and extra editions, their circulation promptly doubled and their financial success was guaranteed. Although John Wentworth sold his *Chicago Democrat* to the *Tribune* to avert what he thought was certain failure, he became a witness of substantial journalistic prosperity, while Horace White, Joseph Medill, and Dr. C. H. Ray came to the forefront in the editorial world. Charles L. Wilson, the veteran editor of the *Chicago Journal*, continued to uphold the conservative republican standpoint and was joined in 1865 by the *Republican*, for a time under the editorial direction of Charles A. Dana, which voiced the dissatisfaction of certain republican forces offended by the *Tribune*. The *Chicago Times*, having absorbed the *Herald* when Cyrus H. McCormick secured control of both papers, aggressively championed the cause of the peace democracy and had a checkered career during the Civil War under the editorial management of Wilbur F. Storey; the war democrats found an organ in the *Morning Post*, which was established in December, 1860, by

[49] Open opposition was voiced on grounds of conscience to the Mexican War. *Gem of the Prairie*, January 29, February 19, 21, 1848.
[50] See *ante*, p. 143. An attempt in 1857 to establish a new republican organ at Springfield, the *Daily Republican*, ended in failure. *Daily Springfield Republican*, February 9, 1857.

the former *Times* editor, James W. Sheahan, a protégé of Douglas, whose advice on the sectional crisis he followed.

The Springfield papers continued their work but seem to have lost much of their ancient prestige, particularly the *Register* after the withdrawal of Lanphier. The Civil War gave Cairo what had previously been denied to it—prosperous newspapers with a degree of stability. For a time the democratic *Gazette* and the *Democrat* had the field, but in 1864 the former was purchased by a republican company and converted into the *Daily News*.

In the closing years of the Civil War decade a tendency found expression among republican papers to revolt against the hide-bound allegiance to party which the zeal and trials of early republicanism had established as a tradition. " One of the most disagreeable features of editorial life," complained the editor of the *Belleville Advocate,* " is the performance of what too many are apt to consider 'duty,' although the term is a misnomer. The party expects its editors to indorse all its actions, to support its nominees, to cover up its frauds and to pervert the aims of its opponents. If the most incompetent men succeed in getting nominated, it matters not; if its conventions are managed by cliques, and the voice of the people hushed by pot-house politicians, we are expected to salve their wounds and expatiate on the necessity of accepting the less of two evils, and abiding by the ' regular nomination,' although it may be the greatest irregularity." " In many cases their papers are owned by county clerks, circuit clerks or other men in office who wish to continue their lucrative positions, and the editors are their 'men in bonds.' "[51] Those country editors who owned their papers were threatened as the price of independence with the competition of a " new organ " ready to do the bidding of party leaders. Under such a slavery many a republican editor squirmed pitifully.

Democratic journalism was perhaps even less fortunate in its outlook. The party was generally out of power and its leaders shared in little of the spoils of politics; as a result its papers were given little support. In places like Dixon, Lee

[51] *Belleville Advocate,* November 27, 1868; however note the policy of the *Chicago Tribune* for 1869 for independence of action.

county, it was "almost dangerous to be called a democrat," and a democratic paper was mobbed there during the canvass of 1868. Editors complained bitterly of this situation; "There is not a democratic local print in Illinois that is realizing for its publisher more than a hand-to-mouth living," commented the *Carthage Republican*. As a result, "auxiliary" newspapers with "patent" outside or inside pages were printed in Chicago or St. Louis and sold to country newspapers at a figure below the cost of home production. Ninety-three county papers, mainly democratic organs, secured their inside pages from the "slop shop" of A. N. Kellogg of Chicago, the principal auxiliary publisher in the west. Such a system, attacked by republican editors and by some democrats as "swindling" journalism, probably did not raise the standards of the independence if it did of the excellence of democratic journalism.

The journalistic development of Illinois is a fair index to the growth of the commonwealth. In 1870 over five hundred newspapers and periodicals were published in the state: 340 political organs pandered to the prejudices of 738,420 subscribers; the next largest circulation, that of 671,600, was boasted by a corporal's guard of nine publications of benevolent secret societies; fifty-eight illustrated and literary periodicals had a following of 339,625; thirty-seven religious organs reached 300,326 subscribers; while twenty-two commercial and financial, sixteen technical and professional, eleven advertising, and ten agricultural journals bespoke the growing professionalization of every branch of industry. Illinois, therefore, was not only growing in population, production, commerce, and wealth, but was also making progress in the realm of refinement, comfort, intellectuality, and religion. "Our civilization, enlightenment and spirituality," boasted a proud editor, "are as progressive as are our elements of commercial and industrial vitality. The school, the church and the arts are doing for the rising generation what energy, practical shrewdness and hard work have done and are doing for the present."[52]

[52] *Aurora Beacon*, April 25, 1867.

BIBLIOGRAPHY

I

MANUSCRIPTS

Mason Brayman manuscripts in Chicago Historical Society autograph collection. A large collection of particular value for railroad building, 1850-1860.

Salmon P. Chase manuscripts in Library of Congress. Contains letters from Jonathan Blanchard, Ichabod Codding, E. B. Washburne, and other Illinoisians.

Thomas Corwin manuscripts in Library of Congress. A dozen letters from Illinoisians, including Richard Yates and S. Lisle Smith.

John J. Crittenden manuscripts in Library of Congress. Several letters from Illinoisians.

J. True Dodge manuscripts in possession of J. True Dodge, Alton, Illinois. Consists of several interesting Civil War letters.

Zebina Eastman manuscripts in Chicago Historical Society autograph collection. Correspondence from his associates in the antislavery cause.

Thomas Ewing manuscripts in Library of Congress. A few dozen letters from Illinoisians.

Augustus C. French manuscripts in McKendree College library. Several thousand letters from democratic correspondents all over the state; a very important collection bound in three volumes.

Joseph Gillespie manuscripts in Chicago Historical Society autograph collection. A large and important collection, including letters from Herndon, Bissell, Reynolds, and others.

Illinois Election Statistics manuscripts in the secretary of state's office, Springfield.

Andrew Johnson manuscripts in Library of Congress. A number of Illinoisians represented among Johnson's correspondence.

Gustave Koerner manuscripts. Transcripts in Illinois Historical Survey, University of Illinois. Seven letters from Lincoln, Douglas, and John Hay.

Charles H. Lanphier manuscripts in possession of Mrs. James W. Patton, Springfield, Illinois. A large file of letters written to Lanphier by Douglas.

William R. Lawrence manuscript interview on "That 'Northwestern

Confederacy'" in Library of Congress. A description of the northwestern conspiracy in 1863-1864.
D. L. Phillips manuscripts in possession of Judson Phillips, Jonesboro, Illinois. Includes letters from Senator Trumbull.
Caleb B. Smith manuscripts in Library of Congress. Letters dated 1849 and 1850 from Justin Butterfield, S. A. Hurlbut, S. Lisle Smith, E. B. Washburne.
W. H. Swift manuscripts, in Chicago Historical Society autograph collection. Valuable for transportation history.
Lyman Trumbull manuscripts in Library of Congress. One of the largest and richest collections of Civil War material extant. Includes correspondence from every prominent republican leader in Illinois except Lincoln.
Jonathan B. Turner manuscripts in collections of Illinois Historical Survey. A rich fund for material on the industrial university.

II

NEWSPAPERS AND PERIODICALS

For the reconstruction of no period of Illinois history does the newspaper play so important a rôle as for the dozen years before and the decade after the election of Lincoln to the presidency. The files used have been preserved in the Illinois State Historical Library, and in the libraries of the Chicago Historical Society and the University of Illinois besides collections in the Newberry Library in Chicago, the Belleville Public Library, the Jacksonville Public Library, the Joliet Public Library, the Rockford Public Library, Reddick's Library of Ottawa in the possession of the trustees of the Cairo Trust Property, and in various newspaper offices scattered over the state. For a survey of journalism in Illinois, 1848-1870, see *ante* pp. 448-458. For a complete bibliography of Illinois newspapers, as well as for additional data on those here listed, see: Scott, Franklin W., *Newspapers and Periodicals of Illinois, 1814-1879* (Springfield, 1910) [*Collections of the Illinois State Historical Library*, volume 6].

Alton Courier, 1852-1855, 1858-1859, Alton, Illinois.
Alton Telegraph, 1847-1852, Alton, Illinois.
Alton Truth Seeker, 1848, Alton, Illinois.
Atlantic Monthly, volume 14, 1864, Boston.
Aurora Beacon, 1848-1869, Aurora, Illinois.
Aurora Guardian, 1852-1857, Aurora, Illinois.
Bankers' Magazine, volumes 1-24, 1846-1870, New York.

BIBLIOGRAPHY

Beardstown Gazette, 1847-1852, Beardstown, Illinois.
Belleville Advocate, 1841, 1846-1869, Belleville, Illinois.
Belleville Democrat, 1858-1869, Belleville, Illinois.
Bloomington Pantagraph, 1854, Bloomington, Illinois.
Cairo City Times, 1854-1855, Cairo, Illinois.
Cairo Daily News, 1863-1865, Cairo, Illinois.
Cairo Democrat, 1863-1868, Cairo, Illinois.
Cairo Evening Bulletin, 1869, Cairo, Illinois.
Cairo Gazette, 1859-1863, Cairo, Illinois.
Cairo Journal, 1857-1858, Cairo, Illinois.
Cairo Sun, 1851-1852, Cairo, Illinois.
Cairo Times and Delta, 1855-1858, Cairo, Illinois.
Cairo Weekly Delta, 1848-1849, Cairo, Illinois.
Cairo Weekly Democrat, 1863-1865, Cairo, Illinois.
Cairo Weekly Times and Delta, 1857-1858, Cairo, Illinois.
Canton Weekly Register, 1852-1868, Canton, Illinois.
Carlinville Democrat, 1868, Carlinville, Illinois.
Carthage Republican, 1863-1870, Carthage, Illinois.
Central Illinois Gazette, 1858-1861, 1864-1866, Champaign, Illinois.
Champaign County Democrat, 1862, Urbana, Illinois.
Champaign County Patriot, 1862-1865, Urbana, Illinois.
Champaign County Union and Gazette, 1861-1870, Champaign, Illinois.
Chester Picket Guard. See *Picket Guard.*
Chicago American, 1840, Chicago, Illinois.
Chicago Daily Commercial Advertiser, 1849-1851, Chicago, Illinois.
Chicago Daily Democratic Press, 1852-1858, 1865, Chicago, Illinois.
Chicago Daily Journal, 1847-1852, Chicago, Illinois.
Chicago Daily Times, 1854-1860, Chicago, Illinois.
Chicago Democrat, 1847-1861, Chicago, Illinois.
Chicago Evening Journal, 1862, 1865-1866, Chicago, Illinois.
Chicago Morning Post, 1862-1864. Became *Chicago Evening Post,* 1865-1867, Chicago, Illinois.
Chicago Press and Tribune, 1857-1860, Chicago, Illinois.
Chicago Record, 1857-1858. Became *Church Record,* 1858-1862, Chicago, Illinois.
Chicago Times, 1857-1870, Chicago, Illinois.
Chicago Tribune, 1860-1870, Chicago, Illinois.
Church Record. See *Chicago Record.*
The Crisis, 1861-1866, Columbus, Ohio.
Daily Constitutionist, 1852-1855, Jacksonville, Illinois.
Daily Springfield Republican, 1857, Springfield, Illinois.

BIBLIOGRAPHY

DeBow's Review and Industrial Resources, Statistics, etc., volumes 9-24, 1847-1862, New Orleans, Louisiana.
Democratic Review, volumes 30-31, 1852, New York.
Du Quoin Recorder, 1866, Du Quoin, Illinois.
Du Quoin Tribune, 1868-1870, Du Quoin, Illinois.
Free West, 1853-1855, Chicago, Illinois.
Gem of the Prairie, 1847-1849, Chicago, Illinois.
Harper's New Monthly Magazine, volumes 1-42, 1850-1870, New York.
Harper's Weekly; a journal of civilization, volumes 1-14, 1857-1870, New York.
Hunt's Merchants' Magazine. See *Merchants' Magazine.*
Illinois Democrat, 1861-1862, 1867-1868, Champaign, Illinois.
Illinois Globe, 1849, Charleston, Illinois.
Illinois Journal, 1847-1855. Became *Illinois State Journal,* 1855-1870, Springfield, Illinois.
Illinois Organ, 1848-1851, Springfield, Illinois.
Illinois Republican, 1849-1852, Belleville, Illinois.
Illinois Staats-Zeitung, 1848-1870, Chicago, Illinois.
Illinois State Register, 1847-1870, Springfield, Illinois.
Illinois Teacher, volumes 1-18, 1855-1872, Peoria, Illinois.
Jacksonville Constitutionist, 1852, Jacksonville, Illinois.
Jacksonville Journal, 1861-1871, Jacksonville, Illinois.
Joliet Republican, 1867-1869, Joliet, Illinois.
Joliet Signal, 1846-1870, Joliet, Illinois.
Jonesboro Gazette, 1851, 1861-1870, Jonesboro, Illinois.
Merchants' Magazine and Commercial Review, conducted by Freeman Hunt, volumes 18-63, 1848-1870, New York.
Mississippi Blätter, 1862-1869, St. Louis, Missouri.
Morgan Journal, 1850-1854, Jacksonville, Illinois.
Mound City Emporium, 1857-1859, Mound City, Illinois.
The Nation, volumes 1-11, 1865-1870, New York.
National Live-Stock Journal, volume 1, 1870-1871, Chicago, Illinois.
Ottawa Free Trader, 1850-1872, Ottawa, Illinois.
Ottawa Weekly Republican, 1854-1870, Ottawa, Illinois.
Our Constitution, 1856-1859, Urbana, Illinois.
Paxton Record, 1865-1870, Paxton, Illinois.
Peoria Transcript, 1861, Peoria, Illinois.
Peru Daily Chronicle, 1853-1854, Peru, Illinois.
Picket Guard, 1865-1866, Chester, Illinois.
Prairie Farmer, 1848-1850, 1853-1855, 1861, 1863, 1864, 1866-1870, Chicago, Illinois.

BIBLIOGRAPHY

Presbytery Reporter, volumes 3-6, 1856-1860, Alton; 1860-1871, Chicago and Alton, Illinois.
Quincy Weekly Herald, 1854-1855, Quincy, Illinois.
Quincy Whig, 1848-1870, Quincy, Illinois.
Rockford Democrat, 1864, 1865, Rockford, Illinois.
Rockford Forum, 1848-1854, Rockford, Illinois.
Rockford Gazette, 1866-1870, Rockford, Illinois.
Rockford Register, 1856-1867, Rockford, Illinois.
Rockford Republican, 1855-1865, Rockford, Illinois.
Rock River Democrat, 1852-1865, Rockford, Illinois.
Rushville Times, 1856-1858, 1868-1870, Rushville, Illinois.
Sangamo Journal, 1847, Springfield, Illinois. In the fall of 1848 it became the *Illinois Journal.*
Scientific American, volume 9, 1853-1854, New York.
St. Clair Tribune, 1854-1857, Belleville, Illinois.
Star of Egypt, 1858, Belleville, Illinois.
Southern Illinois Advocate, 1849, Shawneetown, Illinois.
Urbana Clarion, October 29, 1859, Urbana, Illinois.
Urbana Union, 1854-1858, Urbana, Illinois.
Washington Union, 1848-1860, Washington, D. C.
Western Agriculturist, volumes 6, 9-20, 1874, 1877-1888, Quincy, Illinois.
Western Citizen, 1848-1853, continued as *Free West.*
Western Journal of Agriculture, Manufactures, Mechanics, Arts, Internal Improvement, Commerce, and General Literature, 1848-1851, 5 volumes, St. Louis, Missouri.
Western Manufacturer, volumes 6-7, 1879-1880, Chicago, Illinois.
Miscellaneous Illinois newspapers, 1846-1871, Illinois Historical Survey.

III

FEDERAL AND STATE DOCUMENTS

ILLINOIS

Adjutant General of Illinois, *Report,* volumes 1-8, 1861-1866 (Springfield, 1900-1902).
Blue Book of the State of Illinois, 1909. Compiled by James A. Rose, Secretary of State (Danville, 1909).
Journal of the Convention, Assembled at Springfield, June 7, 1847, in Pursuance of an Act of the General Assembly of the State of Illinois

BIBLIOGRAPHY

... *for the Purpose of Altering, Amending, or Revising the Constitution of the State of Illinois* (Springfield, 1847).
Journal of the Constitutional Convention of the State of Illinois, Convened at Springfield, January 7, 1862 (Springfield, 1862).
Journal of the Constitutional Convention of the State of Illinois, Convened at Springfield, December 13, 1869 (Springfield, 1870).
Journal of the House of Representatives of the State of Illinois, 1849-1869 (Springfield, 1849-1869).
Journal of the Senate of the State of Illinois, 1849-1869 (Springfield, 1849-1869).
[*Law*] *Reports. Reports of Cases at Common Law and in Chancery, argued and determined in the Supreme Court of the State of Illinois*, volumes 5-10 by Charles Gilman (Chicago, 1886-1888), volumes 11-30 by E. Peck (Chicago, 1870-1886), volumes 31-151 by Norman L. Freeman (Chicago, 1866-1886; Springfield, 1870-1894).
Laws of the State of Illinois, 1849-1869 (Springfield, 1849-1869).
Reports made to the Senate and House of Representatives of the State of Illinois, 1849-1869 (Springfield, 1849-1869) [cited as *Reports General Assembly*].
Superintendent of Public Instruction of the State of Illinois, *Biennial Reports*, 1850-1886, volumes 1-36 (Springfield, 1851-1887).

UNITED STATES

Agriculture of the United States in 1860; compiled from the original returns of the Eighth Census (Washington, 1864).
Congressional Globe ... containing sketches of the debates and proceedings of ... congress, volumes 17-42 (Washington, 1848-1870).
Executive Documents of the House of Representatives (Washington, 1853-1870).
Journal of the House of Representatives of the United States (Washington, 1848-1870).
Journal of the Senate of the United States of America (Washington, 1848-1870).
Manufactures of the United States in 1860; compiled from the original returns of the Eighth Census (Washington, 1865).
Population of the United States in 1860; compiled from the original returns of the Eighth Census (Washington, 1864).
Reports of the Commissioner of Agriculture, 1848-1870 (Washington, 1848-1870).

BIBLIOGRAPHY

Richardson, James D. (compiler), *A Compilation of the Messages and Papers of the Presidents, 1789-1897,* 10 volumes (Washington, 1896-1899).

Senate Executive Documents (Washington, 1848-1870).

Seventh Census of the United States: 1850. Embracing a statistical view of each of the states and territories (Washington, 1853).

Statistics of the Population of the United States, embracing the tables of race, nationality, sex, selected ages, and occupations; compiled from the original returns of the Ninth Census (Washington, 1872).

Statistics of the Wealth and Industry of the United States, embracing the tables of wealth, taxation, and public indebtedness; of agriculture; manufactures; mining; and the fisheries. Compiled from the original returns of the Ninth Census (Washington, 1872).

Statistics of the United States (including mortality, property, &c.) in 1860; compiled from the original returns and being the final exhibit of the Eighth Census (Washington, 1866).

Statutes at Large and Treaties of the United States of America, volumes 9-16 (Boston, 1851-1871).

United States Patent Office, *Annual Report of the Commissioner of Patents,* 1861 (Washington, D. C.).

Vital Statistics of the United States, embracing the tables of deaths, births, sex, and age; compiled from the original returns of the Ninth Census (Washington, 1872).

War of the Rebellion: A Compilation of the Official Records of the Union and Confederate Armies. Published under the direction of the Hon. Elihu Root, Secretary of War, by Brig. Gen. Fred C. Ainsworth, Chief of the Record and Pension Office, War Department, and Mr. Joseph W. Kirkley, series I, 53 volumes, series II, 8 volumes, series III, 5 volumes, series IV, 3 volumes, index, 1 volume (Washington, 1881-1901).

IV

CONTEMPORARY ACCOUNTS

An Appeal to Congress by the Citizens of Rock Island and Moline, Illinois, and Davenport, Iowa, in favor of a National Armory on the Site of Fort Armstrong, on the Island of Rock Island, Illinois, 1861.

Annual Review of the Trade and Commerce of Chicago for 1870 (Chicago, 1870).

Ayer, I. Winslow, *The Great Treason Plot in the North during the war. Most dangerous, perfidious, extensive and startling plot ever devised! Imminent hidden perils of the republic. Astounding developments never before published* . . . . (Chicago, 1865).

Bailey, John C. W., *Illinois State Gazetteer and Business Directory, for the years 1864-5, embracing descriptive sketches of all the cities, towns and villages throughout the state* (Chicago, 1864).

Board of Trade of Peoria, *Fourth Annual Report of the Trade and Commerce of the City of Peoria for the Year ending December 31, 1873* (Peoria, 1874).

Breese, Judge Sidney, "Some Old Letters" [Letters from correspondents of Judge Breese], Illinois Historical Society, *Journal*, volume 2 (Springfield, 1909).

Chicago Board of Trade Report, 1858-1875 (Chicago, 1859-1876).

Chamberlin, Everett, *Chicago and its Suburbs* (Chicago, 1874).

City of Quincy, Illinois, Its Trade and Manufactures (Quincy, 1881).

Colby, Charles, *Hand-Book of Illinois, accompanying Morse's new map of the state* (New York, 1855).

Doolittle, James Rood, "Gleanings from the Private Letters and Documents of a Senator of the Civil War Period," Illinois State Historical Society, *Journal*, volume 4 (Springfield, 1911).

Dwyer, James T., "Manufactures in Illinois," Department of Agriculture of Illinois, *Transactions*, volume 9 (Springfield, 1872).

Eastman, Zebina, *History of Anti-Slavery Agitation in Illinois* (Chicago, n. d.).

Eddy, T. M., *The Patriotism of Illinois. A record of the civil and military history of the state in the war for the Union, with a history of the campaigns in which Illinois soldiers have been conspicuous* . . . 2 volumes (Chicago, 1865).

Exhibits and proof of the Illinois war claim and laws in reference to the same. H. J. Hamlin, attorney general, solicitor for claimant (Springfield, 1902).

Forney, John W., *Anecdotes of Public Men* (New York, 1873-1881).

French, Governor A. C., "Letter of Governor A. C. French to Professor J. B. Turner in Regard to the Affairs for the Hospital for the Insane." Illinois State Historical Society, *Journal*, volume 3 (Springfield, 1912).

Greene, Evarts Boutell, and Charles Manfred Thompson, *Governors' Letter-Books, 1840-1853* (Springfield, 1911) [*Collections of the Illinois State Historical Library*, volume 7].

Greeley, Horace, and John F. Cleveland, *A Political Text-Book for 1860. Comprising a brief view of presidential nominations and*

BIBLIOGRAPHY 467

elections: including all the national platforms ever yet adopted: also, a history of the struggle respecting slavery in the territories, and of the action of Congress as to the freedom of the public lands, with the most notable speeches and letters . . . (New York, 1860).

Halstead, Murat, *Caucuses of 1860. A history of the National Political Conventions of the current presidential campaign being a complete record of the business of all the conventions* (Columbus, 1860).

History of Springfield, Illinois. Its attractions as a home and advantages for business, manufacturing, etc. (Springfield, 1871).

Howe, S. F., *Yearbook of Chicago* (n. p., 1885-1886).

Illinois State Agricultural Society, *Transactions*, see *Transactions*.

Jones, John, *The Black Laws of Illinois and a few reasons why they should be repealed* (Chicago, 1864).

Kelley, O. H., *Origin and Progress of the Order of Patrons of Husbandry in the United States; a History from 1866 to 1873* (Philadelphia, 1875).

Lincoln, Abraham, *The Writings of Abraham Lincoln*, federal edition, 8 volumes (New York, 1905-1906).

Lincoln-Douglas Debates, see *Political Debates*.

Lincoln-Douglas Debates of 1858, edited by Edwin Erle Sparks (Springfield, Illinois, 1908) [*Collections of the Illinois State Historical Library*, volume 3].

The Logan Monument Memorial. Edited by George Francis James (Chicago, 1898).

McPherson, Edward, *Political History of the United States of America, during the Great Rebellion* (Washington, 1876).

Minutes of the Annual Conference of the Methodist Episcopal Church, 1846-1869 (New York, 1856-1869).

Moore, Frank (ed.), *The Rebellion Record: A diary of American events, with documents, narratives, illustrations, incidents, poetry, etc.*, 7 volumes (New York, 1862-1864).

Norton, W. T., *Resources of Alton in 1873* (Alton, 1874).

Political debates between Hon. Abraham Lincoln and Hon. Stephen A. Douglas in the celebrated campaign of 1858, in Illinois; including the preceding speeches of each, at Chicago, Springfield, etc.; also, the two great speeches of Mr. Lincoln in Ohio, in 1859, as carefully prepared by the reporters of each party, and published at the times of their delivery (Columbus, 1860).

Printer's Scrap Book, 1846-1853, in Shurtleff College library.

Poor, H. V., *Manual of Railroads of the United States, 1869-1870* (New York, 1870).

BIBLIOGRAPHY

Proceedings of the National Union Republican Convention, held at Chicago, May 20 and 21, 1868 (Chicago, 1868).

Review of the Commerce of Chicago: Her Merchants and Manufactures (Chicago, 1856).

Shuman, Andrew, to James R. Doolittle, August 13, 1862, Illinois State Historical Society, *Journal*, volume 8 (Springfield, 1915-1916).

Tracy, Gilbert A., *Uncollected Letters of Abraham Lincoln Now First Brought Together* (Boston and New York, 1917).

Transactions of the Illinois State Agricultural Society, with notices and proceedings of county societies and kindred associations, volumes 1-8 (Springfield, 1856-1871).

Tribune Almanac for the years 1838 to 1868, inclusive; comprehending The Politicians' Register and The Whig Almanac, containing annual election returns by states and counties . . . . together with political essays, addresses, party platforms, &c. . . . . (New York, 1868).

Trumbull, Lyman, "A Statesman's Letters of the Civil War Period" [Letters of Lyman Trumbull to James R. Doolittle], Illinois State Historical Society, *Journal*, volume 2 (Springfield, 1909).

Turner, Jonathan B., *A Plan for an Industrial University for the State of Illinois*. Submitted to the Farmers' Convention at Granville, held November 18, 1851 (n. p., 1851).

United States Sanitary Commission; Financial Report of the United States Sanitary Commission, from June, 1861, to October 1, 1864 (n. p., 1864) [number 83].

United States Sanitary Commission, Statement of Objects and Methods of the Sanitary Commission, Appointed by the Government of the United States, June 13, 1861 (New York, 1863) [number 69].

United States Sanitary Commission, What the United States Sanitary Commission is doing in the Valley of the Mississippi. Letter from Dr. J. S. Newberry to Hon. W. P. Sprague (n. p., 1863) [number 64].

V

Biography and Reminiscence

Arnold, Isaac N., *Abraham Lincoln: A paper read before the Royal Historical Society, London, June 16, 1881* (Chicago, 1881).

Arnold, Isaac N., *The Life of Abraham Lincoln* (Chicago, 1885).

Barnet, James (ed.), *The Martyrs and Heroes of Illinois in the Great Rebellion. Biographical Sketches* (Chicago, 1866).

BIBLIOGRAPHY

Carriel, Mary Turner, *The Life of Jonathan Baldwin Turner* (Jacksonville, 1911).
Cartwright, Peter, *Autobiography of Peter Cartwright, the backwoods preacher.* Edited by W. P. Strickland (Cincinnati, 1856).
Caton, John Dean, *Early Bench and Bar of Illinois* (Chicago, 1893).
Cook, Frederick Francis, *Bygone Days in Chicago. Recollections of the "Garden City" of the sixties* (Chicago, 1910).
Dawson, George Francis, *Life and services of Gen. John A. Logan as soldier and statesman* (Chicago, 1887).
Eddowes, T. H., and Frances Le Baron and George Brayton Penney (eds.), *Fifty Years of Unitarian Life. Being a record of the proceedings on the occasion of the fiftieth anniversary of the organization of the first Unitarian society of Geneva, Illinois, celebrated June tenth, eleventh and twelfth, 1892* (Geneva, 1892).
Flint, H. M., *The Life of Stephen A. Douglas, United States Senator from Illinois. With his most important speeches and reports* (New York, 1860).
Graff, Reverend Franklin L., *The Record of Fifty Years, historical sermon delivered at the semi-centennial celebration of the First Congregational Church, Champaign, Illinois, Sunday, November 1, 1903* (Champaign, 1904).
Grant, Ulysses S., *Personal Memoirs of U. S. Grant*, 2 volumes (New York, 1885-1886).
Herndon, William H., and Jesse W. Weik, *Abraham Lincoln; the True Story of a Great Life . . . . The History and Personal Recollections of Abraham Lincoln* (New York, 1908).
Johns, Jane Martin, *Personal Recollections of early Decatur, Abraham Lincoln, Richard J. Oglesby, and the Civil War* (Decatur, 1912).
Johnson, Allen, *Stephen A. Douglas. A Study in American Politics* (New York, 1908).
Johnson, Charles Beneulyn, *Illinois in the Fifties* (Champaign, 1918).
Koerner, Gustave, *Memoirs of Gustave Koerner, 1809-1896. Life sketches written at the suggestion of his children.* Edited by Thomas J. McCormack, 2 volumes (Cedar Rapids, Iowa, 1909).
Linder, Usher F., *Reminiscences of the early Bench and Bar of Illinois. With an introduction and appendix by the Hon. Joseph Gillespie* (Chicago, 1879).
Logan, Mrs. John A., *Reminiscences of a Soldier's Wife. An autobiography* (New York, 1913).
Nicolay, John G., and John Hay, *Abraham Lincoln, a History*, 10 volumes (New York, 1890).

BIBLIOGRAPHY

Palmer, John M. (ed.), *The Bench and Bar of Illinois. Historical and Reminiscent*, 2 volumes (Chicago, 1899).

Palmer, John M., *Personal Recollections of John M. Palmer; the Story of an earnest life* (Cincinnati, 1901).

Sheahan, James W., *The Life of Stephen A. Douglas* (New York, 1860).

Smith, Laura Chase, *The Life of Philander Chase, first bishop of Ohio and Illinois, founder of Kenyon and Jubilee Colleges* (New York, 1903).

Sturtevant, Julian M., *Julian M. Sturtevant: An Autobiography.* Edited by J. M. Sturtevant, Jr. (New York, 1896).

Wallace, Isabel, *Life and Letters of General W. H. L. Wallace* (Chicago, 1909).

Welles, Gideon, *Diary of Gideon Welles, Secretary of the Navy under Lincoln and Johnson, with an Introduction by John T. Morse, Jr.* (Boston, 1911).

White, Horace, *The Life of Lyman Trumbull* (Boston, 1913).

VI

Monographs and Special Works

Ackerman, William K., *Early Illinois Railroads* (Chicago, 1884) [Fergus' Historical Series, number 23].

Ackerman, William K., *Historical Sketch of the Illinois Central Railroad, together with a brief biographical record of its incorporators and some of its early officers* (Chicago, 1890).

Ahern, M. L., *The Political History of Chicago*, first edition [covering the period from 1837 to 1887] (Chicago, 1886).

Andreas, A. T., *History of Chicago from the earliest Period to the present Time*, 3 volumes (Chicago, 1884-1886).

Babcock, Kendric C., *The Scandinavian Element in the United States* (Urbana, 1914) [*University of Illinois Studies in the Social Sciences*, volume 3].

Baldwin, Eugene F., "The Dream of the South — Story of Illinois during the Civil War," Illinois State Historical Society, *Transactions*, 1911 (Springfield, 1913).

Bateman, Newton, and Paul Selby (ed.), *Historical Encyclopedia of Illinois*, volume 2, *History of Peoria County*. Edited by David McCulloch, 2 volumes (Chicago and Peoria, 1902).

Beinlich, B. A., "The Latin Immigration in Illinois," Illinois State Historical Society, *Transactions*, 1909 (Springfield, 1910).

BIBLIOGRAPHY

Bess, F. B., *Eine populäre Geschichte der Stadt Peoria* (Peoria, 1906).

Bost, Ernest Lesley, *Current Ideas respecting Slavery and Secession in Illinois in 1860 and 1861* [Thesis submitted for the degree of master of arts, University of Illinois, 1909].

Breese, Sidney, *The Early History of Illinois from its discovery by the French in 1673, until its cession to Great Britain in 1763, including the narrative of Marquette's discovery of the Mississippi* (Chicago, 1884).

Brownson, Howard Gray, *The History of the Illinois Central Railroad to 1870* (Urbana, 1915) [*University of Illinois Studies in the Social Sciences,* volume 4].

Bruncken, Ernest, " Political Activity of Wisconsin Germans," Wisconsin Historical Society, *Proceedings,* volume 49 (Madison, Wis., 1902).

Buck, Solon J., *The Granger Movement. A study of agricultural organization and its political, economic and social manifestations, 1870-1880* (Cambridge, Mass., 1913).

Church, Charles A., *History of Rockford and Winnebago County, Illinois, from the first settlement in 1834 to the Civil War* (Rockford, 1900).

Cole, Arthur C., " President Lincoln and the Illinois Radical Republicans," *Mississippi Valley Historical Review,* volume 4 (Cedar Rapids, Iowa, 1918).

Cook, John Williston, *Educational History of Illinois. Growth and progress in educational affairs of the state from the earliest day to the present.* With portraits and biographies (Chicago, 1912).

County histories have in general been found useful for local information. For complete bibliography of Illinois counties see: Buck, Solon J., *Travel and Description 1765-1865 together with a List of County Histories, Atlases, and Biographical Collections and a List of territorial and state Laws* (Springfield, 1914) [*Collections of the Illinois State Historical Library,* volume 9].

Cunningham, J. O, " The Bloomington Convention of 1856 and Those Who Participated in It," Illinois State Historical Society, *Transactions,* 1905 (Springfield, 1906).

Debel, Niels H., *The Veto Power of the Governor of Illinois* (Urbana, 1917) [*University of Illinois Studies in the Social Sciences,* volume 6].

Dodd, William E., " The Fight for the Northwest, 1860," *American Historical Review,* volume 16 (Lancaster, Pa., 1911).

BIBLIOGRAPHY

Dowrie, George W., *The Development of Banking in Illinois, 1817-1863* (Urbana, 1913) [*University of Illinois Studies in the Social Sciences*, volume 2].

Fairlie, John A., *County and Town Government in Illinois* [Reprinted from the *Annals of the American Academy of Political and Social Science*, Philadelphia, May, 1913].

Faust, Albert B., *The German Element in the United States, with special reference to its political, moral, social, and educational influence* (Boston, 1909).

Fesler, Mayo, "Secret Political Societies in the North during the Civil War," *Indiana Magazine of History*, volume 14 (Bloomington, Ind., 1918).

Finerty, John F., *Ireland; the People's History of Ireland* (New York, 1907).

Fishback, Mason McCloud, "Illinois Legislation on Slavery and Free Negroes, 1818-1865," Illinois State Historical Society, *Transactions*, 1904 (Springfield, 1904).

Fite, Emerson David, *Social and Industrial Conditions in the North during the Civil War* (New York, 1910).

Fleming, Herbert E., "The Literary Interests of Chicago," *American Journal of Sociology*, volumes 11 and 12 (Chicago, 1906-1907).

Guyer, Isaac D., *History of Chicago; its commercial and manufacturing interests and industry. Sketches of manufacturers . . . . glances at . . . . the best hotels; also the principal railroads which center in Chicago* (Chicago, 1862).

Hale's History of Agriculture by Dates. A simple record of historical events and victories of peaceful industries (St. Louis, 1915).

Harris, Norman D., *History of Negro Slavery in Illinois and of the Slavery Agitation in that State* (Chicago, 1906).

Haynes, Reverend N. S., "The Disciples of Christ in Illinois and their Attitude toward Slavery," Illinois State Historical Society, *Transactions*, 1913 (Springfield, 1914).

Hodder, Frank Heywood, "Genesis of the Kansas-Nebraska Act," Wisconsin State Historical Society, *Proceedings*, volume 60 (Madison, Wis., 1913).

Jahrbuch der Deutsch-Amerikanischen Historischen Gesellschaft von Illinois, edited by Julius Goebel, volumes 12, 14, 16 (Chicago, 1912, 1914, 1916).

Journal of the Illinois State Historical Society (Springfield, 1908-date).

Kiner, Henry L., *History of Henry County, Illinois* (Chicago, 1910).

BIBLIOGRAPHY

Koerner, Gustave P., *Das deutsche Element in den Vereinigten Staaten von Nordamerika, 1818-1848* (Cincinnati, 1880).

Kofoid, Carrie P., "Puritan Influences in the Formative Years of Illinois History," Illinois State Historical Society, *Transactions*, 1905 (Springfield, 1906).

Lansden, John M., *A History of the City of Cairo, Illinois* (Chicago, 1910).

Lee, Judson Fiske, "Transportation. A Factor in the Development of Northern Illinois previous to 1860," Illinois State Historical Society, *Journal*, volume 10 (Springfield, 1917).

Lippincott, Isaac, *A History of Manufactures in the Ohio Valley to the Year 1860* (New York, 1914).

Logan, John A., *The Great Conspiracy: its Origin and History* (New York, 1886).

The Lumber Industry of Chicago. Under this caption we review this great industry in detail, from the time Captain Carver brought in the first cargo, in 1834, to the ending of the year 1881. Embracing many facts, figures, and dates supposed to have been lost in the great fire of 1871 and is hitherto an unwritten chapter (Chicago, 1882).

McLean County Historical Society, *Transactions*, Bloomington, Illinois. Meeting of May 29, 1900, commemorative of the convention of May 29, 1856, that organized the republican party in the state of Illinois, volume 3 (Bloomington, 1900).

Mikkelson, Michael A., *The Bishop Hill Colony, a religious communistic Settlement in Henry County, Illinois* (Baltimore, 1892). [*Johns Hopkins University Studies in Historical and Political Science*, volume 10].

Moses, John, and Joseph Kirkland, *History of Chicago, Illinois*, 2 volumes (Chicago, 1895).

Moses, John, *Illinois Historical and Statistical, Comprising the Essential Facts of its Planting and Growth as a Province, County, Territory and State*, 2 volumes (Chicago, 1889).

Nevins, Allan, *Illinois* (New York, 1917) [American College and University Series].

Newton, Fred Earle, *Railway Legislation in Illinois from 1828 to 1870* [Thesis submitted for the degree of master of arts, University of Illinois, 1901].

Pease, Theodore C., *The County Archives of the State of Illinois* (Springfield, 1915) [*Collections of the Illinois State Historical Library*, volume 12].

BIBLIOGRAPHY

Pease, Theodore C., *The Frontier State* (Springfield, 1918) [*Centennial History of Illinois*, volume 2].

Pitman, Benn (ed.), *Trials for Treason at Indianapolis, disclosing Plans for Establishing a Northwestern Confederacy* (n. p., 1892).

Pooley, William V., *Settlement of Illinois, 1830-1850* (Madison, 1908) [Reprinted from *Bulletin of University of Wisconsin*, history series, volume 1].

Powell, Burt E., *The Movement for Industrial Education and the Establishment of the University 1840-1870* (Urbana, 1918) [*Semi-Centennial History of the University of Illinois*, volume 1].

Putnam, James W., *Illinois and Michigan Canal. A study in economic history* (Chicago, 1917) [Chicago Historical Society's *Collections*, volume 10].

Ray, Perley Orman, *The Convention that Nominated Lincoln*. An address delivered before the Chicago Historical Society on May 18, 1916, the fifty-sixth anniversary of Lincoln's nomination for the presidency (Chicago, 1916).

Ray, Perley Orman, *Repeal of the Missouri Compromise, its Origin and Authorship* (Cleveland, 1909).

Rhodes, James Ford, *History of the Civil War 1861-1865* (New York, 1917).

Rhodes, James Ford, *History of the United States from the Compromise of 1850 to the Final Restoration of Home Rule at the South to 1877*, 7 volumes (New York, 1906).

Ryan, John H., "Anti-Slavery Struggle in Illinois as it affected the Methodist Episcopal Church," Illinois State Historical Society, *Transactions*, 1913 (Springfield, 1914).

Schneider, George, "Lincoln and the Anti-Know-Nothing Resolutions," McLean County Historical Society, *Transactions*, volume 3 (Bloomington, 1900).

Schoff, S. S., *The Industrial Interests of Chicago*. Comprising a classified list, with locations and brief description, capital invested, number of men employed, and amount of annual production of the principal manufacturing establishments in the city (Chicago, 1873).

Scott, Franklin William, *Newspapers and Periodicals of Illinois 1814-1879* (Springfield, 1910) [*Collections of the Illinois State Historical Library*, volume 6].

Selby, Paul, "Lincoln and German Patriotism," *Jahrbuch der Deutsch-Amerikanischen Historischen Gesellschaft von Illinois*, volume 12 (Chicago, 1912).

BIBLIOGRAPHY

Selby, Paul, "The Part of Illinoisians in the National Educational Movement 1850-1862," Illinois State Historical Society, *Transactions,* 1904 (Springfield, 1904).

"A Short History of the Church in Illinois," in *The Springfield Churchman* (Springfield, August, 1916—March, 1917).

Smith, Theodore Clarke, *The Liberty and Free Soil Parties in the Northwest* (New York, 1897) [Toppan prize essay of 1896, *Harvard Historical Studies,* volume 6].

Stahl, Katherine, "Early Women Preachers of Illinois," Illinois State Historical Society, *Journal,* volume 9 (Springfield, 1917).

Stoneberg, "The Bishop Hill Colony," Kiner, *History of Henry County, Illinois* (Chicago, 1910).

Transactions of the Illinois State Historical Society (Springfield, 1900-1917).

Wilde, Arthur Herbert, *Northwestern University, a History,* 4 volumes (New York, 1905) [Semi-Centennial Edition].

Wilson, Buford, "Southern Illinois in the Civil War," Illinois State Historical Society, *Transactions,* 1911 (Springfield, 1913).

Wisconsin Historical Collections, volumes 1-12 (Madison, 1855-1892).

INDEX

Abner, Henry, 443
Abolitionists, *see* politics
Adams, Charles Francis, 59
Adams county, 14, 439
Agricultural College, Northern Illinois, *see* education
Agriculture, animal products, 83-85, 375-378; banking system needed for, 93; Buel Institute, 242; Durham and Northumberland Farmers' Club of England, 341; farmers' organized regiments, 279; field products, 75-83, 373-375, 378-381; Fox River Dairy Club, 376; Illinois and Wisconsin Dairymen's Association, 376; Illinois State Agricultural Society, 78, 84, 140, 243, 280, 379, 381, 383, 384, 434, 453; Illinois State Horticultural Society, 82, 374; Illinois State Sugar Cane Convention, 82; Illinois Stock Importing Company, 83; immigrants interested in, 9-14, 21, 330, 338, 339, 341; Industrial League, 384; La Salle County Agricultural Society, 242; machinery for, 79-80, 382; National Agricultural Society, 79, 242; Northwestern Agricultural Society, 79; Northwestern Fruit Growers' Association, 82; Northwestern Pomological Association, 242; Patrons of Husbandry, 386; Sangamon County Agricultural Society, 78; Southern Illinois Fruit Growers' Association, 374; transportation and, 27, 32, 49, 52, 355, 384-386; Turner advocated university for, 231, 240-245, 431-435; United States Agricultural Fair, 80; Wool Growers' Association, 378. *See* education
Alabama, 38, 330
Aldrich, Cyrus, 108
Alexander county, 279n, 341
Alexander, George D., 377
Alexander, John T., 376, 377, 383
Allen, George T., 135n, 352
Allen, James C., 118, 131, 196, 297, 299, 335
Allen, William Joshua, 297, 302, 309, 327, 328, 400, 411

Allen, Willis, 118
Alton, 7, 9, 11, 81, 85, 166, 213, 220, 248, 250n, 371n, 399, 433, 438, 440, 442, 445, 447, 453; anti-Nebraska forces in, 108, 118, 122, 123, 126; congressional election 1854 in, 131; education in, 430; encampment at, 262; know nothing movement in, 137; Lincoln-Douglas debate at, 169, 173; population of, 1, 2, 23; railroad connections with, 33, 42, 43, 44, 45, 46, 49, 51, 52; republican strength in, 173, 200
Alton and Mt. Carmel railroad, *see* transportation
Alton railroad, Chicago and, *see* transportation
Alton railroad, Springfield and, *see* transportation
Alton railroad, Terre Haute and, *see* transportation
American Baptist Free Mission Society, *see* religion
American Bible Society, *see* religion
American Board of Commissions for Foreign Missions, *see* religion
American Emigrant Company, *see* immigration
American Home Missions Society, *see* religion
American Missionary Association, *see* religion
American Tract Society, *see* religion
Ames, Alfred E., 61
Ames, E. B., 95
Amusements, Chicago parks, 349; Independent Baseball Club of Cairo, 447; kinds of, 436-449; National Association of Baseball Players of the Northwest, 447; National Baseball Player's Association, 447
Ancient Order of American Knights, *see* politics
Andover, 20
Anna, 286, 331
Anthony, Elliott, 269
Anthony, Susan B., 428
Antietam, battle of, 288, 296

477

478 INDEX

Antislavery Convention, Christian, *see* religion
Antislavery Convention, Northwestern Christian, *see* religion
Antislavery Society, Illinois State, *see* politics
Appomattox (Va.), 289
Archer, William R., 131, 149
Arenz, Francis, 105, 110
Arkansas, 271
Army of Potomac, 277, 322
Arnold, Isaac N., 59, 237, 304, 355, 356
Arntzen, Bernard, 196, 200
Art, development of, 437
Ashland (Ky.), 66
Ashmun, George, 195
Atchison, David R., 113-116
Athens, 19
Atkins, Jerome, 79
Atlanta (Ga.), 289, 324
Atlantic and Mississippi railroad, *see* transportation
Atlantic ocean, 356
Audubon Club, *see* clubs
Augusta, 367
Aurora, 41, 43, 51, 71, 128, 130, 161, 210, 213n, 351, 445
Aurora railroad, Chicago and, *see* transportation
Avoca, 252

Bailhache, John, 453
Bailhache, William Henry, 453
Baker, Edward D., 57, 67, 68
Baker, Edward L., 453
Baker, Edwin S., 82
Baker, Jehu, 126, 212n
Balatka, Hans, 444
Baltimore conventions: 1848, 55, 59, 60; 1852, 106, 107, 108, 130; 1860, 188, 195-196, 199; 1864, 317-318
Bancroft, George, 394
Banking, bank bill, 95-96, 103; facilities for, 92-95; issue of, in presidential election of 1868, 411; organization of, 97-100; panics of 1854 and 1857, 98, 100; problems of, 361-364; proposed anti-bank provision, 268, 270, 271; State Bank, 93
Banks, Nathaniel P., 142, 147, 161n
Baptist church, abolition, slavery, and, 220, 222, 224
Baptists, French, 17; Negro, 337; schools of, 237-238; strength of, 245, 246, 249, 424; women's rights movements and, 213

Baptist Free Mission Society, American, *see* religion
Baptist University of Chicago, *see* education
"Barnburners," 54
Barnum's Grand Colossal Museum and Menagerie, 438
Bascom, Flavel, 223
Baseball Player's Association, National, *see* amusements
Batavia, 380
Bateman, Newton, 163, 395, 396, 429, 430
Bates, Edward, 189, 191, 192, 194, 298
Bates, General Erastus N., 411
Baton Rouge (La.), 289
Beardstown, 1, 8, 18, 28, 85, 248, 249
Bebb, William, 15
Beecher, Henry Ward, 438
Beet Sugar Company, Germania, 381
Beet Sugar Company, Illinois, 381
Bell, John, 195, 200
Belleville, 25, 34n, 46, 81, 118, 215, 226, 258, 292, 369n, 421; bank in, 97; education in, 236, 430; enlistment in, 280; know nothing influence in, 137; opposed Kansas-Nebraska act, 122, 123; population of, 8, 23; temperance movement in, 204, 209, 210; union meeting at, 69
Belleville and Illinoistown railroad, *see* transportation
Belleville and Southern railroad, *see* transportation
Belmont, battle of, 266, 285, 399
Belvidere, 41
Benton, 201
Benton, Thomas H., 70, 106, 113
Berlin, 20
Bernadotte, 221
Betts, Charles A., 105
Bible Society, American, *see* religion
Biblical Institute, Northwestern, *see* education
Birney, James G., 59n
Bishop Hill, 20-21, 150n
Bissell, William H., 38, 44, 65; congressional aspirant, 108-109; congressman 1858, 57, 65; favored agricultural university, 244; governor 1856, 92, 100, 145-146, 151, 152, 181, 258; opposed Kansas-Nebraska act, 118, 122, 142; supported Fremont 1856, 147
Blackburn Theological Seminary, *see* education
Blackwell, Robert S., 130, 149

INDEX   479

Blair, Francis P., 147, 199, 298, 354, 411
Blair, Montgomery, 324
Blanchard, Jonathan, 218, 222, 223, 224, 231, 238-239, 240, 444-445
Blanchard, Mrs., 402
Bloody Island, 51
Bloomer, Mrs., 213
Bloomington, 28, 83, 87, 129, 177, 232, 283, 334, 360, 367, 375, 382n, 398, 426, 430, 432, 433, 434, 435n, 440; anti-Nebraska meeting in, 123, 128; Douglas and Lincoln in, 1858, 168, 171; growth of, 366; normal school at, 234, 235, 236; population of, 1, 2; republican convention 1856 at, 144-146, 148, 149, 150, 176, 190; state farmers' convention at, 384-385
Bloomington and Western railroad, Indianapolis, *see* transportation
Blue Island, 431
Bluffdale, 292, 294, 449
Board of Commissioners for Foreign Missions, American, *see* religion
Bond, Benjamin, 44, 228, 302
Boon, Levi D., 303
Booth, Edwin, 443
Borden and Company, Gail, 375
Bradley, Furst and, *see* Furst and Bradley
Bradwell, James B., 428
Bradwell, Mrs. Myra, 427, 428
Bragg, Braxton, 287
Brainard, Daniel, 59
Breckinridge, John C., 195, 196, 200, 411
Breckinridge, T. L., 403
Breese, Sidney, congressional aspirant 1852, 108-109; debated with Douglas, 132-133; opposed Kansas-Nebraska act, 126; proposed for president 1868, 410; railroad policies of, 36-38, 45; senatorial candidate 1849, 61-62, 63; senatorial candidate 1858, 162, 165, 166
British, *see* English
Brockway, James W., 337
Brooks, Thorndike, 402
Bross, William, 317
Brough, Colonel John, 44, 52
Brown, Antoinette L., 213
Brown, George T., 145, 449, 454
Brown, John, raid of, 182-183, 187
Browning, Orville H., 297, 403; leader at Bloomington convention 1856, 145, 146; secretary of the interior, 397-398; supported Fremont 1856, 149;

supported Kansas-Nebraska act, 127; supported Lincoln, 191, 192, 194, 298n, 314n, 323n
Bryce, James, 313
Buchanan, James, 106; break between Douglas and, 157-166, 174, 178, 179, 184-185, 187-188, 196; president 1856, 26, 91, 146-150, 151; presidential aspirant 1848, 53, 54; vetoed land grant bill for colleges, 244, 431
Buckmaster, Samuel A., 196
Buel Institute, *see* agriculture
Buena Vista (Mexico), 56, 57
Buffalo (N. Y.), 59, 60, 345
Buford, General N. B., 331, 335
Bull, Ole, 442
Bullock, L. L., 242
Bull Run, battle of, 264, 274
Bunsen, George, 25, 233
Bureau county, 218
Burlingame, Anson, 147
Burlington, and Quincy railroad, Chicago, *see* transportation
Burnett, Henry C., 174
Burnside, General Ambrose E., 303-304
Burritt, Elihu, 438
Bushnell, General Washington, 411
Butz, Caspar, 25, 317

Cabet, A. Charles, 18
Cairo, 118, 201, 226, 283, 354, 360, 368, 377, 397, 399, 401, 417n, 447, 448, 450, 457; congressional election of 1854 in, 131; crime in, 420; education in, 430; encampment in, 262, 304; enlistment in, 279, 306; Grant in command at, 266, 285; growth of, 7-8, 16, 351-353; immigrants in, 331, 332, 334, 335, 336, 337n, 339, 340, 344; kidnapping Negroes in, 228; railroad connections with, 32, 33, 36, 37, 38, 52; secession strength in, 253, 260, 262
Cairo City and Canal Company, *see* transportation
Cairo Emigrant Aid Society, *see* immigration
Calhoun, John, 111, 133, 173, 174n, 187, 317
California, 9-10, 12, 64, 66-68, 147, 348
Cambridge University, 240
Cameron, Daniel, 455
Cameron Guards, 281
Cameron, Simon, 191, 192, 193, 194, 264
Campbell, Alexander, 246, 372
Campbell, George H., 196
Campbell, James M., 121
Campbell, Thomas H., 103

INDEX

Canada, 17, 228, 229, 278, 310, 333, 345, 346-347, 355
Canisius, Theodore, 342
Canton, 28, 137, 210, 211n, 236, 251, 399
Carbondale, 210n, 374, 379, 402, 431
Carlinville, 51, 177, 210n, 250
Carlyle, 108
Carpenter, Philo, 218
Carthage, 283n, 285, 335, 423
Cartwright, Peter, 246, 249
Casey, Zadoc, 45, 104n
Caseyville, 262
Cass, General Lewis, 53, 54, 55, 58, 60, 61, 106, 147
Cassell, William M., 377
Catholics, 26; French, 17; strength, 245, 248, 425-426; temperance and, 206
Caton, John D., 31, 299, 327n, 366
Central America, 184
Central Commercial College, Sloan's, *see* education
Central Illinois Methodist Conference, *see* religion
Central Military Tract railroad, *see* transportation
Centralia, 21, 76, 331, 403, 425
Champaign, 50, 177, 407, 434
Champaign county, 78, 83, 373, 376, 377, 382, 383, 434
Chancellorsville (Va.), 288
Charleston, 169, 172, 306-308
Charleston (S. C.), 187-188, 199, 259
Chase, Philander, 247, 248
Chase, Salmon P., 118, 133, 192, 194, 315, 317, 323
Chatsworth, 381
Chattanooga (Tenn.), 284, 286, 288
Cheney, the Reverend Charles E., 425
Chicago, 31, 55, 59n, 60, 61, 73, 80, 108, 112, 118, 125, 195, 200, 212, 213n, 229, 243n, 257, 270, 292, 328, 338n, 342, 377, 381, 389, 396, 407, 428, 433, 434, 435n; amusements in, 436, 439, 440, 441, 442, 446, 447-448; antislavery meetings in, 219, 223, 224; art exhibit in, 437; banking in, 97, 99, 363; canal convention in, 355; churches in, 221, 222, 245, 247, 248, 249, 250, 251, 425, 445; commercial center, 29, 30, 46, 50, 51, 52, 76, 77, 85, 367, 374, 375, 384, 385; compromise of 1850 in, 71-72; congressional election of 1854 in, 129-130; crime in, 420; democratic convention at, 1864, 323, 326; Douglas in, 1855, 141; Douglas monument in, 398; Douglas' reception in, September 1, 1854, 132; education in, 230, 236, 237, 241, 242, 250, 429, 440; emancipation forces in, 295; enlistment in, 280-281; favored Bloomington convention 1856, 146; Fenian movement in, 344-347, 403; free soil meeting at, 69; growth of, 1, 2, 5-6, 16, 17, 19, 20, 21, 23-25, 348-353, 365; health conditions in, 216, 217; immigrants in, 11, 12, 332, 334, 336, 339, 340, 341n; industrial congress in, 89-90; insurance companies in, 94; Johnson clubs in, 397, 399; labor troubles in, 203, 369-372; land conventions at, 89, 90, 91; medical schools in, 217, 218; municipal election 1856, 144; municipal election 1859, 182; musical center, 442-444; Nebraska and anti-Nebraska forces in, 122, 123, 126, 140; Negroes in, 333; Negro organizations in, 227; newspapers in, 26, 304, 417, 419, 450, 453, 455, 456, 458; Northwestern Agricultural Society in, 79; Northwestern Fair at, 283; panics of 1854 and 1857 in, 98, 100; presidential election of 1860 in, 189, 190-195, 197; public utilities in, 3-4, 5, 6; republican national convention in 1868, 410, 412; Sabbath convention at, 214-215; secret political societies in, 308-310; senatorial election in, 1858, 158n, 159, 161, 162, 166, 167, 168, 173, 177, 179; strength of know nothings in, 138n, 139; temperance movement in, 205, 206, 208, 210; terminus of underground railroad, 228; transportation and, 28, 33, 34, 37, 38, 40, 41, 42, 43, 46, 47, 48, 50, 51, 52, 357, 361, 416; war democrats met at, 1863, 321n
Chicago Academy of Music, *see* music
Chicago Academy of Natural Sciences, *see* education
Chicago and Alton railroad, *see* transportation
Chicago and Aurora railroad, *see* transportation
Chicago and Galena railroad, *see* transportation
Chicago and Milwaukee railroad, *see* transportation
Chicago and Mississippi railroad company, *see* transportation
Chicago and Mobile railroad, *see* transportation

INDEX

481

Chicago and Northwestern railroad, *see* transportation
Chicago Arbeiter Verein, *see* labor
Chicago Board of Trade, 93, 278n, 303, 386, 354, 361n
Chicago, Burlington, and Quincy railroad, *see* transportation
Chicago Cotton Manufacturing Company, 367
Chicago Emigrant Agency, *see* immigration
Chicago Fire and Marine Insurance Company, 94
Chicago Hibernian Benevolent Emigrant Society, *see* immigration
Chicago Historical Society, *see* education
Chicago Jaegers, 281
Chicago Ladies Loyal League, 336
Chicago Mercantile Association, 278n
Chicago Musical Union, *see* music
Chicago Philharmonic Society, *see* music
Chicago railroad, Rock Island and, *see* transportation
Chicago railroad, St. Louis, Jacksonville, and, *see* transportation
Chicago, Rock Island, and Pacific railroad, *see* transportation
Chicago, St. Paul, and Fond du Lac Railway Company, *see* transportation
Chicago Theological Seminary, *see* education
Chicago Times, suppression of, 303-304
Chicago, University of, *see* education
Chinese Sugar Manufacturing Company, Northwestern, 380
Chiniquy, Father, 17
Christian Antislavery Convention, *see* religion
Christian church, 246, 424
Christian Commission, United States, *see* Civil War
Christian Union, *see* religion
Christy, William H., 127
Cincinnati (Ohio), 33, 35, 46, 146, 162, 185, 187, 223, 311
Civil liberties, suppression of, 300-305
Civil War, battles of, 266, 274, 284-289, 296, 324; conclusion of, 289, 387-390; desertion in, 305-306; Freemen's Aid Society, 283; German support of, 342; guerilla warfare, 306-308; Illinois agencies for relief, 282-284; Illinois enlistment and the draft, 263, 273-282, 305; Illinois Soldiers' Orphans' Home, 283; Illinois Soldiers' Relief Association, 282; Ladies' War Committee, 283; Lincoln's call to arms, 261; outbreak of, 259; stimulated prices, 363, 364; United States Christian Commission, 283; United States Sanitary Commission, 283, 332, 427
Clark county, 89
Clay, Cassius M., 133
Clay, Henry, 55-57, 60, 66-74, 101, 149, 176, 388n, 453
Clayton amendment, 123
Cleveland (Ohio), 227, 263, 317, 367n, 378
Clingman, Thomas L., 307
Clinton county, 26, 148
Clubs, Audubon, 446; Excelsior Society, 444; German, 25, 444; Hibernian Society, 444; Masonic order, 444, 445; New England societies, 444; Odd Fellows, 444; secret organizations, 444-445; Société Française, 444; Sons of Penn, 444; Sons of the Pilgrims, 444; St. Andrew's Society, 444; St. George's, 444; Young Men's Christian Association, 250, 303
Cobden, 374
Cochrane, John, 317
Cockle, Washington, 296
Codding, Ichabod, 128, 129, 131, 132, 133, 141, 218
Coffing, Churchill, 150, 175
Coles county, 307, 308
Colfax, Schuyler, 410, 413
Colleges, *see* education
Colorado, 9, 12
Colored National Convention, *see* Negroes
Columbus (Ohio), 14
Comiskey, John, 346, 347
Commerce, banking system needed for, 93-95; railroads stimulate, 49-52; water transportation stimulates, 29-30. *See* Chicago
Commissioners for Foreign Missions, American Board of, *see* religion
Compromise of 1850, 66-74, 103, 119
Congregational General Association, *see* religion
Congregationalists, 13, 220-224, 245, 247, 250, 424, 445
Conkling, James C., 105, 149
Conley, Philip, 161
Constable, Charles H., 149, 302
Constitutional union party, *see* politics
Cook, Burton C., 121, 134, 146, 258

482 INDEX

Cook county, 61, 102, 103n, 123, 190, 267, 269, 364, 365, 419, 431, 439
Cook, Isaac, 162, 188, 455
Cook, John, 421
Cooley, Horace S., 230, 235
Copperas Creek, 28
Copperheads, *see* politics
Corinth (Miss.), 287, 387
Cottage Hill, 432n
Coulterville, 224
Council Bluffs (Iowa), 361
Crane and Company's Great Oriental Circus, 438
Cravath, J. M., 382n
Cravath, M. A., 382n
Crawford county, 196
Crebs, John M., 398
Crimean War, 77
Crittenden, John J., 176n, 257, 291
Cromwell, Oliver, 313
Cuba, 184
Culture, amusements indulged in, 436-449; Chicago living conditions, 350; crime in the fifties, 203-204; during the war, 420-427; German, 24-26, 214-215, 343; of foreign population, 17. *See* education and religion
Cumberland Presbyterians, 246
Cumberland river, 7, 285
Cummings, Professor, 241
Cummins, Associate Bishop David, 425
Cunningham, Hibert B., 401, 402
Currency, demand for improved, 361-364; kinds of, 97-99; small circulation of, 93
Curtis, Benjamin R., 153, 154

Daggy, Professor, 442
Dahn, A. W., 443
Dana, Charles A., 456
Danenhower, William Weaver, 139, 150n, 176, 448, 449
Danville, 15, 360
Davis, David, 191
Davis, Jefferson, 68n, 184, 188, 294, 302, 308, 326
Davis, William M., 402
Dawson, Thomas H., 201n
Dayton, William L., 146, 150n, 185
Dayton, 367
Decatur, 4, 15, 43, 80, 283, 284, 328, 332, 351, 371, 378, 402, 407, 431, 456; anti-Nebraska convention at, 1856, 143-144, 145; congressional election 1854 in, 131; convention at, 1860, 190, 192, 196; Union League organized in, 396-397

Defiance, Camp, 262
De Kalb county, 130, 380
Delahay, Mark W., 166
Delavan, and Nathan's Circus, Welch, 438
Dement, John, 102, 103
Democratic party, *see* politics
Denmark, 342
Dental Convention, Western, *see* Western Dental Convention
Denton, Charles, 79
Detrich, John E., 296
Dickey, H. T., 228
Dickey, Theophilus Lyle, 150, 175, 398, 399, 402-403
Dickinson, Anna, 428
Dillman and Company, 371
District of Columbia, 69, 294, 318n
Dixon, Archibald, 117
Dixon, Arthur, 347
Dixon, 356, 457
Doblebower, John C., 303
Dodge, Augustus C., 115
Doggett, Kate M., 428
Donelson, Andrew J., 146
Donelson, Fort, 284, 285, 286, 387
Doolittle, James R., 199
Dougherty, John, 162, 166, 411
Douglas, Camp, 304, 310
"Douglas Invincibles," 258
Douglas, Stephen A., 25, 61, 62, 65, 136, 139n, 149n, 150n, 152, 279, 297, 398, 401, 454, 457; anti-Lecompton position of, 157-160; attempted to save the union, 257, 261; contributed land to University of Chicago, 237-238; debated with Lincoln, 169-173, 197; failed to avert anti-Nebraska victories 1854, 131-135; Grant follower of, 286; homestead bill of 1849, 90; interest in Pacific railroad, 361; internal improvement policies of, 31, 36-39, 44; Kansas-Nebraska act and, 113-127, 146, 455; objected to New England teachers, 235; opinion of, on Dred Scott decision, 154, 155, 156, 184; presidential aspirant 1852, 102, 105-107; presidential aspirant 1856, 146-147; presidential campaign 1860, 183-201; senator, 111, 160-180, 445; sought to unite democratic party, 141-142; supported Lincoln 1861, 259-260; urged compromise measures 1850, 65-72; Wentworth advocated, for president, 54
Douglass, Frederick, 133, 438

INDEX

Dred Scott decision, 153-155, 156, 163, 164, 171, 184, 187
"Driskells, the," 22
Dubois, Jesse K., 100, 191, 199
Duff, Andrew D., 302, 309
Duggan, Bishop James, 345, 425
Dunlap, Mathias L., 81
Dunne, P. W., 344n
Du Page county, 439
Du Quoin, 360, 399, 426
Durham and Northumberland Farmers' Club of England, *see* agriculture
Dutch, Alfred, 108, 453, 454
Dyer, Charles V., 59, 218, 219
Dyhrenfurth, Julius, 443

Earlville, 51
East St. Louis, 351. *See* Illinoistown
Eastman, Zebina, 146n, 218, 448
Economic conditions, among laborers, 202-204; influenced by growth of cities, 1-5; health conditions, 216-218; inadequate banking system and, 92; Negroes and, 227-229; railroads affect, 48-52
Eden, John R., 299, 307, 411
Edgar county, 218, 307, 308, 335
Edgewood, 360
Education, agricultural college agitation, 231, 232, 240-245, 407, 408, 431-435; Chicago Academy of Natural Sciences, 440; Chicago Historical Society, 440; colleges: Baptist University of Chicago, 237; Blackburn Theological Seminary, 250; Chicago Theological Seminary, 250; Eureka College, 431; Garrett Institute, 250; Hahnemann Medical College, 217; Illinois College, 217, 236, 256, 294, 433; Illinois Industrial University, 428, 431; Illinois Soldiers' College and Military Academy, 396n; Illinois State Normal University, 280, 336, 431, 440; Illinois Wesleyan University, 237; Jacksonville College, 231, 239, 240, 241, 439; Jubilee College, 247; Knox College, 218, 222, 231, 236, 238, 240, 433, 444; Lebanon College, 241; Lind University, 217; Lombard College, 336; McCormick Theological Seminary, 250; McKendree College, 238, 241; Mechanics' Institute of Chicago, 448; Northern Illinois Agricultural College, 244; Northwestern University, 237, 241, 250; Quincy College, 431; Rush Medical College, 217; Shurtleff College, 238, 336, 433; Sloan's Central Commercial College, 213n; Southern Illinois Normal University, 431; University of Chicago, 237-238, 432n; University of Illinois, 237, 239-245; Wheaton College, 239n; elementary, 230-236, 429-430; German interest in, 25, 340; higher, 236-245, 250, 431-435; Illinois Natural History Society, 440; Illinois Historical Society, 451; Illinois State Educational Society, 230-231, 235; Industrial League of the State of Illinois, 242; libraries, 440; National Educational Society, 234-235; Negro, 228, 336-337; regiment formed from Normal University, 280; State Teachers' Association, 440; State Teachers' Institute, 236
Edwards, Cyrus, 175
Edwards, Ninian W., 105, 232-233, 243
Edwardsville, 69, 248
Effingham county, 89
Elections, *see* politics
Elgin, 28, 40, 41, 200n, 246, 366, 375, 376
Ellis, R. F., 213
Ellis Island, 331
Elsinore (Denmark), 342
Elyutt, Archie J., 379
Emancipation proclamation, 296, 298, 300, 301, 335
Emerson, Ralph Waldo, 438
Emigrant Agency, Chicago, *see* immigration
Emigrant Aid Society, Cairo, *see* immigration
Emigrant Aid Society, German, *see* immigration
Emigrant Association, Vermont, *see* emigration
Emigrant Company, American, *see* immigration
Emigration, California, 9, 348; Emigrant Aid Society, 11; Kansas and Nebraska, 10-12, 348; Kansas Settlers' Society, 11; Kansas Women's Aid and Liberty Association, 12; Nebraska Colonization Company, 11; Vermont Emigrant Association, 13
Emporium, 8
England, 84, 118, 176, 339, 344, 365
Englewood, 431
English, 109, 443. *See* population
Episcopalians, 220, 247-249, 425

INDEX

Erie railroad, New York and, *see* transportation
Eureka College, *see* education
Evangelical church, 247
Evans, John, 241
Evanston, 250
Evarts, William M., 194
Everett, Edward, 120, 195
Excelsior Society, *see* clubs

Fairbury, 367
Farmington, 137, 211n
Farragut, Admiral David J., 324, 327, 398, 399
Fell, Jesse, 435n
Fenian movement, 344-346, 403
Ferree, Reverend, 201
Ficklin, Orlando B., 53
Field, Thomas, 228
Fillmore, Millard, 56, 107, 108, 110, 146, 149-150, 176, 302
Finance, business interests need system of, 92; need of new system of, 361-364; railroad construction and land sales affect, 91-92, 98. *See* banking and currency
Fink and Company, *see* transportation
Fire and Marine Insurance Company, Chicago, *see* Chicago
Flagg, Willard C., 374
Fleishman, Charles L., 23
Florence, 28
Florida, 254
Fond du Lac Railway Company, Chicago, St. Paul and, *see* transportation
Fondey, William B., 162
Fontenelle (Kansas), 11
Ford county, 377
Foreign Missions, American Board of Commissioners for, *see* religion
Forrest, Edwin, 443
Foster, Lemuel, 221n
Foster, R. G., 237
Fouke, Philip B., 109, 131
Fox river, 41
Fox River Dairy Club, *see* agriculture
France, 17, 381
Francis, Allen, 453
Francis, Simeon, 453
Frederic, 28
Fredericksburg, 288
Freedman's Aid Commission, Northwestern, *see* immigration
Freeman, J. D., 218
Freeman's Aid Society, *see* Civil War
Free Mission Society for the Northwest, *see* religion

Freeport, 79, 80, 127n, 258, 403, 413; doctrine, 170-172, 183, 184, 185, 187; Lincoln-Douglas debate at, 169
Free soil party, *see* politics
Fremont, General John C., possible presidential candidate, 189; presidential aspirant 1864, 315, 316, 317, 323, 324, 342; presidential candidate 1856, 146-148, 150n, 151, 200, 201; reason for being relieved of command, 291-292; relieved of command at St. Louis, 263, 264-266, 285, 318
French, 177, 341. *See* population
French, Augustus C., 3, 51, 54, 62, 65, 91, 162, 215n, 240, 241, 242; attitude toward banking, 94, 95, 97, 98; gubernatorial candidate 1848, 55, 56-57; land interests of, 88-89; railroad policy of, 34-35, 40, 44, 45
French Canadian, *see* population
Fruit Growers' Association, Northwestern, *see* agriculture
Fruit Growers' Association, Southern Illinois, *see* agriculture
Fry, James B., 276n
Fuller, General Allen C., 276n, 359, 395
Fuller, Henry W., 367
Fulton, 41, 396n
Fulton county, 305, 408
Funk, Isaac, 83, 150
Furst and Bradley Company, 365

Galena, 1, 7, 23, 33, 40, 41, 42, 161, 217, 250, 281, 286, 303, 351, 437
Galena railroad, Chicago and, *see* transportation
Galesburg, 20, 43, 169, 172, 245, 282, 336, 351, 433
Galva, 20, 150
Garrett Institute, *see* education
Garrison, William Lloyd, 133, 176, 218, 317, 439, 456
Geneseo, 280, 356
Geneva, 132
Gennert, Theodore, 381
Georgetown (Ky.), 238
Georgia, 61, 99, 178, 330
Georgian Bay, 30
German Emigrant Aid Society, *see* immigration
German guides, 281
Germania Beet Sugar Company, 381
Germans, 247, 292; amusements and, 215, 441; attitude toward Johnson, 394; customs of, 343-344; educational interest of, 233; enlistment among,

INDEX 485

263, 280-281; immigration of, 23-26, 340, 341; interested in music, 443-444; labor, 369; Lincoln's reëlection and, 316-317, 323, 327-328; political value of, 58, 110, 123-124, 137, 139, 148, 150-151, 177, 186, 189, 190, 200, 341-344; temperance movement and, 209-210. *See* population
Germany, 16, 23, 381
Gettysburg (Pa.), 288, 298
Giddings, Joshua R., 133, 141
Gillespie, Joseph, 44n, 109, 131, 149, 176
Glover, Joseph O., 59
Gooding, A. M., 218
Goodman, Epaphras, 223
Gordon, Joseph, 250n
Goudy, William C., 299
Government, bank measures, 362; bills passed 1863, 299; constitutional convention 1869, 418; educational reforms, 232-234; Negro laws, 333, 335-336; proposed constitution rejected, 259, 267-272; war measures passed, 262
Grand Army of the Republic, 396, 397, 399, 403
Grant, Ulysses S., 341n, 387, 389, 398, 399; battle of Belmont, 266; charges against, 295; general, 263; military achievements of, 285-289, 318, 327; president 1868, 408, 410-414; proposed presidential candidate, 322
Granville, 223, 241
Grau, J., 443
Grayville, 137
Great Britain, *see* England
Great Lakes, 29, 30, 37, 41, 42, 354, 355
Great Western, Illinois, *see* transportation
Great Western railroad, Toledo, Wabash, and, *see* transportation
Great Western Railway Company, *see* transportation
Greeley, Horace, 133, 160, 186, 253, 295, 319-320, 438
Green, Amos, 321
Green, David K., 403
Green, William H., 260, 273, 302, 403
Gregg, David L., 102, 103, 104
Gregory and Hastings, 377
Gregory, John M., 434
Grierson, Benjamin H., 289
Grierson's band, 442
Griggs, Clark R., 433, 434
Griggsville, 28
Grimshaw, Jackson, 317
Grove, 248

Grover, Leonard, 443
Grundy, 384

Hahnemann Medical College, *see* education
Hale, John P., 147
Haley, W. D., 122
Halleck, Henry W., 285, 287
Hamilton, 247
Hamlin, Hannibal, 194-195, 197, 201, 355
Haney, Richard, 423
Hannibal (Mo.), 360
Harney, William S., 263
Harper's Ferry, 182, 187
Harris, B. Frank, 78, 83
Harris, Onesimus, 333
Harris, Thomas L., 57, 67, 73, 131
Harvard University, 237, 451
Hastings, Gregory and, 377
Hawkins, John, 205
Hay, C. D., 156
Haynie, Isham W., 297, 317
Hayti, 227
Healy, G. P. A., 437
Hecker, Friedrich, 23, 25, 146, 151, 177, 274, 280, 316
Henry county, 20, 341n
Henry, Fort, 285
Herndon, William H., 145, 146n, 159, 290, 292, 314, 427
Hibernian Benevolent Emigrant Society, Chicago, *see* immigration
Hibernian Society, *see* clubs
Hillsboro, 35, 51, 237
Hinchcliffe, John, 369n
Hobbs, Mrs. Amelia, 428
Hodnett, John Pope, 346, 347
Hoffman, Francis, 26, 123, 151, 177, 190
Holbrook, Darius, 38, 39
Holly Springs (Miss.), 306
Home Missions Society, American, *see* religion
Homer, 382
Horticultural Society, Illinois State, *see* agriculture
Hossack, John, 229
Hovey, Charles E., 280
Howe, Julia Ward, 439
Hoyleton, 13
Hubbard, Mrs., 213
Humphreys, Truman, 84
Hunter, C. W., 218
Hunter, General David, 285
Hurlbut, General Stephen A., 263, 285, 288, 289, 303, 335, 397
Hussey, Obed, 79

486 INDEX

Icaria, 18-19
Idaho, 348
Illinois and Wisconsin Dairymen's Association, *see* agriculture
Illinois Beet Sugar Company, 381
Illinois Central, *see* transportation
Illinois College, *see* education
Illinois Conference, *see* Methodists
Illinois Congregationalist associations, *see* religion
Illinois Great Western, *see* transportation
Illinois Historical Society, *see* education
Illinois Industrial University, *see* education
Illinois Labor Convention, *see* labor
Illinois Natural History Society, *see* education
Illinois Order of American Knights, *see* politics
Illinois river, 28, 29, 30, 31, 52, 75, 80, 85, 109, 354, 416, 437
Illinois Soldiers' College and Military Academy, *see* education
Illinois Soldiers' Orphans' Home, *see* Civil War
Illinois Soldiers' Relief Association, *see* Civil War
Illinois State Agricultural Society, *see* agriculture
Illinois State Antislavery Society, *see* politics
Illinois State Educational Society, *see* education
Illinois State Horticultural Society, *see* agriculture
Illinois State Normal University, *see* education
Illinois State Sugar Cane Convention, *see* agriculture
Illinois State University, *see* education
Illinois Stock Importing Company, *see* agriculture
Illinois Wesleyan Missionary Conference, *see* religion
Illinois Wesleyan University, *see* education
Illinois Woman Suffrage Association, *see* women's movement
Illinoistown, 8, 34n, 44, 45, 46, 247, 262, 351
Illinoistown railroad, Belleville and, *see* transportation
Illinoistown railroad, Terre Haute and, *see* transportation
Immigration, American born, 12-16, 330-338; American Emigrant Company, 339; Cairo Emigrant Aid Society, 339; Chicago Emigrant Agency, 339; Chicago Hibernian Benevolent Emigrant Society, 21; effect of, upon agriculture, 75; foreign, 16-26, 338-344; German Emigrant Aid Society, 339; Northwestern Freedman's Aid Commission, 336; Prairie Land and Emigration Company, 21; railroads affect, 48, 51; Scandinavian Aid Society, 340; Women's Protective Immigration societies, 15
Independent Baseball Club of Cairo, *see* amusements
Indiana, 14, 43, 95, 176, 177, 192-194, 197, 200, 257, 263, 308, 310, 339
Indianapolis (Ind.), 33, 310
Indianapolis, Bloomington, and Western railroad, *see* transportation
Indians, 113
Industrial Congress, 90
Industrial League, *see* agriculture
Industrial League of the State of Illinois, *see* education
Ingersoll, Eben C., 296
Ingersoll, Robert, 427, 428
Iowa, 18, 42, 52, 83, 115, 194, 263, 330, 340, 357, 361
Ireland, 16, 62, 339, 344, 346, 398
Irish, 248, 425; enlistment among, 281; Fenian movement and, 344, 348; immigration of, 16, 21-23, 339n, 340, 341; National Fair, 344; political value of, 58, 136, 137, 150-151, 177, 200, 341, 344-348, 403; temperance movement and, 210. *See* population
Iroquois county, 377
Island Number 10, 286, 335
Italians, 341, 443. *See* population

Jackson, Andrew, 31, 74, 96, 101, 255, 314, 357
Jackson county, 368
Jacksonville, 10, 19, 190, 348, 376, 423, 426, 433, 439, 449; amusements in, 438, 442, 447; education in, 429; guerrilla bands in, 306; Illinois College in, 217, 236; Negroes in, 336; size of, 351; temperance movement in, 205, 210; Trumbull supports Lincoln in, 173; Turner from, 240, 314; union meeting at, 69
Jacksonville, and Chicago railroad, St. Louis and, *see* transportation
Jacksonville College, *see* education
Janson, Eric, 20

INDEX 487

Jefferson, Thomas, 54, 74
Jersey county, 428
Jerseyville, 218, 232, 303
Jessup, William, 192
Jews, 281, 341
Jo Daviess county, 303n
Johns, H. V., 84
Johnson, Andrew, 342, 346, 404, 410, 424n; impeached, 408-409; politicians' attitude toward, 391-403; vetoed Trumbull's bills, 395; visited Illinois, 398-399
Johnson, Herschel V., 201
Johnson, Madison T., 303, 321
Johnson, Moses, 228
Johnson, Professor, 442
Joliet, 29, 41, 249, 344, 371, 403, 421; abolition convention at, 147; know nothing movement in, 137; temperance movement in, 210
Jones, James C., 178
Jones, John, 338n
Jones, J. Russell, 333
Jones, William, 238
Jonesboro, 169, 172, 210n, 306n, 331, 374, 379
Jubilee College, *see* education
Judd, Norman B., 59, 121, 123, 134, 135, 186; campaigned for Lincoln 1860, 191, 193, 199; defeated for governor, 190

Kalamazoo (Mich.), 434
Kane county, 200n, 368, 375, 419
Kankakee, 17, 34, 177, 399
Kankakee river, 17
Kansas, 147, 156, 183, 239; emigration to, 7, 9, 10-12, 348; influence of Lecompton constitution on election of 1858, 157-180; Kansas-Nebraska act and, 113-124; republicans on in campaign of 1856, 148
Kansas-Nebraska act, 74, 158, 172, 176, 183, 190, 209, 219, 224, 455, 456; provisions and passage of, 113-124; republican party and, 125-152
Kansas Settlers' Society, *see* emigration
Kansas Women's Aid and Liberty Association, *see* emigration
Keep, Henry, 359
Kellogg, A. N., 458
Kellogg, L. D., 335
Kellogg, William, 256
Kendall county, 426
Kennicott, John A., 241, 245
Kennison, David, 60
Kenosha, 71

Kentucky, 15, 174, 175, 176n, 191, 194, 195, 238, 263, 271, 285, 291, 310, 331, 335n, 425
Killpatrick, Thomas M., 231
King, William R., 109
Kinkel, Gottfried, 24
Kinney, William C., 135n
Knapp, Anthony, 296
Knights of the Golden Circle, *see* politics
Know nothing party, *see* politics
Knox College, *see* education
Knox county, 20, 172
Knox, James, 111, 118, 131, 137
Knox, John T., 73
Knoxville, 131
Koerner, Gustave, 44, 46, 326n; commissioner 1861, 258; gubernatorial aspirant, 139; lieutenant governor, 26, 45n, 103, 110, 134, 135n; minister to Spain, 342; opinion on Dred Scott decision, 155; opinion on secession, 255n; opposed Kansas-Nebraska act, 123, 142-144; raised regiment, 280-281; republican leader, 25, 226, 262; supported Fremont, 147, 151, 265; supported Lincoln, 177, 191, 192, 199
Kroh, J. M., 82
Kuykendall, Andrew J., 261, 296, 317, 328, 336n, 397, 417n

Labor, affected industrial development, 368-369; Chicago Arbeiter Verein, 369; colored, 334; emigration affects, 15; European, 339, 381-382; Illinois Labor Convention, 370; National Labor Union, 419; political value of, 325, 370-372; protection of home, 410; shortage of farm, during war, 373; wages and unemployment of, 202-204
Lacon, 367
Ladies' War Committee, *see* Civil War
Lafayette, 20
Lake Forest, 217
Land, railroads, and speculators in, 47-48, 85; reform, 89-91, 102; sale of, 85-89
Lane, Henry S., 193
Lanphier, Charles H., 454
La Salle, 8, 10n, 22, 28, 29, 42, 241, 340, 366, 372, 433
La Salle county, 13, 78, 128, 218, 267, 373, 384, 419
La Salle County Agricultural Society, *see* agriculture
Latshaw, W. D., 454

INDEX

Lawrence, 12
Lawrence county, 368
League of Universal Brotherhood, *see* religion
Lebanon, 201, 225
Lebanon College, *see* education
Lecompton constitution, 157-180
Lee county, 102, 457
Lee, Robert E., 289, 390
Leib, Charles, 166
Lemen, James, 246
Lexington, 423n
Liberty, 211n
Libraries, *see* education
Lima, 423
Lincoln, 211n
Lincoln, Abraham, 57, 101, 121, 137n, 181, 182, 219, 285, 288, 388n, 389, 398, 399, 421-422, 423, 439; answered Douglas 1854, 133; attended anti-Nebraska convention 1856, 143-144; attitude toward slavery and the war, 291-295; called for volunteers, 260, 261; debated with Douglas, 169-173, 197; defeated for senate 1858, 161, 163-180; difficulty of position, 290; disagreement with Fremont, 265, 291-292, 318; effect of assassination of, 390-391; effect of election of, 253, 254, 333; emancipation proclamations, 296, 298, 300, 301, 313, 335; German vote in election of, 341-342; inaugural address of, 259; misunderstanding between Illinois republicans and, 263-266, 290, 292-293, 297-298; offered governorship of Oregon, 64n; opinion of, on Dred Scott decision, 154-155, 156; policy of regarding secession, 255-256, 257-258, 259; policy toward disloyalists, 302-303; presidential campaign 1860, 91, 185-201, 229, 361; reconstruction policy of, 392-393, 397; reëlected 1864, 312-329; refused alignment with republican party 1854, 128-129, 135; religious views of, 426-427; revoked suppression of *Chicago Times*, 304; ridiculed Cass, 58; senatorial aspirant 1854, 134-135; signed land grant bill for colleges, 245; spoke at Bloomington convention 1856, 145, 146; supported Fremont 1856, 147, 149; Taylor supported, 56, 60; Yates demanded credit for Illinois army from, 277
Lincoln-Douglas debates, 168-173, 185
Lincoln Rifles, 281
Lind, Jenny, 442

Lind, University, *see* education
Lippincott, General Charles E., 396, 411
Literature, 439-440; periodicals, 448-449
Livermore, Mary A., 427, 428
Liverpool (England), 28
Livingston county, 18, 381
Lockport, 29
Logan county, 175, 230
Logan, General John A., 45, 296, 297, 328, 397; approved Johnson's impeachment, 409; author of black laws of 1855, 336n; congressional candidate 1868, 44; elected to congress, 1866, 396, 399-403; in presidential campaign 1860; 200-201; joined army, 262, 279; made general, 287; nominated Grant 1868, 410; opposed Trumbull, 404; supported Lincoln 1864, 327; supported secession, 260, 261n, 262, 302
Logan, Mrs. John A., 401, 402
Logan, Stephen T., 57, 191, 258, 298
Lombard College, *see* education
London (England), 3, 21
Long, Annie, 335
Lord, Amasa, 251
Loss, L. H., 223
Louisiana, 18, 288, 289, 380
Louisville (Ky.), 284, 298, 438
Lovejoy, Owen, abolitionist, 133, 218, 270; at republican convention, 128, 129; attended Bloomington convention 1856, 146; "barnburner," 59; congressman 1856, 150, 175; supported Fremont 1856, 147
Lowe, Samuel J., 59
Lutherans, 24, 26, 237, 245, 247
Lyons, Nathaniel, 285

Mabies' Grand Olympic Arena, E. F., and J., 438
Macalister and Stebbins bonds, 92
Macomb, 28, 210
Macoupin, 233n
Macoupin county, 145
Madeira Island, 19
Madison county, 148, 149, 175, 176, 212, 374
Maher, Hugh, 196
Maine, 194, 195, 285
Maine law, 204, 207-209
Malcolm, Howard, 238
Maloney, Richard S., 73
Manly, Uri, 88
Manny, J. H., 79

Manufactures, growth of, 364-367; railroads stimulate, 50
Marion, 260, 400, 401
Marmaduke, Vincent, 311
Marshall, Samuel S., 131, 298, 299
Mason and Dixon line, 185
Mason county, 175, 408
Mason, J., 247
Masonic order, *see* clubs
Massac county, 273, 279n, 302
Massachusetts, 40, 147, 161n, 186, 194, 282, 289, 338
Matteson, Joel A., 44, 92, 96; candidate for United States senate, 134-135; governor 1852, 45, 98, 102-103, 104, 112, 177, 232
Mattoon, 51, 177, 286, 308, 399
Mayo, E. L., 130
McCarthy, Owen, 161
McChesney, J. H., 432n
McClellan, General George B., 322-323, 324, 326, 327, 328
McClernand, General John A., 38, 45, 398; adhered to democratic party, 143; advice to French, 65-66; attitude toward Kansas-Nebraska act, 126; commissioned general, 263, 285; congressman, 57, 182; debated with Douglas, 132-133; joined army, 262, 279; opinion on secession, 256; presented Douglas' plan, 67; resigned commission, 287, 288; senatorial candidate, 63; supported McClellan, 327
McClun, John L., 129
McConnell, James, 84
McCormick, Cyrus H., 79, 223n, 328, 365, 370, 425
McCormick Theological Seminary, *see* education
McCorrisk, Father, 211n
McHenry county, 376
McKendree College, *see* education
McLean county, 87, 373
McLean, John, 146, 153, 154
McMasters, S. Y., 122
McMurty, William, 55
McVicker, James H., 441
Mebrille, L. F., 135n
Mechanics' Institute, *see* education
Medical Society, State, *see* State Medical Society
Medill, Joseph, 314n, 410, 418n, 456
Memphis (Tenn.), 285, 286, 287, 303
Menard county, 442
Menard, Pierre, 56
Mendelssohn society, *see* music

Mendon, 14
Mendota, 41, 43, 380
Mercer county, 20
Merchants' Grain Forwarding Association, 76
Meredosia, 33
Meredosia railroad, Springfield and, *see* transportation
Mersy, Augustus, 280
Methodist Conference, Central Illinois, *see* religion
Methodists, 423, 424; abolition, slavery, and, 220, 224; Negro, 337; schools of, 237, 239n; strength of, 245-246, 249, 250; Swedish, 340
Metropolis, 210n
Mexican War, 55, 56, 57, 62, 86, 101, 178, 286
Mexico, 83, 178, 184, 308
Michigan, 128, 142, 147, 316, 350, 435
Michigan Central, *see* transportation
Michigan City, 167
Michigan, Lake, 5, 37, 42, 109, 350, 437
Milford, 211n
Military Tract railroad, Central, *see* transportation
Militia, reorganization of, 1861, 258-259, 273
Miller, James, 92, 129, 163
Milliken, Isaac L., 132
Milwaukee (Wis.), 247, 446
Milwaukee and St. Paul railroad, *see* transportation
Milwaukee railroad, Chicago and, *see* transportation
Mining, growth of, 368; railroads stimulate, 32, 50
Minnesota, 52, 194, 263, 340, 348, 357
Mission societies, *see* religion
Missionary association, American, *see* religion
Mississippi, 38, 289, 401
Mississippi railroad, Atlantic and, *see* transportation
Mississippi Railroad Company, Chicago and, *see* transportation
Mississippi railroad, Ohio and, *see* transportation
Mississippi river, 1, 5, 7, 12, 13, 15, 16, 29, 30, 32, 33, 34, 37, 41, 42, 51, 52, 65, 66, 109, 148, 204, 246, 263, 264, 284, 286, 288, 289, 330, 334, 350, 351, 352, 354, 355, 356, 357, 373, 379, 409, 427, 437
Missouri, 11, 52, 82, 83, 98, 99, 106, 147, 164, 189, 199, 228, 292, 307, 310,

332, 333, 360, 366, 411; Illinois troops in, 271, 274, 276, 280, 285; presidential vote 1860, 194; secession strength in, 263, 264, 266, 285, 330-331
Missouri Compromise, 64; repeal of, 113, 116, 119, 120, 122, 123, 127, 134, 139, 144
Missouri river, 65, 113
Mitchell, John, 438
Mobile (Ala.), 324
Mobile railroad, Chicago and, *see* transportation
Moline, 20
Monmouth, 414
Monroe county, 148
Montgomery county, 307, 398
Moore, Jesse H., 422
Moore, John, 73, 133
Morgan county, 69, 83, 126, 128, 175, 281, 376, 383, 442
Morgan, James D., 327
Morgan railroad, Sangamon and, *see* transportation
Mormons, 18, 60, 426
Morrill, Justin S., 244
Morrill land grant act, 383, 431, 432
Morris, 3, 356
Morris, Buckner S., 72n, 149, 150, 176, 196, 311
Morris, Colonel Isaac N., 256, 296, 414
Morrison, A. L., 344
Morrison, Colonel James Lowery Donaldson, "Don," 45, 46, 56, 105, 149, 196
Morrison, Colonel William R., 300n
Moses, Adolph, 414
Moses, John, 143
Moulton, Samuel W., 336n
Moultrie county, 411
Mound City, 8, 227
Mt. Carmel railroad, Alton and, *see* transportation
Mulkey, John H., 302, 309
Mulligan, James A., 281
Murfreesboro, 287
Murray, Bronson, 243n
Music, Chicago Academy of Music, 444n; Chicago Musical Union, 443; Chicago Philharmonic Society, 443, 444; growth of appreciation for, 440-444; Mendelssohn society, 443; North American Sängerbund, 444; Oratorio Society, 444; Orchestral Union, 443; Union Musical Association, 442

Naperville, 28, 97

Naples, 43
Nashville (Tenn.), 284
Nathan's Circus, Welch, Delavan, and, 438
National Agricultural Society, *see* agriculture
National Association of Baseball Players of the Northwest, *see* amusements
National Baseball Player's Association, *see* amusements
National Educational Society, *see* education
National Labor Union, *see* labor
"National Reform" Association of Chicago, 91
National Union party, *see* politics
National Watch Company, 366
Native American movement, *see* politics
Natural History Society, Illinois, *see* education
Nauvoo, 18, 19, 375, 426
Nebraska, 361; immigration into, 9-12, 348; Kansas-Nebraska act and, 113-124
Nebraska Colonization Company, *see* emigration
Negroes, Chicago Literary Society, 227; Colored National Convention, 227; enlistment among, 281-282; influx of, 333-338; laws concerning, 71, 74, 225-229, 268, 270, 271, 299, 335, 387, 388, 412, 417-418; number of 1860, 225; political rights of, 337, 388. *See* slavery
New England, 11, 13-15, 96, 105, 189, 199, 204, 205, 209, 218, 230, 234, 235, 238, 247, 310, 316, 323, 338, 364, 366n, 409, 449
New England societies, *see* clubs
New Jersey, 192
New Mexico, 64, 66, 68, 70, 116
New Orleans (La.), 49, 77, 285, 289
Newspapers, 201n; attitude of, toward Kansas-Nebraska act, 119-121, 123, 143-144; Chicago, 6; development of, 449-458; fight for freedom of press, 1862-1863, 301, 303-305; German, 26; influence of editors in senatorial election 1858, 175-176; Nauvoo, 18; Norwegian, 19; Swedish, 20, 340; temperance, 205
New York, 14, 58, 89, 93, 95, 96, 105, 147, 189, 205, 213, 252, 275, 316, 322, 323, 339, 411, 440, 444

INDEX

New York and Erie railroad, *see* transportation
New York City, 6, 15, 16, 42, 47, 49, 81, 83, 91, 178, 213, 246, 338, 339, 344, 349, 350, 352, 359, 364, 369, 376, 410, 451
Niagara (N. Y.), 320
Niagara Falls, 356
Nicholson letter, 117
Nicolay, John G., 156
Noble, Harrison, 371
Normal, 42
Normal University, *see* education
North American Sängerbund, *see* music
North Carolina, 15, 105
Northern Cross railroad, *see* transportation
Northern Illinois Agricultural College, *see* education
Northern Pacific railroad, *see* transportation
Northumberland Farmers' Club of England, Durham and, *see* agriculture
Northwestern Agricultural Society, *see* agriculture
Northwestern Biblical Institute, *see* education
Northwestern Chinese Sugar Manufacturing Company, 380
Northwestern Christian Antislavery Convention, *see* religion
Northwestern Fair, 283
Northwestern Freedman's Aid Commission, *see* immigration
Northwestern Fruit Growers' Association, *see* agriculture
Northwestern Manufacturing Company, 371
Northwestern Pomological Association, *see* agriculture
Northwestern railroad, Chicago and, *see* transportation
Northwestern Sabbath Convention, *see* religion
Northwestern University, *see* education
Norton, Jesse O., 150, 175, 219, 403; congressman, 111, 130, 137; opposed Kansas-Nebraska act, 118
Norway, 19
Norwegians, *see* Scandinavians

O'Brien, W. W., 411
Odd Fellows, *see* clubs
Odell, 18
Ogden, Mahlon D., 59
Ogden, William B., 40
Ogle county, 22
Oglesby, General Richard J., 288, 346, 403, 433; called special sessions, 407; governor 1864, 328, 339, 349, 371, 377, 381, 387, 405, 409, 415, 426, 433; opinion on reorganizing militia, 273; opposed Trumbull, 404; Palmer succeeded as governor, 414
O'Hair, John, 308
Ohio, 14, 15, 93, 94, 133, 141, 146, 185, 186, 194, 200, 257, 263, 296, 322, 326, 366, 376, 410, 411, 453
Ohio and Mississippi railroad, *see* transportation
Ohio river, 7, 13, 30, 65, 263
Oliver, A. R., 341
Olmstead, C. E., 381
Olney, 305
Omaha (Neb.), 361
Omelveny, Harvey K. S., 121, 268, 298
Ontario, Lake, 30
Oquawka railroad, Peoria and, *see* transportation
Oratorio Society, *see* music
Orchestral Union, *see* music
Order of American Knights, Illinois, *see* politics
O'Reagan, Bishop Anthony, 248
Oregon, 64, 348, 365, 453
Orphans' Home, Illinois Soldiers', *see* Civil War
Osgood, Uri, 121, 134
Osman, Moses, 454
Osman, William, 454
Ottawa, 8, 28, 29, 41, 69, 79, 150, 221, 243n, 254, 258, 340, 371n, 380, 398, 447; anti-Nebraska meetings in, 122, 128; antislavery convention at, 223; enlistment in, 281; free soil convention at, 59; growth of, 18, 366-367; know nothing movement in, 137; Lincoln-Douglas debate at, 169, 170; schools in, 236; slave rescue case in, 182, 229; temperance movement in, 206-207, 210, 211n
Overland trail, 9
Oxford University, 240

Pacific railroad, Chicago, Rock Island, and, *see* transportation
Palestine, 248
Palmer, General John M., 232, 302; anti-Nebraska democrat, 134, 144n; attended Bloomington convention, 145; attitude toward Kansas-Nebraska act, 121, 126; bills vetoed by, 1869, 416; campaigned for Lincoln 1860,

INDEX

191, 199; commissioned general, 285; debates with Douglas, 132-133; defeated for congress, 182; governor 1868, 337, 359, 411, 414, 428; Illinois commander of G. A. R., 397; inaugural speech of, 414-415; not commissioned general, 263-264; opinion of Grant, 287; opinion of Lincoln, 313; opposed Trumbull, 404-405; supported Fremont 1856, 148
Pana, 314, 360, 399
Paris, 221, 307
Paris (France), 79, 339, 383
Parkman, Dr., 451
Parks, Gavion D. A., 403
Pasedeloup, Francis, 341n
Patrons of Husbandry, *see* agriculture
Patti, Adelina, 442
Paxton, 340
Peck, Ebenezer, 108
Peck, Ira L., 242
Peck, John Mason, 23, 122, 241, 246
Pekin, 1, 5, 28, 123, 127, 309, 360
Pendleton, George H., 322, 328n, 364, 410, 411
Peninsular campaign, 288
Pennsylvania, 14, 60, 192, 194, 200, 264, 364, 409, 440
Peoria, 28, 30, 52, 79, 81, 84, 85, 148, 177, 200n, 248, 256, 289n, 296, 321, 344n, 375, 399, 411, 423, 434; growth of, 1, 5, 7, 23, 351, 366
Peoria and Oquawka railroad, *see* transportation
Peoria county, 267, 408
Perry county, 81, 148, 419
Peru, 8, 10n, 23, 28, 29
Peru and Rock Island railroad, *see* transportation
Petersburg, 236
Philadelphia (Pa.), 15, 139, 146-147, 149, 185, 399, 425
Phillips, David L., 395
Phillips, Colonel Jesse J., 398
Phillips, L. D., 80
Phillips, Wendell, 319, 439
Piatt county, 383
Piccolomini, Marietta, 442
Pickering, William H., 47
Pierce, Franklin, 101; consents to Kansas-Nebraska proposal, 117; president 1852, 107, 109-110, 112
Pike county, 360
Pike's Peak, 12
Pitman, James M., 426
Pittsburg (Pa.), 146
Pittsburg Landing (Tenn.), 284, 286-287
Pittsfield, 28
Plano, 211n, 426
Poles, 341. *See* population
Politics, abolition movement, 136, 139, 147, 218-220, 235, 239, 246, 291-310; acts and influence of copperheads, 296, 302-303, 305-310, 332; Ancient Order of American Knights, 310; and religion, 423; compromise agitation of 1850, 63-74; congressional elections: 1852, 108-109; 1854, 129-135, 137; 1856, 150; 1862, 296-298; 1866, 396, 398-403; constitutional or national union party, 195; death of Lincoln and attitude toward Johnson, 390-403; democratic party: candidates and platform 1848, 53-55, 57; defeated in congressional elections 1854, 129-135, 137; Nebraska issue and, 125-127; organization 1864, 320-323, 324-328; strength in constitutional convention 1862, 266-269; temperance causes break in, 208; victories, 1862-1863, 296-301, 312; view of secession, 256-257, 258-259; finance and, 93-96, 103; free soil party, 59-64, 70, 73, 110, 111, 218-219; growth of labor power and, 370-372; gubernatorial elections: 1852, 102-105; 1856, 143-146, 151-152; 1860, 190, 196; 1864, 387; 1868, 411-414; Illinois Order of American Knights, 321; influence of foreign vote, 25-26, 341-348; Kansas-Nebraska act and, 113-124; Knights of the Golden Circle, 308-310; know nothing party, 136-141, 149, 444; land reform and, 89-91; Lecompton constitution and senatorial election of 1858, 153-180; legislative session 1867, 405-407; legislative session 1869, 415-418; native American movement, 136, 137, 138, 139; Negro vote, 337; newspapers for, 452-458; party organization 1855, 141-143; presidential elections: 1848, 57-61; 1852, 102, 105-108, 109-110; 1856, 146-151; 1860, 183-189, 191-201; 1864, 312-329; 1868, 408-414; reconstruction, 318-319, 325; republican party: disintegration of, 418-419; effect of Negro importations on, 334-336; formed from anti-Nebraska forces, 127-129, 141; friction in, 312-320, 323; inspired by war victories 1864, 324-329; misunderstanding between Lincoln and, 264-266, 290, 292-293, 297-298, 312, 314; offered new constitu-

INDEX

tion, 268-272; supported war, 262; view of secession, 254-256, 257; senatorial election 1867, 404-405; Sons of Liberty, 310; Union League, 309-310, 396, 403; whig party; candidates and platform 1848, 53, 55-56, 57; decline of, 101, 111, 112-113, 135, 140; Kansas-Nebraska act and, 127; "Wide awake" organization, 197-198, 258; women's suffrage movement, 428-429
Polk, James K., 31, 53-54, 58, 64, 101
Pomological Association, Northwestern, *see* agriculture
Pool, O., 414
Pope county, 260
Pope, General John, 263, 286
Popular sovereignty, Dred Scott decision and, 153-154; in 1854, 113-124; in Lincoln-Douglas debates, 155-180
Population, English, 21, 341; foreign born, 16-26, 338-344; French, 17-19; French Canadian, 17; German, 23-26, 340-341; increase of, 1-2, 5-9, 12-26; Irish, 21-23, 340-341; Italian, 341; Negro, 225; Polish, 341; Portuguese, 19; Scandinavian, 19-20, 340-341; Scotch, 341; southern white and Negro, 330-338
Portuguese, 19, 281, 341
Potawatomi, 436
Potomac, *see* army of
Powell, William H., 234, 241
Prairie Land and Emigration Company, *see* immigration
Prentice, George D., 438
Prentiss, General Benjamin M., 262, 263, 285, 401
Presbyterians, 17, 425; abolition, slavery, and, 220-222, 223, 224; strength of, 245, 246, 247, 249, 250
Price, Sterling, 292
Price, William, 159
Princeton, 210
Pruessing, Ernest, 317
Puget Sound, 361n
Pulaski county, 341
Pulley, James D., 262n, 401
Putnam county, 128, 223, 244

Quarter, Bishop William, 248
Quimby, Judge, 414
Quincy, 5, 9, 11, 117, 218, 250, 258, 282, 375, 414, 426, 439, 446; churches in, 245, 248; congressional election 1854 in, 131; democratic victory in, 144; education in, 236; growth of, 1, 8, 23, 351, 366; know nothing influence in, 137, 138n; land office closed at, 87; Lincoln-Douglas debate at, 169; Negroes in, 334, 336; support of Kansas-Nebraska act in, 127; public utilities in, 5; republican victory in municipal election, 182; temperance movement in, 207
Quincy College, *see* education
Quincy railroad, Chicago, Burlington, and, *see* transportation

Rafferty, Patrick, 347
Raith, Julius, 281
Randolph county, 148
Randolph, James W., 127
Rantoul, Robert, 40
Raum, Green B., 396
Ray, Dr. Charles H., 144, 393, 395, 409, 417n, 456
Raymond and Company's Mammoth Menagerie, 438
Reconstruction, *see* politics
Redman, Jackson, 226
Reformed Episcopal Church, 425
Reformed Presbyterians, 246
Religion, 3n; abolition, slavery, and the church, 220-225; activities, 248-252; American Baptist Free Union Society, 222; American Bible Society, 250-251; American Board of Commissioners for Foreign Missions, 222; American Home Missions Society, 250; American Missionary Association, 222, 250; American Tract Society, 222, 250, 251; campaign against secret societies, 445; Central Illinois Methodist Conference, 423, 424n; Christian Antislavery Convention, 223-224; Christian Union, 423; Congregational General Association, 445; during and after the war, 422-427; Free Mission Society for the Northwest, 222; growth of churches, 245-248; Illinois Congregationalist associations, 223; Illinois Wesleyan Missionary conference, 222; League of Universal Brotherhood, 224; ministers denounced Kansas-Nebraska act, 122; ministers formed company, 280; Negro churches, 337; Northwestern Biblical Institute, 250; sabbath observance and churches, 214-216; temperance and churches, 206, 211; United States Christian Commission, 283; Western Tract Con-

vention, 222; Western Unitarian Conference, 220; women's rights movement and churches, 213. *See* education and various denominations
Republican party, *see* politics
Reynolds, John, 45, 46, 69, 122, 321, 400; adhered to democratic party, 143; opposed Kansas-Nebraska act, 126, 162; opposed new constitution, 271; supported secession, 261
Reynolds, John P., corresponding secretary of State Agricultural Society, 379, 381, 383
Rhode Island, 282
Rice, John B., 371
Rice's Hippodrome, Dan, 438
Richardson, Colonel William A., attitude toward war, 296, 299, 300; congressman, 57, 131; defeated for governor 1856, 145, 149, 151; Douglas follower, 67, 90; managed Douglas campaign 1860, 188; senator, 298, 328; voted for Kansas-Nebraska bill, 117, 118
Richmond, James C., 247
Richmond (Va.), 277, 289, 320, 387, 389
Robinson, Charles, 147
Robinson, James C., 296, 299, 328
Rochester Mills, 82
Rockford, 11, 12, 20, 250, 340, 376, 447; anti-Nebraska meetings in, 122, 127; enlistment in, 281; growth of, 366, 367; railroad connections with, 33, 41, 48; republican convention in, 128; republican strength in, 151; republican victory in municipal election, 182; strength of know nothings in, 138n; temperance movement in, 207, 210; volunteers from, 277
Rockford, Rock Island and St. Louis railroad, *see* transportation
Rock Island, 1, 34, 41, 42, 52, 356
Rock Island and Chicago railroad, *see* transportation
Rock Island, and Pacific railroad, Chicago, *see* transportation
Rock Island, and St. Louis railroad, Rockford, *see* transportation
Rock Island county, 334
Rock Island railroad, Chicago and, 349
Rock Island railroad, Peru and, *see* transportation
Rock river, 354, 356
Rock River Conference, *see* Methodists
Rock Spring, 122
Rockton, 5
Rockwell and Company's Mammoth Circus, 438
Rodgers, the Reverend, 335n
Roe, Dr. Edward R., 196, 240, 241, 449
Rosecrans, General William S., 287, 288
Ross, Lewis W., 196
Roy, J. E., 237
Rugg, G. H., 79
Rush Medical College, *see* education
Rushville, 28
Russell, John, 292, 294, 449
Russia, 341
Rutherford, Reuben C., 243
Rutland, 13
Rutland (Vt.), 13
Ryan Guards, 281

Sabbath Convention, Southwestern Illinois, *see* religion
Safford, Dr. Mary J., 428
Salem, 34, 45, 79, 141
San Francisco (Cal.), 350, 361
Sangamon and Morgan railroad, *see* transportation
Sangamon county, 84, 105, 128, 175, 378
Sangamon County Agricultural Society, *see* agriculture
Sanitary Commission, United States, *see* Civil War
Savannah, 289n, 387
Sawyer, J. L., 374
Sawyer, S. S., 374
Scandinavian Aid Society, *see* immigration
Scandinavians, 150, 177, 247. *See* population
Scanlon, J. F., 347
Scanlon, Michael, 344
Schlaeger, Edward, 123
Schmidt, Ernest, 317n
Schneider, George, 25, 26, 123, 144, 151, 342
Schröder, Dr. H., 375
Schurz, Carl, 177, 192n, 199, 342
Schuttler, Peter, 365
Scotch, 281, 341. *See* population
Scotch regiments, 281
Scott, General Winfield, 56, 107, 109-110
Scripps, John L., 455
Secession, 102; accomplished, 259; Douglas tried to prevent, 199; Illinois' attitude toward, 260, 267; opinions on, 253-258, 290, 299n, 302; threatened in 1849, 63-66, 102
Sedgwick, C., 59
Selby, Paul, 143, 453

INDEX

Seymour, Horatio, 147, 322, 411-413
Seward, William H., 110, 120, 161n, 182, 185-186, 189, 191, 192-194, 198, 298, 398
Shawneetown, 87, 141n, 360, 414, 450
Sheahan, James W., 161, 303, 455, 457
Sheean, David, 303, 321
Shelby county, 308n
Shenandoah river, 324
Sheridan, General Philip, 324, 327
Sherman, Francis C., 334
Sherman, General William T., 287, 288, 289, 324, 327, 387
Shields, General James, 34; attitude toward Kansas-Nebraska act, 126-127; compromise vote of, 67, 68; defeated for senate 1854, 134-135, 138; Fenian, 22; senator, 38, 39, 72, 62-63, 117
Shiloh (Tenn.), 287
Sigel, Franz, 280, 285
Singleton, General James W., 144, 149, 176, 268, 321; opinion on secession, 256; voted for Kansas-Nebraska bill, 127
Shurtleff College, *see* education
Slade, William, ex-governor of Vermont, 235
Slavery, abolition movement and, 209, 219-225; abolition of, in District of Columbia, 294; and the church, 246, 247; constitutional amendments concerning, 325, 337, 388; constitutional rights of, 313; emancipation movement, 290-298, 423; emancipation proclamation, 296, 298, 300, 301, 313, 335; founding of republican party and, 125-152; Fremont's proclamation, 264-265, 342; influence of, on politics 1848-1852, 53-74; issue of, in Dred Scott decision and Lincoln-Douglas debates, 153-180; issue of, in presidential election 1860, 182-201; Kansas-Nebraska act and, 113-124; newspapers and, 455-456; question of, in Kansas, 11. *See* Negroes and religion
Sloan, Walter, 449
Sloan's Central Commercial College, *see* education
Smith, Caleb B., 193
Smith, General G. W., 396
Smith, George, 94, 99
Smith, Gerrit, 89, 147
Smith, Joseph, Jr., 426
Smith, Melancthon, 326
Smith, Robert, 57, 62n

Smith, William, congressman from Virginia, 174
Smith, W. L. G., 448
Smithsonian Institution, 451
Snelling, Fort, 437
Société Française, *see* clubs
Soldiers' Orphans' Home, Illinois, *see* Civil War
Soldiers' Relief Association, Illinois, *see* Civil War
Sons of Liberty, *see* politics
Sons of Penn, *see* clubs
Sons of Temperance, 205-206, 444, 445
Sons of the Pilgrims, *see* clubs
South Butler (N. Y.), 213
South Carolina, 254, 318n
South Chicago, 337
Southern Illinois Fruit Growers' Association, *see* agriculture
Southern Illinois Normal University, *see* education
Southern railroad, *see* transportation
Southwestern Illinois Sabbath Convention, *see* religion
Speculation, and banking, 99; in Cairo, 7; in land, 85-89; railroad, 31-52
Springer, Francis, 231, 237
Springfield, 10, 15, 25, 31, 34, 48, 54, 57, 61, 63, 69, 72, 73, 96, 101, 103, 104, 111, 112, 119, 144, 156, 182, 249, 250, 251, 258, 267, 268, 270n, 286, 300, 304, 309, 321, 346, 366, 369, 372, 377, 388, 393, 398, 399, 422, 426, 428, 432, 434, 440, 450, 454, 456n, 457; advocates insurance companies, 94; amusements in, 438, 440, 441, 442; banks in, 97; colored mass meeting in, 337; congressional election of 1854, 131; crime in, 420; democratic convention in 1861, 256; democratic peace meeting at, 299-300; democratic victory in, 144; Douglas in 1854, 132-133; Douglas' letters to confidants in, 115; Douglas urged union loyalty at, 261; enlistment in, 281; favored Bloomington convention 1856, 146; growth of, 1, 2, 6, 19, 351; health conditions in, 216-217; immigrants in, 332, 336; know nothing convention in, 139; presidential election 1860 in, 185, 186, 195, 198; public utilities in, 4, 5, 6-7; railroads, connections with, 33, 42, 48; religious fervor at, 424; republican state convention 1854, 128-129, 143; republican convention 1858, 190; schools in, 230, 231, 237, 240,

241, 242, 243; senatorial election 1858 in, 158-180; state fair at, 79; Stock Importing Company at, 83-84; sugar cane convention at, 82; temperance movement in, 205, 207, 208, 210; women's rights movement in, 212
Springfield and Alton railroad, *see* transportation
Springfield and Illinois Southeastern railroad, *see* transportation
Springfield and Meredosia railroad, *see* transportation
St. Andrew's society, *see* clubs
St. Anne, 17
St. Anthony, 437
Stark county, 20, 234
Starne, Alexander, 103
State Agricultural Society, *see* agriculture
State Antislavery Society, Illinois, *see* politics
State Bank, *see* banking
State Educational Society, Illinois, *see* education
State Medical Society, 218
State Sanitary Fair, 284
State Sugar Cane Convention, Illinois, *see* agriculture
State Teachers' Association, *see* education
State Teachers' Institute, *see* education
St. Clair county, 51, 97, 105, 135n, 146, 226; education in, 230, 233; republican following in, 148, 151
Stebbins bonds, Macalister and, 92
Stephens, Alexander H., 178
Stephenson, Benjamin F., 397
Sterling, 356
Stevens, Thaddeus, 318
St. George's Society, *see* clubs
St. Louis, 16, 31, 220, 442, 445; bank circulation from, 95; commerce and railroad connections with, 29, 33, 34, 35, 36, 41, 42, 43, 45, 46, 51, 52, 177, 360; commercial center, 5, 7, 8, 18, 19, 350, 351, 357, 374; Fremont in, 265; influence of press of, 450, 458; secession strength in, 262-263
St. Louis and Terre Haute railroad, *see* transportation
St. Louis, Jacksonville, and Chicago railroad, *see* transportation
St. Louis railroad, Rockford, Rock Island, and, *see* transportation
St. Louis, Vandalia, and Terre Haute railroad, *see* transportation

Stock Importing Company, Illinois, *see* agriculture
Stock Yard and Transit Company, Union, 385
Stone, Lucy, 212, 438
Stoneman, George, 289
Storey, Wilbur F., 456
Stowe, Harriet Beecher, 448
St. Paul (Minn.), 41
St. Paul, and Fond du Lac Railway Company, Chicago, *see* transportation
St. Paul railroad, Milwaukee and, *see* transportation
"St. Paul's," 437
Strawn, David, 78
Strawn, Jacob, 83, 376
Stringer, Mrs. C. T. F., 428
Stuart, John T., 176, 196, 388n
Sturtevant, Julian M., antislavery leader, 239, 256n; critic of Lincoln, 294
Stuttgart (Germany), 23
Suffrage Association, Illinois Woman, *see* women's movement
Sugar Cane Convention, Illinois State, *see* agriculture
Sullivant, Joseph, 14
Sullivant, Michael L., 14, 78, 382
Sumner, Charles, Massachusetts senator, 294, 318
Sumter, Fort, 259, 274
Superior, Lake, 36ın
Sweat, Peter, 95
Swedenborgians, 245
Swedes, *see* Scandinavians
Swedish Lutherans, 247
Swedish Methodists, 245
Swedona, 20
Sweeney, Thomas W., 345
Swett, Leonard, 190, 334
Swiss, 441
Sycamore, 380

Tammany Society, 178
Taney, Roger B., chief justice, 154
Tariff, 101, 366n, 367, 409-410
Taylor, Colonel Edmund D., attitude toward Kansas-Nebraska act, 126, 133
Taylor, General Zachary, 62, 64; president 1848, 56-58, 60, 61; proposal of, 1850, 67, 69
Tazewell county, 123, 309
Teachers' Institute, State, *see* education
Telegraph, extension of, 31
Temperance movement, 204-211, 421
Tennessee, 15, 175, 178, 195, 271, 289, 330, 331

INDEX

Tennessee river, 7, 285, 286
Terre Haute (Ind.), 7, 14, 33, 46
Terre Haute and Alton railroad, *see* transportation
Terre Haute and Illinoistown railroad, *see* transportation
Terre Haute railroad, St. Louis and, *see* transportation
Terre Haute railroad, St. Louis, Vandalia, and, *see* transportation
Texas, 65, 83, 288, 365, 376, 377
Theological Seminary, Blackburn, *see* education
Theological Seminary, Chicago, *see* education
Theological Seminary, McCormick, *see* education
Third Industrial Convention, 243n
Thomas, William, 57
Thornton, Anthony, 299
Thurston, Sherman, 228
Tilton, Theodore, 338
Toledo, Wabash and Great Western, *see* transportation
Tolono, 377
Tonica, 211n
Toombs, Robert, Georgia senator, 173
Towanda, 211n
Tract Society, American, *see* religion
Transportation, agriculture and, 27, 32, 49-50, 355, 384-386; bills for improved 1869, 416; Cairo City and Canal Company, 38-39; Chicago center of, 349, 350; Douglas' interest in Pacific railroad, 114; Fink and Company, 48; growth of railroad, 2, 5, 7, 14, 27, 31-52, 357, 361, 364; Illinois and Michigan canal, 5, 8, 29, 32, 33, 36, 85, 92, 354, 356, 407, 416; of immigrants, 330-334; plank roads, 28; railroad construction affects finance, 91-92, 98; railroad men organized brigade, 280; railroads: Alton and Mt. Carmel, 47; Alton and Terre Haute, 46, 51; Atlantic and Mississippi, 33, 44, 46, 48, 88; Belleville and Southern, 360; Central Military Tract, 43; Chicago and Alton, 18, 45, 48, 49n, 360; Chicago and Aurora, 41; Chicago and Milwaukee, 47, 359; Chicago and Mississippi Railroad Company, 42; Chicago and Mobile, 38; Chicago and Northwestern, 47, 48, 359, 361; Chicago and Rock Island, 359, 361; Chicago, Burlington and Quincy, 43, 51, 360; Chicago, Rock Island, and Pacific, 360, 361; Chicago, St. Paul, and Fond du Lac Railway Company, 359; Galena and Chicago, 8, 40-41, 46, 48, 52, 130, 303, 359, 361; Great Western Railway Company, 36-40; Illinois Central, 7, 8, 13, 18, 21, 33, 36-40, 41, 42, 43, 48, 50, 51, 52, 86-89, 91, 92, 108, 114, 177, 208n, 270, 330, 331, 332, 334, 339, 351, 374, 375, 416; Illinois Great Western, 43; Indianapolis, Bloomington, and Western, 360; Michigan Central, 33; Michigan Southern, 349n; Milwaukee and St. Paul, 359; New York and Erie, 40; Northern Cross, 33, 43, 46-47; Northern Pacific, 361n; Ohio and Mississippi, 33, 34, 44, 45, 46, 52; Pacific, 147, 163n, 350, 361; Peoria and Oquawka, 43; Peru and Rock Island, 41; Rockford, Rock Island, and St. Louis, 360; Rock Island and Chicago, 8, 41, 349n; Sangamon and Morgan, 43; Springfield and Alton, 42-43; Springfield and Illinois Southeastern, 360; Springfield and Meredosia, 43; St. Louis and Alton, 177; St. Louis and Terre Haute, 360; St. Louis, Jacksonville, and Chicago, 360; St. Louis, Vandalia, and Terre Haute, 360; Terre Haute and Alton, 45-46, 52; Terre Haute and Illinoistown, 46; Toledo, Wabash and Great Western, 43, 360; sabbath observance and, 214; water, 27, 29-30, 33, 354-357
Trapp, Albert H., 135n
Treat, Samuel H., 309
Trumbull, Lyman, 255, 421; aided in war legislation, 262; bills of, 1866, 395; campaigned for Lincoln, 173-175, 198-199; debated with Douglas, 132-133, 141; favored Negro enlistment, 282; in congressional canvass 1866, 403-404; leader at Bloomington convention 1856, 145; opinion on Dred Scott decision, 155; opinion of Palmer, 264; opposed Kansas-Nebraska act, 126, 142; radical war position of, 291, 293-294, 297-298, 302, 304, 312, 314, 315; senator, 131, 134-137, 163, 166, 200, 259, 399, 404-405; supported conscription, 275; supported Fremont, 147, 265; voted for Johnson's acquittal, 409
Turner Cadets, 281
Turner, Jonathan B., 80-81, 239, 247n, 314; advocated agricultural and industrial university, 231, 232, 233n,

498 INDEX

240-245, 431-435; congressional candidate 1854, 130; lecturer, 439
Turner, Thomas J., 62, 209n, 258, 397, 398, 403, 413
Tuttle, James H., 334
Twain, Mark, 439

Uncle Tom's Cabin, 226
Underhill, Isaac, 81
Underwood, William H., 143, 215, 421
Unger, Julius, 443
Union county, 279n, 306, 374
Union League, *see* politics
Union Musical Association, *see* music
Union Stock Yard and Transit Company, 385
Unitarian Conference, Western, *see* religion
Unitarians, 220, 248, 426
United Presbyterians, 246
United States Agricultural Fair, *see* agriculture
United States Christian Commission, *see* Civil War
United States Sanitary Commission, *see* Civil War
Universal Brotherhood, League of, *see* religion
Universalists, 245, 248, 249, 426, 427
University of Chicago, *see* education
University of Illinois, *see* education
Upper Alton, 238, 436
Urbana, 4, 15, 42, 79, 81, 304; agricultural university at, 408, 433-435
Usrey, William J., 143
Utah, 64, 66, 68, 70, 116, 184

Vallandigham, Clement L., 296, 323, 326
Van Amringe, H., 18, 90, 212
Van Buren, John, 121, 147
Van Buren, Martin, 59-61, 89, 219
Vandalia, 306
Vandalia, and Terre Haute railroad, St. Louis, *see* transportation
Van Deren, D. J., 220
Van de Velde, Right Reverend James Oliver, 248
Van Meter, "Professor," 442
Vaudois, 18
Vaughan, J. C., 146
Vermilion county, 377
Vermont, 13, 137, 235, 244
Vermont Emigrant Association, *see* emigration
Vicksburg (Miss.), 284, 287, 288, 298, 399

Victoria, 20
Vincennes (Ind.), 31, 33, 35, 44, 46, 360
Vinton, James E., 205
Virginia (Ill.), 28, 177
Virginia, 15, 98, 147, 174, 175, 257, 263, 271, 331

Wabash, and Great Western railroad, Toledo, *see* transportation
Wabash county, 82
Wabash river, 7, 14
Wade-Davis bill, 319, 323
Wait, Olive Starr, 212
Wait, William S., 89, 212
Waite, C. B., 428
Waldenses, 18
Walker, George, 454
Walker, James B., 223n
Walker, Mrs. Mary L., 427
Ward, B. C., 280
Ward, S. G., 200n
Washburne, Elihu B., abolition and, 219; attended Bloomington convention 1856, 145; congressman, 111, 130, 131, 242; favored Douglas, 161; opposed Kansas-Nebraska act, 118; supported Lincoln, 319
Washington county, 26
Washington, D. C., 38, 39, 62, 68, 72, 91, 102, 114, 131, 156, 157, 161, 166, 184, 185, 188, 255, 256, 257, 259, 262, 263, 264, 265, 277, 282, 288, 315, 317, 318, 339, 355, 409, 447, 451
Waukegan, 69
Wayne county, 230
Webb, Edwin B., 105, 149, 176
Webster, Daniel, 66, 70, 108
Webster, John W., 451
Weed, Thurlow, 161n
Welch, Delavan, and Nathan's circus, 438
Welles, Gideon, 318, 398
Wells, C. D., 59
Wentworth, John, 38, 103n, 125, 229, 453, 454, 456; abolition and, 219; anti-Nebraska democrat, 142, 144n; campaigned for Lincoln 1860, 199; congressional aspirant 1854, 129-130; congressman, 111, 328; influence of, 54-55, 57, 59-60, 61, 63, 67, 68, 73, 108, 109, 112, 190; land reform advocated by, 89; opposed Kansas-Nebraska act, 117, 118; prominent editor, 455; supported Douglas, 105-106; supported Fremont 1856, 148; supported new constitution, 270; urges united action in north, 140

INDEX

Wesleyan Missionary Conference, Illinois, *see* religion
Wesleyan University, Illinois, *see* education
West Belleville, 217
Western Dental Convention, 218
Western Tract Convention, *see* religion
Western Unitarian Conference, *see* religion
West Urbana, 50, 149, 249
West Virginia, 263
Wheaton College, *see* education
Whig party, *see* politics
White county, 105, 398
White, Horace, 255, 410, 456
White, J. G., 426
Whitehouse, Bishop Henry J., 248, 425
Whiteside county, 396n
Whitney, Alfred M., 149n
Whittier, John Greenleaf, 456
"Wide awake" organization, *see* politics
Wilderness campaign, 289
Will county, 28, 79, 128, 267, 341, 419
Williams, Archibald, 127, 131
Williams, Isaac, 57
Williamson county, 260, 400
Wilmington, 375
Wilmot, David, 60
Wilmot proviso, 54, 55, 58, 60, 61, 62, 63, 64, 67, 69, 70, 74, 90, 102, 103, 113
Wilson, Charles L., 108, 453, 456
Wilson, Henry, 16:n
Wilson, Thomas, 401
Wilson's Creek, 285
Winnebago, 211n
Winnebago county, 15, 151, 210
Winona (Minn.), 357
Wisconsin, 41, 47, 52, 128, 142, 177, 199, 263, 316, 330, 340, 350, 357, 359
Wisconsin Dairymen's Association, Illinois and, *see* agriculture
Wisconsin Marine and Fire Insurance Company, 94
Wise, Henry A., 147

Women's Aid and Liberty Association, Kansas, *see* emigration
Women's movement, 211-214, 427-429; Illinois Woman Suffrage Association, 428
Women's Protective Immigration societies, *see* immigration
Wood, John, 258, 268
Woodward, James H., 69, 130
Wool Growers' Association, *see* agriculture
Wool Tariff Convention, 378
Wright, Erastus, 128
Wright, Horatio G., 306n

Yale College, 237
Yates, Camp, 262
Yates, Richard, 268, 387, 403; advanced Grant, 286; called for volunteers, 274, 275; called special legislative session, 261; campaigned for Lincoln 1860, 191, 199; comments on secession strength, 267; congressman, 73, 111, 242; defeated for congress 1854, 131, 137; defeated for senate, 298; favored Negro enlistment, 282; governor 1860, 190, 200, 346, 355, 432, 433; inaugural address of, 255-256; opposed Kansas-Nebraska act, 118; opposed new constitution, 270, 272; prorogued legislature 1863, 299; recommended reorganization of militia, 273; senator 1864, 328, 417; succeeded by Oglesby, 328; supported Fremont 1856, 148, 149; supported Lincoln 1864, 327; war interest of, 257-258, 276-277, 281, 283, 284, 295, 297, 307, 314
Yates, William, 81
Yocum, William, 335n
York, Major, 307
York, Shubal, 218
Young Men's Christian Association, *see* clubs
Young, Timothy R., 57

Ziegfeld, Dr. Florence, 444n